# STRATEGY AND FORCE PLANNING

## Second Edition

Edited by

The Strategy and Force Planning Faculty
National Security Decision Making Department
Naval War College

Dr. Richmond M. Lloyd—Course Director
Dr. Henry C. Bartlett
CAPT Michael J. Filkins, USNR
LTC James J. Maye, USA
Col Kevin E. McHugh, USAF
Dr. Mackubin T. Owens, Jr.
AMB Lauralee Peters
Dr. Andrew L. Ross
Prof. Timothy E. Somes
Lt Col James A. Stevens, USAF
Prof. David W. Swindle

NAVAL WAR COLLEGE PRESS
NEWPORT, RI

Naval War College Press
Newport, RI
1997

Second Printing

**Library of Congress Cataloging-in-Publication Data**

Strategy and force planning / edited by the Strategy and Force
  Planning Faculty, National Security Decision Making Department,
  Naval War College . Richmond M. Lloyd, course director ; Henry C.
  Bartlett ... [et al.]. — 2nd ed.
      p.    cm.
  Includes index.
  1. Military planning—United States. 2. National security—United
States.  I. Lloyd, Richmond M.  II. Bartlett, Henry C.  III. Naval
War College (U.S.).  Strategy and Force Planning Faculty.
U153.S77  1997
355´.033073—dc21                                                    97-5303
                                                                    CIP

For sale by the Superintendent of Documents, U.S. Government Printing Office
Washington, DC 20402
ISBN 1-884733-08-5

# STRATEGY AND FORCE PLANNING

## Table of Contents

28AUS

# Acknowledgments

The purpose of this book is to provide the very best in thinking about national security in support of the Strategy and Force Planning course within the National Security Decision Making Department of the Naval War College. It explores the economic, political, and military components of national security strategy; examines broad force planning concepts; and analyzes the development of specific force structures in support of the National Military Strategy.

This second edition of *Strategy and Force Planning* presents a wide range of articles on national security requirements, strategy, and resources. We thank the authors and copyright holders for their permission to republish their works and expose their ideas to another audience.

As teachers, we depend crucially upon the new insights, professional experience, and critical commentary of our students—representing the U.S. Navy, Marine Corps, Army, Air Force, Coast Guard, and many civilian agencies, as well as the navies of over 40 friendly and allied countries. We are grateful to all of them for their many invaluable insights without which this volume would not have been possible.

Nor would this book have been possible without the hard work of the Naval War College staff. We wish to express our profound thanks for their essential support.

Rear Admiral James R. Stark, USN, President of the Naval War College, provided the personal leadership, endless encouragement, and intellectual stimulus so necessary to undertaking and completing an effort of this kind. Captain Mack A. Thomas, USN, Deputy to the President and Chief of Staff, ensured the financial support required to produce this book.

The Dean of Academics, William M. Calhoun, enthusiastically championed opportunities for faculty research and publication. Dr. William E. Turcotte, Chairman of the National Security Decision Making Department, has a gift for asking hard questions and rejecting easy answers. Without his zeal for curriculum development and scholarly endeavor, we would not have benefited from the academic environment that fosters teaching and research excellence. His Executive Assistant, Professor Kevin Kelley, carried the heavy burden of departmental administration, leaving the faculty free to think, research, and write. Chris Anderson, the Department's Academic Coordinator, deserves special mention for her superb administrative support and indispensable coordination. We are also grateful to Genevieve Pietraszek and Jane Lutz for their prompt and cheerful assistance in handling secretarial services for the department.

Carole Boiani, Head of Publications Division, supervised the unusually large task of coordinating the overall word processing/typesetting effort. Special thanks goes to Gina Vieira who performed all desktop publishing, incorporated our numerous changes, made many significant suggestions to improve format, and ensured that the manuscript was consistent in format. Our heartfelt thanks to Jackie Cayer who, as Head of the Copyright and Editorial Division, supervised copyright approval and the paste-up of graphic material. She was adeptly assisted by Teresa Clements who negotiated copyright releases and was responsible for graphic layouts.

Jerry Lamothe, Division Head of Graphic Arts, deserves our deepest gratitude. He managed the reproduction of all visual materials, relying upon the services of Joe Nunes, Joan Mikosh-Johnson, Andy Small, Pat Rossoni, and Gina Atkins. The overall quality of this book reflects their creative energy and their determination to maintain the highest professional standards.

We would like to take this opportunity to thank our many colleagues at the Naval War College and other institutions. We have all greatly benefited from their work. Their thoughts and writings have passed the ultimate test of critical scrutiny in the classroom, deepening our understanding of the enduring concepts and current issues that must be confronted. We are also indebted to the visiting scholars who have served with our department. Ambassador Lauralee Peters, State Department Advisor to the President and a member of the Strategy and Force Planning Faculty, has been particularly helpful in providing professional insights and editing skills. Finally, we wish to thank Dr. Henry C. Bartlett, project manager of *Strategy and Force Planning*, Second Edition, as well as Professor Timothy Somes. Without their countless hours of work and attention to detail, this book would never have seen the light of day.

We close by thanking our families for their essential support and understanding.

# Preface

The purpose of this book is to assist those interested in the art of strategy and force planning: students, practitioners, and concerned citizens. It develops a rational sequence of concepts, from the highest level of strategic thinking to visions of military forces for the future. Its overarching thesis is that strategy must serve as a guide to force planning.

This is the seventh book in a continuing series by the Strategy and Force Planning Faculty, National Security Decision Making Department, of the U.S. Naval War College. Previous volumes have dealt with the same general subjects of national goals, national security strategy, military strategy, and the allocation of defense resources.

The book is organized into eight parts. Part One, "Strategy and Force Planning Concepts," sets the stage. It focuses on broad frameworks for thinking about national defense, stressing their use in developing strategy, sizing and structuring future forces, and allocating scarce defense resources. Part Two, "Perspectives on International Relations," articulates various perspectives on how the world works.

Part Three, "National Interests and Grand Strategy," marks the starting point of the arduous task of thinking through America's global role on the eve of the twenty-first century. It stresses the need to select a grand strategy that will support U.S. national interests. Part Four, "Economic Strategy," examines the component of grand strategy that many believe may have the greatest prominence over the coming decade.

Part Five, "Diplomatic Strategy," assesses the future of diplomacy, taking a hard look at alliances, coalitions, and multilateral organizations. Part Six, "Geostrategic Planning," adopts a geopolitical perspective for interpreting the shifts in global trends and power centers.

Part Seven, "Military Strategy and Force Planning," analyzes the approaches of past administrations, examining how military strategy was developed to support grand strategy. Finally, Part Eight, "The Military in the Future," considers the implications of strategic decisions for developing future defense capabilities. This section combines analytical concepts and some controversial judgments about force requirements. The book ends with several different perspectives on the nature of future war, stressing the technological implications for the Department of Defense.

# Chapter 1

**\* \* \***

# Strategy and Force Planning Framework

Richmond M. Lloyd

*Richmond Lloyd presents a conceptual framework for organizing and evaluating the essential factors involved in making future strategy and force planning decisions. The framework begins with national interests and objectives and the formulation of a national security strategy which includes all elements of national power. It then proceeds to more detailed assessments of alternative national military strategies and defense forces for the future. What are the most important factors and how are they interrelated? How can you use such a framework to guide and evaluate the formulation of alternative strategies and forces?*

## Introduction

The United States continues to reassess its national priorities and the fundamental elements of its national security strategy. It is important for the nation to take advantage of this moment in time, but to do so well requires quality and clarity in decisions about strategy and force planning. Lacking a clear set of objectives and a focused, robust national security strategy, the United States will only be able to react to, rather than control, world events affecting its interests. Muddling through will not do. Today's decisions about strategy and force planning will fundamentally influence our national security strategy and force posture well into the next century. Properly done, such decisions will be a powerful investment in the future. To avoid the consequences of planning errors, it is useful to revisit the basics of strategy and force planning in their fullest dimensions.[1]

Making the best strategic and force choices in a free society is a difficult and lengthy process. The strategist and force planner must consider numerous

Dr. Richmond M. Lloyd is Director of the Strategy and Force Planning course in the National Security Decision Making Department at the Naval War College and holds the Theodore Roosevelt Chair of Economics. He received a Ph.D. in business adiminstration from the University of Rochester, has a M.B.A. from the University of Chicago, and a B.S. in mechanical engineering from the University of Rochester. His current research and teaching interests include strategy and force planning, defense and international economics, and logistics.

international and domestic factors, including political, economic and military influences. The sheer number of ideas, concepts, opinions and differing points of view can be confusing, especially if you do not have a useful framework for organizing key factors. Because planning involves preparing for the future, there is considerable uncertainty and much room for disagreement about preferred strategy and how forces should be structured, organized, and equipped. Unfortunately, there rarely is a single right answer. Equally valid arguments are often made for widely different choices, each depending on the objectives sought and the assumptions made about threats, challenges, opportunities, technological advances, and future political and economic conditions. This tendency is exacerbated by various advocates who focus on the single factor most important to them, such as the threat or budget, without a balanced attempt to explore the full dimensions of the problem. A framework helps the strategist and force planner to ask the right questions and to seek the best solutions through a comprehensive treatment of all the important factors.

While recognizing that organizational interests, bureaucratic behavior, and politics play significant roles in the final selection of defense forces, this article presents a rational framework for the formulation of national security requirements and the evaluation of alternative strategy and force choices. This article does not describe the Joint Strategic Planning System (JSPS) and the Planning, Programming, and Budgeting System (PPBS), which are the organizational processes used within the Department of Defense to develop a national military strategy, select future forces and update the Future Years Defense Program (FYDP). Nor does it review the weapons acquisition process. Rather, the framework is intended to highlight the major factors that should be considered within these processes. This framework therefore represents a compromise between the complexity of reality and simplicity as an aid to understanding. It attempts to identify the most essential elements in strategy and force planning and their dominant relationships. The framework takes a top-down approach by starting with national interests and objectives and proceeds down to the detailed assessments that assist decision makers in the selection of future strategy and forces. These elements and relationships are illustrated in Figure 1.[2]

The purpose of presenting this framework is to provide a tool for understanding the fundamental concepts of strategy and force planning. It provides an approach for organizing the decision maker's thinking as he or she goes about the task of planning future strategy and forces. Taken in that light, it can be used as: (1) a guide to developing alternative strategies and future forces; (2) an aid to evaluating the arguments of strategists or force planners; and (3) a starting point for developing alternative approaches to structuring major force planning decisions.[3]

Figure 1
Strategy and Force Planning Framework

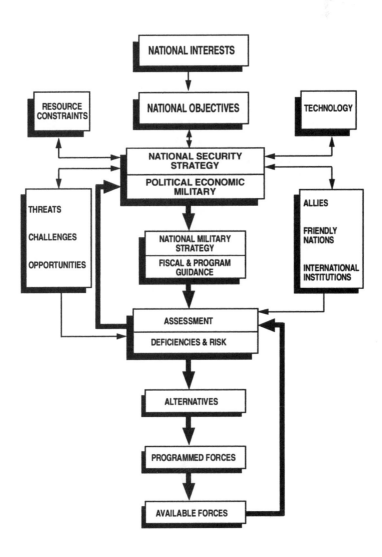

## Scope

Two main themes underlie this discussion of strategy and force planning concepts: (1) the allocation of scarce resources, and (2) the relationship among ends, means and risks. There will never be enough resources to satisfy all the nation's wants. Thus, we must make strategic choices, establish requirements, set priorities, make decisions, and allocate scarce resources to the most critical needs.

Strategy is the most important guide for force planning. To obtain the most from our limited national resources (means), we must determine where we want to go (objectives), and how we plan to get there (strategy). The importance of these ideas sometimes gets lost in the process of making detailed assessments and specific weapon system decisions. It may be necessary to adjust our security objectives (ends) to fit within the bounds of our nation's political, economic, and military power (means). A mismatch between these two strategy and force planning elements poses some danger (risk) to our overall security interests.

Force planning can be defined as the process of establishing military require-ments based on an appraisal of the security needs of the nation, and selecting military forces to meet those requirements within fiscal limitations. These requirements are sometimes divided into broad defense planning cases such as weapons of mass destruction, major war, regional conflicts, terrorism, operations other than war, and overseas presence. Alternatively, one can take a regional focus aligned with that of each of the major unified commanders, who are responsible for developing plans to deal with the full spectrum of potential threats within their areas of responsibility. The individual military services are responsible for organizing, training, and equipping the forces provided to the unified commanders. Thus, service-oriented and mission area categories are also used. In any case, the scope of military force planning is so vast that it is generally treated in manageable components. But, once these have been dealt with, it is always imperative that the planner return to view the whole. A comprehensive joint/combined perspective is necessary to ensure that service-specific force structuring decisions are considered within a national (joint) and allied (com-bined) context.

For purposes of discussion, the strategy and force planning framework is divided into two sections: *strategic choices* (the top) *and force choices* (the bottom). Strategic choices involve the identification of national interests, na-tional objectives, and the national security strategy with its political, economic, and military components. The security environment must be assessed to include consideration of future threats, challenges, and opportunities shown on the left and the expected role of allies, friendly nations, and international institutions shown on the right. Resource constraints and technology are important factors that further shape and influence final development of the preferred national security strategy. The resulting national military strategy along with fiscal and policy guidance leads to more detailed military strategy and force choices in the bottom half of the framework.

Force choices involve an assessment of the ability of available forces to support the national military strategy in meeting future threats and challenges. Deficiencies are identified that result when specific fiscal constraints are applied to the acquisition of future defense forces. Alternative force choices are evaluated to address deficiencies and reduce risks resulting in programmed forces for the future. As the programmed forces are fielded, they become available to support the strategy.

Both choices have major feedback loops as depicted by the heavier lines in Figure 1, indicating the iterative nature of the strategy and force planning process. Assessments also play a crucial role in strategy and force planning, as this is where both strategic and force choices come together.

## Strategic Choices

*National Interests*. At the highest level of abstraction, national interests are the "wellspring" from which national objectives and a grand strategy flow. National interests are the most important wants and needs of a nation.[4]

The overriding national interests are normally stated in terms of national survival and well-being. Preservation of our territorial integrity, freedom, independence, political institutions and honor are fundamental to our survival as a nation. Maintenance of the economic well-being and overall quality of life of the American people are also important national interests. Another national interest is the survival of our allies. We are a nation whose national interests are inextricably linked to those of our allies by historic, political, economic and cultural ties.

President George Bush in his 1991 National Security Strategy of the United States summarized our national interests as:

> The survival of the United States as a free and independent nation, with its fundamental values intact and its institutions and people secure. . . .
> A healthy and growing U.S. economy to ensure opportunity for individual prosperity and resources for national endeavors at home and abroad. . . .
> Healthy, cooperative and politically vigorous relations with allies and friendly nations. . . .
> [and] A stable and secure world where political and economic freedom, human rights, and democratic institutions flourish.[5]

President Bill Clinton in his 1996 National Security Strategy of Engagement and Enlargement states:

> Protecting our nation's security—our people, our territory and our way of life—is my Administration's foremost mission and constitutional duty. . . .
> The preamble to the Constitution sets out the basic objective: 'to provide for the common defense, promote the general welfare, and secure the blessings of liberty to ourselves and our posterity.' The end of the Cold War does not alter these fundamental purposes. . . .
> In all cases, the nature of our response must depend on what best serves our own long-term national interests. Those interests are ultimately defined by our security requirements. Such requirements start with our physical defense and economic well-being. They also include environmental

security as well as the security of our values achieved through expansion of the community of democratic nations.[6]

Donald Nuechterlein suggests that national interests can be viewed in terms of four broad categories: (1) defense of the homeland; (2) economic well-being; (3) favorable world order; and (4) promotion of values. He further suggests that the intensity of the nation's interest in some issue can be scaled from high to low as: (1) survival, (2) vital, (3) major, and (4) peripheral.[7] The threat of a possible nuclear attack on the United States has always been treated as a survival interest.

In his 1980 State of the Union address, President Jimmy Carter indicated that free world access to foreign oil was a vital interest of the United States. Such judgments have important influences on strategy and force planning. Throughout the 1980s, a Southwest Asia focus was used, among others, to determine the level and mix of future U.S. power projection capabilities and to establish the U.S. Central Command. These investments paid off when the U.S. with its allies and friends successfully expelled Iraqi forces from Kuwait during the 1991 Persian Gulf War. It should be recognized that there will be a continuous debate over the use of U.S. forces arising from differing views of interests as vital, major or peripheral.

*National Objectives.* Whereas national interests define the basic, nonnegotiable needs of a nation, national objectives "spell out what a country is trying to do." National objectives are the specific goals that a nation seeks in order to advance, support or defend its national interests. They are generally described in three broad categories—political, economic, and security—although other categories such as social, ideological, or technological are also used.[8]

A few examples of political, economic, and security objectives articulated by President George Bush are:

> strengthen and enlarge the commonwealth of free nations that share a commitment to democracy and individual rights;
> establish a more balanced partnership with our allies and a greater sharing of global leadership and responsibilities;
> promote a strong, prosperous, and competitive U.S. economy;
> ensure access to foreign markets, energy, mineral resources, the oceans, and space;
> deter any aggression that could threaten the security . . . and—should deterrence fail—repel or defeat military attack and end conflict on terms favorable to the United States, its interests and allies.[9]

Similarly, President Bill Clinton identifies three primary goals:

> Enhancing Our Security. Taking account of the . . . array of new threats, a military capability appropriately sized and postured to meet the diverse needs of our

strategy, including the ability, in concert with regional allies, to win two nearly simultaneous major regional conflicts . . . continue to pursue a combination of diplomatic, economic and defense efforts, including arms control agreements, to reduce the danger of nuclear, chemical, biological and conventional conflict and to promote stability.

Promoting Prosperity at Home. A vigorous and integrated economic policy designed to put our own economic house in order, work toward free and open markets abroad and promote sustainable development.

Promoting Democracy. A framework of democratic enlargement that increases our security by protecting, consolidating and enlarging the community of free market democracies . . . strengthening democratic processes in key emerging democratic states including Central and Eastern Europe, Russia, Ukraine and other new independent states of the former Soviet Union.[10]

These brief examples address the *highest* level of abstraction and provide only a starting point for the strategist. Detailed objectives must be formulated and prioritized for each region and particular situation in which U.S. interests are involved.

Too often stated objectives are vague, misdirected, overly ambitious or miss opportunities. It is essential that they be focused and clearly stated. In John Collins' words, "If you don't know what you want to do, you can't plan how to do it."[11]

*National Security Strategy*. Strategy is a word often used but little understood. It has taken on so many meanings in different publications that it is important to set the context for its use here. André Beaufre defines strategy as:

> The art of applying force so that it makes the most effective contribution toward achieving the ends set by political policy. . . . The aim of strategy is to fulfill the objective laid down by policy, making the best use of the resources available. . . . The art of strategy consists in choosing the most suitable means from those available and so orchestrating their results that they combine to produce a psychological pressure sufficient to achieve the moral effect required.[12]

John Collins states that:

> National strategy fuses all the powers of a nation, during peace as well as war, to attain national interests and objectives. Within that context, there is an overall political strategy, which addresses both international and internal issues; an economic strategy, both foreign and domestic; a national military strategy; and so on. Each component influences national security immediately or tangentially.[13]

National security strategy, as used here refers to the overall approach or master plan for accomplishing national objectives through a combination of political, economic, military or psychological means. These tools are the basic instruments of national power. The terms grand strategy or national strategy are also used. The key point is that strategic choices indicate how a nation will employ *all* of these instruments in the pursuit of national objectives. These strategic choices, and the assumptions made about them, provide guidance and establish limits on lower level decisions. The framework in Figure 1 explicitly shows the national military strategy flowing from and in support of the national security strategy. This same relationship holds for the political and economic elements of the national security strategy, but such detail is omitted to allow further treatment of force planning. Thus, in the top-down strategy and force planning approach suggested by this framework, the national security strategy that is initially selected sets the bounds in which successive force choice decisions are made.

*National Military Strategy.* A nation's military strategy should flow from its objectives and overall national security strategy. The significant changes in the security environment of the 1990s have required that all elements of U.S. national military strategy be reviewed. To help in such a review, it is sometimes useful to view the elements of this strategy as fundamental choices concerning alternative courses of action. These elements or "descriptors" outline how we intend to use our military means to achieve our ends. Some of these fundamental choices are: a coalition strategy vs. a go-it-alone strategy; deterrence vs. warfighting; forward deployed forces vs. U.S.-based strategic reserve; globally flexible forces vs. regionally tailored forces; and active vs. reserve force components. The degree to which the national military strategy is modified by these and other parameters will greatly influence the types of forces required.

Such evolutions in the U.S. military strategy have been very evident in the years since the end of the Cold War. The 1992 U.S. National Military Strategy had four key descriptors: strategic deterrence and defense, forward presence, crisis response, and reconstitution.[14] More recently, the U.S. National Military Strategy of Flexible and Selective Engagement is intended to achieve two national military objectives—"Promote Stability through regional cooperation and constructive interaction," and "Thwart Aggression through credible deterrence and robust warfighting capabilities." The three components of this strategy are peacetime engagement, deterrence and conflict prevention, and fight and win. These in turn are supported by the two complementary strategic concepts of overseas presence and power projection.[15] The Chairman, Joint Chiefs of Staff in 1996 published Joint Vision 2010 to serve as an "operationally based template" to help further guide the development of future forces in a joint context. It emphasizes the growing importance of information superiority and emerging operational concepts of dominant maneuver, precision engagement, focused logistics and full-dimensional protection.[16]

***Fiscal and Program Guidance.*** The strategy and force planning process can be viewed in one sense as a resource allocation problem. Early in the U.S. Defense Department's JSPS and PPBS processes, policy, strategy, fiscal and programming guidance is issued. The Secretary of Defense's Defense Planning Guidance provides the administration's specific defense priorities for the next several years.

Two different levels of resource allocation affect the amount of resources applied to defense. At the highest level there is consideration of the nation's total resources and how they are to be shared between the private and public sectors. This is an integral part of the debate over the choice of grand strategy, and the allocation of resources to implement it. The focus of debate at this level is concerned with growth, employment, inflation, budget and trade deficits, and overall productivity of the economy.

The second level of resource allocation occurs between defense and non-defense programs within the federal budget. Competing political, economic and security objectives strongly influence these resource allocation decisions. Thus, defense planners must articulate well their legitimate needs to meet the nation's security objectives. Realistic appraisals must be made of the future availability of defense funds. Too often, defense plans assume budgets will rise in the future to correct current deficiencies. The U.S. continues to reassess its national priorities in light of the changing nature of threats, challenges, opportunities and fiscal realities.

### Force Choices

Once overall national security strategy and national military strategy are determined, it is necessary to assess our ability to carry out our chosen strategy given the availability of forces and the projected threats and challenges. These assessments take various forms, from detailed analytical treatments of opposing forces to intuitive judgements about the nonquantifiable factors of war. But whatever the form, any strategy and force assessment should somehow include the essential elements of objectives, strategy, threats, available forces and risk. The fundamental standard is simply:

> Do the military forces support the national security strategy such that national objectives are achieved, at acceptable risk, in face of the threats?

Deficiencies identified by this overall assessment are often described in terms of risks. These risks may be reduced by judicious selection from among alternative forces. Final decisions about which forces to include in the next Future Years Defense Program are conditioned by overall national objectives and strategy, fiscal and program guidance, and the risk assumed by not investing in foregone opportunities.

The entire force choice process should be dynamic in order to adapt to changing conditions. Different force planning elements are considered in varying degrees both inside and outside the Department of Defense. By design, the entire process must come together at least once a year with the preparation of the Future Years Defense Program. This, however, is not the final word, as Congress will modify choices to reflect its evaluation of the proposed strategy and forces, as well as the public and political moods of the time.

Each of the force choice elements is considered in more detail in the following sections.

*Threats, Challenges, and Opportunities*. An essential task for the strategist and force planner is to assess the security environment in terms of future threats, challenges and opportunities. During the Cold War the United States and its allies faced a well-defined threat and much strategy and force planning was driven explicitly by traditional nation-specific threat assessments. The hoped-for peace of the 1990s was short-lived as forces of disintegration clashed with forces of integration. Ambiguity and uncertainty now complicate the task.[17]

At some point, however, the force planner must consider the full spectrum of conflict ranging from weapons of mass destruction, major conventional war, and regional conflicts to peace operations, terrorism, drug trafficking, humanitarian assistance, and presence. Henry Bartlett, Paul Holman, and Timothy Somes suggest that the most important task is to evaluate fully the nature of such conflicts, their likelihood of occurrence, and their consequences for the national interests. Ultimately such judgements lead to further decisions as to how military forces should be structured and applied across the spectrum.[18]

Traditional threat assessments continue to have an important though modified role in the strategy and force planning process. Consideration of a specific nation's capabilities, intentions, and circumstances, as well as vulnerabilities, are important.[19] Capabilities refer to the physical ability of a potential enemy to impose its will on other nations. Military capability is often measured by the number and quality of weapons and armed forces personnel, command and control features, deployment patterns, readiness level, and mobilization ability, though assessing overall effectiveness is inherently complex and difficult. Information about an adversary's important economic and political factors is often more difficult to obtain and even more challenging to interpret.

The intentions and plans of a potential adversary are usually more vague and uncertain than is knowledge of its capabilities. Specific circumstances of the time can alter a nation's capabilities and intentions in unexpected ways. And identification of vulnerabilities allows weaknesses of a threatening nation to be exploited in the development of strategy.

*Allies, Friendly Nations, and International Institutions*. A major strategic choice is the extent to which our strategy will be linked to other nations either through broad alignments, specific alliances such as NATO, collective or cooperative security through international institutions such as the United Nations, or ad hoc coalitions. The expected contributions of allies and friendly nations are critically important to our ultimate strategy and our allocating of limited resources. This inevitably raises the issues of the effectiveness of such relationships as well as the division of labor and overall burdensharing. Other nations' capabilities, intentions, circumstances and vulnerabilities must also be taken into account. Their national interests and objectives will come first, and it is only when those interests and objectives are compatible with our own that we can expect to include allied forces in the accomplishment of our objectives. Such evaluations are critical to the fundamental choice between a go-it-alone versus a coalition strategy.

*Available Forces*. Another major input to the continuing assessment process is a description of the military forces that would be available to engage in future conflicts. These forces include: (1) existing forces (active and reserve) minus those that are scheduled for retirement; (2) forces programmed to become operational during the time of interest; and (3) force contributions that can be expected from allies and friendly nations in specific situations.

Existing forces provide an initial starting point to which additions and deletions are made. Given the extended life and long procurement lead times for many weapon systems, existing forces inevitably form a major part of the force structure far into the future. Since our force structure is not built from the ground up each year, force-modernization choices are most often made "on the margin." Thus, although national security objectives and military strategy should determine our selection of forces, it is also true that existing forces largely determine today's strategy and our ability to meet today's contingencies.

Operational planners tend to emphasize readiness and sustainability, since they must plan for the possibility of fighting with today's existing forces. Force planners tend to focus on modernization and force structure issues since their goal is to create future forces capable of supporting the nation's future strategy and objectives. Both perspectives are important, and the best strategist and force planner strikes a balance between operating existing forces and investing in future capability.

*Assessment*. Strategy and force planning assessments comprise a complex series of analyses that evaluate the capabilities of U.S. and allied forces to support the national security strategy when opposed by potential threats. The results of these assessments are the identification of deficiencies in available forces and an indication of risks to interests inherent in current programs. These assessment exercises serve as a basis for formulating changes to the programmed forces. This appraisal process leads to the decisions that eventually reallocate funds among various programs within fiscal guidelines. Deficiencies are corrected by making changes in the various weapon procurement, manpower, operations and maintenance, research and development, and other supporting programs. The revised programs are then used as the basis for future force posture.

In making these assessments, defense planners must consider:

> what we want to do (objectives);
> how we plan to do it (strategy);
> what we are up against (threats and challenges);
> what is available to do it (forces);
> and what are the mismatches (risks).

Both qualitative and quantitative assessments are useful in comparing opposing forces and strategies. Qualitative factors include such things as leadership, doctrine, training, morale, logistics, intelligence, technology, and initiative. Quantitative factors include order of battle, firepower, mobility, survivability, accuracy, range, weapons effects, and a host of other measurable quantities. In the analysis of quantitative factors, use is made of counting, modeling and gaming. By adding the human element, political-military simulations, wargames, and exercises can provide very useful insights to the strategist and force planner.[20]

***Deficiencies and Risk.*** Through qualitative and quantitative assessments of objectives, strategy, forces, and threats, deficiencies in our strategy or force posture are identified. After the Persian Gulf War it was determined that strategic mobility capabilities should be increased dramatically to ensure a more rapid deployment of a larger force during the early stages of a future crisis. The net result of such deficiencies is that risks must be assumed until improvements can be made.

Risk can be broadly described as the difference between desired ends (national security objectives) and what can be achieved with available means (strategy and forces). To choose military forces effectively, risks must be analyzed, assessed, and managed. In particular, the likelihood of failure and the consequence of failure should be addressed. How risks are to be measured and described must be decided.

To minimize their effect, risks must be managed. For crucial uncertainties, additional information may be sought to reduce them. Budgets may be raised to lower the overall risk of failure. Limited resources may be reallocated among mission areas, accepting increased risks in some areas in order to reduce the risk in others. At the highest level of planning, a nation may accept higher levels of security risks to achieve other political or social development objectives.

*Alternatives and Programmed Forces.* The next step in force planning is to select from alternative forces the number, type, and mix of military capabilities needed to correct deficiencies and minimize risks, keeping in mind balanced force levels and fiscal realism. The resulting programmed force is fiscally constrained but hopefully fulfills the most critical aspects of the national military strategy.

There are three general levels of resource allocation that occur at this stage of force planning. The first occurs when defense fiscal and policy guidance is refined and each service's share of the defense budget is determined. Concerns over roles, missions and functions can surface at this time. Changing defense priorities should have an important effect. How should defense dollars be allocated across the spectrum of conflict? How should the elements of the overall national military strategy such as overseas presence, power projection and regional conflict be supported? What are the needs for each of the unified and specified commands? Is readiness or modernization a top priority?

Within each service a second major resource allocation must be made among each of the appropriation accounts. Here the concern is over how much should be allocated to force structure, modernization, readiness and operational tempo, and support infrastructure. Does the force structure support the national military strategy, are readiness and operational tempos sustainable today, is there sufficient modernization for the future, and is the support infrastructure appropriately sized?

A final level of allocation occurs when alternative force choices are made within and among mission areas of each service. Should Army divisions be heavy or light? Should the Navy emphasize carriers, submarines, strategic sealift or amphibious lift? Should the Air Force modernize fighter/attack aircraft or strategic airlift? What should be the mix between active and reserve forces? Issues at all three levels of resource allocation must be addressed from a joint and combined perspective.

## Feedback and Iteration

This description of the strategy and force planning framework considered each element in a step-by-step fashion. This is not meant to imply that strategy and force planning is a rigid, sequential process. In reality, elements are considered in varying degrees by different groups at different times. Feedback and iteration exist at all levels and are crucial to ensure a comprehensive treatment of all elements.

The heavy lines in the upper portion of Figure 1 emphasize the need for feedback and iteration in making strategic choices. Military, political, and economic assessments may indicate the need to revise the initial choice of national security strategy in order to better satisfy the national objectives. It may also be necessary to review the national objectives to ensure that more has not been attempted than the strategy can accomplish with available resources and technology.

The heavy lines in the lower portion of the framework indicate the need to reassess the ability of available forces to carry out the national military strategy after the programmed forces are added. Alternative forces can be evaluated in order to determine the most effective choice within resource limits.

Finally, assessment forms the link between choices about strategy and force structure. Limitations or deficiencies of a military strategy may become apparent only after forces needed to carry it out are determined. Where a strategy-force mismatch exists, either the forces must be adjusted, the strategy strengthened, the objectives revised, or the additional risks accepted.[21]

## Summary

This article presents an organized framework for choosing strategy and defense forces. Political, bureaucratic and organizational factors often obscure the important rational elements of strategy and force planning decisions. In light of today's dynamic security environment and increasing competition for scarce resources, choosing the best strategy and defense forces is more crucial now than ever before. Errors made now will only result in strategy and defense forces ill-suited to the nation's future needs. Precise and thorough consideration must be given to all the key elements of strategy and force planning.

Because of the complexities involved and the numerous uncertainties that make precise evaluation difficult, clear-cut choices are seldom achieved. Consequently, final decisions are often made in an atmosphere of political bargaining and organizational advocacy. It is incumbent upon those involved in national defense to use some rational approach for considering the numerous planning elements as they make timely and informed judgments on complex strategic and force choice issues. In addition, it is essential that they clearly and concisely communicate their reasoning to the American public.

## Notes

1. This article updates Richmond M. Lloyd, "Strategy and Force Planning Framework" in Strategy and Force Planning Faculty, eds., *Strategy and Force Planning* (Newport, RI: Naval War College Press, 1995), pp. 1-14., Richmond M. Lloyd, "Force Planning for the 1990s" in Force Planning Faculty, eds., *Fundamentals of Force Planning*, Vol. I, *Concepts* (Newport, RI: Naval War College Press, 1990), pp.105-126, and Richmond M. Lloyd and Lt Col Dino A. Lorenzini, US Air Force, "A Framework for Choosing Defense Forces," *Naval War College Review*, January/February 1981, pp. 46-58. Significant portions of the original articles are used in their entirety without further citation. I want to thank my colleagues on the Strategy and Force Planning faculty at the Naval War College, Dino Lorenzini, and my students who have reconfirmed the importance of a framework and have provided innumerable suggestions which have been incorporated here.

2. This diagram is a modification of that originally appearing in the Lloyd and Lorenzini, 1981 article which was an adaptation of the Force Structure Assessment Methodology given in NWP-1 (Rev. A), *Strategic Concepts of the U.S. Navy,* (Washington: Dept. of the Navy, 1978).

3. This framework is intended to comprehensively include the most important strategy and force planning factors. Within each broad category, many concepts, principles, ideas and methods may be used. Clearly, certain factors will be more important than others depending on the circumstances. The art of strategy and force planning is to know which factors are most relevant to the issues at hand. Quite often, alternative approaches give greater emphasis to what is considered a key variable such as the threat, technology, or the budget. At some time, however, the planner must review and synthesize all factors in a comprehensive manner. See Henry C. Bartlett, G. Paul Holman, Jr. and Timothy E. Somes, "The Art of Strategy and Force Planning," Chapter 2 in this collection of readings for another framework and discussion of the strengths and weaknesses of alternative approaches.

4. John M. Collins, *Grand Strategy* (Annapolis: Naval Institute Press, 1974), pp. 1-3.

5. George Bush, *National Security Strategy of the United States* (Washington, DC: The White House, August, 1991), pp. 3-4.

6. Bill Clinton, *A National Security Strategy of Engagement and Enlargement* (Washington, DC: The White House, February, 1996), pp. i, 3, and 11.

7. For a more detailed discussion of these concepts see Donald E. Nuechterlein, "America Recommitted: United States National Interests in a Restructured World," Chapter 7 in this collection of readings.

8. Collins, *Grand Strategy*, pp. 2-3.

9. Bush, p. 3.

10. Clinton, pp. 11-12.

11. John M. Collins, *U.S. Defense Planning, A Critique* (Boulder, CO: Westview Press, 1982), p. 6.

12. André Beaufre, *An Introduction to Strategy* (New York: Praeger, 1965), pp. 22 and 24.

13. Collins, *Grand Strategy*, p. 14.

14. Colin L. Powell, Chairman, Joint Chiefs of Staff, *National Military Strategy of the United States* (Washington, DC: U.S. Government Printing Office, January, 1992), pp. 6-8.

15. John M. Shalikashvili, Chairman, Joint Chiefs of Staff, *National Military Strategy of the United States of America, 1995: A Strategy of Flexible and Selective Engagement* (Washington, DC: U.S. Government Printing Office, 1995), pp. 4-7.

16. John M. Shalikashvili, Chairman, Joint Chiefs of Staff, *Joint Vision 2010* (Washington, DC: Department of Defense, 1996), pp. ii, and 19-25.

17. Peter Schwartz advises decision makers to develop scenarios that focus on driving forces, predetermined elements and critical uncertainties, not to predict the future, but to challenge conventional wisdom and better prepare for an uncertain future. See Peter Schwartz, "The Art of the Long View," Chapter 3 in this collection of readings.

18. See Henry C. Bartlett, G. Paul Holman, Jr., and Timothy E. Somes, "The Spectrum of Conflict: What Can It Do for Force Planners?," Chapter 29 in this collection of readings.

19. See Frederick H. Hartmann, *The Relations of Nations,* (New York: Macmillan, 1978), pp. 259-262 for an excellent discussion on why military officers prefer to focus on capabilities while diplomats tend to concentrate on intentions and circumstances.

20. For a comprehensive treatment of wargaming principles, and its history, especially at the Naval War College, see Peter P. Perla, *The Art of Wargaming, A Guide for Professionals and Hobbyists* (Annapolis: Naval Institute Press, 1990).

21. General André Beaufre describes the planner's challenge: "The most difficult military problem to resolve is that of establishing a security system, as inexpensively as possible in time of peace, capable of transforming itself very rapidly into a powerful force in case of the danger of aggression." André Beaufre, *Strategy for Tomorrow* (New York: Crane, Russak, 1974), p. 71.

# Chapter 2

## * * *

# The Art of Strategy and Force Planning

Henry C. Bartlett, G. Paul Holman, Jr.
and Timothy E. Somes

*Henry C. Bartlett, G. Paul Holman, Jr. and Timothy E. Somes point out that strategists and force planners deal with a wide array of variables when they formulate national security goals, strategies and future military requirements. A simple model can help the process by focusing on key variables and stressing interactions among them. The authors present their version of such a model and explain how it can be used by planners and decision makers. In the second half of the article, they focus more narrowly on alternative approaches to force planning and their respective strengths and weaknesses. After studying the first part of the article, would you modify the "Bartlett" model in any way to help in strategic development and force planning? Specifically, what would you change and why? How are the various approaches to force planning in the second part of the article related to the model? Should one of them dominate force planning, or can they be melded together to improve decision making?*

A n ancient cliche holds that strategy is an art, not a science. Specifically, strategy is the linking of ends and means—a "game plan" that tells how finite resources will be employed to accomplish declared objectives. Coherent strategy is the key to institutional success; it is as important for businesses and universities as it is for countries.

Force planning, like strategy, is also an art. It is the process of appraising the security needs of a nation, establishing the military requirements that result

Professors Bartlett and Somes are members of the Strategy and Force Planning course, National Security Decision Making Department of the Naval War College. Professor Holman is at the George C. Marshall Center in Garmisch, Germany. They teach and conduct research on global security issues, national military strategy, and future military force requirements. Portions of this article are adapted from Henry C. Bartlett, "Approaches to Force Planning," NWC Force Planning Faculty, ed., *Fundamentals of Force Planning* (Newport, RI: Naval War College Press, 1990), v. 1, pp. 443-53.

Reprinted from *Naval War College Review*, Spring 1995, pp. 114-126 (with minor modifications).

from them, and selecting, within resource constraints, military forces to meet those requirements.

Practitioners of strategy and force planning come from a wide variety of academic disciplines and professional backgrounds. Some have particular knowledge of geopolitics, others have extensive experience in economics, diplomacy, or political office. Many have spent years in operational military billets. Some are especially comfortable with abstract concepts; others prefer practicalities. The challenge is to blend this array of perspectives and approaches so as to devise the best strategies and capabilities to support a nation's security aims.

The first half of this article presents a simple model that addresses the key variables in the art of strategy and force planning. This part stresses logical decisions about ends, means, and strategy; it identifies potential mismatches among the variables, repeating the process as necessary. The second half of the article focuses more narrowly on military force planning. It examines commonly used approaches, whose strengths and weaknesses are then weighed in terms of the model.

## A Model of Strategic Development

Practitioners of strategy and force planning constantly struggle to achieve a balance among many competing variables. The art of strategy and force planning is made evident by how well the inevitable tensions among these variables are resolved.

***The Key Variables***. The "Bartlett model" in figure 1 illustrates this dynamic process. It can be used to explore substantive controversies and to facilitate national security decision making. The model reveals the interaction among what we consider the key variables, and thereby represents a comprehensive approach to strategy development and force planning.

*Ends and objectives*. Strategists and force planners usually think in terms of levels of objectives. At the highest level are national interests, which endure over time and command broad support. The survival of the country and the health of its economy are interests that appear on any such list. Strategists also agree, by and large, about the desirability of global peace, although they may disagree about the impact of any specific conflict on national interests. Less tangible—and as a result, more controversial—goals arise from the concern for such values as democracy and human rights.

Lower-level goals must be reconciled with these highest-level, national interests. Global objectives must be weighed against regional, and long-term goals against short-term. Assuring such consistency demands a high degree of intellectual rigor and discipline from all strategists. As examples, the U.S. commitments to preservation of open markets and freedom of the seas are long-term objectives that flow from the national interest of economic well-being.

Others, such as preventing Iraq and Iran from dominating the Persian Gulf, may be more sensitive to rapid changes.

---

Figure 1
Bartlett Model[1]

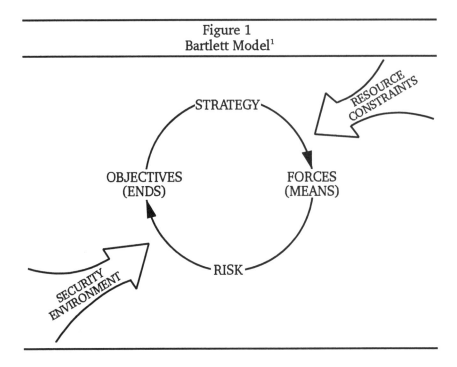

---

*Security environment.* Assessing the security environment is one of the most difficult tasks of strategists and force planners. Sudden changes in the security environment may radically alter national objectives in particular regions of the world. An assessment of the security environment should include a wide range of considerations, such as shifting international power centers, dominant trends, critical uncertainties, evolving economic interdependence, changing domestic requirements, cultural, religious and demographic trends, ethnic warfare, ecological challenges, and advancing technology. All of these, and other considerations, are factors that determine a nation's security environment.

*Strategies* are often conceived as "game plans" for achieving desired goals with limited means. The art of the strategist is not only to select the best plan among alternatives but to be sure the game itself is worth playing. At the highest level of national thinking, such a game plan is often referred to as grand, or national security, strategy. It reflects the structure of international relations—not merely a country's sense of who its allies and rivals are but also its strengths, weaknesses, and the capacity of its body politic to accept challenges. Grand strategy should provide a clear concept of how economic, diplomatic, and military instruments of national power will be used to achieve national goals and policy.[2]

Lower levels of strategy, for each of the major instruments of national power, are more prescriptive. An economic strategy should explain, for example, how a country intends to change its rate of growth or its role in the world marketplace. A diplomatic strategy should describe how a nation expects to implement its highest goals through communication with foreign governments, directly and in international forums. Finally, a military strategy should support the others, explaining how, and under what circumstances, the military instrument of national power will be used to achieve influence, deterrence, defense, or compellence.

The *means or tools* available to execute the chosen strategy comprise, theoretically, the total resources of the country. In practice, however, strategists and force planners usually think in terms of three basic sets of tools. The economic instruments of national power include trade agreements, foreign aid, the money supply, taxes, government expenditures, and subsidies. Among the diplomatic means are alignments, alliances, ad hoc coalitions, treaties, good offices, sanctions, and negotiations of every conceivable kind and complexity. Military instruments include the full array of armed might, from the capabilities for nuclear war and large-scale conventional war to nation building. The changing world security environment will alter the relative utility of these instruments and will add others. Different instruments of power already affect international and domestic arenas. Some authorities would emphasize psychology—which reflects the ability of national leaders to use the "bully pulpit" to dominate the communications media, and thus to mobilize public opinion at home and abroad. Still others include technological, informational, environmental, social, cultural, ethnic, and other forms of interaction and influence. Strategists must not overlook these additional varieties of influence.

*Constrained resources.* Wants almost always exceed resources, for governments as well as individuals. Any country must choose among rival demands and mutually exclusive alternatives. The armed forces compete for resources against many other government agencies, against nongovernmental demands, and against each other, especially when a democratic country is at peace. As a result, strategy and force planning entail resource allocation, deciding which objectives and courses of action are most important, and setting priorities.

*Risk of failure.* Uncertainty is the dominant characteristic of the international and domestic security environments. As a result, strategists and force planners must weigh their hopes for success against the possibility of failure. They do so by reexamining the security environment, goals, strategies, available resources, and tools needed to achieve stated objectives. This is a continuous, iterative process. Perhaps the single most important value of risk assessment is that it results in a constant effort to identify and correct imbalances among the key variables. Strategists, for instance, tend to focus on ends-means mismatches, because of their concern that national objectives not become too ambitious for the resources available. Force planners tend to emphasize strategy-force incongruities, hoping to ensure that the level and mix of future forces will in fact adequately support a given military strategy.

***Realigning the Key Variables***. As strategists and force planners consider the twenty-first century, they face a constant need to adjust their thinking. The model suggests that a change in one variable will usually result in the modification of others, and accordingly in mismatches. To restore the balance, strategists and planners must be ready to realign the key variables. There are a number of ways of doing so.

*Modify the ends*. In a rational world, strategists would first assess the international security environment in terms of shifting power centers, dominant trends, and critical uncertainties; then they would articulate specific national ends or objectives. Thus the most logical place to begin correcting a mismatch between the security environment and the means is to reconsider the national ends.

*Change the means*. Political alterations may generate substantial changes in the means available. Such changes are sometimes quantitative. The Korean War, for instance, caused large increases in U.S. defense spending beginning in 1950, while the collapse of the Soviet Union has prompted sharp declines. A qualitative change in means may necessitate shifting priority from some instruments of national power to others. Consider two illustrations of an adjustment in means precipitated by the recent change in the security environment. First, many observers believe that in an interdependent world economic tools for achieving national objectives have become more effective than military ones, so greater attention must be paid to the strategic use of tools such as boycotts, most-favored-nation status, free-trade agreements, and technological advantage. Second, in both of the post–Cold War efforts to adjust the military means to the security environment (the Cheney-Powell "Base Force" and the 1993 "Bottom-Up Review"), the means were adjusted before a new military strategy was fully developed.[3]

*Revise the strategy*. Containment, the grand strategy that guided the West through the Cold War, is no longer applicable. Replacing it has been difficult. Some favor a strategy of collective security, with broad reliance on international institutions such as the United Nations. Others advocate a strategy of selective engagement, focusing more narrowly on critical threats to U.S. national interests. Whatever the ultimate result, such a shift in U.S. strategy will have major implications for all the other variables. In theory, there are many possible ways to achieve any given objective with the resources available; the strategist must pick the best one.

*Reevaluate the risk of failure*. It is inevitable that national security analysts will disagree about the risks. As an example, a planner assuming that

National Guard brigades can be activated and fully trained in a short period of time will see little risk in reducing active-duty units; a colleague who rejects that assumption will be uneasy about such cuts. Another source of discomfort is the potential for "war stoppers," obstacles that make impossible a vital course of action. For example, over the coming decade logistical constraints could well frustrate otherwise brilliant plans and strategies. Finally, the degree of confidence also depends crucially on the nature of the threats and the national interests at stake. Weapons of mass destruction, for example, tend to create greater levels of anxiety than terrorism or conventional conflict. Such examples suggest that risk, as used in this model, cannot be quantified; rather, it is the "comfort level" that senior planners experience as they assess the key variables.

## Alternative Approaches to Force Planning

Although the Bartlett model provides a structure for examining national security, practitioners routinely approach force planning and strategic development from different perspectives. Each approach accentuates one variable or aspect at the expense of others. These alternatives have evolved over the years and are given different relative emphasis in different sectors of the national security assessment and decision-making process.

*Top-Down.* National interests and objectives "drive" the "top-down" approach to force planning; it, in turn, focuses principally on a nation's grand or national security strategy. This approach is strongly hierarchical, dominated by a downward flow of key documents through successive levels of decision making. A top-down approach has several strengths. First, it helps strategists and force planners concentrate on ends. Second, it provides a systematic way to think through requirements from a broad, or "macro," perspective. Third, it emphasizes the relationship among the supporting instruments of national power—economic, political, and military—each of which requires its own strategy for achieving the higher-level goals.

Finally, a great virtue of the top-down approach is that strategies can be broken down into sets of key "descriptors." If rightly selected, these are more than mere labels or slogans. They should crystallize *how* the strategy will be executed, using only a few words that are as precise and crisp as possible. Higher-level descriptors should serve as criteria for lower-level choices, strategies, and evaluations of force structure, all of which then create lower-level descriptors. For example, the 1994 National Security Strategy made effective use of two important descriptors: Engagement and Enlargement. They were chosen to replace the Cold War descriptor of Containment, and they reflected months of intense debate within the administration.

Whether or not one agrees with that strategy and these descriptors, they provided guidance on how national security objectives would be achieved. The 1996 National Security Strategy declared that the "three central components" (which we would call descriptors) of the strategy of Engagement and Enlargement were: "maintaining a strong defense capability and employing effective diplomacy to promote cooperative security measures"; to "open foreign markets and spur global economic growth"; and "promotion of democracy abroad." For the purposes of military strategists and force planners, "maintaining a strong defense capability" led to such lower-level descriptors as "Credible Overseas Presence," "Countering Weapons of Mass Destruction," "Contributing to Multilateral Peace Operations," "Supporting Counterterrorism Efforts," and maintaining forces "sufficient, in concept with regional allies, to help defeat aggression in two nearly simultaneous regional conflicts."[4] The challenge to the force planner is then to craft a force structure that will support these descriptors.

There are certain pitfalls associated with this approach. First, it generally considers possible constraints only late in the planning process. Consequently, when dollar, technological, or other limits are applied, the distance between desires and constraints is likely to be so great that major adjustments among the ends and means become necessary. A second concern is rigidity; because this approach is hierarchical, it can lead lower-level planners to take for granted the validity of higher-level objectives and strategy—even when they deserve to be challenged. A final problem is the degree of openness, or public awareness, of national security strategies. On the one hand, public exposure and debate are essential for achieving consensus and support in a democracy; they are even legally mandated by the Congress. Yet at the same time, specific details may be so sensitive that, for reasons of security, they cannot be publicly stated.

*Bottom-Up.* Existing military capability drives the "bottom-up" approach to force planning.[5] It tends to emphasize improving existing capabilities and weapon systems, with particular regard to current operational issues. It is related to military operational planning, since both concepts use current force structure as a basic reference; however, the differences between them are important. The matrix of table 1 shows how force planning and operational planning interrelate.

A major advantage of the bottom-up approach is that it emphasizes the "real" world. Strategists and planners are compelled to focus on how potential adversaries can be handled with existing forces; doing so militates against presuming future capabilities that may never materialize. Focusing on current capability can also improve strategies and operational plans. On the other hand, too much emphasis on a bottom-up approach can result in neglect of the future and may frustrate long-term goals or creativity. Another pitfall is a tendency to lose sight of the "big picture"; local or theater considerations may be allowed to dominate when an integrated global view is required.

*Scenario.* The "scenario" approach to force planning is situationally driven. The planner starts with a well defined set of conditions at the national, theater, regional, or global level and then postulates a problem or crisis. A fully developed scenario usually combines a large amount of current, real-world information with elements or assumptions of established plans. These frequently include warning and mobilization times, force levels, and, where appropriate, military campaign intentions.

## Table 1
### Force Planning Compared to Operational Planning

| Criteria | Force Planning | Operational Planning |
|---|---|---|
| Purpose | Structuring Forces | Fighting Forces |
| Orientation | Global/Regional | Theater/Local |
| Input | Future: | Existing: |
|  | Forces | Forces |
|  | Threats | Threats |
|  | Objectives | Objectives |
|  | Strategies | Strategies |
|  | Risk of Failure | Risk of Failure |
| Output | Planned and | Contingency/ |
|  | Programmed Forces | War Plans |
| Biases | Development | Deployment |
|  | Modernization | Employment |
|  | Force Structure | Readiness |
|  | Research & Development | Sustainability |

The scenario approach has three clear strengths. The first is its specific and tangible focus. If the scenario is a conventional Iraqi attack against Kuwait, fairly precise planning can be undertaken once major assumptions are made. If simultaneous scenarios are anticipated, such as Korea and Iraq, even more specific planning can result. A further advantage is that it encourages clear priorities; national interests dictate that some regions, theaters, or countries be considered more important than others. A third strength is the dynamic nature of a scenario, in which events are sequential and time lines are specified. However, there are limitations to this approach. The world rarely conforms to a planner's expectations. Also, scenarios tend to take on a life of their own; after all the work involved in planning them, there is a natural reluctance to challenge their basic rationales. Thus such key assumptions as warning times and mobilization rates may become absolutes, and hypotheses about enemy doctrine may be treated as facts. Finally, scenarios tend to be retrospective, reliving old crises rather than exploring new challenges.

***Threat.*** The "threat" approach involves identifying potential opponents and assessing their capabilities. The point of departure is often an assessment of the balance of capabilities between adversaries. Recent changes in the security environment make the threat approach to force planning more difficult than during the Cold War. It does, however, have three strengths, the most important being that it keeps the focus on potential adversaries. Secondly, it considers both the "macro" level of the global balance of power and the "micro" level of specific conflict situations. Finally, the threat approach reminds both strategists and force planners that military capabilities do count in warfare; it requires them to consider serious assessments and devise realistic scenarios.

Of its pitfalls, the most prominent is the difficulty of determining what constitutes a valid threat. Perhaps no other single aspect of the art of the strategist and force planner is more controversial. To deal with this challenge, other terms (such as "danger," employed in the *Bottom-Up Review*) have sometimes been used. Threat-based planning is inherently reactive, and analysts may have grave difficulty adapting to sudden changes in the international environment. An additional problem of the threat-driven technique lies in its bias toward quantitative data, such as numbers of people, units of energy, or types and quantities of weapon systems. These figures can be misleading in terms of overall unit or weapon system combat power, and this tendency may result in overlooking, underrating, or overestimating important qualitative factors such as training, experience, leadership, morale, or strategy. A related weakness is a superficial accounting of military force; any war is an extraordinarily complex interaction of people, equipment, and organizations, but threat assessments often employ simplistic numerical comparisons such as tank-versus-tank or tanks-versus-antitank weapons.

***The Capability/Mission.*** The "mission" approach is functionally based, examining the capabilities of friendly forces irrespective of plausible threats or of crisis or combat conditions. The force planner starts with such broad categories of military activities as strategic deterrence, power projection, or overseas presence. These categories may then be broken down into more specific activities, such as joint strike, air superiority, strategic mobility, sea control, and ground maneuver. Even more specific mission subsets might be suppression of enemy air defenses, counter-battery artillery fire, and mine countermeasures. This approach provides a way of looking at capabilities across general categories of wartime activity.

The capabilities/mission approach has a number of advantages. First, it fosters realistic and detailed appraisal of the capabilities of any military

**Table 2**
**Summary of Alternatives**

| Approaches | "Drivers" | Strengths | Pitfalls |
|---|---|---|---|
| Top-Down | Interests/ Objectives/ Strategies | Concentrates on ends Systematic (macro-view) Integrates tools of power | Ignores constraints too long Fear of challenging higher levels Public awareness of strategy |
| Bottom-Up | Current military capability | Emphasizes real world Helps improve current war plans | Neglects future Loses big picture |
| Scenario | Situation/ Circumstances | Specific focus Encourages priorities Dynamic—handles time well | World is unpredictable Takes on life of its own Tends to be retrospective |
| Threat | Opponents | Focus on future Balance of power Emphasizes military capability | Too simplistic Adapts poorly to sudden change Inherently retrospective Biased by quantitative data |
| Capability/ Mission | Function | Realistic appraisal of capabilities Sets priorities Confronts uncertainty | Tendency toward suboptimization May ignore higher goals Understates friendly strengths |
| Hedging | Minimizing risk | Assures balance and flexibility | Exaggerates rivals' capabilities Worst-case scenarios/high cost |
| Technology | Superior systems | Stresses knowledge and creativity Saves lives and cuts casualities Force multiplier | Often costly for small gain High risk Works against balanced forces |
| Fiscal | Budget | Supports democratic process Requires setting priorities | May not reflect security environment Worsens cyclical spending Leads to "fair sharing" |

organization, which is especially useful with respect to future threats, since it allows friendly forces to maximize their strengths and exploit enemy weaknesses in advance. Even if no threat can be identified, this approach allows force planners to set priorities and correct apparent imbalances. The primary shortcoming of the capability/mission approach is a tendency toward suboptimization. Higher-level goals may be ignored and more creative ways of fighting dismissed through institutional inertia or infatuation with traditional warfare specialties.

*Hedging.* The idea here is to prepare fully (indeed, over-prepare) for any conceivable tasking of military force. This technique seeks redundancy of systems, anticipates a wide range of employment options, and demands a balanced force, i.e., one that can deal with a wide range of contingencies. Different countries facing diverse threats will hedge their strategies and force structures in different ways. The U.S. tends to hedge its force structure by providing for capabilities across the entire spectrum of conflict, from humanitarian assistance operations to nuclear war.

An emphasis on hedging has merit in that it directly confronts uncertainty about the future. History provides examples of forces tailored for specific purposes that were overcome by unforeseen events. Consequently, hedging seeks to assure both balance and flexibility. On the other hand, it tends to understate friendly strengths, exaggerate the capabilities and the hostility of potential rivals, and thus drive planners toward worst-case scenarios. Its biggest fault, not surprisingly, is that its recommendations are very costly.

*Technology.* The "technology" emphasis rests upon the belief that conflict can best be deterred and aggression stopped by fielding systems superior to those of potential enemies. The Manhattan Project of World War II, the post–Vietnam War development of precision-guided munitions, and current enthusiasm for "information warfare" all illustrate the technological optimism of U.S. strategists and force planners. The greatest advantage of this approach is that it capitalizes on knowledge and individual creativity, basic strengths of a post-industrial economy. Moreover, it offers the potential of saving lives and reducing casualties. Finally, skillful development of advanced technology may provide significant military leverage (that is, a "force multiplier" or "force enhancer").

There are, nonetheless, definite pitfalls. One is the risk of paying too much money for too small a gain, especially once a technology matures. The opposite problem is that huge investments are required to achieve revolutionary breakthroughs but do not guarantee such successes. Even when development is successful, the technological approach often leads to a dramatically smaller force of much costlier platforms. For all these reasons, it may channel too great a proportion of defense resources into too few, overly specialized programs at the expense of balance, flexibility, and greater numbers.

*Fiscal.* The "fiscal" approach is driven by the budget. Overall dollar constraints are fixed at the outset by such nonmilitary considerations as some maximum permissible percentage of Gross Domestic Product, the exigencies of deficit reduction, or the demands of other sectors of the federal budget (e.g., entitlements). The strength of the fiscal approach is that it supports the democratic process—that is, it specifies defense resources in light of the overall economy, competing national requirements, and public perceptions of the security environment. It also requires planners to set priorities, thus avoiding uncon-strained thinking and fostering fiscal discipline both within and among a nation's armed services. A major weakness is that the fiscal approach may not reflect the international security environment, resulting in a significant lag between military capabilities and emerging threats. Secondly, reassessment of threats to national interests—which happens regularly in a democratic country—tends to worsen the cyclical character of defense spending, which frustrates rational long-term planning. At its worst, this technique may lead to the unwise retention of a traditional "fair share" apportionment of funds among the services and defense agencies rather than an integrated and rational allocation that takes account of the greatly changed security situation. Thus it may increase the potential for interservice rivalry and suboptimization.

Practitioners of strategy and force planning should be sensitive to the strengths and pitfalls of each of these approaches. The various planning focuses tend to produce different solutions and choices. Awareness of these differences can help strategists and planners stay in touch with reality. Table 2 summarizes these alternatives, what drives them, and their strengths and pitfalls.

## A Challenging Art

The primary purpose of this article has been to provide a simple but powerful tool (the Bartlett model) to help students of strategy and force planning. There are many strengths to the model: its very simplicity makes it easy to remember; it focuses on the most important variables and helps in their analysis; and, finally, it stresses the iterative nature of the national security decision making process. The second purpose has been to consider some of the approaches to strategy and force planning actually used by practitioners. Each was taken in isolation to make clear its individual merits and limitations. However, during an actual planning cycle all of the ap-proaches will probably be used to arrive at, or review, decisions. To use this model and these approaches wisely can constitute a real and challenging art.

Finally, the article argues that strategists and force planners must keep a number of practical considerations in mind:
- Be sure the game is worth playing;
- Integrate a full range of strategic perspectives;
- Meld force planning approaches;
- Identify key strategy and force planning "descriptors;"
- Set priorities, resolve conflicting demands upon resources, and eliminate mismatches;
- Assess the risk of failure and subsequent action;

- Select the best solution, considering economic, political, and military tools of national power.

That strategy and force planning is an art is a fact worth remembering. It implies that students, practitioners, and critics should recognize that there is more than one approach to formulating strategy and making decisions about future military force structure. Secondly, it underscores the fact that different approaches may lead to alternative solutions. The authors believe that using the Bartlett model and the other ideas described in this article will contribute to the development of better national security strategies, plans, decisions, and force choices.

---

## Notes

1. Referring to this figure as a "model" springs from the authors' view of its value as a simple graphic representation of a very complex, highly dynamic, continually iterating process. We use the word in the sense of a "description or analogy used to help visualize something (as an atom) that cannot be directly observed"—in this case the complex strategy and force planning process. (See *Webster's Ninth New Collegiate Dictionary*, Springfield, MA: Merriam-Webster, 1983, p. 762.) It is a simplification that permits analysis and understanding of a far more complex reality (in this case the process this article attempts to describe). Our "model," like many models, conveys the sense of the changes that must result when one or more of the variables or parameters in the real world is modified. A model can sometimes be helpful in predicting what will occur in the real world in response to changes (but often scaling problems or non-quantifiable parameters inhibit this type of use.) The word "framework," a possible alternative term—defined as "a basic structure (as of ideas)" (see *Webster's* p. 489)—we believe is a more passive term which does not as successfully convey the sense of dynamic interplay in the process, which is what we are attempting to capture in our "model."

2. For the most recent edition, see William J. Clinton, *A National Security Strategy of Engagement and Enlargement* (Washington: The White House, February 1996).

3. Secretary of Defense Dick Cheney stated in his *Annual Report to the President and the Congress, January 1991*, "Force reductions were begun in FY [fiscal year] 1990–1991 and will continue during the Department's multiyear defense program. Projected force structure reductions from FY 1990 to FY 1995 include a drop in Army divisions from 28 (18 active) to 18 (12 active), and a drop in Air Force tactical fighter wing equivalents from 36 (24 in the active component) to 26 (15 active). Battle force ships will be reduced to 451, compared to the old goal of 600 ships." (Washington: U.S. Govt. Print. Off. [hereafter GPO], 1991, p. ix). This force structure was called the "Base Force." The Chairman of the Joint Chiefs of Staff, Colin Powell, did not issue the supporting *National Military Strategy* until a year later, in January 1992. Moving away from the Cold War stress on a global strategy, it shifted to a "regionally oriented" strategy. It declared that "this new strategy is built upon the four key foundations of the National Defense Strategy: Strategic Deterrence and Defense, Forward Presence, Crisis Response, and Reconstitution" (p. 6. and Powell's introduction). For the final details of the Base Force see Cheney's *Annual Report to the President and the Congress, February 1992* (Washington: GPO, 1992), pp. vii and 1.

The "Bottom-Up Review" (BUR) was a product of the new Clinton administration. It further reduced the force structure to 10 active Army divisions (37 National Guard brigades—15 with enhanced readiness), 13 active Air Force wings (7 reserve wings), and 346 Navy ships by FY 1999. The initial concepts underlying this force structure appeared in Les Aspin, Secretary of Defense, *Report on the Bottom-Up Review* (Washington: Department of Defense, October 1993). It briefly sketched a strategy "to win two major regional conflicts that occur nearly simultaneously." More specific numbers for the BUR force structure appeared in Les Aspin, *Annual Report to the President and the Congress, January 1994* (Washington: GPO, 1994), p. 27. However, a fully developed National Military Strategy of the United States (signed by the Chairman of the JCS) was late in coming.

4. Clinton, pp. 3, and 13–14.

5. The reader will notice that we use the term "bottom-up" in a different sense than did the BUR. We would characterize the BUR as a combination of "threat" and "scenario" approaches to force planning.

and how could agencies make money at it? What would be the effect of suddenly popular new communications media, such as fax machines? A set of scenarios would have described the range of worlds that might emerge by looking carefully at important elements of the world in the early 1980s.

In 1987, the shock began to hit. Ad agency profits began to decline, people found themselves laid off, and more and more agencies had to haggle over fees with their clients. Most ad people assumed the crisis was temporary; that it would be followed by a new status quo. Today, in 1990, ad agencies are in yet deeper economic trouble, still hoping for a turnaround, and still refusing to look at the opportunities—as well as the pitfalls—in the rise of new technology. I know this because, along with several other people, I began work in the late 1980s on a set of scenarios about the effects of new technologies on the media business. We found clients from every conceivable segment: a broadcast network, a telephone company, a movie production studio, and a consumer products company that places major advertisements. All but one of the advertising agencies we invited to join us in this study of its own future weren't interested. To judge from our conversations with them, they are afraid of what they might learn, as if the cost of ignorance were smaller.

Scenarios are *not* predictions. It is simply not possible to predict the future with certainty. An old Arab proverb says that, "he who predicts the future lies even if he tells the truth." Rather, scenarios are vehicles for helping people learn. Unlike traditional business forecasting or market research, they present alternative images; they do not merely extrapolate the trends of the present. One common trend, for instance, is the U.S. birthrate. In the early 1970s, it hovered around 3 million births per year; forecasters at the U.S. Census Bureau projected that this "trend" would continue forever. Schools, which had been rushed into construction during the baby boom of the fifties and early sixties, were now closed down and sold. Policymakers did not consider that the birthrate might rise again suddenly. But a scenario might have considered the likelihood that original baby boom children, reaching their late thirties, would suddenly have children of their own. In 1979, the U.S. birthrate began to rise; it is now, in 1990, almost back to the 4 million of the fifties. Demographers also failed to anticipate that immigration would accelerate. To keep up with demand, the state of California (which had been closing schools in the late 1970s) must build a classroom every day for the next seven years.

Often, managers prefer the illusion of certainty to understanding risks and realities. If the forecaster fails in his task, how can the manager be blamed? But in the long run, this denial of uncertainty sets the stage for surprises, shattering the manager's confidence in his or her ability to look ahead. Scenarios allow a manager to say, "I am prepared for whatever happens." *It is this ability to act with a knowledgeable sense of risk and reward that separates both the business executive and the wise individual from a bureaucrat or a gambler.*

## The Explorations of Pierre Wack

Scenarios first emerged following World War II, as a method for military planning. The U.S. Air Force tried to imagine what its opponents might do, and to prepare alternative strategies. In the 1960s, Herman Kahn, who had been part of the Air Force effort, refined scenarios as a tool for business prognostication. He became America's top futurist, predicting the inevitability of growth and prosperity. But scenarios reached a new dimension in the early 1970s, with the work of Pierre Wack. In 1968, Wack was a planner in the London offices of Royal Dutch/Shell, the international oil enterprise, in a newly formed department called Group Planning.

Pierre and other planners at Royal Dutch/Shell (notably his colleague Ted Newland) were looking for events that might affect the price of oil, which had been more or less steady since World War II. Oil was, in fact, seen as a strategic commodity; consuming nations would do what they could to keep the price low, since the prosperity of their economies depended on oil. But there were several significant events in the air. First, the United States was beginning to exhaust its oil reserves. Meanwhile, American demand for oil was steadily rising. And the emerging Organization of Petroleum Exporting Countries was showing signs of flexing its political muscle. Most of these countries were Islamic, and they bitterly resented Western support of Israel after the 1967 six-day Arab-Israeli war.

Looking closely at the situation, Pierre and Ted realized that Arabs *could* demand much higher prices for their oil. There was every reason that they *would*. The only uncertainty was when. One could not know for sure, but it seemed likely to happen before 1975, when old oil price agreements were due to be renegotiated. They wrote up two sets of scenarios—each a complete set of stories about the future, with tables of projected price figures. One story presented the conventional wisdom at Royal Dutch/Shell: somehow, the oil price would stay stable. In order for that to happen, a miracle would have to occur; new oil fields, for instance, might have to appear in non-Arab countries. The second scenario looked at the more plausible future—an oil price crisis sparked by OPEC. Shell's directors listened carefully as Pierre presented these two scenarios. The directors understood the implications: they realized that they might have to change their business drastically.

Pierre waited for a change in behavior at Royal Dutch/Shell; but no change in behavior came. That's when he developed his breakthrough: scenarios, as he later put it, should be "more than water on a stone." To be truly effective, they had to "change our managers' view of reality."

In this new type of scenario, there were no more simple tales of possible futures. Instead, Pierre described the full ramifications of possible oil price shocks. He tried to make people feel those shocks. "Prepare!" he told oil refiners and marketers. "You are about to become a low-growth industry." He warned the drillers and explorers who sought new oil to get ready for the possibility that OPEC countries would take over their oil fields. Most importantly, Pierre vividly pointed to the forces in the world, and what sorts of influences those forces had to have. He helped managers imagine the decisions they might have to make as a result.

And he was just in time. In October 1973, after the "Yom Kippur" war in the Middle East, there *was* an oil price shock. The "energy crisis" burst upon the world. Of the major oil companies, only Shell was prepared emotionally for the change. The company's executives responded quickly. During the following years, Shell's fortunes rose. From one of the weaker of the "Seven Sisters," the seven largest global oil companies, it became one of the two largest (after Exxon) and, arguably, the most profitable. Pierre was no longer concerned with prognostication; his concern was the mind-set of decision-makers. It was no accident that his 1985 article on scenarios in the *Harvard Business Review* was titled, "The Gentle Art of Reperceiving," rather than "How to Predict the Future." To operate in an uncertain world, people needed to be able to *reperceive*—to question their assumptions about the way the world works, so that they could see the world more clearly. The purpose of scenarios is to help yourself change your view of reality—to match it up more closely with reality as it is, and reality as it is going to be.

*The end result, however, is not an accurate picture of tomorrow, but better decisions about the future.* The planner and the executive are partners in taking a long view. Thus, while Pierre Wack's seminal role is at the heart of this story, it is thoughtful and farsighted Shell executives who invited him into that role in the first place, provided him with the resources he needed, and paid him the compliment of listening to him and taking him seriously. Surrounding Pierre was an exceptionally able team, including Ted Newland and Napier Collyns, who were critical to the success of the scenario process. In this book I will focus more on the role of those whose day-to-day activities lead them to spend time taking a long view. The real value comes from the interaction with those who must decide and act.

Pierre Wack was not interested in predicting the future. His goal was the liberation of people's insights. His methods were the inspiration for the art of the long view. . . .

## Creating Scenario Building Blocks

In the days when pharaohs ruled Egypt, a temple stood far up the Nile, beyond the cataracts in Nubia, in what is now the northern deserts of the Sudan. Three tributaries joined together in that region to form the Nile, which flowed down one thousand miles to produce a miraculous event each year, the flooding of its river basin, which permitted Egyptian farmers to grow crops in the hot, rainless midsummer.

Every spring, the temple priests gathered at the river's edge to check the color of the water. If it were clear, the White Nile, which flowed from Lake Victoria through the Sudanese swamps, would dominate the flow. The flooding would be mild, and late; farmers would produce a minimum of crops. If the stream appeared dark, the stronger waters of the Blue Nile, which joined the White Nile at Khartoum, would prevail. The flood would rise enough to saturate the fields and provide a bountiful harvest. Finally, if the stream showed dominance by the green-brown waters of the Atbara, which rushed down from the Ethiopian highlands, then the floods would be early and catastrophically high. The crops might drown; indeed, the Pharaoh might have to use his grain stores as a reserve.

Each year, the priests sent messengers to inform the king of the color of the water. They may also have used lights and smoke signal to carry word downstream. The Pharaoh then knew how prosperous the farmers in his kingdom would be, and how much he could raise in taxes. Thus, he knew whether he could afford to conquer more territory. As Pierre Wack (who often told this story at Shell) would say, the priests of the Sudanese Nile were the world's first long-term forecasters. They understood the meaning of predetermined elements and critical uncertainties.

The process of building scenarios starts with the same thing that the priests did—looking for driving forces, the forces that influence the outcome of events. In this case, one such force was the rain. It fell upstream on the Nile's tributaries, and affected the balance between them. That, in turn, influenced the fate of thousands of people whom the Pharaoh might conquer that year. There was a second driving force, as well—the dependence on Nile flooding to grow crops. Had the Egyptians had irrigation canals and fertilizer, they could have planted crops further out in the desert. They would not have had to worry about the river flow at all.

***Driving Forces: What We Know We Care About***. Every enterprise, personal or commercial, is propelled by particular key factors. Some of them are within the enterprise: your workforce and goals. Others, such as government regulation, come from outside. But many outside factors, in particular, are not intuitively obvious. The color of the water's stream made it easy to guess its effect on the floods downstream; if all the rivers were the same color, the priests might never have understood. Similarly, the impact of government regulation on businesses is obvious, but there are many less obvious external factors as well.

Identifying and assessing these fundamental factors is both the starting point and one of the objectives of the scenario method.

In other words, driving forces are the elements that move the plot of a scenario, that determine the story's outcome. In a mystery story, the motive is a driving force; indeed much fictional detective work consists of figuring out a credible driving force for an otherwise unexplainable murder. In adventure stories, one driving force is the quest that propels the journey. Another is the opposition—a villain, force of nature, or opposing tribe that resists the hero's quest. In *Romeo and Juliet*, the romantic love of the two young principals is one driving force. Another is the concept of filial responsibility which binds them. The third is the rivalry between the families. Without all three forces, there would be no story.

Without driving forces, there is no way to begin thinking through a scenario. They are a device for honing your initial judgment, for helping you decide which factors will be significant and which factors will not.

As a business executive thinking about the future of your company, you know that interest rates, energy prices, new technology, the behavior of the markets, and your competitors' actions all come from the outside to affect your business. But how do you find the significant driving forces among them, and the forces which underlie them? You start by taking another look at the decisions you have to make.

You will quickly see that some driving forces are critical to that decision, while others don't require much attention. Gravity and the laws of physics affect everyone's life. But you will rarely have to ponder them for scenarios. Few forces could be more boring, for example, than the fact that British Commonwealth countries speak English—until you investigate the future of French Canada or Pakistan. Trust your instincts; it is part of human nature to be interested in factors that affect the decisions we need to make.

When the founders of Smith & Hawken tools . . . asked: *Should we open a small business?* we looked first at what would affect the outcome of our decision. Our answers were all driving forces: the demographics of the United States; the availability of tools from abroad (which, in turn, was driven by the balance of payments); the importance of a home and garden in American values; and the American economy. There were other driving forces in the world at that time—for instance, the growing enmity among Arab nations—which had little to do with our story.

Often, identifying driving forces reveals the presence of deeper, more fundamental forces behind them. . . . Shell planners asked: *"Should we build a giant off-shore gas drilling platform?"* Among the driving forces we considered were the European gas market and the European gas supply. What forces influenced the European gas supply? One clear factor was European-U.S.S.R. relations. And what force influenced those relationships? One was the totalitarian, seemingly rigid politics of the Soviet Union.

Driving forces often seem obvious to one person and hidden to another. That is why I almost always compose scenarios in teams. Often, we begin this stage (after we have individually done our research) by standing before a large sheet of white paper, and brainstorming together. A year ago, I did this with a group of Pacific Gas and Electric executives. They were considering a perennial power utility question: Should they invest in building more power plants? Or should they instead try to reduce the need for more power by promoting energy-efficiency? Both paths would cost the same, and result in the same amount of available energy. But they needed to know which driving forces existed, to make one choice or the other preferable.

Some factors were obvious. Every executive in the room was keenly aware of twenty-year-old environmentalist resistance to nuclear power in California. After years of bitter antagonism, the PG&E executives were now coming to accept the fact that the movement would not go away, and that it would have long-lasting political impact.

Less obvious was the force of immigration—the fact that California was becoming a more multicultural society. If the company promoted energy-efficiency, it would henceforth depend more on the nature of its customer than on the economics of nuclear technology. Promoting energy-efficiency would mean communicating with millions of Philippine, Vietnamese, and El Salvadoran homeowners. That meant the human capital of the company had to change. There was not a single Tagalog speaker, for example, among PG&E's executive ranks—so far. If the company chose energy-efficiency, it might need to hire some.

Another driving force was economic volatility. Everyone in the room could see signs of distress: the stock market turbulence, the U.S. deficits, increasing inflation. As large borrowers of capital, big power projects are keenly sensitive to inflation and interest rates. The economic volatility increased the risk of massive investments—it made the energy-efficiency side look better.

Finally, the company's own growing appreciation of the greenhouse effect was another driving force. PG&E had come to realize that a large-scale investment in energy-efficiency—in which it would help customers make individual investments in, for example, insulation—would not only help its public relations, but would stabilize California's energy demands. Whatever happened to oil prices or nuclear power, the state would be able to manage. Ultimately, PG&E decided that it could handle the necessary cultural change. The effects of this decision will increasingly change California. In other words, PG&E's decision will itself become a driving force.

Whenever I look for driving forces I first run through a familiar litany of categories:

- Society

- Technology
- Economics
- Politics
- Environment

In nearly every situation, I find forces from each of these arenas which make a difference in the story.

For example, consider a decision which many large book publishing companies are making. Today, publishers print massive overruns of popular "mass-market" paperback books. Bookstores order more than they can sell, and place them on shelves for a few weeks, knowing that a few books will take off as bestsellers. The rest are returned to publishers, which refund their cost to bookstores and pulp the books. It's a wasteful, costly practice which puts pressure (some feel unnecessary pressure) on writers, bookstores, *and* publishers.

But under what scenarios could that practice be different? To answer, we need to analyze the driving forces which exist to keep the practice going—and the potential forces which could influence it to change:

- **Social**: The continuing wave of population growth is perhaps the strongest driving force of our time. It suggests a continuing market for books, especially because people tend to read more as they get older. Literacy in America, while hard to measure, is generally considered to be declining: another growing force. A third force is the increasing cultural diversity of America, which continues to affect book publishing by opening new markets and changing the demographics of old ones.

- **Technological**: The continuous improvement and innovation in electronic media may shrink the audience for books. It may also have more subtle effects on the distribution of books; on the ability, for instance, to build high-speed laser printers in bookshops that download books over telephone wires, print them, and bind them while people wait. Meanwhile, improvements in paper shredding and recycling technologies may make it less expensive to shred books.

- **Economic**: The cost of transportation may add to the cost of printing and pulping excess books. It, in turn, depends on the cost of oil and on inflation. The 1980s brought another economic driving force in some companies: the amount of the debt added to publishing expenses after a leveraged buyout.

- **Political:** Laws affect every endeavor. One important ruling affecting U.S. book sales is the Thor Power Tools vs. Internal Revenue Service decision of 1981. By allowing the IRS to tax publishers on their back inventory in warehouses, it added pressure to destroy unsold books, instead of saving them to sell later. Another might be restrictions placed by countries (such as Great Britain) on importing American books for sale. Internal politics can matter as well. Thus a third political force would be the pressure within any corporation to continue existing practices, rather than experimenting with new ones. Book publishers have invested heavily in developing and promoting these mass-market distribution channels.

• **Environmental:** The impact of ecological damage on human affairs, and the increasing public perception of ecological harm. In the long run the cost of paper and the resulting books will be significantly affected by the growing pressure to restrict logging practices.

Having identified driving forces, I usually step back to sort through them. Which are significant and will actually influence events? Which are irrelevant? The international restrictions on imports, for example, can be ignored for this domestic book publishing problem—*unless* it's plausible to think that these restrictions might change, and books returned from bookstores can be shipped profitably to other countries.

Some forces are clearly significant: the cost of transportation, and declining literacy rates. But their effects may be ambiguous. Declining literacy rates, for example, could imply a shrinking market for paperback books—or a growing market, compared with hardback books. To learn which effect it will have, you will probably have to return to the hunting and gathering phase, researching whether book outlets are expanding in the United States. If they *are* expanding, are mass-market outlets growing more quickly or slowly than independent specialty shops?

You may not immediately see any influence from some forces, but don't rush to discard them. Environmental influences, for example, seem remote from book publishing considerations; but conceivably a forest shortage would raise the price of paper. Even more conceivably, a *perceived* deforestation crisis could lead to public pressure for more efficient publishing. A few farsighted publishers, realizing that more efficient practices would save money for them in the long run, might find themselves promoting environmentalism for the most self-interested reasons.

As individuals, or even as companies, we have little control over driving forces. Our leverage for dealing with them comes from recognizing them, and understanding their effect. Little by little, then, as we act within society, our actions contribute to new driving forces which in turn will change the world once more.

*Warning: Ambiguity Ahead*. After "identifying and exploring the driving forces," one must uncover the "predetermined elements" and the "critical uncertainties." There is a temptation to assume that these are all separate categories, painted in three distinct colors. That, alas, is not the case. (I say "alas" because then scenarios would be much easier to explain. However, they would also be much less illuminating to use.) There are overlaps among them. But you mull over them for different purposes, in different ways. Weaving together these conceptual building blocks you are deepening your understanding of the world by considering the elements of your scenarios. Once your understanding of the dynamics and patterns of the situation is clearer, then you go on to write the scenarios.

Some scenario-builders—including Pierre Wack—refuse to give definitions for any elements at all. They believe that any definition would trivialize the subtleties of the process. Scenario creation is not a reductionist process; it is an art, as is story-telling.

I am willing to try to offer a few definitions. But as I go on to describe the other two building blocks—predetermined elements and critical uncertainties—I warn you not to focus on the definitions. Focus, instead, on how you perceive elements in various situations. There is indeed something almost mystical about human understanding of events. If you have trouble distinguishing driving forces from predetermined elements, and those from uncertainties, think of a story important to *your* life and business. Create an image of the elements in that story. They will come to you. For example in my business the spread of sophisticated desktop electronics is a key driving force. I can be sure that over the coming decade our technological capabilities will continue to accelerate as new computing technology becomes ever smaller, faster, and cheaper. However, I can't be sure how rapidly that new technology will appear on the desktops of the companies we work with. My strategy will be governed by the intersection of the predetermined elements of accelerating technology and the critical uncertainty of the pace of innovation in the giant multinationals we work with.

*Predetermined Elements: What We Know We Know*. Put yourself now in the position of a priest on the river, watching the water turn brown and green. To warn the Pharaoh of a devastating flood required supreme confidence. Being wrong was breaking a religious sacrament and would also, no doubt, have meant losing one's life. They had that confidence, however, because the fate of the floods that year was predetermined. Nothing could change its impact on the crops, even though the impact would not be felt for months later. The priests may or may not have known *why* the color of the water affected the power of the flood. They may or may not have been aware of the driving force—the rainfall pattern which caused one river, or another, to dominate. But they knew the predetermined elements of flooding as well as they knew anything.

The modern era has its predetermined elements as well. General Motors and American Telephone and Telegraph both tried to reshape their businesses during the 1980s. Both lived out their troubles in a public, almost humiliating way. Analysts have predicted deeper troubles for both. Yet their situations are very different. General Motors could collapse from its current troubles, but AT&T could not. It has a guaranteed flow of cash from its long-distance telephone network. It so dominates the long-distance market, and that market is so profitable, that any time AT&T's top management need capital they can merely slow down their long-distance equipment maintenance. Soon, they have enough cash to cover their crisis and speed up their maintenance again. Thus, in any scenario we can think of for AT&T during the next few years, its survival is assured. In order to imagine AT&T failing, you have to imagine something happening to destroy that predetermined flow of money. Imagining such a change, in turn, would mean looking more closely at the forces that drive the system.

Predetermined elements do not depend on any particular chain of events. If it seems certain, no matter which scenario comes to pass, then it is a predetermined element. In 1982 at Shell, we came to believe that there would be a substantial United States Government budget deficit throughout the 1980s. We reached that conclusion after examining the prevailing American political logic of the day. The two largest components of the American government budget, defense spending and Social Security, were rising uncontrollably. The American public supported both increases. Four months after Reagan took office, he tried to propose a slight delay in cost-of-living increases for Social Security. The proposal was defeated in the Senate, one hundred votes to none. The third biggest budget component—interest payments on the deficit itself—could not be controlled.

Other governments might have raised taxes, but American anti-tax feeling was (and remains) too strong. The origins of this anti-tax feeling, incidentally, probably stemmed from another driving force: the reality that, for most middle-class Americans, purchasing power had hardly changed in ten (now almost twenty) years. The Reagan administration cut everything it could: space, education, welfare, transportation, nondefense research, infrastructure maintenance. The net result of the cuts was insignificant in a 200-billion-dollar deficit. America was caught in political gridlock: Americans wanted to cut taxes and increase spending. If that continued, interest on the deficit would have to become the largest single element of the budget. The government would be forced to borrow abroad. As a result of that, the dollar would eventually fall, interest rates would rise, and government bonds would be devalued.

That, ultimately, is exactly what happened. The Japanese bought the U.S. bonds, let them be devalued, and have supported the U.S. deficit ever since. Once our assumption was in place we could agree to assume a big deficit in every scenario we wrote for the 1980s. This contradicted every economist we talked to; they all said the deficit could not be sustained past 1984.

Identifying such elements is a tremendous confidence builder—not in the U.S. political system, but in your own decisions. You can commit to some policies and feel sure about them. There are several useful strategies for looking for predetermined elements:

• **slow-changing phenomena:** such things include the growth of populations, the building of physical infrastructure, and the development of resources.

• **constrained situations:** for example, the Japanese must (and will) maintain a positive trade balance because they have 120 million people on four islands who do not possess the resources to feed, clothe, warm, or transport themselves.

• **in the pipeline:** today, for example, we know almost exactly how large the teenage population of the nineties in the United States will be. All of them have been born already. They are all in the pipeline already. The only uncertainty is immigration and we have a pretty good feel for that now . . . it will be high.

• **inevitable collisions:** in the deficit discussion above the inevitability of an enduring federal imbalance was created by the collision of the American voting public's absolute refusal to provide the government with higher taxes at the same time that they also refused to forego any public benefits. Once the gridlock was created there was no way out.

The most commonly recognized predetermined element, of course, is demographics, a slowly changing phenomenon. As soon as the baby boom began, it was obvious that its members would eventually age. The effects of this aging are still unclear, and many members of the "Don't trust anyone over thirty" generation denied that they too would one day be gray. Deep in their hearts, however, the baby boomers knew of the inevitability. "Will you still need me," they asked, "will you still feed me, when I'm sixty-four?"

I first realized the impact of the aging of the baby boomers in the early 1970s, while creating a scenario on new businesses for the lumber company Weyerhauser. We knew that, no matter what happened, there would be a massive opportunity in houseplants. Our three scenarios were similar to those we used to inform Smith & Hawken . . . but the outlook was even better for houseplants than for high-quality garden tools. If the economy boomed, baby boomers would invest more in their homes; along with the paintings and furniture, they'd buy plants as "indoor landscaping." If the economy collapsed into violence and incoherence, houseplants would allow frightened nature lovers to avoid the risks of going outside. Finally, if a social transformation took place, houseplants would be as much a part of it as meditation and health food. Reality turned out to be a combination of all three scenarios. Weyerhauser went into the commercial nursery business with considerable success. And I came away with a new understanding of how the marketplace of things and ideas in America was about to change.

Demographics also made it clear why perestroika was inevitable. The Soviet Union experienced a sharp decline in births during and immediately after World War II. During the 1960s and 1970s the original "baby bust" was echoed by an even greater decline than we saw in the United States. In the mid-eighties therefore it was certain that the U.S.S.R. would experience a decline in its labor force as fewer and fewer young people came of age. That would begin to turn around in the early nineties, but a short-term decline was predetermined. Gross national product depends on the size of the labor force, and the level of productivity. The Soviet Union's productivity was declining, and people were trying to get out of, not into, the U.S.S.R. When the labor force shrank, it meant the collapse of the Soviet economy.

Pundits [kept] asking why Gorbachev [was] having so much trouble jump-starting the Soviet economy. Demographics [made] it clear that he [wouldn't] succeed until after 1991. At that point, the number of twenty-year-olds [began] to rise once again.

Predetermined elements are fearful sometimes because people tend to deny them. The chickens coming home to roost is a predetermined element. So is the next payment on our loan, or a project deadline that we hoped might never arrive. Gridlock is also predetermined. To calculate the amount of gridlock in [1995], look at the number of people of driving age. Multiply it by the average number of cars per person in America. Then calculate the increase in highway mileage, based on construction projects started in the last five years. (It takes at least five years, and usually more, to build an urban highway.) Even if tomorrow the United States embarked on an unprecedented effort to build highways and mass transit systems, it would be too late; we can be certain that seven or eight large urban areas in the United States will be frozen with gridlock in the mid-1990s. . . .

***Critical Uncertainties: Dwelling-places of Our Hopes and Fears.*** For five thousand years, the waters of the Nile rose and fell predictably. The dynasty of the pharaohs declined; other governments emerged and they too declined, but the means for predicting floods remained basically the same. Then, in the early 1960s, the Aswan High Dam was built. It was a remarkable feat of engineering, five hundred miles downstream from where the fierce Atbara joined the Nile. Now if priests had still kept vigil at their temple (or government clerks a monitoring station at the same locale upstream), they would have lost their ability to foretell. Whether the water was blue, white, or green-brown, the result would be the same: the flow would reach the Aswan Dam and stop. The fate of the flood plains below is now in human hands.

One could perhaps, based on a knowledge of Egyptian politics, make an educated guess about the flooding level. It would now depend on two competing driving forces: the farmers' same need for water, and a new need by Egyptian consumers for electricity from the dam. Regulating the dam was a political act, subject to pressure from both sides. The flooding, as a result, became an "uncertainty." If you wanted to know how much money the Egyptian Government could raise in taxes from farmers this year, you could not simply tell from the color of the water. You had to find out what the people in the dam's control tower would do.

In every plan, critical uncertainties exist. Scenario-planners seek them out to prepare for them, an approach that hearkens back to old military scenarios: "We know they have to come from the east, General, but we don't know if they're traveling up the mountain or through the forest. Here's what we'll do in either case."

A critical uncertainty for Smith & Hawken was the degree to which the U.S. economy would recover from the shocks of the seventies. Although we knew the approximate numbers of our potential market, we didn't know how many of them would be prosperous enough to buy imported garden tools. In the Shell scenario, we knew the demographic pressures on the Soviet Government. We didn't know how responsive their political system could be.

*Critical uncertainties are intimately related to predetermined elements. You find them by questioning your assumptions about predetermined elements: what might cause the price of oil to rise again?* What might AT&T do to *lose* its domination over the long-distance business, and its resulting cash cow? Shell's scenarios, for example, *still* include the U.S. deficit as a predetermined element. But Shell also asks: what might happen to change the deficit? It would have to involve drastic cuts in defense spending and Social Security. Thus, the American debate over military cutbacks and the "peace dividend" is a critical uncertainty when considering scenarios for the late 1990s. Another critical uncertainty is real income growth in America. If it returned to the levels of the 1960s, people might feel more generous about taxes.

We've already seen such "miracles" take place in recent history. In the 1970s, futurists said that oil reserves would be exhausted by the 1990s. They were right about the predetermined elements: population growth and an on-going level of energy consumption at the current price. There was, however, an uncertainty that few futurists considered: would people (and institutions) be willing to change their habits if the price of oil rose? People and institutions did, and that change made a critical difference.

If gridlock, for example, becomes too onerous, could a similar change of habit occur? Would businesses institute flexible hours en masse? Would they allow "telecommuting?" Would real estate prices decline enough that people could afford to move closer to work? Or would car telephones and fax machines turn the automobile, stuck in traffic, into a portable office? We cannot know for sure, and any look ahead at gridlock could include two scenarios: one where many cities are paralyzed, and one where commuting undergoes a transformation.

I sometimes think of the relationship between predetermined elements and critical uncertainties as a choreographed dance. You cannot experience the dance just by knowing the sequence of steps that must take place. Each dancer will interpret them differently, and add his or her unpredictable decisions. Similarly (for example), you cannot completely know the nature of a labor force from the population demographics. It is uncertain how many people will pursue a job. This figure has varied a great deal in recent years, especially as more and more women began working. If boom times break out and incomes rise quickly again, will more women (or men) elect to raise families and drop out of the labor pool?

Or consider the publishing industry again. The readership population is mostly predetermined—it depends on demographics. Increasing competition from electronic media is also predetermined. Literacy is also a crucial element—but it is far from predetermined. It depends on decisions made about education during the next few years. Thus, the quality of education now will influence the print media market in the next twenty years. Yet how many book publishers have bothered to invest in improving education in any significant way?

We might create two scenarios for the publishing industry, depending on the degree of literacy. In Scenario A, a large number of literate people spend some of their time reading. Scenario B is the opposite; people become more oriented to television and radio because reading is unable to hold their attention. There is also a third possible scenario—even faster growth for print media, because more people spend their time with a variety of media which mutually reinforce each other in an increasingly closed and mediated world.

Driving forces, predetermined elements, and critical uncertainties give structure to our exploration of the future. . . .

# Chapter 4

## * * *

# The Theory & Practice of International Relations: Contending Analytical Perspectives

Andrew L. Ross

*Andrew Ross provides a brief overview of the three analytical perspectives that inform the work of international relations analysts. Realism assumes that states are the most important actors, that they are unitary as well as rational, and that national security dominates the hierarchy of international issues. Liberalism puts greater stress on the role of non-state actors, contends that the state is neither unitary nor rational, and broadens the agenda of international politics to include economic and social issues. Marxism focuses on the capitalist nature of the international system, its historical development, the dominance of advanced industrial societies and the subordination of less developed societies, and how economics shapes political events. Are realism, liberalism, and marxism mutually exclusive? Which of the three perspectives have most influenced U.S. decision makers? Which should most influence U.S. strategic choices?*

The passing of the cold war does not spell the end of the state system, nor does it mean that states will have to worry less about security than they did during the cold war. International politics will remain a fundamentally competitive activity involving states that have the capacity to inflict massive harm on each other.—John J. Mearsheimer[1]

The end of the Cold War has brought no mere adjustment among states but a novel redistribution of power among states, markets, and civil society. National governments are not simply losing autonomy in a globalizing economy. They are sharing powers—including political, social, and security roles at the core of sovereignty—with businesses, with international organizations, and with a multitude of citizens groups, known as nongovernmental organizations. . . . The absolutes of the Westphalian system—territorially fixed states where everything of value lies within some state's borders; a single, secular authority governing each territory and representing it outside its borders; and no authority above states—are all dissolving.—Jessica T. Mathews[2]

---

Andrew L. Ross is Professor of National Security Affairs at the U.S. Naval War College.

Welcome to the analytical anarchy of international relations, where no one conceptual paradigm rules. The disagreement between Mearsheimer and Mathews is only the tip of the iceberg. There is, and long has been, considerable debate among analysts about the nature of past, present, and likely future international relations. The end of the cold war has only served to heighten long-running disputes. Whether one focuses on the actors thought to be most significant, the relative importance of systemic, national, or individual levels of analysis, the evolving structure of the international system, the salience of national attributes such as democracy, the relationship between politics and economics, or the issue areas argued to be of greatest import, controversy abounds.

This controversy cannot easily be dismissed. It is not attributable simply to the unfortunate contrarieties, even perversities, exhibited by occasionally iconoclastic analysts and sporadically quirky academics. Rather, it is rooted in the contending intellectual traditions that inform analyses of international political, economic, and security affairs. The analysis of international relations is not now, indeed has never been, governed by a single dominant conceptual paradigm.[3] Instead, it has been shaped by three contending perspectives: realism, liberalism, and marxism. The conflicting and even contradictory assumptions that provide the foundation upon which these three perspectives have been erected are responsible for the analytical controversies evident in contemporary work in international relations.

International relation's three analytical traditions and the ensuing controversies are of no little import. They are not merely academic curiosities that can be safely ignored by men and women of action. Directly or indirectly, the three intellectual traditions shape perceptions of what matters and what does not in international affairs, inform analyses of how the world works, serve as the source of strategic alternatives for dealing with international problems, and, in the end, inform the choices taken by decision makers.[4] Thus decision makers as well as analysts, whether explicitly or implicitly, are influenced by these intellectual frameworks. And decision makers, no less than analysts, must be aware of the assumptions upon which their choices are founded. To paraphrase the economist John Maynard Keynes, "Practical men, who believe themselves to be quite exempt from any intellectual influences, are usually the slaves of some defunct . . . academic scribbler of a few years back." Realism, liberalism, and marxism require the attention of any who would seriously turn their talents to international affairs. Ideas matter.

The arguments made by Mearsheimer and Mathews nicely illustrate the differences between realism and liberalism, the two analytical perspectives that shape the on-going strategic debate in the United States. Though, as in the past, only infrequently encountered in the United States, marxism is no stranger elsewhere. Marxism, or perhaps more accurately neo-marxism, has long informed debates and choices around the world. An adequate under-standing, therefore, of the issues, debates, and choices confronting not only the United States but also the international community requires an awareness of the fundamental principles that underlie each of the three analytical traditions.

The purpose here is not to attempt to resolve the differences among realism, liberalism, and marxism or to make the case for one over the others. Some of the differences, arguably, are insurmountable;[5] even if they were not, they would require more than these few pages to surmount. In addition, the author is of at least two minds, and perhaps three, on the virtues of the three approaches to understanding. Therefore, the objective here is more mundane: to convey the essence of each of the three analytical traditions, to identify the core assumptions of each of the perspectives, and to bring out the tensions among them.

## Realism

While no one paradigm has governed the theory and practice of international relations, proponents of one of the three intellectual traditions have if not exercised at least aspired to a near-hegemonic domination. As one prominent warrior in both theoretical and policy debates observed, "Realism has been the dominant tradition in thinking about international politics."[6] The ascendance of realism is due in part to its long and illustrious tradition. Long before the emergence of the term *realpolitik*, the essence of realist thought and behavior was captured in the Renaissance concept of *raison d'état*. Realism's distin-guished intellectual lineage includes the likes of Thucydides, Machiavelli, and Hobbes.[7] This rich heritage has informed the writings of more recent analysts such as Hans Morgenthau,[8] Kenneth Waltz,[9] and John Mearsheimer[10] as well as the actions of political figures such as Richard Nixon and Henry Kissinger.

The central concern of realism is war and peace. Since it is war that most threatens the survival of peoples and states, realists focus on war, particularly major power war, the causes of war, and how it might be prevented. Realist practitioners, consequently, are preoccupied with maintaining national security against external military threats.

Realism revolves around six core assumptions about how the world works. The first is that international politics is anarchic. Anarchy here should not be equated with chaos. Realists characterize the international system as anarchic because, unlike domestic political systems, there is no central political authority that rules over the units that make up the international system. The interna-tional political system consists of independent, sovereign political units—states—that are not subject to, or governed by, a higher political author-ity. Sovereignty, indeed, resides in states precisely because of the absence of a central political authority with the capability to impose order. State sovereignty means that "Formally, each is the equal of all the others. None is entitled to command; none is required to obey."[11] That is why anarchy prevails in the international system.

The second core assumption is that the state is the most important political unit, the central actor, in the international system. International relations consists of relations among states. Realists recognize, of course, the existence of other, non-state, actors. But they argue that non-state actors possess neither the independence nor capabilities of states, particularly major states. They are either comprised of states (international organizations) or subject to them (nongovernmental organizations). Non-state actors have yet to attain the status of states. Only states are sovereign actors. And it is sovereign states that continue to make the critical decisions in international relations—decisions about war and peace.

Third, states are unitary actors. For analytical purposes, realists assume that states are unitary, integrated actors that speak with one voice in their dealings with other states. Countries confront the rest of the world united; it is the state, or the central government, that deals with other states. State and society are one, with states speaking for the societies they represent. Domestic, or societal, actors such as political parties, classes, interest groups, and private individuals do not have the standing to represent the country as a whole in international affairs; their interests are subservient to the larger national interest. Similarly, components of the state are assumed to coordinate their behavior and not act independently of each other. As Viotti and Kauppi put it, "The state is a unitary actor in that it is usually assumed by realists to have one policy at any given time on any particular issue."[12] Once decisions are made, disagreements are put aside and the government speaks with one voice. Neither the executive, legislative, or judicial branches of government nor the various bureaucracies that comprise the executive branch have interests independent of the broader state, or national, interest.

Realists are aware of the occasional exception to the rule here. Infrequently, perhaps when the issues are minor and the stakes low, or when no official position exists, components of the government may publicly disagree or societal actors may speak out or act independently. Realists insist, however, that if the issues are important and the stakes are high, efforts at independent, uncoordinated dealings with the rest of the world either do not occur or are quickly squashed. Thus the assumption that states are unitary actors remains a valid working assumption.

Fourth, realists also assume that, for the purposes of analysis, states are rational actors as well as unitary actors.[13] States are presumed to have the ability to identify their interests and objectives, to recognize challenges or threats to their interests and objectives, to evaluate the alternatives for dealing with challenges or threats, and to select the alternative that maximizes their interests and objectives. Thus this rationality is an instrumental rationality: states are capable of performing cost-benefit calculations in the context of their interests and objectives.

Realists are careful to note that despite the assumed rationality of states, success is not guaranteed. Rationality does not insulate states from the mistakes and miscalculations that result from incomplete or inaccurate information. It also offers little protection against the deliberate efforts of some states to deceive other states about their intentions and strengths and weaknesses.

The fifth core assumption of realism is that the international system is the most important determinant of state behavior. In an anarchical system of sovereign states interacting without the benefit of a central authority able to impose order, provide security, resolve disputes, and enforce decisions, states must fend for themselves. The international system, in other words, is a self-help system.[14] In a self-help system, states seek to ensure their survival by accumulating the capabilities, or power, needed to maintain their national security. The power that matters most to states is not absolute but relative power, especially offensive and defensive military power. As Mearsheimer explains, ". . . the greater the military advantage one state has over other states, the more secure it is. Every state would like to be the most formidable military power in the system because this is the best way to guarantee survival in a world that can be very dangerous."[15] Competition for power, and therefore conflict, is inherent in an anarchic, self-help system—it is impossible for each state to be "the most formidable military power in the system." Thus, for realists, conflict is inevitable and international politics is a zero-sum game. When what matters is not absolute power but relative power, states can only increase their power at the expense of others. If one state gains, another state must lose.

No state is immune from the system-induced struggle for survival and power. Whether states pursue power by building up internal capabilities or by entering into external alliances and/or coalitions, they are motivated by this struggle. Even states that attempt to insulate themselves by acquiring defensive rather than offensive military capabilities will find no refuge. Others will not fail to perceive malign intent and respond by enhancing their own military capabilities, leading our defensively inclined state to a response of its own. This security dilemma is inevitable under anarchy.[16] There is no escape from the threat of war in realism's anarchical world.

Realist explanations of international relations clearly highlight the implications of systemic anarchy for state behavior. The characteristics of states and leaders are of little consequence. It is not the characteristics of states—whether they are democratic, authoritarian, or totalitarian, republics or monarchies—or leaders—whether they are idealistic or pragmatic, moral, amoral, or immoral—but the anarchical nature of the international system, its structure, and a state's position in the system that accounts for state behavior. According to one of realism's leading lights, ". . . realism does not distinguish between 'good' states and 'bad' states, but essentially treats them like billiard balls of varying size."[17]

The sixth and final assumption of realism is that of all the issues states deal with in international relations, issues of military security matter most. Security issues top state agendas. Grand strategy and national security, for realists, constitute the substance of high politics; everything else, including economics, is relegated to low politics. That is not to say that economic issues do not matter. Rather, it is to say that realists argue that security issues and related political issues have priority over economic issues, no matter how vital. Indeed high politics dominates and shapes low politics; politics determines economics—economics is subject to the logic of politics. Mearsheimer is characteristically blunt on this point: ". . . states operate in both an international political environment and an international economic environment, and the former dominates the latter in cases where the two systems come into conflict. . . . Since a state can have no higher goal than survival, when push comes to shove, international political considerations will be paramount in the minds of decision-makers."[18] In an anarchical, self-help system, states are inevitably preoccupied with national security, territorial integrity, and the utility and fungibility of military power. For realists, as Wayman and Diehl note, "Economic capability is important only as a means of shoring up, improving, and sustaining military capability."[19]

## Liberalism

Realism's leading intellectual challenger, particularly in the United States and Western Europe, is liberalism.[20] Liberalism's intellectual lineage, which includes Plato, Aristotle, Grotius, Montesquieu, Locke, Rousseau, Kant, and, from economics, Adam Smith and David Ricardo, is no less distinguished than that of realism.[21] And its contemporary proponents—Graham Allison,[22] Robert Keohane,[23] Joseph Nye,[24] and John Ruggie,[25] for instance—are every bit as renowned as the contemporary advocates of realism. As for twentieth century political leaders who subscribe to liberalism rather than realism, liberals put forward Woodrow Wilson and Franklin Roosevelt as opposed to the realists' Richard Nixon and Henry Kissinger. Take your pick.

While realists focus on war and peace, the central problem for liberals is conflict and cooperation. Liberals have explicitly adopted a broader perspective than realists, whose perspective, they argue, is too constrictive, even myopic. International relations is about more than war and peace; war is not the only form of conflict and peace is not the only form of cooperation. Economic, ideological, cultural, social, religious, and ethnic as well as military conflict pervade international politics. War is not the only threat to the survival of peoples and states; pestilence, famine, and plagues too put the survival of peoples and states at risk.[26] And cooperation occurs not only when peace breaks out but also when conflict is prevalent. Even the United States and Soviet Union and NATO and the Warsaw Pact during the cold war were able to cooperate; at times, arms control cooperation served to take the edge off of U.S.-Soviet, NATO-Warsaw Pact conflict. Liberal practitioners, consequently, are not as fixated on narrow national security issues as their realist counterparts.

Liberals go on to contest virtually every precept, or assumption, that realists hold dear. First, they qualify the realist characterization of the international system as anarchic. Liberal analysts agree with their realist counterparts that there is no central political authority in the international system that imposes order, provides security, resolves disputes, and enforces decisions. But they point out that states and other actors cooperate, even under anarchy, to impart order, enhance their security, resolve disputes, and enforce decisions. An international society is possible even in an anarchical system of states.[27] Principles, norms, rules, conventions, and procedures, some of them codified in international law, have been developed that constrain, even govern, the behavior of states and other actors.[28] States have pooled and invested their sovereignty in establishing the international institutions and international regimes in which these principles, norms, rules, conventions, and procedures are embodied.[29] State sovereignty is not inviolate; it is frequently and deliberately surrendered in an effort to create and maintain the institutions that serve as the foundation of international order and international society. Thus states, according to liberals, hold sovereignty less dear than do realists. It would appear that sovereignty is more jealously guarded by realists than by states.

Second, liberals reject what they see as realism's narrow focus on the state as the central actor. States are not always the most important actors, particularly in international economic affairs, where billions of dollars a day in financial transactions take place without the benefit of state involvement. The scope of international relations is much broader than realists recognize; international relations is about more than the interactions of states. It includes as well the activities of a veritable alphabet soup of universal, regional, and functional international organizations established by states (such as the UN, EU, OSCE, OAU, OAS, ASEAN, APEC, British Commonwealth, WTO, OECD, and OPEC), nongovernmental organizations (Amnesty International, CARE, Greenpeace, Oxfam, and Red Cross, for instance), multinational corporations, crime syndicates, drug cartels, and private individuals that operate across state boundaries. These different and increasingly numerous non-state actors interact with both state and non-state actors. They put issues on the international agenda with which states must then contend; they confront states and constrain their behavior; they frequently circumvent state authority; and they at times exert an independent influence on events. Some non-state actors are in command of resources that dwarf those of some of the states with which they deal.

Third, the assumption that states are unitary actors is also discarded. States do not always speak with one voice in their dealings with other actors. Countries do not necessarily confront the rest of the world as a united whole. State and society may not act as one. As Viotti and Kauppi put it, ". . . the realist view of the state as a unitary actor is an abstraction that masks the essence of politics that is found principally within the state. The state is not some reified entity—an abstraction to be treated as if it were a physical being that acts with single-mindedness determination, always in a coherent manner."[30] The behavior of states cannot be explained without disaggregating the state and examining the behavior both of components, and even subcomponents, of the government and of groups and individuals in society. To explain state behavior, liberal analysts turn to the political process of decision making and the actors that participate in that often messy process.

Neither the state nor the government is an abstract entity; within the realist's black box of the state is a government that consists of organizations and bureaucracies, legislatures and legislative committees, and individuals. States act when organizations, bureaucracies, and individuals act. Government decisions are the output of parochial and at times imperial organizations that often are only loosely coordinated. These organizations rely heavily on standard operating procedures; their repertoires, and consequently their flexibility, are limited; they tend to adapt slowly and incrementally to change. Within these organizations are bureaucracies peopled by hierarchically positioned players. Jettisoning realism's notion of a unitary actor, liberals see many actors, or players:

> players who focus not on a single strategic issue but on many diverse intra-national problems as well; players who act in terms of no consistent set of strategic objectives but rather according to various conceptions of national, organizational, and personal goals; players who make government decisions not by a single, rational choice but by the pulling and hauling that is politics.[31]

The perceptions of these players and the positions they stake out on the issues of the day are highly colored by their positions in the decision making process—where you stand depends on where you sit.[32]

Societal actors—political parties, classes, interest groups, the media, and private individuals—also seek to influence governmental decisions. These societal actors clash, compete, bargain, and compromise with each other and with governmental players in an effort to sway government decisions and actions. Foreign policy as well as domestic policy is the result of the pluralist give and take of politics. Many liberal analysts, indeed, reject the realist distinction between foreign and domestic.

This array of public and private actors—governmental organizations, bureaucracies, and officials and political parties, classes, interest groups, the media, and private individuals—have their own interests and objectives. The resulting conglomeration of conflicting and frequently contradictory public and private interests does not conveniently add up to the realist conception of "national interests." There are many interests, but few meaningful national interests. Thus the realist concept of national interest is, for liberal analysts, an ambiguous, if not hollow, construct. Indeed, as discussions of national interest move from the abstract to the concrete, the more difficult it is to achieve consensus.

In the end, therefore, liberals argue that the realist conception of the state as a unitary actor only serves to ensure that realists fail to examine how decisions are actually made and implemented. According to liberals, realists simply miss (or are too lazy to attend to) the essence, and the complexity, of politics within and among states.

Having taken apart the black box of the state, liberals must question as well realism's fourth assumption—that states are rational actors. If state behavior is the result of political pulling and hauling and conflict and compromise among a multitude of public and private actors, conventional notions of rationality must be discarded. States do not simply rationally and logically proceed from their interests and objectives to challenges or threats, the alternatives for responding to challenges or threats, to, finally, selection of the alternative that maximizes their interests and objectives. Politics infuses each step of the decision making process. As Allison puts it, ". . . what happens is not chosen as a solution to a problem but rather results from compromise, conflict, and confusion of officials with diverse interests and unequal influence."[33] Thus we are left not with rationality but with "bounded rationality;" not with value maximization or optimization, but with "satisficing."[34]

Their emphasis on the politics of decision making also leads liberal analysts to reject realism's fifth assumption. The international system is not necessarily the most important determinant of state behavior. National and individual level determinants compete with system level determinants of international politics. The characteristics of states and their leaders may be profoundly important. Democracies, it seems, do not go to war against each other.[35] Indeed, we have seen the emergence of a democratic security community. Democratic Britain and France behaved differently than Nazi Germany during the 1930s. Political leaders in the United States during the cold war made much of the fact that the United States was a democratic, free market country while the Soviet Union was an authoritarian, communist country. A united democratic Germany does not raise the same fears that a united monarchical or totalitarian Germany did. At the individual level, Churchill and Hitler behaved differently, as did Roosevelt and Stalin and Gandhi and Pol Pot.[36] State behavior is not simply the result of the anarchical nature of the international system, its structure, and a state's position in the system. The nature of states and their leaders matters as well.

Liberal analysts reject as well the realist argument that international relations is inherently conflictual. Despite the anarchical nature of the international system, cooperation as well as conflict is evident among states. States do not always live in harmony with each other, but neither are they perpetually at war with one another. More often than not, they find ways to resolve their differences short of war. States cooperate both to enhance their security and their economic well-being. International institutions, international economic interdependence, and democracy work to mitigate the conflict-inducing effects of anarchy. The mutual gains that result from cooperation demonstrate that international politics is not a zero-sum game but a positive-sum game.

Finally, liberals see an extensive array of issues on national and international agendas and employ a broader, more inclusive, conception of security. Traditional national security issues do not always top national and international agendas.[37] Economic issues vie with security issues for top billing; and a variety of other issues—social, cultural, ideological, religious, environmental, and welfare—are in contention. In the words of one liberal analyst, "A nation's economic strategy is now at least as important as its military strategy."[38] The realist distinction between high and low politics and the argument that politics determines economics are both rejected. The distinction between high and low politics is artificial and outmoded. And it is the interaction between politics and economics that drives events; indeed the distinction between politics and economics is as artificial as the distinction between high and low politics.[39]

Liberals contend that realists have long harbored an unnecessarily narrow conception of national security. Security, for liberals, is about more than protecting the country from external military threats.[40] Non-military concerns about, for instance, economic security, energy security, and environmental security all fall within the purview of the broader, liberal conception of national security. Non-military threats pose as great a threat to life and limb as military threats. According to one report, "In 1996, alone, between 1 million and 3 million people died of malaria. . . Between 300 million and 500 million people now get malaria each year, and someone dies of it about every 15 seconds. . . Over the last decade, malaria has killed about 10 times as many children as all wars combined have in that period."[41] By what logic does war deserve pride of place in national security at the expense of killers such as malaria, dengue hemorrhagic fever, and AIDS?

## Marxism

Marxism[42] offers a radical departure from both realism and liberalism.[43] Traditional realist and liberal assumptions and analytical categories are discarded or are turned on their heads. Probably no intellectual tradition has been more vilified and less understood, especially by uninformed politicians and their many followers in the United States.[44] Yet marxism has been tremendously influential, politically as well as intellectually. The powerful intellectual writings of Marx, Engels, and Lenin continue to resonate in the more contemporary work of eminent neo-marxist economists, historians, political scientists, and sociologists such as Theotonio Dos Santos,[45] Eric Hobsbawm,[46] William Appleman Williams,[47] Peter Evans,[48] Fernando Henrique Cardoso,[49] and Immanuel Wallerstein.[50]

The central problem for marxism is not war and peace or even conflict and cooperation. War and peace and conflict and cooperation, for marxists, are merely manifestations of a deeper, underlying reality. Marxists are preoccupied with the material structures of domination and subordination, and the consequent inequities, evident both within and across societies.

The set of assumptions that underlies marxism differ significantly from those upon which realism and liberalism are based. Marxists, first, accept realism's emphasis on the importance of the international context within which interactions occur. But their characterization of that international context differs fundamentally from that advanced by realists. Marxists focus not on the implications of an anarchic international system but on the world political economy. The most important feature of the international system is neither realism's anarchy nor liberalism's institutionalism and interdependence; rather, the critical characteristic of the international system is that it is capitalist. Thus it is not the political logic of either realism's or liberalism's international political system but the economic logic of the capitalist world system that is the key to understanding.

Second, the historical development of the capitalist world economy is central to an understanding of its logic and functioning. In short, the dominant position of some societies and the subordinate position of others is a result of the development and functioning of the capitalist world system. Some societies have benefited from the development and functioning of the capitalist world system; others have not.

The history of the capitalist world system is the story of its emergence out of a feudal Europe, its transformation from its agricultural to industrial and then financial modes, and its expansion. That expansion from an initially European base to the incorporation of the rest of the world was brought about by the mercantilistic imperialism of the capitalist states of Europe. The two waves of European imperial conquest brought first the western hemisphere and then Asia and Africa under the sway of capitalism. During the development and expansion of the capitalist system, the early capitalist societies of Europe and North America emerged as centers of industrial and financial power. Latecomers to capitalism in Latin America, Africa, and Asia served the dominant societies as sources of agricultural products, natural resources, and cheap labor and as markets for their manufactured products.

The asymmetrical positions of different societies in the capitalist world order are the result of the uneven development of capitalism. The historical development and expansion of the capitalist world system left the advanced industrial societies of the "North" ascendant over the less developed (or, more optimistically, developing) societies of the "South." According to the materialistic logic of marxism, less developed societies are undeveloped not, as classical liberal economists would have us believe, because they have failed to adopt capitalist ways and to allow themselves to be fully integrated into the capitalist world system, but because of the manner in which capitalism developed and expanded to absorb them. Consequently, less developed societies in the capitalist world economy have been subordinate to and dependent upon advanced industrial societies. Even the more advanced developing societies have not been able to exercise any meaningful measure of influence over their economic destiny; their development remains dependent upon the portfolio investment of Northern capitalists and the direct investment of Northern multinational corporations.

Third, the most important actors for marxists are not states but classes. As Marx and Engels wrote, "The history of all hitherto existing society is the history of class struggles."[51] Classes are defined by their relationship to the means of production. The owners of the means, of factors, or production—land, technology, and capital—are society's dominant class—the bourgeoisie, or capitalists. Those employed by the owners of the means of production constitute society's subordinate class—the proletariat, or workers. Thus we have parallel structures of domination and subordination on the domestic and the international levels. Furthermore, owners of the means of production and workers in advanced industrial societies share greater interests with their counterparts in developing societies than with each other; but both capitalists and workers in advanced industrial societies are in a superior position to their compatriots elsewhere, and will strive to maintain their advantages.

The actors that realists and liberals focus on are, for marxists, little more than tools of the dominant capitalist class. States, international institutions, political parties, and interest groups exist to serve the interests of capitalism's ruling elite. States are used by the capitalist ruling class to manage the domestic and international affairs of capitalism, particularly by guaranteeing and enforcing property rights. While realists see states clashing as they attempt to maximize national interests, marxists see classes in conflict as they attempt to maximize class interests. In the words of Marx and Engels, "The executive of the modern State is but a committee for managing the common affairs of the whole bourgeoisie."[52] National interests are dictated by the interests of the owners of the means of production.

Fourth, as the historical experience and asymmetrical positions of the bourgeoisie and the proletariat and of the advanced industrial and less developed societies illustrate, there are winners and losers in the capitalist world system. Within societies, wealthy, politically powerful capitalists dominate, exploit even, poor, politically weak workers. [53] At the international level, wealthy, politically powerful advanced industrial societies dominate poor, politically weak less developed societies. Thus for marxists as for realists, international relations is a zero-sum game.

| | Realism | Liberalism | Marxism |
|---|---|---|---|
| **Table 1** *Realism, Liberalism, & Marxism: Analytical Assumptions* | | | |
| Intellectual Precursors | Thucydides, Machiavelli, Hobbes | Plato, Aristotle, Montesquieu, Locke, Rousseau, Kant | Marx, Engels, Lenin |
| Central Problem | War & Peace | Conflict & Cooperation | Domination & Subordination |
| Nature of International System | Anarchic | Constrained Anarchy | Capitalist |
| Actors | States | International & Nongovernmental Organizations, States, Organizations, Bureaucracies, Political Parties, Classes, Interest Groups, Media, Individuals | Classes |
| Behavior of Actors | Unitary, Rational, Interest Maximizing | Political: Transnational & National Pulling & Hauling, Bargaining, & Compromising in Pursuit of Public & Private Interests | Interest Maximizing |
| Type of Game | Zero-Sum | Positive-Sum | Zero-Sum |
| The Agenda | Dominated by National Security Issues | Extensive; Socioeconomic Issues Contend with National Security Issues for Top Billing | Dominated by Economic Issues |
| Relationship Between Politics & Economics | Politics Determines Economics | The Interaction of Politics & Economics Drives Events | Economics Determines Politics |

Fifth, and finally, while politics determines economics for realists and the interaction between politics and economics drives events for liberals, for marxists, economics determines politics—politics is subject to the logic of economics. Economics is the base, or foundation, of society; all else, including the political (and the state), is mere superstructure. Economics is the key that unlocks the door to an understanding of the dynamics of the world system. Thus while realists ignore the ravages of malaria and liberals contend that it should be regarded as a threat to national security, marxists, more radically, point out that "Money for malaria research is meager in part because the disease primarily afflicts poor people, and Western drug companies doubt that Third World villagers would be able to pay much for a new malaria vaccine even if it was developed."[54]

## Realism, Liberalism, Marxism & System Structure

The divergent conceptions of the structure of the international system advanced by realists, liberals, and marxists serve as a concrete illustration of the real differences among the three analytical perspectives.

For realists, system structure is determined by the distribution of resources across states. The structure of the international system depends on the number of states with the greatest power resources. In the eighteenth and nineteenth centuries, the European state system is said to have been multipolar, with five major powers—Britain, France, Russia, Prussia/Germany, and the Austro-Hungarian empire—contending for power and influence. More recently, during the cold war of the second half of the twentieth century, when two powers, or superpowers, dominated international politics, the international system was considered to be bipolar. With the end of the cold war and the consequent early end of the twentieth century, the structure of the international system has been characterized as, alternatively, unipolar, with the United States as the only remaining superpower; multipolar, with the United States having to contend with other powers such as Russia, China, Japan, and either the "Europe" of the European Union or the "Europe" of Britain, France, and a newly reunited Germany; or as in transition from a unipolar structure to a multipolar structure.

Liberals, typically, provide a more nuanced and complex conceptualization of contemporary system structure. The world is not simply unipolar, bipolar, or multipolar. According to Joseph Nye, "Power is becoming more multidimensional, structures more complex and states themselves more permeable. This added complexity means that the world order must rest on more than the traditional balance of power alone."[55] Nye portrays the post-cold war international system as a layer cake. The top layer is military and therefore unipolar; the United States remains the only full-service military power. In the middle is an economic layer that has been tripolar since the early 1970s. On the bottom is a layer of transnational interdependence that reflects the diffusion and fragmentation of power. Here one finds "transnational relations that cross borders outside the control of government, and that include actors as diverse as bankers and terrorists. . . ."[56]

For marxists, the end of the cold war has not altered the structure of the world system. The structure of the system is economically determined. It can be portrayed as a set of three concentric circles. In the center is the core, which is made up of the dominant advanced industrial societies. Located on the outer ring is the periphery, the less developed societies found in Latin America, Africa, and Asia. In between is the semiperiphery, a combination of those societies progressing from the periphery to the core and those that have dropped from the core. According to Wallerstein, this structure has been in place since 1640.[57] It has survived greater upheavals than that posed by the end of the cold war and remains firmly in place.

Realists remain most concerned about war among the great powers. Since they generally argue that bipolar systems are more stable than multipolar systems, the shift from bipolarity to multipolarity seen by some has been greeted with alarm.[58] Liberals, more convinced than realists of the pacifying effects of international institutions, economic interdependence, and the emergence of a democratic security community, are less concerned about major power conflict than about regional and communal conflicts.[59] Marxists point to the growing chasm between core and periphery, the haves and the have-nots, as the central fault line in the international system. Realists respond that regional conflicts, internal communal conflicts, and challenges from have-nots are unlikely to upset the balance of power among the major states. For realists, major power war remains the only significant threat to international stability.

## In Lieu of Closure

While there are linkages among the three analytical perspectives—realism's major powers reside in the core of marxism's capitalist world system, for instance—the differences among realism, liberalism, and marxism overwhelm the similarities. Realists and marxists provide relatively lean, parsimonious explanations of how the world works. But realists begin their causal arguments with politics while marxists begin with economics. Liberals feel compelled to amend the parsimony of realism with several layers of explanatory complexity, and their causal arguments emphasize the interaction of politics and economics. Divergent, frequently conflicting, assumptions about the central problems of international relations, the nature of the international system, the most important actors, the nature of the game, and the relationship between politics and economics abound.

The disagreements among realists, liberals, and marxists cannot be ignored. The intellectual and theoretical debates among the three traditions continue to be reflected in political debates. In the United States, where realism and liberalism dominate political discourse about the U.S. role in the world, the four post-cold war grand strategy alternatives that have emerged are shaped by variants of realism and liberalism.[60] The Clinton administration's strategy of "Engagement and Enlargement" reads like a dialogue between realists and liberals.[61] Robert Dole's criticisms of the Clinton defense and foreign policy record during the 1996 presidential campaign were informed by realism.[62] Institutionally, the Department of Defense leans toward realism while the

Department of State tends to favor liberalism.[63] And marxism, though it does not shape strategic debates in the United States, emerges in critiques of realist and liberal strategic proposals.[64]

The following two chapters provide examples of realist and liberal analysis. As you read these chapters, look for the assumptions that inform the arguments. And think about whether you would prefer the president to view the world through a realist or a liberal (or a marxist) lens.

---

## Notes

The author thanks Mackubin T. Owens, Jr., for his insightful comments on an earlier draft of this essay. This chapter was completed in January 1997. The author is not responsible for any paradigm shifts that have occurred since then.

1. John J. Mearsheimer, "Disorder Restored," in Graham Allison and Gregory F. Treverton, eds., *Rethinking America's Security: Beyond Cold War to New World Order*, (New York: W. W. Norton & Company, 1992), p. 235.

2. Jessica T. Mathews, "Power Shift," *Foreign Affairs*, Vol. 76, No. 1 (January/February 1997), p. 50.

3. The concept of "paradigm" has recently entered our political vocabulary; it has been thoroughly misunderstood and abused. For the real thing, see Thomas S. Kuhn, *The Structure of Scientific Revolutions*, 2nd ed., (Chicago: University of Chicago Press, 1970).

4. On how realism and liberalism have shaped U.S. foreign policy, see David Callahan, *Between Two Worlds: Realism, Idealism, and American Foreign Policy After the Cold War*, (New York: HarperCollins, 1994).

5. On the difficulties of reconciling conflicting visions, see Thomas Sowell, *A Conflict of Visions*, (New York: Morrow, 1987).

6. Joseph S. Nye, Jr., *Understanding International Conflicts: An Introduction to Theory and History*, (New York: HarperCollins, 1993), p. 3. Other labels used for this analytical perspective include classical realism, neorealism, and structural realism.

7. On realism's intellectual roots, see Mark V. Kauppi and Paul R. Viotti, *The Global Philosophers: World Politics in Western Thought*, (New York: Lexington Books, 1992); and Benjamin Frankel, ed., *Roots of Realism*, special issue, *Security Studies*, Vol. 5, No. 2 (Winter 1995). Alexander Hamilton is usually put forward as an example of a realist practitioner during the early American Republic. See Robert W. Tucker and David C. Hendrickson, *Empire of Liberty: The Statecraft of Thomas Jefferson*, (New York: Oxford University Press, 1990).

8. Hans J. Morgenthau, *Politics Among Nations: The Struggle for Power and Peace*, (New York: Alfred A. Knopf, 1978).

9. Kenneth N. Waltz, *Man, the State, and War: A Theoretical Analysis*, (New York: Columbia University Press, 1959); and Waltz, *Theory of International Politics*, (Reading, MA: Addison-Wesley, 1979).

10. John J. Mearsheimer, "Back to the Future: Instability in Europe After the Cold War," *International Security*, Vol. 15, No. 1 (Summer 1990), pp. 5-56; and Mearsheimer, "The False Promise of International Institutions," *International Security*, Vol. 19, No. 3 (Winter 1994/95), pp. 5-49.

11. Waltz, *Theory of International Politics*, p. 88.

12. Paul R. Viotti and Mark V. Kauppi, *International Relations Theory: Realism, Pluralism, Globalism*, 2nd ed., (New York: Macmillan, 1993), p. 6.

13. This assumption is critical to the deductive theorizing that pervades the realist enterprise. See Frank W. Wayman and Paul F. Diehl, "Realism Reconsidered: The Realpolitik Framework and Its Basic Propositions," in Wayman and Diehl, eds., *Reconstructing Realpolitik*, (Ann Arbor: The University of Michigan Press, 1994). p. 10.

14. As Waltz, *Theory of International Politics*, p. 111, explains, "To achieve their objectives and maintain their security, units in a condition of anarchy . . . must rely on the means they can generate and the arrangements they can make for themselves. Self-help is necessarily the principle of action in an anarchic order. A self-help situation is one of high risk—of bankruptcy in the economic realm and of war in a world of free states."

15. Mearsheimer, "The False Promise of International Institutions," pp. 11-12.

16. On the security dilemma, see Waltz, *Theory of International Politics*, pp. 186-187; and Robert Jervis, "Cooperation Under the Security Dilemma," *World Politics*, Vol. 30, No. 2 (January 1978), pp. 167-214.

17. Mearsheimer, "The False Promise of International Institutions," p. 48.

18. Mearsheimer, "Back to the Future," p. 44.

19. Wayman and Diehl, "Realism Reconsidered," p. 12.

20. Other terms used as labels for this analytical tradition include idealism, optimism, neoliberalism, and pluralism.

21. On liberalism's intellectual roots, see Kauppi and Viotti, *The Global Philosophers*. As Hamilton is seen as the exponent of realism at the beginnings of the American Republic, Jefferson is seen as the advocate of liberalism. See Tucker and Hendrickson, *Empire of Liberty*.

22. Graham T. Allison, *Essence of Decision: Explaining the Cuban Missile Crisis*, (Boston: Little, Brown, 1971).

23. Robert O. Keohane and Joseph S. Nye, Jr., eds., *Transnational Relations and World Politics*, (Cambridge, MA: Harvard University Press, 1979, 1971); Keohane and Nye, *Power and Interdependence*, 2nd ed., (Glenview, IL: Scott, Foresman, 1989); Keohane, *After Hegemony: Cooperation and Discord in the World Political Economy*, (Princeton: Princeton University Press, 1984); and Keohane, ed., *Neorealism and Its Critics*, (New York: Columbia University Press, 1986).

24. Joseph S. Nye, Jr., *Bound to Lead: The Changing Nature of American Power*, (New York: Basic Books, 1990).

25. John Gerard Ruggie, ed., *The Antinomies of Interdependence: National Welfare and the International Division of Labor*, (New York: Columbia University Press, 1983); and Ruggie, *Winning the Peace: America and World Order in the New Era*, (New York: Columbia University Press, 1996).

26. See William H. McNeill, *Plagues and Peoples*, (New York: Anchor Press/Doubleday, 1976); Laurie Garrett, *The Coming Plague: Newly Emerging Diseases in a World Out of Balance*, (New York: Farrar, Straus and Giroux, 1994); and Richard Preston, *The Hot Zone*, (New York: Random House, 1994).

27. See Hedley Bull, *The Anarchical Society: A Study of Order in World Politics*, (New York: Columbia University Press, 1977).

28. See Robert O. Keohane, *International Institutions and State Power: Essays in International Relations Theory*, (Boulder: Westview Press, 1989); Stephen D. Krasner, ed., *International Regimes*, (Ithaca: Cornell University Press, 1983); and James N. Rosenau and Ernst-Otto Czempiel, eds., *Governance Without Government: Order and Change in World Politics*, (Cambridge: Cambridge University Press, 1992).

29. According to Keohane, *International Institutions and State Power*, p. 2, ". . . the institutionalization of world politics exert significant impacts on the behavior of governments. In particular, patterns of cooperation and discord can be understood only in the context of the institutions that help define the meaning and importance of state action. . . . [S]tate actions depend to a considerable degree on prevailing institutional arrangements. . ."

30. Viotti and Kauppi, International Relations Theory, p. 7.

31. Allison, *Essence of Decision*, p. 144.

32. "Each participant, depending on where he sits, will see a somewhat different face of an issue, because his perception of the issue will be heavily shaded by his particular concerns." Morton H. Halperin, with the assistance of Priscilla Clapp and Arnold Kanter, *Bureaucratic Politics and Foreign Policy*, (Washington, DC: The Brookings Institution, 1974), p. 16.

33. Allison, *Essence of Decision*, p. 162.

34. See Allison, *Essence of Decision*, pp. 71-72.

35. See Michael W. Doyle, "Liberalism and World Politics Revisited," in Charles W. Kegley, Jr., ed., *Controversies in International Relations Theory: Realism and the Neoliberal Challenge*, (New York: St. Martin's, 1995), pp. 83-106); and Bruce M. Russett, *Grasping the Democratic Peace: Principles for a Post-Cold War World*, (Princeton: Princeton University Press, 1993).

36. And Dan Quayle is no John Kennedy.

37. "No longer can all issues be subordinated to military security." Keohane and Nye, Power and Interdependence, p. 26.

38. Richard Rosecrance, "The Rise of the Virtual State," *Foreign Affairs*, Vol. 75, No. 4 (July/August 1996), p. 46.

39. See Andrew L. Ross, "The Political Economy of Defense: The Nature and Scope of the Inquiry," in Ross, ed., *The Political Economy of Defense: Issues and Perspectives*, (Westport, CT: Greenwood Press, 1991), pp. 1-21.

40. See Joseph J. Romm, *Defining National Security: The Nonmilitary Aspects*, (New York: Council on Foreign Relations Press, 1993); and Theodore H. Moran, *American Economic Policy and National Security*, (New York: Council on Foreign Relations Press, 1993).

41. Nicholas D. Kristof, "Malaria Makes a Comeback, Deadlier Than Ever," *The New York Times*, January 8, 1997.

42. Other terms used as labels for this intellectual tradition include neo-marxism, radicalism, structuralism, and, less appropriately, globalism.

43. Despite the fall of communism in the former Soviet Union and in Eastern Europe, analytical marxism is far from dead. Marx and Engels never reigned in the Soviet Union. Its leaders adopted what was, at best, a rather corrupt form of marxism.

44. For an evenhanded account of marxism, see Robert L. Heilbroner, *Marxism: For and Against*, (New York: W.W. Norton & Company, 1980). See also Shlomo Avineri, *The Social and Political Thought of Karl Marx*, (Cambridge: Cambridge University Press, 1968).

45. Theotonio Dos Santos, "The Structure of Dependence," *American Economic Review*, Vol. 60, No. 2 (May 1970), pp. 231-236.

# 62    Perspectives on International Relations

46. E. J. Hobsbawm, *The Age of Revolution: Europe 1789-1848*, (New York: Praeger, 1969); Hobsbawm, *The Age of Capital*, 1848-1875, (New York: Scribner, 1975); Hobsbawm, *The Age of Empire, 1875-1914*, (New York: Pantheon, 1987); Hobsbawm, *The Age of Extremes: A History of the World, 1914-1991*, (New York: Pantheon, 1995).

47. William Appleman Williams, *The Tragedy of American Diplomacy*, 2nd rev. ed., (New York: Dell. 1972).

48. Peter Evans, *Dependent Development: The Alliance of Multinational, State, and Local Capital in Brazil*, (Princeton: Princeton University Press, 1979).

49. Fernando Enrique Cardoso and Enzo Faletto, *Dependency and Development in Latin America*, (Berkeley: University of California Press, 1979)

50. Immanuel Wallerstein, *The Modern World System I: Capitalist Agriculture and the Origins of the European World-Economy in the Sixteenth Century*, (San Diego: Academic Press, Inc., 1974); Wallerstein, *The Modern World System II: Mercantilism and the Consolidation of the European World-Economy, 1600-1750*, (New York: Academic Press, Inc., 1980); Wallerstein, *The Modern World System III: The Second Era of Great Expansion of the Capitalist World-Economy*, (San Diego: Academic Press, Inc., 1989); and Wallerstein, *The Capitalist World-Economy*, (Cambridge: Cambridge University Press, 1979).

51. Karl Marx and Friedrich Engels, *The Communist Manifesto*, (Harmondsworth: Penguin Books, 1967), p. 79.

52. Marx and Engels, *The Communist Manifesto*, p. 82.

53. The ". . . interests of classes stand opposed. The degree to which one class achieves its material interest measure the degree to which the other fails." James A. Caporaso and David P. Levine, *Theories of Political Economy*, (Cambridge: Cambridge University Press, 1992), p. 57.

54. Kristof, "Malaria Makes a Comeback, Deadlier Than Ever."

55. Joseph S. Nye, Jr., "What New World Order?" *Foreign Affairs*, Vol. 71, No. 2 (Spring 1992), p. 88.

56. Joseph S. Nye, Jr., "Conflicts after the Cold War," *The Washington Quarterly*, Vol. 19, No. 1 (Winter 1996), p. 9.

57. Wallerstein, *The Capitalist World-Economy*, p. 18. On the core-periphery structure, see also Barry Buzan, "New Patterns of Global Security in the Twenty-First Century," *International Affairs*, Vol. 67, No. 3 (July 1991), pp. 431-451.

58. See Mearsheimer, "Back to the Future."

59. See Nye, "Conflicts after the Cold War."

60. See Barry R. Posen and Andrew L. Ross, "Competing Visions for U.S. Grand Strategy," *International Security*, Vol. 21, No. 3 (Winter 1996/97), pp. 5-53.

61. *A National Security Strategy of Engagement and Enlargement*, (Washington, D.C.: U.S. Government Printing Office, February 1996).

62. See Bob Dole, "Shaping America's Global Future," *Foreign Policy*, No. 98 (Spring 1995), pp. 29-43.

63. Here at the Naval War College, the National Security Decision Making Department's Policy Making and Implementation subcourse is the embodiment of analytical liberalism.

64. For an intriguing example, see Christopher Layne and Benjamin Schwarz, "American Hegemony—Without an Enemy," *Foreign Policy*, No. 92 (Fall 1993), pp. 5-23.

# Chapter 5

**\* \* \***

# Existential Realism After the Cold War

Robert J. Lieber

*Robert J. Lieber provides an assessment of contemporary international relations that is thoroughly grounded in the realist school of thought. He argues that what he terms "existential realism" is about "what exists" or "what is'." For Lieber, as for other realists, the international system is anarchic and the state is the most important actor. Is there any threat to the primacy of states in world politics? Might it be that economic competition is becoming more important than military competition and that war is becoming obsolete as economic interdependence and integration increase? What post-Cold War order will replace the Cold War order? Will the post-Cold War order be more or less stable than the Cold War order? What do you think of the policy implications Lieber draws from existential realism?*

The end of the Cold War and the collapse of the Soviet Union have triggered a fundamental reexamination of world politics and the future of American foreign policy. This burgeoning debate among scholars, practitioners, and politicians involves two related but ultimately separate levels of analysis. One concerns the nature of international relations and the other of the United States within it.

The discussion has begun to produce an outpouring of analysis and prescription. At its best, this dialogue has the potential for being the most fruitful in the past 45 years, that is, since a consensus on U.S. Cold War policies was achieved in the spring of 1947. The policy debate has, however, also been accompanied by misconceptions about the world in which policy

Robert J. Lieber is professor and chairman of the Department of Government at Georgetown University. His most recent book, co-edited with Kenneth Oye and Donald Rothchild, is *Eagle in a New World: American Grand Strategy in the Post—Cold War Era* (New York: HarperCollins, 1992).

Robert J. Lieber, "Existential Realism After the Cold War," *The Washington Quarterly,* 16:1, Winter 1993, pp. 155-168. Copyright © 1993 by the Center for Strategic and International Studies (CSIS) and the Massachusetts Institute of Technology. Minor modifications to the text have been made.

choices must be made. In this context, a reconsideration of the nature of post-cold war international relations seems especially important. No analysis, let alone prescription, can be of much use if it is not grounded in reality. Indeed, even the most idealistic, normative prescriptions (i.e., of what "ought" to be) can have little bearing unless they are grounded in an understanding of what exists (i.e., what "is").

In this light, the notion of *realism* bears reexamination. It is an approach to the understanding of international relations that becomes prevalent among scholars and policymakers in the aftermath of World War II and that was most commonly associated with the thought of authors such as E. H. Carr and Hans J. Morgenthau,[1] as well as policymakers such as George Kennan. Their approach was conditioned by the experiences of Allied appeasement of fascism and the trauma of the war, and subsequently by the threat posed by Stalin and the Soviet Union. More than four decades later, however, in the aftermath of the disintegration of the USSR and the end of the East-West conflict, and in conjunction with the development of a burgeoning and interdependent international economy, pervasive communication linkages, and the growth of international and regional institutions, there has been a tendency to question the precepts of realism and their continued relevance.

Properly understood, however, the essential components of realism remain central to an understanding of international relations. This requires separating what has been particular to a given era (in this case, the threat from the Soviet Union that precipitated the Cold War) from what is more enduring. It also requires avoiding excessive emphasis on the particular versions of realism identified with specific authors such as Morgenthau or Kenneth Waltz.[2] In essence, neither the passing of the Cold War, as momentous a development as that has been, nor the strengths or weaknesses of specific variants of realism (among them "neorealism"[3] and "structural realism"[4]), should distract attention from the essential characteristics of international relations and the realist appreciation to which these give rise.

There is also a need to avoid the kind of time-bound critiques to which realism has been subject. For example, during the height of the Cold War, and indeed, as late as the early 1980s, realists were sometimes criticized from the right for not embracing strategies to achieve the "rollback" of Soviet communism from Eastern Europe (Dean Acheson's "College of Cowardly Communist Containment," in Richard Nixon's memorable 1952 slogan), for not supporting the Vietnam War (opposed by realists such as Morgenthau), or for not embracing concepts of nuclear war fighting (advocated by some strategists in the late 1970s and early 1980s). More recently, realism has been described as failing to take into account long-term changes, such as the growing importance of nationalism, democratization, transnational communications, migration, and economic interdependence.[5]

Realism has also been attacked from the left of the political and academic spectrum on the grounds, for example, that it is antithetical to a world order based on democracy that could lead to peace and prosperity, and that it favors the development of a national security apparatus capable of being used to suppress individual freedom at home and abroad.[6] In addition, at an international scholarly meeting, the author of this article was criticized for his *description* of international realities, with a European participant depicting the presentation as a manifestation of "American intellectual imperialism."[7]

In order to avoid entanglement in these debates, and the sometimes overly specific and time-bound variants they represent, it seems appropriate to employ the term *existential realism* in an attempt to achieve a durable understanding of the international system. There is a valuable antecedent for this designation. In writing about strategic nuclear deterrence in the early 1980s, Robert Jervis observed that "mutual assured destruction exists as a fact, irrespective of policy,"[8] and he cited what has elsewhere been termed "existential deterrence."[9] Adopting this terminology, I use *existential realism* here to designate a series of realities about the international system in which states exist.

## The Components of Existential Realism

In essence, states exist in an international system that lacks a central authority. In this sense the system is anarchic. This is not to suggest that it is chaotic, but that it subsists in the absence of governance.[10] This characteristic means that politics in the international arena differs profoundly from politics in the domestic realm. Specifically, there is no authoritative arbiter to resolve disputes—which are inevitable in human affairs. Nor is there a central power with the means to provide security for the members of the system.

As a consequence of the anarchy problem, states find that they dwell in a kind of self-help system. They either must be prepared to defend their own interests and those of their people, or to seek means of doing so through alliances. These realities of existential realism do not yield iron laws, but they do create a series of propensities shaping state behavior. Recognition of these propensities, and appreciation that they are not rigidly deterministic but that they condition the environment in which states and their leaders act, is crucial to an understanding of international relations.

One of these propensities involves what has been widely described as the security dilemma. In an anarchic international environment, states tend to arm themselves for self-protection. This has the effect of stimulating others to do likewise and thus causing all states to be potentially threatened. The problem has been presented concisely by Glenn Snyder:

> Even when no state has any desire to attack others, none can be sure that others' intentions are peaceful, or will remain so; hence each must accumulate power for

defense. Since no state can know that the power accumulation of others is defensively motivated only, each must assume that it might be intended for attack. Consequently, each party's power increments are matched by the others, and all wind up with no more security than when the vicious cycle began, along with the costs incurred in having acquired and having to maintain their power.[11]

If the security dilemma causes states to feel insecure and to arm themselves, the anarchy problem and self-help system to which it gives rise create a propensity for states to resort to force when they find that their vital interests or even their existence are at stake. Cases in point here include Israel's preemptive attack on Egypt in the 1967 war, Britain's military campaign to regain control of the Falkland Islands from Argentina, and the tragedy of war in Yugoslavia among Serbs, Croats, and Muslims.

In the 1967 case, Israel faced a situation in which President Gamal Abdel Nasser of Egypt had demanded the withdrawal of United Nations (UN) forces from Sinai, and Secretary General U Thant had immediately complied. The UN "policemen" having left the scene (thereby providing a vivid illustration of the weaknesses of international constraints on conflict), and with Nasser having pledged to destroy Israel and having moved massive armored forces into Sinai, the Israelis opted to strike first, rather than risk awaiting a first strike from the Egyptians.

Britain's action in the Falklands is also instructive. In this case, after Argentina's seizure of the islands on April 2, 1982, the UN Security Council passed a resolution condemning the invasion and demanding immediate Argentine withdrawal. Despite the Council's vote of ten to one in its favor, however, the Thatcher government was well aware that the UN resolution carried no enforcement powers. Instead, in order to regain the islands, the British resorted to self-help—sending a task force some 8,000 miles into the South Atlantic in order to reconquer the territory from Argentina.

Yugoslavia presents a different type of case. In this instance, the absence of an external authority able to resolve disputes or maintain order created conditions conducive to military conquest by Serbia after the republics of Croatia and Bosnia-Herzegovina declared independence. The remnants of the Serb-led central government, together with Serbian groups in the republics, could embark on the conquest of large areas of Croatia and Bosnia, as well as threaten dangerous actions against Kosovo and Macedonia in the knowledge that no international power or organization was likely to have the ability or the will to intervene decisively. To be sure, the conflict rested on a long and bloody inter-ethnic history, including the legacy of World War II, during which a fascist regime in Croatia had slaughtered more than a half million Yugoslavs of other ethnic groups. Moreover, initiatives within Croatia and Bosnia were often taken by local groups and militias. Nonetheless, the Serbian government under Slobodan Milosevic was able to pursue a deliberate policy of conquest and "ethnic cleansing."

In the face of the slaughter in Yugoslavia, the European states remained divided and uncertain. The institutions of the European Community (EC) provided no institutional basis for collective action. The Conference on Security and Cooperation in Europe (CSCE) was too weak and unwieldy. And the North Atlantic Treaty Organization (NATO) lacked the internal agreement that would have been necessary for it to act in a conflict for which it was not designed.

In turn, the involvement of UN forces for humanitarian purposes was slow and of modest scale. The forces lacked the authority and numbers to impose order, their efforts to negotiate cease-fires were flagrantly violated, and their measures to feed starving populations in cities such as Sarajevo did not prevent the Serbian regime from carrying out its bombardment of civilian populations and deliberate campaign to force vast numbers of Croats and Muslims from their homes.

UN sanctions efforts against Yugoslavia also had only limited effect. The embargo was widely flouted by Serbia's eastern neighbors, particularly Romania, whose own precarious economic and political situations made them indifferent to UN policies. Moreover, the weapons embargo had the unintended effect of favoring the Serbs over their victims in Bosnia. Local Serbian forces were amply supplied with heavy weapons from the central government, while the Bosnians had only light weapons with which to defend themselves against the Serbian onslaught.

Ironically, the limited UN measures may have actually worsened the situation on the ground. In the absence of an effective intervention by the international community, it is at least conceivable that the Bosnians (who substantially outnumbered the Serbs within the borders of the republic), might have been able to procure sufficient arms to defend themselves and achieve a rough balance of power. Had this not been sufficient to cause the Serbs to halt their onslaught and seek to negotiate, it is at least conceivable that it would have allowed the Bosnians to protect their people from the worst bombardments, starvation, and human rights abuses, as well as to halt the massive population exodus that has created the worst refugee crisis in Europe since the end of World War II. In essence, policies more attentive to existential realism might have done more to reduce the incentives for Serbian aggression and to reduce overall human suffering. The cases of Israel in 1967, Britain in the Falklands, and Yugoslavia provide diverse illustrations of the way in which the absence of central authority and the nature of the international system create a propensity for states to use force in situations of conflict. To be sure, states and their decision makers retain a degree of choice, and not every conflict must culminate in war. In acute situations, however, where the interests of states are at risk and they find themselves without external guarantees of protection or enforcement, the resort to force becomes a significant factor.

## Challenges to Existential Realism and the Role of the State

Existential realism does not require its adherents to ignore the impact of other forces shaping international relations. Indeed, a number of forces other than the state play a significant role. But their effect must be carefully gauged.

One such force is the growth of a vast and open international economy, in which states find themselves enmeshed and their borders increasingly permeable. Moreover, the more developed the state, the more it tends to find that the needs of this population can only be met though active participation in international economic activity that the state may have only limited capacity to influence.

Economic interdependence can, however, be the source of conflict as well as cooperation. Trade disputes, or even neomercantilist trade wars, provide a case in point. As an additional illustration, the European currency crisis of late September 1992 found countries such as Italy and Britain facing fluctuations in exchange values and interest rates that were largely determined by market forces and the actions of the German Bundesbank, over neither of which they had much influence. Here too, however, it would be wise not to exaggerate the element of international cooperation. Despite consultations among governmental officials, the European exchange rate mechanism began to break down under the strain of these events. In essence, much of the problem stemmed from the situation within the border of Germany. There, in response to the massive costs of absorbing the former German Democratic Republic (estimated at $130 billion in 1992 alone), the Bonn government and the Bundesbank had adopted high interest rates. This policy, in response to a serious domestic problem, had the effect of harming economic growth among Germany's EC partners and creating havoc with their exchange rates.

Second, the development of international institutions has had a noticeable impact. At the global level, the United Nations has gained increasing visibility, although its capacity to act effectively remains severely constrained. Other global bodies are more focused in their agendas, particularly in the case of organizations devoted to economic activity, as in the case of the International Monetary Fund (IMF), the World Bank, and the General Agreement on Tariffs and Trade (GATT). Compared to their global counterparts, regional institutions have on occasion had a greater effect, in some cases a very significant one. The European Community is an example. Here too, however, the limits are as evident as the possibilities. The initial euphoria of many Europeans—and especially of outside observers—over the movement toward Europe 1992 (the package of integration measures planned to take effect as of mid-night on December 31, 1992) has given way to a growing realization of the obstacles to the deepening of regional integration. The uncertain fate of the Maastricht treaty, meant to move the Community toward more extensive integration in monetary policy as well as in foreign and defense policy and institutional procedures, reflects these obstacles, as does the increasingly bitter controversy over German monetary policy. More broadly, both global and regional bodies remain tied to states for their funding and basic authority. This tends to limit their ability to affect national actions.

Third, democratization can operate to mitigate the anarchic nature of the international system. In this case, genuinely democratic states have had a laudable record of not making war against one another. Why this should be so is a matter of conjecture, but one evident factor is that by making policy processes more transparent, democracy eases some of the uncertainty about state intentions that drives the security dilemma. The spread of democratization thus holds the potential for very significantly reducing the level of interstate violence. Indeed, at a conceptual level, democratization may represent a profound challenge to the assumptions on which existential realism is based. At the same time, however, it is essential to note that democratic states do continue to find themselves in conflict and sometimes at war with nondemocratic states. Moreover, the idea of democratization implies the adoption of a genuinely effective constitutional democracy as widely understood in the West, and not the kind of plebiscitary charade that authoritarian systems sometimes adopt in a bid to provide their rulers with greater legitimacy. Nor does the concept of democracy really include instances when elections are not more than a means by which a group or movement consolidates power and then closes off the process against other competing groups ("one man, one vote, one time").

Fourth, forces both above and below the state tend to erode its authority and control. Internally, there are claims from subnational groups, especially those that are regionally or ethnically based. These claims can, under the rubric of self-determination, result in calls for the creation of new forms of government or even statehood. This is exemplified in the disintegration of the USSR into its constituent republics, as well as the growing fissiparous tendencies within many of these new states, as well as in the fragmentation of Yugoslavia. Conversely, the state is often too small to meet the needs of its own people, especially in the economic realm. Here, the activity of bodies such as the EC, and the patterns of global activity in trade, investment, financial flows, labor migration, and communications present a direct challenge to customary state sovereignty.

Fifth, nuclear weapons may inhibit conflict. Despite more than four decades of Cold War, the confrontation between the United States and the Soviet Union did not escalate into a major superpower war. An important reason for restraint was the existence of nuclear weapons and the accompanying pattern of assured destruction. This acted to inhibit the behavior of both countries in times of crisis and was a factor in shaping what John Gaddis termed the "long peace" between them.[12] Here, however, what was applicable to the superpowers would, in all probability, be inapplicable for most others. The stabilizing characteristics of assured destruction, massive internal restraints, and geographic distance all acted as inhibitors. A world of growing nuclear proliferation, however, would be one of lethal danger.

Sixth, the behavior of states within the international system can be shaped by a learning process, a phenomenon that has received increasing attention from scholars.[13] This may be a matter of shared historical experience, as in the traumatic experience of Europeans in two world wars. It may also be a matter of values, for example, attention to human rights or the claims of Islamic Fundamentalism. The question remains, however, why learning seems to have an impact in some circumstances but not others, for example, in Germany after World War II but not after World War I.

Together, these factors (the global economy, international institutions, democratization, transnational and subnational forces, nuclear weapons, and learning) have been significant either in eroding the ability of states to act autonomously, or in shaping state behavior. Frequently, they have the effect of mitigating or even precluding conflict and war, although they are not always necessarily conducive to cooperation. Nevertheless, authority still resides with the state, hence the propensities described by existential realism continue to condition state behavior. Moreover, subnational regional and ethnic groups typically speak in the language of statehood and often see this as the goal for which they strive.

Finally, despite noteworthy societal changes, the durability of the state remains evident. As Robert Gilpin has noted, the state has for more than three centuries remained the focal point for economic development, military power, and human identity.[14] To be sure, each of these functions has been subject to significant challenge. States, however, have nonetheless remained both durable and adaptable, and alternate claimants are not in evidence. Thus, as long as humans are organized in states, and while there is a general absence of effective, legitimate authority at the regional or global level, the anarchy problem, and the properties to which it gives rise, will persist.

## Implications for the Post-Cold War System

In the immediate aftermath of the Cold War, it was widely hoped and assumed that there would be a major reduction in international conflict. The argument stated for example by Kenneth Oye,[15] held that the East-West confrontation had the unfortunate effect of causing local wars to be exacerbated by the participation of the superpowers or their proxies. Conflicts such as those in Angola, Ethiopia, and Vietnam were seen as cases in point. Thus, it was argued, with the ebbing of the Cold War, the threshold level of violence would tend to be significantly reduced.

An alternative conception, and one grounded more explicitly in existential realism, suggests a less optimistic conclusion. This approach acknowledges that superpower involvement often inflamed local conflicts, but it also notes the extent to which the superpowers acted to restrain the behavior of regional actors and proxies. The restraint was a product of the dominance, or hegemony, of each superpower within its respective sphere, and its effects were particularly evident in Europe and the Middle East. It is thus conceivable that, given problems of ethnicity, national identity, territorial disputes, and the ambitions of individual leaders, the international system may now experience as much or more conflict than during the Cold War.[16]

In the case of Eastern Europe, the brutal imposition of Soviet domination after 1945 had the side effect of temporarily imposing order. That is, it suppressed bitter and long-standing national and ethnic rivalries that had been exacerbated after the post-World War I breakup of the Ottoman, Austro-Hungarian, German, and Russian empires. From the vantage point of existential realism, the problem of anarchy in state to state and inter-ethnic relations within the region was temporarily held in abeyance by the imposition of a Soviet-dictated order. The point here is not to offer any kind words for what was a cruel hegemonic regime, but to observe that it had the result of imposing a degree of order on the actors.[17]

With the breathtaking changes of 1989-1991, in which the government of Mikhail Gorbachev abandoned the East European governments, which quickly fell, and the collapse of the Warsaw Pact and the disintegration of the USSR itself followed, the fabric of relations between and within the East European states also began to unravel. Although Yugoslavia had not been subject to Soviet domination since 1948, it is doubtful that the violent disintegration and ethnic civil war there would have occurred had the older pattern of Soviet regional domination been in effect.

Moreover, the decomposition of the USSR into its constituent republics, each of which has acquired formal attributes of statehood, has also unleashed fissiparous forces within the republics themselves. The mostly weak central governments have had difficulty in dealing with these challenges, and the increased level of violence that has already occurred (for example in Georgia, Armenia, and Azerbaijan) may be difficult to contain.

In the case of Western Europe, the post-1945 Soviet threat provided the need and opportunity both for U.S. leadership of the Atlantic Alliance and the creation of series of institutions for security and economic cooperation. Moreover, these conditions also proved conducive to ending the historic confrontation between France and Germany that had been the focal point for three major wars in 75 years, and for establishing unprecedented cooperation among the industrial democracies of Western Europe.

In existential realist terms, the American-led security and economic arrangements, motivated by the Soviet threat, provided a basis for order in Europe above the level of the state and thus made possible a mitigation and then resolution of the conflicts that had torn the continent for three centuries.

Despite periods of détente in the 1960s and 1970s, as well as frequent disagreements among the Western allies over such matters as the 1956 Suez crisis, the Cuban missile crisis, Vietnam, the 1973 Middle East war and oil crisis, and a series of economic policy disagreements, the postwar pattern of West European and Atlantic cooperation remained durable as long as three realities obtained: first, the Soviet military occupation of Eastern Europe, with its potential threat to the West; second, the continuing imposition of Marxist-Leninist regimes upon the East Europeans; and, third, an unchanging Soviet regime.[18]

With the end of the Soviet threat, much of the original impetus that gave rise to the Western cooperative institutions has disappeared. Among the West Europeans themselves, however, and distinctly unlike the situation among the East Europeans, four decades of working together have permitted the implantation of institutions and behavior that seem robust enough to withstand the change. These include an extensive web of economic interdependence; democratization; the institutions of the EC and of the Western-led world economy; the learning experiences derived from twentieth-century history; and the self-interest of the governments and populations of Western Europe. Moreover, cooperation and common institutions among the West Europeans have been entered into voluntarily, not imposed from above, and they thus retain a basic legitimacy that was absent from the Soviet-imposed arrangements in Eastern Europe. Future expansion and deepening of the European Community remain more problematic, but the risks of conflict and war among the West Europeans can be effectively excluded.

The relationship between Western Europe and the United States, however, has been placed in question by the transformation of East-West relations, as well as by a tendency toward consolidation of regional trade blocks. The postwar economic and security order was created by the Western Alliance in reaction to the Soviet threat, and the disintegration of the USSR dissolved the original rationale for its existence. The diminished security threat also removed a key motivation for the United States to support a relatively open international economic order.[19] This potential impetus for a U.S. retreat was further exacerbated by the erosion of the U.S. ability to pay the costs of maintaining the existing security and economic regimes, that is, to sustain military expenditures disproportionately greater than those of its European and Japanese competitors, as well as to tolerate what is frequently depicted as unfair trade competition by the same countries.

The end of the Cold War has thus affected Eastern and Western Europe differently. It has also had different effects outside the main arenas of East-West competition. In Ethiopia, Angola, and South Africa, the end of the Cold War helped to reduce the level of violence in local conflicts. In Central America, the change helped bring a series of brutal internal wars to an end. Not every change brought about by the end of the Cold War has been peaceful, however. In the cases of Somalia and Afghanistan, external involvement has given way to internally based strife that is as bad or worse as anything preceding it. For Afghanistan, this has meant a bloody struggle among competing factions. In the case of Somalia, disintegration of the local government and the struggle among armed clans has produced what comes as close to the Hobbesian war of all against all as anything to be seen on the face of the earth.

Finally, the Middle East has provided an especially pertinent case in point. It is doubtful that Saddam Hussein would have been willing or able to invade Kuwait in August 1990 had it not been for the reduced Soviet role in the region. In that sense, the immediate aftermath of the end of the East-West conflict brought more rather than less regional conflict.

It is also the case, however, that Russian support in the UN Security Council made it possible for the United States to organize and lead the coalition countries in their effort to isolate Saddam and then to oust him militarily from Kuwait. Moreover, the initiation of Arab-Israeli peace talks, beginning at Madrid in October 1991 under the sponsorship of the United States and (nominally) the USSR, would have been impossible during the Cold War. Syrian behavior in particular, was shaped by an appreciation that the United States has become the dominant power in the Middle East, and in the absence of Soviet support and protection, President Hafez Assad altered his behavior accordingly.

### International Organizations as Challenges to Realism

Existential realism is largely an empirical description of reality.[20] But rudimentary institutions and practices do exist that, if sufficiently enlarged, would begin to change the realities upon which that realism is based. Perhaps the most obvious agent of this potential change is the United Nations. The world organization appeared to play an unprecedented role in the Persian Gulf crisis and war. Security Council resolutions provided the legitimacy for economic sanctions and then for the use of force against Saddam, as well as for the subsequent effort to identify and destroy Iraq's nuclear, chemical, biological, and missile programs. Moreover, with the end of the Cold War, the role played by the UN in expanded peacekeeping arrangements in regional conflicts has contributed to a sense of the UN's broader possibilities.

The change in Russian behavior and the willingness of Moscow to collaborate with the United States, Britain, and France in the Security Council (along with the passive acquiescence of the People's Republic of China) seemed to suggest that the UN finally would be able to function in the role its founders had hoped for in 1945, with the permanent members of the Security Council functioning as the world's policemen. Until that point, the cold war division among the permanent members of the Security Council had paralyzed the UN's capacity to act decisively. The obstacles to effective operation of the UN continue to remain daunting, however, nor is there much practical possibility of developing longer-term efforts to achieve a workable system of collective security in which members of the institution would come to the defense of all the others.[21]

First, the world has changed since 1945. Then, great power agreement really did carry with it the ability to impose conditions on lesser countries. In the world of the 1990s, however, there has been extensive diffusion of power, so that important regional states have far greater autonomous capability to defy the Security Council. States such as Iran, India, Brazil, and Nigeria, not to mention Japan and Germany, cannot easily be directed or intimidated by the Security Council. Moreover, even in the remarkable case of a near universal agreement to act against Iraq in its flagrant violation of international law, the liberation of Kuwait nonetheless took an unprecedented degree of effort by countries whose size and wealth dwarfed those of Iraq.

In addition, without the leadership of the United States, neither the political nor military components of the coalition response would have been feasible. It is inconceivable that the initiative would have been seized by the countries of the United Nations collectively, let alone by an important regional grouping such as the European Community or the Arab League. None of the other potential actors had the political coherence to act or the military capability to project power halfway around the world against a medium-sized state equipped with a large army, modern weapons, and a demonstrated capacity for the most ruthless application of violence. Indeed, the alternative to U.S. leadership in the crisis would have been inaction.

Although the UN role was significant, it consisted mainly of providing a useful legitimacy for the actions of individual states. This made it easier domestically for a number of countries to take part in the sanctions and in the coalition's military effort; it helped to make feasible the large German and Japanese monetary contributions to finance the war; and it even aided the Bush administration in gaining majority support in Congress for a resolution authorizing the use of force. These are not unimportant considerations, but they are modest enough given Saddam's egregious violation of international law.

Elsewhere, when the permanent members of the Security Council agree, and in circumstances where local forces are prepared to cooperate, the post-cold war environment has permitted the UN to play an important role in peacekeeping, and the number of calls for its intervention have multiplied. The limits of the UN response to Serbian aggression in Yugoslavia and to starvation on a massive scale in Somalia have, however, been evident. Both cases involve[d] appalling and quite evident human suffering, yet— . . .—the UN lack[ed] the structure, forces, money, institutional base, and political consensus to act decisively in either case. In consequence, the insight of existential realism remains useful, even while it highlights the grim reality that there does not exist an effective authority above the level of the state that would be capable of acting effectively to promote order and resolve disputes among or within states.

Regional institutions [have been] comparably deficient or inadequate in responding to the scale of these challenges. In the case of Somalia, neither the Arab League nor the Organization of African Unity [was] able to act. As for Yugoslavia, the European Community, and the Europeans more broadly, [were] unable to reverse the Serbian onslaught or halt policies of "ethnic cleansing." Germany and Italy [were] inhibited from intervening militarily as a consequence of their aggressive role in the Balkans during World War II, and the principal European countries [were] divided and in disarray over what course of action to take. . . . The European [Union] itself simply does not possess the authority or capacity to undertake an effective role in Yugoslavia in any case. Moreover, efforts to enhance the [EU's] capacity to act in the realm of foreign and security policy, as well as to strengthen its centralized institutions, have met with growing domestic opposition throughout the [Union].

## Implications for U.S. Foreign Policy

Emphasis here on the insights that realism continues to provide does not dictate cynical disregard for international cooperation or for efforts to limit conflict or to foster democratization and protection of human rights. Nor, in light of the extensive changes in international economics, communications, and society, should realism be seen as sufficient unto itself as an all-encompassing theory of internal relations.[22] Nonetheless, through its appreciation of the realities of the international system, existential realism provides insights into the way in which state behavior is shaped by this environment, and the understanding remains essential both for theory and policy. Such an approach is consistent with an appreciation both for the role of international institutions—as mechanisms for mitigating the effects of anarchy as well as for providing both domestic and international legitimacy for collective action—and for the need to maintain national and alliance capabilities powerful enough to deal with threats.

Realism's implications for the United States include avoiding a post-cold war utopian belief that the United Nations and other international institutions can provide the means for effective collective security and the solution of common problems if Americans are only sufficiently ardent in their support for them. Such an approach risks confusing "ought" with "is."

International organizations can, indeed, play an increasingly useful role, but there is little prospect that by themselves they can deal effectively with the most serious threats to the peace. The weakness of these bodies makes them especially vulnerable to members who deliberately transgress. As but one illustration, let us look at the International Atomic Energy Agency (IAEA) and its monitoring of the Iraqi nuclear program. Under the terms of the Nuclear Non-Proliferation treaty, the IAEA was responsible for inspecting Iraqi facilities. By any reasonable standard, a country such as Iraq presented a prima facie risk of both deception and proliferation. Given the weakness of the inspection procedures and the IAEA's institutional culture, however, some 70 percent of its budget was devoted to inspections in Japan, Germany, and Canada. Moreover, the ineffectual nature of its inspections in Iraq meant that the IAEA missed detecting the massive but covert Iraqi nuclear program. In consequence, prior to the onset of the Gulf crisis, the IAEA provided a kind of legitimacy for Iraq, and its officials developed a bureaucratic self-interest in defending their assessment. Indeed, following the war, the UN-mandated inspection, and the discovery of the covert Iraqi program, a leading IAEA official rushed to Baghdad in an effort to convince the inspectors that what they had discovered was not actually what they knew it to be.[23]

A dangerous alternative to overreliance on international institutions is a retreat into isolationism. . . , an attitude toward the external world that fail[s] to take into account the need for an active and internationalist foreign policy. In reality, problems such as nuclear and missile proliferation; instability in Eastern Europe and the former Soviet Union; flows of trade, money, and investment; and even problems of labor migration and the environment can only be dealt with on an international basis and not by policies conducted on a narrowly national basis.

As a means of making sense of the external world and the requirements of foreign policy, realism provides no iron laws of human behavior, but it does offer an approach to reality in which both theory and policy can be grounded. In the post-cold war world, patterns of interdependence and significant areas of cooperation among states are of fundamental importance. But a continuing realm for power politics exists simultaneously as an enduring feature of the  same world, and international relations remain subject to the basic existential problems identified by realism: states exist in an international system without an overall authority to provide order; this "self-help" system creates imperatives that shape foreign policy behavior, especially in security matters, and sometimes in other realms; conflicts, which are inevitable in human affairs, and for which externally devised solutions are unavailable, have the potential for erupting into violence and war. Recognition of these realities is a precondition both for understanding the dynamics of international affairs and for developing policies that are to have any hope of achieving peace and protecting the national interest.

## Notes

1. E. H. Carr, The Twenty Years' Crisis, 1919-1939: *An Introduction to the Study of International Relations* (New York: St. Martin's, 1939, rev. ed., 1946); Hans J. Morgenthau, *Politics Among Nations: The Struggle for Power and Peace* (New York: Knopf, 1948).

2. Kenneth N. Waltz, *Theory of International Politics* (New York: Random, 1979).

3. See Robert O. Keohane, ed., *Neorealism and Its Critics* (New York: Columbia University Press, 1976).

4. Structural realism is identified with the approach taken by Waltz in *Theory of International Politics*.

5. Joseph S. Nye, Jr., "What New World Order?" *Foreign Affairs* 71 (Spring 1992), p. 89.

6. See Alan Gilbert, "Must Global Politics Constrain Democracy: Realism, Regimes and Democratic Internationalism," *Political Theory* 20 (February 1992), pp. 9-37, and Stephen D. Krasner, "Realism, Imperialism, and Democracy: A Response to Gilbert," *Political Theory* 20 (February 1992), pp. 38-52, especially 38-39.

7. Roundtable, "Is There a Global International Relations Theory?" Annual Convention of the International Studies Association, Atlanta Georgia, April 2, 1992.

8. Robert Jervis, *The Illogic of American Nuclear Strategy* (Ithaca, N.Y.: Cornell University Press, 1984), p. 146.

9. *Ibid.*, p. 155, quoting McGeorge Bundy, "The Bishops and the Bomb," *New York Review of Books*, June 16, 1983, pp. 3-8.

10. See the discussion in Lieber, *No Common Power: Understanding International Relations*, 2d ed. (New York: HarperCollins, 1991), pp. 5-6.

11. Glenn H. Snyder, "The Security Dilemma in Alliance Politics," *World Politics* 36 (July 1984), p. 461. The original use of the term "security dilemma" was made by John H. Herz in his *Political Realism and Political Idealism* (Chicago: University of Chicago Press, 1951).

12. John Gaddis, "The Long Peace: Elements of Stability in the Postwar International System," *International Security* 10 (Spring 1986). The assumption that the spread of nuclear weapons to Germany would be a force for stability is made by John Mearsheimer (although it is not shared by most other analysts). See "Back to the Future: Instability in Europe After the Cold War," *International Security* 15 (Summer 1990).

13. See Richard E. Neustadt and Ernest R. May, *Thinking in Time: The Uses of History for Decision Makers* (New York: The Free Press, 1986); George W. Breslauer and Philip E. Tetlock, eds., *Learning in U.S. and Soviet Foreign Policy* (Boulder, Colo.: Westview, 1991); and Joseph S. Nye, Jr., "Nuclear Learning and U.S. Soviet Security Regimes," *International Security* 41 (Summer 1991).

14. Robert Gilpin, *The Political Economy of International Relations* (Princeton, N.J.: Princeton University Press, 1987): also, "The Richness of the Tradition of Political Realism," *International Organization* 38 (Spring 1984), pp. 287-304.

15. Kenneth A Oye, "Beyond Postwar Order and New World Order: American Foreign Policy in Transition," in Oye, Lieber, and Donald Rothchild, eds., *Eagle in a New World: American Grand Strategy in the Post-Cold War Era* (New York: HarperCollins, 1992), pp. 18-19.

16. Stanley Hoffman makes a comparable point: "While the world no longer lives under the shadow of a superpower nuclear confrontation, the numbers of actual possible conflicts, both among and within states, seem bound to grow, whether because of aggressive ambitions, as with Saddam Hussein, or border disputes and rival claims over the same territory, as in the case of Palestine, or domestic crises and policies that have effects abroad, causing other states to threaten external intervention, as with Yugoslavia," "Delusions of World Order," *New York Review of Books*, April 9, 1992, p. 37.

17. Anton DePorte has previously argued that, at the time it occurred, the forced division of Germany had the effect of eliminating a principal source of European instability. *Europe Between the Superpowers: The Enduring Balance* (New York: Yale University Press, 1979).

18. For an elaboration of this argument, see Laeber, "The United States and Western Europe in the Post-Cold War World," in Oye, Lieber, and Rothchild, *Eagle in a New World*, p. 318.

19. See *Ibid.*, p. 320.

20. Richard K. Betts makes a similar point in "Systems for Peace or Causes of War: Collective Security, Arms Control, and the New Europe," *International Security* 17 (Summer 1992), p. 11.

21. Betts makes this point effectively in "Systems for Peace or Causes of War?" pp. 7-8 and 17-20.

22. Nye makes a comparable point, although with more emphasis on the limits of realism and a definition emphasizing its military dimension: "The realist view of world order, resting on a balance of military power, is necessary but not sufficient, because it does not take into account the long term societal changes that have been slowly moving the world away from the Westphalian system." "What New World Order?" p. 89.

23. This account is from the author's interview on April 20, 1992, with a scientist from the Lawrence Livermore National Laboratory, who had served as a leader of one of the UN nuclear inspection teams.

# Chapter 6

### ★ ★ ★

# Power Shift

Jessica T. Mathews

*Jessica T. Mathews argues that the international system is undergoing a profound transformation, that the significance of state boundaries and authority is diminishing, and that the salience of traditional threats is on the decline while that of non-traditional threats is on the rise. Do you agree that states are becoming less important and nonstate actors more important? How should we deal with the nongovernmental organizations (NGOs) Mathews focuses on here? Can states effectively counter the increasing globalization of economic activity? What role will international organizations play in the future? Are states no longer "the natural problem-solving unit"?*

## The Rise of Global Civil Society

The end of the Cold War has brought no mere adjustment among states but a novel redistribution of power among states, markets, and civil society. National governments are not simply losing autonomy in a globalizing economy. They are sharing powers—including political, social, and security roles at the core of sovereignty—with businesses, with international organizations, and with a multitude of citizens groups, known as nongovernmental organizations (NGOs). The steady concentration of power in the hands of states that began in 1648 with the Peace of Westphalia is over, at least for a while.[1]

The absolutes of the Westphalian system—territorially fixed states where everything of value lies within some state's borders; a single, secular authority governing each territory and representing it outside its borders; and no authority above states—are all dissolving. Increasingly, resources and threats that matter, including money, information, pollution, and popular culture, circulate and shape lives and economies with little regard for political boundaries. International standards of conduct are gradually beginning to override claims of national or regional singularity. Even the most powerful states find

Jessica T. Mathews is a Senior Fellow at the Council on Foreign Relations.

Reprint by permission of *Foreign Affairs*, vol. 76, no. 1, January/February 1997, pp. 50-66. Copyright © 1996 by the Council on Foreign Relations, Inc.

the marketplace and international public opinion compelling them more often to follow a particular course.

The state's central task of assuring security is the least affected, but still not exempt. War will not disappear, but with the shrinkage of U.S. and Russian nuclear arsenals, the transformation of the Nuclear Nonproliferation Treaty into a permanent covenant in 1995, agreement on the long-sought Comprehensive Test Ban treaty in 1996, and the likely entry into force of the Chemical Weapons Convention in 1997, the security threat to states from other states is on a downward course. Nontraditional threats, however, are rising—terrorism, organized crime, drug trafficking, ethnic conflict, and the combination of rapid population growth, environmental decline, and poverty that breeds economic stagnation, political instability, and, sometimes, state collapse. The nearly 100 armed conflicts since the end of the Cold War have virtually all been intrastate affairs. Many began with governments acting against their own citizens, through extreme corruption, violence, incompetence, or complete breakdown, as in Somalia.

These trends have fed a growing sense that individuals' security may not in fact reliably derive from their nation's security. A competing notion of "human security" is creeping around the edges of official thinking, suggesting that security be viewed as emerging from the conditions of daily life—food, shelter, employment, health, public safety—rather than flowing downward from a country's foreign relations and military strength.

The most powerful engine of change in the relative decline of states and the rise of nonstate actors is the computer and telecommunications revolution, whose deep political and social consequences have been almost completely ignored. Widely accessible and affordable technology has broken governments' monopoly on the collection and management of large amounts of information and deprived governments of the deference they enjoyed because of it. In every sphere of activity, instantaneous access to information and the ability to put it to use multiplies the number of players who matter and reduces the number who command great authority. The effect on the loudest voice—which has been government's—has been the greatest.

By drastically reducing the importance of proximity, the new technologies change people's perceptions of community. Fax machines, satellite hookups, and the Internet connect people across borders with exponentially growing ease while separating them from natural and historical associations within nations. In this sense a powerful globalizing force, they can also have the opposite effect, amplifying political and social fragmentation by enabling more and more identities and interests scattered around the globe to coalesce and thrive.

These technologies have the potential to divide society along new lines, separating ordinary people from elites with the wealth and education to command technology's power. Those elites are not only the rich but also citizens groups with transnational interests and identities that frequently have more in common with counterparts in other countries, whether industrialized or developing, than with countrymen.

Above all, the information technologies disrupt hierarchies, spreading power among more people and groups. In drastically lowering the costs of communication, consultation, and coordination, they favor decentralized networks over other modes of organization. In a network, individuals or groups link for joint action without building a physical or formal institutional presence. Networks have no person at the top and no center. Instead, they have multiple nodes where collections of individuals or groups interact for different purposes. Businesses, citizens organizations, ethnic groups, and crime cartels have all readily adopted the network model. Governments, on the other hand, are quintessential hierarchies, wedded to an organizational form incompatible with all that the new technologies make possible.

Today's powerful nonstate actors are not without precedent. The British East India Company ran a subcontinent, and a few influential NGOs go back more than a century. But these are exceptions. Both in numbers and in impact, nonstate actors have never before approached their current strength. And a still larger role likely lies ahead.

## Dial Locally, Act Globally

No one knows how many NGOs there are or how fast the tally is growing. Published figures are badly misleading. One widely cited estimate claims there are 35,000 NGOs in the developing countries; another points to 12,000 irrigation cooperatives in South Asia alone. In fact, it is impossible to measure a swiftly growing universe that includes neighborhood, professional, service, and advocacy groups, both secular and church-based, promoting every conceivable cause and funded by donations, fees, foundations, governments, international organizations, or the sale of products and services. The true number is certainly in the millions, from the tiniest village association to influential but modestly funded international groups like Amnesty International to larger global activist organizations like Greenpeace and giant service providers like CARE, which has an annual budget of nearly $400 million.

Except in China, Japan, the Middle East, and a few other places where culture or authoritarian governments severely limit civil society, NGOs' role and influence have exploded in the last half-decade. Their financial resources and—often more important—their expertise, approximate and sometimes exceed those of smaller governments and of international organizations. "We have less money and fewer resources than Amnesty International, and we are the arm of the U.N. for human rights," noted Ibrahima Fall, head of the U.N. Centre for Human Rights, in 1993. "This is clearly ridiculous." Today NGOs deliver more official development assistance than the entire U.N. system (excluding the World Bank and the International Monetary Fund). In many countries they are delivering the services—in urban and rural community development, education, and health care—that faltering governments can no longer manage.

The range of these groups' work is almost as broad as their interests. They breed new ideas; advocate, protest, and mobilize public support; do legal, scientific, technical, and policy analysis; provide services; shape, implement, monitor, and enforce national and international commitments; and change institutions and norms.

Increasingly, NGOs are able to push around even the largest governments. When the United States and Mexico set out to reach a trade agreement, the two governments planned on the usual narrowly defined negotiations behind closed doors. But NGOs had a very different vision. Groups from Canada, the United States, and Mexico wanted to see provisions in the North American Free Trade Agreement on health and safety, transboundary pollution, consumer protection, immigration, labor mobility, child labor, sustainable agriculture, social charters, and debt relief. Coalitions of NGOs formed in each country and across both borders. The opposition they generated in early 1991 endangered congressional approval of the crucial "fast track" negotiating authority for the U.S. government. After months of resistance, the Bush administration capitulated, opening the agreement to environmental and labor concerns. Although progress in other trade venues will be slow, the tightly closed world of trade negotiations has been changed forever.

Technology is fundamental to NGOs' new clout. The nonprofit Association for Progressive Communications provides 50,000 NGOs in 133 countries access to the tens of millions of Internet users for the price of a local call. The dramatically lower costs of international communication have altered NGOs' goals and changed international outcomes. Within hours of the first gunshots of the Chiapas rebellion in southern Mexico in January 1994, for example, the Internet swarmed with messages from human rights activists. The worldwide media attention they and their groups focused on Chiapas, along with the influx of rights activists to the area, sharply limited the Mexican government's response. What in other times would have been a bloody insurgency turned out to be a largely nonviolent conflict. "The shots lasted ten days," José Angel Gurría, Mexico's foreign minister, later remarked, "and ever since, the war has been . . . a war on the Internet."

NGOs' easy reach behind other states' borders forces governments to consider domestic public opinion in countries with which they are dealing, even on matters that governments have traditionally handled strictly between themselves. At the same time, cross-border NGO networks offer citizens groups unprecedented channels of influence. Women's and human rights groups in many developing countries have linked up with more experienced, better funded, and more powerful groups in Europe and the United States. The latter work the global media and lobby their own governments to pressure leaders in developing countries, creating a circle of influence that is accelerating change in many parts of the world.

## Out of the Hallway, Around the Table

In international organizations, as with governments at home, NGOs were once largely relegated to the hallways. Even when they were able to shape governments' agendas, as the Helsinki Watch human rights groups did in the Conference on Security and Cooperation in Europe in the 1980s, their influence was largely determined by how receptive their own government's delegation happened to be. Their only option was to work through governments.

All that changed with the negotiation of the global climate treaty, culminating at the Earth Summit in Rio de Janeiro in 1992. With the broader independent base of public support that environmental groups command, NGOs set the original goal of negotiating an agreement to control greenhouse gases long before governments were ready to do so, proposed most of its structure and content, and lobbied and mobilized public pressure to force through a pact that virtually no one else thought possible when the talks began.

More members of NGOs served on government delegations than ever before, and they penetrated deeply into official decision-making. They were allowed to attend the small working group meetings where the real decisions in international negotiations are made. The tiny nation of Vanuatu turned its delegation over to an NGO with expertise in international law (a group based in London and funded by an American foundation), thereby making itself and the other sea-level island states major players in the fight to control global warming. *ECO,* an NGO-published daily newspaper, was negotiators' best source of information on the progress of the official talks and became the forum where governments tested ideas for breaking deadlocks.

Whether from developing or developed countries, NGOs were tightly organized in a global and half a dozen regional Climate Action Networks, which were able to bridge North-South differences among governments that many had expected would prevent an agreement. United in their passionate pursuit of a treaty, NGOs would fight out contentious issues among themselves, then take an agreed position to their respective delegations. When they could not agree, NGOs served as invaluable back channels, letting both sides know where the other's problems lay or where a compromise might be found.

As a result, delegates completed the framework of a global climate accord in the blink of a diplomat's eye—16 months—over the opposition of the three energy superpowers, the United States, Russia, and Saudi Arabia. The treaty entered into force in record time just two years later. Although only a framework accord whose binding requirements are still to be negotiated, the treaty could force sweeping changes in energy use, with potentially enormous implications for every economy.

The influence of NGOs at the climate talks has not yet been matched in any other arena, and indeed has provoked a backlash among some governments. A handful of authoritarian regimes, most notably China, led the charge, but many others share their unease about the role NGOs are assuming. Nevertheless, NGOs have worked their way into the heart of international negotiations and into the day-to-day operations of international organizations, bringing new priorities, demands for procedures that give a voice to groups outside government, and new standards of accountability.

## One World Business

The multinational corporations of the 1960s were virtually all American, and prided themselves on their insularity. Foreigners might run subsidiaries, but they were never partners. A foreign posting was a setback for a rising executive.

Today, a global marketplace is developing for retail sales as well as manufacturing. Law, advertising, business consulting, and financial and other services are also marketed internationally. Firms of all nationalities attempt to look and act like locals wherever they operate. Foreign language skills and lengthy experience abroad are an asset, and increasingly a requirement, for top management. Sometimes corporate headquarters are not even in a company's home country.

Amid shifting alliances and joint ventures, made possible by computers and advanced communications, nationalities blur. Offshore banking encourages widespread evasion of national taxes. Whereas the fear in the 1970s was that multinationals would become an arm of government, the concern now is that they are disconnecting from their home countries' national interests, moving jobs, evading taxes, and eroding economic sovereignty in the process.

The even more rapid globalization of financial markets has left governments far behind. Where governments once set foreign exchange rates, private currency traders, accountable only to their bottom line, now trade $1.3 trillion a day, 100 times the volume of world trade. The amount exceeds the total foreign exchange reserves of all governments, and is more than even an alliance of strong states can buck.

Despite the enormous attention given to governments' conflicts over trade rules, private capital flows have been growing twice as fast as trade for years. International portfolio transactions by U.S. investors, 9 percent of U.S GDP in 1980, had grown to 135 percent of GDP by 1993. Growth in Germany, Britain, and elsewhere has been even more rapid. Direct investment has surged as well. All in all, the global financial market will grow to a staggering $83 trillion by 2000, a 1994 McKinsey

& Co. study estimated, triple the aggregate GDP of the affluent nations of the Organization for Economic Cooperation and Development.

Again, technology has been a driving force, shifting financial clout from states to the market with its offer of unprecedented speed in transactions—states cannot match market reaction times measured in seconds—and its dissemination of financial information to a broad range of players. States could choose whether they would belong to rulebased economic systems like the gold standard, but, as former Citicorp chairman Walter Wriston has pointed out, they cannot withdraw from the technology-based marketplace, unless they seek autarky and poverty.

More and more frequently today, governments have only the appearance of free choice when they set economic rules. Markets are setting de facto rules enforced by their own power. States can flout them, but the penalties are severe—loss of vital foreign capital, foreign technology, and domestic jobs. Even the most powerful economy must pay heed. The U.S. government could choose to rescue the Mexican peso in 1994, for example, but it had to do so on terms designed to satisfy the bond markets, not the countries doing the rescuing.

The forces shaping the legitimate global economy are also nourishing globally integrated crime—which U.N. officials peg at a staggering $750 billion a year, $400 billion to $500 billion of that in narcotics, according to U.S. Drug Enforcement Agency estimates. Huge increases in the volume of goods and people crossing borders and competitive pressures to speed the flow of trade by easing inspections and reducing paperwork make it easier to hide contraband. Deregulation and privatization of government-owned businesses, modern communications, rapidly shifting commercial alliances, and the emergence of global financial systems have all helped transform local drug operations into global enterprises. The largely unregulated multi-trillion-dollar pool of money in supranational cyberspace, accessible by computer 24 hours a day, eases the drug trade's toughest problem: transforming huge sums of hot cash into investments in legitimate business.

Globalized crime is a security threat that neither police nor the military—the state's traditional responses—can meet. Controlling it will require states to pool their efforts and to establish unprecedented cooperation with the private sector, thereby compromising two cherished sovereign roles. If states fail, if criminal groups can continue to take advantage of porous borders and transnational financial spaces while governments are limited to acting within their own territory, crime will have the winning edge.

## Born—Again Institutions

Until recently, international organizations were institutions of, by, and for nation-states. Now they are building constituencies of their own and, through

NGOs, establishing direct connections to the peoples of the world. The shift is infusing them with new life and influence, but it is also creating tensions.

States feel they need more capable international organizations to deal with a lengthening list of transnational challenges, but at the same time fear competitors. Thus they vote for new forms of international intervention while reasserting sovereignty's first principle: no interference in the domestic affairs of states. They hand international organizations sweeping new responsibilities and then rein them in with circumscribed mandates or inadequate funding. With states ambivalent about intervention, a host of new problems demanding attention, and NGOs bursting with energy, ideas, and calls for a larger role, international organizations are lurching toward an unpredictable, but certainly different, future.

International organizations are still coming to terms with unprecedented growth in the volume of international problem-solving. Between 1972 and 1992 the number of environmental treaties rocketed from a few dozen to more than 900. While collaboration in other fields is not growing at quite that rate, treaties, regimes, and intergovernmental institutions dealing with human rights, trade, narcotics, corruption, crime, refugees, antiterrorism measures, arms control, and democracy are multiplying. "Soft law" in the form of guidelines, recommended practices, nonbinding resolutions, and the like is also rapidly expanding. Behind each new agreement are scientists and lawyers who worked on it, diplomats who negotiated it, and NGOs that back it, most of them committed for the long haul. The new constituency also includes a burgeoning, influential class of international civil servants responsible for implementing, monitoring, and enforcing this enormous new body of law.

At the same time, governments, while ambivalent about the international community mixing in states' domestic affairs, have driven some gaping holes in the wall that has separated the two. In the triumphant months after the Berlin Wall came down, international accords, particularly ones agreed on by what is now the Organization for Security and Cooperation in Europe and by the Organization of American States (OAS), drew explicit links between democracy, human rights, and international security, establishing new legal bases for international interventions. In 1991 the U.N. General Assembly declared itself in favor of humanitarian intervention without the request or consent of the state involved. A year later the Security Council took the unprecedented step of authorizing the use of force "on behalf of civilian populations" in Somalia. Suddenly an interest in citizens began to compete with, and occasionally override, the formerly unquestioned primacy of state interests.

Since 1990 the Security Council has declared a formal threat to international peace and security 61 times, after having done so only six times in the preceding 45 years. It is not that security has been abruptly and terribly threatened; rather, the change reflects the broadened scope of what the international community now feels it should poke its nose into. As with Haiti in 1992, many of the so-called Chapter VII resolutions authorizing forceful intervention concerned domestic situations that involved awful human suffering or offended international norms but posed little if any danger to international peace.

Almost as intrusive as a Chapter VII intervention, though always invited, election monitoring has also become a growth industry. The United Nations monitored no election in a member state during the Cold War, only in colonies. But beginning in 1990 it responded to a deluge of requests from governments that felt compelled to prove their legitimacy by the new standards. In Latin America, where countries most jealously guard their sovereignty, the OAS monitored 11 national elections in four years.

And monitoring is no longer the passive observation it was in earlier decades. Carried out by a close-knit mix of international organizations and NGOs, it involves a large foreign presence dispensing advice and recommending standards for voter registration, campaign law, campaign practices, and the training of clerks and judiciaries. Observers even carry out parallel vote counts that can block fraud but at the same time second-guess the integrity of national counts.

International financial institutions, too, have inserted themselves more into states' domestic affairs. During the 1980s the World Bank attached conditions to loans concerning recipient governments' policies on poverty, the environment, and even, occasionally, military spending, a once sacrosanct domain of national prerogative. In 1991 a statement of bank policy holding that "efficient and accountable public sector management" is crucial to economic growth provided the rationale for subjecting to international oversight everything from official corruption to government competence.

Beyond involving them in an array of domestic economic and social decisions, the new policies force the World Bank, the International Monetary Fund, and other international financial institutions to forge alliances with business, NGOs, and civil society if they are to achieve broad changes in target countries. In the process, they have opened themselves to the same demands they are making of their clients: broader public participation and greater openness in decision-making. As a result, yet another set of doors behind which only officials sat has been thrown open to the private sector and to civil society.

## Leaps of Imagination

After three and a half centuries, it requires a mental leap to think of world politics in any terms other than occasionally cooperating but generally competing states, each defined by its territory and representing all the people therein. Nor is it easy to imagine political entities that could compete with the emotional attachment of a shared landscape, national history, language, flag, and currency.

Yet history proves that there are alternatives other than tribal anarchy. Empires, both tightly and loosely ruled, achieved success and won allegiance. In the Middle Ages, emperors, kings, dukes, knights, popes, archbishops, guilds, and cities exercised overlapping secular power over the same territory in a system that looks much more like a modern, three-dimensional network than the clean-lined, hierarchical state order that replaced it. The question now is whether there are new geographic or functional entities that might grow up alongside the state, taking over some of its powers and emotional resonance.

The kernels of several such entities already exist. The European Union is the most obvious example. Neither a union of states nor an international organization, the EU leaves experts groping for inadequate descriptions like "post-sovereign system" or "unprecedented hybrid." It respects members' borders for some purposes, particularly in foreign and defense policy, but ignores them for others. The union's judiciary can override national law, and its Council of Ministers can overrule certain domestic executive decisions. In its thousands of councils, committees, and working groups, national ministers increasingly find themselves working with their counterparts from other countries to oppose colleagues in their own government; agriculture ministers, for example, ally against finance ministers. In this sense the union penetrates and to some extent weakens the internal bonds of its member states. Whether Frenchmen, Danes, and Greeks will ever think of themselves first as Europeans remains to be seen, but the EU has already come much further than most Americans realize.

Meanwhile, units below the national level are taking on formal international roles. Nearly all 50 American states have trade offices abroad, up from four in 1970, and all have official standing in the World Trade Organization (WTO). German *Länder* and British local governments have offices at EU headquarters in Brussels. France's Rhône-Alpes region, centered in Lyon, maintains what it calls "embassies" abroad on behalf of a regional economy that includes Geneva, Switzerland, and Turin, Italy.

Emerging political identities not linked to territory pose a more direct challenge to the geographically fixed state system. The WTO is struggling to find a method of handling environmental disputes in the global commons, outside all states' boundaries, that the General Agreement on Tariffs and Trade, drafted 50 years ago, simply never envisioned. Proposals have been floated for a Parliamentary Assembly in the United Nations, parallel to the General Assembly, to represent the people rather than the states of the world. Ideas are under discussion that would give ethnic nations political and legal status, so that the Kurds, for example, could be legally represented as a people in addition to being Turkish, Iranian, or Iraqi citizens.

Further in the future is a proposed Global Environmental Authority with independent regulatory powers. This is not as far fetched as it sounds. The burden of participating in several hundred international environmental bodies is heavy for the richest governments and is becoming prohibitive for others. As the number of international agreements mounts, the pressure to streamline the system—in environmental protection as in other areas—will grow.

The realm of most rapid change is hybrid authorities that include state and nonstate bodies such as the International Telecommunications Union, the International Union for the Conservation of Nature, and hundreds more. In many of these, businesses or NGOs take on formerly public roles. The Geneva-based International Standards Organization, essentially a business NGO, sets widely observed standards on everything from products to internal corporate procedures. The International Securities Markets Association, another private regulator, oversees international trade in private securities markets—the world's second-largest capital market after domestic government bond markets. In another crossover, markets become government enforcers when they adopt treaty standards as the basis for market judgments. States and NGOs are collaborating ad hoc in large-scale humanitarian relief operations that involve both military and civilian forces. Other NGOs have taken on standing operational roles for international organizations in refugee work and development assistance. Almost unnoticed, hybrids like these, in which states are often the junior partners, are becoming a new international norm.

## For Better or Worse?

A world that is more adaptable and in which power is more diffused could mean more peace, justice, and capacity to manage the burgeoning list of humankind's interconnected problems. At a time of accelerating change, NGOs are quicker than governments to respond to new demands and opportunities. Internationally, in both the poorest and richest countries, NGOs, when adequately funded, can outperform government in the delivery of many public services. Their growth, along with that of the other elements of civil society, can strengthen the fabric of the many still-fragile democracies. And they are better than governments at dealing with problems that grow slowly and affect society through their cumulative effect on individuals—the "soft" threats of environmental degradation, denial of human rights, population growth, poverty, and lack of development that may already be causing more deaths in conflict than are traditional acts of aggression.

As the computer and telecommunications revolution continues, NGOs will become more capable of large-scale activity across national borders. Their loyalties and orientation, like those of international civil servants and citizens of non-national entities like the EU, are better matched than those of governments to problems that demand transnational solutions. International NGOs and cross-border networks of local groups have bridged North-South differences that in earlier years paralyzed cooperation among countries.

On the economic front, expanding private markets can avoid economically destructive but politically seductive policies, such as excessive borrowing or overly burdensome taxation, to which governments succumb. Unhindered by ideology, private capital flows to where it is best treated and thus can do the most good.

International organizations, given a longer rein by governments and connected to the grassroots by deepening ties with NGOs, could, with adequate funding, take on larger roles in global housekeeping (transportation, communications, environment, health), security (controlling weapons of mass destruction, preventive diplomacy, peacekeeping), human rights, and emergency relief. As various international panels have suggested, the funds could come from fees on international activities, such as currency transactions and air travel, independent of state appropriations. Finally, that new force on the global scene, international public opinion, informed by worldwide media coverage and mobilized by NGOs, can be extraordinarily potent in getting things done, and done quickly.

There are at least as many reasons, however, to believe that the continuing diffusion of power away from nation-states will mean more conflict and less problem-solving both within states and among them.

For all their strengths, NGOs are special interests, albeit not motivated by personal profit. The best of them, the ablest and most passionate, often suffer most from tunnel vision, judging every public act by how it affects their particular interest. Generally, they have limited capacity for large-scale endeavors, and as they grow, the need to sustain growing budgets can compromise the independence of mind and approach that is their greatest asset.

A society in which the piling up of special interests replaces a single strong voice for the common good is unlikely to fare well. Single-issue voters, as Americans know all too well, polarize and freeze public debate. In the longer run, a stronger civil society could also be more fragmented, producing a weakened sense of common identity and purpose and less willingness to invest in public goods, whether health and education or roads and ports. More and more groups promoting worthy but narrow causes could ultimately threaten democratic government.

Internationally, excessive pluralism could have similar consequences. Two hundred nation-states is a barely manageable number. Add hundreds of influential nonstate forces—businesses, NGOs, international organizations, ethnic and religious groups —and the international system may represent more voices but be unable to advance any of them.

Moreover, there are roles that only the state—at least among today's polities—can perform. States are the only nonvoluntary political unit, the one that can impose order and is invested with the power to tax. Severely weakened states will encourage conflict, as they have in Africa, Central America, and elsewhere.

Moreover, it may be that only the nation-state can meet crucial social needs that markets do not value. Providing a modicum of job security, avoiding higher unemployment, preserving a livable environment and a stable climate, and protecting consumer health and safety are but a few of the tasks that could be left dangling in a world of expanding markets and retreating states.

More international decision-making will also exacerbate the so called democratic deficit, as decisions that elected representatives once made shift to unelected international bodies; this is already a sore point for EU members. It also arises when legislatures are forced to make a single take-it-or-leave-it judgment on huge international agreements, like the several-thousand-page Uruguay Round trade accord. With citizens already feeling that their national governments do not hear individual voices, the trend could well provoke deeper and more dangerous alienation, which in turn could trigger new ethnic and even religious separatism. The end result could be a proliferation of states too weak for either individual economic success or effective international cooperation.

Finally, fearsome dislocations are bound to accompany the weakening of the central institution of modern society. The prophets of an internetted world in which national identities gradually fade, proclaim its revolutionary nature and yet believe the changes will be wholly benign. They won't be. The shift from national to some other political allegiance, if it comes, will be an emotional, cultural, and political earthquake.

## Dissolving and Evolving

Might the decline in state power prove transitory? Present disenchantment with national governments could dissipate as quickly as it arose. Continuing globalization may well spark a vigorous reassertion of economic or cultural nationalism. By helping solve problems governments cannot handle, business, NGOs, and international organizations may actually be strengthening the nation-state system.

These are all possibilities, but the clash between the fixed geography of states and the nonterritorial nature of today's problems and solutions, which is only likely to escalate, strongly suggests that the relative power of states will continue to decline. Nation-states may simply no longer be the natural problem-solving unit. Local government addresses citizens' growing desire for a role in decision-making, while transnational, regional, and even global entities better fit the dimensions of trends in economics, resources, and security.

The evolution of information and communications technology, which has only just begun, will probably heavily favor nonstate entities, including those not yet envisaged, over states. The new technologies encourage noninstitutional, shifting networks over the fixed bureaucratic hierarchies that are the hallmark of the single-voiced sovereign state. They dissolve issues' and institutions' ties to a fixed place. And by greatly empowering individuals, they weaken the relative attachment to community, of which the preeminent one in modern society is the nation-state.

If current trends continue, the international system 50 years hence will be profoundly different. During the transition, the Westphalian system and an evolving one will exist side by side. States will set the rules by which all other actors operate, but outside forces will increasingly make decisions for them. In using business, NGOs, and international organizations to address problems they cannot or do not want to take on, states will, more often than not, inadvertently weaken themselves further. Thus governments' unwillingness to adequately fund international organizations helped NGOs move from a peripheral to a central role in shaping multilateral agreements, since the NGOs provided expertise the international organizations lacked. At least for a time, the transition is likely to weaken rather than bolster the world's capacity to solve its problems. If states, with the overwhelming share of power, wealth, and capacity, can do less, less will get done.

Whether the rise of nonstate actors ultimately turns out to be good news or bad will depend on whether humanity can launch itself on a course of rapid social innovation, as it did after World War II. Needed adaptations include a business sector that can shoulder a broader policy role, NGOs that are less parochial and better able to operate on a large scale, international institutions that can efficiently serve the dual masters of states and citizenry, and above all, new institutions and political entities that match the transnational scope of today's challenges while meeting citizens' demands for accountable democratic governance.

---

## Notes

1. The author would like to acknowledge the contributions of the authors of ten case studies for the Council on Foreign Relations study group, "Sovereignty, Nonstate Actors, and a New World Politics," on which this article is based.

# Chapter 7

\* \* \*

# America Recommitted: United States National Interests in a Restructured World

### Donald E. Nuechterlein

*Donald E. Nuechterlein argues that the term "national interest" has long been invoked as a rationale for state action, but is nonetheless characterized by a great deal of ambiguity. Accordingly, he attempts to provide a framework for defining "national interest." He distinguishes between national, strategic and private interests and concludes that four long-term, enduring national interests have conditioned the way in which U.S. policy makers have viewed the international arena: defense of the homeland; enhancement of the nation's economic well-being; creation of a favorable world order; and promotion of democratic values. He then develops four criteria by which to assess the intensity of an interest: survival, vital, major and peripheral. He combines the four basic interests and the intensity criteria into a matrix which, he contends, enables a policymaker to, for instance, assess and compare the competing interests of the various parties involved in a crisis. Is Nuechterlein's matrix a useful framework for assessing national interests? Do his four interests suggest a hierarchy? What value does his intensity criteria have?*

### Defining U.S. National Interests:
### An Analytical Framework

The term "national interest" has been applied by statesmen, scholars, and military planners since the Middle Ages to the foreign policy and national security goals of nation-states. American presidents and their secretaries of state have invoked the term since the beginning of the republic, and today it is widely used to define the broad purposes of U.S. foreign policy.

Dr. Donald E. Nuechterlein has written on the subject of national interests for many years. He was Professor of International Affairs at the Federal Executive Institute from 1968 to 1988.

For example, Ronald Reagan's report to Congress in 1987, titled *National Security Strategy of the United States*, included a section that described: U.S. Interests, Major Objectives in Support of U.S. Interests, and Principal Threats to U.S. Interests. This presidential statement asserted that the strategy it contained "reflects our national interests and presents a broad plan for achieving the national objectives that support those interests."[1] Although the concept is not new, however, there has been much ambiguity about the meaning of the term in scholarly writing. Most scholars have preferred to offer their own definitions of national interest rather than accept formulations proposed by others. Consequently, many definitions may be found in the international relations literature, many of them not particularly useful to clear thinking about the actual formulation of foreign and national security policies.[2]

During the early 1950s a great debate raged in academic circles between the "realist" school, epitomized by Hans J. Morgenthau, and the "idealist" view of national interests, often associated with a former president, Woodrow Wilson. The idealists believed that ethics and morals must play an important part in defining the national interest, and they rejected the realists' assertion that the pursuit of power should be the primary goal of a nation-state. Another debate emerged among the realists about whether there is an objective, unchanging national interest which a nation's leaders pursue, or whether, in American-style democracy, the definition of national interest (or interests) is the end product of a political process and thus subject to periodic change based on national experience.

In the 1960s some American scholars took issue with the "elitist" view that an objective national interest for any country can be identified and acted upon, as Morgenthau and others maintained. Dissenters argued that nations have multiple general interests and that in the American political context they are the result of long debate and negotiation between the president and Congress and among various political groups that hold different views of America's international goals. Among the most prominent of these "constitutionalists" was Paul Seabury, who published *Power, Freedom, and Diplomacy* in 1963. Seabury summed up his view this way: "We might thus conceive of the national interest as a kaleidoscopic process by which forces latent in American society seek to express certain political and economic aspirations in world politics through the highest organs of state. To comprehend this process, we must not merely understand something of the formal governmental processes by which foreign policy is made, but also penetrate into the depth of the nation itself to discern the wellsprings of thought, ideology, and smaller interests that feed into the mainstreams of American policy abroad."[3]

In 1973 I contributed to this debate in a volume titled *United States National Interests in a Changing World*. In reflecting on the intense discussion then taking place over whether Vietnam should have been considered a "vital" U.S. interest, requiring the use of large American forces, I argued that the intensity of an interest in any international dispute, particularly when a vital interest might be at stake, is ultimately decided by debate within the U.S. constitutional system and that the president has the primary, but not exclusive, role in defining the level of an interest.[4] The Vietnam experience proved that Congress possesses the power to override a president's (in this case Lyndon Johnson's) view of the national interest, and this fact was underscored again in the 1980s when Ronald Reagan was unable to persuade Congress that his perception of a vital U.S. interest in Central America should prevail.

Yet another group of scholars think that "national interest" is too nebulous, too egocentric, or too outdated a concept to contribute anything significant to our understanding of an emerging interdependent world in which the nation-state is losing importance. One of the most influential skeptics in the 1970s was James N. Rosenau, who argued in his book, *The Scientific Study of Foreign Policy*, that neither the "objectivists" nor the "subjectivists," as he labeled proponents of the contending viewpoints, offered an effective rationale for using national interest as a research tool. He concluded: "Despite the claims made for the concept and notwithstanding its apparent utility, the national interest has never fulfilled its early promise as an analytic tool." Attempts by objectivists and subjectivists to use and apply it, he asserted, have proved fruitless or misleading, with the result that although "textbooks on international politics continue to assert that nations act to protect and realize their national interests, the research literature of the field has not been increased and enriched."[5]

Rosenau's criticism is partially correct: few scholars and few practitioners in the foreign policy field have looked systematically at why the United States pursues certain international objectives instead of others. It is too simple to suggest that bureaucratic politics, historical precedent, or economic determinism is the primary basis for deciding what American foreign policy should be. It is more reasonable to conclude, I suggest, that American policymakers are influenced by geographical, cultural, political, and economic factors that are deeply embedded in the national experience and in the particular ideology of the American people. While it may be true that certain major countries in Europe seem willing to qualify their national sovereignty in the interest of an emergent supranational entity called the European Community, which may give rise at some point to a new "nation" and a new set of national interests, this fact refers to a process by which nations disappear and emerge but does not detract from the very notion of national interest itself. The issue here is not what constitutes interests but what constitutes a "nation." So long as any nation has the authority to refuse the demands of another state or international body, one must conclude that it is acting under some notion of what constitutes its national interest. We are now seeing the proliferation of national entities within states—Lithuania, the Ukraine, Quebec, and Croatia are examples—which demand, in the name of national identity, independence from their larger countries. Furthermore, so long as political leaders continue to speak in terms of national interests and national priorities, scholars ought to accept some responsibility to help define those interests instead of ignoring the issue.

## Nature and Kinds of National Interests

In simplest terms, the fundamental national interest of the United States is the defense and well-being of its citizens, its territory, and the U.S. constitutional system. National interest can be distinguished from the public interest because the latter deals primarily with the internal well-being of the society. The public interest is protected by a set of laws that elected officials are pledged to uphold. The national interest, on the other hand, deals with the external environment, and most sovereign states reserve to themselves the ultimate authority to decide how to function in the international arena—or system, as some prefer to call it. Under the U.S. constitutional system, the president has the primary responsibility to define national interests with the advice and consent of the Senate and with financial support from the Senate and House. In matters involving the public interest, national authority is more evenly divided among the president, the Congress, and the courts. Public interest and national interest are not mutually exclusive, however. The public interest is heavily influenced by the international environment at a given time, especially during international tensions; the national interest is influenced by the degree of social stability and political unity prevailing in the country, as demonstrated by the post-Vietnam political climate in the United States.

Strategic interests are second-order interests: they are concerned with the political, economic, and military means of protecting the country against military threats. They may be defined in terms of geography, military power, availability or scarcity of resources, science and technology, and damage limitation in time of war. Occasionally, strategic interests tend to determine national interests, rather than the reverse, and in these cases confusion about goals and an overemphasis on military security may result. Private interests are those pursued by business and other organizations operating abroad and needing U.S. government support. As the United States trade deficit grew in the 1980s, private business interests assumed a larger role in the assessment of national interests than they had during the 1960s and 1970s.

The United States, like most major powers, has both unchanging and changing national interests: some it has pursued consistently over long periods of time, and others it has followed for shorter periods and then altered because of changing world conditions or a new domestic political environment. Throughout the nation's history four long-term, enduring national interests have conditioned the way the U.S. government viewed the external world and this country's place in it:

(1) defense of the United States and its constitutional system;

(2) enhancement of the nation's economic well-being and promotion of U.S. products abroad;

(3) creation of a favorable world order (international security environment);

(4) promotion abroad of U.S. democratic values and the free market system.

For all practical purposes, defending the United States includes defending Canada, Greenland, Iceland, Mexico, and the Caribbean Basin. Within this defense perimeter the United States will exert great pressure, including the use of military force, to prevent a foreign power from establishing military bases, and it will employ covert actions as well as economic sanctions against local governments that may be tempted to ally themselves with a foreign power. President John F. Kennedy's confrontation with General Secretary Nikita Khrushchev in October 1962 over Soviet medium-range nuclear missiles in Cuba demonstrated the importance of this basic interest.

The U.S. interest in economic well-being includes the freedom of Americans to trade and invest abroad, access to foreign markets and natural resources, maintenance of the value of U.S. currency in international financial markets, and preservation of a high standard of living for American citizens. Current concerns about persistent trade deficits, foreign ownership of American businesses and real estate, and the emergence of the United States as a major debtor country all reflect this interest.

Efforts to create a favorable world order flowed from America's disillusionment with isolationism after 1941 and its determination, following World War II, to create a new international environment in which Europe and East Asia would be peaceful and friendly to the United States. Sponsorship of the United Nations, containment of Soviet power, formation of NATO, military interventions in Korea, Vietnam, and Lebanon (1958) were results of the U.S. postwar interest in building a favorable world order within which Americans could feel secure.

Promoting democratic government and individual rights has been an objective of American diplomacy over much of its history. Between 1945 and 1975, however, this interest received little attention from policymakers, who were so preoccupied with creating a new world order that they did not care much about what kinds of governments the United States allied itself with. In the mid-1970s Congress prevailed on the president, through amendment of foreign aid legislation, to give greater emphasis to human rights when determining foreign assistance policy.

These four basic interests are long-term concerns that rise and fall in importance over decades, rather than months or years, and compete for public attention and government resources. During the forty-year Cold War period, U.S. world-order interests dominated the time and thinking of American policymakers; in the 1990s, this interest will probably be less important, and economic well-being more important, than they were in the 1980s.

## The National Interest Matrix

A correct determination of U.S. national interests lies not primarily in identifying which of the four basic, enduring interests is involved in a given international dispute but in assessing the intensity of the interest or stake the United States has in a specific issue or crisis. To differentiate levels of intensity, four additional terms are used in the matrix format shown in Table 1.[6] These terms, if carefully defined, provide policymakers a clear choice when deciding what is at stake in any foreign policy issue.

**Table 1**
**National Interest Matrix**

| Basic national interest | Intensity of interest | | | |
| --- | --- | --- | --- | --- |
| | Survival (critical) | Vital (dangerous) | Major (serious) | Peripheral (bothersome) |
| Defense of homeland | | | | |
| Economic well-being | | | | |
| Favorable world order | | | | |
| Promotion of values | | | | |

"Survival" interests are rare and are relatively easy to identify. A survival interest is at stake when there is an imminent, credible threat of massive destruction to the homeland if an enemy state's demands are not countered quickly. Such crises are easy to recognize because they are dramatic and involve an armed attack, or threat of attack, by one country on another's home territory: Hitler's invasion of Poland in 1939, Germany's bombing of Britain in 1940-41, North Korea's attack on South Korea in 1950, the Soviet Union's invasion of Afghanistan in 1979, and the U.S. invasion of Grenada in 1983. Iraq's invasion of Kuwait in August 1990 is a dramatic example of a survival interest—for Kuwait. Among the great powers that entered World War II, the United States was the only one whose survival interest was not threatened, even though some argue that Japan's attack on Pearl Harbor falls into this category. All the other powers were either invaded or, in the case of Britain, heavily bombed.

A "vital" interest differs from a survival one principally in the amount of time a country has to decide how it will respond to an external threat. It may involve economic, world-order, and ideological issues, in addition to defense of homeland, and may ultimately be as dangerous to the country as a military attack. But threats to a country's vital interests are potential, even probable, but not imminent dangers. They provide policymakers time to consult allies, to bargain with an adversary, to employ political and economic actions that may alter a trend, and to engage in a show of force warning an adversary that its course may lead to war. These were the policies pursued by President Bush toward Iraq in the summer of 1990.

A vital interest is at stake when an issue is so important to a nation's well-being that its leadership refuses to compromise beyond the point that it considers tolerable. If political leaders decide that they cannot compromise on an issue beyond a certain point and are willing instead to risk economic and military sanctions, the interest is probably vital. Examples are Harry Truman's decision in June 1950 to confront North Korea over its invasion of South Korea; John Kennedy's decision not to permit Soviet missiles in Cuba or elsewhere in the Caribbean; Richard Nixon's decision to take the United States off the gold standard in August 1971 and force U.S. trading partners to accept a devaluation of the dollar; Nixon's decision in October 1973 to alert U.S. forces when the Soviet Union threatened to send paratroopers to Egypt to defend that country against Israel; Jimmy Carter's effort in April 1980 to rescue American hostages in Iran; Ronald Reagan's decision in April 1986 to bomb Libya; and George Bush's retaliation against Iraq in August 1990. In sum, a vital stake may involve defense-of-homeland, economic well-being and world-order interests. Rarely, however, would a promotion-of-values interest by itself be viewed at the vital level.

It is important to emphasize that a vital interest is not defined by the kind of policy actions a president chooses in a crisis or serious international dispute; actions are symptoms of the interest's intensity rather than its governor. Occasionally a country's leadership will conclude after deliberation that an issue is a vital one—that is, it has reached the intolerable point—but that no dramatic action is warranted or even possible. Conversely, force may sometimes be used even though the issue involved is not viewed as intolerable, provided a realistic calculation indicates that the costs of using force will be low and the benefits considerable. This was probably the situation when President Reagan decided in October 1983 to invade the Caribbean island of Grenada. It may also have been true of his decision in the summer of 1987 to send more than thirty warships to the Persian Gulf to prevent Iran from establishing its control over shipping there. Fundamentally, a vital interest exists when a country's leadership believes that serious harm will come to the country if it fails to take dramatic action to change a dangerous course of events. Such action may include using economic sanctions and/or conventional military force. The use of nuclear and other weapons of massive destruction, however, would not be authorized unless a survival interest is at stake.

A "major" interest is one that a country considers to be important but not crucial to its well-being. Major interests involve issues and trends, whether they are economic, political, or ideological, that can be negotiated with an adversary. Such issues may cause serious concern and even harm to U.S. interests abroad, but policymakers usually come to the conclusion that negotiation and compromise, rather than confrontation, are desirable—even though the result may be painful. Examples illustrating major interests for the United States have been the Arab oil embargo in 1973, which was a serious but not dangerous threat to the U.S. economy; the 1979 Sandinista revolution in Nicaragua; Moscow's invasion of Afghanistan in 1979; President Reagan's decision not to use force in Lebanon in 1983; and President Bush's choice in 1989 not to request additional military assistance for the Nicaraguan Contras. Each case involved a serious challenge to important U.S. interests, but in each one the president decided that the United States could live with an unsatisfactory outcome.

Deciding whether an issue is vital or major is a crucial choice for policymakers, specifically the president. (Table 1 highlights this choice.) In the final analysis, the difference between a major and a vital interest is what top policymakers believe to be tolerable or intolerable. If the president and his National Security Council believe they can accommodate an undesirable but nevertheless acceptable solution, the issue probably is a major interest. But if a situation becomes so distressing that they are unwilling to compromise further in order to find a solution, then the issue probably is vital. President Bush's demand that Iraq withdraw from Kuwait was that kind of choice in 1990.

A "peripheral" interest is one that does not seriously affect the well-being of the United States as a whole, even though it may be detrimental to the private interests of Americans conducting business abroad. These issues bear watching by the State Department and other government agencies, but they are a lower order of political, economic, and ideological magnitude. Examples are the imprisonment abroad of American citizens on drug charges, and isolated cases of infringement on U.S. business interests located abroad. The infringement of human rights in other countries was perceived as a peripheral interest by policymakers until the 1970s, when Congress insisted it be accorded a higher priority. President Carter agreed, and Presidents Reagan and Bush continued the policy, albeit with less public display. Two cases in which human rights were accorded a major-interest priority involved South

Africa and the Philippines, where serious human rights violations occurred in the 1970s and 1980s.

## Utilizing the Interest Matrix

The core of this conceptual framework for assessing national interests is contained in the matrix shown in Table 1 above. The policymaker's task is to determine how large a stake the United States has in a specific international issue or crisis—for each of the four basic interests—and then to estimate the intensity of interest that other principal countries have in that issue. Comparing these levels of interest for the major players involved in a dispute permits one to calculate whether the issue at hand is likely to end with negotiations or lead to armed confrontation. Estimates of the interests and intentions of leaders in other countries are, of course, subjective judgments made by diplomats, intelligence specialists, scholars, businessmen, journalists, and others possessing detailed knowledge of the nations involved. Policymakers, especially the president and the National Security Council, need to make the fundamental judgment about the intensity of the U.S. interest and then decide whether it is desirable to negotiate further or to threaten hostilities. In the case of a trade issue, the option would more likely be to use economic sanctions rather than military force.

The interest matrix should be viewed as a guide to making wise policy choices in a systematic manner rather than as a sure means of finding the "right" answer. Key foreign policy decisions result from a process in which political leaders make subjective judgments based on their different perceptions of reality. The value of the interest matrix to decisionmaking is that it encourages policymakers to think through the important criteria they should take into account before deciding that an interest is vital and may therefore require the use of economic and military sanctions.

## Notes

1. National Security Strategy of the United States, Special White House Report, January 1987, p. 4.

2. For a comprehensive survey of writers on "national interest," see Elmer Plischke, *Foreign Relations: Analysis of Its Anatomy* (Westport, Conn.: Greenwood Press, 1988), chaps. 2-3.

3. Paul Seabury, *Power, Freedom, and Diplomacy* (New York: Random House, 1963), p. 87.

4. Donald E. Nuechterlein, *United States National Interests in a Changing World* (Lexington: Univ. Press of Kentucky, 1973), chap. 6: "Changing Perceptions of U.S. Interests in Southeast Asia—A Case Study."

5. James M. Rosenau, *The Scientific Study of Foreign Policy* (New York: Free Press, 1971), p. 248.

6. The first version of this matrix was published in my article "National Interests and Foreign Policy: A Conceptual Framework for Analysis and Decision-Making," *British Journal of International Studies*, Oct. 1976, p. 247.

# Chapter 8

## ✦ ✦ ✦

# Competing Visions for U.S. Grand Strategy

Barry R. Posen and Andrew L. Ross

Barry R. Posen and Andrew L. Ross identify, develop, refine, and critique four alternative U.S. grand strategies: neo-isolationism, selective engagement, cooperative security, and primacy. The basic premises and assumptions of each grand strategy alternative are identified and assessed. Posen and Ross also examine the positions of each strategy on particular issues and discuss their force structure implications. Which of these grand strategies should shape U.S. policy and strategic choices today? How do nuclear weapons and their spread affect the strategies? What are the force planning implications of the four alternatives? Can a political consensus be built around any of these post-Cold War strategic alternatives?

The dramatic events that marked the end of the Cold War and the subsequent early end of the twentieth century require the United States to reconsider its national security policy. What are U.S. interests and objectives? What are the threats to those interests and objectives? What are the appropriate strategic responses to those threats? What principles should guide the development of U.S. policy and strategy? In short, what should be the new grand strategy of the United States?

Barry R. Posen is Professor of Political Science in the Defense and Arms Control Studies Program at MIT. Andrew L. Ross is Professor of National Security Affairs at the U.S. Naval War College. The original version of this essay was submitted by Barry R. Posen as written testimony for the House Armed Services Committee on March 3, 1993. Earlier versions of this piece appeared in Strategy and Force Planning Faculty, eds., *Strategy and Force Planning* (Newport, R.I.: Naval War College Press, 1995), pp. 115-134; and in Robert J. Lieber, ed., *Eagle Adrift: American Foreign Policy At the End of the Century* (New York: Longman, 1997), pp. 100-134. The views expressed here are those of the authors and do not necessarily reflect the views of the Naval War College, the Department of the Navy, or any other U.S. government department or agency.

Barry R. Posen and Andrew L. Ross, "Competing Visions for U.S. Strategy," *International Security*, 21:3, Winter 1997, pp. 5-53. Copyright © 1996 by the President and Fellows of Harvard College and the Massachusetts Intitute of Technology.

Four grand strategies, relatively discrete and coherent arguments about the U.S. role in the world, now compete in our public discourse. They may be termed neo-isolationism; selective engagement; cooperative security; and primacy (see Table 1 for a summary presentation of the four alternative visions). Below, we describe each of these four strategies in its purest form; we borrow liberally from the academics, government officials, journalists, and policy analysts who have contributed to this debate, but on issues where others have kept silent, or been inconsistent, we impose consistency in the interest of clarity. Our purpose is not advocacy; it is transparency. We hope to sharpen the public debate, not settle it. We then offer our characterization and critique of the evolving grand strategy of the Clinton administration, an uneasy amalgam of selective engagement, cooperative security, and primacy. Finally, we speculate on what might cause the United States to make a clearer grand strategy choice.

The state of the U.S. economy, the national finances, and persistent social problems largely drove foreign and defense policy out of the 1992 presidential race. The 1996 campaign was little different. The first months of the first Clinton administration were characterized by indirection, later by a near single-minded focus on economic issues. Security matters were dealt with sequentially and incrementally; no obvious grand scheme emerged until Assistant to the President for National Security Affairs Anthony Lake proposed in September 1993 that U.S. policy shift "From Containment to Enlargement." Not until July 1994 were the ideas initially advanced by Lake codified in the administration's *National Security Strategy of Engagement and Enlargement.* Those ideas remain intact in the February 1996 version of that White House document.[1] Yet the Clinton administration, like the Bush administration before it, has failed to build a domestic political consensus in support of its strategic vision. Thus the post-Cold War grand strategy debate continues.

We distinguish the four alternative strategies in four ways. We ask, first, what are the major purposes or objectives each identifies for the United States in international politics? These range from a narrow commitment to the basic safety of the United States to an ambitious effort to secure permanent U.S. global preeminence.

Second, we ask: what are each strategy's basic premises about international politics? Though advocates are seldom explicit, underlying disagreements among the strategies on basic questions help to explain their other disagreements. In particular, the four strategies disagree on the "fragility" of international politics—the propensity for developments unfavorable to the United States to cascade rapidly in ever more unfavorable directions, and for developments favorable to the United States to move in ever more favorable directions. A fragile international political system both requires and responds to U.S. activism. Answers to three central questions of modern international relations theory affect each strategy's assessment of the fragility of international politics: (1) Do

## Table 1. Competing Grand Strategy Visions.

|  | Neo-Isolationism | Selective Engagement | Cooperative Security | Primacy |
|---|---|---|---|---|
| **Analytical Anchor** | Minimal, defensive realism | Traditional balance of power realism | Liberalism | Maximal realism/ unilateralism |
| **Major Problem of Int'l Politics** | Avoiding entangle-ment in the affairs of others | Peace among the major powers | The indivisibility of peace | The rise of a peer competitor |
| **Preferred World Order** | Distant balance of power | Balance of power | Interdependence | Hegemonic |
| **Nuclear Dynamics** | Supports status quo | Supports status quo | Supports aggression | Supports aggression |
| **Conception of National Interests** | Narrow | Restricted | Transnational | Broad |
| **Regional Priorities** | North America | Industrial Eurasia | Global | Industrial Eurasia & the home of any potential peer competitor |
| **Nuclear Proliferation** | Not our problem | Discriminate prevention | Indiscriminate prevention | Indiscriminate prevention |
| **NATO** | Withdraw | Maintain | Transform & expand | Expand |
| **Regional Conflict** | Abstain | Contain; discriminate intervention | Intervene | Contain; discriminate intervention |
| **Ethnic Conflict** | Abstain | Contain | Nearly indiscriminate intervention | Contain |
| **Humanitarian Intervention** | Abstain | Discriminate intervention | Nearly indiscriminate intervention | Discriminate intervention |
| **Use of Force** | Self-defense | Discriminate | Frequent | At will |
| **Force Posture** | Minimal self-defense force | Two-MRC force | Reconnaissance strike complex for multilateral action | A two-power-standard force |

states tend to balance against, or bandwagon with, expansionists? That is, will most states, faced with a neighbor growing in power and ambition, take steps to improve their power through some combination of internal military preparation and external alignment? (2) Do nuclear weapons make conquest easier or harder? If secure retaliatory nuclear deterrent forces are easy to get, and the risks they impose for ambitious aggressors are easy for those aggressors to grasp, then they make it difficult for aspiring hegemons to improve their power position through intimidation or conquest. If, on the other hand, they cause hegemons to perceive themselves as invulnerable to attack, such states may be emboldened to aggressive acts. (3) How much potential influence does the United States actually have in international politics? How do we measure relative power in international politics; is it reasonable to speak of a unipolar world? Here, there are two subsidiary issues. Measured globally, how much international political influence can the current U.S. "share" of gross world power resources—economic, technological, and military capabilities—buy? How much money, and how many lives, are the American people willing to pay for influence in international politics in the absence of a major threat? If the United States is relatively quite powerful in international politics, then it can think in terms of great objectives. If not, its objectives will need to be limited. If the United States is inherently much more powerful than is often believed, then the American people may not need to sacrifice much more than they already do for the United States to undertake ambitious policies successfully.[2]

We ask, third, what are the preferred political and military instruments of each strategy? Do advocates prefer to work multilaterally or unilaterally? Do they favor international organizations or prefer traditional alliances? How much military force does the United States require, and what kind? Our force structure analysis is indicative rather than comprehensive; as a heuristic device we rely substantially on the array of alternative force structures developed by the late Les Aspin during his tenure as Chairman of the House Armed Services Committee and then as Secretary of Defense early in the Clinton administration.[3] The force structures (see Table 2) were developed with an eye to the number and variety of contingencies they could support—the "business end" of grand strategy.[4]

Fourth, to illustrate the real world implications of each grand strategy, we ask: what are their positions on a number of basic issues now on the United States agenda, including nuclear proliferation, NATO enlargement, and regional conflict?

After describing each strategy along these four dimensions, we offer a short critique, which reflects both our own specific concerns and what we believe are the most credible counter-arguments that the proponents of the other strategies might offer.

The essay closes with a brief review and analysis of the Clinton administration's grand strategy, which consists of a core of cooperative security principles and impulses, drawn toward primacy as it has faced a less tractable international environment that it expected, but constrained toward selectivity by a U.S. citizenry whose support for ambitious foreign projects seems shallow at best. We explain why this compromise has proven necessary, and offer some hypotheses about what could cause this grand strategy to change.

## Table 2. Comparison of Alternative Future Force Structures.

| | Force A[1] | Force B[2] | Force C[3] | Force D[4] | Base Force [5] | Clinton-BUR[6] |
|---|---|---|---|---|---|---|
| **ARMY** | | | | | | |
| Active divisions | 8 | 8 | 9 | 10 | 12 | 10 |
| Reserve divisions | 2 | 2 | 6 | 6 | 6 | 8 |
| **MARINES[7]** | | | | | | |
| Active divisions | 2 | 2 | 2 | 3 | 2 1/3 | 3 |
| Reserve divisions | 1 | 1 | 1 | 1 | 1 | 1 |
| **AIR FORCE** | | | | | | |
| Active wings | 6 | 8 | 10 | 11 | 15 | 13 |
| Reserve wings | 4 | 6 | 8 | 9 | 11 | 7 |
| **NAVY** | | | | | | |
| Total ships | 220 | 290 | 340 | 430 | 450 | 346 |
| Carriers | 6 | 8 | 12 | 15 | 13 | 12 |
| Attack subs | 20 | 40 | 40 | 50 | 80 | 45-55 |
| Amphibious assault ships[8] | 50 | 50 | 50 | 82 | 50 | 44 |
| **PERSONNEL** | | | | | | |
| Active | 1,247,000 | 1,312,000 | 1,409,000 | 1,575,000 | 1,626,000 | 1,450,000 |
| Reserve | 666,000 | 691,000 | 904,000 | 933,000 | 920,000 | 905,000 |
| 1997 BUDGET AUTHORITY, billions 97$ (DOD+DPE)[9] | 231 | 246 | 270 | 295 | 291-301 | 253 |

NOTES

[1]Alternatives A,B,C, and D were devised by the House Armed Services Committee under the leadership of then Chairmen Les Aspin. Force A: A "foundation" of nuclear, forward presence, special operations, and continental defense forces, and an industrial mobilization base, plus forces for one "major regional contingency" (MRC) such as the 1991 war against Iraq, and a modest humanitarian intervention capability.

[2]Force B: Preceding plus sufficient airpower to support heavily an ally in a second major regional contingency.

[3] Force C: Preceding plus sufficient forces in reserve to sustain comfortably a large new forward deployment for a major regional contingency, plus the capability to mount simultaneously a small invasion similar to the attack on Panama in 1989.

[4]Force D: Preceding with "a more robust response," plus a second humanitarian intervention and naval "power projection" for the second MRC.

[5]Base Force: Proposed by President Bush and Former Chairman of the Joint Chiefs of Staff Colin Powell. General Powell was attempting to develop a force structure that accommodated the widespread expectation of a "peace dividend," and at the same time clearly preserved the image and the fact of U.S. superpower status.

[6]Clinton Bottom-Up Review: Two "near simultaneous regional contingencies" plus a moderate peace-keeping operation and substantial forward presence; objective for the year 2000; 1997 force structure is close but not identical. The "Bottom-Up Review" was developed by Secretary of Defense Les Aspin early in the Clinton administration. It relied substantially on the analysis that he had conducted as a Congressman to generate Options A-D. The BUR Force Structure is meant to be able to fight two Desert Storm-scale "Major Regional Contingencies" (MRCs) "nearly" simultaneously, and to sustain a high level of forward military presence in peacetime. The BUR force structure has the unusual attribute of being slightly larger, but costing somewhat less than Force C, Aspin's earlier preference.

[7] Marine divisions and Navy Carriers each have associated air wings, respectively slightly larger and slightly smaller than their Air Force counterparts, which number 72 aircraft.

[8]These transport Marine units to their attack positions; some of these ships (10-12 in the current force) are very large, roughly half the size of a standard Nimitz class carrier, and carry VSTOL aircraft, helicopters, and hovercraft.

[9]Totals include roughly ten billion dollars of DOE funding to maintain the nuclear weapons complex. Among budget analysts, it is generally agreed that the available defense dollars that the Bush administration projected and the Clinton administation projects after the turn of the century would be inadequate to support their preferred force structures. By 2005, $20-65 billion more than the projected 1997 budget would be required to fund the Base Force; see Congessional Budget Office, "Fiscal Implications of the Base Force," p. 11. The CBO estimates that after the turn of the century the modernization of the smaller Bottom-Up Review Force Structure with new technology weapons currently in development or production would require between $7 billion and $31 billion more per year than the current budget plans for the year 1999, which is little different from the 1997 plan. See CBO, *An Analysis of the Administration's Future Years Defense Program for 1995-1999* (Washington, D.C.: Congressional Budget Office, January 1995), p. 50.

## Neo-Isolationism

Neo-isolationism is the least ambitious, and, at least among foreign policy professionals, probably the least popular grand strategy option.[5] The new isolationists have embraced a constricted view of U.S. national interests that renders internationalism not only unnecessary but counterproductive. National defense—the protection of "the security, liberty, and property of the American people"[6]—is the only vital U.S. interest.

The new isolationism subscribes to a fundamentally realist view of international politics and thus focuses on power.[7] Its advocates ask: who has the power to threaten the sovereignty of the United States, its territorial integrity, or its safety? They answer that nobody does.[8] The collapse of the Soviet Union has left a rough balance of power in Eurasia. If either Russia or China begins to build up its military power, there are plenty of wealthy and capable states at either end of Eurasia to contain them. Indeed, Russia and China help to contain one another. Thus no state has the capability to conquer the rest and so agglomerate enough economic capability and military mobilization potential to threaten the American way of life. Like traditional isolationism, this strategy observes that the oceans make such a threat improbable in any event. The United States controls about one quarter of the gross world product, twice as much as its nearest competitor, Japan, and while not totally self-sufficient, is better placed than most to "go it alone." U.S. neighbors to the north and south are militarily weak and destined to stay that way for quite some time. The United States is inherently a very secure country.[9] Indeed, the United States can be said to be strategically immune.[10]

The new isolationism is strongly motivated by a particular understanding of nuclear weapons. It concedes that nuclear weapons have increased the potential capacity of others to threaten the safety of the United States. But nuclear weapons make it very hard, indeed nearly inconceivable, for any power to win a traditional military victory over the United States. Nuclear weapons assure the political sovereignty and the territorial integrity of the United States. The collapse of the Soviet Union has so reduced the military resources available to its successor states that a counterforce attack on U.S. nuclear forces, an old and exaggerated fear, is out of the question. There can be no politically rational motive for any country large or small to explode a nuclear weapon on North America. U.S. retaliation would be devastating. Moreover, the fact that Britain, France, the People's Republic of China, and Russia have nuclear retaliatory forces makes it quite likely that these powers will deter each other, further reducing the risk that an ambitious hegemon could dominate and militarily exploit the economic resources of the Eurasian landmass.

***Issues and Instruments***. Given the absence of threats to the U.S. homeland, neo-isolationism holds that national defense will seldom justify intervention abroad. The United States is not responsible for, and cannot afford the costs of, maintaining world order. The pursuit of economic well-being is best left to the private sector. The promotion of values such as democracy and human rights inspires ill-advised crusades that serve only to generate resentment against the United States; consequently, it is a poor guide to policy and strategy.

The new isolationism would concede, however, that our great capabilities are a magnet for trouble so long as we are involved in any way in various political disputes around the world. Intervention in these disputes is thus a good way to attract attention to the United States. The strong try to deter the United States; the weak to seduce it; the dispossessed to blame it. Neo-isolationism would argue that those who fear terrorism, especially terrorism with nuclear, biological, or chemical weapons, can increase U.S. safety by keeping it out of foreign conflicts. Middle Eastern terrorists, for instance, whether sponsored by Syria, Iran, Iraq, or Libya, would find little reason to target the United States and its citizens, either abroad or at home, if the United States refrained from meddling in the Middle East.

Neo-isolationism advises the United States to preserve its freedom of action and strategic independence. Because neo-isolationism proposes that the United States stay out of political conflicts and wars abroad, it has no particular need for political instruments. Even traditional alliance relationships that obligate the United States in advance, such as NATO, ought to be dismantled. International organizations are a place to talk, perhaps to coordinate international efforts to improve the overall global quality of life, but not to make or keep peace. This would implicate the United States and draw it into conflicts.

Most of the foreign policy issues now facing the United States would disappear under the new isolationism. The future of NATO, for instance, would be left to Europe. Neo-isolationists would have the United States abandon that anachronistic alliance, not lead the way in its ill-conceived expansion. Bosnia, too, is a European problem in which the United States has no concrete, material stake. The United States would no longer be preoccupied with Russian political and economic reform, or the lack thereof. Arabs and Israelis would have to sort out their affairs (or not) without U.S. meddling. Islamists would be deprived of the Great Satan. The North Korean threat would be left to South Korea, the country whose interests are actually threatened. In Latin America and Africa, the United States would no longer rescue Haitis and Somalias. Humanitarian assistance, if and when provided, would be confined to disasters—famines, epidemics, earthquakes, and storms. The United States might be willing to help clean up the mess after foreign wars have sorted themselves out. But intervention of any kind during wars would be viewed as a mistake, since at least one side is likely to be disadvantaged by humanitarian assistance to the others and would thus come to view the United States as an enemy.

*Force Structure*. Neo-isolationism generates a rather small force structure. It is unlikely to cost more than two percent of GDP.[11] First and foremost, the United States would need to retain a secure nuclear second-strike capability to deter nuclear attacks from any quarter. Modest air and missile defenses might be put in place to deal with low-grade threats. Second, the U.S. intelligence community would have the task of watching worldwide developments of weapons of mass destruction in order to forestall any terrorist threats against the United States. If such threats occurred, it would be their job to find an address against which retaliation could be directed. Third, the United States would probably wish to retain a capable navy (perhaps a third to a half the current size), and diverse special operations forces. The purpose would largely be to protect U.S. commerce abroad from criminal activity—piracy, kidnapping, and extortion. The remainder of U.S. forces would be structured to preserve skills at ground and tactical air warfare in the event that the balance of power on the Eurasian land mass eroded, perhaps requiring a return to a more activist U.S. policy. Since the burden of defending wealthy allies can be discarded in the aftermath of the Soviet Union's fortuitous collapse, those forces need not be forward-deployed in Europe and Asia. A major mission of the intelligence community would be to provide timely warning of strategic developments in Eurasia that would warrant a return to a more activist foreign and security policy. The U.S. force structure would no longer be driven either by demanding and costly forward presence requirements or by the need to prepare to engage in multiple foreign contingencies. American military forces would be used only to defend narrowly construed U.S. interests. Given these limited requirements, even "Force A" (see Table 2), the smallest of Aspin's notional force structures, is larger than necessary.

*Critique*. The United States can, more easily than most, go it alone. Yet we do not find the arguments of the neo-isolationists compelling. Their strategy serves U.S. interests only if they are narrowly construed. First, though the neo-isolationists have a strong case in their argument that the United States is currently quite secure, disengagement is unlikely to make the United States more secure, and would probably make it less secure. The disappearance of the United States from the world stage would likely precipitate a good deal of competition abroad for security. Without a U.S. presence, aspiring regional hegemons would see more opportunities. States formerly defended by the United States would have to look to their own military power; local arms competitions are to be expected. Proliferation of nuclear weapons would intensify if the U.S. nuclear guarantee were withdrawn. Some states would seek weapons of mass destruction because they were simply unable to compete conventionally with their neighbors. This new flurry of competitive behavior would probably energize many hypothesized immediate causes of war, including preemptive motives, preventive motives, economic motives, and the propensity for miscalculation. There would likely be more war. Weapons of mass destruction might be used in some of these wars, with unpleasant effects even for those not directly involved.

Second, if these predictions about the international environment are correct, as competition intensified U.S. decision-makers would continuously have to reassess whether their original assumptions about the workings of the balance of power in Eurasia and the deterrent power of nuclear weapons were still valid. Decision-makers require both good political intelligence and compelling cause-effect knowledge about international politics to determine that a policy shift is in order. More importantly, decision-makers would have to persuade the country that a policy reversal is necessary, but U.S. foreign policy is a tough thing to change. Given these problems, how much trouble would have to occur before the United States returned to a more active role? Would the United States return in time to exert its influence to help prevent a great power war? If the United States did decide that a more active role was necessary, how much influence would it have after years of inactivity? Would the United States return in time to prevent an aspiring hegemon from getting a jump ahead, as Nazi Germany did in World War II? If not, the costs of containment or rollback could prove substantial.

Third, though the United States would save a great deal of money in its defense budget, perhaps 1-1.5 percent of GDP, or $70-100 billion per year relative to the budgets planned by the Clinton administration, these annual savings do not seem commensurate with the international influence the strategy would forgo. Though this is a lot of money, which has many worthy alternative uses, the redirection of these resources from the military is unlikely to make the difference between a healthy and an unhealthy economy that is already some seven trillion dollars in size. Neo-isolationists seem willing to trade away considerable international influence for a relatively modest improvement in domestic welfare. Given the potential stakes in international politics, the trade-off is imprudent. Engagement in international politics imposes obvious burdens and risks. Shedding an active role in international politics, however, increases the risks of unintended consequences and reduces U.S. influence over the management of those consequences, and over issues that we can hardly anticipate.

## Selective Engagement

Selective engagement endeavors to ensure peace among powers that have substantial industrial and military potential—the great powers.[12] By virtue of the great military capabilities that would be brought into play, great power conflicts are much more dangerous to the United States than conflicts elsewhere. Thus Russia, the wealthier states of the European Union, the People's Republic of China, and Japan matter most. The purpose of U.S. engagement should be to affect directly the propensity of these powers to go to war with one another. These wars have the greatest chance of producing large-scale resort to weapons of mass destruction, a global experiment that the United States ought to try to prevent. These are the areas of the world where the world wars have originated, wars that have managed to reach out and draw in the United States in spite of its strong inclination to stay out.

Like the new isolationism, selective engagement emerges from the realist tradition of international politics and its focus on large concentrations of power.[13] Like cooperative security, it is also interested in peace. Though some of its proponents agree with the neo-isolationist premise that U.S. geography and nuclear deterrence make the United States so secure that a Eurasian hegemon would not pose much of a security problem for the United States,[14] selective engagement holds that any great power war in Eurasia is a danger to the United States.[15] On the basis of both the increased destructive power of modern weaponry and the demonstrated inability of the United States to stay out of large European and Asian wars in the first half of this century, selective engagement argues that the United States has an interest in great power peace.

Selective engagement shares the neo-isolationist expectation that states balance, and that nuclear weapons favor the defender of the status quo. However, selective engagers also recognize that balancing may be tardy, statesmen may miscalculate, and nuclear deterrence could fail. Given the interest in great power peace, the United States should engage itself abroad in order to ensure against these possibilities in the places where the consequences could be the most serious. Balancing happens, but it happens earlier and more easily with a leader. Nuclear weapons deter, but why not place the weight of U.S. strategic nuclear forces behind the status quo powers, just to simplify the calculations of the ambitious? Selective engagement tries to ensure that the great powers understand that the United States does not wish to find out how a future Eurasian great power war might progress, and that it has sufficient military power to deny victory to the aggressor.

Advocates of selective engagement do start from the premise that U.S. resources are scarce: it is simply impossible to muster sufficient power and will to keep domestic and international peace worldwide, or to preserve the United

States as the undisputed leader in a unipolar world.[16] The United States does have 22 percent of gross world product, at least half again as much as Japan, its closest economic competitor, but only 4.6 percent of global population. Global economic development will gradually reduce the U.S. economic advantage, and demographics already limit U.S. capacity for intervention in labor intensive civil wars. Desert Storm does not suggest a permanent, overwhelming U.S. military superiority; other wars may not be so easy. Moreover, short of a compelling argument about an extant threat, the people of the United States are unlikely to want to invest much money or many lives either in global police duties—cooperative security—or in trying to cow others into accepting U.S. hegemony—primacy.

*Issues and Instruments*. Selective engagement advocates are worried about nuclear proliferation, but proliferation in some countries matters more than in others.[17] Countries seeking nuclear weapons who have no conflict of interest with the United States or its friends are viewed more favorably than those who do. The Nuclear Non-Proliferation Treaty (NPT) is viewed as an instrument to permit countries who have neither the wealth to support nuclear forces, nor the political insecurity or ambition to need or want them, to find a refuge from a race that they would rather not run. Selective engagement advocates may be willing to try to cajole India, Israel, Pakistan, or Ukraine into surrendering their nuclear capabilities and joining the NPT, but they hold that it would be absurd to turn neutrals or friends into enemies on this issue alone.

Proliferation really matters in politically ambitious countries that have demonstrated a certain insensitivity to risks and costs. North Korea, Iraq, and Iran fall into this category. The most important response is to convince them that they are being watched, and that the United States intends to stand against any nuclear ambitions they might have. Depending on the pace of their weapons programs, and the extent of their bellicosity, stronger measures may be warranted. There is no consensus on the use of force, however. Advocates of selective engagement are always sensitive to costs; preventive attacks may not be feasible.

Regional competitions among small states matter to the extent that they could energize intense great power security competition. This risk preserves the Persian Gulf as a core U.S. security interest.[18] The problem is not so much U.S. dependence on Gulf oil as the far greater dependence on it by many other great powers. A struggle over the control of the Gulf could draw in great powers on opposing sides, or set off competition elsewhere to expropriate energy resources. Moreover, should most of the economic potential associated with this oil fall into the hands of one ambitious actor, it could provide the underpinnings for a substantial regional military challenge. If Iraq could achieve the military development it did on its own oil revenues, how much more might it have achieved with the revenues of Kuwait or Saudi Arabia?

Even if such a power would not pose a direct threat to the United States, it would certainly be in a position to pose a threat to many of its neighbors. A great war in the Persian Gulf, with the risk of large-scale use of weapons of mass destruction, is the kind of experiment that the United States probably ought not to wish to run.

For the advocates of selective engagement, then, the parts of the world that matter most are the two ends of Eurasia—Europe and East Asia—and the Middle East/Southwest Asia. Traditional alliances are the appropriate vehicle to pursue these interests. Selective engagement especially favors the preservation of NATO, though not its expansion. That is not to say that the rest of the world can be completely ignored. Some countries may matter more than others for particular reasons. For example, proximity alone makes Mexico an important U.S. foreign policy interest. Moreover, if selective engagement is to remain a viable strategy, it will need to adapt to the likely emergence of sizeable new powers, and the potential for conflict among them.[19]

Advocates of selective engagement are concerned with ethnic conflict where it runs the risk of producing a great power war. Fortunately, there are not many places where this seems likely. Arguably, there is only one dangerous potential conflict of this type in Eurasia today—the currently dormant rivalry between Russia and Ukraine. Conflicts elsewhere in Eurasia may tempt one or more great powers to intervene, and thus they merit a certain degree of judicious diplomatic management. Most of these conflicts do not engage the vital interests of any state; they are strategically uninteresting. The former Yugoslavia, for instance, contains no military or economic resources that would affect the security of any European great power.

Advocates of selective engagement view humanitarian intervention as a question to be settled by the normal processes of U.S. domestic politics. There is no clear strategic guide that tells which interventions are worth pursuing and which are not. Their perspective does suggest several critical considerations. The most important strategic question is the opportunity cost. Given one's best estimate of the plausible course of the humanitarian intervention, what will be its consequences for U.S. material and political ability to intervene in more strategically important areas if trouble should arise during or after the humanitarian intervention? An intervention to bring sufficient order to Somalia to permit the distribution of humanitarian assistance required the equivalent of a single division of ground forces and involved the risk of relatively modest U.S. casualties. But even the horror of what had transpired earlier in Somalia proved insufficient to preserve U.S. public support through the relatively modest U.S. casualties that ensued. To preserve by force the unitary, multi-ethnic, ethnically intermingled Bosnia-Herzegovina that existed at the moment of Yugoslavia's dissolution could have required three or more U.S. divisions for the indefinite future, plus European forces.[20] There would likely have been more than a few casualties. Intervention in Yugoslavia would have made it more difficult to intervene elsewhere. As the casualties mount in any intervention, and the bloodshed begins to make the U.S. position more morally ambiguous to the American public, the political will to act in more important regions could erode.

*Force Structure*. A selective engagement policy probably requires a force structure similar to those proposed by the late Secretary of Defense Les Aspin in 1992 as "Force B" or "Force C" (see Table 2). A strong nuclear deterrent is still needed to deter nuclear attack on the United States and to protect its freedom of action in a world of several nuclear powers. Since the United States has an interest in stability in three critical areas of the world (both ends of Eurasia and the Persian Gulf), and since simultaneous trouble in two or more areas cannot be ruled out, it is reasonable to retain a "two regional wars" capability. Both force structures have sufficient air and ground forces for one major regional contingency ("MRC"), and sufficient air forces to support a regional ally in a second contingency. "Force C" places additional emphasis on sea and air lift and on aircraft carrier task forces, perhaps more than is truly necessary given that the United States ought to be able to identify in advance the location of the interests over which it might be willing to threaten or wage war. "Force C" also assumes that the United States must maintain sufficient reserve forces to sustain with ease a new major forward deployment of indeterminate duration, and at the same time conduct a small offensive operation such as the invasion of Panama. These additions seem an overly conservative interpretation of the forces necessary for selective engagement; "Force B" may be adequate.

*Critique*. Selective engagement has its own problems. First, the strategy lacks a certain romance: will the cool and quiet, steady, long-term exercise of U.S. power in the service of stable great power relations win the political support of any major constituency in the United States? Compared to other strategies, there is relatively little idealism or commitment to principle behind the strategy. It lacks the exuberant U.S. nationalism of primacy, or the commitment to liberal principle of cooperative security. It focuses rather narrowly on interests defined in terms of power. Can such a strategy sustain the support of a liberal democracy long addicted to viewing international relations as a struggle between good and evil?

Second, the strategy expects the United States to ignore much of the trouble that is likely to occur in the world. America's prestige and reputation might suffer from such apparent lethargy, however, which could limit its ability to persuade others on more important issues. Great power rivalries are currently muted, and if successful, the strategy will quietly keep them so. This would be an enormous contribution to the welfare of the entire world. However, it is an open question whether a regular tendency to avoid involvement in the issues that do arise will ultimately affect the ability of the United States to pursue its more important interests. Arguably, it was fear of such a result that provided one of the impulses for the ultimate U.S. involvement in trying to end the war in Bosnia.

Third, selective engagement does not provide clear guidance on which ostensibly "minor" issues have implications for great power relations, and thus merit U.S. involvement. It posits that most will not matter, but admits that some will. Some connections are more obvious than others, but all will be the subject of debate. Since trouble in peripheral areas is likely to be more common than trouble in core areas, the selective engagement strategy gives its least precise positive guidance on matters that will most commonly figure prominently in the media, and hence in the public debate on U.S. foreign policy. The responsible practice of selective engagement will thus require considerable case-by-case analysis and public debate.

Fourth, selective engagement is not as selective as its advocates would have us believe. Europe and Asia matter because that is where the major powers reside; and the Middle East matters because of its oil resources. Much of the world, therefore, matters. Developments on the periphery of this rather large expanse of the earth will invariably and regularly produce intense media coverage and committed partisans of intervention. The argument will often prove tempting that the frontiers of "what matters" need to be pacified to protect "what matters." NATO enlargement is a good example; advocates want to pacify eastern Europe "preventively" even though Russia is weak and there is no obvious simmering major power conflict there. Few advocates of selective engagement favor this policy, in part because they believe in balancing behavior, and fear that Russia will be catalyzed into reactions that will cause exactly the kind of trouble the United States hopes to avoid. It is likely that those who subscribe to selective engagement would be doomed to spend their careers arguing against grand strategy "mission creep," even if U.S. policymakers explicitly chose selective engagement as the national strategy.[21]

Finally, neo-isolationists would argue that there is one huge tension in the selective engagement argument. The United States must maintain substantial military forces, threaten war, and risk war largely for the purpose of preventing war. A traditional realist position accepts the risk of war, and the costs of waging war, to prevent aggressors from building sufficient power to challenge the United States directly. Neo-isolationists, however, argue that if you want to avoid war, you must stay out of the affairs of others. They remind us that it is quite unlikely that the results of even a great power war could decisively shift the balance of power against the United States. If the United States goes out into the world to prevent hypothetical wars, it will surely find some real ones. Advocates of selective engagement resist this deductive logic for two reasons: the United

States was drawn against its intentions into two costly world wars that started in Eurasia; and the United States pursued an activist policy during the Cold War which both contained Soviet expansionism and avoided great power war.

## Cooperative Security

The most important distinguishing feature of cooperative security is the proposition that peace is effectively indivisible.[22] Cooperative security, therefore, begins with an expansive conception of U.S. interests: the United States has a huge national interest in world peace. Cooperative security is the only one of the four strategic alternatives that is informed by liberalism rather than realism.[23] Advocates propose to act collectively, through international institutions as much as possible. They presume that democracies will find it easier to work together in cooperative security regimes than would states with less progressive domestic polities.

Cooperative security does not view the great powers as a generic security problem. Because most are democracies, or on the road to democracy, and democracies have historically tended not to fall into war with one another, little great power security competition is expected.[24] A transitional Russia and an oligarchical China remain troublesome, but the answer there is to help them toward democracy as in the Clinton administration formulation, "Engagement and Enlargement." The motives for great powers to collaborate are presumed to be greater than in the past, and the barriers to cooperation are presumed to be lower.

The cooperative security enterprise represents an effort to overcome the shortcomings of traditional collective security.[25] For both, aggression anywhere, and by anyone, cannot be allowed to stand. Both place a premium on international cooperation to deter and thwart aggression. It is to be "all for one and one for all." Cooperative security advocates do not rely on spontaneous power balancing because this is only likely when traditional vital interests are engaged. Instead, international institutions, particularly the United Nations, are to play a critical role in coordinating the deterrence and defeat of aggression. Regional institutions, particularly a transformed NATO, have an important role to play where international institutions are weak. Institutions respond to imminent threats, and deter all who would break the peace.

Previously, great powers could view small wars as unlikely threats to their national security. But the emergence of weapons of mass destruction means that any arms race or war can produce a world-class disaster.[26] The United States, and indeed the rest of the industrialized world, simply cannot live with these risks indefinitely. Nuclear weapons do not favor the status quo, except for the very small number of great powers who have them. Most states do not have the resources or organizational skills to deploy secure retaliatory forces. Most do not yet have, and many will not be able to acquire, nuclear weapons. The casualty-sensitivity of the democracies suggests that the risk of even a small nuclear attack might discourage them from coming to the assistance of a country in trouble. Aggressors are expected to be undemocratic, greedy, and casualty-insensitive; nuclear weapons favor them. Thus nuclear arms control, particularly non-proliferation, is at the heart of cooperative security.

Cooperative security subscribes to one premise that, for the most part, the other three strategies do not even consider. A high level of what one might term "strategic interdependence" is posited. Wars in one place are likely to spread; unsavory military practices employed in one war will be employed in other wars. The use of weapons of mass destruction will beget their use elsewhere; ethnic cleansing will beget more ethnic cleansing. Refugees fleeing the nationalist violence of one country will energize xenophobia in countries of refuge. The organization of a global information system helps to connect these events by providing strategic intelligence to good guys and bad guys alike; it connects them politically by providing images of one horror after another in the living rooms of the citizens of economically advanced democracies.[27] The result is a chain of logic that connects the security of the United States and its more traditional allies to a host of distant troubles. Thus, these distant troubles cannot be ignored.

*Issues and Instruments*. Cooperative security advocates believe that they now have more effective means to achieve their goals. The United States is presumed, based on the Desert Storm victory, to hold decisive military-technological superiority and thus to be able to wage speedy, low-casualty wars. In the past, advocates of collective security relied on world public opinion, and on economic sanctions. They understood that it is difficult to get self-interested states to support military intervention on the side of peace in distant places, so they stressed the impact of these less costly measures. Cooperative security advocates still like these mechanisms, but history has taught them to be skeptical that they will prove sufficient. Instead it is argued that real military action is cheaper than it once was.[28]

Advocates of cooperative security have added the arms control mechanisms developed in the last three decades to the traditional collective security repertoire. With enough arms control agreements, transparency, and confidence- and-security-building measures (CSBMs), and enough intrusive verification, states around the world will be able to avoid conflicts arising from misperception or first-strike advantages. The offensive military capabilities that enable states to engage in aggression will thus be acquired by few countries. Peace-loving states will adopt defensive military postures and an international military division of labor that will provide only their combined forces with an offensive capability. The few "rogue states" left after all this arms control and institution-building can either be intimidated by the threat of high technology warfare or decisively defeated in short order.

A cooperative security strategy depends on international organizations to coordinate collective action. They are part of the complicated process of building sufficient credibility to convince all prospective aggressors that they will regularly be met with decisive countervailing power. The threat of great powers to intervene—even when they have no immediate interests at stake—must be made credible. A standing international organization with substantial domestic and international legitimacy is necessary to coordinate multilateral action and to create the expectation of regular, effective intervention for peace.

Its advocates stress that cooperative security is a work in progress.[29] Global cooperative security structures will not emerge fully developed. Indeed it is argued that they need not: existing "overlapping, mutually reinforcing arrangements" provide the foundation upon which cooperative security can be built. As three leading proponents have written, "military establishments around the world already are entangled in a large web of internationally sanctioned restraints on how they equip themselves and operate in peacetime. Cooperative security means making the effort to thicken and unify this web."[30] That, clearly, entails a long term project.

In at least one area of the world, the project is seen as already well under way. Europe has begun to practice cooperative security with a web of diplomatic, economic, and security arrangements, particularly the arms control, transparency, and CSBMs associated with the Organization for Security and Cooperation in Europe. The Clinton administration views NATO enlargement, in part, as an extension of the cooperative security project.[31] If Europe, even during the Cold War, could develop such arrangements, the proponents of cooperative security ask, can other regions not do the same now that the distractions of the Cold War are behind us?

Proliferation is a key issue for cooperative security advocates. They support very strong measures to prevent and reverse it.[32] They supported not only the indefinite extension of the Nuclear Non-Proliferation Treaty in 1995 but also the strengthening of its safeguards. The demonstration effect of any new proliferation is presumed to be great. It is therefore reasonable to oppose any new nuclear power beyond those declared nuclear weapons states in the original treaty. Moreover, the policy must be pursued equally versus friends, enemies, and neutrals. Israeli, Indian, and Ukrainian nuclear weapons are all bad, regardless of the fact that the United States has no political conflict of interest with any of these countries. Proliferation must also be headed off for another reason: the more nuclear powers there are in the world, the more dangerous it will be for international organizations to act aggressively against miscreants, the less likely they will be to act, and the more likely it is that the entire cooperative security edifice will collapse.[33] War to prevent new nuclear powers from emerging would be reasonable in some circumstances.[34]

Regional conflicts among states are of critical interest to cooperative security advocates. Cross-border aggression has always been the most clear-cut problem; it is never acceptable. Conflicts within states emerge as a new, serious problem for a cooperative security strategy.[35] Historically, collective security tried to establish the conditions for peace among a small number of great powers and empires. Today we have many more states, and even more groups aspiring to statehood. Politically conscious groups often span the boundaries of several territorially defined states. Thus inter-group conflict may become inter-state conflict. Even when irredenta are not involved, civil wars may attract outside intervention by the greedy, and thus precipitate international wars. Finally, ethnic conflict tends to be ferocious. The brutal behavior portrayed on the television screens of the world creates a malign precedent.

Cooperative security advocates favor military action for humanitarian purposes.[36] But the connection between immediate humanitarian concerns and the task of building sufficient credibility to deter future aggressors is tenuous. Indeed, the goals may conflict, as often seemed the case in Bosnia-Herzegovina. In the first phase of that war, the United States and other democratic states could have supplied arms to the Bosnian Muslims with relative ease to help them fend off the military attacks of the Serbs. They might even have flown tactical air sorties to assist the Muslims. This would have made the point that aggression does not pay. But it is unlikely that UN humanitarian efforts would have survived such a policy. A large-scale intervention with several hundred thousand troops might have been necessary both to stop the Serbs and to sustain the UN humanitarian effort to care for those in need of the everyday necessities of life. Despite such difficulties, cooperative security advocates seem to want to pursue short term humanitarianism and long-term political principle at the same time. This makes for demanding military operations.

*Force Structure*. What kind of U.S. force structure is required to support a cooperative security strategy? While cooperative security envisions the adoption of defensive military postures, "a small number of nations, including the United States, must maintain certain elements of their armed forces beyond that required for territorial defense and make those elements available to multinational forces when needed."[37] The U.S. contribution to this multinational force would emphasize the country's comparative advantage in aerospace power: the three elements of the reconnaissance strike complex—command, control, communications and intelligence; defense suppression; and precision-guided munitions—that were employed in Desert Storm.

Advocates have suggested that this force would be smaller than the "Bottom-Up Review" force advocated by the Clinton administration (see Table 2).[38] But their assessment focuses on means, while assuming that others will cooperate to the maximum extent of their ability—i.e., that they will maintain larger forces than they currently plan. Moreover, it ignores the necessity for a period of regular and consistent military action if there is to be any hope of building the international credibility necessary to affect the calculations of prospective aggressors everywhere.

A true cooperative security strategy could involve the United States in several simultaneous military actions. U.S. forces were recently engaged in Iraq and in Somalia simultaneously, while advocates clamored for a third U.S. military action in Bosnia. Haiti subsequently replaced Somalia on this list, even as the U.S. military role in Bosnia expanded. UN forces were deployed in several other places—arguably in insufficient numbers to accomplish their missions completely. The experiences in Desert Shield/Desert Storm and in the Somali relief operation suggest that U.S. leadership is often the key ingredient for substantial international cooperation.[39] It is not the subtle diplomacy of the United States that proves critical, but rather its military reputation, which depends on large, diverse, technologically sophisticated, and lushly supplied military forces capable of decisive operations. At least initially, the United States would have to provide disproportionate military power to launch a global cooperative security regime. A force structure in the range of the Clinton administration's "Bottom-Up Review" force and the "Base Force" (see Table 2) may be necessary to pursue a true cooperative security policy with a good chance of success.

*Critique*. Cooperative security is vulnerable to a range of criticisms. First, individual states are still expected to be able to rise above narrow conceptions of national interest in response to appeals for action on behalf of the collective good, and to engage in what will seem to them as armed altruism. In theory, some collective action problems associated with collective security[40] may be ameliorated by cooperative security. In particular, the combination of intensive arms control, military technological superiority, and U.S. leadership is meant to reduce substantially the costs of cooperation for any given member of the cooperative security regime. Nevertheless, there will still be defectors and free riders. Major power aggression would still be a problem for cooperative security, as it was for collective security, if some powers perceive the intrinsic stakes as small and the aggressor as far away and difficult to fight. It seems unlikely, for example, that the NATO allies would ever fight the People's Republic of China over Taiwan, even if the United States wanted to do so. States concerned about the possible competitions of the future will still ask if any given opportunity for current cooperation to achieve a common good, or oppose a common bad, changes their power position relative to all other potential challengers, including one another.

Second, the task of building sufficient general multilateral credibility to deter a series of new and different potential aggressors seems very difficult. Regular

U.S. action to oppose the Soviet Union during the Cold War did not entirely dissuade that regime from new challenges. Since this was an iterative bipolar game, credibility should have accumulated, but that does not seem to have happened. Although U.S. credibility appears to have been quite high in Europe, where direct interests were great and deployed military power was strong, elsewhere Soviet behavior was often mischievous. It is quite likely, therefore, that a true cooperative security strategy would involve the UN, designated regional organizations, and effectively the United States, in a number of wars over many years if it is to have any hope of establishing the ability to deter the ambitious and reassure the fearful. This would, however, serve to further strain public support for a demanding strategy.

Third, democracies are problematical partners in a cooperative security project in a crucial respect: their publics must be persuaded to go to war. Since the publics in modern liberal democracies seem to be quite casualty sensitive, the case for risking the lives of their troops in *distant* wars is inherently difficult to make. This is one reason why the decisive military superiority of a technologically dominant coalition of peace-loving states is a necessary condition for cooperative security to work. This in turn depends on the military power of the United States.

Fourth, cooperative security places a heavy burden on arms control. It is not clear that arms control can bear that burden. Nonproliferation efforts have met with mixed success. Verification and, especially, enforcement remain problematic. The open international economic system, which most cooperative security advocates strongly favor, inevitably accelerates the diffusion of the economic and technological underpinnings of military power. While arms control can increase the economic costs and political risks of engaging in proscribed activities, determined states will continue to acquire and employ military forces. Thus the members of a cooperative security regime are likely to have to respond to aggression more often than the proponents of such a regime predict. Cooperative security must oversell the probability and magnitude of an international happy ending in order to elicit political support for an indeterminate period of high activism.

## Primacy

Primacy, like selective engagement, is motivated by both power and peace. But the particular configuration of power is key: this strategy holds that only a preponderance of U.S. power ensures peace.[41] The pre-Cold War practice of aggregating power through coalitions and alliances, which underlies selective engagement, is viewed as insufficient. Peace is the result of an imbalance of power in which U.S. capabilities are sufficient, operating on their own, to cow all potential challengers and to comfort all coalition partners. It is not enough, consequently, to be *primus inter pares,* a comfortable position for selective engagement. Even the most clever Bismarckian orchestrator of the balance of power will ultimately fall short. One must be *primus solus.* Therefore, both world order and national security require that the United States maintain the primacy with which it emerged from the Cold War. The collapse of bipolarity cannot be permitted to allow the emergence of multipolarity; unipolarity is best. Primacy would have been the strategy of a Dole administration.

Primacy is most concerned with the trajectories of present and possible future great powers. As with selective engagement, Russia, China, Japan and the most significant members of the European Union (essentially Germany, France, and Britain), matter most. War among the great powers poses the greatest threat to U.S. security for advocates of primacy as well as those of selective engagement. But primacy goes beyond the logic of selective engagement and its focus on managing relations among present and potential future great powers. Advocates of primacy view the rise of a peer competitor from the midst of the great powers to offer the greatest threat to international order and thus the greatest risk of war. The objective for primacy, therefore, is not merely to preserve peace among the great powers, but to preserve U.S. supremacy by politically, economically, and militarily outdistancing any global challenger.

The Bush administration's draft Defense Planning Guidance (DPG), leaked to the press in March of 1992, provides the most fully developed blueprint for precluding the rise of such a peer competitor. The DPG is the high-level strategic statement that launches, and in theory governs, the Pentagon's annual internal defense budget preparation process. Subsequent published commentary by former Secretary of Defense Richard Cheney suggests that the Bush administration broadly subscribed to the principles suggested by the leaked passages.[42] The authors of the draft DPG were unyielding in their insistence that the United States maintain its status as the world's sole superpower:

> Our first objective is to prevent the reemergence of a new rival, either on the territory of the former Soviet Union or elsewhere, that poses a threat on the order of that posed formerly by the Soviet Union. This is a dominant consideration... and requires that we endeavor to prevent any hostile power from dominating a region whose resources would, under consolidated control, be sufficient to generate global power.... Our strategy must now refocus on precluding the emergence of any potential future global competitor.[43]

Those parts of the world identified as most likely to harbor potential peer competitors were Western Europe, East Asia, the territories of the former Soviet Union, and Southwest Asia..

Strategic planners in the Department of Defense and more recent advocates argue that others already believe, or can be lead to believe, that the United States is a benign hegemon. Thus the project is expected to meet with global support rather than opposition.[44] Other states will not balance against the United States. Thus:

> the U.S. must show the leadership necessary to establish and protect a new order that holds the promise of convincing potential competitors that they need not aspire to a greater role or pursue a more aggressive posture to protect their legitimate interests.... In the non-defense areas, we must account sufficiently for the interests of the advanced industrial nations to discourage them from challenging our leadership or seeking to overturn the established political and economic order.... We will retain the pre-eminent responsibility for addressing selectively those wrongs which threaten not only our interests, but those of our allies or friends, or which could seriously unsettle international relations.[45]

Present and aspiring major powers are to be persuaded, it seems, that they can rest easy, and need not bother investing in the political, economic, and military means they might otherwise require to safeguard their interests. Indeed, any assertion of strategic independence by the likes of Germany and Japan would only erode the global and regional stability sought by all.[46]

In addition to maintaining U.S. primacy by reassuring others of the purity of its intentions, the draft DPG envisioned the United States seeking to prevent the rise of challengers by promoting international law, democracy, and free-market economies, and precluding the emergence of regional hegemons. It is important to note that though primacy focuses on the maintenance of overwhelming U.S. power and influence, it remains strongly committed to liberal principles. It is simply more judicious about the commitment of U.S. military power to particular liberal projects than is the cooperative security strategy. Support for political and economic transformation are seen as the best way to ensure that Russia will not revert to the authoritarian, expansionist habits of old, though the United States should hedge against the failure of such reform. In Europe, the United States would work against any erosion of NATO's preeminent role in European security and the development of any security arrangements that would undermine the role of NATO, and therefore the role of the United States, in European security affairs. The countries of East and Central Europe would be integrated into the political, economic, and even security institutions of Western Europe. In East Asia, the United States would maintain a military presence sufficient to ensure regional stability and prevent the emergence of a power vacuum or a regional hegemon. The same approach applied to the Middle East and Southwest Asia, where the United States intended to remain the preeminent extraregional power. The United States would also endeavor to discourage India's hegemonic ambitions in South Asia. The regional dimension of the strategy outlined in the draft DPG is thus consistent with the global dimension: the aspirations of regional as well as global hegemons are to be thwarted.

Proponents of primacy are more than a little upbeat about the post-Cold War international position of the United States. Even though all too few Americans recognize their good fortune, "they have never had it so good."[47] In this best of all possible worlds, the United States today is the only world superpower. It "enjoys strategic and ideological predominance" and exercises hegemonic influence and authority.[48] The U.S share of gross world product is considered to be more than sufficient to maintain primacy. According to primacy advocates, this is in line with its share at the outset of World War II, in which the United States led a global war and simultaneously enjoyed the highest standard of living in the world.[49] Moreover, looking only at GDP masks the extent of U.S. dominance. The United States has more hard-to-measure "soft power"—domination of the news media, mass culture, computers, and international communications—than any other nation.[50] And the United States is the master of the most advanced military technologies, especially intelligence and command and control capabilities and precision-guided munitions. This technological advantage renders traditional military organizations vastly less capable against the United States than traditional military analysis would suggest. (Primacy and cooperative security share this premise.) Advocates of primacy, like those of selective engagement, do recognize that U.S. resources are limited, but they contend that the United States is a wealthy country that all too often acts as if it were poor.[51] The problem is not a lack of resources, but a lack of political will. Advocates of primacy are quite optimistic, however, that the U.S. public can be induced to sacrifice for this project.[52]

***Issues and Instruments***. Certainly the most serious threat to U.S. primacy would be an across-the-board political, economic, and military challenger. Yet even a power that rivaled the United States in only one or two of these three dimensions of national power could erode U.S. preponderance. That the Soviet Union during the Cold War was unable to issue a credible challenge in the economic realm, as well as the political and military, did little to allay U.S. fears. It is generally the one-dimensional challenge that is seen as providing the near-term threat to continued U.S. primacy.[53] Some fear a resurgence of a militarily capable Russia. Others argue that the United States is most vulnerable in the economic realm. For a time, Japan was viewed as the main contender. Others worry about the rise of China, fearing an imminent, mutually reinforcing growth of its economic and military power.

The debate on NATO enlargement has shown that some still view Russia as strong and dangerous. Though smaller and weaker than its Soviet predecessor, it is presumed to be on the move again.[54] The remedy is a revived policy of containment. This "new containment," however, is little more than a stalking horse for primacy. Whether targeted at Russia or China, the new containment, like the old containment, identifies a threat that provides the rationale for remaining heavily involved in Eurasia and for maintaining the political, economic, and especially military capabilities needed to pursue an intense global strategic competition. One advocate of primacy who wants the United States "to be the global hegemon of the regional hegemons, the boss of all the bosses" has explicitly called for the "potential" or "latent" containment of both Russia and China, while others prefer a more active version.[55]

Calls for containing Russia are most prominently identified with Zbigniew Brzezinski and Henry Kissinger, and have surfaced with the greatest clarity in the debate on whether NATO should formally expand and offer membership and protection to former Eastern European members of the Warsaw Pact. Both fear the seductive effect of a "security vacuum" in Eastern (newly re-christened "Central") Europe. "A Russia facing a divided Europe would find the temptation to fill the vacuum irresistible."[56] Observers should not be lulled by the relative decline in capability precipitated by the dissolution of the Soviet Union, the collapse of the Soviet economy, and the deterioration of the Soviet (now Russian) military. Containment advocates cite a new Russian assertiveness, demonstrated in diplomatic, military, and economic interventions large and small around its periphery.[57] Russia brings three dangerous qualities to the table: it possesses tremendous inherent strategic reach; considerable material reserves; and the largest single homogeneous ethnic-cultural population in Europe. Brzezinski asserts that Russian culture somehow contains within it the seeds of expansion.[58] (One notes here echoes of Cold War logic, which viewed Communism as inherently aggressive.)

Because the new containment is so closely tied to NATO expansion, advocates say little about other regions of the world. It seems, however, that NATO expansion is part of a much more ambitious policy. Brzezinski adds a more forward U.S. policy around the Russian periphery.[59] In some recent work, he describes an "oblong of maximum danger," which extends from the Adriatic to the border of the Chinese province of Sinkiang and from the Persian Gulf to the Russian-Kazakh frontier.[60] Here he expects a stew of ethnic and nationalist conflict and proliferation of weapons of mass destruction—a "whirlpool of violence"—although the precise nature of U.S. interests here is not well developed. Similarly, Kissinger alludes to the role of a revived NATO in the resolution of the crises that will surely attend the adjustment of Russia, China, and Japan to the changed circumstances of the post-Cold War world; Kissinger has also alluded to a NATO role in Korea, Indonesia, Brazil, and India.[61]

Two elements in the case for NATO expansion suggest that its advocates perceive the Russian threat as less imminent than they often imply. First, they think that Russia's fears of an expanded NATO can be rather easily assuaged. Second, they see the Russian military threat as quite manageable. Advocates of NATO expansion usually advocate a simultaneous diplomatic approach to Russia in the form of some sort of "security treaty."[62] They concede that NATO should not move large forces forward onto the territory of new members.[63] The combination of a formal diplomatic act of reassurance and military restraint is expected to ameliorate the possibility that the eastward march of a mighty and formerly adversarial military coalition could be perceived by Russia to pose a threat. These expectations seem inconsistent with the image of a looming Russian threat.

Similarly, advocates of NATO expansion are relaxed about its costs because they are relaxed about the current Russian military threat. As of late 1996, NATO had yet to release a public estimate of the costs of expansion.[64] One general statement of the threat has been offered by a team of political and military analysts from the Rand Corporation:

> One should avoid assuming worst-case scenarios. Even a re-armed Russia would not be the military Leviathan the Soviet Union once was. It would have an imposing military force, but probably not a great deal more than that of Iran, Iraq, or North Korea—in short, a major regional contingency-sized threat. Defending against such a threat would be very different than against the theater-wide challenge posed by the Warsaw Pact during the Cold War.[65]

Thus, there is no imminent or even remote military threat to these Eastern European countries that NATO cannot deal with rather comfortably with its current capabilities.

Given the politically and militarily relaxed image of the Russian threat expressed by NATO expansion advocates, one wonders what is actually driving them. In our judgment, it is first the desire to anchor the United States in a diplomatic enterprise that will preserve and widen its involvement in European and international affairs, simply because this is viewed as an unalloyed good in its own right. Second, it is to forestall even a hint of an independent German foreign policy in the east.[66] A revived containment policy in Europe may be nothing more than the adaptation of a politically familiar vehicle to the task of preserving U.S. primacy.

Another candidate for future peer competitor, and therefore long-term threat, is China.[67] Current economic trends in that country suggest that it could become a formidable economic competitor in the first quarter of the next century. Its new economic capability could easily be translated into not only regional but also perhaps global military might.[68] The admission of Vietnam into ASEAN (the Association of Southeast Asian Nations) can be read in part as reflecting regional concerns about China's intentions. China's rapid economic growth, improving military capabilities, stridency on Taiwan, and interest in the South China Sea have led to the suggestion that it would be prudent to hedge against the failure of engagement with China by means of a strategy of "hidden containment." Such a strategy would include maintaining U.S. military presence in the region, establishing a robust diplomatic relationship with Vietnam, and perhaps even reviving something along the lines of SEATO.[69] According to *The*

*Economist,* containment "should mean recognizing that China is a destabilizing force and impressing upon it the need to forswear force in trying to settle its grievances."[70]

Advocates of primacy share with the new isolationists and selective engagers a healthy skepticism of international organizations.[71] International organizations have little if any power and therefore can do little to maintain or, particularly, restore peace. Yet international organizations should not be entirely rejected because of fears that they may draw the United States into conflicts or concerns that they cannot credibly deter aggression. Even a hegemonic power will, from time to time, find it useful to exploit the diplomatic cover provided by international organizations. If the facade of multilateralism renders the rule of an extraordinary power more palatable to ordinary powers, as it did during the Gulf War, international organizations are a strategic asset.

Proliferation is as much a concern for primacy as it is for cooperative security.[72] The threat to U.S. interests posed by the proliferation of nuclear and other weapons of mass destruction and their means of delivery was highlighted in the draft DPG. Proliferation is a problem because it undermines U.S. freedom of action by increasing the costs and risks of U.S. military interventions around the world. Because they serve to perpetuate a U.S. military advantage, current nonproliferation efforts should be continued. But while prevention is a useful first line of defense in combating proliferation, by itself it is inadequate to the task. The United States must also be able to deter and defend against the use of nuclear, biological, or chemical weapons by present and future powers which might develop such capabilities.

Proponents of primacy view regional conflict, ethnic conflict, and humanitarian intervention in much the same light as do the advocates of selective engagement. Regional conflict matters most when it impinges on major power relations and the rise of potential peer competitors and regional hegemons. Outside of the Persian Gulf, most conflicts in what was once referred to as the Third World will be of little concern. Much the same can be said for ethnic conflict, however reprehensible it may be, and the need for U.S. humanitarian intervention.[73] There is no obvious security rationale, under primacy, for humanitarian military operations, though some operations (such as Bosnia) may offer opportunities to demonstrate and assert U.S. power and leadership.

*Force Structure.* The forces needed to support a grand strategy of primacy should inspire a sense of *déjà vu.* A nearly Cold War-size force, in particular the Bush administration's "Base Force," would do just fine (see Table 2). The draft DPG was intended to provide the classified rationale for a 1.62 million person Base Force. General Colin Powell apparently saw this force as essential if U.S. primacy was to be preserved.[74] Two advocates of primacy recently called for increasing defense spending by as much as $80 billion above current levels, to roughly the level required to support the "Base Force." They propose that the adequacy of U.S. military forces be measured against "a two- (or three-, or four-) power standard," analogous to Britain's two-power standard of old, in which the Royal Navy was meant to be superior to the two next strongest navies in the world combined. This would serve to perpetuate the current disparity in military capabilities between the United States and other powers.[75] Presumably, the disparity to be maintained is qualitative rather than quantitative.

Military modernization is a high priority for the advocates of primacy. Indeed, if the objective is actually to deter any state from considering a challenge to U.S. preeminence, then it is logical for the United States military to pursue a level of qualitative superiority over potential challengers that would discourage them from entering the competition. That requires higher levels of research and development and procurement funding. The force must also be capable of what the Bush administration termed reconstitution: the ability to expand U.S. military capabilities in order to deter, and if necessary respond to, the rise of a global challenger. Thus the level of defense spending required to support a grand strategy of primacy would likely be greater in the future than it would be now, as a consequence of both modernization and expansion.

American military preeminence should ensure that U.S. forces could be used at will, but would seldom have to be, since threats to U.S. interests would be deterred by overwhelming military capabilities. Advocates of primacy, perhaps in an effort to reassure the rest of the world, have counseled that the United States use force sparingly. They advise against the use of military force on behalf of purely economic interests, or to promote American values, reverse setbacks to democracy, support the United Nations, or resolve civil wars. Protracted military involvement in non-critical regions is to be avoided. Because world order and stability are to be maintained, however, the United States is to look favorably on the use of force to resist aggression.[76] Despite the lip service given to restraint, this self-appointed mission could involve a lot of fighting.

*Critique.* One of the foremost advocates of primacy has argued that "it matters which state exercises the most power in the international system"; that U.S. primacy is to be preferred to that of another power and is superior to a world in which no one is able to exercise primacy (the balance-of-power world implicitly embraced by selective engagement); and that primacy enables a state to achieve its objectives without resorting to war.[77] However, although primacy may offer many benefits for the United States and even for the world, the quest for primacy is likely to prove futile for five reasons.

First, the diffusion of economic and technological capabilities—precipitated in part by the open international economic system that the United States supports, in part by the spread of literacy, and in part by the embrace of market economics—suggests that other countries will develop the foundations to compete in international politics. New great powers will rise in the future. Indeed, though there is no recognized rule of thumb that specifies the share of gross world product a state must command in order to bid for hegemony, it seems peculiar to suggest that the situation today is not much different from the end of World War II, when an unbombed United States produced 40 percent of gross world product.[78]

Second, contrary to the expectations of primacy advocates, it is likely that some states will balance against the United States. They will not wish to remain in a permanent position of military inferiority, just as the United States would struggle to reverse the position if it were imposed even by a benevolent state. Primacy underestimates the power of nationalism. Some states, simply out of national pride, may not accept U.S. leadership. States coalesce against hegemons rather than rally around them. Primacy is therefore a virtual invitation to struggle.

Third, American insistence on hegemonic leadership can engender resistance that may undermine the long-term effectiveness of any multilateral mechanisms that the United States may wish to exploit should challengers actually emerge. If a rising power such as China cannot be accommodated, as Britain accommodated the rise of the United States, the collective defense mechanisms of selective engagement or the collective security component of cooperative security would ensure that the United States need not alone bear the burden of taking on those who would undermine international order and stability: primacy may make this remedy unavailable.

Fourth, primacy carries the logical implication that the United States should be willing to wage preventive war. For now, such discussions focus on depriving "rogue" states of their nascent capabilities to assemble weapons of mass destruction. However difficult this may be, it is easy compared to the problem of restraining larger states. Will U.S. domestic politics permit a preventive war to forestall the rise of a challenger if other measures have proven insufficient? How will other major powers react to preventive war?

Fifth, the pursuit of primacy poses the constant risk of imperial overstretch. Primacy is inherently open-ended. A little bit more power will always seem better. Selective engagement is vulnerable to this temptation; primacy is even more so. Attempting to sustain an image of such overwhelming power that others will not even think of making the effort to match U.S. capabilities, or challenge U.S. leadership, seems a good recipe for draining the national treasury. Primacy may be affordable today, but it is less likely to be had on the cheap in the future. Ultimately, primacy is probably unsustainable and self-defeating. Primacy is little more than a rationale for the continued pursuit of Cold War policy and strategy in the absence of an enemy.[79]

## The Clinton Administration's Grand Strategy:
## Selective (But Cooperative) Primacy

The Clinton administration came to office strongly inclined to pursue a cooperative security policy. Several of its senior national security officials were identified with the development of cooperative security ideas before the 1992 election.[80] The international and domestic constraints that the administration has encountered in its efforts to execute the strategy have forced both real and rhetorical compromises.

*A National Security Strategy of Engagement and Enlargement* (February 1996), the most complete statement of the administration's grand strategy vision, prominently contains within it the language of cooperative security and selective engagement, plus a dash of primacy.[81] The document reveals a curiously dialectical quality, alternating between cooperative security rhetoric and selective engagement rhetoric. The administration has adopted an avowedly internationalist posture founded on a broad conception of national interests. The phrase "engagement and enlargement" conveys both the mode and the purpose, or vision, of the strategy: the United States must be engaged in the world to enlarge the community of democratic free-market countries. Neo-isolationism is explicitly rejected. The repeated calls for U.S. leadership may be interpreted as a bow in the direction of primacy, as is the stress on U.S. unilateral military capabilities.[82]

The document promotes, on the one hand, "cooperative security measures." On the other hand, it acknowledges "limits to America's involvement in the world—limits imposed by careful evaluation of our fundamental interests and frank assessment of the costs and benefits of possible actions," and notes that "we cannot become involved in every problem." The array of transnational threats and challenges confronting the post-Cold War world "demand cooperative, multilateral solutions." Arms control is unequivocally embraced as "an integral part of our national security strategy" and seen as becoming increasingly multilateral. But the country's force structure must enable the United States to deal with threats not just multilaterally but unilaterally. "Our leadership must stress preventive diplomacy... in order to help resolve problems, reduce tensions and defuse conflicts before they become crises," yet "our engagement must be selective, focusing on the challenges that are most important [to] our own interests and focusing our resources where we can make the most difference."[83]

While the document issues calls for strengthening the United Nations, and for the United States to be prepared to participate in a wide variety of multilateral peace operations, that participation is nevertheless subject to a restrictive set of conditions that, if taken at face value, would ensure that the United States is seldom actually engaged in such operations. Economic multilateralism too is championed, but a self-regarding emphasis on "enhancing

American competitiveness," which might be expected of selective engagement or primacy, is present as well.[84] Democracy must be promoted, but a selective approach prevails: some parts of the world and some countries, particularly the states of the former Soviet Union and Eastern and Central Europe, matter more than others. The United States will intervene in the morass of ethnic and other intrastate conflicts only if there is an exit strategy. Humanitarian interventions too will occur under the strategy, but only under "certain conditions."[85] More generally, decisions on whether, when, and how to use military force are subject to stringent guidelines that, if consistently adhered to, ensure that it will be used quite selectively. The administration's highest-priority regions—the two ends of Eurasia—are the same as those of selective engagement and primacy.

The Clinton administration has been forced to water down a commitment to cooperative security because its purposes proved too grand and its premises faulty; the U.S. power necessary to pursue the strategy proved greater than expected. The liberal internationalist rhetoric that accompanies cooperative security generates a long agenda and great expectations for action. But to succeed without the commitment of substantial U.S. power, both international and multilateral institutions need to be strong and cohesive. And, more generally, very extensive international cooperation would be required. Both assumptions were flawed.

The UN remains a weak institution. Though it has been remarkably busy at peacekeeping over the last five or six years, it has proven ineffectual wherever the local parties have been even moderately resistant. Regional institutions did not do much better: the European Union and to a lesser extent the Organization for Security and Cooperation in Europe made attempts to help manage the dissolution of Yugoslavia, but they were unable to produce any results. The UN was able to organize some humanitarian relief in Yugoslavia, but was unable to bring about a settlement, or even to ameliorate the brutality of the fighting. Moreover, all three of these institutions contained ample numbers of democratic, peace-loving states. The EU is made up entirely of such states. Democracies may not fight one another, but this does not mean that they will always cooperate to settle disputes at the margins of traditional national interests.

The Clinton administration discovered that although international institutions are weak, the forces of U.S. domestic politics are not particularly supportive of strengthening them. The rhetoric of U.S. "leadership" that both the Democrats and the Republicans have adopted in their foreign policy statements is as much an expression of what the U.S. public seems to be against in international affairs as what it is for. It is against giving up much U.S. autonomy. As several observers have noted, the freshmen Republicans elected in 1994 are not so much isolationist as "unilateralist."[86] This means that the United States is in no position to strengthen weak international institutions. The only multilateral organization that is loved across the U.S. political spectrum seems to be NATO, which is why it is carrying so much U.S. foreign policy weight.

The Clinton administration also discovered that international cooperation is not so easy to arrange. Even the good guys can conceptualize their national interests in opposition to one another. Three conflicts with liberal democratic allies have surfaced during the Clinton administration. While all of these conflicts cannot be attributed to cooperative security projects, they nevertheless illustrate the broader problem: democracies can be "uncooperative." First, the Clinton administration itself pursued a strangely "non-cooperative" economic policy with the Japanese for most of 1993-96. This caused many in Asia to wonder if the United States was abandoning its commitment to a multilateral trading system.[87] Second, the United States vehemently disagreed with the policy pursued in Bosnia by Britain and France. U.S. policymakers believed that there was some way to produce a unified, pluralist, democratic Bosnia-Herzegovina. The British and French believed that once the war got going, some variant of a partition solution was the right answer. Privately, both British and U.S. officials admit that differences over Bosnia brought U.S.-British relations to their lowest point since the 1956 Suez crisis. In the end, the United States and the allies compromised on a Bosnia settlement: the United States agreed to commit troops to support an effort to achieve a Bosnia settlement more to its liking, while the allies agreed to support such a settlement so long as it included a very high level of autonomy for the three communities of Bosnia. Finally, in August 1996 the United States initiated a dispute with its allies and trading partners over their economic relations with countries that the United States intended to sanction economically. The U.S. proposed unilaterally to punish the citizens of countries who do business with Cuba, Iran, and Libya. While in the latter two cases the allies may broadly agree with the anti-terrorism principles that motivate U.S. actions, they do not consider these actions to be commensurate with their own national interests. More importantly, they recoil from what they perceive as the arrogance of U.S. policy.

If friends and allies have their own interpretations of U.S. actions, "rivals" are even more likely to be suspicious, and less likely to prove cooperative. Though the Clinton administration has gone to great lengths to portray NATO expansion in cooperative security terms, Russian political figures and policymakers do not seem to accept the notion that NATO expansion is good for their country. Clinton administration officials remain optimistic that the Russians will accommodate themselves to NATO expansion. This is probably true in the sense that since there is nothing they can do about it, at some point they have nothing to gain by opposition. This does not mean, however, that a positive Russian consensus will develop around the project. Indeed, it seems equally plausible that the fact of NATO expansion will be a continuing sore point in Russian domestic politics. Similarly, the United States initially pursued a very energetic policy of "engagement" with the People's Republic of China, "engaging" the Chinese simultaneously on their domestic politics, their economic policies, and several aspects of their foreign policy. Engagement usually took the form of the United States explaining to Chinese officials how they should change their behavior, and ignoring Chinese sensitivities about interference in their internal affairs, and the status of Taiwan. The result was a generally non-cooperative China.

Because international and regional security institutions are weak, more U.S. leadership is required to make things happen than cooperative security advocates had hoped. Resources are necessary to supply this leadership, and resources for international affairs have become more scarce than they were during the Cold War. In particular, foreign aid and the State Department budget have been cut in half since 1984, largely at the instigation of the Congress, and are destined to fall another 20 percent by 2002.[88] The defense budget remains large, even by Cold War standards; real defense spending nearly equals the outlays of the 1970s, and is roughly 80 percent of the early 1960s. It is also very large relative to the rest of the world, equaling the total defense spending of the next five major military powers in 1994 (Russia, China, Japan, France, and Germany).[89] Yet these resources, which would be more than adequate to support a policy of selective engagement, seem to produce a military that is not quite capable of the range of projects that it now faces.

The Clinton administration's defense program faces persistent tensions among force size, activity, readiness, and modernization. Most observers believe that the force structure cannot be funded for the level of resources planned after the turn of the century. The "Bottom-Up Review" avowedly sized the military for two nearly simultaneous Major Regional Contingencies (MRCs), and then added extra capabilities to support a vigorous forward presence. The quest for permanent military-technological dominance has proven expensive. In contrast to many doubters, it does seem to us that the force structure may well be able to deal with two simultaneous MRCs today, but it appears that both "Major" and "Minor" Regional Contingencies (MaRCs and MiRCs?) are difficult to end definitively. This high level of activity seems to have imposed stresses and strains on the organization that may require additional resources to resolve. The United States today deals with two simultaneous MiRCs on a daily basis: the military containment of Iraq, including protection of the Kurds, and the combined ground, naval, and air operation in Bosnia. For a brief period, the U.S. military was also simultaneously involved in Haiti. Calls are occasionally heard for forcible intervention in Rwanda and Burundi; humanitarian military assistance was provided in Rwanda; and logistical military support has been offered for multilateral military interventions in both places. The U.S. military presence in the Republic of Korea has an edgy quality to it that makes the mission anything but garrison duty, arguably a "MiRC" that could quickly turn into a "MaRC."

The U.S. military is busy, and new missions are suggested daily. Finally, resources that were expected from the "downsizing" of the U.S. military have not materialized. Cuts in the infrastructure that supported the Cold War effort have not been proportional to the cuts in the divisions, wings, and warships that are the "business end" of the force. Neither the Congress nor the executive have shown much discipline in this matter. Thus, though the financial resources to remedy many problems may be present within the defense budget, they are fenced off politically. In sum, pursuit of the objectives of cooperative security, with weak or non-existent cooperative security institutions, probably requires more U.S. resources than advocates projected.

The Clinton administration's grand strategy is the result, therefore, of four conflicting sets of pressures. Its own ambitious purposes impel considerable activism. The constraints presented by the current realities of international politics make these purposes difficult to achieve without the exercise of U.S. leadership and power. A substantial portion of the U.S. political elite, in particular congressional Republicans, displays an erratic impulse toward unilateral U.S. actions on selected issues, particularly those that have to do with perceived unfinished Cold War business, such as national ballistic missile defense, Cuba, and Taiwan's independence. The general public is far from isolationist, but is nevertheless not particularly interested in foreign affairs. The Clinton administration has moved toward a grand strategy that tries to address these conflicting pressures. The accommodations that the Clinton administration strategy has made with the obstacles it has encountered have been incremental, rhetorical, disjointed, and incomplete. In theory, the incoherence of the current strategy could produce a series of new difficulties for the administration, and conceivably a disaster. In practice, the Clinton administration may succeed in avoiding a disaster through its well-known skills at "triangulation." At the first sign of serious resistance on the domestic or international front, they adapt or back away in order to keep costs under control. The second Clinton administration may muddle through.

*Long Term Prospects for Change.* What is the longer-term prognosis for U.S. grand strategy? What could cause this strategy to change and in what direction might it change? The answer depends upon a number of contingencies.

Ironically, the Clinton administration grand strategy has already evolved to a point where it has many of the trappings of primacy. Indeed, Clinton's foreign and defense policy team has discovered that considerable U.S. leadership and major commitments of U.S. power are necessary for the pursuit of the transformed world order they seek. The Republicans would probably follow a somewhat purer version of primacy, and move even further away from cooperative security than the Clinton administration already has, if they could take back the presidency.[90] What might cause U.S. foreign policy makers in both parties to abandon primacy?

One likely source of a major change in U.S. grand strategy is change in U.S. domestic politics. The aging of the "baby boomers" will put substantial pressure on the federal budget after the turn of the century. An increasing portion of the politically active adult population will have dim memories of the Cold War. Even the Persian Gulf War is beginning to fade into the past. The combination of these developments could produce decreasing budgetary and political support for an activist U.S. foreign policy. U.S. leaders will have to husband these scarce resources; selective engagement may become the U.S. grand strategy by default.

Primacy could die the death of a thousand cuts. The overall U.S. share of global power will decline a little. Scientific, technological, and productive capacities will spread across the world. Niche players will develop in economics, warfare, and even ideology. Close allies will grow tired of incessant U.S. demands. Traditional adversaries will balk as the United States tries to set the criteria for responsible membership in the "international community." A series of not very costly but ultimately indecisive interventions could exhaust the patience of the U.S. public. Selective engagement again could be the default strategy, but retreat to isolationism is also possible.

Alternatively, the U.S. share of gross world power could decline significantly. Though some skepticism is in order on this score, the prospect ought not to be ruled out entirely. Russia may recover economically and politically; the Japanese economy could improve, the Chinese economy might continue to enjoy very high growth rates. Global statistical comparisons may increasingly conform to the description "multipolar world." In such a world the United States would be constrained by other powers. Selective engagement, again, seems a plausible fall-back position.

The temptations of U.S. power could prove too strong in the short term. Many Democrats and many Republicans believe that democratic principles and liberal values are universal, or should be, and that this country should act to spread them. Moreover, the end of the Cold War left a lot of foreign policy and security specialists without much to do; they will find new dragons to slay. Thus, it is plausible that the United States will get itself into a major war over these values and principles. The United States is quite powerful militarily, and it is possible that the war would be another Desert Storm. On the other hand, it is just as likely, given the kind of world we face and beliefs we carry, that the war will be a Vietnam, or Boer War, or Algeria, or "the troubles" of Northern Ireland. Such a war could easily produce a retreat to neo-isolationism. This is no great insight, and responsible foreign policy professionals will try to avoid this war, because they understand its risks. But blunders are possible.

Finally, a change in a more ambitious direction would result if an aspiring peer competitor jumped the gun, like Saddam Hussein did, challenging the United States before its power was adequate. The behavior of such a state could create threats to many while the United States is still strong and active, and the challenger is still too weak. Such a threat could permit primacy to evolve into "containment." The fearful would once again be eager to embrace U.S. leadership. The people of the United States would allocate plenty to military preparedness and to foreign aid. In a host of small and large ways, medium and great powers would encourage and subsidize U.S. leadership.

## Conclusions

This brief overview cannot do justice to the full range of argumentation about which the advocates of neo-isolationism, selective engagement, cooperative security, primacy, and engagement and enlargement disagree. But it is a start. By way of conclusion we offer three general points.

First, it should be clear that these strategic alternatives produce different advice about when the United States should use force abroad, and the advice is not equally explicit. The new isolationism suggests "almost never." Cooperative security could imply "frequently." Selective engagement advises "it all depends," but suggests some rough criteria for judgment. Primacy implies the employment of force whenever it is necessary to secure or improve the U.S. relative power position, but permits it whenever the United States is moved to do so. An understandable desire for clear decision rules on when to use force should not, however, outweigh the more fundamental concerns that ought to drive the U.S. choice of strategy.

Second, these alternative strategies generate different force structures, two of which may prove attractive because of the money they save. But leaders should understand that these force structures constrain future political leaders—or ought to constrain them. A neo-isolationist force structure cannot quickly be recast for cooperative security or humanitarian intervention. A force structure designed for selective engagement may prove inadequate for the full range of cooperative security missions. A true cooperative security force structure may include more intervention capabilities than needed for strategic weight in great power wars, perhaps at some cost to the ability of the United States to wage high intensity warfare, unless the defense budget grows accordingly. A force structure tailored for primacy permits most kinds of military operations but may be so imposing that it causes some states to compete more rather than less with the United States.

Finally, although the alternatives are not entirely mutually exclusive, for the most part one cannot indiscriminately mix and match across strategies (as both post-Cold War administrations have attempted to do) without running into trouble. They contain fundamental disagreements about strategic objectives and priorities, the extent to which the United States should be engaged in international affairs, the form that engagement should assume, the means that should be employed, the degree of autonomy that must be maintained, and when and under what conditions military force should be employed. Some combinations just do not go together. One cannot expect to reap the rewards of isolationism if one still intends to engage on behalf of friends such as Israel. One cannot wage war in the name of cooperative security in Bosnia-Herzegovina, fail to do the same if Russia helps destabilize the Georgian Republic, and still expect to establish a well-founded fear of international reaction on the part of aggressors everywhere. Selective engagement may ultimately draw the United States into strategically unimportant conflicts if its leaders consistently try to wrap their actions in the rhetoric and institutions of cooperative security. Those who dream of cooperative security, but practice primacy, must understand that they may gradually erode the international institutions upon which their dream depends, postponing it to an ever more distant future. And the rhetoric and diplomacy of a new containment strategy, even if it is only a convenient vehicle for the pursuit of primacy, probably does not permit, as the advocates would claim, particularly friendly relations with the objects of the policy. The Clinton administration has found it expedient to draw opportunistically from three grand strategies. It seems plausible that a future Republican administration would succumb to the same temptations, and for similar reasons. Though primacy figures prominently in the strategic inclinations of both parties, elements of other strategies pop up as needed. Given the realities of U.S. politics, such an *ad hoc* approach is probably inevitable until a crisis impels a choice. And the failure to develop a clearer consensus on grand strategy may hasten the arrival of that crisis. Perhaps the best we can do now is to lay out those choices.

## Notes

1. Anthony Lake, "From Containment to Enlargement," *U.S. Department of State Dispatch*, Vol. 4, No. 39 (September 27, 1993), pp. 658-664; *A National Security Strategy of Engagement and Enlargement* (Washington, D.C.: U.S. Government Printing Office [U.S. GPO], July 1994); and *A National Security Strategy of Engagement and Enlargement* (Washington, D.C.: U.S. GPO, February 1996).

2. Each grand strategy should have an economic component. Most of the literature, however, treats the economic component in a cursory way, if at all. As we began to consider the possible economic elements of each alternative we determined that a separate essay would be required to offer more than a superficial treatment. Therefore, this essay confines itself to the political and military aspects of alternative U.S. grand strategies.

3. We also rely on these options because they have the unusual attribute that five of them largely employ the same basic methodology to develop force structure and to estimate the costs of those force structures. Representative Les Aspin, "An Approach to Sizing American Conventional Forces for the Post-Soviet Era," February 25, 1992 (unpublished manuscript); Secretary of Defense Les Aspin, *Report on the Bottom-Up Review* (Washington, D.C.: Department of Defense, 1993); Congressional Budget Office (CBO), Staff Memorandum, "Fiscal Implications of the Administration's Proposed Base Force," December, 1991 (unpublished manuscript); see also Andrew F. Krepinevitch, *The Bottom-Up Review: An Assessment* (Washington, D.C.: Defense Budget Project, 1994); and Dov S. Zakheim and Jeffrey M. Ranney, "Matching Defense Strategies to Resources: Challenges for the Clinton Administration," *International Security,* Vol. 18, No. 1 (Summer 1993), pp. 51-78. The Bush-Cheney-Powell "Base

Force" was probably generated by a somewhat different methodology. The individuals who made the budget estimates in every case had access to the best available cost information. Other analysts have developed force structures and estimated costs on the basis of their individual methodologies; we chose not to employ them because we could not be sure they were strictly comparable.

4. However, there are reasons why the cost estimates in Table 2 could be too high or too low. Most estimates, particularly those for the Base Force and Clinton Bottom-Up Review (BUR) force, probably underestimate the cost of major procurement after the turn of the century. On the other hand, many estimates of the costs of smaller forces probably do not take credit for the savings that ought to accrue from proportional reductions in defense infrastructure that ought to accompany reductions in force structure. This tends to occur for two reasons. First, because U.S. defense politics focuses on the Future Years Defense Plan, or FYDP, most policy-oriented budget analysts focus primarily on the near-term budgetary consequences that would directly arise from incremental reductions in existing forces. Second, infrastructure, particularly bases and depots, are often politically protected. It is only slightly absurd to suggest, therefore, that nearly all the conventional combat power in the U.S. military could be eliminated, and still leave us with a defense budget of $100 billion a year, which is the implication of the trend of costs versus force structure in Options A-D.

5. The new isolationists seldom refer to themselves as isolationists. Indeed, they often vociferously deny isolationist tendencies. Earl Ravenal, "The Case for Adjustment," *Foreign Policy*, No. 81 (Winter 1990-91), pp. 3-19, prefers "disengagement." Patrick J. Buchanan, too, in "America First—and Second, and Third," *National Interest*, No. 19 (Spring 1990), pp. 77-82, uses "disengagement." Doug Bandow, "Keeping the Troops and the Money at Home," *Current History*, Vol. 93, No. 579 (January 1994), pp. 8-13, prefers "benign detachment." Eric A. Nordlinger, however, in the most sophisticated, and perhaps least conventional version of the new isolationism, *Isolationism Reconfigured: American Foreign Policy for a New Century* (Princeton, N.J.: Princeton University Press, 1995), embraces "isolationism."

6. Bandow, "Keeping the Troops and the Money at Home," p. 10.

7. The version of realism that underlies the new isolationism is minimal. Its strategic imperatives are even more limited than those of the minimal realism outlined by Christopher Layne, "Less is More: Minimal Realism in East Asia," *National Interest*, No. 43 (Spring 1996), pp. 64-77. Layne distinguishes between maximal and minimal realism. He views a balance of power approach (which we call "selective engagement") as minimal realism. Layne links primacy with maximal realism. For an earlier version of minimal realism and neo-isolationism, see Robert W. Tucker, *A New Isolationism: Threat or Promise?* (New York: Universe Books, 1972). Nordlinger, *Isolationism Reconfigured*, is the most significant exception to the generalization that neo-isolationism is driven by a realist interpretation of international politics. His eclectic approach to developing a national strategy of isolationism and its concurrent foreign policy is, in the end, informed more by liberalism than realism.

8. Alan Tonelson, "Superpower Without a Sword," *Foreign Affairs*, Vol. 72, No. 3 (Summer 1993), p. 179, observes that "few international conflicts will directly threaten the nation's territorial integrity, political independence or material welfare."

9. Christopher Layne, "The Unipolar Illusion: Why New Great Powers Will Rise," *International Security*, Vol. 17, No. 4 (Spring 1993), p. 48, makes this point. He uses it to support an argument for a grand strategy that he calls "strategic independence." It bears some similarity to the selective engagement strategy outlined below, albeit a rather inactive version of it.

10. Nordlinger, *Isolationism Reconsidered*, pp. 6 and 63-91.

11. Ravenal, "The Case for Adjustment," pp. 15-19, develops a force structure and defense budget within these parameters which is explicitly geared to support a grand strategy quite similar to what we label isolationism. He suggests an active force of 1.1 million people, with six Army and two Marine divisions, eleven tactical air wings, six carriers with five air wings, and a strategic dyad of submarines and bombers, which could be funded for about $150 billion in constant 1991 dollars, perhaps $175 billion in 1997 dollars, or roughly 2.5 percent of GDP. See Force A in Table 1, which is roughly the same size, but which then-Congressman Aspin estimated would cost considerably more, $231 billion in 1997 dollars, roughly 3 percent of GDP. See also Tonelson, "Superpower Without a Sword," pp. 179-180, who argues for a similar force structure, but who seems to subscribe to a conservative version of selective engagement. The Center for Defense Information has proposed that an even smaller force structure would be sufficient to support a strategy of disengagement. For $104 billion in constant 1993 dollars, CDI proposed to field a force of only 500,000 people, one Marine and three Army divisions, four Air Force tactical wings, two carriers and 221 other combat vessels, and a nuclear force of 16 submarines. See "Defending America: CDI Options for Military Spending," *The Defense Monitor*, Vol. 21, No. 4 (1992). Nordlinger, *Isolationism Reconfigured*, p. 46, suggested that forces at half the levels sustained during the Cold War and early post-Cold War years would be sufficient.

12. Robert Art, "A Defensible Defense: America's Grand Strategy After the Cold War," *International Security*, Vol. 15, No. 4 (Spring 1991), pp. 5-53; and Stephen Van Evera, "Why Europe Matters, Why the Third World Doesn't: American Grand Strategy After the Cold War," *Journal of Strategic Studies*, Vol. 13, No. 2 (June 1990), pp. 1-51, are the two most complete expositions of selective engagement. See also Ronald Steel, *Temptations of a Superpower*, (Cambridge, Mass: Harvard University Press, 1995).

13. Selective engagement is informed neither by the minimal realism that underlies the new isolationism nor the maximal realism that drives primacy; it is instead based on the traditional mainstream balance-of-power realism evident in Hans J. Morgenthau, *Politics Among Nations: The Struggle for Power and Peace*, 5th ed., rev. (New York: Alfred A. Knopf, 1978).

14. Posen classifies himself as a "selective engagement" advocate. He does believe, however, that the United States should not only act to reduce the probability of great power war, it should also pursue the traditional policy of opposing the rise of a Eurasian hegemon who would conquer or even dominate the world's centers of industrial and economic power. The latter risk seems very low in the short term, but preserving the political division of industrial Eurasia remains a U.S. interest.

15. On this point see Van Evera, "Why Europe Matters," pp. 8-10; and Art, "Defensible Defense," pp. 45-50.

16. Art, "Defensible Defense," p. 45. See also Jonathan Clarke, "Leaders and Followers," *Foreign Policy* No. 101 (Winter 1995-96), pp. 37-51, arguing both that the U.S. share of global power is too small to support cooperative security or primacy, and that U.S. public support for such strategies is too weak.

17. See Art, "Defensible Defense," pp. 23-30.

18. Art, "Defensible Defense," p. 47. Stephen Van Evera, "The United States and the Third World: When to Intervene?" in Kenneth A. Oye, Robert J. Lieber, and Donald Rothchild, eds., *Eagle in a New World* (New York: Harper Collins, 1992), pp. 127-131, makes a comprehensive case for U.S. intervention in the Persian Gulf in 1990, Operation Desert Shield, but expresses skepticism about the necessity for Operation Desert Storm.

19. Robert S. Chase, Emily B. Hill, and Paul Kennedy, "Pivotal States and U.S. Strategy," *Foreign Affairs*, Vol. 75, No. 1 (January/February 1996), p. 33, have singled out Mexico, Brazil, South Africa, Algeria, Egypt, Turkey, India, Pakistan, and Indonesia as pivotal states "whose future will profoundly affect their surrounding regions." The list is long, the adjective "pivotal" seems premature, and systematic attention to these states in addition to the great powers is hardly selective. Nevertheless, the list does highlight states that may pose special problems today, or which may become serious contenders for regional power in the future.

20. Barry R. Posen, "A Balkan Vietnam Awaits 'Peacekeepers'," *Los Angeles Times*, February 4, 1993, p. B7. The article assesses the force requirements to police the "Vance-Owen Plan," which intended to preserve a unitary Bosnia-Herzegovina. The three principal ethnic and religious groups in Bosnia would have remained intermingled, as they were at the outset of the war. Thus the police problem would have been quite complex and demanding, similar to the British problem in Northern Ireland.

21. Chase, Hill, and Kennedy, "Pivotal States and U.S. Strategy," provide an illustration of how the project grows. See also James A. Baker, III, "Selective Engagement: Principles for American Foreign Policy in a New Era," *Vital Speeches of the Day*, Vol. 60, No. 10 (March 1, 1994), pp. 299-302. The former secretary of state argues for an expansive strategic agenda that looks more like primacy than selective engagement.

22. Inis L. Claude, *Swords into Plowshares: The Problems and Progress of International Organization*, 4th ed. (New York: Random House, 1971), p. 247; Arnold Wolfers, *Discord and Collaboration: Essays on International Politics* (Baltimore: Johns Hopkins University Press, 1962), pp. 183-184: "'any aggressor anywhere' is in fact the national enemy of every country because in violating the peace and law of the community of nations it endangers, if indirectly, the peace and security of every nation."

23. On the differences between realism and liberalism, see David A. Baldwin, ed., *Neorealism and Neoliberalism: The Contemporary Debate* (New York: Columbia University Press, 1993); Michael E. Brown, Sean M. Lynn-Jones, and Steven E. Miller, eds., *Debating the Democratic Peace* (Cambridge, Mass.: MIT Press, 1996); Michael E. Brown, Sean M. Lynn-Jones, and Steven E. Miller, eds., *The Perils of Anarchy: Contemporary Realism and International Security* (Cambridge, Mass.: MIT Press, 1995); Robert Gilpin, *The Political Economy of International Relations* (Princeton, N.J.: Princeton University Press, 1987); Charles W. Kegley, Jr., ed., *Controversies in International Relations Theory: Realism and the Neoliberal Challenge* (New York: St. Martin's Press, 1995); Robert O. Keohane, ed., *Neorealism and Its Critics* (New York: Columbia University Press, 1986); and Richard Ned Lebow and Thomas Risse-Kappen, eds., *International Relations Theory and the End of the Cold War* (New York: Columbia University Press, 1995).

24. Charles A. Kupchan and Clifford A. Kupchan, "Concerts, Collective Security, and the Future of Europe," *International Security*, Vol. 16, No. 1 (Summer 1991), pp. 149-150; and Richard Ullman, *Securing Europe* (Princeton, N.J.: Princeton University Press, 1991), p. 76.

25. For the core works see Ashton B. Carter, William J. Perry, and John D. Steinbruner, *A New Concept of Cooperative Security*, Occasional Paper (Washington, D.C.: Brookings Institution, 1992); Janne E. Nolan, ed., *Global Engagement: Cooperation and Security in the 21st Century* (Washington, D.C.: Brookings Institution, 1994); Paul B. Stares and John D. Steinbruner, "Cooperative Security and the New Europe," in Stares, ed., *The New Germany and the New Europe* (Washington, D.C.: Brookings Institution, 1992), pp. 218-248. For a shorter exposition, see Randall Forsberg, "Creating a Cooperative Security System," in *After the Cold War: A Debate on Cooperative Security*, Institute for Defense and Disarmament Studies (Reprint, Cambridge, Mass.), first published in *Boston Review*, Vol. 17, No. 6 (November/December 1992).

26. "Proliferation of destructive technology casts a shadow over future U.S. security in a way that cannot be directly addressed through superior force or readiness. Serious economic and environmental problems point to an

inescapable interdependence of U.S. interests with the interests of other nations." Carter, Perry, and Steinbruner, *A New Concept of Cooperative Security*, p. 4.

27. Madeleine K. Albright, U.S. Permanent Representative to the United Nations, "Realism and Idealism in American Foreign Policy Today," *U.S. Department of State Dispatch*, Vol. 5, No. 26 (June 27, 1994), pp. 434-437, offers an explicit and comprehensive statement of these views.

28. See Carter, Perry, and Steinbruner, *A New Concept of Cooperative Security*, pp. 24-30.

29. Ross, who is sympathetic to cooperative security, emphasizes this point.

30. Carter, Perry, and Steinbruner, *A New Concept of Cooperative Security*, pp. 8 and 9.

31. Strobe Talbott, "Why NATO Should Grow," *New York Review of Books*, Vol. 42, No. 13 (August 10, 1995), p. 28: "Enlargement of NATO would be a force for the rule of law both within Europe's new democracies and among them.... An expanded NATO is likely to extend the area in which conflicts like the one in the Balkans simply do not happen." The administration's case for expansion incorporates the logic of containment as well as that of cooperative security. As Talbot put it, "among the contingencies for which NATO must be prepared is that Russia will abandon democracy and return to the threatening patterns of international behavior that have sometimes characterized its history" (p. 29). See also Ronald Asmus, Richard Kugler, and Stephen Larrabee, "NATO Expansion: The Next Steps," *Survival*, Vol. 37, No. 1 (Spring 1995), p. 9; and the systematic critique offered by Michael E. Brown, "The Flawed Logic of NATO Expansion," *Survival*, Vol. 37, No. 1 (Spring 1995), pp. 38-39.

32. Commission on America and the New World, *Changing Our Ways: America and the New World* (Washington, D.C.: Carnegie Endowment for International Peace, 1992), pp. 73-75.

33. Advocates seldom make this point explicitly, but a similar point is made by Carter, Perry, and Steinbruner, *A New Concept of Cooperative Security*, p. 51: "many countries that feel threatened by an intrusive reconnaissance strike capability they cannot match can aspire to chemical agents as a strategic counterweight."

34. "The Commission believes that the use of military force to prevent nuclear proliferation must be retained as an option of last resort." Commission on America and the New World, *Changing Our Ways*, p. 75.

35. See Gareth Evans, "Cooperative Security and Intrastate Conflict," *Foreign Policy*, No. 96 (Fall 1991), pp. 3-20. Comments by cooperative security advocates on the war in Yugoslavia reveal a strong desire for some cooperative security organization to intervene militarily. See Forsberg, "Creating a Cooperative Security System," p. 3; and Jonathan Dean, "Moving Toward a Less Violent World—Test Case, Europe," *Boston Review*, Vol. 17, No. 6 (November/December 1992), p. 7.

36. Commission on America and the New World, *Changing Our Ways*, p. 51: "The United States should be more actively engaged in strengthening the collective machinery to carry out humanitarian actions. In this way we can reduce the likelihood of having to choose between unilateral military intervention and standing idle in the face of human tragedy."

37. William J. Perry, "Military Action: When to Use It and How to Ensure Its Effectiveness," in Nolan, *Global Engagement*, p. 235.

38. See William W. Kaufmann and John Steinbruner, *Decisions for Defense* (Washington, D.C.: Brookings Institution, 1991), pp. 67-76, which offers a cooperative security force structure that would cost roughly $150 billion (1992 dollars, excluding Department of Energy expenses on nuclear weaponry) annually by the end of the century. Their recommended force structure is quite similar to Aspin's "Force A," Table 2. The authors seem to argue that the adequacy of such a force structure would depend on a series of prior diplomatic developments in the world that would, for all intents and purposes, put a functioning cooperative security regime in place. Jerome B. Wiesner, Philip Morrison, and Kosta Tsipis, "Ending Overkill," *Bulletin of the Atomic Scientists*, Vol. 49, No. 2 (March 1993), pp. 12-23, offer a force structure, costing $115 billion per year, which they seem to believe is consistent with a collective security strategy. Though small, the air and naval forces they recommend are quite capable; the Army they recommend, however, with a total active personnel strength of 180,000, would barely be adequate for a repetition of Operation Desert Shield/Desert Storm. It is difficult to see how it could support a collective security strategy. More recently, Michael O'Hanlon, *Defense Planning For the Late 1990s: Beyond the Desert Storm Framework* (Washington, D.C.: Brookings Institution, 1995), pp. 32-40, has proposed a force structure estimated to cost about $20 billion a year less than the Bottom-Up Review force.

39. Laying out the realist theoretical argument for why coalitions need leaders, and why leaders are defined by great power, is Josef Joffe, "Collective Security and the Future of Europe: Failed Dreams and Dead Ends," *Survival*, Vol. 34, No. 1 (Spring 1992), pp. 40-43.

40. See Richard K. Betts, "Systems for Peace or Causes of War? Collective Security, Arms Control, and the New Europe," *International Security*, Vol. 17, No. 1 (Summer 1992), pp. 5-43; Joffe, "Collective Security and the Future of Europe"; and John J. Mearsheimer, "The False Promise of International Institutions," *International Security*, Vol. 19, No. 3 (Winter 1994/95), pp. 5-49.

41. This is the maximal realism of hegemonic stability theory. See Robert Gilpin, *War and Change in World Politics* (Cambridge, U.K.: Cambridge University Press, 1981).

42. See Dick Cheney, "Active Leadership? You Better Believe It," *New York Times*, March 15, 1992, Section 4, p. 17. The draft DPG is placed in the larger contexts of the Bush administration's national security policy and

strategy, and a discussion of primacy in U.S. policy and strategy, by David Callahan, *Between Two Worlds: Realism, Idealism, and American Foreign Policy After the Cold War* (New York: HarperCollins, 1994).

43. "Excerpts from Pentagon's Plan: 'Prevent the Emergence of a New Rival'," *New York Times*, March 8, 1992, p. 14.

44. The notion that U.S. hegemony is benevolent and perceived as such by others is evident also in William Kristol and Robert Kagan, "Toward a Neo-Reaganite Foreign Policy," *Foreign Affairs*, Vol. 75, No. 4 (July/August 1996), pp. 18-32; and Joshua Muravchik, *The Imperative of American Leadership: A Challenge to Neo-Isolationism* (Washington, D.C.: AEI Press, 1996).

45. "Excerpts from Pentagon's Plan: 'Prevent the Emergence of a New Rival'," p. 14.

46. The Assistant Under Secretary of Defense for Policy Planning when the draft DPG was prepared, Zalmay Khalilzad, has suggested that "the United States would not want Germany and Japan to be able to conduct expeditionary wars." Khalilzad, "Losing the Moment? The United States and the World After the Cold War," *Washington Quarterly*, Vol. 18, No. 2 (Spring 1995), p. 105.

47. Kristol and Kagan, "Toward a Neo-Reaganite Foreign Policy," p. 22.

48. Ibid., p. 20.

49. Muravchik, *The Imperative of American Leadership*, pp. 32-33.

50. Kristol and Kagan, "Toward a Neo-Reaganite Foreign Policy," p. 21. The term "soft power" is associated with Joseph Nye, Dean of the Kennedy School of Government and former Assistant Secretary of Defense for International Security Affairs. He and former Vice Chairman of the Joint Chiefs of Staff William A. Owens develop the notion of U.S. dominance in these new tools of power in Nye and Owens, "America's Information Edge," *Foreign Affairs*, Vol. 75, No. 2 (March/April 1996), pp. 20-36.

51. According to Muravchik, *The Imperative of American Leadership*, p. 36: "We can afford whatever foreign policy we need or choose. We are the richest country in the world, the richest country the world has ever known. And we are richer today than we have ever been before. We command not fewer but more resources than ever." He calls for spending 5 percent of GDP on what he calls foreign policy ("defense, foreign aid, and everything else"); p. 44.

52. Kristol and Kagan, "Toward a Neo-Reaganite Foreign Policy," pp. 26-27, 30-32; and Muravchik, *The Imperative of American Leadership*, pp. 36-50. Muravchik argues both that the United States allocates too few resources to the military and to foreign aid to support a strategy of primacy and that it requires a balanced budget. He suggests that to remedy these deficiencies the U.S. should solve the problem of rising medical costs and social security solvency, and add revenues, and in just two pages, he explains how (pp. 42-43).

53. As the Cold War drew to a close, some saw an economic challenge from Japan as the principal threat to U.S. primacy. See, e.g., Samuel P. Huntington, "America's Changing Strategic Interests," *Survival*, Vol. 33, No. 1 (January/February 1991), p. 10; Huntington, "The Economic Renewal of America," *The National Interest*, No. 27, Spring 1992, p. 15; and Huntington, "Why International Primacy Matters," *International Security*, Vol. 17, No. 4 (Spring 1993), pp. 71-81. Huntington's concern about U.S. economic strength and how it might be preserved and strengthened are echoed in Zalmay Khalilzad, "Losing the Moment?" pp. 103-104.

54. Zbigniew Brzezinski, "The Premature Partnership," *Foreign Affairs*, Vol. 73, No. 2 (March/April 1994), p. 76. Oddly, though he presents many of the same arguments for NATO expansion in a subsequent article, he is somewhat less alarmist there about the extent of the current danger emanating from Russia. See Zbigniew Brzezinski, "A Plan for Europe," *Foreign Affairs*, Vol. 74, No. 1 (January/February 1995), p. 34.

55. James Kurth, "America's Grand Strategy: A Pattern of History," *National Interest*, No. 43 (Spring 1996), pp. 3-19; the quotation is from p. 19.

56. Henry Kissinger, "Expand NATO Now," *Washington Post*, December 19, 1994.

57. See Brzezinski, "The Premature Partnership," pp. 72-73. A disturbing account of Russian actions is found in Fiona Hill and Pamela Jewett, *Back in the USSR: Russia's Intervention in the Internal Affairs of the Former Soviet Republics and the Implications of United States Policy Toward Russia*, Strengthening Democratic Institutions Project (Cambridge, Mass.: John F. Kennedy School of Government, Harvard University, January 1994).

58. Brzezinski, "The Premature Partnership," pp. 71-75, calls this "the imperial impulse." See also Brzezinski, *Out of Control: Global Turmoil on the Eve of the Twenty-First Century* (New York: Collier, 1993), pp. 173-181.

59. Brzezinski, "The Premature Partnership," pp. 79-82. He urges "political assurances for Ukraine's independence and territorial integrity"; "a more visible American show of interest in the independence of the Central Asian states, as well as of the three states in the Caucasus"; and "some quiet American-Chinese political consultations regarding the area."

60. Brzezinski, *Out of Control*, pp. 163-166.

61. Kissinger, "Expand NATO Now."

62. Brzezinski, "Premature Partnership," pp. 81-82; Kissinger, "Expand NATO Now."

63. Ibid.; and Zbigniew Brzezinski, "A Bigger—and Safer—Europe," *New York Times*, December 1, 1993.

64. The Congressional Budget Office has estimated that NATO expansion would cost from $61 billion to $125 billion over the years 1996-2010. See Congressional Budget Office, CBO Papers, "The Costs of Expanding the NATO Alliance" (Washington, D.C.: Congressional Budget Office, March 1996).

65. Asmus, Kugler, and Larrabee, "NATO Expansion," p. 32.

66. Ronald Asmus, Richard Kugler, and Stephen Larrabee, "Building a New NATO," *Foreign Affairs*, Vol. 72, No. 4 (September/October 1993), p. 34: "While Germany remains pre-occupied with the staggering challenge of the political and economic reconstruction of its Eastern half, the need to stabilize its eastern flank is Bonn's number one security concern." See also Brzezinski, "A Plan for Europe," p. 42: "Most important, a united and powerful Germany can be more firmly anchored within this larger Europe if the European security system fully coincides with America's."

67. Khalilzad, an ardent proponent of primacy, has written that China "... is the most likely candidate for global rival." Zalmay Khalilzad, *From Containment to Global Leadership? America and the World After the Cold War* (Santa Monica: RAND, 1995), p. 30.

68. Karen Elliott House, "The Second Cold War," *Wall Street Journal*, February 17, 1994. She alludes to "the looming threat of a militarizing, autocratic China" and observes that "a resurgent China flexes its muscles at increasingly fearful neighbors."

69. Thomas L. Friedman, "Dust Off the SEATO Charter," *New York Times*, June 28, 1995, p. A19.

70. "Containing China," *Economist*, July 29, 1995, pp. 11 and 12.

71. See, for instance, Muravchik, *The Imperative of American Leadership*, pp. 71-82.

72. Charles Krauthammer, "The Unipolar Moment," *Foreign Affairs*, Vol. 70, No. 1 (1991), pp. 31-32. In previous versions of this essay we classified Krauthammer as a "cooperative security" advocate, but his emphasis on the dominant role of the U.S. warrants his inclusion here.

73. At least one advocate of primacy, however, sees the United States as having been, from the start, insufficiently active in Bosnia. See Muravchik, *The Imperative of American Leadership*, pp. 85-131.

74. Callahan, *Between Two Worlds*, p. 135.

75. Kristol and Kagan, "Toward a Neo-Reaganite Foreign Policy," pp. 25-26. Similarly, Muravchik, *The Imperative of American Leadership*, p. 138, calls for defense spending that would be "somewhere around 4 percent of GDP." Khalilzad, "Losing the Moment," p. 102, offers a less ambiguous, and less demanding, multipower standard than do Kristol and Kagan. He proposes that U.S. forces be able to defeat simultaneously "the *two* next most powerful military forces in the world that are not allied with the United States."

76. On these issues see Khalilzad, "Losing the Moment?" pp. 104-105; and Muravchik, *The Imperative of American Leadership*, pp. 152-170.

77. Huntington, "Why International Primacy Matters," p. 70. Huntington more specifically argues that "power enables an actor to shape his environment so as to reflect his interests. In particular it enables a state to protect its security and prevent, deflect, or defeat threats to that security. It also enables a state to promote its values among other peoples and to shape the international environment so as to reflect its values"; pp. 69-70.

78. Muravchik, *The Imperative of American Leadership*, p. 32: "America is even more powerful today than it was in the immediate aftermath of World War II, although that moment is cited by many heralds of American decline as the apogee of American power."

79. See Christopher Layne and Benjamin Schwarz, "American Hegemony—Without an Enemy," *Foreign Policy*, No. 92 (Fall 1993), pp. 5-23; and Benjamin Schwarz, "Why America Thinks It Has to Run the World," *Atlantic Monthly*, June 1996, pp. 92-102. Layne and Schwarz draw heavily on Melvyn P. Leffler, *A Preponderance of Power: National Security, the Truman Administration, and the Cold War* (Stanford, Calif.: Stanford University Press, 1992). More extended critiques of primacy are provided by Callahan, *Between Two Worlds*; Robert Jervis, "International Primacy: Is the Game Worth the Candle?" *International Security*, Vol. 17, No. 4 (Spring 1993), pp. 52-67; Layne, "The Unipolar Illusion"; and Nordlinger, *Isolationism Reconfigured*, pp. 134-141.

80. Prominent members of the administration who were associated with the theoretical development of cooperative security ideas include Ashton Carter, Morton Halperin, Catherine Kelleher, and William Perry; see works cited in footnote 25. John Deutsch participated in the development of a similar approach to U.S. foreign policy; see Commission on America and the World, *Changing Our Ways*.

81. *A National Security Strategy of Engagement and Enlargement*. Since the adminstration's presentation of its strategy has been more consistent than its actions, we focus here solely on the third version of this Clinton White House document (February 1996).

82. U.S. leadership appears to be necessary in every class of international problem; the word "leadership" appears four times on p. 2 alone. See *A National Security Strategy of Engagement and Enlargement*, p. 2. Military requirements are discussed on p. 14, where the language of primacy also emerges: "A strategy for deterring and defeating aggression in more than one theater ensures we maintain the flexibility to meet unknown future threats, while our continued engagement represented by that strategy helps *preclude* such threats from developing in the first place" (emphasis added).

83. Ibid., pp. 3, 9-12, 21.

84. Ibid., p. 27.

85. Ibid., p. 18.

86. Dick Kirschten, "Mixed Signals," *National Journal,* May 27, 1995, pp. 1274-1277; see also Robert Greenberger, "Dateline Capitol Hill: The New Majority's Foreign Policy," *Foreign Policy,* No. 101 (Winter 1995-96), pp. 159-169.

87. Jeffrey Garten, "Is America Abandoning Multilateral Trade?" *Foreign Affairs,* Vol. 74, No. 6 (November/December 1995), pp. 50-62. For the most part, economic tensions did not directly affect the security relationship, but former Ambassador to Japan Michael H. Armacost suggests that "trade frictions generated mistrust and resentment that threatened to contaminate our security relations." Armacost, *Friends or Rivals? The Insider's Account of U.S.-Japan Relations* (New York: Columbia University Press, 1996), p. 194.

88. Casimir Yost and Mary Locke, "The Raid on Aid," *Washington Post,* July 28, 1996, p. C1.

89. See Congressional Budget Office, *Reducing the Deficit: Spending and Revenue Options* (Washington, D.C.: CBO, August 1996), Figure 3-1, p. 98; U.S. Arms Control and Disarmament Agency, *World Military Expenditures and Arms Transfers, 1995* (Washington, D.C.: U.S. GPO, 1996), Figure 4, p. 4.

90. See Bob Dole, "Shaping America's Global Future," *Foreign Policy,* No. 98 (Spring 1995), pp. 29-43. One quotation reveals much: "From Bosnia to China, from North Korea to Poland, our allies and our adversaries doubt our resolve and question our commitment"; p. 31. See also "Remarks by Senate Majority Leader Dole, March 1, 1995," *Foreign Policy Bulletin,* Vol. 5, No. 6 (May/June 1995), pp. 33-35; and Baker, "Selective Engagement."

# Chapter 9

## ✴ ✴ ✴

# Toward Strategic Independence:
# Protecting Vital American Interests

Ted Galen Carpenter

*Ted Galen Carpenter asserts that U.S. interests dictate that it seek to attain a high degree of "strategic independence." The strategic autonomy he favors requires the dramatic changes in U.S. strategy and policy called for by the neo-isolationists. The United States is to abstain from involvement in UN operations, withdraw from anachronistic Cold War alliances, refuse to be the world's policeman, and play the role of "balancer of last resort." Do you agree that the United States is strategically overextended? How does Carpenter characterize U.S. vital interests? What are the opportunity costs of Carpenter's strategic approach?*

America's security policy is adrift without a compass in a turbulent post-Cold War world. The Clinton administration has shown little understanding of the necessary balance between military capabilities and military commitments. Even worse, the administration has failed to understand that even the United States—an economic and military superpower—cannot police the world. The Prussian leader Frederick the Great once warned that he who attempts to defend everything defends nothing. U.S. security policy exhibits precisely that defect.

Instead of continuing to pursue an expensive and dangerous policy of global interventionism, the United States has the opportunity to adopt a new approach: strategic independence. This new policy would mean that the US would use military forces solely for defending America's vital security interests. Implementing strategic independence would entail several dramatic changes in Washington's foreign policy: 1) the United States would decline to participate militarily in UN peacekeeping operations—indeed, America's political and financial commitment to the United Nations would be greatly circumscribed;

Ted Galen Carpenter is Director of the Foreign Policy Program at the Cato Institute.

Reprint "Toward Strategic Independence: Protecting Vital American Interests" by Ted Galen Carpenter reprinted by permission of the *Brown Journal of World Affairs*, Summer 1995, Volume II, pp. 7-13.

2) US Cold War alliances would be phased out before the end of the decade, in most cases; 3) the United States would explicitly reject a global policing role, whether acting unilaterally, in combination with regional allies, or through the Untied Nations; and 4) perhaps most important, the United States would adopt the role of the balancer of last resort in the international system rather than the intervenor of first resort.

## America's Strategic Overextension

The Clinton administration shows a disturbing inability to discriminate between those developments in the international system that are essential to America's security, and those that are peripheral or irrelevant. U.S. policymakers frequently act as though everything, everywhere is important to U.S. interests. Thus, the administration has preserved all of Washington's Cold War security obligations, and has even sought to upgrade some of them, such as the mission of policing the Persian Gulf region. The administration has also sought to add new security commitments, proposing to enlarge NATO to include the nations of Central and Eastern Europe. Additionally, the administration has involved the United States in multilateral peacekeeping and nation-building missions in places such as Somalia and Haiti. The inevitable result is strategic overextension.

Such an approach is unnecessary, as well as undesirable. Given the absence of a superpower adversary, the United States has no need to continue subsidizing the defense of allies in Western Europe and East Asia. Although these allies prefer to rely on the United States, they have the population and economic resources to build whatever military forces they need to protect themselves from lesser threats. Just as domestic welfare expenditures foster an unhealthy mentality of dependence on the part of recipients, so too do international military welfare subsidies foster unhealthy mentalities of dependence.

The financial benefits that Washington's security dependents receive are considerable—and it is understandable that they wish to continue the arrangement—but the benefits to the United States are less apparent. The principal justification offered by U.S. policymakers is that a dominant U.S. role around the world helps preserve "stability," and prevents the reemergence of the great destructive power rivalries that led to previous wars.[1] Accordingly, the United States does not want Japan or the major powers of Western Europe to even aspire to play more active military roles, because such assertiveness might prove disruptive.[2]

Although there is some validity to that argument, the costs and risk entailed in preserving U.S. dominance are extremely high. Not only does a "smothering" strategy require U.S. forces to risk involvement in actual or potential conflicts which have little direct relevance to America's security, but such a strategy requires that the United States maintain a much larger—and more costly— military than would otherwise be necessary. It is Washington's global-policing role that accounts for the huge disparity between U.S. military spending and the spending levels of other industrial countries.

If, instead of encouraging the prosperous West European and East Asian nations to remain forever dependent on the United States for their security, Washington would encourage them to take responsibility for their own defense, the United States could then grasp the opportunity to take advantage of a post-Cold War world in which there are new, multiple centers of power. America can receive indirect benefits from more vigorous defense efforts by other major democratic nations which, to protect their own vital interests, will be compelled to contain threats and promote stability in their respective regions.

Preserving Washington's Cold War alliances is a dubious decision from the standpoint of American interests; expanding those commitments is even more ill-advised. Proposals to enlarge NATO, for example, would entangle the United States in the myriad disputes of Central and Eastern Europe. Enlarging NATO would fatally undercut the position of Russia's democratic faction and give the ultranationalists an ideal issue to exploit; it would risk a confrontation with Moscow over a region in which Russia has political, economic, and security interests going back generations; and, it would involve the United States in quarrels and conflicts among the Central and East European nations themselves.[3]

America's legitimate European interests do not warrant taking such risks. The primary interest of the United States is preventing a hostile power from dominating the Continent and thereby posing a serious threat to America's own security. Such a danger is utterly improbable in the foreseeable future. In any case, it is imperative to distinguish between a conflict which threatens to undermine the European balance of power, and the assortment of petty conflicts now taking place in portions of Eastern Europe that have little relevance outside the immediate region. For the United States to become entangled in such wars would be a misguided attempt to micromanage the Continent's security.

## Defining Vital Interests

The European example illustrates a larger point. U.S. policymakers must be more cautious and discriminating about the concept of vital interests. When President Clinton contended that the United States had vital interest at stake in Haiti—citing the desire to promote democracy in the Western Hemisphere as an example—he demonstrated a failure to grasp the concept.

To constitute a vital U.S. interest, a development must have a direct, immediate, and substantial connection to America's physical survival, political independence, or domestic liberty. Anything that does not reach that threshold is a secondary interest, a peripheral interest, or, in many cases, not a valid security interest at all.[4] It is also important to stress that "vital" means essential or indispensable, not merely relevant or desirable. Democracy in Haiti and elsewhere in the hemisphere is indeed desirable, but it is hardly indispensable to America's well-being. There have been dictatorships in Haiti—as well as in Caribbean and Latin American countries—without any discernible adverse impact on the security of the United States.

The concept of a vital interest also has an operational definition. A vital interest is something for which the United States must be prepared to wage a major war, if necessary. That sobering factor alone should be enough to discourage U.S. policymakers from using the term in a casual fashion, or in making security commitments that the United States would be unwise to fulfill.

## The Significance of the Demise of the Soviet Threat

Although the collapse of the Soviet Union did not change the nature of America's vital interests, it did radically alter the global-threat environment. During the Cold War, it was possible to argue that conflicts which appeared to have only local or regional importance were, in fact, much more significant because they frequently involved Soviet surrogates. Whatever validity that argument may have had, it is no longer relevant. Without the Soviet factor, most conflicts that are taking place in various regions are parochial. They may be of importance to the parties involved— and perhaps to neighboring states—but they have no serious potential to menace the United States.

The demise of the Soviet threat altered the global-threat environment in another important way. Throughout the Cold War, conventional wisdom held that only the United States could neutralize the military threat posed by another superpower. That argument was probably overdone, even during the Cold War. Although no single nation other than the United States had the wherewithal to counter the power of the USSR, an alliance of several medium-size nations might well have been able to do so. In particular, the major countries of Western Europe, once they had recovered from the devastation of World War II, should have been capable of containing Soviet expansionism—at least in Europe.

In any case, the argument has no relevance today. There is no superpower threat, and regional powers are capable of neutralizing lesser threats without the aid of the United States. The notion that the European Union—with a collective population of more then 370 million, a gross domestic product of $7.5 trillion a year, and more than 2 million troops—cannot contain Serb expansionism strains credulity. Similarly, the argument that Japan, South Korea, Russia, China, and the other powers of East Asia cannot address the threat posed by North Korea's nuclear program is unfounded. Americans who contend that only the United States can solve such problems exhibit a disturbing national hubris. The leaders of other countries who make the same contention have the ulterior motive of wanting the United States to continue assuming an unwarranted portion of the costs and risks of international security.

America should position itself as the balancer of last resort in the international system. In other words, the United States should maintain sufficient forces to backstop the efforts of other powers were an unusually potent expansionist threat to emerge, and were those powers unable to contain it with their own resources. Such a breakdown of regional containment efforts is rare, and, given the absence of any credible candidate to become a global hegemonic threat comparable to Nazi Germany or the Soviet Union, the need is remote for the United States to use military force to implement the balancer role in the foreseeable future.

## Avoiding Unnecessary UN Entanglements

A security strategy based on the defense of vital American interests would leave no room for signing on to peacekeeping or nation-building enterprises directed by the United Nations. The Clinton administration has retreated somewhat from its initial enthusiasm for UN military missions. At one time, the administration considered contributing U.S. troops to a permanent UN peacekeeping force, and seemed willing to subordinate U.S. military person- nel to UN command. The ineptitude that the United Nations displayed in conducting its missions in Somalia and Bosnia has apparently caused admini- stration officials to advocate a more cautious policy.

Nevertheless, the administration remains too willing to commit U.S. troops to dubious UN missions that have little relevance to the security of the United States. The debacle in Somalia was a warning of the dangers entailed by involvement in such operations. Yet the administration indicates that the United States is willing to provide forces—perhaps including ground troops—to extri- cate UN peacekeepers from Bosnia if that mission is terminated.

In addition to problems of excessive costs and risks, the United States would be wise to avoid involvement in UN peacekeeping operations for another reason: it is important to maximize America's decision-making autonomy and preserve the widest array of policy alternatives whenever possible. An interventionist policy within a global collective security arrangement may be the worst of all possible options. Unilateral interventionism, at least, leaves U.S. officials com- plete latitude to determine when, where, and under what conditions to use the nation's armed forces. Working through the UN Security Council to reach such decisions reduces that flexibility and creates another layer of risk. That hin- drance is especially troublesome if Washington is serious about collaborating in collective security operations, and is not merely seeking to use the United Nations as a multilateral facade for U.S. objectives. Other powers are going to insist on *quid pro quos* for supporting measures desired by Washington. The calls by Britain and France—Western Europe's two permanent members on the Security Council—for the United States to assume its "fair share" of the risks in the UN's Bosnia peacekeeping mission are omens of such pressures.

## Rejecting the "Light-Switch" Model of US Engagement

Whenever dissident policy experts suggest pruning Washington's overgrown global security commitments, defenders of the *status quo* invariably cry "isolationism."[5] That view is essentially the light-switch theory of America's engagement in the world—that there can be only two possible positions: on or off. According to this theory, either the United States continues to pursue an indiscriminate global interventionist policy, which requires putting American military personnel at risk in such places as Somalia, Haiti, and Bosnia, or it adopts a "Fortress America" strategy and "cuts itself off from the world."

Such a contention is a red herring. No serious analyst advocates creating a hermit republic. It is entirely possible to adopt a security policy between the extremes of global interventionism—which is essentially the current U.S. policy—and Fortress America. Moreover, there are different forms of engagement in world affairs, of which the political-military version is merely one form. Economic connections and influence are crucial, and seem to be growing in importance. Diplomatic and cultural engagement is also significant, especially in the age of the information revolution.

There is no reason why the United States must have identical positions along each axis of engagement. It is entirely feasible to have extensive economic and cultural relations with the rest of the world—and have an active and creative diplomacy—without playing the role of world policeman. It is only in the area of military engagement that the United States needs to retrench.

A policy of strategic independence is based on a more modest and sustainable world-role for the United States. It takes into account the fundamental changes that have occurred in the world in recent years, and seeks to position the United States to benefit from an emerging multi-polar political, economic, and military environment. It would end the promiscuously interventionist policy that requires a military budget larger than those of all other industrial powers combined, and that has placed American military personnel at risk in such strategically irrelevant places as Somalia and Haiti. A new security strategy would enable the United States to substantially reduce its military budget and force structure while more-than-adequately protecting national security.

Strategic independence also would be a policy consistent with the values of a constitutional republic based on the principle of limited government. The lives, freedoms, and financial resources of the American people are not rightfully available for whatever missions suit the whims of political leaders. The U.S. government has constitutional and moral responsibilities to protect the security and liberty of the American republic. It has neither constitutional nor moral writs to risk lives and resources to police the planet, promote democracy, or advance other aims on the bureaucracy's foreign policy agenda.

---

## Notes

1. For examples of such reasoning, see Richard Holbrooke, "America, A European Power," *Foreign Affairs* 74, no. 2 (March-April 1995): 38-51; White House, "A National Security Strategy of Engagement and Enlargement," February 1995, 1-2, 25-28; and Department of Defense, Office of International Security Affairs, "United States Security Strategy for the East Asia-Pacific Region," February 1995, 9-10, 23-24, 31.

2. This point was expressed explicitly in the initial draft of the Pentagon's defense planning guidance document that was leaked to the press in early 1992. Patrick E. Tyler, "US Strategy Plan Calls for Insuring No Rivals Develop," *New York Times*, 8 March 1992: A1; and Patrick E. Tyler, "Excerpts from Pentagon's Plan: Prevent the Emergence of a New Rival," *New York Times*, 8 March 1992: A14. For discussions of Washington's long-standing policy of attempting to keep the major West European and East Asian powers subordinate by meshing them into US-dominated security organizations, see Benjamin Schwarz, "'Cold War' Continuities: US Economic and Security Strategy Toward Europe," *Journal of Strategic Studies* 17, no. 4 (December 1994): 82-104; and Christopher Layne and Benjamin C. Schwarz, "American Hegemony—Without an Enemy," *Foreign Policy* 92 (Fall 1993).

3. For detailed discussions of the many problems associated with NATO expansion, see Ted Galen Carpenter, *Beyond NATO: Staying Out of Europe's Wars* (Washington: Cato Institute, 1994); Jonathan G. Clarke, "Beckoning Quagmires: NATO in Eastern Europe," *Journal of Strategic Studies* 17, no. 4 (December 1994): 42-60; Hugh De Santis, "Romancing NATO: Partnership for Peace and East European Stability," *ibid.*, 61-81; Owen Harries, "The Collapse of 'The West,'" *Foreign Affairs* 72 (September-October, 1993): 41-42; and Michael E. Brown, "The Flawed Logic of NATO Expansion," *Survival* 37, no. 1 (Spring 1995): 34-52.

4. For a more detailed discussion which distinguishes among the various classes of security interests, see Ted Galen Carpenter, *A Search for Enemies: America's Alliances after the Cold War* (Washington: Cato Institute, 1992) 170-79.

5. An egregious example of this attitude was President Clinton's depiction of even his mildest foreign policy critics as proponents of isolationism. White House, Office of the Press Secretary, Remarks by the President to the Nixon Center for Peace and Freedom Policy Conference, Washington, DC, 1 March 1995, 2-4, 7. Eric A. Nordlinger was one of the few scholars or policy experts who did not use the term "isolationism" as a pejorative. See his *Isolationism Reconfigured: American Foreign Policy for a New Century* (Princeton, NJ: Princeton University Press, 1995).

# Chapter 10

## ✱ ✱ ✱

## Losing the Moment?
## The United States and the
## World After the Cold War

Zalmay Khalilzad

*Zalmay Khalilzad rejects neo-isolationist and balance of power approaches in favor of "U.S. leadership." He calls for the United States "to retain global leadership and to preclude the rise of a global rival or a return to multipolarity for the indefinite future." The United States, in other words, must maintain its primacy as the world's sole superpower. What do you think of Khalilzad's policy guidelines? Should the United States adopt the two-power force planning standard he recommends? Does U.S. security require U.S. primacy? What are the opportunity costs of pursuing primacy? How would the rest of the world react to the strategic approach advocated here?*

Three years after the collapse of the Soviet Union, the United States is heading toward squandering a once-in-a-lifetime opportunity to shape the future of the world because it still does not have a broadly agreed upon vision and a grand strategy for the new era. The United States cannot succeed in shaping the post-cold war world unless it knows what shape it wants the world to take, understands what it takes to mold international relations in accordance with that vision, and has the will to see the task through. Without a strategy, the United States will tend to lose the initiative in world affairs and be placed in a reactive mode.

The lack of vision endangers the completion of even modest tasks. An administration can neither evaluate specific policy decisions adequately, nor reach an

Zalmay Khalilzad is program director for strategy, doctrine, and force structure of RAND's Project AIR FORCE. From 1990 to 1993 he was assistant under secretary of defense for policy planning.

Zalmay Khalilzad, "Losing the Moment? The United States and the World After the Cold War," *The Washington Quarterly*, 18:2, Spring 1995, pp. 87-107. Copyright © 1995 by the Center for Strategic and International Studies (CSIS) and the Massachusetts Institute of Technology.

effective consensus with respect to them, without first constructing a framework for guiding policy, setting priorities, and deciding what constitute vital U.S. interests. Absent such a framework it will be more difficult to decide what is important and what is not, to determine which threats are more serious than others, and to develop coherent approaches to respond to new challenges. Policy on many issues will be ambivalent and uncertain and will lack staying power. Short-term and parochial interests will take priority over longer-term, national interests.

Without a broadly agreed architectural framework, gaining widespread bipartisan support for policy also becomes harder, as has been evident in recent discussions of foreign and security policy. Sustaining popular support and staying the course for particular policies become harder if the costs of implementation increase but the commitment cannot be explained in terms of a national interest and a strategy on which broad agreement has been achieved.

### The Search for a New Vision

Despite efforts by both the Bush and Clinton administrations, three years after the end of the Soviet Union, no grand strategy has yet jelled and there is no consensus on overarching national security objectives. It appears that the United States is still trying to get its strategic bearings.

With the disintegration of the Soviet Union, Secretary of Defense Dick Cheney's department put forward a new defense strategy—the "Regional Defense Strategy"—which emphasized precluding any hostile power from dominating a region critical to U.S. interests; strengthening and extending the alliances among democratic and like-minded powers; and helping reduce the likelihood of conflict by reducing the sources of instability.[1] The Regional Defense Strategy did not jell as the nation's grand strategy. There was an intense but brief debate when versions of the document were leaked. Although President George Bush appeared supportive of the concept as indicated in some of his statements, he did not try actively to build political support for it. Given the dangers involved in any systemic shift in power, President Bush managed the disintegration of the Soviet Union extremely well. But because of the deteriorating domestic economic situation during the last year of his presidency, he did not push for a broad political consensus on a new grand strategy. Besides, an election year may not be the best time for generating such a consensus.

In July 1994, a year and a half after coming to power, the Clinton administration published its *National Security Strategy of Engagement and Enlargement*. Like the Regional Defense Strategy of the previous administration, President Bill Clinton's document proposes strengthening and adapting the alliances among the market democracies. Similarly, it emphasizes regional threats. It goes further, however, in its emphasis on peacekeeping operations, in highlighting the importance of economic issues and the global expansion of democracy, and in its concern about environmental issues. It also emphasizes a readiness to "participate in multilateral efforts to broker settlements of internal conflicts." Similarly, it states that "our forces must prepare to participate in peacekeeping, peace enforcement and other operations in support of these objectives." Other than globalizing democracy, the document does not have a unifying concept. It does not deal with some of the tough issues such as how to hedge against Russian reimperialism and Chinese expansionism. It also does not provide a clear sense of priorities.[2]

For most of his presidency, Clinton's handling of foreign and security policy has been controversial. Although the president has committed himself to building a "new public consensus" for "active engagement abroad" no determined effort toward achieving that consensus has been made so far.

Besides the problems with the content of what has been proposed and inadequate efforts to build consensus on a new grand strategy, two other broader factors have played a role in the absence of broadly agreed upon grand strategy. One is the fact that American culture is disinclined toward great strategic design. The task is made even harder by a second reason: an underlying and widely held belief that the world is more uncertain now compared to the cold war period—making both the development and broad acceptance of a grand strategy more difficult.

But this assumption of greater uncertainty is only partially and only retrospectively correct. The cold war world was not truly much more certain than the world of today—at least not to those who were players in the struggle. Even though the enemy was known, it was never easy to predict Soviet behavior and developments around the world. "Kremlinology" was an almost mystical science, and as developments showed, U.S. information and understanding of what was really happening in the Soviet Union were often well off the mark. Nor was there always a consensus over policy; there were major disagreements about issues such as arms control and Vietnam. Even so, during the Cold War the United States was relatively certain of its overall objectives and priorities among them. Now it is not. This is the critical difference between the Cold War and the current era.

## The United States' Possible Visions

Given the opportunity costs, the United States should no longer delay the development of a vision and a national grand strategy. The shift in the tectonics of power confronts Washington with several options. The choice that the United States makes is not only important for setting the country's global direction for this new era, but also for the major impact it will have on the calculations of others.

As the victor in the Cold War, the United States can choose among several strategic visions and grand strategies. It could abandon global leadership and turn inward. Alternatively, it could seek to give up leadership gradually by reducing the U.S. global role and encouraging the emergence of a seventeenth- to nineteenth-century style balance of power structure with spheres of influence. Third, it could seek, as its central strategic objective, to consolidate its global leadership and preclude the rise of a global rival.

*Neo-Isolationism*. In the short run, abandoning global leadership and turning inward could be an attractive option. It would result in a significant reduction in defense expenditures—although how much money the United States would really save over either the short or the long run should it adopt such a strategy has not been seriously studied.[3] Such a policy would also mean that U.S. servicemen and servicewomen would be less likely to be put in harm's way in places like Bosnia or Iraq, Haiti or Somalia. The reduction in defense burden could help deal with the budget deficit and improve U.S. economic competitiveness, especially because, at the same time, many foreign competitors would have to increase their defense expenditures. Ignoring foreign issues would enable the United States to concentrate on and solve its many domestic problems more effectively.

Furthermore, in many cases, allies to whose defense the United States has been committed no longer need it (e.g., the Soviet threat to Western Europe has disappeared and the current threats to Europe are much smaller by comparison) and should be able to manage on their own (e.g., South Korea has over twice the population and many times the gross national product [GNP] of North Korea). The commitment of the United States to the defense of an ally like South Korea may only serve to enable its government to spend less on defense and focus more on strengthening its economy.

Realistically and over the longer term, however, a neo-isolationist approach might well increase the danger of major conflict, require a greater U.S. defense effort, threaten world peace, and eventually undermine U.S. prosperity. By withdrawing from Europe and Asia, the United States would deliberately risk weakening the institutions and solidarity of the world's community of democratic powers and so establishing favorable conditions for the spread of disorder and a possible return to conditions similar to those of the first half of the twentieth century.

In the 1920s and 1930s, U.S. isolationism had disastrous consequences for world peace. At that time, the Untied States was but one of several major powers. Now that the United States is the world's preponderant power, the shock of a U.S. withdrawal could be even greater.

What might happen to the world if the United States turned inward? Without the United States and the North Atlantic Treaty Organization (NATO), rather than cooperating with each other, the West European nations might compete with each other for domination of East-Central Europe and the Middle East. In Western and Central Europe, Germany—especially since unification—would be the natural leading power.

Either in cooperation or competition with Russia, Germany might seek influence over the territories located between them. German efforts are likely to be aimed at filling the vacuum, stabilizing the region, and precluding its domination by rival powers. Britain and France fear such a development. Given the strength of democracy in Germany and its preoccupation with absorbing the former East Germany, European concerns about Germany appear exaggerated. But it would be a mistake to assume that U.S. withdrawal could not, in the long run, result in the renationalization of Germany's security policy.

The same is also true of Japan. Given a U.S. withdrawal from the world, Japan would have to look after its own security and build up its military capabilities. China, Korea, and the nations of Southeast Asia already fear Japanese hegemony. Without U.S. protection, Japan is likely to increase its military capability dramatically—to balance the growing Chinese forces and still-significant Russian forces. This could result in arms races, including the possible acquisition by Japan of nuclear weapons. Given Japanese technological prowess, to say nothing of the plutonium stockpile Japan has acquired in the development of its nuclear power industry, it could obviously become a nuclear weapon state relatively quickly, if it should so decide. It could also build long-range missiles and carrier task forces.

With the shifting balance of power among Japan, China, Russia, and potential new regional powers such as India, Indonesia, and a united Korea could come significant risks of preventive or preemptive war. Similarly, European competition for regional dominance could lead to major wars in Europe or East Asia. If the Unites States stayed out of such a war—an unlikely prospect—Europe or East Asia could become dominated by hostile power. Such a development would threaten U.S. interests. A power that achieved such dominance would seek to exclude the United States from the area and threaten its interests—economic and political—in the region. Besides, with the domination of Europe or East Asia, such a power might seek global hegemony and the United States would face another global Cold War and the risk of a world war even more catastrophic than the last.

In the Persian Gulf, U.S. withdrawal is likely to lead to an intensified struggle for regional domination. Iran and Iraq have, in the past, both sought regional hegemony. Without U.S. protection, the weak oil-rich states of the Gulf Cooperation Council (GCC) would be unlikely to retain their independence. To preclude his development, the Saudis might seek to acquire, perhaps by purchase, their own nuclear weapons. If either Iraq or Iran controlled the region that dominates the world supply of oil, it could gain a significant capability to damage the U.S. and world economies. Any country that gained hegemony would have vast economic resources at its disposal that could be used to build military capability as well as gain leverage over the United States and other oil-importing nations. Hegemony over the Persian Gulf by either Iran or Iraq would bring the rest of the Arab Middle East under its influence and domination because of the shift in the balance of power. Israeli security problems would multiply and the peace process would be fundamentally undermined, increasing the risk of war between the Arabs and the Israelis.

The extension of instability, conflict, and hostile hegemony in East Asia, Europe, and the Persian Gulf would harm the economy of the United States even in the unlikely event that it was able to avoid involvement in major wars and conflicts. Higher oil prices would reduce the U.S. standard of living. Turmoil in Asia and Europe would force major economic readjustment in the United States, perhaps reducing U.S. exports and imports and jeopardizing U.S. investments in these regions. Given that total imports and exports are equal to a quarter of U.S. gross domestic product, the cost of necessary adjustments might be high.

The higher level of turmoil in the world would also increase the likelihood of the proliferation of weapons of mass destruction (WMD) and means for their delivery. Already several rogue states such as North Korea and Iran are seeking nuclear weapons and long-range missiles. That danger would only increase if the United States withdrew form the world. The result would be a much more dangerous world in which many states possessed WMD capabilities; the likelihood of their actual use would increase accordingly. If this happened, the security of every nation in the world, including the United States, would be harmed.

At present, mainstream sentiment in the two major U.S. political parties rejects isolationism as a national strategy, even though both have elements favoring it. It is possible, however, that without a vision and grand strategy, the United States might follow policies that result in at least some of the consequences of a neo-isolationist strategy.

***Return to Multipolarity and Balance of Power***. Another option for the United States would be to rely on a balance of power to preclude the emergence of a "superpower" that could threaten U.S. security. This approach has some positive features, but it is also dangerous. Based on current realities, the other potential great powers are Japan, China, Germany (or the European Union [EU]), and Russia. In the future this list could change. A new great power—such as India, Brazil, or Indonesia—could emerge, or one of the existing ones—such as Russia or China—could decline or disintegrate and cease to be a great power.

Some argue that the world is inevitably heading toward a multiplicity of roughly equal great powers and that the United States should facilitate such a development. This approach starts from the assertion that, based on economic indices, the world already consists of several great powers and assumes that the diffusion of wealth and technology will continue. It is further assumed that, over time, the current economic powers will become political and military powers commensurate with their economic strength; they will be obliged to do so because, in the post-cold war world, others will not perceive threats in the same way and so will not be willing to run risks for them.[4]

In a balance of power regime, NATO would gradually decline in importance and would ultimately disappear, or it would be subsumed, as the Russians now advocate, into a broader but less muscular organization such as the Organization on Security and Cooperation in Europe (OSCE). The U.S. presence in Western Europe would end as the West Europeans built up their capability and a balance of power emerged on the continent. The United States could affect the pace of such a development by, for example, announcing that it intended to withdraw from Europe by a specific date—thus giving impetus to a European military buildup to balance Russia.

For such a balance of power system to work, either Germany would have to substantially increase its military power or the EU would have to strengthen its internal unity and become a kind of superstate. The United States would continue to have a vital interest in preventing the domination of Europe—including Russia—by a single power. So, if the Germans decided to build up militarily to a force that appeared to threaten the rest of Europe, the United States could play its part by forming alliances with any European country or countries that sought to prevent German hegemony and by maintaining adequate forces in the United States and perhaps in Great Britain. Problems unrelated to any attempt to establish hegemony over Europe, however, such as instability in the Balkans, East-Central Europe, or North Africa, would be the responsibility of the Europeans alone and the United States would not get militarily involved in conflicts in these regions.

Similarly, the United States would be unlikely to get involved militarily on the territory of the former Soviet Union; in general, it would accept a Russian sphere of influence there. The other European great powers (and perhaps also the United States) would not want Russia to reincorporate Ukraine, however, because, combined, Russia and Ukraine would have a military potential so much greater than any European state as to threaten to destroy the possibility of achieving a balance of power. Western Europe and Russia would both have interests in East-Central Europe and would have to try to work out rules for regulating their interactions.

In East Asia, the United States would similarly become a balancer against either China or a Japan that had built up its military capability. In the event of a serious imbalance between Japan and China, the United States could play a balancing role with forces based in the United States or possibly in some of the smaller states in the region. As in the case of Europe, the United States would seek to prevent the emergence of regional hegemony by shifting alliances; it would cooperate with other powers to protect common interests and be prepared to protect specific interests in the region, such as the lives and property of U.S. citizens.

In the Persian Gulf, in this framework, the United States and other major powers would oppose the domination of the region by any one power, because such a power would acquire enormous leverage over states that depend on the region's oil. At the regional level, the United States and other major powers could rely on a balance between Iran and Iraq to prevent regional hegemony. Assuming the great powers were willing to pursue a joint policy toward the Persian Gulf, the fact that the United States is relatively less dependent on the Gulf than either Western Europe or Japan would give it a strong bargaining position when the time came to allocate the burdens required by such a policy among the great powers. On the other hand, one or more great powers might be tempted to abandon the great power coalition and to support a potential hegemony in the Gulf in return for favorable access to the Gulf's resources and markets. Finally, the United States would have to be the dominant power affecting important security issues in the Americas.

Aside from the question of inevitability, a balance of power system would have certain advantages for the United States. First, the U.S. government could reduce defense expenditures (probably not by as much as with a neo-isolationist strategy) and deploy U.S. military force less often to world hot spots, because it would let other great powers take the lead in dealing with problems in their regions. Second, the United States would be freer to pursue its economic interests, even when they damaged its political relations with countries that had been, but were no longer, allies; only in the particular case that required the United States to ally with another great power to ward off a specific threat would it be constrained.

It is possible that in a balance of power system the United States would be in a relatively privileged position as compared to the other great powers. Given the relative distance of the United States from other power centers, it might be able to mimic the former British role of an offshore balancer. As in the nineteenth century, the United States and other great powers would compete and cooperate to avoid hegemony and global wars. Each great power would protect its own specific interests and protect common interests cooperatively. If necessary, the United States would intervene militarily to prevent the emergence of a preponderant power.

But there are also several serious problems with this approach. First, there is a real question whether the major powers will behave as they should under the logic of a balance of power framework. For example, would the West European powers respond appropriately to a resurgent Russian threat, or would they behave as the European democracies did in the 1930s? The logic of a balance of power system might well require the United States to support a non-democratic state against a democratic one, or to work with one undesirable state against another. For example, to contain the power of an increasingly powerful Iran, the United States would have to strengthen Iraq. The United States may, however, be politically unable to behave in this fashion. For example, after the Iraqi victory against Iran in 1988, balance of power logic indicated that the United States should strengthen Iran. However, because of ongoing animosity in U.S. -Iranian relations, the nature of Iran's regime, and moral concerns, the United States could not implement such a strategy. There are many other examples. To expect such action is therefore probably unrealistic.

Second, this system implies that the major industrial democracies will no longer see themselves as allies. Instead, political, and possibly even military, struggle among them will become not only thinkable but legitimate.[5] Each will pursue its own economic interest much more vigorously, thereby weakening such multilateral economic institutions as the General Agreement on Tariffs and Trade (GATT) and the liberal world trading order in general. This would increase the likelihood of major economic depressions and dislocations.

Third, the United States is likely to face more competition from other major powers in areas of interest to it. For example, other powers might not be willing to grant the United States a sphere of influence in the Americas, but might seek, as Germany did in World War I, to reach anti-U.S. alliances with Latin American nations. Similarly, as noted above, another great power might decide to support a potential hegemon in the Persian Gulf.

Finally, and most important, there is no guarantee that the system will succeed in its own terms. Its operation requires subtle calculations and indications of intentions in order to maintain the balance while avoiding war; nations must know how to signal their depth of commitment on a given issue without taking irrevocable steps toward war. This balancing act proved impossible even for the culturally similar and aristocratically governed states of the nineteenth-century European balance of power systems. It will be infinitely more difficult when the system is global, the participants differ culturally, and the governments of many of the states, influenced by public opinion, are unable to be as flexible (or cynical) as the rules of the system require. Thus, miscalculations might be made about the state of the balance that could lead to wars that the United States might be unable to stay out of. The balance of power system failed in the past, producing World War I and other major conflicts. It might not work any better in the future—and war among major powers in the nuclear age is likely to be more devastating.

*Global Leadership.* Under the third option, the United States would seek to retain global leadership and to preclude the rise of a global rival or a return to multipolarity for the indefinite future. On balance, this is the best long-term guiding principle and vision. Such a vision is desirable not as an end in itself, but because a world in which the United States exercises leadership would have tremendous advantages. First, the global environment would be more open and more receptive to American values—democracy, free markets, and the rule of law. Second, such a world would have a better chance of dealing cooperatively with the world's major problems, such as nuclear proliferation, threats of regional hegemony by renegade states, and low-level conflicts. Finally, U.S. leadership would help preclude the rise of another hostile global rival, enabling the United States and the world to avoid another global cold or hot war and all the attendant dangers, including a global nuclear exchange. U.S. leadership would therefore be more conducive to global stability than a bipolar or a multipolar balance of power system.

Precluding the rise of a hostile global rival is a good guide for defining what interests the United States should regard as vital and for which of them it should be ready to use force and put American lives at risk. It is a good prism for identifying threats, setting priorities for U.S. policy toward various regions and states, and assessing needs for military capabilities and modernization.

To succeed in the long term in realizing this vision, the United States should adhere to the following principles as guidelines for its policies. It must:

• maintain and strengthen the "zone of peace"[6] and incrementally extend it;

• preclude hostile hegemony over critical regions;

• hedge against reimperialization by Russia and expansion by China while promoting cooperation with both countries;

• preserve U.S. military preeminence;

• maintain U.S. economic strength and an open international economic system;

• be judicious in the use of force, avoid overextension, and develop ways of sharing the burden with allies; and

• obtain and maintain domestic support for U.S. global leadership and these principles.

Why are these principles important and how can the United States pursue them effectively? The remainder of this article will focus on these issues.

## Maintain, Strengthen, and Extend the Zone of Peace

In the course of building up the Western alliance, the United States helped create a community of nations in Western Europe and East Asia that was held together by more than just the Soviet threat. These nations shared common values, most important among them democracy and a commitment to free markets. War among these nations became unthinkable. This commonality of interests was expressed in the creation of organizations such as NATO and the Group of Seven (G-7), and in bilateral treaties such as that between the United States and Japan. Under U.S. leadership, this group of nations pursued a policy of containing the Soviet Union until its collapse; in the post-cold war era, it is clear that, given continued unity, these nations will be strong enough to overpower any threat from outside their ranks. Thus, this community of nations may be called the "zone of peace." Maintaining, strengthening, and extending the zone of peace should be the central feature of U.S. post-cold war grand strategy.

Maintaining the zone of peace requires, first and foremost, avoiding conditions that can lead to renationalization of security policies in key allied countries such as Japan and Germany. The members of the zone of peace are in basic agreement and prefer not to compete with each other in realpolitik terms. But this general agreement still requires U.S. leadership. At present there is greater nervousness in Japan than in Germany about future ties with Washington, but U.S. credibility remains as strong in both countries. The credibility of U.S. alliances can be undermined if key allies such as German and Japan believe that the current arrangements do not deal adequately with threats to their security. It could also be undermined if, over an extended period, the United States is perceived as either lacking the will or the capability to lead in protecting their interests.

In Europe, besides dealing with balancing Russian military potential and hedging against a possible Russian reimperialization, the near-term security threat to Germany comes form instability in East-Central Europe and to a lesser degree from the Balkans. For France and Italy, the threats come from conflicts in the Balkans, Islamic extremism, and the spread of WMD and ballistic and cruise missiles to North Africa and the Middle East. For example, at present the Germans fear that conflicts and instability in East-Central Europe might "spill out" or "spill in." Such crises could set the stage for a bigger conflict and/or send millions of refugees to Germany. The Germans are divided on how to deal with the threat from the east. For now, however, they are focused on integrating the former East Germany and favor a U.S.-led alliance strategy rather than filling the vacuum themselves, as indicated in their substantial defense cuts. This is in part because of their confidence in the United States and the common values and interests they perceive among the allies, and in part because an alliance-based policy is cheaper for Germany than a unilateral approach. But should the Germans come to believe that the alliance will not or cannot deal with threats to their interests, they might well consider other options.

In East Asia, too, Japan favors alliance with the United States to deal with uncertainty about Russia, future Chinese military capability, including power projection, and the threat of nuclear and missile proliferation on the Korean peninsula. For the same reasons as Germany, Japan currently prefers to work with the United States. But the loss of U.S. credibility could also change Japan's calculations; the test will be how well the United States deals with North Korea's nuclear program.

As long as U.S.-led allied actions protect their vital interests, these nations are less likely to look to unilateral means. This implies that the United States needs a military capability that is larger than might be required based on a definition of U.S. interests based on isolationism or the balance of power.

U.S. power and willingness to lead in protecting vital joint interests in Europe, East Asia, and the Middle East are necessary to preserve the zone of peace. In Europe these interests can be best served if NATO remains the primary entity to deal with the security challenge from instability and conflict to the south and the east and a possible revanchism in Russia. To perform this role, NATO must adapt by maintaining a robust military capability as a hedge against Russia's going bad; by preparing for the eventual membership of the nations of East-Central Europe in the alliance in coordination with EU expansion; and by developing the capability to deter and defeat threats from the south. NATO allies need to increase their ability to project power to perform these tasks. West Europeans have ample capability for self-defense but their capability for projecting power eastward or southward is far more limited. Even with increased European power projection capabilities, the United States would need to maintain a significant military force on the continent for an indefinite period—both because of military needs and to demonstrate its commitment and resolve.

Asia has no NATO-like multilateral alliance. The core security relationships are the U.S.-Japanese and U.S.-South Korean ties. Maintaining security ties with each other is important for both the United States and Japan, even though trade relations between the two have a greater potential to create mutual antagonism than trade relations between the United States and Germany. While North Korea remains hostile and military powerful and, in any case, in order to hedge against uncertainties in Russia and China, the United States needs to station sufficient force in the region to deter all three countries and, with reinforcements, defend critical U.S. interests while running only limited risks. At present the main military threat is a possible North Korean attack against South Korea. The United States and its Asian allies should explore the possibility of establishing multilateral security arrangements that can promote stability by increasing mutual trust and providing for effective burden sharing.

Within these constrains, it is in the U.S. interest and the interests of the other members of the zone of peace that the zone ultimately encompass the whole world. Unfortunately, this is not a near-term proposition. Many regions and states are not ready. The United States should seek to expand the zone selectively and help others prepare for membership.

The most important step that the United States and the other prosperous democracies can take is to assist others in adopting the economic strategies that have worked in North America, Western Europe, and East Asia and are being successfully implemented in parts of Latin America and elsewhere in Asia. Economic development and education are the most effective instruments for solving the problems of the nations outside the zone of peace.

## Preclude Hostile Hegemony over Critical Regions

A global rival could emerge if a hostile power or coalition gained hegemony over a critical region, defined as one that contains economic, technical, and human resources such that a power that controlled it would possess a military potential roughly equal to, or greater than, that of the United States. It is, therefore, a vital U.S. interest (i.e., one that the United States should be willing to use force to protect) to avoid such a development. Although this could change in the future, two regions now meet this criterion: East Asia and Europe. The Persian Gulf is critically important for a different reason—its oil resources are vital for the world economy.

In the long term, the relative importance of various regions can change. A region that is critical to U.S. interests now might become less important, while some other region might gain in importance. For example, Southeast Asia appears to be a region whose relative importance is likely to increase if the regional economies continue to grow as impressively as they have done in the past several years. The Gulf might decline if the resources of the region became less important for world prosperity because technological developments provided economically feasible alternative sources of energy.

At present, the risks of regional hegemony in Europe and East Asia are very small. This is due in large part to the alliance of the key states of these regions with the United States, which endorses the presence of U.S. forces and the credibility of U.S. commitments. It is thus vital that U.S. alliances in Europe and East Asia be maintained but adapted to meet the challenges of the new era. During the Cold War, the U.S. role in these two regions not only deterred threats from the Soviet Union but also contained rivalries. In Europe, it is not in the U.S. interest for the EU either to become a superstate or to disintegrate. The former could ultimately pose a global challenge—Western Europe's economy is bigger than the U.S. economy. The latter could encourage mutual suspicion and contribute to renationalization and a possible repeat of the first half of the twentieth century.

At this point, the United States is the preponderant outside power in the Persian Gulf. Its position there helps to discourage the rise of a rival and will put it in a strong position to compete should one arise. U.S. preponderance serves the interests of the members of the zone of peace because it helps diminish the threat of interruption of oil supplies from the region. But the threat of hostile regional hegemony remains. The United States, with support from its allies, needs to maintain adequate military capability to deter and defeat the threat of regional hegemony from Iraq or Iran. The United States should seek greater contributions from its NATO allies and Japan in meeting the security challenges in this region. Washington and its allies must also encourage regional cooperation among the GCC states and help them cope with the contradictory pressures—liberal and fundamentalist—for domestic change that beset them. Given the recent progress in the Arab-Israeli conflict, U.S. security ties with Israel can help in dealing with threats from Iran or Iraq in the Gulf.

## Hedge against Reimperializtaion in Russia

Russia is still trying to find a place for itself in the world. Although still weakening militarily and economically, as heir to the Soviet strategic nuclear arsenal it is capable of conducting an all-out nuclear attack on the United States. Consequently, it requires special attention under any circumstances. In the near term—10 years—Moscow is unlikely to pose a global challenge. Even in its current weakened condition, however, Russia can pose a major regional threat if it moves toward reimperialization. This scenario has been dubbed "Weimar Russia," denoting the possibility that, embittered by its economic and political troubles and humiliations, Russia may attempt to recover its past glory by turning to ultranationalist policies, particularly the reincorporation of—or he-gemony over—part or all of the old "internal" empire. In the aftermath of the December 1993 parliamentary elections and Vladimir Zhirinovsky's strong showing in them, many Russians indicated a strong preference for reincorpora-tion of the so-called near abroad—the states on the territory of the former Soviet Union. But, more recently, concerns about costs and negative international reaction have resulted in a shift in favor of hegemony—Russian geopolitical and economic domination of weak but nominally independent states.

To avoid Russian hegemony over the near abroad, to say nothing of creating the groundwork for future cooperation on a whole range of international mat-ters, the United States and the other members of the democratic zone of peace have a substantial interest in helping Russia become a "normal" country, that is, a country that does not hanker for an empire and whose domestic life is not distorted by overmilitarization. Ideally, it would become a prosperous, free market, Western-style democracy. Whether Russia will succeed in becoming a normal state is difficult to predict, but the stakes justify a major Western effort. Even so, the key determinant is Russian domestic politics, over which, under the circumstances, the United States can have only limited influence, and the domestic trends are not very hopeful.

As the United States encourages Russia to join the zone of peace and cooperate on specific issues based on common concerns, it is in the U.S. interest that Russia's neighbors, such as Ukraine, Kazakhstan, and Uzbekistan, be able to make any attempt by Russia to recreate the empire very costly, thereby deterring it. And should deterrence fail, such an approach would help sap its energies, undermining its prospects for becoming an effective global challenge. This does not mean that the United States needs hostile relations between these countries and Moscow; good economic and political relations between Russia and its neighbors are not inconsistent with U.S. interests. But discouraging the emergence of a very robust Commonwealth of Independent States and consolidating Ukrainian, Kazakh, and Uzbek independence should be the primary U.S. objective in dealing with these countries.

The United States and its allies have lost some opportunities here because economic problems and pressure from Russia have reduced support for independence in some of the newly independent states. To discourage Russian reincorporation of Ukraine by force, NATO must make it clear to Russia, and must convince its own publics and parliaments, including the U.S. Congress, that such an action would lead to a cutoff of economic assistance to Russia, to NATO membership for the nations of East-Central Europe on a much faster track—perhaps at once—than would be the case otherwise, and possibly to material support to a Ukrainian resistance movement and Russian isolation from the West. Without such preparations now, there is danger that, in the face of a possible Russian takeover of Ukraine, NATO expansion to East-Central Europe would not be politically supported because it would appear to be too provocative. Unfortunately, at times in the past the United States has appreciated its stake in a situation too late to express its intentions clearly enough to deter an aggressor. A clear and strong Western posture now should also strengthen those Russians who do not consider reimperializaton to be in their country's interests.

But this is not only a military matter. The key for Ukraine and others is to carry out economic and political reforms to increase internal stability and reduce their vulnerability to Russian interference and domination. The United States, the EU countries, and Japan have a stake in helping Ukraine and others adopt significant economic reforms. To encourage such a development, the G-7 states should be willing to meet some of the costs of the transition to a market-oriented system.

## Discourage Chinese Expansionism

China is another major power that might, over the long term and perhaps sooner than Russia, emerge as a global rival to the United States. China's economic dynamism, now also being reflected in its military development, ensures that—if domestic turmoil can be avoided—China will become an increasingly important player on the global scene in coming decades. The country has had dramatic economic growth. Between 1978 and 1992 its GNP increased by 9 percent annually. In 1992, that rate increased to 12 percent. Its foreign trade increased from $21 billion in 1978 to $170 billion in 1992. According to the International Monetary Fund, Chinese output may have exceeded $1.6 trillion dollars in 1992. The World Bank gives an even higher estimate: $2.3 trillion. Militarily, China has been increasing its power projection capability—both naval and air—in part by purchasing advanced equipment from Russia. If China continues to grow at a higher rate than the United States, at some point in the next century it could become the world's largest economy.[7] Such a development would produce a significant shift in relative economic power, with important potential geopolitical and military implications.

China, however, faces significant political uncertainties in its domestic politics, including a possible succession crisis on the death of Deng Xiaoping and the centrifugal tendencies unleashed by differential economic growth among the provinces. Indeed, Chinese weakness, not excluding a possible civil war that could disrupt economic prosperity and create refugee flows, may cause significant problems for its neighbors and the world community.

Assuming these difficulties can be avoided, the world will have to deal with the fact that China is not a "satisfied" power. Among the major powers, China appears more dissatisfied with the status quo than the others. Beyond Hong Kong and Macau, which will be ceded to China by the end of the century, it claims sovereignty over substantial territories that it does not now control, such as Taiwan, the Spratly Islands and the South China Sea generally, and the Senkaku Islands between China and Japan. Although China has abandoned communism as a global ideology and seems to have accepted the economic imperative of the global economy, it is still seeking its "rightful" place in the world geopolitically. How will China define its role as its power grows beyond its territorial interests? China appears to be seeking eventual regional predominance, a prospect opposed by Japan, Russia, and several other rising regional powers such as Indonesia and India.

Even without regional domination, China might become interested in becoming the leader of an anti-U.S. coalition based on a rejection of U.S. leadership generally or as it is expressed in such policies as nonproliferation and human rights. This is evident in its assistance to Pakistani and Iranian nuclear programs. It is also clear that China is not as opposed to the North Korean nuclear program as the United States is. Some Chinese writing on strategy and international security expresses hostility to U.S. preponderance and implies the need to balance it. But China recognizes the importance of the United States—as a market for Chinese goods and as a source for technical training and technology. Without U.S. help China is less likely to achieve its economic and military objectives.

China, however, is decades away from becoming a serious global rival either by itself or in coalition with others, and its internal political development is likely to influence the type of foreign policy it pursues. In particular, its degree of democratization is likely to determine how much money and effort China is willing to devote to improving its international standing in the light of its immense development tasks at home. This provides the United States with ample strategic warning. For the near term, economic considerations are likely to be dominant in Chinese calculations. Nevertheless, China by itself or as the leader of a coalition of renegade states could complicate U.S.-led efforts to deal with issues such as proliferation and stability in the Persian Gulf and Northeast Asia. Chinese economic success confronts the United States with a dilemma. On the one hand, it increases Chinese potential to become a global rival. On the other, it might produce democratization, decentralization, and a cooperative China.

The United States should continue to pursue economic relations with China and encourage its integration in global economic and security regimes. It should also use the leverage of economic relations, which are very important to China, to continue to encourage Chinese cooperation in restraining nuclear and missile proliferation in places like Korea and Iran. But Chinese cooperation is likely to remain limited. While the United States continues to cooperate with China, it should be cautious in transferring to it technologies that have important military implications. It should also ensure that China's neighbors, such as Taiwan and the member states of the Association of Southeast Asian Nations, have the means to defend themselves. Working with other powers, especially Japan, Korea after unification, and Indonesia, the United States should preclude Chinese regional hegemony by maintaining adequate forces in the region. Without a U.S. presence in the region, as Chinese power grows, some states in the region are likely to appease China and move closer to it, while others such as Indonesia, Japan, and Vietnam would seek to balance it.

### Preserve U.S. Military Preeminence

A global rival to the United States could emerge for several reasons. Because the main deterrent to the rise of another global rival is the military power of the United States, an inadequate level of U.S. military capability could facilitate such an event. This capability should be measured not only in terms of the strength of other countries, but also in terms of the U.S. ability to carry out the strategy outlined here. U.S. tradition makes the prospect of defense cuts below this level a serious possibility: historically, the United States has made this error on several occasions by downsizing excessively. It faces the same danger again for the longer term.

The issue is not only what levels of resources are spent on defense but also on what, for what, and how they are spent. For the United States to maintain its military preeminence, in addition to meeting possible major regional contingencies (MRCs), it needs specific capability in three areas.

First, besides maintaining a robust nuclear deterrent capability because of concerns with Russian and Chinese existing or potential nuclear postures, the United States needs to acquire increased capability to deter, prevent, and defend against the use of biological, chemical, and nuclear weapons in major conflicts in critical regions. The regional deterrence requirements might well be different form those with regard to the Soviet Union during the Cold War because of the character and motivations of deferent regional powers. U.S. ability to prevent and defend against use is currently very limited. In the near term, therefore, to deter use of WMD against its forces and allies, the United States may have to threaten nuclear retaliation.

To counter the spread of WMD and their means of delivery (especially ballistic and cruise missiles), the United States should seek to develop the capability to promptly locate and destroy even well-protected facilities related to biological, chemical, and nuclear weapons and their delivery systems. Equally important will be the ability to defend against the use of these weapons, including both active and passive defense. Deploying robust, multilayered ballistic missile defenses is vital for protecting U.S. forward-deployed forces and extending protection to U.S. allies, thus gaining their participation and cooperation in defeating aggression in critical regions.

Second, the United States needs improved capability for decisive impact in lesser regional crises (LRCs)—internal conflicts, small wars, humanitarian relief, peacekeeping or peacemaking operations, punitive strikes, restoration of civil order, evacuation of noncombatant Americans, safeguarding of security zones, and monitoring and enforcement of sanctions. Given the end of the Cold War, the United States can be more selective in deciding when to become involved militarily. It has not been selective enough during the past three years. Getting involved in LRCs can erode U.S. capabilities for dealing with bigger and more important conflicts. Nevertheless, some crises may occur in areas of vital importance to the United States—e.g., in Mexico, Cuba, South Africa, or Saudi Arabia—and others might so challenge American values as to produce U.S. military involvement. The United States might also consider participating with allies in some LRCs because of a desire either to extend the zone of peace or to prevent chaos from spreading to a critical region and thereby threatening the security of members of the zone of peace.

At present, LRCs are treated as lesser included cases of major regional conflicts, in the same way that some thought about regional conflicts in relation to a global conflict during the Cold War. It has been suggested that the United States "underestimated and misestimated the MRC requirements during the Cold War."[8] It would be a mistake to treat LRCs the same way now, especially because in the future U.S. forces will be much smaller than in the past and will provide a smaller margin for error. Even small LRCs can impose substantial and disproportionate demands on the support elements of U.S. forces—such as airborne warning and control systems (AWACS), SEAD (suppression of enemy air defenses), airlift, and communications. To be prepared for its MRC commitments and to have some increased LRC capabilities, the United States needs more airlift and changes in the MRC-driven training and organization of U.S. forces.

Third, it is essential to retain a mobilization base to reconstitute additional military capability in a timely fashion if things go badly in any major region. Without such a capability the United States is unlikely to be able to take prompt action, given the amount of strategic warning it is likely to receive.

To discourage the rise of another global rival or to be in a strong position to deal with the problem should one arise, focusing U.S. military planning for the future on Korea and the Persian Gulf, plus increased ability for LRC operations, is inadequate. Over time, although the threat from North Korea will probably disappear, other larger threats could emerge. As an alternative, the United States should consider moving toward sizing its forces largely by adopting the requirement that they be capable of simultaneously defeating the most plausible military challenges to critical U.S. interests that might be created by the *two* next most powerful military forces in the world that are not allied with the United States. Such a force should allow the United States to protect its interests in Asia, Europe, and the Persian Gulf. Such a force-sizing principle does not mean that U.S. forces have to be numerically as large as the combined forces of these two powers. It means that they should be capable of defeating them given relatively specific near-simultaneous scenarios of great importance to the United States—a Gulf and Asia scenario; a Europe and Asia scenario; or Asian and Gulf scenarios nearly simultaneously. Such an approach would give the United States a flexible global capability for substantial operations.

U.S. superiority in new weapons and their use would be critical. U.S. planners should therefore give higher priority to research on new technologies, new concepts of operation, and changes in organization, with the aim of U.S. dominance in the military-technical revolution that may be emerging. They should also focus on how to project U.S. systems and interests against weapons based on new technologies.

The Persian Gulf War gave a glimpse of the likely future. The character of warfare will change because of advances in military technology, where the United States has the lead, and in corresponding concepts of operation and organizational structure. The challenge is to sustain this lead in the face of the complacency that the current U.S. lead in military power is likely to engender. Those who are seeking to be rivals to the United States are likely to be very motivated to explore new technologies and how to use them against it. A determined nation making the right choices, even though it possessed a much smaller economy, could pose an enormous challenge by exploiting breakthroughs that made more traditional U.S. military methods less effective by comparison.

For example, Germany, by making the right technical choices and adopting innovative concepts for their use in the 1920s and 1930s, was able to make a serious bid for world domination. At the same time, Japan, with a relatively small GNP compared to the other major powers, especially the United States, was at the forefront of the development of naval aviation and aircraft carriers. These examples indicate that a major innovation in warfare provides ambitious powers an opportunity to become dominant or near-dominant powers. U.S. domination of the emerging military-technical revolution, combined with the maintenance of a force of adequate size, can help to discourage the rise of a rival power by making potential rivals believe that catching up with the United States is a hopeless proposition and that if they try they will suffer the same fate as the former Soviet Union.

Although, based on the strategy proposed here, the United States needs increased capabilities in some areas, it can cut back elsewhere and do things differently to free up resources for them. The United States still has too many bases. The country does not have the most effective process for making informed decisions for allocating resources for various types of force elements—that is, those forces that are required for current and future objectives and operational requirements. As things currently stand there is too much duplication in some key areas and capabilities that are not as relevant now as they were before. This is especially true in the maintenance and support area. For example, the navy, the air force, and industry all provide maintenance for military aircraft engines. Greater centralization here could save significant resources. The Defense Department is still being forced to buy weapon systems that it says it does not need and will not be needed under the proposed strategy. The current acquisition system is very costly and can save resources if streamlined.

## Preserve U.S. Economic Strength

The United States is unlikely to preserve its military and technological dominance if the U.S. economy declines seriously. In such an environment, the domestic economic and political base for global leadership would diminish and the United States would probably incrementally withdraw from the world, become inward-looking, and abandon more and more of its external interests. As the United States weakened, others would try to fill the vacuum.

To sustain and improve its economic strength, the United States must maintain its technological lead in the economic realm. Its success will depend on the choices it makes. In the past, developments such as the agricultural and industrial revolutions produced fundamental changes positively affecting the relative position of those who were able to take advantage of them and negatively affecting those who did not. Some argue that the world may be at the beginning of another such transformation, which will shift the sources of wealth and the relative position of classes and nations. If the United States fails to recognize the change and adapt its institutions, its relative position will necessarily worsen.

To remain the preponderant world power, U.S. economic strength must be enhanced by further improvements in productivity, thus increasing real per capita income; by strengthening education and training; and by generating and using superior science and technology. In the long run the economic future of the United States will also be affected by two other factors. One is the imbalance between government revenues and government expenditure. As a society the United States has to decide what part of the GNP it wishes the government to control and adjust expenditures and taxation accordingly. The second, which is even more important to U.S. economic well-being over the long run, may be the overall rate of investment. Although their government cannot endow Americans with a Japanese-style propensity to save, it can use tax policy to raise the savings rate.

Another key factor affecting the global standing of the United States is its current social crisis: the high rate of violence in cities, the unsatisfactory state of race relations, and the breakdown of families. Although it faces no global ideological rival, and although movements such as Islamic fundamentalism and East Asian neo-Confucian authoritarianism are limited in their appeal, the social problems of the United States are limiting its attractiveness as a model. If the social crisis worsens, it is likely that, over the long term, a new organizing principle with greater universal appeal will emerge and be adopted by states with the power and the desire to challenge the erstwhile leader.

## Use Force Judiciously; Avoid Overextension; Share the Burden with Allies

Overextension is a mistake that some of the big powers have made in the past. Such a development can occur if the United States is not judicious in its use of force and gets involved in protracted conflicts in non-critical regions, thereby sapping its energies and undermining support for its global role. And when the United States uses force in critical regions, its preference should be to have its allies and friends contribute their fair share. Having the capability to protect U.S. vital interests unilaterally if necessary can facilitate getting friends and allies of the United States to participate—especially on terms more to its liking. It is quite possible that if the United States cannot protect its interests without significant participation by allies, it might not be able to protect them at all. For example, in the run-up to the Gulf war, several allies did not favor the use of force to evict Iraqi forces from Kuwait. If the military participation of these allies had been indispensable for military success against Iraq, Saddam Hussein's forces might still be in Kuwait and Iraq might now possess nuclear weapons.

When it comes to lesser interests the United States should rely on non-military options, especially if the stakes involved do not warrant the military costs. It has many options: arming and training the victims of aggression; providing technical assistance and logistic support for peacekeeping by the Untied Nations, regional organizations, or other powers; and economic instruments such as sanctions and positive incentives. The effectiveness of these non-military options can be enhanced by skillful diplomacy.

The members of the zone of peace have a common interest in the stability of Europe, North America, East Asia, and the Persian Gulf. Japan, for example, imports oil from the Gulf and exports to and invests in the other critical regions. The same is true of Europe. The U.S. global role benefits these other members as well as the United States. But there is a danger (known as the "free rider" problem) that the other members of the zone of peace will not do their fair share. This was a problem during the Cold War and it is unlikely to go away. It is a potentially important political issue in the United States, which does face a dilemma: As long as the United States is able and willing to protect common interests, other countries may be happy to rely on it, thereby keeping their political opposition under control, accepting no risk for their youth, and continuing to focus on their economies. But on the other hand, the United States would not want Germany and Japan to be able to conduct expeditionary wars. The United States will probably therefore be willing to bear a heavier military burden than its allies, but fairness and long-term public support require that this disproportion not be excessive.

A balance needs to be struck and a formula has to be found to balance each country's contribution of "blood and treasure." In the Gulf war a substantial degree of burden sharing was realized. But the allies can do more. For the long term, one possible solution is to institutionalize burden sharing among the G-7 nations for the security of critical regions, including sharing the financial costs of military operations. Questions of out-of-area responsibility are important in peacetime, both on a day-to-day basis and in times of crisis and war. Burden-sharing steps would not obviate a significant and perhaps disproportionate U.S. military role in major crises in critical regions, but this is a price the United States should be willing to pay.

## Obtain and Maintain Domestic Support for U.S. Leadership

Some might argue that, given the costs involved, the American people will not support a global leadership role for the United States. It can also be argued that the public might not support the level of defense expenditure required to pursue a global leadership strategy because domestic priorities are in competition for the same dollars. Public opinion polls indicate that Americans are focused on domestic concerns. Such a perception discouraged a serious debate on national security issues in the last presidential debate.

According to a recent poll, however, Americans support both U.S. involvement in world affairs (90 percent) and also want more attention to domestic issues (84 percent). A majority of Americans support peace "through strength."[9] Whether the public would in fact support a global leadership strategy as outlined here is not known. Such a role is indeed not without costs. The cost of sustaining U.S. leadership is, however, affordable. At present the burden imposed by U.S. defense efforts, approximately 4 percent of GNP, is lighter than at any time since before the Korean War. The burden will shrink further as the economy expands, and the costs of leadership can be kept at a sustainable level by avoiding overextension and by more effective burden sharing among the members of the zone of peace.

Moreover, a global leadership role serves the economic interests of the United States. For example, it can facilitate U.S. exports, as recently seen in U.S. contracts with Saudi Arabia for the sale of aircraft and the modernization of Saudi telecommunication systems. As discussed earlier, the costs of alternative approaches to U.S. global leadership can ultimately be higher. Rather than undermining domestic prosperity, such a role can in fact facilitate it. The economic benefits of U.S. leadership have not been focused on either analytically or in the statements made to the public.

Global leadership and building a more democratic and peaceful world should also appeal to American idealism, a defining American characteristic. For sustaining domestic political support, this appeal might well be as important as appeals to more selfish and material American interests. In fact, having such a lofty goal can be a spur to the kinds of social and educational reforms that are necessary, rather than being an alternative to them.

## Conclusion

As a nation, the United States is in a position of unprecedented military and political power and enjoys a unique leadership role in the world. Maintaining this position and precluding the rise of another global rival for the indefinite future is the best long-term objective for the United States. It is an opportunity the United States may never see again.

In the long run, this situation will not last if Americans turn inward or make the wrong choices. The question is whether the country will accept its responsibility—for reasons of self-interest and historical necessity—and meet the challenge of the new era with vision and resolve. The time has come for President Bill Clinton to make a compelling case for U.S. leadership and to seek to shape public attitudes. Without a vision, a strategy, and bipartisan support, he will fail to win public approval for U.S. global leadership, and his country will fail to seize this historic moment.

*This article is drawn from a larger RAND study, "From Containment to Global Leadership? America and the World After the Cold War." The author would like to thank Cheryl Benard, Abe Shulsky, Andrew Marshall, David Chu, Paul Davis, Brent Bradley, Kevin Lewis, Scooter Libby, Chuck Miller, Craig Moore, Chris Bowie, Dan Drezner, and Ken Watman for their comments on the earlier drafts.*

## Notes

1. Dick Cheney, *Defense Strategy for the 1990s: The Regional Defense Strategy* (Washington, D.C.: Department of Defense, 1993).

2. William J. Clinton, *A National Strategy of Engagement and Enlargement* (Washington, D.C.: The White House, July 1994).

3. Among the questions that would have to be addressed are: Would the defense of the United States include the defense of North America or the Americas generally? How far into the Atlantic and Pacific Oceans would the defensive perimeter extend? Would the United States need a robust anti-ballistic missile defense?

4. Henry Kissinger, *Diplomacy* (New York, N.Y.: Simon & Schuster, 1994), p. 809.

5. It is, however, an interesting question whether the governments of modern industrial democracies would be able to convince their populations to support preparations for (let alone, actually fight) major wars against each other on purely realpolitik terms, or whether ideological or nationalist motives would have to be adduced.

6. The concept of a "democratic zone of peace" was used in U.S. Defense Department documents in 1992. See Dick Cheney, *The Regional Defense Strategy* (Washington, D.C.: Department of Defense, January 1993). The concept was also used by Max Singer and Aaron Wildavsky in their 1993 book, *The Real World Order: Zones of Peace/Zones of Turmoil* (Chatham, N.J.: Chatham House Publishers, 1993).

7. *Economist*, October 1, 1994, p. 70. According to the *Economist*, if current trends hold by the year 2020 the Chinese economy might well be 40 percent larger than the U.S. economy.

8. Kevin Lewis, "The Discipline Gap and Other Reasons for Humility and Realism in Defense Planning," in Paul Davis, ed., *New Challenges for Defense Planning* (Santa Monica, Calif.: RAND, 1994), p. 103.

9. Times Mirror Center for People and the Press, *The People, the Press and Politics* (Washington, D.C., September 21, 1994), p. 37.

# Chapter 11

## ✱ ✱ ✱

## Bottom-Up
## Foreign Policy

Charles William Maynes

*Charles William Maynes provides a critique of the Bush and Clinton post-Cold War foreign policies. He then suggests an alternative that exhibits characteristics of a selective engagement strategy and a realist perspective. He defines four fundamental purposes of American foreign policy. The first is to defend the heartland from attack. He focuses on future threats from great powers such as China, Russia and India. He concludes that, "The principle challenge for the international system in the coming decades is the peaceful inclusion of rising states like China and India." The second is to create an environment in which U.S. democracy will thrive. Third is to improve the welfare of the American people followed by maintaining America's postwar role as "steward of the international system without incurring disproportionate costs." What are the key diplomatic, economic and military elements of his proposed alternative for each of his four purposes? To what extent do his proposals imply a blending of the realist and pluralist perspectives for assessing the evolving security environment?*

More than six years since the fall of the Berlin Wall, two administrations have tried and failed to construct a post-Cold War foreign policy that enjoys intellectual support among specialists and political acceptance within the country at large. Neither the "new world order" of the Bush administration nor the Clinton administration's doctrine of democratic and free market "enlargement" has endured as an organizing concept. As a result, both administrations have repeatedly been driven to a pattern of reactive diplomacy. Pronouncements have been made or actions have been taken on an ad hoc basis. The aim has been to deflect public pressure or protect the image of the president.

In the Bush administration this pattern was evident in the development of policy toward Russia. The collapse of communism in Eastern Europe offered

Charles William Maynes is the editor for *Foreign Policy*.

Reprinted with permission from *Foreign Policy*, 104, Fall 1996, pp. 35-53. Copyright © 1996 by the Carnegie Endowment for International Peace.

America the most plastic moment in international relations since 1917, but America was without an appropriate doctrine to help it respond to the new opportunity. As a result, the Bush administration seemed essentially a spectator to events in Moscow. That approach changed only when the Democtractic challenger, Bill Clinton, was poised to announce his own plan for responding to events in Russia. Suddenly, the White House organized an emergency press conference so the president could announce his plan—a few minutes before the Democratic challenger was to speak. The purpose appeared less to aid the new republics in the former communist states than to preempt the Democratic nominee.

There were other examples of reactive diplomacy in the Bush administration. Throughout 1992, it watched chaos develop in Somalia. Its assistant secretary for African affairs warned his superiors that without preventive diplomacy Somalia would blow apart within the year. He was ordered to stay out of the affair. At the United Nations, the Bush administration blocked all efforts to provide help, because it wanted to avoid paying the American share (31 per cent) of United Nations peacekeeping expenditures. Then media coverage of the trauma in Somalia became too heart-wrenching to bear; the administration abruptly reversed course and accepted sole responsibility for attempting to restore order in that country at a cost of more than $1 billion. Again, the absence of a post-Cold War vision left the United States without an appropriate policy guide.

The Clinton administration has followed a similar reactive pattern. Events—and not doctrine—have driven diplomatic responses. Most of the key decisions have been made not in fulfillment of some carefully developed post—Cold War strategy but rather as last-minute efforts to head off criticism of the president. Lacking a clear Somalia strategy, for example, the Clinton team allowed the mission there to acquire a logic of its own. Soon disaster struck: 18 U.S. soldiers were killed in a firefight, and the administration had no compelling explanation for the deaths. The political storm at home forced the administration to withdraw from Somalia in humiliation.

In Haiti, months of fruitless diplomacy closed off all options except invasion if the president's credibility was to be salvaged. Only Jimmy Carter's last-minute intervention spared the administration the embarrassment of invading this hemisphere's poorest country.

In Bosnia, the United States assumed leadership to bring about peace only when the alternative became unpalatable: fulfillment of a pledge to help extract British and French peacekeepers from Bosnia, perhaps under combat conditions. As of mid-1996, the military side of the American-led NATO effort in Bosnia was proceeding well—ironically, only because the U.S.—led force was adopting a neutral stance toward the parties, a stance that the United States had earlier denounced the U.N. for favoring. And although the administration contends that

Dayton represents the first chapter in a comprehensive new vision of America's post—Cold War role in Europe, that seems unlikely. Even the administration must doubt that it could attract political support at home to take up comparable defense responsibilities elsewhere in ethnically troubled Central or Eastern Europe. Few expect to see American peacekeepers in Transylvania or Moldova, whether under NATO command or not. In this respect, the Dayton success must be seen as America's attempt to hold onto its old Cold War role in NATO rather than defining a new role for itself in Europe.

## Four Purposes of Foreign Policy

If both the "new world order" and the doctrine of "enlargement" have been found wanting, is there an alternative vision of foreign policy that the country might consider? How would it compare with the course we have been following?

An attempt to answer those questions must begin with an examination of the fundamental purposes of American foreign policy. They are four:

- to defend the heartland from attack,
- to conserve or create an environment in which U.S. democracy can thrive,
- to protect and, if possible, improve the welfare of the American people, and
- to maintain America's postwar role as steward of the internatonal system without incurring disproportionate costs.

How do we measure current policy against this template?

***Defending the Heartland***. Today the heartland faces no traditional military threat but rather the impact of outside influences against which military power is largely irrelevant—drugs, crime, terrorism, and economic competition. Valiant efforts made by some former Cold War strategists and Pentagon supporters to prove the relevance of the military for dealing with some or all of these issues are not convincing. Diplomats, spies, and police—and not the military—are the nation's first line of defense against these contemporary threats.

What about future threats? China is the power that over the long run appears to pose the most serious challenge. It has demographic mass, economic dynamism, critical geographic placement, and growing military might. It is the one great power still trapped in the mindset of the Cold War, maintaining a communist ideology that, while weak among the masses, justifies the elite's hold on power. China's economic modernization will transform it into the world's greatest export power, dwarfing even Japan's influence in the world economy.

There are historical reasons to be concerned about China's rise that have nothing to do with ideology. Every major country, including the United States, that arrived at a stage when it was able to project its military power internationally has done so, usually with unfortunate consequences for its neighbors. It was at such a point in their development that Britain, France, and the United States established colonial empires, both formal and informal, and Germany and Japan made bids for regional or world mastery. The Soviet Union at the apogee of its power promoted mischief worldwide. Will China also conform to this unsettling pattern?

Another reason to follow events in China carefully is that it is the only great power that does not appear to be exhausted demographically. Old men may declare wars, but young men and now women fight them. Today, all of the major states except China face serious demographic problems. Russia is in a demographic free fall, its birthrate plummeting. Western Europe, Japan, and the United States are witnessing a progressive aging of their populations as young people have fewer children and older people enjoy longer lives. The wealth of these societies is steadily being transferred to their older members, leaving less available for other activities, including international commitments. In 1995, for example, 45 per cent of China's population was under 25 compared with 36 per cent in the United States. Only 6 per cent of China's population was over 65, compared with 13 per cent in the United States, where, in 1995, Social Security and Medicare together consumed 40 per cent of noninterest outlays. By its very size, its demographic mass, and its growing wealth, China confronts an entirely different set of pressures.

India is another state that could pose special problems in the coming decades. Its surging population, economic potential, regional aspirations, and military might suggest a power that will increasingly exert its influence in the region. That is not necessarily a problem for the United States, but it may be for India's neighbors, some of which have been close friends of the United States.

Today no great power, actual or potential, is hostile to the United States, though U.S.-Chinese relations are increasingly strained. Nor is there any reason why relations with current or future great powers must inexorably develop in an antagonistic direction. But the rise of new powers like China and India poses a strategic challenge to the current international system. As these states become more powerful, they will seek their place in the sun, and unless they are accorded a role that is also in the interests of other major powers, conflict could develop. Regrettably, the record of the international system in accommodating new powers is terrible: Challengers like pre-World War II Germany and Japan invariably overreach, and established powers like the United States and Great Britain respond inadequately. The principal challenge for the international system in the coming decades is the peaceful inclusion of rising states like China and India.

A plausible criticism of current policy is the degree to which relations with the rising or excluded powers have deteriorated. The United States regularly and publicly calls for the integration of Russia and China into the international system, but there is no practical substance to its calls. No U.S. proposal has ever offered Russia early or realistic membership in a European organization that counts, and America's approach to China is basically to ask it to accept rules drawn up by others—as in the fields of trade and nonproliferation. It should not be a surprise that Beijing and Moscow find this approach unsatisfactory, even insulting. Of course, by their actions, officials in Moscow and Beijing have seriously complicated the process of integration. A strategic approach to U.S. foreign policy would require that American policymakers devote more time to developing international arrangements that offer Russia and China a place at the decision table without challenging the interests of other powers.

What about other current or future threats to the United States? U.S. officials have occasionally suggested that rogue states or anarchy are conceivable replacements for the Soviet menace as America's principal international concern. The rogue states are Cuba, Iran, Iraq, Libya, and North Korea. A review of the list suggests how insignificant that threat really is. All have basket-case economies. All are bordered by states possessing great military potential. All are diplomatically isolated. Such states are not threats, but problems. Even if they were to acquire weapons of mass destruction, these states could not pose, in the foreseeable future, an existential threat to the United States. They might over the course of several years acquire the power to strike back at the U.S. heartland in a limited way, but it will be at the price of their own extinction.

It is certainly a high priority for the West to retard the development of weapons of mass destruction within such states, but even that threat must be put in perspective. The leaders of these states are not suicidal. Saddam Hussein was armed with chemical weapons during the Persian Gulf war. He did not use them, because he feared an American response that might doom his regime. We can expect similar restraint from the others. These states are not crazy. They are cornered, and American should remember that each one of them has suffered from U.S. efforts to overthrow or attack them. Their cornered conditions may occasionally render them dangerous. Regrettably, American policy continues to confirm their paranoia and make them even more dangerous. For example, a "covert" American program to overthrow the Iranian government was proposed by Congress and discussed publicly. With the possible exception of Iraq, each of the rogue states is ripe for integration with the outside world.

America should be working to expose these states to greater outside influence and pressure. In the current international climate, rogue regimes, lacking plausible great-power patrons, are trapped in a political cul-de-sac from which they can emerge only by taking steps of accommodation toward international norms. Political analyst Jude Wanniski has compared such states to the stranded Japanese soldiers after World War II who struggled on in the jungles of Asia for years after Tokyo's defeat. Finally, they were lured to surrender. Sooner or later, the rogue states—the stranded survivors of the Cold War—must also surrender. That is, they must join the international system from which they are now shunned. American policy should aim to make that transition as peaceful as possible. Current policy perversely works to make the transition extremely difficult.

Is anarchy a strategic threat? The collapse of several states in Africa and the unrest in the former Soviet Union have caused some to embrace anarchy as the new strategic threat. Senior officials in both the Bush and Clinton administrations have suggested that chaos could replace Moscow as the "enemy." Certainly, it is possible to imagine scenarios where anarchy could pose a danger to American security. If Russian society collapsed and various groups seized parts of the nuclear weapons stock, perhaps to sell to the highest bidder, or if China failed to pass through its coming leadership change without a crippling civil war, the foundations of the current international system might totter. For the moment, however, the main pillars of the international system are remarkably stable.

To be seriously threatened, the international system must be challenged by one of the great powers in a bid for hegemony, or the collapse of a great state must set off a bit for advantage among the remaining powers. The only power with the military capability today to make a bid for world hegemony is the United States; yet it has no such aspirations and is entering a period of financial stringency. What happens in Liberia or even Bosnia cannot affect the underlying stability of the international system so long as the great powers refuse, as they have to date, to intervene in these crises for diplomatic advantage, which would renew the kind of struggle for supremacy that unsettled Europe prior to 1914. It is to the great credit of the Clinton administration that Russia was brought into the Bosnian settlement, thus minimizing this danger.

New crises may develop. If the United States were to support independence for Taiwan or the return of Kaliningrad to Germany, a new great-power confrontation could develop. China, which is the most isolated of the great powers, may also mismanage its entry on the world scene. But none of these possibilities is inevitable.

*Cultivating Democracy.* What can we say about the success of U.S. foreign policy in conserving or creating an environment in which American democracy can thrive? Here the signals are mixed. The United States accords the promotion of democracy pride of place in its rhetoric, but the key to this goal is the future of Russia—and it appears that two administrations have missed the opportunity to exert a positive influence on the development of Russian democracy. Instead of opening their markets and developing a new security structure in Europe that could include Russia and the other republics of the former Soviet Union, the United States and its allies offered aid under conditions that undermined the political stability of the recipient states—and in amounts always unequal to the tasks. When the radical democrats were in power in Moscow in 1992 and 1993, for example, the West found it difficult to come up with an aid package of $1 billion. By 1996, after the political situation had deteriorated significantly, the West encouraged the International Monetary Fund to provide aid in the amount of $10 billion. Lacking vision when the moment was plastic, the West responded in fear after the opportunity for true partnership had receded.

A possible alternative to a significant aid program would have been a decision to accept Russia as a full partner politically and economically the way that Germany and Japan were embraced after World War II. The United States would then have opened its markets to Russian goods and invited Russia (and China) to participate as equals in the tasks of global management. Instead, the West, led by the United States, demanded that Russia pass a number of severe political and economic tests before it could attain the status of full partner. During the early years of the Cold War, the United States was ready to rehabilitate the fascists in Germany and Japan. Later the United States was willing to make China, in the midst of the bloody Cultural Revolution, its strategic partner. Yet in the post-Cold War era it could not accept Russia, which no longer poses a threat to European security, as a political equal. History will record this bipartisan decision as a massive failure of American statecraft. American politicians, locked in Cold War attitudes, were terrified of paying the domestic cost of perceived sympathy toward Moscow long after the Warsaw Pact had disappeared and the Soviet Union had collapsed.

Yet the current international order is uniquely favorable to the United States and other major powers, including Russia and China. None of these powers is threatening the others and all have need for a period of external calm in order to attend to domestic deficiencies. Thus the common goal should be the defense of that benign order, not the preservation of Cold War alliances. The West should, therefore, even at this late date, search for ways to offer all major powers access to the globe's decision tables. The Group of Seven (G-7) has timidly reached out to Russia by inviting President Boris Yeltsin to a brief discussion at the end of their meetings. China is excluded. A forum is needed that accords these two powers, and others, an international voice equal to their importance. It could be either a reformed G-7 or a totally new forum.

Some in the administration have argued that China, even more than Russia, is not ready for such a role, because it is not democratic and violates international standards of human rights. On these points, Americans must develop a sense of perspective. During the Cold War, the United States was willing to offer trade and even military support to a China that was drenched in blood and whose citizens lived in terror and misery. The abandonment of the Cultural Revolution and the reforms that the current regime in China has undertaken have immensely improved the lives of China's 1.2 billion people. Indeed, no single step has done more to improve the human rights of more people than this set of reforms. Many countries in the international system can be crudely pressured to conform to international standards; because of its size and history, China cannot. It can be nudged. It can be encouraged. And through its own development, it can change. But the United States will thwart the cause of democracy and human rights in the world if it proceeds on the assumption that China is another state like Nicaragua that can be compelled rather than persuaded to accept international standards. The United States must judge China primarily in terms of its external policy and press it domestically to accept international standards of law and practice. In this regard, we should judge our policy toward the mainland by the same standard we once applied to Taiwan, whose external policy mattered more to us than its internal order, which was far from democratic but was improving.

*Advancing the Welfare of Americans*. What about the welfare of the American people? Is current policy, which might be described as continued Cold War military vigilance combined with unregulated markets, designed to improve that welfare? The economic difficulties of the bottom 50 per cent of the population do not allow an affirmative answer.

In fact, America's current course seems ill chosen to promote the general welfare unless some way can be found to achieve important changes in the country's internal policies. Both political parties have placed their bets on the invisible hand internationally and an increasingly unfettered capitalist system domestically. They have continued to open the American market to international competition while hamstringing organized labor and setting the country on a course that will steadily increase pressure on the American worker, particularly anyone without a graduate degree. There is growing evidence to suggest that this combination of policies is crushing those without exceptional skills.

The 1994 *Economic Report of the President*, for example, points out that between 1979 and 1990 all levels of the American male work force lost ground except for those with a graduate degree. Those with a high school diploma lost a shocking 21 per cent in real income. Those without a high school degree lost even more. (Those with a bachelor's degree lost 1 per cent.) According to the report, one important cause of this decline was the growing internationalization of the American economy: The open economy cows labor unions, which have become hesitant to press wage demands for fear that the owners will simply move operations abroad or at least find less costly foreign workers who can perform some of the same work overseas. Business executives have become fiercely antilabor; they know that in the new global economy they cannot grant wage increases to workers or they will invite a flood of more competitively priced imports. The restraint on wages leads to higher corporate profits and to growing income disparities. In 1995, the Organization for Economic Cooperation and Development published a study titled *Income Distribution in OECD Countries*. The results showed that the gap between rich and poor was greater in the United States than in *any* of the other 16 member states included in the study. Census studies indicate that, in the United States, only the top quintile of U.S. households has experienced increases in income since 1974.

The social tensions resulting from these wage trends are beginning to influence American politics. In the 1992 election, the candidacy of Ross Perot advanced a blend of America First sentiments and protectionism that might well have swept him into the While House had he not committed a few avoidable gaffes. In the 1996 campaign, Pat Buchanan picked up and darkened the same rhetoric and, though he lost the nomination, profoundly changed the country's political agenda. American society is increasingly separating into two classes—those hammered by the globalized economy and those profiting from it. The resultant resentments threaten to polarize political debate and to deepen anger in the country. When a country has part of its urban population constantly threatening to riot and part of its rural population undergoing combat training through a spreading militia movement, it is fair to say that social conditions in that country are troubled.

***Stewarding the International System.*** What about American stewardship of the international system? Here, paradoxically, the United States suffers from a bipartisan consensus that overextends the country militarily and underextends it diplomatically. With no serious threat, the United States in fiscal year 1995 maintained a defense budget of $263.8 billion. In real terms, this figure is greater than that of 1980, after the late Carter buildup and while the Cold War raged. The United States acts as if the Warsaw Pact still existed and the Soviet Union were still in place. The U.S. military effort remains vastly larger than that of any other major power. The United States has accepted responsibility for the ground defense of South Korea, if necessary, although North Korea is one-tenth as rich as only one-half as populous as its neighbor to the south. America is the lone gendarme of the Persian Gulf, even though the oil flows primarily to Europe and Japan. Meanwhile, the United States, the U.N.'s largest deadbeat, is slashing its contributions to international development organizations, is forced to shut off the air conditioning in some of its tropical embassies in order to save money, and is engaged in a severe downsizing of its foreign policy establishment owing to budget pressures.

In late 1995, Secretary of State Warren Christopher contended that 1995 was one of the best years in American diplomacy since the end of the Cold War. He had in mind the administration's registered gains—the Dayton accord, the ceasefire in Northern Ireland, and the successful presidential election in Haiti. Yet the historical record of this administration and its Republican opposition will rest less on what happens in these areas, important as they are, than on

America's declining ability to serve as the responsible steward of the post-Cold War international system.

## An Emboldened Foreign Policy

If Americans were to abandon their bipartisan post-Cold War conceptual timidity, what might an alternative foreign policy look like? It could rest on the following elements:

• The United States could rhetorically abandon its hegemonic pretension (as the world's only superpower), which creates a subconscious barrier to greater efforts at cooperation with other major powers. It is psychologically satisfying for American politicians to speak constantly about the United States as the world's only remaining superpower, but the urgent goal of American foreign policy should be to find a balance between commitments, which are expanding in places like Bosnia, Eastern Europe, Haiti, and South Korea, and resources, which are shrinking. In Europe, this would mean that, following the Bosnia mission, the principal military goal of the United States would again be to prevent the rise of another hegemonic power on the continent. Washington would make it clear that the Dayton accord does not mean that the United States intends to become involved in internal European conflicts. The United States would contribute to the resolution of these conflicts primarily through diplomatic efforts to calm, cajole, and control the spread of ethnic conflict in Europe, but it would not attempt to police Europe internally. In Asia, the United States would progressively move away from its current posture as a land power. It would offer air and sea protection in support of its Asian allies, who have the resources and population to carry out their own land defense. (Some might object that this is a recipe for an arms race in Asia, since no one wants to see Japan again pose a major military threat to its neighbors. But what Asian states fear is Japan's ability to project military power, which requires a blue-water navy and a long-range air force. America can provide regional balance by remaining the preeminent air and naval power there.)

• The United States would center its foreign policy on the countries that determine the overall character of the international system—China, Japan, Russia, members of the European Union, and some of the emerging powers, such as India and Indonesia. Only states of this size and power can mount or prevent the kind of regional or global struggle that could jeopardize world peace. So long as such states are at peace, surface turmoil in the international system can continue without shaking its foundations. It is only when such states engage in the type of "great game" that was played before World War I or when some great power seeks a hegemonic role that regional or global peace is endangered. America's goal should be to work for a concert of powers, involving Russia and China at the decision table. The United States should be more patient with these states as they make their transitions to modernity. The United States need not drop its concerns about democracy and human rights, but it can apply the same standard to Russia and China that it applies to American allies or friends like Turkey or Egypt. Today, for example, Turkey, with a population of 63 million, has imprisoned more than twice as many journalists as China (20), with a population of 1.2 billion, yet one would not know this from official U.S. statements. Egypt's elections are less fair than those in Russia. This is not a call for the United States to hammer Turkey or Egypt, but for a single standard of judgment, one that reflects the new reality that China and Russia are no longer enemies.

• The United States would nudge Europe and Japan to assume larger military responsibilities, but it would do this in the context of renewed efforts to further reduce the levels of armaments in both regions. Despite the impressive reductions in conventional armaments that have taken place, there are still more tanks in Europe now than there were when Adolf Hitler launched his assault on the Soviet Union. Although it is inevitable that Japan's military responsibilities will grow—it is already edging into U.N. peacekeeping—this new role need not be threatening to others, provided an effort can be made to establish balance among the major powers at the lowest possible level of forces. That is not possible without a strategic understanding with China, which will likewise be impossible without an effort to create a peacetime structure in the region that accords China a place of real influence.

• The United States would work for commitments to principles and multilateral structures that constrain imperialistic behavior and contain dangerous great-power rivalry. In their immediate neighborhood, great powers inevitably assume disproportionate responsibilities and influence. The task is to prevent this fact of life from justifying either imperialism or conflicts among the great powers as they perhaps attempt to act in disputed spheres of influence. The Nixon administration's much ridiculed attempt to negotiate an international code of conduct that would have disciplined U.S. and Soviet behavior in the Third World was in fact an initial step in this direction. It failed because international conditions were not yet ripe. Now they may be.

Is an effort to work for a concert of powers realistic? The German foreign policy commentator Josef Joffe has assumed that the nature of states cannot change and that, in the end, U.S. options in Europe (and presumably in Asia) will turn out to be, to use his shorthand, either Britain or Bismarck, i.e., either bloodless balancing à la Britain or a complicated security structure controlled by the preeminent international power—then Germany, now the United States.[1] In fact, the current U.S. proposals for NATO expansion seem to be following the path of Bismarck: They call for expansion to the east with some kind of unspecified special relationship with Russia. Bismarck's system of simultaneous alliances with Austria and Russia was another effort to square the circle. It required a political genius to manage, and it broke down soon after Bismarck retired, paving the way for World War I. An unexamined question is whether any of the powers today posses the quality of political leadership necessary to manage the kind of Bismarckian structure that American leaders, both Republican and Democratic, are willy-nilly pursuing.

In fact, Joffe is wrong in his assumption—that the behavior of states can never change. Were he right, Soviet troops would have crushed the East Germans when they tore down the Berlin Wall. Or Germany would be as great a threat today as it was in 1914. Japan would not be a civilian power. And the goal of most states would again be to seize territory rather than to acquire wealth through internal development.

• The United States would work with the major European powers to create a pan-European security organization to carry out the kinds of functions now being performed by the U.N. and NATO in the former Yugoslavia. NATO's stated purpose would be reformulated to be one of providing stability to Europe, in particular to reassure Germany that it is protected against nuclear blackmail. If NATO is to be expanded, it must develop formal mechanisms to ensure that non-member states like Russia and Ukraine will have a policy voice equal to NATO members on European security issues that do not involve the protection of member states against physical attack. Under such arrangements, for example, it would be understood that NATO alone could not make a decision to send a peacekeeping force to a European state that was not a member. It would be understood that NATO would move military assets into a new member's territory only in response to an explicit threat from a nonmember. Finally, any effort toward NATO expansion should be in the context of further efforts to reduce the still excessive conventional armaments of Europe. Current plans for NATO expansion call for massive increases in the defense expenditures of the new member states. Needed, instead, is an effort to reduce further the conventional burden they are carrying.

• The United States would announce as a long-term policy objective the progressive denuclearization of the world, because the spread of nuclear weapons is the greatest threat to America's current position of almost total security. It would open talks with the other nuclear powers for the creation of a minimum deterrent of a few hundred weapons for each state. Because other states will not indefinitely tolerate a privileged position for the nuclear states, it would begin a study on the long-run—in all likelihood *very* long-run—steps required to rid the world of nuclear weapons. To begin the process of delegitimizing nuclear weapons and in recognition of the fact that Russia no longer enjoys conventional superiority in Europe, it would announce a no-first-use doctrine for weapons of mass destruction. The administration's reluctance to address the relevance of Cold War nuclear strategy to America's current international challenges is an example of the conceptual timidity of the American foreign policy elite in both parties. As Fred Iklé, former under secretary of defense for policy in the Reagan administration, has pointed out, no state has a greater interest in delegitimizing the use of nuclear weapons than the United States in the post-Cold War era, for the most serious threat to U.S. security is the possibility that some smaller power will break the taboo against the use of nuclear weapons and expose the United States to attack. Iklé therefore urges that the United States press for a consensus among the nuclear powers in favor of a no-first-use doctrine, except in response to an attack by another weapon of mass destruction.

One step that would stimulate debate on this subject would be a more honest discussion of the dangers of America's current nuclear policy. In his call for a no-first-use consensus, Iklé notes, for example, that during the Cold War there were "several accidents and mistakes that could have sparked a large-scale nuclear war," but those "horrid details are still largely shrouded in secrecy."[2] Congress should press the administration to release these "horrid details" so that we can finally have a frank debate about the risks of our current posture.

• America would contribute more to fostering the development of international institutions. If America's goal is to create a system that reduces the current propensity of others to look to it to assume a disproportionate burden, then the United States must reverse its current policy of paring back contributions to international institutions and adopt the more realistic policy of giving them the resources needed to accomplish the new tasks they are being asked to carry out. The past four years have demonstrated both that the permanent members of the Security Council are not willing to shoulder this responsibility at the global level and that, if only because of media attention, they also cannot adopt an official position of indifference. The United States should press for the strengthening of regional organizations in Africa, Europe, and Latin America so that they can respond to the Bosnias and Rwandas of the world at the regional level. In this regard, the United States would favor the earmarking of national units for peacekeeping operations at either the global or the regional level. The U.S. goal would be to create greater respect at all levels of the international system for international law and processes. Finally, the United States would support efforts to identify new sources of revenue for the international system, because the current system of financing the U.N. and other international activities is no longer reliable. Any new source of income must still be subject to strict control by the member states. There can be no question of granting international bureaucrats control of the new funding sources, but it is also true that traditional means of funding international activities are proving inadequate.

• An alternative foreign policy would also involve a strategy to improve the welfare of the average American. The main crisis the United States faces today is internal, not external, but that reality does not mean that America can turn its back on the world. The solution to America's internal crisis must be a combination of internal reform and external engagement. America cannot turn its back on foreign markets, because, overall, jobs directly related to exports generate wages nearly one-fifth higher than jobs that are domestically based. Export-related jobs are also the fastest growing sector of our economy.

Nevertheless, the country cannot continue on the current course, which involves growing income disparities, without adverse effects on the social fabric. Some theorists believe that reversing these internal trends is almost impossible. Economist James Heckman of the University of Chicago has developed complicated estimates[3] that, when extrapolated, suggest that a national training program sweeping enough to return the earnings differential between skilled and unskilled workers to the level of 1979 would cost roughly $170 billion a year. That appears to be an impossible goal. It would be impossible even if training were the only answer, but a multipart program is needed. America's goal need not be a restoration of 1979 levels but a reversal of current trends and a series of steps that can rebuild labor's place in American life, as much for social as economic reasons.

If the United States were at war, it would try to use the talents of every young man and woman in the country. They would be inducted and educated to carry out the tasks required for national survival. In the global economy, the national goal must also be "not a talent wasted." This approach should be viewed as a requirement for national survival as a leading civilian power. The United States should make the long-overdue post-Cold War cuts in its military budget and channel most of the money into a national training program, perhaps run by American industry, which may understand better than the government the skills that must be promoted. The goal would be to equip American workers to compete in the twenty-first century economy.

But there must also be an effort to strengthen labor, and the president's economic advisers have identified the reason for this reality: Industries with a strong labor movement have a more equitable wage structure than those without such a movement. Consequently, unless we can find other ways to reduce the income disparities that are developing, it is in everyone's political interest to see a revival of the American labor movement. Senator Jesse Helms (R-North Carolina), chairman of the Senate Foreign Relations Committee, recently stated his belief that the age of unions is over and that the United States should therefore get out of the International Labor Organization, a U.N. agency that brings labor, business, and government together. No one of significance in either party denounced this statement. This kind of bashing of American labor must stop. The stability of the country may well depend on a revival of American unionism.

Great powers can fall from mistakes at home just as easily as from setbacks abroad. The international positions of Britain and Russia declined more because of internal policy failures than foreign policy mistakes. The dominance that America has enjoyed since 1945 has rested fundamentally on its economic system, which has delivered a steadily improving standard of living for a majority of its citizens. That sense of progress created confidence among the American people and tolerance for their leaders' international ambitions. Thus empowered, those leaders were able to accomplish remarkable policy feats. Restoring that faith in the American system and its ability to deliver for every citizen is now the highest priority of American statecraft, but the path of reform must proceed in a way that does not close America off from the world. Such an approach is possible, but only if both parties abandon the Cold War blinders that still block real consideration of alternative policies.

---

## Notes

1. See Josef Joffe, "'Bismarck' or 'Britain'? Toward an American Grand Strategy after Bipolarity," *International Security* 19 (Spring 1995): 94-117.

2. Fred Charles Iklé "The Second Coming of the Nuclear Age," *Foreign Affairs* 75 (January/February 1996): pp. 119-128.

3. See James J. Heckman, "Is job training oversold?" *The Public Interest* 115 (Spring 1994): 91-115.

# Chapter 12

\* \* \*

# A New Concept of
# Cooperative Security

Ashton B. Carter, William J. Perry
and John D. Steinbruner

*A cooperative security strategy focuses on collective actions with other nations to promote peace and prevent war. Consequently, multilateralism is central to cooperative security. So is the need for international institutions like the United Nations. In this article, Ashton B. Carter, William J. Perry, and John D. Steinbruner develop their concept of cooperative security. The central purpose is to prevent war "primarily by preventing the means for successful aggression from being assembled." They point out that, "Cooperative security differs from the traditional idea of collective security as preventive medicine differs from acute care. Cooperative security is designed to ensure that organized aggression cannot start on any large scale. Collective security, however, is an arrangement for deterring aggression through counterthreat and defeating it if it occurs." How would they attempt to limit the means of aggression? Is it possible to reconcile the concept of defensive forces with the need for an international power projection capability if aggression takes place? What are the force planning implications of their concept for the U.S. military?*

## The Concept of Cooperative Security

The central purpose of cooperative security arrangements is to prevent war and to do so primarily by preventing the means for successful aggression from being assembled, thus also obviating the need for states so threatened to

Ashton B. Carter, a Harvard professor, was formerly Director of the Center for Science and International Affairs at Harvard University and Assistant Secretary of Defense for International Security Policy. William J. Perry is a former Secretary of Defense who has written widely about national security matters. John D. Steinbruner is a noted expert and author on national security affairs at the Brookings Institute.

make their own counterpreparations. Cooperative security thus displaces the centerpiece of security planning from preparing to counter threats to preventing such threats from arising—from deterring aggression to making preparation for it more difficult. In the process, the potential destructiveness of military conflict—especially the use of weapons of mass destruction—is also reduced. Cooperative security differs from the traditional idea of collective security as preventive medicine differs from acute care. Cooperative security is designed to ensure that organized aggression cannot start on any large scale. Collective security, however, is an arrangement for deterring aggression through counterthreat and defeating it if it occurs.

Clearly the one idea does not preclude the other and both are, in fact, mutually reinforcing. A fully developed cooperative security framework would include provisions for collective security as a residual guarantee to its members. Systematic prevention of dangerous or aggressive military postures would make these residual guarantees easier to convey because they would be less likely to be required and, in the event, easier to underwrite. The cooperative security idea assumes that war is not inevitable, as disease and death are, and that commitment to prevention can aspire to be indefinitely effective.

To meet this aspiration, it is presumed that cooperation would ideally be comprehensive, including all important features of military capability as well as all major military establishments. The arrangement would restrain the ground forces and tactical air assets that provide the firepower for offensive operations. It would less stringently limit systems that are more or less unambiguously defensive and that can only be used to resist offensive intrusion on national territory. It would restrict nuclear weapons deployments to background deterrent functions only, ensure high standards of safety for the security and control of these weapons, and constrain further innovation and deployment of nuclear weapons to existing types and to existing nuclear weapons states. It would eliminate all other weapons of mass destruction. It would provide transparency so that all military establishments are informed of the military preparations of others and significant violations of the arrangement cannot be concealed. It would have enforceable sanctions and positive incentives to induce compliance and to halt attempted violations. The resulting limits on equipping and operating military forces would be consensual and universally shared.

Since they are to be established by consent rather than imposed by threat of force, cooperative security arrangements must be based on premises that can be widely accepted as legitimate. Such arrangements should also be inclusive in the sense that all countries are eligible to belong to them as long as they conform to its rules. Indeed the spirit of cooperative security is to ensure that all countries do belong and do conform. This requires incentives to induce voluntary compliance and also careful construction of the rules to be sure they can be reasonably judged to be equitable from a universal perspective.

Such a cooperative security order need not take the form of a single, all-encompassing legal regime or arms control agreement, but would probably begin with a set of overlapping, mutually reinforcing arrangements derived from agreements already in force. In fact, a look at the rich fabric of constraints that have grown up in more or less unconnected fashion indicates that ingredients of cooperative security are not hard to find on the international landscape. These range from limits on military operations, such as various confidence and security building measures (CSBMs) in Europe and the Middle East and agreements covering accidents, hotlines, and crisis centers between the superpowers, to limits on force size and weapons types—for example, START, CFE, and INF agreements and the nuclear, biological, and chemical weapons nonproliferation regimes. They extend to cooperative verification and transparency measures, such as the data exchanges and on-site inspections required by arms control agreements, the U.N. Permanent Five arms sale registry, and the new Open Skies agreement. They are embodied in formal agreements like START and CFE and in informal regimes like COCOM and the London and Australia groups. And they are embodied in tacit but firmly established norms of international behavior, such as those condemning use of weapons of mass destruction or changing of borders by force.

Military establishments around the world already are entangled in a large web of internationally sanctioned restraints on how they equip themselves and operate in peacetime. Cooperative security means making the effort to thicken and unify this web. Spinning the web must become a more conscious, central objective of international security policy. Many of the existing restraints grew up in the cold war. The end of the cold war is not an occasion to abandon the spinning of this web, but an opportunity to make the web more comprehensive. Though the rules embodied in the web will require adaptation to the peculiar security dilemmas of different regions, all regions should be encompassed by it.

Thus, cooperative security is, and probably will remain, an aspiration that will be only incompletely fulfilled. It is not a description of the world system, a prediction about the future, or a theory of international relations. But aspirations give coherence to security policy. They define what is desirable and partly, if incompletely, achievable. Organizing principles like deterrence, nuclear stability, and containment embodied the aspirations of the cold war, and they were invaluable in guiding thought and action. Cooperative security is the corresponding principle for international security in the post-cold war era.

For the United States, Russia, and the European powers previously locked in military confrontation, cooperative security is the right principle with which to guide their disengagement and the massive demobilization of their military establishments and industries. Cooperative security also offers a new and shared framework for the major powers to influence regional conflict and stem proliferation. For many other states long engaged in regional confrontation, cooperative security provides a new framework for the international community to provide reassurance and stability, replacing the rigid East-West alignments of the past and preempting reliance on a superpower-led collective security that many smaller countries fear and distrust. And for new nations born from the breakup of the USSR, for newly powerful nations like Japan and Germany seeking a security identity, and for emerging regional powers, cooperative security defines a responsible path of self-expression.

It would be easy to gain consensus that an international security arrangement characterized by these various elements of cooperation would be a superior form of international order. With immediate military threats reduced and their development made more controllable, the traditional objectives of deterring war and protecting national territory could be accomplished with substantially smaller forces at a far lower cost. Moreover, direct cooperation would allow more legitimate international influence on the looming restructuring of military establishments in the former blocs of East and West, as well as on the intensifying competition between economic and military investment in the developing world. Prevailing judgment will be highly skeptical, however, on the achievability of such a comprehensive form of cooperative security. It is widely believed, with ample historical support, that sovereign nations cannot be made to conform to cooperative standards.

Like containment and deterrence, therefore, the usefulness of the cooperative security principle depends on establishing its limits. Cooperative security does not aspire to create an international government, to eliminate all weapons, to prevent all forms of violence, to resolve all conflicts, or to harmonize all political values. The focus is on preventing accumulation of the means for serious, deliberate, organized aggression—that is, the seizing of territory by force or the destruction of vital assets by remote bombardment. Focused on restraining the organized preparations of established militaries, cooperative security does not address itself directly to substate violence, which is a principal source of chronic conflict and human misery in the world. But cooperative security provides a framework—indeed, a necessary framework—for the international community to organize responses to civil violence.

## Ingredients of a Cooperative Order

An international arrangement incorporating the concept of cooperative security and accepting the consequent constraints must begin with the central principle that the only legitimate purpose of national military forces is the defense of national territory or the participation in multinational forces that enforce U.N. sanctions or maintain peace. That principle is consistent with the declared military doctrines of the major military establishments and is now believed consistent with their real expectations as well. Since it requires that any effort to change borders by force be disavowed, there are political difficulties with it in some parts of the world, particularly in the Middle East. Nonetheless, it is accepted broadly enough and seriously enough to be the most promising foundation for international consensus.

Full adoption of this principle would lead immediately to important conclusions for cooperative design of military forces. National ground forces would be structured for defense of national territory and their territory-taking capabilities would be minimized. National capabilities for deep strike at rear and homeland targets inside the territory of others by missile or long-range aircraft would be constrained. Some of the ground and air forces that are in excess of national requirements could be configured for use in a multinational military force that could enforce U.N. sanctions when necessary. As an egregious form of offensive capability, nuclear weapons would be relegated to a background deterrent role only and their spread stemmed. Chemical and biological weapons would be banned entirely. Mutual restraint would be verified and reassurances given among cooperating parties through extensive transparency in force deployment and operations and in production, sale, and purchase of weapons. . . .

## Defensive Configuration of Conventional Forces

If defense of national territory is the sole purpose of nationally controlled military forces, then they should be so configured that they cannot be readily dislodged from their home territory but also cannot effectively attack anyone else's. That implication provides a natural standard for regulating the allowed size and peacetime operations of conventional forces, but it also presents immediate practical difficulties. The distinction between offensive and defensive capability cannot be clearly drawn in physical terms. Nearly all weapons can support offensive or defensive purposes depending on how they are utilized. Overall defensive and offensive force configurations are not discrete categories but a continuous spectrum, and the determination of where any given military deployment might fall on that spectrum involves judgments about firepower, weapons mix, operational doctrine, training history, and underlying intention. Such judgements cannot be reduced to a formula that would withstand analytic dispute and political suspicion.

Moreover, the scope and the apparent incentive for dispute over such limits are substantial. In order to align the existing military establishments with a defensive standard, it appears that prevailing operational doctrines would have to be reversed or at least severely contained. Although the major military establishments assertively and sincerely declare their defensive intentions, over recent decades their technological development and operational planning have come to emphasize rapidly executed deep interdiction missions against an opponent's organizational structure rather than its frontline firepower. These doctrines, which are believed to be dictated by the technical imperatives of modern warfare, invariably rely on surprise and strongly encourage preemption. They have the politically appealing effect of displacing much of the destruction caused by one's own forces onto the opponent's territory and the emotionally appealing effect of justifying strong initiative and bold military leadership. And they have been demonstrated to be effective, most notably in the recent Persian Gulf War. Effective implementation of the principle of defensive configuration contests this tradition and demands revisions that are not incremental in character. A revolution in military practice seems to be required.

To compound this difficulty, the revolution also seems particularly difficult to justify for two of the leading cases. The U.S. military establishment, which currently possesses the most advanced capacity for global power projection, experiences no contiguous military threat to its home territory. There is no need for large military forces in the continental United States, and most of their value would be forfeited if they could not be projected to geographically remote situations. Israeli military forces, which have superior power projection capabilities in the most turbulent region of the world, are driven by a different calculus to a similar operational commitment. The military posture of the Israelis is designed to defend a small amount of territory against a number of contiguous states that are perceived to be intensely hostile and that in the aggregate outnumber them. Unwilling to risk any penetration of their limited space, Israeli military forces have developed a doctrine of rapid mobilization and preemptive offense that is deeply ingrained and would be very difficult to redirect.

If the most capable military establishments appear at the outset to be so intractable, then even those countries whose security requirements are most compatible with a defensive configuration of forces—notably Russia and China—might be reluctant to accept a defensive configuration as an international standard. Fortunately, however, a practical arrangement can achieve the essential purposes of defensive configuration without indisputably exact measurement or a radical reversal of prevailing operational doctrine. The situation is less intractable than it seems at first.

There is a major advantage in the fact that seizing territory and establishing political control over it requires large ground force movements. With advanced reconnaissance methods, preparations for ground assaults are extremely difficult to conceal, and cooperative rules could readily make tactical surprise impossible. And tactical air operations, which now provide the decisive elements of a successful preemptive offensive, are dependent on coordinated air traffic control. Internationalizing the function of military air traffic control offers a practical means of imposing a meaningful buffer between normal peacetime activity and the preemptive air operations that would initiate an aggressive war.

The key to such international control would be the creation of an international surveillance system that maintained a current "order of battle" of military aircraft on a worldwide basis. Such a surveillance system, to be effective, would have to consist of continuous, routine inputs from three and possibly four generic subsystems: the extensive system of ground-based radars in the international civil air traffic control network, international inspectors established in the manner of CSCE, the satellite reconnaissance systems employed by several nations, most notably the United States, and possible new internationally developed and operated space reconnaissance systems. The creation of such an information system would require the solution of at least two problems: the distillation, transmission, and synthesis of data from the extensive air traffic control network to some central control station and the declassification and transmission to this control station of certain data from the nationally controlled satellite systems, so these data could be integrated with the air traffic control data.

By imposing controls on the location and movement of ground forces in peacetime and on tactical air operations, a practical cooperative arrangement can keep national military establishments disengaged from immediate confrontation and unable to make the extensive preparations necessary to mount a ground force offensive without triggering international reactions. However, even with such controls, it is possible to envision preemptive, surprise attacks of strike aircraft when the distance separating the opposing nations is as short as it is in the Mideast and when the strike aircraft are kept in shelters until shortly before the attack. Therefore the control mechanism must include the threat of sanctions, which, as a last resort, would entail an internationally organized air attack that could very credibly promise to disrupt the intricate coordination required to sustain a successful ground offensive. That strategy of control concentrates restrictions on the most vulnerable part of an offensive operation—ground force movements—and seeks to appropriate the most capable part—tactical air operations—to defend the cooperative arrangement against any major challenge. The strategy also implies the availability of the U.S. reconnaissance strike complex capability to the international forces executing the military sanctions.

A successful ground offensive normally requires that a significant firepower advantage be brought to bear at the point of attack in order to dislodge the defending force. In order to seize territory, an offensive force has to move and thereby expose itself more than the defending force that can operate from concealed and protected positions. That usually results in higher attrition rates for the offensive force in competitively contested battles. A firepower advantage is necessary to offset the higher expected rate of attrition and to make the offensive succeed. Cooperative control provisions covering ground forces should therefore seek to equalize available firepower and to prevent unbalanced concentration at any point of potential attack.

Since sovereign countries have substantially different amounts of territory to defend, different-sized populations, and different military traditions, exact equality on each frontier is not a feasible aspiration. It is possible to imagine, however, common standards for the density of forces (a standard military unit for a given territorial perimeter to be defended); concentration (the force allowed to be assembled at any given location); movement (the force allowed to be moved from one location to another in a given time); and transparency (basic information about force size, location, movement, and rates of investment provided to the international community). If international rules were established in these terms, the major ground force establishments could be set in configurations that are reasonably accepted as defensive. The precise details would matter less than the fact that common rules were defined and enforced, and that they were accompanied by extensive transparency.

While a comprehensive set of military force restraints has never been established on a global basis, the precursor of such a global set of restraints on ground and air forces can be seen clearly in Europe. The CFE agreement imposes national ceilings on ground force equipment (tanks, armored personnel carriers, and artillery pieces) and tactical aircraft and helicopters. These ceilings, while not derived from a requirement to make all national borders defensible but rather to restrict the offensive potential of the former Eastern and Western alliances, nonetheless go a long way toward establishing the principle of defensive postures in Europe. The extensive CSBMs established by the CSCE in 1990, which restrict the peacetime movement and concentration of the armies limited by the CFE, also further constrain offensive potential. The Open Skies agreement, together with the inspections that are part of the CFE and the CSBMs, establishes a higher standard of transparency. Finally, negotiations are under way to provide integrated air traffic control over the whole of Europe.

Major ingredients of a cooperative security regime therefore already exist in Europe. This evolving regime provides all states with a reassuring cap on the threat from their neighbors. It furnishes an internationally shared rationale for the economically and socially disruptive process of rapid demobilization faced by all European governments. It establishes a cooperative benchmark for the size and structure of their military establishments for new states emerging from the former Soviet Union that are defining their security postures, as well as for old states realigning their postures to their post-cold war situation. It establishes a framework in which violators of the rules or the peace are sanctioned and—less directly but importantly—it establishes a habit of cooperative engagement among military establishments that makes collective security peacekeeping operations more likely to succeed when needed. Continuing to build this European web of restraint, and extending it to other regions, with suitable adjustment for their special needs, is a principal aim of cooperative security.

## Internationalized Response to Aggression

Most security relationships throughout the world would be decisively stabilized by common rules that restrict national military forces to a defensive configuration and even the difficult cases would become less dangerous. Nonetheless even the most exacting rules would have too much ambiguity to carry the full burden of international security. Clever exploitation of the common rules, variations in geography that make defense more difficult for some countries than others, and the possibility of a rogue nation secretly developing an offensive capability in violation of the rules would provide some scope for aggression. Therefore an integral part of any cooperative security regime must be the capability to organize multinational forces to defeat aggression should it occur. This capacity would provide a background deterrent effect as well as physical protection. The United Nations Security Council can authorize multinational military forces for this purpose; indeed, the U.N. is authorized to form its own military force. It is more immediately realistic, however, to focus on U.N. authorization of multinational forces to deal with major acts of aggression on an ad hoc basis.

In a cooperative security regime, the use of military force by the United Nations—or any nation—is a last resort, to be invoked only after political pressure and economic sanctions have failed. The threat of military force should be sufficient to obviate the need to use it if the right military and political conditions are met. The threat will be maximally effective when political conditions permit the military force to be a broadly based coalition.

This broad international support makes the U.N. threat of military action politically credible. The threat also will be militarily credible if the coalition military force is organized around the reconnaissance strike complex employed by the United States in Desert Storm. Organizing the force around conventional armored combined forces could lead to a long and bloody ground war, and an aggressor might believe that he could wear down the resolve of the coalition governments (as Saddam Hussein believed at the beginning of the Gulf War). Organizing the threat of military force around nuclear weapons would not be credible, particularly if the aggressor had some nuclear weapons of his own. Nuclear nations in a cooperative security regime must maintain a sufficient nuclear capability that no aggressor nation could ever see an advantage by initiating a nuclear attack; on the other hand, they should not regard their nuclear weapons as a deterrent to aggression with conventional weapons.

In any multinational military force organized around a reconnaissance strike complex, the United States military would have a special role to play. It would provide most of the airlift required to quickly transport coalition military forces to the theater; it would provide most of the tactical intelligence data required to support the precision strike weapons; and it would supply most of the stealth aircraft used to suppress enemy air defenses. On the other hand, coalition partners would participate on an equal basis in achieving air and naval superiority in the theater, and would play a dominant role in the ground forces of the coalition. In this view of cooperative security, the special military capability of the United States would be used to give coalition forces an advantage that not only insured a military victory, but one that could be achieved with minimal losses to coalition forces. Therefore it should provide maximum deterrent to any potential aggressor.

Precisely because of the great deterrent effect of this military capability, any potential aggressor would be seeking ways to defeat it. Therefore we should expect to see efforts to emulate it, efforts to finesse it, and efforts to counter it. This capability could indeed be emulated by a half dozen of the advanced industrial nations of the world, but at great expense and with a very visible effort. It is unlikely to be emulated by any of the regional powers that we presently consider to be potential aggressors.

A more likely strategy for a potential aggressor is to try to finesse this military capability by developing weapons of mass destruction, especially nuclear weapons. While this response would be essentially suicidal, an aggressor might convince itself that it could succeed in such a bluff—certainly the self-destructive actions of Iraq suggest that Saddam Hussein was basing much of his strategy on bluffs or gross misconceptions about the resolve of coalition nations. Therefore a cooperative security regime should place a very high priority on actions designed to prevent the proliferation of weapons of mass destruction, especially nuclear weapons. Another possible strategy for a potential aggressor is to develop countermeasures to the reconnaissance strike force, which can be done to some degree by many nations. This prospect suggests that the United States should dedicate a portion of its defense effort to appropriate counter-countermeasures.

More generally, the United States would require a major restructuring and downsizing of its defense forces under a cooperative security regime. Such restructuring would have three major objectives:

a. to effect a significant reduction in the size of U.S. ground and naval forces (with a concomitant reduction in the defense budget). The new ground and naval forces would be sized to deal with credible military threats to U.S. territory; to provide the cadre for reconstitution of U.S. forces if a new superpower military threat emerged (that is, if the cooperative security regime collapsed); and to provide whatever (minimal) ground and naval support the United States might be requested to provide to multinational military forces;

b. to maintain a capability to provide a core contribution to the strategic intelligence evaluations that assess the emergence of new threats to the cooperative security regime, as well as key inputs to the verification of treaties or U.N. sanctions (limits on weapon developments or force deployments, for example); and

c. to maintain a capability to provide key elements of the reconnaissance strike military forces that would be used in multinational military actions whenever diplomacy and economic sanctions proved to be insufficient.

Other nations belonging to the cooperative security regime would also restructure and downsize their defense forces. Their objectives in restructuring would be conceptually similar to the objectives of the United States, but these objectives would manifest themselves in different ways depending on their circumstances. Objective (a) would be the same for all members of the regime. For some of these nations, providing for their territorial defense would involve maintaining significant ground forces. Russia, Germany, France, China, and India, for example, would have the bulk of the ground forces, and would therefore be expected to make up the bulk of the ground forces needed in any multinational expeditionary force. Similarly, the United Kingdom, Italy, and Japan would place a greater emphasis on naval forces for their territorial defense and would therefore make the major contributions to the naval arm of a multinational force. Only a few nations besides the United States (Russia and the United Kingdom, for example) have developed and deployed global strategic intelligence assets that permit them to make a significant contribution to global threat evaluation and verification assessment (Objective (b)). These nations would be expected to make such a contribution to the appropriate international coalition. A handful of nations have military capabilities that would be of special importance to the reconnaissance strike force (Objective (c)). Russia has significant capability in airlift, sealift, and air superiority aircraft; France, Germany, and the United Kingdom have a significant capability in air superiority aircraft. Therefore these nations, along with the United States, would provide the reconnaissance strike elements of any multinational expeditionary force.

Thus, in the interest of maintaining the power projection capability needed when major military actions must be undertaken by the cooperative security regime, some nations will end up with national defense forces larger than needed for territorial defense. This asymmetry will likely cause two related political problems. Some nations will fear that the nations with the larger defense forces will apply their military forces to achieve national or hegemonic objectives. Others will fear that the nations with the larger forces will let this special military capability erode or be reluctant to use it, so that it will not be available when needed for multinational forces. Each of these fears has some historical justification; indeed, both could be realized at the same time. Thus a substantial challenge for a cooperative security regime would be to work out the political measures that minimize these risks. For example, the nations with the reconnaissance strike forces could establish dual command channels (analogous to those established in NATO for nuclear weapons) for these forces. Also, the U.N. could establish funding to assist in the maintenance of certain of these national forces. Finally, the nations with these special forces could agree not to use them in violation of the U.N. charter.

As difficult as it will be to meet these political challenges, the two logical alternatives are even less attractive. One alternative is for the United States, for example, to disband its airlift and reconnaissance strike forces, since arguably they are not needed for territorial defense. However, this would greatly weaken the ability of any multinational force to decisively defeat a military threat posed by an aggressor nation with sizable armored forces. The other alternative would be for the United States and other relevant nations to turn over these special forces to the U.N., giving the U.N. a large (several hundred thousand men) permanent military force. For a variety of reasons, such a move would probably be impractical to implement. In any event, the U.N. would probably be better served with a relatively small permanent military force, designed for peacekeeping duties, as proposed by the present secretary general. Peacekeeping U.N. forces would likely be called into action many times. The special expeditionary force would be assembled only on an ad hoc basis, and this would occur rarely if the cooperative security regime is effective. . . .

# Chapter 13

## ✶ ✶ ✶

## The Myth of
## Post-Cold War Chaos

### G. John Ikenberry

*Ikenberry argues that recent attempts to describe the new post-Cold War order have failed because "there is no such creature." He reminds us that toward the end of World War II the liberal powers agreed to manage security, trade, and other important matters cooperatively. At war's end, they started building an international structure designed to solve the internal problems of Western industrial capitalism. The world order they created has grown stronger and it has shaped the Germany and Japan of today. Now, most of the rest of the world wants to join. What four principles did the liberal powers pursue in their strategy to build Western solidarity and security? Is cooperative security what America has been embracing for decades after all? Should we simply seek "an agenda of reform and renewal" to protect over 50 years of investment in economic openness and joint governance?*

### The 1945 Order Lives On

A great deal of ink has been shed in recent years describing various versions of the post-Cold War order. These attempts have all failed, because there is no such creature. The world order created in the 1940s is still with us, and in many ways stronger than ever. The challenge for American foreign policy is not to imagine and build a new world order but to reclaim and renew an old one—an innovative and durable order that has been hugely successful and largely unheralded.

The end of the Cold War, the common wisdom holds, was a historical watershed. The collapse of communism brought the collapse of the order that took shape after World War II. While foreign policy theorists and officials scramble

G. John Ikenberry is Co-Director of the Lauder Institute of Management and International Studies and Associate Professor of Political Science at the University of Pennsylvania.

Reprinted by permission of *Foreign Affairs*, Vol. 75, no. 3, May/June 1996, pp. 79-91.

to design new grand strategies, the United States is rudderless on uncharted seas.

The common wisdom is wrong. What ended with the Cold War was bipolarity, the nuclear stalemate, and decades of containment of the Soviet Union—seemingly the most dramatic and consequential features of the postwar era. But the world order created in the middle to late 1940s endures, more extensive and in some respects more robust than during its Cold War years. Its basic principles, which deal with organization and relations among the Western liberal democracies, are alive and well.

These less celebrated, less heroic, but more fundamental principles and policies—the real international order—include the commitment to an open world economy and its multilateral management, and the stabilization of socioeconomic welfare. And the political vision behind the order was as important as the anticipated economic gains. The major industrial democracies took it upon themselves to "domesticate" their dealings through a dense web of multilateral institutions, intergovernmental relations, and joint management of the Western and world political economies. Security and stability in the West were seen as intrinsically tied to an array of institutions—the United Nations and its agencies and the General Agreement on Tariffs and Trade (GATT) only some among many—that bound the democracies together, constrained conflict, and facilitated political community. Embracing common liberal democratic norms and operating within interlocking multilateral institutions, the United States, Western Europe, and, later, Japan built an enduring postwar order.

The end of the Cold War has been so disorienting because it ended the containment order—40 years of policies and bureaucratic missions and an entire intellectual orientation. But the watershed of postwar order predated hostilities with the Soviet Union. The turning point was not a Cold War milestone such as the announcement of the Truman Doctrine in 1947 or the creation of the Atlantic alliance in 1948-49. It might have come as early as 1941, when Roosevelt and Churchill issued the Atlantic Charter declaring the liberal principles that were to guide the postwar settlement. The process became irreversible in 1944, when representatives at the Bretton Woods conference laid down the core principles and mechanisms of the postwar Western economic order and those at Dumbarton Oaks gave the political aspect of the vision concrete form in their proposals for a United Nations. The Cold War may have reinforced the liberal democratic order, by hastening the reintegration of Germany and Japan and bringing the United States much more directly into the management of the system. But it did not call it forth.

In world historical terms, the end of the Cold War is an overrated event. Former Secretary of State James A. Baker III observes in his 1995 memoir, *The Politics of Diplomacy*, "In three and a half years [from the late 1980s to the early 1990s] . . . the very nature of the international system as we know it was transformed." To be sure, large parts of the non-Western world are undergoing a tremendous and difficult transformation. A great human drama is playing itself out in the former communist states, and the future there hangs in the balance. But the system the United States led the way in creating after World War II has not collapsed; on the contrary, it remains the core of world order. The task today is not to discover or define some mythic new order but to reclaim the policies, commitments, and strategies of the old.

## A Tale of Two Doctrines

World War II produced two postwar settlements. One, a reaction to deteriorating relations with the Soviet Union, led to the containment order, which was based on the balance of power, nuclear deterrence, and political and ideological competition. The other, a reaction to the economic rivalry and political turmoil of the 1930s and the resulting world war, can be called the liberal democratic order. It culminated in a wide range of new institutions and relations among the Western industrial democracies, built around economic openness, political reciprocity, and multilateral management of an American-led liberal political system.

Distinct political visions and intellectual rationales animated the two settlements, and at key moments the American president gave voice to each. On March 12, 1947, President Truman delivered his celebrated speech before Congress announcing aid to Greece and Turkey, wrapping it in an American commitment to support the cause of freedom worldwide. The declaration of the Truman Doctrine was a founding moment of the containment order, rallying Americans to a new great struggle, this one against what was thought to be Soviet communism's quest for world domination. A "fateful hour" had struck, Truman said, and the people of the world "must choose between two alternate ways of life." If the United States failed to exercise leadership, he warned, "we may endanger the peace of the world."

It is often forgotten that six days before, Truman had delivered an equally sweeping speech at Baylor University. On this occasion he spoke of the lessons the world must learn from the disasters of the 1930s. "As each battle of the economic war of the Thirties was fought, the inevitable tragic result became more and more apparent," said Truman. "From the tariff policy of Hawley and Smoot, the world went on to Ottawa and the system of imperial preferences, from Ottawa to the kind of elaborate and detailed restrictions adopted by Nazi Germany." Truman reaffirmed America's commitment to "economic peace," which would involve tariff reductions and rules and institutions of trade and investment. When economic differences arose, he said, "the interests of all will be considered, and a fair and just solution will be found." Conflicts would be captured and tamed in a cage of multilateral rules, standards, safeguards, and procedures for dispute resolution. According to Truman, "This is the way of a civilized community."

But it was the containment order that impressed itself on the popular imagination. In celebrated American accounts of the early years after World War II, intrepid officials struggled to make sense of Soviet military power and geopolitical intentions. A few "wise men" fashioned a reasoned and coherent response to the global challenge of Soviet communism, and their containment strategy gave clarity and purpose to several decades of American foreign policy. Over those decades, sprawling bureaucratic and military organizations were built around containment. The bipolar division of the world, nuclear weapons of growing size and sophistication, the ongoing clash of two expansive ideologies—all these gave life to and reinforced the centrality of the containment order.

By comparison, the thinking behind the liberal democratic order was more diffuse. The liberal democratic agenda was less obviously a grand strategy designed to advance American security interests, and it was inevitably viewed during the Cold War as secondary, a preoccupation of economists and businessmen. The policies and institutions that supported free trade among the advanced industrial societies seemed the stuff of low politics. But the liberal democratic agenda was actually built on a robust yet sophisticated set of ideas about American security interests, the causes of war and depression, and a desirable postwar political order. Although containment overshadowed it, the postwar liberal democratic order was more deeply rooted in the American experience and an understanding of history, economics, and the sources of political stability.

The proper foundations of political order have preoccupied American thinkers from the nation's founding onward, and innovative institutions and practices were developed in response to independence, continental expansion, civil war, economic depression, and world war. The liberal ideal was held high: open and decentralized political institutions could limit and diffuse conflict while integrating diverse peoples and interests. Moreover, a stable and legitimate political order was assured by its grounding in the Constitution, which specified rights, guarantees, and an institutionalized political process. When American officials began to contemplate postwar order, they were drawing on a wellspring of ideas, experiments, and historical lessons and sifting these with an abiding liberal belief in the possibility of peaceful and mutually beneficial international relations.

The most basic conviction underlying the postwar liberal agenda was that the closed autarkic regions that had contributed to the worldwide depression and split the globe into competing blocs before the war must be broken up and replaced by an open, nondiscriminatory economic system. Peace and security, proponents had decided, were impossible in the face of exclusive economic regions. The challengers of liberal multilateralism, however, occupied almost every corner of the advanced industrial world. Germany and Japan were the most overtly hostile; both had pursued a dangerous path that combined authoritarian capitalism with military dictatorship and coercive regional autarky. But the British Commonwealth and its imperial preference system also challenged liberal multilateral order.

The hastily drafted Atlantic Charter was an American effort to ensure that Britain signed on to its liberal democratic war aims.[1] The joint statement of principles affirmed free trade, equal access to natural resources for all interested buyers, and international economic collaboration to advance labor standards, employment security, and social welfare. Roosevelt and Churchill declared before the world that they had learned the lessons of the interwar years—and those lessons were fundamentally about the proper organization of the Western political economy. America's enemies, its friends, and even America itself had to be reformed and integrated into the postwar economic system.

## The Liberal Manifesto

The postwar liberal democratic order was designed to solve the internal problems of Western industrial capitalism. It was not intended to fight Soviet communism, nor was it simply a plan to get American business back on its feet after the war by opening up the world to trade and investment. It was a strategy to build Western solidarity through economic openness and joint political governance. Four principles pursued in the 1940s gave shape to this order.

The most obvious principle was economic openness, which would ideally take the form of a system of nondiscriminatory trade and investment. As American strategic thinkers of the 1930s watched the world economy collapse and the German and Japanese blocs emerge, they pondered whether the United States could remain a great industrial power within the confines of the western hemisphere. What were the minimum geographical requirements for the country's economic and military viability? For all practical purposes they had their answer by the time the United states entered the war. An American hemispheric bloc would not be sufficient; the United States needed secure markets and supplies of raw materials in Asia and Europe. Experts in a Council on Foreign Relations study group reached a similar conclusion when considering the necessary size of the area on which the United States depended for economic vitality.

American thinking was that economic openness was an essential element of a stable and peaceful world political order. "Prosperous neighbors are the best neighbors," remarked Roosevelt administration Treasury official Harry Dexter White. But officials were convinced that American economic and security interests demanded it as well. Great liberal visionaries and hard-nosed geopolitical strategists could agree on the notion of open markets; it united American postwar planners and was the seminal idea informing the work of the Bretton

Woods conference on postwar economic cooperation. In his farewell remarks to the conference, Secretary of the Treasury Henry Morgenthau asserted that the agreements creating the International Monetary Fund and the World Bank marked the end of economic nationalism, by which he meant not that countries would give up pursuit of their national interest but that trade blocs and economic spheres of influence would no longer be their vehicles.

The second principle was joint management of the Western political-economic order. The leading industrial democratic states must not only lower barriers to trade and the movement of capital but must govern the system. This also was a lesson from the 1930s: institutions, rules, and active mutual management by governments were necessary to avoid unproductively competitive and conflictual economic practices. Americans believed such cooperation necessary in a world where national economies were increasingly at the mercy of developments abroad. The unwise or untoward policies of one country threatened contagion, undermining the stability of all. As Roosevelt said at the opening of Bretton Woods, "The economic health of every country is a proper matter of concern to all its neighbors, near and far."

The belief in cooperative economic management also drew inspiration from the government activism of Roosevelt's New Deal. The postwar Western system was organized at a high tide of optimism about the capability of experts, economic and technical knowledge, and government intervention. The rise of Keynesian economics in Europe in the 1930s had begun to encourage an activist role for the state in the economy and society. International economic governance was a natural and inevitable extension of the policies being tried in individual Western industrial societies.

A third principle of liberal democratic order held that the rules and institutions of the Western world economy must be organized to support domestic economic stability and social security. This new commitment was foreshadowed in the Atlantic Charter's call for postwar international collaboration to ensure employment stability and social welfare. It was a sign of the times that Churchill, a conservative Tory, could promise a historic expansion of the government's responsibility for the people's well-being. In their schemes for postwar economic order, both Britain and the United States sought a system that would aid and protect their nascent social and economic commitments. They wanted an open world economy, but one congenial to the emerging welfare state as well as business.

The discovery of a middle way between old political alternatives was a major innovation of the postwar Western economic order. British and American planners began their discussion in 1942 deadlocked, Britain's desire for full employment and economic stabilization after the war running up against the American desire for free trade. The breakthrough came in 1944 with the Bretton Woods agreements on monetary order, which secured a more or less open system of trade and payments while providing safeguards for domestic economic stability through the International Monetary Fund. The settlement was a synthesis that could attract a new coalition of conservative free traders and the liberal prophets of economic planning.

A final element of the liberal democratic system might be termed "constitutionalism"—meaning simply that the Western nations would make systematic efforts to anchor their joint commitments in principled and binding institutional mechanisms. In fact, this may be the order's most basic aspect, encompassing the other principles and policies and giving the whole its distinctive domestic character. Governments might ordinarily seek to keep their options open, cooperating with other states but retaining the possibility of disengagement. The United States and the other Western nations after the war did exactly the opposite. They built long-term economic, political, and security commitments that were difficult to retract, and locked in the relationships, to the extent that sovereign states can. Insofar as the participating governments attempted to construct a political order based on commonly embraced norms and principles along with institutional mechanisms for resolving conflicts and reaching specific agreements, they practiced constitutionalism.

Democracies are particularly capable of making constitutional commitments to each other. For self-regarding states to agree to pursue their interest within binding institutions, they must perceive in their partners a credible sense of commitment—an assurance that they will not exit at the least sign of disagreement. Because policymaking in democracies tends to be decentralized and open, the character of commitments can be more clearly determined and there are opportunities to lobby policymakers in the other democracies. Democracies do not just sign agreements; they create political processes that reduce uncertainty and build confidence in mutual commitments.

## A Constitution for the West

The constitutional political order was constructed in the West around economic, political, and security institutions. In the economic realm, the Bretton Woods accords were the first permanent international arrangements for cooperation between states. Rule and institutions were proposed to ensure a stable and expansionary world economy and an orderly exchange rate system. Many of the original agreements for a rule-based monetary order gave way to ad hoc arrangements based more on the American dollar, but the vision of jointly managed, multilateral order remained. The organization of postwar trade relations also had an uncertain start, but ultimately an elaborate system of rules and obligations was developed, with quasi-judicial procedures for adjudicating disputes. In effect, the Western governments created an array of transnational political arenas organized by function. The postwar years were filled with economic disputes, but they were largely contained within these arenas.

The constitutional vision informed the creation of the United Nations, which combined political, economic, and security aspirations. To be sure, the U.N. system preserved the sovereign rights of member states. Intent on avoiding the failures of the League of Nations, the architects of the new international body drafted a charter under which the great powers would retain their freedom of action. But despite its weak rules and obligations, the United Nations reflected American and European desires to insure against a relapse of American isolation, to establish principles and mechanisms of conflict resolution, and to mute conflicts between states within a semi-institutionalized political process.

Cold War security structures provided additional constitutional architecture. Lord Ismay's observation that NATO was created to keep the Russians out, the Germans down, and the Americans in encapsulates the alliance's importance in locking in long-term commitments and expectations. The American-Japanese security pact had a similar dual-containment character. These institutions not only served as alliances in the ordinary sense of organized efforts to balance external threats, but offered mechanisms and venues for building relations, conducting business, and regulating conflict. The recent French decision to rejoin NATO can be understood only in this light. If NATO were simply a balancing alliance, the organization would be in an advanced stage of decay. It is NATO's broader political function— binding the democracies together and reinforcing political community—that explains its remarkable durability.

The democratic character of the United States and its partners facilitated construction of these dense interstate connections. The decentralized and open character of domestic institutions encouraged political give-and-take across the advanced industrial world. Thus the Western liberal democratic order was not only defined by a set of institutions and agreements but made for a particular kind of politics—transnational, pluralistic, reciprocal, legitimate.

The constitutional features of the Western order have been especially important for Germany and Japan. Both countries were reintegrated into the advanced industrial world as semisovereign powers that had accepted unprecedented constitutional limits on their military capacity and independence. As such, they became unusually reliant on Western regional and multilateral economic and security institutions. The Western order in which they were embedded was integral to their stability and their very functioning. The Christian Democratic politician Walther Leisler Kiep argued in 1972 that "the German-American alliance . . . is not merely one aspect of modern German history, but a decisive element as a result of its preeminent place in our politics. In effect, it provides a second constitution for our country." Western economic and security institutions were and are for Germany and Japan a political bulwark that provides stability and transcends those institutions' more immediate purposes.

## What Endures

For those who thought cooperation among the advanced industrial democracies was driven primarily by Cold War threats, the last few years must appear puzzling. Relations between the major Western countries have not broken down. Germany has not rearmed, nor has Japan. What the Cold War focus misses is an appreciation of the other, less heralded, postwar American project—the building of a liberal order in the West. Archaeologists remove one stratum only to discover an older one beneath; the end of the Cold War allows us to see a deeper and more enduring layer of the postwar political order that was largely obscured by the more dramatic struggles between East and West.

Fifty years after its founding, the Western liberal democratic world is robust, and its principles and policies remain the core of world order. The challenges to liberal multilateralism both from within and from outside the West have mainly disappeared. Although regional experiments abound, they are fundamentally different from the autarkic blocs of the 1930s. The forces of business and financial integration are moving the globe inexorably toward a more tightly interconnected system that ignores regional as well as national borders. Recent proposals for an Atlantic free trade agreement and a Transatlantic Treaty, whatever their economic merits, reflect the trend toward increased integration across regions. The successful conclusion of the Uruguay Round of international trade talks in 1994 and the launching of the World Trade Organization on January 1, 1995, testify to the vigor of liberal multilateral principles.

Some  aspects of the vision of the 1940s have faded. The optimism about government activism and economic management that animated the New Deal and Keynesianism has been considerably tempered. Likewise, the rule-based, quasi-judicial functions of liberal multilateralism have eroded, particularly in monetary relations. Paradoxically, although the rules of cooperation have become less coherent, cooperation itself has increased. Formal rules governing the Western world economy have gradually been replaced by a convergence of thinking on economic policy. The consensus on the broad outlines of desirable domestic and international economic policies has both reflected and promoted increased economic growth and the incorporation of emerging economies into the system.

The problems the liberal democratic order confronts are mostly problems of success, foremost among them the need to integrate the newly developing and post-communist countries. Here one sees most clearly that the post-Cold War order is really a continuation and extension of the Western order forged during and after World War II. The difference is its increasingly global reach. The world has seen an explosion in the desire of countries and peoples to move toward democracy and capitalism. When the history of the late twentieth century is written, it will be the struggle for more open and democratic polities throughout the world that will mark the era, rather than the failure of communism.

Other challenges to the system are boiling up in its leading states. In its early years, rapid and widely shared economic growth buoyed the system, as working- and middle-class citizens across the advanced industrial world rode the crest of the boom. Today economic globalization is producing much greater inequality between the winners and the losers, the wealthy and the poor. How the subsequent dislocations, dashed expectations, and political grievances are dealt with—whether the benefits are shared and the system as a whole is seen as socially just—will affect the stability of the liberal world order more than regional conflict, however tragic, in places like the Balkans.

To be sure, the Cold War reinforced solidarity and a sense of common identity among the liberal democracies, so it would be a mistake to take these binding forces for granted now. Trade disputes, controversies over burden-sharing, and regional conflict will test the durability of the liberal order. Without a Cold War threat to unite their countries, leaders in the advanced democracies will have to work harder to manage the inevitable conflicts and fissures. An agenda of reform and renewal would be an intelligent move to protect 50 years of investment in stable and thriving relations. Policies, institutions, and political symbols can all be directed at reinforcing liberal order, just as they are in individual liberal polities. At the very least, Western leaders could spend much more time acknowledging and celebrating the political space they share.

It is fashionable to say that the United States after the Cold War faces its third try at forging a durable world order, at reinventing the basic rules of world politics, just as after both world wars. But this view is more rhetorically compelling than historically valid. The end of the Cold War was less the end of a world order than the collapse of the communist world into an expanding Western order. If that order is to be defended and strengthened, its historical roots and accomplishments must be reclaimed. The United States built and then managed the containment order for 40 years, but it also built and continues to enjoy the rewards of an older liberal democratic order. America is not adrift in uncharted seas. It is at the center of a world of its own making.

## Note

1. Churchill insisted that the charter not mandate the dismantling of the British Empire and its system of trade preferences, and only last-minute sidestepping of this controversial issue made agreement possible.

# Chapter 14

\* \* \*

# The Political Economy of National Defense

Mackubin Thomas Owens

*Mackubin Thomas Owens lays out the scope of political economy and its relationship to national security. He argues that economic power is an indispensable element of strategic planning and force planning because a nation's economy underpins its military power: a strong economy is better able to provide resources for defense than a weak one. He contends that how a state ensures the availability of the necessary means to support its strategic choices has two components: the best political-economic approach to achieving the twin goals of prosperity and national security—classical liberalism, modern liberalism, or neo-mercantilism; and the categories affecting how scarce resources are allocated for defense—the strategic element and the structural element. What questions must any economic system answer? What is "opportunity cost" and why is this concept important? What is government's proper role in providing a strong economy? What are the strengths and weaknesses of each of the three systems of political economy that Owens discusses?*

National security and economic prosperity are inextricably linked. To secure its existence in the international system, a state must make strategic choices in both peace and war. To implement a strategy, the state must have access to adequate economic resources. Ultimately, it is impossible to separate economic power and political power. Whatever enhances the commercial, financial, and industrial power of a state increases the military potential of that state.[1]

There is a reciprocal relationship between economic prosperity and military power. As Paul Kennedy observes, ". . . wealth is usually needed to underpin military power, and military power is usually needed to acquire and protect wealth."[2]

Regarding the former, a major constraint on the war-making potential of the European states until the late seventeenth century was the absence of effective capital mobilization. As Fernand Braudel wrote of sixteenth-century Europe,

---

Mackubin Thomas Owens is Professor of Strategy and Force Planning in the National Security Decision Making Department of the Naval War College and Editor-in-Chief of *Strategic Review*.

"The expense of war crippled states. . ."[3] War was financed by such inefficient and counterproductive means as heavy taxation, plunder, conquest and forced tribute. England was the first modern state to transcend the limitations imposed by such primitive methods of capital mobilization. It did so by means of what has come to be called the "financial revolution."[4]

This revolution was characterized by an alliance between governments and commercial interests, which permitted the former to borrow from the latter on a massive scale. "More than any other factor, superior fiscal organization allowed England to challenge and eventually eclipse Bourbon France in the struggle for European mastery."[5] Indeed, as Paul Kennedy has persuasively argued, Alfred Thayer Mahan was wrong to attribute England's dominance in the eighteenth and nineteenth centuries to sea power alone. The financial revolution enabled England to become a sea power in the first place.[6]

The dependence of military power on adequate resources seems clear. But the reverse is also true. Economic well-being and prosperity do not occur in a vacuum. As Thomas Hobbes observed, there is no production without security. Insofar as military forces provide security, they underwrite prosperity. This relationship is nicely summed up by Colin Gray:

> The post-1945 eventual prosperity of OECD members undoubtedly supported security regimes and arrangements of a kind strongly reinforcing of economic progress. But, the entire OECD experience, indeed the whole fabric of what used to be called Western economic life, has been underwritten by the military protection provided largely by the United States.[7]

Problems arise, of course, if security commitments outstrip available economic resources. Examining the "interaction between economics and strategy as each of the leading states in the international system strove to enhance its wealth and its power, to become (or to remain) rich and strong," Kennedy concludes that a mismatch between capabilities and commitments, a state of affairs he calls "imperial overstretch," has been a major factor in the decline of once great powers.[8]

It is possible to take advantage of such a mismatch between an adversary's economic power and military strategy. Some observers attribute the rapid collapse of the USSR in 1990 to a U.S. grand strategy that identified the weakness of communist economic organization as a strategic "center of gravity" upon which to focus. This strategy then exploited the economic mismatch between the U.S. and the Soviet Union: while the U.S. spent a maximum of 6.3 percent of a large and growing gross domestic product (GDP) on defense, the Soviets spent a considerably larger portion of a much smaller one on security.

That U.S. policy makers in the 1980s stressed the economic component of grand strategy to achieve precisely this outcome is suggested by a revealing passage from the 1987 *National Security Strategy of the United States*. According to this document, a major objective of U.S. strategy was "to force the Soviet Union to bear the brunt of its domestic economic shortcomings in order to discourage excessive Soviet military expenditures and global adventurism."[9]

The importance of the economic factor in strategic planning and force planning cannot be denied. How then does a state ensure that the necessary economic means are available to support its strategic choices? This question has two parts: (1) what approach best achieves the goal of prosperity: an economy expanding in "real" (non-inflationary) terms, characterized by a broad increase in a nation's standard of living; and (2) how does a nation allocate resources among competing national goals?

The starting point for examining these issues is to understand the pervasiveness of what economists call "scarcity:" they postulate that productive resources—those resources used to produce goods—are limited, and that therefore goods and services themselves are also limited. In the words of Lionel Robbins, "[Economics is] the science which studies human behavior as a relationship between ends and scarce means which have alternative uses."[10]

Scarcity affects all levels of human activity: individuals, families, firms and governments. Yet, human desires are virtually unlimited. The "goods" we desire outstrip our ability to produce them. For individuals and households, goods might be food, clothing, transportation and leisure time. For a firm, goods are productive resources. For government, goods are national defense and social programs. Ultimately, all of these goods are in competition. Not all things that people desire can be provided to all who desire them; therefore economic actors must make choices: they must give up some goods in order to have other goods. The highest valued alternative given up to obtain some other good is called "cost," more specifically "opportunity cost." Production is the central human response to scarcity. While human beings can never overcome scarcity, they can, through productive work, create wealth and thereby improve their lot in life. There are many ways to organize productive activity. These systems of "political economy"[11] represent a spectrum from total reliance on voluntary market exchanges to "command" type economies in which the state makes all economic decisions.

## Paths to Economic Prosperity: Systems of Political Economy

Any system of political economy must ultimately answer three questions: What goods will be produced? How will goods be produced? For whom will goods be produced? There are two predominant ways to organize economic activity in response to these three questions: a decentralized market mechanism; and a system of collective, public-sector decision-making.[12]

***The Market Approach.*** A market-oriented system of political economy corresponds to what Robert Gilpin calls "liberalism" (more properly, classical liberalism).[13] The market system is characterized by private ownership, voluntary contracts and exchange, and reliance on market prices to allocate scarce resources. It stresses individual freedom (thus the term "liberalism") and views incentives as the motive force of economic well-being.

In the free market view, each individual is the best judge of what he or she wants, and of how to achieve the chosen ends. Thus, individual decisions by consumers and producers provide the answers to the three economic questions. The consumer ultimately determines what will be produced and for whom. Responding to consumer demand, private firms determine how these goods will be produced by combining factors of production (labor, natural resources, land and capital) in order to minimize cost and maximize profit. Liberalism views economic relations, both domestic and international, as essentially harmonious.

*The Collective Action Approach*. The major alternative to the market organization of economic activity is a process of collective decision-making in which the imperatives of politics dominate economic choice. Two major assumptions underlie collective decision-making: (1) reliance on the market leads to an undesirable outcome; and (2) economic relations are *conflictual*: exchange, far from being a positive sum game, is zero-sum—if one party gains from an exchange, the other party must lose. In this system, government, to some degree, allocates resources or distributes the output of production.

The extreme form of collective decision-making—in which the government owns the means of production, determines what will be produced and how, and then distributes the output—is called *socialism*. Socialism has taken many forms, from marxism to national socialism or fascism, to so-called "social democracy." Marxism, in particular, maintains that the principal economic actor is not the individual, but the economic class, and that the goal of economic activity is not the maximization of individual welfare, but the maximization of class interests.[14]

Another form of collective decision-making is *mercantilism*, defined by Robert Gilpin as "the subservience of the economy to the state and its interests—interests that range from matters of domestic welfare to those of international security."[15] In the mercantilist system, the government may permit private ownership in name, but allocate resources and goods by means of taxes, subsidies, and regulations. Domestically, mercantilism seeks to increase the power of the state against other institutions. Internationally, mercantilism seeks to increase the power of one state against other states.

The "mixed economy" of the United States includes elements of both a decentralized market system and public-sector decision-making. Although most economic decisions are made by individuals and private firms, government plays an important role, not only by undertaking economic activities itself, but also by establishing monetary, fiscal, and regulatory policies that influence the choices of private actors.[16] The real question at the heart of the contemporary debate about the American political economy concerns the level of government intervention in the market most consistent with the achievement of economic prosperity and power.

## Paths to Prosperity:
## Contending Views of the Role of Government in the Economy

What is the proper role of government in a political economy? What policies should the United States follow to achieve the twin goals of prosperity and security in the international arena? What economic policies will ensure real economic growth, with low inflation and the creation of high value, high wage jobs? What should be done to reduce the federal deficit, and to increase the national savings rate? What should government do to regulate economic activity?

With the collapse of the Soviet Union and the apparent discrediting of Marxism as a viable guide to economic organization, the debate seems to have been reduced to three competing views: *market liberalism*, a reinvigorated argument on behalf of the free market; a *modern liberal* advocacy of government intervention in the economy to correct *market failures*; and *neo-mercantilism*, a system concerned primarily with the relative decline of U.S. power in the international system.

Advocates of each view generally agree on the goal: a healthy, growing economy. All express concern about such economic problems as inflation, unemployment, large budget and trade deficits, the low savings rate among Americans, and U.S. firms' alleged lack of international competitiveness. But not surprisingly, they differ substantially over the role of government in achieving the goal and dealing with the problems.

*Market Liberalism.* Market liberalism is rooted in the classical liberal political philosophy of John Locke, the American Founders and Adam Smith. The role of government in a system characterized by reliance on the market is limited because of the belief that a strong government poses a significant danger to individual liberty and concern about the waste and inefficiencies associated with government activity.

In a free market system, government is traditionally limited to certain well-defined functions: national defense and the maintenance of good order (the military and police functions); the administration of justice, including protection of property rights and enforcement of contracts (the court system); limited investment in and maintenance of public works (harbors, highways and bridges); and protection of the weakest citizens.

Twentieth-century advocates of the market have added the "non-activist" maintenance of a stable macro-economy, especially a stable currency, as a role of government. Government is not so much a player in the free market system as it is a referee whose job is to maintain a fair game.

Market liberalism extends the limited role of government to international economic transactions as well as domestic. In Gilpin's words:

> Through free exchange of commodities, removal of restrictions on the flow of investment, and an international division of labor, everyone will benefit in the long run as a result of a more efficient utilization of the world's scarce resources.[17]

Market liberalism maintains that just as the public interest is best served by limited government interference in the domestic economy, the national interest is best served by free trade and "a generous and cooperative attitude regarding economic relations with other countries."

Classical liberals believe that reliance on the free market is the best way to promote not only prosperity, but also security, both domestically and internationally. According to Ethan Kapstein:

> Domestically, as states increase their wealth, the relative burdens of defense will weigh less heavily on overall economic activity. Internationally, as commercial and financial flows become global, economic incentives to engage in hostilities will be reduced, paving the way for a peaceful world order.[18]

The latter is a long-standing claim of liberalism, perhaps best expressed by Montesquieu:

> [T]he natural effect of commerce is to lead to peace. Two nations that trade together become mutually dependent; if one has an interest in buying, the other has an interest in selling; and all unions are based on mutual needs.[19]

***Modern Liberalism***. The origins of modern liberalism can be traced to the nineteenth-century reaction against the perceived injustices and failures of "laissez-faire." But the most thorough intellectual justification of the political economy of modern liberalism was provided by John Maynard Keynes, arguably the most influential economist of the twentieth century. His most important book, *The General Theory of Employment, Interest, and Money*, published in 1936 during the midst of the Great Depression, offered a plausible explanation for that economic catastrophe and a strategy for ending it.

The modern liberal justifies government intervention in the market primarily to correct problems he believes to be inherent in the market process itself:

- the unequal distribution of economic power among market participants;
- "market failures," the likelihood that an unfettered market will lead to:

(1) collusion and monopoly;
(2) the existence of "externalities," the "spillover" consequences of many market activities that affect the well-being of a nonconsenting party;

(3) the undervaluing and thus underproduction of "public goods;" and
(4) the possibility that uninformed consumers can be exploited by producers selling unsafe, overpriced goods; and

• macroeconomic instability, the alleged tendency of the free market to swing from a recessionary, high-unemployment state to inflationary "boom," and back again.

The modern liberal believes that government must play a major role in the economy by redistributing wealth; by regulating economic activity; by pursuing an "activist" macroeconomic policy, both fiscal (taxing and government spending), and monetary; and through "public investment" or "industrial policy," designed to enhance the economic welfare of the population.

The modern liberal disagrees with the classical liberal about the performance of the market domestically, but shares the latter's passion for international free trade, both to promote prosperity and, through economic interdependence, to improve international security. Both market liberalism and modern liberalism accept the general proposition that international economic interdependence contributes to global economic welfare, and as such, lessens the likelihood of conflict. Some go so far as to suggest that national boundaries, indeed, the "nation state" itself, have become obsolete in an increasingly interdependent world economy.[20]

**Neo-mercantilism.** Mercantilism, a "system of power politics," dominated economic thought from the sixteenth to the eighteenth centuries. The international goal of mercantilism was to increase the power of the state relative to other states. Thus the state intervened in economic affairs to develop the state's "commercial, financial, military, and naval resources."[21]

Mercantilists held that the power of the state depends upon the capacity to make war. They believed the basis of military power to be "wealth," in the form of "specie" (gold and silver). Thus for the mercantilists, the goal of international trade was to run a balance-of-trade surplus. Since all states could not do so simultaneously, mercantilists saw trade as a source of conflict rather than cooperation. In the words of the arch-mercantilist Colbert, ". . . trade causes perpetual strife both in time of war and in time of peace between all the nations. . ."[22]

Adam Smith's *The Wealth of Nations* was primarily a critique of the mercantilist system. But even as free trade ideas spread, mercantilism retained a certain attraction for states seeking their "place in the sun." Friedrich List's writing represented a counterrevolution against liberalism, and served as the basis of Germany's economic program of the late nineteenth century. The attraction of mercantilism as a policy of governments was diminished by the two world wars.

Recently, some scholars have developed a theory of international trade called "hegemonic stability." Although not strictly a version of neo-mercantilism hegemonic stability shares some important assumptions with the neo-mercantilist approach. In this view:

> . . . international trade based on the liberal principles of comparative advantage and the division of labor does not just occur through the actions of a global "invisible hand." Instead, economic openness only arises in the presence of a hegemonic power, a state willing and able to provide the world with the collective goods of economic stability and international security. A state will only adopt the leadership role of hegemon when it is in its national interest to do so. In short, the theory of hegemonic stability rests on two fundamental propositions: (1) order in world politics is typically created by a single dominant power, and (2) the maintenance of order requires continued hegemony.[23]

Theorists cite two examples of hegemonic stability: *Pax Britannica* (1815-1914) and *Pax Americana* (1945-present).

Some contend that *Pax Americana* began to show signs of strain beginning in the 1970s, and that the United States must now make a concerted effort to maintain its relative advantage in the international system by means of economic, rather than military means.[24] Although neo-mercantilists concede that the *absolute* economic power of the United States is immeasurably greater now than at the end of World War II, they believe that America's *relative* economic power, especially *vis a vis* Japan and Europe, has declined.

Thus Samuel Huntington claims that ". . . in a world in which military conflict between major states is unlikely, economic power will be increasingly important in determining the primacy or subordination of states."[25] Or in Daniel Bell's paraphrase of Clausewitz, "economics is the continuation of war by other means."[26]

The neo-mercantilists argue that the decline in relative U.S. economic power represents another form of "market failure:" while reliance on the market may result in an increasing ability by a nation's citizens to consume in the short run, in the long run, such reliance will cause a nation to lose productive capacity in advanced industries and sophisticated services. In the words of James Fallows, paraphrasing List, "in the long run, . . . a society's well-being and its overall wealth are determined not by what the society can *buy* but by what it can *make*."[27]

In the view of the neo-mercantilist, the resulting decline in high-value, high-wage employment will contribute to a long-term fall in the nation's standard of living as well as its strategic position. This decline could have several likely results: (1) adverse military consequences for the U.S. as a result of the loss of technological superiority; (2) a decline in U.S. international influence; and (3) concomitant increase in the influence of other nations over the U.S.

According to the theory of hegemonic stability, the decline of relative U.S. power could create a more disorderly, less peaceful world, just as the decay of *Pax Britannica* created the necessary, if not sufficient conditions for the two world wars of the twentieth century. As British hegemony declined, small states that previously had incentives to cooperate with Britain "defected" to other powers, causing the international system to fragment. The outcome was depression and war.[28] In the view of some, the decline of American power could lead to a similar outcome. In Huntington's words, "the maintenance of U.S. primacy matters for the world as well as for the United States."[29]

While both neo-mercantilists and some modern liberals agree that government action is necessary to stimulate and protect certain critical industries, they disagree over the purpose. Modern liberals advocate an "industrial policy" primarily to promote the economic welfare of American citizens. Neo-mercantilists do so mainly as a way to maximize U.S. economic power relative to other nation-states.

## Allocating Scarce Resources for Defense

The second aspect of the political economy of national security concerns how best to allocate scarce national resources among competing national ends in order to provide "enough" for defense. Choices among alternative uses of scarce resources and the opportunity costs resulting from those choices pervade the entire process of providing for the common defense, and confirm Friederich von Hayek's characterization of economics as "the study of the unintended consequences of human action."

Allocating resources for defense has two components: what Samuel Huntington has called the *strategic*, concerned with the particular needs to be fulfilled by military force; and the *structural*, decisions "made in the currency of domestic politics. . ." concerned with providing the resources "which go into the strategic units and uses of force."[30]

Taking the structural first, security is a "public good:" goods that will not be provided by the market because there is no way to exclude non-paying consumers. While consumer goods may be limited to those who are willing to pay for them, the opportunity cost of excluding non-paying citizens from consuming such public goods as national defense is too high.

Thus public goods break the market link between consumption and cost. Public goods are available to all at no direct cost. Individuals have no incentive to pay voluntarily for the benefits they derive from a public good; they are "free riders." Thus public goods will be underproduced by the market, if they are produced at all. This constitutes a conflict between the individual self-interest of consumers, as registered by the market allocation of resources, and the public interest of achieving economic efficiency.

The production and distribution of public goods is accomplished through the collective decision-making process. In practice, a choice made in the public sector may have an immense impact, whether intended or not, and for better or worse, on the private sector. How public goods are provided through government action is the subject of a relatively new branch of political economy called "public choice" theory.[31]

Ultimately, allocating resources for defense is only a part of the most fundamental choice about political economy that a nation makes: what portion of the wealth and income of its people will be kept by those who produce it and what portion will go to the public sector. The allocation of national income to the private and public sectors is a public policy choice effected through the collective decision making process.

Citizens, presumably operating through their elected representatives at all levels of government, decide what programs should be publicly funded, who should receive the benefits from them, and how they should be funded—by means of taxes or government borrowing. Income allocated to the public sector entails a fundamental opportunity cost: it is not available to fulfil the private desires of the citizens.

In addition, the way in which income is allocated to the public sector carries costs as well. On the one hand, if the money is raised by taxation, the incentives of wealth producers may be adversely affected. If the rate of taxation is too high, individuals may work less, or divert wealth away from productive enterprises in order to hide it from the tax collector. In any event, economic growth may be slowed by a high level of taxation.

On the other, if the money is borrowed by the government, interest rates may rise, "crowding out" private borrowers who would otherwise invest in wealth producing enterprises. Again, economic growth could be adversely affected. The point is, a nation that diverts a large portion of its national product to public spending may create a burden that its economy is ultimately unable to bear.

Once resources are allocated to the public sector, the next choice is to use them for defense or non-defense purposes. As the functions of government have expanded far beyond those laid out by the classical liberals, the public sector competitors for defense dollars have increased substantially. The opportunity cost of funding a defense program may be to cut a domestic program or to raise taxes to fund both.

No one has ever offered a more eloquent example of the opportunity cost, both private and public, of defense spending than President Dwight D. Eisenhower:

> The cost of one modern heavy bomber is this: a modern brick school in more than 30 cities. It is two electric power plants, each serving a town of 60,000 population. It is two fine, fully equipped hospitals. It is some 50 miles of concrete highway.[32]

But presumably, this opportunity cost will be borne if, in the judgement of policy makers, it is less than the strategic benefits achieved by defense spending.

This observation leads us to the strategic context of resource allocation for defense. The question, "how much is enough?" cannot be answered independently of strategy. Strategic considerations play an important role in determining what resources will go to defense.

In thinking about the relationship between resources and strategy, the decision maker must consider several questions:

(1) Is the chosen strategy adequate to secure the interests of the nation?
(2) Are the resources adequate to achieve the objectives of the chosen strategy?
(3) If not, is the risk of accepting a strategy-resource mismatch manageable?
(4) If the risk is judged to be unmanageable, should the objectives be scaled back, or should resources be increased?
(5) If resources are increased, what is the opportunity cost?

It should be apparent that the strategic and structural factors of allocating resources for defense are closely intertwined.

As Huntington writes:

[I]n practice no sharp line exists between the strategic and structural elements...This is particularly true of the overall magnitude of the military effort. This is determined by many strategic and structural decisions.... The determination of the resources available to the government and the allocation of those resources to military, domestic, and foreign purposes is, indeed, the crux of national policy. The determination of the magnitude of the military effort combines strategy and structure and also transcends them.[33]

## Conclusion: Prosperity and Security

Political economy is concerned with how a political society allocates scarce resources in order to promote prosperity. National security is concerned with how a state employs power to maintain its place in the international arena. This essay has attempted to illustrate the reciprocal relationship between the two.

A more prosperous state is better able to provide resources for defense. But a state is more likely to be prosperous the better it can ensure its own security and protect the security of its citizens.

What is the best path to prosperity? Classical liberals, modern liberals, and neo-mercantilists each offer a different answer to the problem. These different responses constitute the current debate over political economy in general.

Economic power is an important element of national power, but it must be placed in its proper context. A strong economy is a *necessary* but not a *sufficient* condition for success in international affairs. Clearly, to be successful in the international arena, a state must have the necessary resources to implement its chosen strategy. But as the U.S. experience in Vietnam demonstrated, even overwhelming economic might cannot redeem a flawed strategic vision.

# Notes

The author is grateful to his colleague at the Naval War College, Andrew Ross, for his helpful comments on an earlier draft of this chapter.

1. Edward Mead Earle, "Adam Smith, Alexander Hamilton, Friedrich List: The Economic Foundations of Military Power," in Earle, ed., *Makers of Modern Strategy: Military Thought From Machiavelli to Hitler* (Princeton: Princeton University Press, 1943).

2. Paul Kennedy, *The Rise and Fall of the Great Powers* (New York: Random House, 1987), p. xvi.

3. Fernand Braudel, *The Mediterranean and the Mediterranean World in the Age of Philip II* (New York: Harper & Row, 1973), Vol. 2, p. 840.

4. P.G.M. Dickson, *The Financial Revolution in England: A Study of the Development of Public Credit, 1688-1756* (London: Ashgate Publishers, 1993 [First Published, 1967]); John Brewer, *The Sinews of Power: War, Money and the English State, 1688-1783* (New York: Alfred A. Knopf, 1989).

5. Williamson Murray and Mark Grimsley, "Introduction: On Strategy," in Murray *et al.*, eds., *The Making of Strategy: Rulers, States, and War* (Cambridge: Cambridge University Press, 1994), p. 18.

6. Paul M. Kennedy, *The Rise and Fall of British Naval Mastery* (London: Macmillan Press, 1983)

7. Colin Gray, "Global Security and Economic Well-being: A Strategic Perspective," *Political Studies*, Vol. 42, No. 1, March 1994, p. 36. Cf. Robert Art's observation:

> The fact is that we simply do not know whether the world's political economy would experience even greater movement toward economic closure and managed trade if the United States were to withdraw totally into "Fortress America.". . . What we do know is that the current openness was forged during the waging of the Cold War and is a partial by-product of it; that America's provision of security helped bind Western Europe, Japan, and the United States together; and that today's economic openness has been associated with a global American military presence.

Robert J. Art, "Defense Policy," in Art and Seyom Brown, *U.S. Foreign Policy: The Search for a New Role* (New York: Macmillan College Publishing Company, 1993), pp. 112-113.

8. Kennedy, *The Rise and Fall of the Great Powers*, pp. xv, and *passim*.

9. Ronald Reagan, *National Security Strategy of the United States*, January 1987, p. 4.

10. Lionel Robbins, *An Essay on the Nature and Significance of Economic Science, 1932.* Cited in James D. Gwartney and Richard L. Stroup, *Economics: Private and Public Choice* (New York: Harcourt Brace Jovanovich, 1995), Seventh Edition, p. 4. Scarcity is fundamental to modern economic analysis. Cf. Gwartney and Stroup, pp. 4-14.

11. "Political economy" was the term used by the economists of the late eighteenth and early nineteenth centuries to describe the study of "the wealth of nations." Adam Smith, David Ricardo, and John Stuart Mill all employed the term, which is a combination of politics, the affairs of state, and the Greek for "household management" (*oikos nomikos*). When, in the late nineteenth century, both economics and political science began to ape the methodology of the physical sciences, "political economy" fell into disuse, except among Marxists, for whom it expressed the central importance of the relationship between control of the means of production by the dominant economic class, and the political "superstructure" of the state: the institutions of government, law, and culture. Recently the term has enjoyed a renaissance among non-Marxist analysts, referring to, in the words of Andrew Ross,

> . . . a burgeoning field of inquiry that has synthesized economic and political analysis, in the process dramatically transforming the way analysts think about economics and politics, at both the domestic and international levels. Political economy has exposed the artificiality of the scholastic differentiation between economics and political science by directing our attention to how politics influences economic behavior and how economics influences political behavior. . . .

Andrew L. Ross, "The Political Economy of Defense: The Nature and Scope of the Inquiry," in Ross, ed., *The Political Economy of Defense: Issues and Perspectives* (New York: Greenwood Press, 1991), pp. 1-2. Cf. Robert Gilpin, *The Political Economy of International Relations* (Princeton: Princeton University Press, 1987); and Ethan Barnaby Kapstein, *The Political Economy of National Security: A Global Perspective* (New York: McGraw-Hill, 1992).

12. Gwartney and Stroup, pp. 45-48.

13. Robert Gilpin, "The Nature of Political Economy," reprinted in Robert J. Art and Robert Jervis, eds., *International Politics: Anarchy, Force, Political Economy, and Decision-Making* (New York: Harper Collins, 1992), Third Edition, pp. 240-241.

14. Gilpin, "The Nature of Political Economy," pp. 279-282.

15. Gilpin, "The Nature of Political Economy," p. 278.

16 Joseph E. Stiglitz, *Economics of the Public Sector* (New York: W.W. Norton, 1988), Second Edition, pp. 2-4.

17. Gilpin, "The Nature of Political Economy," p. 279.

18. Kapstein, p. 5.

19. Montesquieu, *De L'Esprit des Lois*, XX. 1, in *Oeuvres Completes* (Paris: Editions du Seuil, 1964), p. 651.

20. See, for instance, Richard Rosecrance, "The Rise of the Virtual State," *Foreign Affairs,* Vol. 75, No. 4, July/August 1996, pp. 45-6.

21. Earle, p. 118.

22. Cited in Kapstein, p. 27.

23. Kapstein, p. 3. Cf. Gray and Art, note 7 above. Cf. also Gilpin, *The Political Economy of International Relations*; Gilpin, *War & Change in World Politics* (Cambridge: Cambridge University Press, 1981); Joseph Greico, *Cooperation Among Nations* (Ithaca: Cornell University Press, 1990); Charles P. Kindleberger, *The World in Depression: 1929-1939* (Berkeley: University of California Press, 1973); and Robert Keohane, *After Hegemony* (Princeton: Princeton University Press, 1984).

24. Cf. Edward N. Luttwak, "From Geopolitics to Geo-Economics: Logic of Conflict, Grammar of Commerce," *The National Interest,* No. 20, Summer 1990, and *The Endangered American Dream* (New York: Simon and Schuster, 1993; and James Fallows, "How the World Works," *The Atlantic Monthly,* December 1993, "What Is an Economy For?" *The Atlantic Monthly,* January 1994, and *Looking at the Sun: The Rise of the New East Asian Economic and Political System* (New York: Pantheon, 1994).

25. Samuel Huntington, "Why International Primacy Matters," *International Security,* Vol. 17, No. 4, Spring 1993, p. 72.

26. Daniel Bell, "Germany: The Enduring Fear," *Dissent,* Vol. 37, Fall 1990, p. 466. Cited in Huntington, p. 81.

27. Fallows, "How the World Works," p. 66.

28. Kindleberger, *passim*; Gilpin, *The Political Economy of International Relations,* pp. 127-131; Gilpin, *War & Change in World Politics,* pp. 156-210.

29. Huntington, "Why International Primacy Matters," pp.82-83.

30. Samuel P. Huntington, *The Common Defense: Strategic Programs in National Politics* (New York: Columbia University Press, 1961), pp. 3-5.

31. Public choice involves the application of economic analysis to the collective decision making process. Economists of the "public choice" school have demonstrated that actors in the public sector, just as those in the private sector, respond to incentives. But because the market and collective decision making processes are structurally different, the rewards to the actors in each are also different. Public choice economists argue that, just as there are market failures such as externalities, there are also "government failures" such as "rent-seeking." Both lead to the misallocation of scarce resources. Public choice economists stress the use of *rules* to bring the self-interest of political players into harmony with economic efficiency. The best known public choice economist is James Buchanan, who won the Nobel Prize for economics in 1988. Cf. Buchanan and Gordon Tullock, *The Calculus of Consent* (Ann Arbor: University of Michigan Press, 1962); Buchanan and Richard Wagner, *Democracy in Deficit: The Political Legacy of Lord Keynes* (New York: Academic Press, 1977); James Gwartney and Richard Wagner, eds., *Public Choice and Constitutional Economics* (Greenwich: JAI Press, 1988); and Gwartney and Stroup, pp. 92-109, 802-849.

32. Quoted in Charles J. Hitch and Ronald McKean, *The Economics of Defense in the Nuclear Age* (Cambridge: Harvard University Press, 1960), p. 4.

33. Huntington, *The Common Defense,* p. 5.

# Chapter 15

### * * *

# The Public Sector in a Mixed Economy

### Joseph E. Stiglitz

*Joseph Stiglitz discusses the role of government or the public sector in a "mixed economy." In a mixed economy, many if not most economic activities are undertaken by individual actors and private firms, but government plays an important role, either by its own economic enterprises or by influencing private activity by fiscal, monetary, and regulatory policies. In a primarily capitalist system, the usual rationale for government intervention in economic affairs is to correct "market failures." But the public sector can suffer from "government failures" as well. What criteria should be used to determine the relative weight of government or the market in the allocation of scarce resources? According to these criteria, what would be the advantages and disadvantages of each approach?*

## The Mixed Economy

The United States has what is called a mixed economy: while many economic activities are undertaken by private firms, others are undertaken by the government. In addition, the government alters the behavior of the private sector, either intentionally or unintentionally, through a variety of regulations, taxes, and subsidies. By way of contrast, in the USSR and the Soviet bloc counties, most economic activities [were] undertaken by the government. In many Western European economies, the government is responsible for a much larger share of economic activity than in the United States. For instance, in Britain the government [was] responsible for the production of coal and steel.

Joseph E. Stiglitz is a professor at Princeton University. He has published a number of works on economics, earning widespread recognition for his analyses of the relationship between government and the market.

Reprint from *Economics of the Public Sector*, Second Edition, by Joseph Stiglitz, pp. 2-20, by permission of W.W. Norton & Company, Inc. Copyright © 1988, 1986 by Joseph E. Stiglitz, the Trustee of Edward Hannaway Stiglitz Trust, the Trustee of Julia Hannaway Stiglitz Trust and the Trustee of the Trust for the Benefit of Joseph E. Stiglitz's children. Minor modifications to the text have been made.

What the government is responsible for in the United States has also changed dramatically. One hundred years ago there were some private highways and all railroads were private; today there are no major private roads and most interstate railroad passengers travel by Amtrak, a publicly established and subsidized enterprise. It is because mixed economies are constantly facing the problem of defining the appropriate boundaries between government and private activities that the study of public finance in these countries is both so important and so interesting.

Why does the government do some things and not others? Why has the scope of government activity changed over the past hundred years, and why does it do more in some countries than it does in the United States, while in other countries it does less? Does the government do too much? Does it do what it attempts to do well? Could it do it better? These are the central questions with which public finance is concerned. They have been at the center of political, philosophical, and economic debates for centuries. The debates continue. Even though economists cannot provide definitive answers, they have contributed enormously to our understanding of the issues by making us aware of the strengths and limitations of both the public and private sectors.

## An Impetus for Government Action: Market Failures

In the period between the Great Depression (1930s) and the early 1960s, economists (and politicians) became aware of a large number of ways in which the free-market economy, even the richest free-market economy in the world, seemed to fail to meet certain basic social needs. The economy had always suffered from periodic episodes of unemployment, some of them massive. In the Great Depression, the unemployment rate reached 25 percent and national output fell by about 30 percent from its peak in 1929. The depression brought to the fore problems that, in less severe form, had been there for a long time. Many individuals lost virtually all of their money when banks failed and the stock market crashed. Many elderly people did not have the resources on which to survive. Many farmers found that the prices they received for their products were so low that they could not make their mortgage payments, and defaults became commonplace.

In response to the depression, the federal government not only took a more active role in attempting to stabilize the level of economic activity, but it also passed legislation aimed at alleviating many of the specific problems: unemployment insurance, social security, federal insurance for depositors, federal programs aimed at supporting agricultural prices, and a host of other programs aimed at a variety of social and economic objectives. Together, these programs are referred to as the "New Deal."

After World War II the economy recovered, and the country experienced an unprecedented level of prosperity. But it became clear that the fruits of that prosperity were not being enjoyed by all. Many individuals seemed, by the condition of their birth, to be condemned to a life of squalor and poverty; they received inadequate education, and their prospects for obtaining good jobs were bleak.

These inequities provided the impetus for many of the government programs that were enacted in the 1960s, when President Lyndon B. Johnson declared his "War on Poverty." While some programs were aimed at providing a "safety net" for the needy—for instance, programs to provide food and medical care to the poor—others, such as job retraining programs, were directed at improving the economic opportunities of the disadvantaged.

Could government actions alleviate these problems? How was success to be gauged? The fact that some programs did not live up to the hopes of its most enthusiastic supporters did not, of course, mean that it was a failure. Medicaid, which provides medical assistance to the indigent, was successful in eliminating some of the differences in access to medical care between the poor and the rich, but the difference in life expectancy between these two groups was not eliminated. Medicare, which provides medical care for the elderly, was successful in relieving the elderly and their families of much of the anxiety concerning the financing of their medical expenses, but it left in its place a national problem of rapidly increasing medical expenditures. While the social security program provided the aged with an unprecedented level of economic security, in the late 1970s and early 1980s it ran into financial crises that raised questions about whether future generations would be able to enjoy the same benefits.

Twenty years after the War on Poverty began, it is clear that poverty has not been eradicated from America. But have the expenditures had a significant effect in reducing it? While there is no consensus on the answer to this question, both critics and supporters of the government's programs agree that it is not enough to have good intentions: many of the programs designed to alleviate the perceived inadequacies of the market economy have had effects that differed markedly from those the proponents thought (or hoped) they would have. Urban renewal programs designed to improve the quality of life in inner cities have, in many instances, resulted in the replacement of low-quality housing with high-quality housing that poor people cannot afford, thus forcing them to live in even worse conditions. Though many programs designed to promote integration of public schools have succeeded, some have instead increased residential segregation or led some parents to enroll their children in private schools, which has in turn weakened support for public education. A disproportionate share of the benefits of farm programs has accrued to large farms; government programs have not enabled many of the small farms to survive. There have been allegations that government welfare programs have contributed to the breakup of families and to the development of an attitude of dependency.

Supporters of continued government efforts claim that critics exaggerate the failures of government programs. They argue that the lesson to be learned is not that the government should abandon its efforts to solve the major social and economic problems facing the nation, but that greater care must be taken in the appropriate design of government programs.

## Government Failures

While market failures led to the major government programs of the 1930s and 1960s, in the 1970s the shortcomings of the programs led economists and political scientists to investigate government failure. Under what conditions would government programs not work well? Were the failures of government programs mere accidents, or were they predictable results, following from the inherent nature of governmental activity? Are there lessons to be learned for the design of programs in the future? There are four major reasons for the systematic failures of the government to achieve its stated objectives: the government's limited information, its limited control over private responses to its actions, its limited control over the bureaucracy, and the limitations imposed by political processes.

*1. Limited information.* The consequences of many actions are complicated and difficult to foresee. When the federal government adopted its urban renewal programs, it did not anticipate that they might lead to a decline in the supply of housing available to the poor. Similarly, the government did not anticipate the precipitous increase in expenditures on medical care by the aged that followed the adoption of the Medicare program.

*2. Limited control over private market responses.* The government has only limited control over the consequences of its actions (particularly within a democracy such as ours). When New York City passed its rent control legislation, many advocates overlooked the fact that apartments were supplied by individuals who would turn elsewhere for investment opportunities if the return to their investment declined. Advocates thus failed to anticipate that the supply of rental housing would decrease and that the quality of services provided by landlords would deteriorate. Though the government attempted to control this deterioration by imposing standards on landlords, these attempts were only partially successful and exacerbated the decline in the supply of rental housing. There was little the New York City government could do to stop this, short of repealing the rent control statutes.

*3. Limited control over bureaucracy.* Congress and state and local legislatures design legislation, but delegate implementation to some government agency. This agency may spend considerable time writing detailed regulations; how these detailed regulations are drafted is critical in determining the effects of the legislation. The agency may also be responsible for ensuring that the regulations are enforced. For instance, when Congress passed the Environmental Protection Act, its intent was clear—to ensure that firms did not pollute the environment. But the technical details—for instance, determining the admissible level of pollutants for different industries—were left to the Environmental Protection Agency (EPA). During the first two years of the Reagan administration, there were numerous controversies over whether the EPA had been lax in promulgating and enforcing regulations, thus subverting the intentions of Congress.

In many cases, the failures to carry out the intent of Congress are not deliberate attempts to avoid the wishes of Congress, but are a result of the ambiguities in Congress's intentions. And, there is a further problem of ensuring that administrators whose job it is to execute the law will do so fairly and efficiently. Just as a principal subject of inquiry in standard economics is the analysis of the incentives within the private sector, so one of the subjects of study here is the analysis of incentives within the public sector: What causes bureaucrats to take the actions they take?

**4. *Limitations imposed by political processes*.** Even if government were perfectly informed about the consequences of all possible actions, choosing among those actions through the political process would raise additional difficulties. Government actions affect many persons, but they are decided upon by only a limited group—their elected representatives. The decision makers have to ascertain the preferences of their constituencies and they have to find some way of reconciling or making choices among conflicting preferences. It is often alleged that the government acts in an inconsistent manner. Under certain circumstances this is a natural consequence of democratic decision making. Moreover, our political process is one in which those who are elected to serve the public sometimes have incentives to act for the benefit of special-interest groups. Thus, the failure of politicians to carry out what would seem to be in the public interest is not just the consequence of the greed or malevolence of a few wayward politicians, but it may be the inevitable consequence of the workings of political institutions in democratic societies.[1]

Critics of government intervention in the economy believe the four sources of government failure are sufficiently important that the government should be restrained from attempting to remedy alleged deficiencies in markets. But even if one does not agree with this conclusion, recognition of the four limitations on government action is a prerequisite for the design of successful government policies.

## Earlier Views Concerning the Role of Government

The vacillation in views concerning the role of the government that has occurred during the past fifty years has also occurred frequently in the past.[2] For instance, in the eighteenth century a dominant view, particularly among French economists, was that the government should take an active role in promoting trade and industry. Those who advocated this view were called *mercantilists*.

It was partly in reaction to this view that Adam Smith (who is often viewed as the founder of modern economics) wrote his book *The Wealth of Nations* (1776), in which he advocated a limited role for government. Smith attempted to show how competition and the profit motive would lead individuals—in pursuing their own private interests—to serve the public interest. The profit motive would lead individuals to supply the goods other individuals wanted. Competing against one another, only firms that produced what was wanted and produced it at as low a price as possible would survive. Smith argued that the economy was led, as if by an invisible hand, to produce what was desired and in the best possible way.

Adam Smith's ideas had a powerful influence both on governments and on economists. Many of the most important nineteenth-century economists, such as the Englishmen John Stuart Mill and Nassau Senior, promulgated the doctrine known as laissez faire, which argued that the government should leave the private sector alone; it should not attempt to regulate or control private enterprise. Unfettered competition would serve the best interests of society.

Not all the nineteenth-century social thinkers were persuaded by Smith's reasoning. They were concerned with grave inequalities in income that they saw around them, with the squalor in which much of the working classes lived, and with the unemployment that workers frequently faced. While nineteenth-century writers like Charles Dickens attempted to portray the plight of the working classes in novels, social theorists, like Karl Marx, Sismondi, and Robert Owen, attempted not only to develop theories explaining what they saw but also to suggest ways in which society might be reorganized. To many, the evils in society could be attributed to the private ownership of capital; what Adam Smith saw as a virtue they saw as a vice. Marx, if not the deepest of the social thinkers, was certainly the most influential among those who advocated a greater role for the state in controlling the means of production. Still others saw the solution neither in the state nor in private enterprise but in smaller groups of individuals getting together and acting cooperatively for their mutual interest.

These continuing controversies have stimulated economists to attempt to ascertain the precise sense in which, and the precise conditions under which, the invisible hand guides the economy to efficiency. It is now known that the presumption of the efficiency of the market economy is valid only under fairly restrictive assumptions. The failures we noted above make it apparent that there are many problems with which the market does not deal adequately. Today, among American economists, the dominant view is that *limited* government intervention could alleviate (but not solve) the worst problems: the government should take an active role in maintaining full employment and alleviating the worst aspects of poverty, but private enterprise should play the central role in the economy. There is still considerable controversy about how limited or how active a role the government should take. Some economists, such as Harvard University Professor John Kenneth Galbraith, believe that the government should take a more active role, while others, such as Nobel Laureates Milton Friedman of Stanford University's Hoover Institution and George Stigler of the University of Chicago, believe that the government should take a less active role. Views on this subject are affected by how serious one considers the failures of the market to be and by how effective one believes the government can be in remedying them.

## What or Who Is the Government

. . . What distinguishes those institutions that we have labeled as "government" from private institutions? There are two important differences. First, in a democracy the individuals who are responsible for running public institutions are elected, or are appointed by someone who is elected (or appointed by someone who is appointed by someone who is elected. . . ). The "legitimacy" of the person holding the position is derived directly or indirectly from the electoral process. In contrast, those who are responsible for administering General Motors are chosen by the shareholders of General Motors: while those who are responsible for administering private foundations (such as the Rockefeller and Ford foundations) are chosen by a self-perpetuating board of trustees.

Secondly, the government is endowed with certain rights of compulsion that private institutions do not have. The government has the right to force you to pay taxes (and if you fail, it can confiscate your property and/or imprison you). The government has the right to "force" its young males to serve in the armed forces, at wages below those that would induce them to volunteer. The government has the right to seize your property for public use provided it pays you just compensation (this is called the right of eminent domain).

Not only do private institutions and individuals not have these rights, but the government actually restricts the rights of individuals to give to others similar powers of compulsion. For instance, the government does not allow you to sell yourself into slavery.

In contrast, all private exchanges are voluntary. I may want you to work for me, but I cannot force you to do so. I may need your property to construct an office building, but I cannot force you to sell it. I may think that some deal is advantageous to both of us, but I can not force you to engage in the deal.

This ability to use compulsion means that the government may be able to do some things that private institutions cannot do. And the differences in the processes by which those who administer public and private institutions are chosen may have important implications for the behavior of those institutions. It is important to keep these differences in mind as we discuss . . . alternative views of the role of the government.

## The Public Sector and the Fundamental Economic Questions

Economics is the study of *scarcity*, of how societies make choices concerning how to use their limited resources. Four questions are asked:

What is to be produced?

How is it to be produced?

For whom is it to be produced?

How are these decisions made?

Like any field of economics, the economics of the public sector is concerned with these fundamental questions of choice. But it focuses on the choices made within the public sector itself, on the role of the government, and on the ways that government affects the decisions made in the private sector.

*1. What is to be produced*? How much of our resources should be devoted to the production of public goods, such as defense and highways, and how much of our resources should we devote to the production of private goods, such as cars, TV sets, and video games? We often depict this choice in terms of the production possibilities schedule, which traces the various amounts of two goods that can be produced efficiently with a given technology and resources. In our case, the two goods are public goods and private goods. Figure 1 gives the various possible combinations of public goods and private goods that the society can produce.

Society can spend more on public goods, such as national defense, but only by reducing what is available for private consumption. Thus, in moving from $G$ to $E$ along the production possibilities schedule, public goods are increased, but private goods are decreased. A point such as $I$, which is below the production possibilities schedule, is said to be *inefficient*: society could get more public goods and more private goods. A point such as $N$, which is above the production possibilities schedule, is said to be *infeasible*: it is not possible, given current resources and technology, to have at the same time that quantity of public goods and that quantity of private goods.

*2. How should it be produced*? The second question, how what is produced should be produced, is as important as the first question. When should the government take direct responsibility for production of the goods that are

**Figure 1**
**Society's Production Possibilities Schedule**

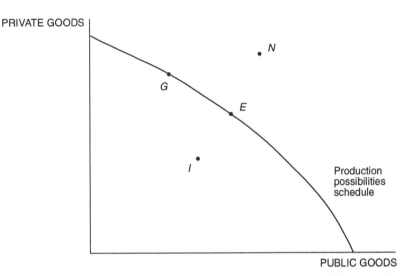

publicly provided, and when should the government procure these goods from private firms? While most of the weapons used by the military are produced by private firms, only a small percentage of public educational expenditures goes to private schools. In many countries, government enterprises produce goods (such as telephone services, steel, and electricity) that are sold to individuals. While some individuals believe that, unless such commodities are directly produced by public enterprises, consumers will be exploited, other individuals believe that state enterprises are inevitably less efficient than private enterprises.

Other issues are subsumed under this second question. Government policy affects how firms produce the goods they produce: environmental protection legislation restricts pollution by firms; payroll taxes that firms must pay on the workers they employ make labor more expensive and thus discourage firms from using production techniques that require much labor; other provisions of the tax code may change the attractiveness of one machine relative to another. Though discussion of these questions seldom comes to the center of political debates, recent debates about the distorting effect of taxation and the desirability of nuclear reactors as energy sources are important exceptions.

*3. For whom? The question of distribution.* Government decisions about taxation or welfare programs affect how much income different individuals have to spend. Similarly, the government must decide what public goods to produce; some groups will benefit from the production of one public good, others from another.

*4. How are collective choices made*? There is one area that is of more concern to public-sector economics than to other branches of economics: the processes by which *collective* choices are made. Collective choices are the choices that we as a society must make together—for instance, concerning our legal structure, the size of our military establishment, our expenditures on other public goods, etc. Economics texts in fields other than public-sector economics focus on how individuals make their decisions concerning consumption, how firms make their decisions concerning production, and how the price system works to ensure that the goods demanded by consumers are produced by firms. Collective decision making is far more complicated, for individuals often disagree about what is desirable. After all, just as some individuals like chocolate ice cream and some like vanilla ice cream, some individuals get greater enjoyment out of public parks than do others. But while with private goods, the individual who likes chocolate ice cream can simply buy chocolate ice cream, and the individual who likes vanilla ice cream can buy vanilla ice cream, with public goods we must make a decision together. Anyone who has lived in a family knows something about the difficulties of collective decision making (should we go the movies or go bowling?). Public decision making is far more complex. One of the objectives of public-sector economics is to study how collective choices (or, as they are sometimes called, social choices) are made in democratic societies.

The recognition of this divergence of views is important in itself. It should make us wary of expressions such as "It is in the public interest" or "We are concerned with the good of society." Different policies may be good for different individuals. One should carefully specify who will benefit from and who will be harmed by each policy.

## Studying the Economics of the Public Sector

The study of the economics of the public sector can be divided into three categories.

*1. Knowing what activities the public sector engages in and how these are organized*. The complexity of the government's operations is so great that it is difficult to assess what its total expenditures are and what they go for. The budget of the federal government alone is a document that is more than 1,000 pages, and within the budget, activities are not easily compartmentalized. Some activities are undertaken in several different departments or agencies. Research, for instance, is funded through the Department of Defense, the National Science Foundation, the National Institutes of Health, and the National Air and Space Administration, among others. Also, a department such as the Department of Health and Human Services undertakes a myriad of activities some of which are only vaguely related to others.

Further, as we have noted, taxes and expenditures occur at several different levels: in some places, individuals pay not only federal and state taxes but a separate tax to the school district, another tax to the township, another tax to the county, still another tax to the jurisdictions that provide water and sewage, and still another tax to support the library.

*2. Understanding and anticipating, insofar as possible, the full consequences of these governmental activities.* When a tax is imposed on a corporation, who bears the tax? It is unlikely that the tax will do nothing more than reduce corporate profits. More likely, at least part of the tax will be passed onto consumers through higher prices. Or, perhaps, onto employees, as wages fall. When the government passes a rent control law, what will be the long-run consequences? Will renters really be better off in the long run? What are the consequences of the government's changing the age of retirement for social security? Of charging tuition in state universities? Of providing free medical care to the aged?

We have already noted that the consequences of government policies are often too complicated to predict accurately. There is often controversy about what the consequences will be. Indeed, even after a policy has been introduced, there is often controversy about what its effects are. . . .[W]e shall attempt not only to present all sides of some of the major controversies, but also to explain why such disagreements have persisted, and why it is difficult to resolve some of these important questions.

*3. Evaluating alternative policies.* To do this, not only do we need to know the consequences of alternative policies, but we need to develop criteria for evaluation. First we must understand the objectives of government policy, and then we must ascertain the extent to which the particular proposal meets (or is likely to meet) those criteria. But even that is not enough. Many proposals have effects other than the intended effects, and one must know how to predict these other consequences and to bring them into the evaluation.

## Normative Versus Positive Economics

The distinction we have just made, between analyzing the *consequences* of a government policy and making *judgments* concerning the desirability of particular government policies, is an important one. The former kind of analysis is often referred to as positive economics, the latter as normative economics (or welfare economics). Positive economics is concerned not only with analyzing the consequences of particular government policies, but with describing the activities of the public sector and the political and economic forces that brought these particular programs into existence. When economists step beyond the pure analysis of positive economics, they move into the realm of normative economics.

Normative economics is concerned with judging how well various policies work and designing new policies that better meet certain objectives.

Normative economics makes statements like, "If the government wishes to restrict the importation of oil in a way that is least costly to the government and consumers, tariffs on the importation of oil are preferable to quotas." Or, "If the objective of the farm program is to assist the poorer farmers, a system of price supports is not as good as a system of appropriately designed income transfers." In other words, in normative economics, economists compare the extent to which various government programs meet desired objectives, and determine which programs better meet these objectives. In contrast, positive economics makes statements like, "The imposition of quotas on oil in the 1950s led to higher domestic prices and the more rapid depletion of our natural resources." Such statements simply describe the effects of a program without evaluating whether intended objectives have been met. No judgments about the desirability or undesirability of the consequences are made.

When economists make such statements, they try not to impose their own criteria, their own values. They often view themselves as providing "technical assistance" to policy makers, helping them to attain their objectives.

At the same time, economists often comment on the objectives that politicians and policy makers put forth; sometimes stated objectives of politicians are not their real objectives. There is a hidden agenda. Economists may use the fact that a program differs from that which would be designed to achieve the stated objective to argue that the "true" objective is different, and they make *inferences* about what the true objectives of a program are by examining its consequences.

Economists also attempt to see, to what extent various objectives may be in conflict with one another and, when they are in conflict, to suggest how these conflicts can be resolved. Economists also try to clarify the full implications of alternative value systems. They attempt to see which values are basic and which values can be derived from other, more fundamental values. Economists' work on these questions often comes close to that of political philosophers.

The two approaches, the positive and the normative, are complementary; to make judgments about what activities the government *should* undertake, one must know the consequences of various government activities. One must be able to describe accurately what will happen if the government imposes one tax or another or attempts to subsidize one industry or another.

Some examples may help clarify the scope of positive and normative economics. Assume Congress is considering increasing a tax on cigarettes or alcohol. Positive economics is concerned with questions such as:

  a) How much will the prices of cigarettes or alcohol rise?

  b) How will this affect the demand for cigarettes or alcohol?

  c) Do lower-income individuals spend a larger proportion of their income on smoking (drinking) than do higher-income individuals?

d) What are the likely consequences of the tax on the profits of the cigarette industry or the liquor industry?

e) What will be the repercussions of a cigarette tax on the prices of tobacco and hence on the income of tobacco farmers? Of an alcohol tax on the price of alcohol and hence on the income of distilleries and breweries?

f) What will be the consequences of reduced smoking for the incidence of lung cancer and heart disease? What fraction of the associated medical expenditures is borne directly or indirectly by the government itself? What will be the consequences of reduced drinking on automobile accidents, and on the associated medical costs? What effect will the increased longevity from reduced smoking have on the social security system?

On the other hand, normative economics is concerned with *evaluating* the various consequences and coming to a judgment concerning the desirability of the tax changes:

a) If our primary concern in the choice of taxes is their impact on the poor, which tax is preferable, the liquor tax or the tobacco tax?

b) If our primary concern in the choice of taxes is how the tax distorts behavior (from what it would be in the absence of the tax), which tax is preferable, the liquor tax or the tobacco tax?

c) If our concern is reducing medical costs, which tax is preferable, the liquor tax or the tobacco tax?

d) Are there better taxes than either of these for attaining any particular objective of the government?

As a second example, assume the government is considering imposing a fine on steel firms generating pollution to discourage them from polluting, or a subsidy on pollution abatement equipment to encourage them to clean up their act. Positive economics is concerned with questions such as:

a) How much of a reduction in pollution will be caused by fines (or subsidies) of different magnitudes?

b) How much of an increase in the price of steel will be caused by the imposition of fines?

c) How much will this price hike reduce the demand for steel produced in the United States?

d) How will these reductions in demand affect employment and profits in the steel industry?

e) How much are those living in the vicinity of steel mills willing to pay for the reduction in the level of pollution? That is, how much is it worth to them?

Again, normative economics is concerned with evaluating the different effects:

a) If our concern is primarily with the poor, which system, a tax or a subsidy, would be preferable? The poor are affected as consumers by the change in prices of all commodities using steel. Since they are more likely to live near steel mills, pollution is more likely to affect them than the rich. But if a fine reduces the demand for steel and employment in the steel industry, the poorer, unskilled workers are the ones who would suffer the most. How do we add up all these effects? And what is the level of tax or subsidy that maximizes the welfare of the poor?

b) If our concern is with maximizing the value of national income, which system, a tax or a subsidy, would be preferable? Or should we have neither? And again, if it is desirable to have one or the other, what is the level of tax or subsidy that maximizes national income?

This example is typical of many such situations that we face in economic policy analysis: there are some gainers (those who can now breathe the cleaner air) and there are some losers (consumers who pay higher prices, producers who have lower profits, workers who lose their jobs). Normative economics is concerned with developing systematic procedures by which we can compare the gains of those who are better off with the losses of those who are worse off, to arrive at some overall judgment concerning the desirability of the proposal.

The distinction between normative statements and positive statements arises not only in discussions of particular policy changes but also in discussions of political processes. For instance, economists are concerned with *describing* the consequences of majority voting. When there are differences in views concerning how much should be spent on national defense, how do the divergent viewpoints get reflected in the outcome of any particular political process? What will be the consequences of requiring a two-thirds majority for increments in public expenditures exceeding a certain amount? What will be the consequences of increasing politicians' pay? Of restricting private contributions to political campaigns? Of public support for political campaigns? But economists are also concerned with *evaluating* alternative political processes. Are some political processes better, in some sense, than others? Are they more likely to produce "consistent" choices? Are some political processes more likely than others to yield equitable or efficient outcomes?

## Disagreements Among Economists

... *Failure to Trace the Full Consequences of a Government Policy*. Many controversies arise because one side or the other (or both) fails to trace the full consequences of a government policy. We have already noted several examples of this: in rent control, where the proponents failed to take into account the consequences for the supply of rental housing, or in Medicare, where some economists failed to take into account the sharp rise in expenditures on medical care by the aged.

An early example of the failure to think through the full consequences of a government policy was the window tax which was enacted in England in 1696 (under the Act of Making Good the Deficiency of the Clipped Money). At the time, windows were a luxury, and wealthy individuals had houses with more windows than those of poor individuals. It would have been administratively difficult to have an income tax; the government did not have the capacity to ascertain what each individual's income was. Indeed, individuals did not keep the kinds of records that would enable them to ascertain what their income was. Thus, the window tax base may have been a good measure of ability to pay. Those who could afford to have many windows were presumably in a better position to pay taxes; windows may have provided, in other words, an equitable basis of taxation. It was undoubtedly not the intention of those who levied the tax that the windows should be blocked up, but this was one of the major consequences of the tax. To avoid the tax, individuals built houses with few windows. The tax led to dark houses.

. . .[W]e shall frequently point out that the consequences of government policies are markedly different from the intended result. In the *long-run*, individuals and firms respond to changes in taxes and other government policies, and these long-run responses need to be taken into account. Moreover, as a result of these adjustments, a tax or subsidy on one good may have consequences for others. Any major tax change is likely to lead to repercussions for the whole economy. Although many of the individual effects may be small, in total, when all the effects are taken into account, these indirect repercussions may indeed be serious. . . . [L]ater . . . we shall point out some dramatic examples of this—where, for instance, a tax on wages turns out to leave workers unaffected but to lower the price of land.

***Differences in Views about How the Economy Behaves***. Economists agree that in evaluating a policy one should take into account all consequences; in fact, they view the identification of these consequences as one of their primary roles in policy analysis. They often disagree, however, about how the economy behaves, and hence about what the consequences of a government policy will be. Unlike other scientists, economists are not able to do controlled experiments. The standard way that science has found to test competing theories of how a system behaves is to carry out an experiment. With luck, the results of the experiment will bear out the predictions of only one theory, while discrediting others. But economists ordinarily do not have the possibility of doing controlled experiments. Instead, the experiments that economists can observe are the uncontrolled experiments that are being done for us in different markets and in different time periods, and the historical evidence often does not permit us to resolve disagreements about how the economy behaves.

In analyzing the consequences of various policies, economists make use of what are called models. Just as a model airplane attempts to replicate the basic features of an airplane, so too a model of the economy attempts to depict the basic features of the economy. The actual economy is obviously extremely complex; to see what is going on, and to make predictions about what the consequences of some change in policy will be, one needs to separate out the essential from the inessential features. What features one decides to focus on in constructing a model depend on what questions one wishes to address. The fact that models make simplifying assumptions, that they leave out many details, is a virtue, not a vice. An analogy may be useful. In going on a long trip, one often uses several maps. One map, depicting the interstate highway system, provides an overview, enabling one to see how to get from the general area where you are to the general area where you wish to go. You then use detailed maps, to see how to get from your point of origin to the expressway and from the expressway to your final destination. If the interstate highway map had every street and road in the country, the map would have to be so large as to limit its usefulness; the extra detail, though important for some purposes, would simply get in the way.

All analysis involves the use of models, of simple hypotheses concerning how individuals and firms will respond to various changes in government policy, and how these responses interact to determine the total impact on the economy. Everybody—politicians as well as economists—uses models in discussing the effects of alternative policies. The difference is that economists attempt to be *explicit* about their assumptions, and to be sure that their assumptions are consistent with each other and with the available evidence.

**1. The degree of competition.** One broad source of disagreement among economists is the extent to which the economy is competitive. . . . [W]e shall assume that the economy is very competitive; that there are many firms in each industry competing actively against each other. Each is so small relative to the market that it has no effect on the market price. There are no barriers to entry into the industry, so that if there are profitable opportunities in the industry, they will be quickly seized upon.

Few economists believe that in all sectors of the economy these assumptions are valid, but many economists believe that the economy is sufficiently competitive that the insights that one obtains from analyzing a competitive economy are relevant to an understanding of the effects of government policy in the American economy. Most economists also agree that there are some industries that are not well described by the competitive model, and that the analysis of the effects of taxation in those industries requires an analysis of how monopolies (industries with a single firm) or oligopolies (industries with a few firms) operate.

But there are other economists, such as Harvard's John Kenneth Galbraith, who believe that the economy is basically not very competitive, and that one obtains little insight into the effects of a tax by assuming that it is. These economists believe that most industries are dominated by three or four large firms; that though they may compete vigorously in some directions—for instance, in attempting to develop new products—in other areas, such as pricing policy, there is often tacit collusion. In their view, the traditional competitive model is likely to give misleading results. They contend that an appropriate model needs to take into account the limitations on the extent of competition.

Still others believe that there is a great deal of competition in the long run, but that in the short run competition is more limited. We cannot resolve these disagreements, but what we can do is to show how and when different views lead to different conclusions.

**2. The magnitude of response.** Even when economists agree about the kind of response that a particular policy will elicit, they may disagree about the magnitude of the response. That is, they may agree that income tax cuts will induce individuals to work harder, but some may feel that the effect is very likely to be small, while others may believe that the effect is likely to be large. This was one of the sources of dispute about the consequences of President Reagan's 1981 tax cut. Proponents of the tax cut believed that the lower rates would provide such a spur to the economy that tax revenues would actually increase. Critics agreed that the tax cut might provide some spur to the economy, but they argued that the increase in national income was likely to be so small that tax revenues would decline.[3] This decline would, in their view, lead to large deficits, which would, in turn, have a deleterious effect on the economy. As it turned out in the short run, the response of the economy was even smaller than some of Reagan's critics had predicted.

Although a central concern of modern economics is ascertaining the magnitude of the response of, say, investment to an investment tax credit, of consumption to a change in the income tax rate, of savings to an increase in the interest rate, etc., it is an unfortunate fact that various studies, using different bodies of data and different statistical techniques, come up with different conclusions. As economists obtain more data and develop better techniques for analyzing the limited available data, some of these disagreements may be resolved.

**Disagreement Over Values.** While the two previous sources of disagreement arise within positive economics, the final source of disagreement lies within normative economics. Even if there is agreement about the full consequences of some policy, there may be a disagreement about whether the policy is desirable. There are frequently *trade-offs*: a policy may increase national output but also increase inequality; a policy may increase employment but also increase inflation; a policy may benefit one group but make another group worse off. There are, in other words, some desirable consequences of the policy and some undesirable consequences. Individuals may weigh these consequences in different ways, some attaching more importance to price stability than to unemployment, others attaching more importance to growth than to inequality.

On questions of values, there is no more unanimity among economists than there is among philosophers. . . .

---

## Notes

1. This view has been particularly argued by George Stigler. See, for instance, his "Theory of Regulation," *Bell Journal*, Spring 1971, pp. 3-21.

2. See A.O. Hirschman, *Shifting Involvements: Private Interest and Public Action* (Princeton, NJ: Princeton University Press, 1982). Hirschman has put forth an interesting theory attempting to explain the constant changes in views on the appropriate role of the government.

3. See, for example, Don Fullerton, "On the Possibility of an Inverse Relationship between Tax Rates and Government Revenues," *Journal of Public Economics*, October 1982, pp. 1-22.

# Chapter 16

## ✴ ✴ ✴

# The Nature of Political Economy

Robert Gilpin

*Robert Gilpin relates "political economy" to international relations. He argues that the relationship between economics and politics in the modern world is reciprocal. Politics determines the framework of economic activity and channels it according to power. But the economic process redistributes power and wealth and thus transforms power both domestically and internationally. Gilpin examines the economic dimensions of realism, liberalism, and Marxism. What is the relationship between power and wealth? How do advocates of mercantilism and economic liberalism differ in their respective views of power and wealth? What role does government play in each approach?*

The international corporations have evidently declared ideological war on the "antiquated" nation state. . . . The charge that materialism, modernization and internationalism is the new liberal creed of corporate capitalism is a valid one. The implication is clear: the nation state as a political unit of democratic decision-making must, in the interest of "progress," yield control to the new mercantile mini-powers.[1]

While the structure of the multinational corporation is a modern concept, designed to meet the requirements of a modern age, the nation state is a very old-fashioned idea and badly adapted to serve the needs of our present complex world.[2]

**T**hese two statements—the first by Kari Levitt, a Canadian nationalist, the second by George Ball, a former United States undersecretary of state—express a dominant theme of contemporary writings on international relations. International society, we are told, is increasingly rent between its

Robert Gilpin is a widely published scholar who has served for many years at the Center of International Studies and the Woodrow Wilson School of Public and International Affairs of Princeton University.

Reprint from *International Politics: Anarch, Force, Political Economy, and Decision Making,* edited by Robert J. Art andRobert Jervis, pp. 275-283; 290. Originally from *U.S. Power and Multinational Corporation* by Robert Gilpin, pp. 20-44. Copyright © 1975 by Basic Books, Inc. Reprinted by permission of Basic Books, a division of HarperCollins Publishers, Inc., NY.

economic and its political organization. On the one hand, powerful economic and technological forces are creating a highly interdependent world economy, thus diminishing the traditional significance of national boundaries. On the other hand, the nation-state continues to command men's loyalties and to be the basic unit of political decision making. As one writer has put the issue, "The conflict of our era is between ethnocentric nationalism and geocentric technology."[3]

Ball and Levitt represent two contending positions with respect to this conflict. Whereas Ball advocates the diminution of the power of the nation-state in order to give full rein to the productive potentialities of the multinational corporation, Levitt argues for a powerful nationalism which could counterbalance American corporate domination. What appears to one as the logical and desirable consequence of economic rationality seems to the other to be an effort on the part of American imperialism to eliminate all contending centers of power.

Although the advent of the multinational corporation has put the question of the relationship between economics and politics in a new guise, it is an old issue. In the nineteenth century, for example, it was this issue that divided classical liberals like John Stuart Mill from economic nationalists, represented by Georg Friedrich List. Whereas the former gave primacy in the organization of society to economics and the production of wealth, the latter emphasized the political determination of economic relations. As this issue is central both to the contemporary debate on the multinational corporation and to the argument of this study, this chapter analyzes the three major treatments of the relationship between economics and politics—that is, the three major ideologies of political economy.

## The Meaning of Political Economy

The argument of this study is that the relationship between economics and politics, at least in the modern world, is a reciprocal one. On the one hand, politics largely determines the framework of economic activity and channels it in directions intended to serve the interests of dominant groups; the exercise of power in all its forms is a major determinant of the nature of an economic system. On the other hand, the economic process itself tends to redistribute power and wealth; it transforms the power relationships among groups. This in turn leads to a transformation of the political system, thereby giving rise to a new structure of economic relationships. Thus, the dynamics of international relations in the modern world is largely a function of the reciprocal interaction between economics and politics.

First of all, what do I mean by "politics" or "economics"? Charles Kindleberger speaks of economics and politics as two different methods of allocating scarce resources: the first through a market mechanism, the latter through a budget.[4] Robert Keohane and Joseph Nye, in an excellent analysis of international political economy, define economics and politics in terms of two levels of analysis: those of structure and of process.[5] Politics is the domain "having to do with the establishment of an order of relations, a structure. . . ."[6] Economics deals with "short-term allocative behavior (i.e., holding institutions, fundamental assumptions, and expectations constant). . . ."[7] Like Kindleberger's definition, however, this definition tends to isolate economic and political phenomena except under certain conditions, which Keohane and Nye define as the "politicization" of the economic system. Neither formulation comes to terms adequately with the dynamic and intimate nature of the relationship between the two.

In this study, the issue of the relationship between economics and politics translates into that between wealth and power. According to the statement of the problem, economics takes as its province the creation and distribution of wealth; politics is the realm of power. I shall examine their relationship from several ideological perspectives, including my own. But what is wealth? What is power?

In response to the question, What is wealth?, an economist-colleague responded, "What do you want, my thirty-second or thirty-volume answer?" Basic concepts are elusive in economics, as in any field of inquiry. No unchallengeable definitions are possible. Ask a physicist for his definition of the nature of space, time and matter, and you will not get a very satisfying response. What you will get is an *operational* definition, one which is usable: it permits the physicist to build an intellectual edifice whose foundations would crumble under the scrutiny of the philosopher.

Similarly, the concept of wealth, upon which the science of economics ultimately rests, cannot be clarified in a definitive way. Paul Samuelson, in his textbook, doesn't even try, though he provides a clue in his definition of economics as "the study of how men and society *choose*. . . to employ *scarce* productive resources . . . to produce various commodities . . . and distribute them for consumption."[8] Following this lead, we can say that wealth is anything (capital, land, or labor) that can generate future income; it is composed of physical assets and human capital (including embodied knowledge).

The basic concept of political science is power. Most political scientists would not stop here; they would include in the definition of political science the purpose for which power is used, whether this be the advancement of the public welfare or the domination of one group over another. In any case, few would dissent from the following statement of Harold Lasswell and Abraham Kaplan:

> The concept of power is perhaps the most fundamental in the whole of political science: the political process is the shaping, distribution, and exercise of power (in a wider sense, of all the deference values, or of influence in general).[9]

Power as such is not the sole or even the principal goal of state behavior. Other goals or values constitute the objectives pursued by nation-states: welfare, security, prestige. But power in its several forms (military, economic, psychological) is ultimately the necessary means to achieve these goals. For this reason, nation-states are intensely jealous of and sensitive to their relative power position. The distribution of power is important because it profoundly affects the ability of states to achieve what they perceive to be their interests.

The nature of power, however, is even more elusive than that of wealth. The number and variety of definitions should be an embarrassment to political scientists. Unfortunately, this study cannot bring the intradisciplinary squabble to an end. Rather, it adopts the definition used by Hans Morgenthau in his influential *Politics Among Nations:* "man's control over the minds and actions of other men."[10] Thus power, like wealth, is the capacity to produce certain results.

Unlike wealth, however, power cannot be quantified; indeed, it cannot be over-emphasized that power has an important psychological dimension. Perceptions of power relations are of critical importance; as a consequence, a fundamental task of statesmen is to manipulate the perceptions of other statesmen regarding the distribution of power. Moreover, power is relative to a specific situation or set of circumstances; there is no single hierarchy of power in international relations. Power may take many forms—military, economic, or psychological—though, in the final analysis, force is the ultimate form of power. Finally, the inability to predict the behavior of others or the outcome of events is of great significance. Uncertainty regarding the distribution of power and the ability of the statesmen to control events plays an important role in international relations. Ultimately, the determination of the distribution of power can be made only in retrospect as a consequence of war. It is precisely for this reason that war has had, unfortunately, such a central place in the history of international relations. In short, power is an elusive concept indeed upon which to erect a science of politics.

Such mutually exclusive definitions of economics and politics as these run counter to much contemporary scholarship by both economists and political scientists, for both disciplines are invading the formerly exclusive jurisdictions of the other. Economists, in particular, have become intellectual imperialists; they are applying their analytical techniques to traditional issues of political science with great success. These developments, however, really reinforce the basic premise of this study, namely, the inseparability of economics and politics.

The distinction drawn above between economics as the science of wealth and politics as the science of power is essentially an analytical one. In the real world, wealth and power are ultimately joined. This, in fact, is the basic rationale for a political economy of international relations. But in order to develop the argument of this study, wealth and power will be treated, at least for the moment, as analytically distinct.

To provide a perspective on the nature of political economy, the next section will discuss the three prevailing conceptions of political economy: liberalism, Marxism, and mercantilism. Liberalism regards politics and economics as relatively separable and autonomous spheres of activities; I associate most professional economists as well as many other academics, businessmen, and American officials with this outlook. Marxism refers to the radical critique of capitalism identified with Karl Marx and his contemporary disciples; according to this conception, economics determines politics and political structure. Mercantilism is a more questionable term because of its historical association with the desire of nation-states for a trade surplus and for treasure (money). One must distinguish, however, between the specific form mercantilism took in the seventeenth and eighteenth centuries and the general outlook of mercantilistic thought. The essence of the mercantilistic perspective, whether it is labeled economic nationalism, protectionism, or the doctrine of the German Historical School, is the subservience of the economy to the state and its interests—interests that range from matters of domestic welfare to those of international security. It is this more general meaning of mercantilism that is implied by the use of the term in this study.

Following the discussion of these three schools of thought, I shall elaborate my own, more eclectic, view of political economy and demonstrate its relevance for understanding the phenomenon of the multinational corporation.

## Three Conceptions of Political Economy

The three prevailing conceptions of political economy differ on many points. Several critical differences will be examined in this brief comparison. (See Table 1.)

Table 1
Comparison of the Three Conceptions of Political Economy

|  | Liberalism | Marxism | Mercantilism |
|---|---|---|---|
| Nature of economic relations | Harmonious | Conflictual | Conflictual |
| Nature of the actors | Households and firms | Economic classes | Nation-states |
| Goal of economic activity | Maximization of global welfare | Maximization of class interests | Maximization of national interest |
| Relationship between economics and politics | Economics *should* determine politics | Economics *does* determine politics | Politics determines economics |
| Theory of change | Dynamic equilibrium | Tendency toward disequilibrium | Shifts in the distribution of power |

***The Nature of Economic Relations.*** The basic assumption of liberalism is that the nature of international economic relations is essentially harmonious. Herein lay the great intellectual innovation of Adam Smith. Disputing his mercantilist predecessors, Smith argued that international economic relations could be made a positive-sum game; that is to say, everyone could gain, and no one need lose, from a proper ordering of economic relations, albeit the distribution of these gains may not be equal. Following Smith, liberalism assumes that there is a basic harmony between true national interest and cosmopolitan economic interest. Thus, a prominent member of this school of thought has written, in response to a radical critique, that the economic efficiency of the sterling standard in the nineteenth century and that of the dollar standard in the twentieth century serve "the cosmopolitan interest in a national form."[11] Although Great Britain and the United States gained the most from the international role of their respective currencies, everyone else gained as well.

Liberals argue that, given this underlying identity of national and cosmopolitan interests in a free market, the state should not interfere with economic transactions across national boundaries. Through free exchange of commodities, removal of restrictions on the flow of investment, and an international division of labor, everyone will benefit in the long run as a result of a more efficient utilization of the world's scarce resources. The national interest is therefore best served, liberals maintain, by a generous and cooperative attitude regarding economic relations with other countries. In essence, the pursuit of self-interest in a free, competitive economy achieves the greatest good for the greatest number in international no less than in the national society.

Both mercantilists and Marxists, on the other hand, begin with the premise that the essence of economic relations is conflictual. There is no underlying harmony; indeed, one group's gain is another's loss. Thus, in the language of game theory, whereas liberals regard economic relations as a non-zero-sum game, Marxists and mercantilists view economic relations as essentially a zero-sum game.

***The Goal of Economic Activity.*** For the liberal, the goal of economic activity is the optimum or efficient use of the world's scarce resources and the maximization of world welfare. While most liberals refuse to make value judgments regarding income distribution, Marxists and mercantilists stress the distributive effects of economic relations. For the Marxist the distribution of wealth among social classes is central: for the mercantilist it is the distribution of employment, industry, and military power among nation-states that is most significant. Thus, the goal of economic (and political) activity for both Marxists and mercantilists is the redistribution of wealth and power.

***The State and Public Policy***. These three perspectives differ decisively in their views regarding the nature of the economic actors. In Marxist analysis, the basic actors in both domestic and international relations are economic classes; the interests of the dominant class determine the foreign policy of the state. For mercantilists, the real actors in international economic relations are nation-states; national interest determines foreign policy. National interest may at times be influenced by the peculiar economic interests of classes, elites, or other subgroups of the society; but factors of geography, external configurations of power, and the exigencies of national survival are primary in determining foreign policy. Thus, whereas liberals speak of world welfare and Marxists of class interests, mercantilists recognize only the interests of particular nation-states.

Although liberal economists such as David Ricardo and Joseph Schumpeter recognized the importance of class conflict and neoclassical liberals analyze economic growth and policy in terms of national economies, the liberal emphasis is on the individual consumer, firm, or entrepreneur. The liberal ideal is summarized in the view of Harry Johnson that the nation-state has no meaning as an economic entity.[12]

Underlying these contrasting views are differing conceptions of the nature of the state and public policy. For liberals, the state represents an aggregation of private interests: public policy is but the outcome of a pluralistic struggle among interest groups. Marxists, on the other hand, regard the state as simply the "executive committee of the ruling class," and public policy reflects its interests. Mercantilists, however, regard the state as an organic unit in its own right: the whole is greater than the sum of its parts. Public policy, therefore, embodies the national interest or Rousseau's "general will" as conceived by the political elite.

***The Relationship between Economics and Politics: Theories of Change***. Liberalism, Marxism, and mercantilism also have differing views on the relationship between economics and politics. And their differences on this issue are directly relevant to their contrasting theories of international political change.

Although the liberal ideal is the separation of economics from politics in the interest of maximizing world welfare, the fulfillment of this ideal would have important political implications. The classical statement of these implications was that of Adam Smith in *The Wealth of Nations*.[13] Economic growth, Smith argued, is primarily a function of the extent of the division of labor, which in turn is dependent upon the scale of the market. Thus he attacked the barriers erected by feudal principalities and mercantilistic states against the exchange of goods and the enlargement of markets. If men were to multiply their wealth, Smith argued, the contradiction between political organization and economic rationality had to be resolved in favor of the latter. That is, the pursuit of wealth should determine the nature of the political order.

Subsequently, from nineteenth-century economic liberals to twentieth-century writers on economic integration, there has existed "the dream ... of a great republic of world commerce, in which national boundaries would cease to have any great economic importance and the web of trade would bind all the people of the world in the prosperity of peace."[14] For liberals the long-term trend is toward world integration, wherein functions, authority, and loyalties will be transferred from "smaller units to larger ones; from states to federalism; from federalism to supranational unions and from these to superstates."[15] The logic of economic and technological development, it is argued, has set mankind on an inexorable course toward global political unification and world peace.

In Marxism, the concept of the contradiction between economic and political relations was enacted into historical law. Whereas classical liberals—although Smith less than others—held that the requirements of economic rationality *ought* to determine political relations, the Marxist position was that the mode of production does in fact determine the superstructure of political relations. Therefore, it is argued, history can be understood as the product of the dialectical process—the contradiction between the evolving techniques of production and the resistant sociopolitical system.

Although Marx and Engels wrote remarkably little on international economics, Engels, in his famous polemic, *Anti-Duhring*, explicitly considers whether economics or politics is primary in determining the structure of international relations.[16] E.K. Duhring, a minor figure in the German Historical School, had argued, in contradiction to Marxism, that property and market relations resulted less from the economic logic of capitalism than from extraeconomic political factors: "The basis of the exploitation of many by man was an historical act of force which created an exploitative economic system for the benefit of the stronger man or class."[17] Since Engels, in his attack on Duhring, used the example of the unification of Germany through the Zollverein or customs union of 1833, his analysis is directly relevant to this discussion of the relationship between economics and political organization.

Engels argued that when contradictions arise between economic and political structures, political power adapts itself to the changes in the balance of economic forces; politics yields to the dictates of economic development. Thus, in the case of nineteenth-century Germany, the requirements of industrial production had become incompatible with its feudal, politically fragmented structure. "Though political reaction was victorious in 1815 and again in 1848," he argued, "it was unable to prevent the growth of large-scale industry in Germany and the growing participation of German commerce in the world market."[18] In summary, Engels wrote, "German unity had become an economic necessity."[19]

In the view of both Smith and Engels, the nation-state represented a progressive stage in human development, because it enlarged the political realm of economic activity. In each successive economic epoch, advances in technology and an increasing scale of production necessitate an enlargement of political organization. Because the city-state and feudalism restricted the scale of production and the division of labor made possible by the Industrial Revolution, they prevented the efficient utilization of resources and were, therefore, superseded by larger political units. Smith considered this to be a desirable objective; for Engels it was an historical necessity. Thus, in the opinion of liberals, the establishment of the Zollverein was a movement toward maximizing world economic welfare;[20] for Marxists it was the unavoidable triumph of the German industrialists over the feudal aristocracy.

Mercantilist writers from Alexander Hamilton to Frederich List to Charles de Gaulle, on the other hand, have emphasized the primacy of politics; politics, in this view, determines economic organization. Whereas Marxists and liberals have pointed to the production of wealth as the basic determinant of social and political organization, the mercantilists of the German Historical School, for example, stressed the primacy of national security, industrial development, and national sentiment in international political and economic dynamics.

In response to Engels's interpretation of the unification of Germany, mercantilists would no doubt agree with Jacob Viner that "Prussia engineered the customs union primarily for political reasons, in order to gain hegemony or at least influence over the lesser German states. It was largely in order to make certain that the hegemony should be Prussian and not Austrian that Prussia continually opposed Austrian entry into the Union, either openly or by pressing for a customs union tariff lower than highly protectionist Austria could stomach."[21] In pursuit of this strategic interest, it was "Prussian might, rather than a common zeal for political unification arising out of economic partnership, [that] ... played the major role."[22]

In contrast to Marxism, neither liberalism nor mercantilism has a developed theory of dynamics. The basic assumption of orthodox economic analysis (liberalism) is the tendency toward equilibrium; liberalism takes for granted the existing social order and given institutions. Change is assumed to be gradual and adaptive—a continuous process of dynamic equilibrium. There is no necessary connection between such political phenomena as war and revolution and the evolution of the economic system, although they would not deny that misguided statesmen can blunder into war over economic issues or that revolutions are conflicts over the distribution of wealth; but neither is inevitably linked to the evolution of the productive system. As for mercantilism, it sees change as taking place owing to shifts in the balance of power; yet, mercantilist writers such as members of the German Historical School and contemporary political realists have not developed a systematic theory of how this shift occurs.

On the other hand, dynamics is central to Marxism; indeed Marxism is essentially a theory of social *change*. It emphasizes the tendency toward *disequilibrium* owing to changes in the means of production and the consequent effects on the everpresent class conflict. When these tendencies can no longer be contained, the sociopolitical system breaks down through violent upheaval. Thus war and revolution are seen as an integral part of the economic process. Politics and economics are intimately joined.

*Why an International Economy?* From these differences among the three ideologies, one can get a sense of their respective explanations for the existence and functioning of the international economy.

An interdependent world economy constitutes the normal state of affairs for most liberal economists. Responding to technological advances in transportation and communications, the scope of the market mechanism, according to this analysis, continuously expands. Thus, despite temporary setbacks, the long-term trend is toward global economic integration. The functioning of the international economy is determined primarily by considerations of efficiency. The role of the dollar as the basis of the international monetary system, for example, is explained by the preference for it among traders and nations as the vehicle of international commerce.[23] The system is maintained by the mutuality of the benefits provided by trade, monetary arrangements, and investment.

A second view—one shared by Marxists and mercantilists alike—is that every interdependent international economy is essentially an imperial or hierarchial system. The imperial or hegemonic power organizes trade, monetary, and investment relations in order to advance its own economic and political interests. In the absence of the economic and especially the political influence of the hegemonic power, the system would fragment into autarkic economies or regional blocs. Whereas for liberalism maintenance of harmonious international market relations is the norm, for Marxism and mercantilism conflicts of class or national interests are the norm. . . .

## Notes

1. Kari Levitt, "The Hinterland Economy," *Canadian Forum 50* (July-August 1970): 163.
2. George W. Ball, "The Promise of the Multinational Corporation," *Fortune*, June 1, 1967, p. 80.
3. Sidney Rolfe, "Updating Adam Smith," *Interplay* (November 1968): 15.
4. Charles Kindleberger, *Power and Money: The Economics of International Politics and the Politics of International Economics* (New York: Basic Books, 1970), p. 5.
5. Robert Keohane and Joseph Nye, "World Politics and the International Economic System," in *The Future of the International Economic Order: An Agenda for Research*, ed. C. Fred Bergsten (Lexington, Mass: D.C. Heath, 1973), p. 116.
6. *Ibid.*
7. *Ibid.*, p. 117.
8. Paul Samuelson, *Economics: An Introductory Analysis* (New York: McGraw-Hill, 1967), p. 5.
9. Harold Lasswell and Abraham Kaplan, *Power and Society: A Framework for Political Inquiry* (New Haven: Yale University Press, 1950), p. 75.
10. Hans Morgenthau, *Politics Among Nations* (New York: Alfred A. Knopf), p. 26. For a more complex but essentially identical view, see Robert Dahl, *Modern Political Analysis* (Englewood Cliffs, N.J.: Prentice-Hall, 1963).
11. Kindleberger, *Power and Money*, p. 227.
12. For Johnson's critique of economic nationalism, see Harry Johnson, ed., *Economic Nationalism in Old and New States* (Chicago: University of Chicago Press, 1967).

13. Adam Smith, *The Wealth of Nations* (New York: Modern Library, 1937).

14. J.B. Condliffe, *The Commerce of Nations* (New York: W.W. Norton, 1950), p. 136.

15. Amitai Etzioni, "The Dialectics of Supernational Unification," in *International Political Communities* (New York: Doubleday, 1966), p. 147.

16. The relevant sections appear in Ernst Wangerman, ed., *The Role of Force in History: A Study of Bismarck's Policy of Blood and Iron*, trans. Jack Cohen (New York: International Publishers, 1968).

17. *Ibid.*, p. 12.

18. *Ibid.*, p. 13.

19. *Ibid.*, p. 14.

20. Gustav Stopler, *The German Economy* (New York: Harcourt, Brace and World, 1967), p. 11.

21. Jacob Viner, *The Customs Union Issue*. Studies in the Administration of International Law and Organization. no. 10 (New York: Carnegie Endowment for International Peace, 1950), pp. 98-99.

22. *Ibid.*, p. 101.

23. Richard Cooper, "Eurodollars, Reserve Dollars, and Asymmetrics in the International Monetary System," *Journal of International Economics 2* (September 1972): 325-44.

# Chapter 17

## ✱ ✱ ✱

# The Rise of the Virtual State

Richard Rosecrance

*Richard Rosecrance asserts that a new reality is emerging in the international arena: the virtual state—a state that has downsized its territorially-based productive capability making its economy reliant on mobile factors of production. Recognizing that its own production does not have to take place at home, it plays host to capital and labor of other nations. States, in effect, cultivate human capital. Of particular importance is that a nation's size and land holdings no longer determine the economic potential of the state. Production by domestic industries takes place abroad. Land becomes less valuable than technology, knowledge and direct investments. The state negotiates with foreign and domestic capital and labor to lure them into its own economic sphere. A state's economic strategy is now at least as important as its military strategy. Among the ramifications may be a world increasingly divided into "head" and "body" nations, where a country like Canada stresses the headquarters functions and China will be the model for a body nation. Do virtual states, as the author declares, hold the competitive key to greater wealth in the 21st century? Will the rise of the virtual state force a fundamental rethinking of past theories of power in international politics? If virtual states need other states' production capabilities will this result in a reduced danger of conflict?*

## Territory Becomes Passé

Amid the supposed clamor of contending cultures and civilizations, a new reality is emerging. The nation-state is becoming a tighter, more vigorous unit capable of sustaining the pressures of worldwide competition. Developed states are putting aside military, political, and territorial ambitions as they struggle not for cultural dominance but for a greater share of world output. Countries are not uniting as civilizations and girding for conflict with one another. Instead, they are downsizing—in function if not in geographic form.

Richard Rosecrance is Professor of Political Science and Director of the Center for International Relations at the University of California, Los Angeles.

Reprinted by permission of *Foreign Affairs*, Vol. 75, No. 4, July/August 1996, pp. 45-61. Copyright © 1996 by the Council on Foreign Relations, Inc.

Today and for the foreseeable future, the only international civilization worthy of the name is the governing economic culture of the world market. Despite the view of some contemporary observers, the forces of globalization have successfully resisted partition into cultural camps.

Yet the world's attention continues to be mistakenly focused on military and political struggles for territory. In beleaguered Bosnia, Serbian leaders sought to create an independent province with an allegiance to Belgrade. A few years ago Iraqi leader Saddam Hussein aimed to corner the world oil market through military aggression against Kuwait and, in all probability, Saudi Arabia; oil, a product of land, represented the supreme embodiment of his ambitions. In Kashmir, India and Pakistan are vying for territorial dominance over a population that neither may be fully able to control. Similar rivalries beset Rwanda and Burundi and the factions in Liberia.

These examples, however, look to the past. Less developed countries, still producing goods that are derived from land, continue to covet territory. In economies where capital, labor, and information are mobile and have risen to predominance, no land fetish remains. Developed countries would rather plumb the world market than acquire territory. The virtual state—a state that has downsized its territorially based production capability—is the logical consequence of this emancipation from the land.

In recent years the rise of the economic analogue of the virtual state—the virtual corporation—has been widely discussed. Firms have discovered the advantages of locating their production facilities wherever it is most profitable. Increasingly, this is not in the same location as corporate headquarters. Parts of a corporation are dispersed globally according to their specialties. But the more important development is the political one, the rise of the virtual state, the political counterpart of the virtual corporation.

The ascent of the trading state preceded that of the virtual state. After World War II, led by Japan and Germany, the most advanced nations shifted their efforts from controlling territory to augmenting their share of world trade. In that period, goods were more mobile than capital or labor, and selling abroad became the name of the game. As capital has become increasingly mobile, advanced nations have come to recognize that exporting is no longer the only means to economic growth; one can instead produce goods overseas for the foreign market.

As more production by domestic industries takes place abroad and land becomes less valuable than technology, knowledge, and direct investment, the function of the state is being further redefined. The state no longer commands resources as it did in mercantilist yesteryear; it negotiates with foreign and domestic capital and labor to lure them into its own economic sphere and stimulate its growth. A nations's economic strategy is now at least as important as its military strategy; its ambassadors have become foreign trade and investment representatives. Major foreign trade and investment deals command executive attention as political and military issues did two decades ago. The frantic two weeks in December 1994 when the White House outmaneuvered the French to secure for Raytheon Company a deal worth over $1 billion for the management of rainforests and air traffic in Brazil exemplifies the new international crisis.

Timeworn methods of augmenting national power and wealth are no longer effective. Like the headquarters of a virtual corporation, the virtual state determines overall strategy and invests in its people rather than amassing expensive production capacity. It contracts out other functions to states that specialize in or need them. Imperial Great Britain may have been the model for the nineteenth century, but Hong Kong will be the model for the 21st.

The virtual state is a country whose economy is reliant on mobile factors of production. Of course it houses virtual corporations and presides over foreign direct investment by its enterprises. But more than this, it encourages, stimulates, and to a degree even coordinates such activities. In formulating economic strategy, the virtual state recognizes that its own production does not have to take place at home; equally, it may play host to the capital and labor of other nations. Unlike imperial Germany, czarist Russia, and the United States of the Gilded Age—which aimed at nineteenth-century omnicompetence—it does not seek to combine or excel in all economic functions, from mining and agriculture to production and distribution. The virtual state specializes in modern technical and research services and derives its income not just from high-value manufacturing, but from product design, marketing, and financing. The rationale for its economy is efficiency attained through productive downsizing. Size no longer determines economic potential. Virtual nations hold the competitive key to greater wealth in the 21st century. They will likely supersede the continent-sized and self-sufficient units that prevailed in the past. Productive specialization will dominate internationally just as the reduced instruction set, or "RISC," computer chip has outmoded its more versatile but slower predecessors.

## The Trading State

In the past, states were obsessed with land. The international system with its intermittent wars was founded on the assumption that land was the major factor in both production and power. States could improve their position by building empires or invading other nations to seize territory. To acquire land was a boon: a conquered province contained peasants and grain supplies, and its inhabitants rendered tribute to the new sovereign. Before the age of nationalism, a captured principality willingly obeyed its new ruler. Hence the Hapsburg monarchy, Spain,

France, and Russia could become major powers through territorial expansion in Europe between the sixteenth and nineteenth centuries.

With the Industrial Revolution, however, capital and labor assumed new importance. Unlike land, they were mobile ingredients of productive strength. Great Britain innovated in discovering sophisticated uses for the new factors. Natural resources—especially coal, iron, and, later, oil—were still economically vital. Agricultural and mineral resources were critical to the development of the United States and other fledgling industrial nations like Australia, Canada, South Africa, and New Zealand in the nineteenth century. Not until late in the twentieth century did mobile factors of production become paramount.

By that time, land had declined in relative value and become harder for nations to hold. Colonial revolutions in the Third World since World War II have shown that nationalist mobilization of the population in developing societies impedes an imperialist or invader trying to extract resources. A nation may expend the effort to occupy new territory without gaining proportionate economic benefits.

In time, nationalist resistance and the shift in the basis of production should have an impact on the frequency of war. Land, which is fixed, can be physically captured, but labor, capital, and information are mobile and cannot be definitively seized; after an attack, these resources can slip away like quicksilver. Saddam Hussein ransacked the computers in downtown Kuwait City in August 1990 only to find that the cash in bank accounts had already been electronically transferred. Even though it had abandoned its territory, the Kuwaiti government could continue to spend billions of dollars to resist Hussein's conquest.

Today, for the wealthiest industrial countries such as Germany, the United States, and Japan, investment in land no longer pays the same dividends. Since mid-century, commodity prices have fallen nearly 40 percent relative to prices of manufactured goods.[1] The returns from the manufacturing trade greatly exceed those from agricultural exports. As a result, the terms of trade for many developing nations have been deteriorating, and in recent years the rise in prices of international services has outpaced that for manufactured products. Land prices have been steeply discounted.

Amid this decline, the 1970s and 1980s brought a new political prototype: the trading state. Rather than territorial expansion, the trading state held trade to be its fundamental purpose. This shift in national strategy was driven by the declining value of fixed productive assets. Smaller states—those for which, initially at any rate, a military-territorial strategy was not feasible—also adopted trade-oriented strategies. Along with small European and East Asian states, Japan and West Germany moved strongly in a trading direction after World War II.

Countries tend to imitate those that are most powerful. Many states followed in the wake of Great Britain in the nineteenth century; in recent decades, numerous states seeking to improve their lot in the world have emulated Japan. Under Mikhail Gorbachev in the 1980s, even the Soviet Union sought to move away from its emphasis on military spending and territorial expansion.

In recent years, however, a further stimulus has hastened this change. Faced with enhanced international competition in the late 1980s and early 1990s, corporations have opted for pervasive downsizing. They have trimmed the ratio of production workers to output, saving on costs. In some cases productivity increases resulted from pruning of the work force; in others output increased. These improvements have been highly effective; according to economist Stephen Roach in a 1994 paper published by the investment banking firm Morgan Stanley, they have nearly closed the widely noted productivity gap between services and manufacturing. The gap that remains is most likely due to measurement problems. The most efficient corporations are those that can maintain or increase output with a steady or declining amount of labor. Such corporations grew on a worldwide basis.

Meanwhile, corporations in Silicon Valley recognized that cost-cutting, productivity, and competitiveness could be enhanced still further by using the production lines of another company. The typical American plant at the time, such as Ford Motor Company's Willow Run factory in Michigan, was fully integrated, with headquarters, design officers, production workers, and factories located on substantial tracts of land. This comprehensive structure was expansive to maintain and operate, hence a firm that could employ someone else's production line could cut costs dramatically. Land and machines did not have to be bought, labor did not have to be hired, medical benefits did not have to be provided. These advantages could result from what are called economies of scope, with a firm turning out different products on the same production line or quality circle. Or they might be the result of small, specialized firms' ability to perform exacting operations, such as the surface mounting of miniaturized components directly on circuit boards without the need for soldering or conventional wiring. In either case, the original equipment manufacturer would contract out its production to other firms. SCI Systems, Solectron, Merix, Flextronics, Smartflex, and Sanmina turn out products for Digital Equipment, Hewlett-Packard, and IBM. In addition, AT&T, Apple, IBM, Motorola, MCI, and Corning meet part of their production needs through other suppliers. TelePad, a company that makes pen-based computers, was launched with no manufacturing capability at all. Compaq's latest midrange computer is to be produced on another company's production line.

Thus was born the virtual corporation, an entity with research, development, design, marketing, financing, legal, and other headquarters functions, but few or no manufacturing facilities: a company with a head but no body. It represents the ultimate achievement of corporate downsizing, and the model is spreading rapidly from firm to firm. It is not surprising that the virtual corporation should catch on. "Concept" or "head" corporations can design new products for a range of different production facilities. Strategic alliances between firms, which increase specialization, are also very profitable. According to the October 2, 1995, *Financial Times*, firms that actively pursue strategic alliances are 50 percent more profitable than those that do not.

## Toward the Virtual State

In a setting where the economic functions of the trading state have displaced the territorial functions of the expansionist nation, the newly pruned corporation has led to the emerging phenomenon of the virtual state. Downsizing has become an index of corporate efficiency and productivity gains. Now the national economy is also being downsized. Among the most efficient economies are those that possess limited production capacity. The archetype is Hong Kong, whose production facilities are now largely situated in southern China. This arrangement may change after 1997 with Hong Kong's reversion to the mainland, but it may not. It is just as probable that Hong Kong will continue to govern parts of the mainland economically as it is that Beijing will dictate to Hong Kong politically. The one country-two systems formula will likely prevail. In this context, it is important to remember that Britain governed Hong Kong politically and legally for 150 years, but it did not dictate its economics. Nor did this arrangement prevent Hong Kong Chinese from extending economic and quasi-political controls to areas outside their country.

The model of the virtual state suggests that political as well as economic strategy push toward a downsizing and relocation of production capabilities. The trend can be observed in Singapore as well. The successors of Lee Kuan Yew keep the country on a tight political rein but still depend economically on the inflow of foreign factors of production. Singapore's investment in China, Malaysia, and elsewhere is within others' jurisdictions. The virtual state is in this sense a negotiating entity. It depends as much or more on economic access abroad as it does on economic control at home. Despite its past reliance on domestic production, Korea no longer manufactures everything at home, and Japanese production (given the high yen) is now increasingly lodged abroad. In Europe, Switzerland is the leading virtual nation; as much as 98 percent of Nestlé's production capacity, for instance, is located abroad. Holland now produces most of its goods outside its borders. England is also moving in tandem with the worldwide trend; according to the Belgian economic historian Paul Bairoch in 1994, Britain's foreign direct investment abroad was almost as large as America's. A remarkable 20 percent of the production of U.S. corporations now takes place outside the United States.

A reflection of how far these tendencies have gone is the growing portion of GDP consisting of high-value-added services, such as concept, design, consulting, and financial services. Services already constitute 70 percent of American GDP. Of the total, 63 percent are in the high-value category. Of course manufacturing matters, but it matters much less than it once did. As a proportion of foreign direct investment, service exports have grown strikingly in most highly industrialized economies. According to a 1994 World Bank report, *Liberalizing International Transactions in Services*, "The reorientation of [foreign direct investment] towards the services sector has occurred in almost all developed market economies, the principal exporters of services capital: in the most important among them, the share of the services sector is around 40 percent of the stock of outward FDI, and that share is rising."

Manufacturing, for these nations, will continue to decline in importance. If services productivity increases as much as it has in recent years, it will greatly strengthen U.S. competitiveness abroad. But it can no longer be assumed that services face no international competition. Efficient high-value services will be as important to a nation as the manufacturing of automobiles and electrical equipment once were.[2] Since 1959, services prices have increased more than three times as rapidly as industrial prices. This means that many nations will be able to prosper without major manufacturing capabilities.

Australia is an interesting example. Still reliant on the production of sheep and raw materials (both related to land), Australia has little or no industrial sector. Its largest export to the United States is meat for hamburgers. On the other hand, its service industries of media, finance, and telecommunications—represented most notably by the media magnate Rupert Murdoch—are the envy of the world. Canada represents a similar amalgam of raw materials and powerful service industries in newspapers, broadcast media, and telecommunications.

As a result of these trends, the world may increasingly become divided into "head" and "body" nations, or nations representing some combination of those two functions. While Australia and Canada stress the headquarters or head functions, China will be the 21st-century model of a body nation. Although China does not innately or immediately know what to produce for the world market, it has found success in joint ventures with foreign corporations. China will be an attractive place to produce manufactured goods, but only because sophisticated enterprises from other countries design, market, and finance the products China makes. At present China cannot chart its own industrial future.

Neither can Russia. Focusing on the products of land, the Russians are still prisoners of territorial fetishism. Their commercial laws do not yet permit the delicate and sophisticated arrangements that ensure that "body" manufacturers deliver quality goods for their foreign "head." Russia's transportation network is also primitive. These, however, are temporary obstacles. In time Russia, with China and India, will serve as an important locus of the world's production plant.

## The Vestiges of Serfdom

The world is embarked on a progressive emancipation from land as a determinant of production and power. For the Third World, the past unchangeable strictures of comparative advantage can be overcome through the acquisition of a highly trained labor force. Africa and Latin America may not have to rely on the exporting of raw materials or agricultural products; through education, they can capitalize on an educated labor force, as India has in Bangalore and Ireland in Dublin. Investing in human capital can substitute for trying to foresee the vagaries of the commodities markets and avoid the constant threat of overproduction. Meanwhile, land continues to decline in value. Recent studies of 180 countries show that as population density rises, per capita GDP falls. In a new study, economist Deepak Lal notes that investment as well as growth is inversely related to land holdings.[3]

These findings are a dramatic reversal of past theories of power in international politics. In the 1930s the standard international relations textbook would have ranked the great powers in terms of key natural resources: oil, iron ore, coal, bauxite, copper, tungsten, and manganese. Analysts presumed that the state with the largest stock of raw materials and goods derived from land would prevail. CIA estimates during the Cold War were based on such conclusions. It turns out, however, that the most prosperous countries often have a negligible endowment of natural resources. For instance, Japan has shut down its coal industry and has no iron ore, bauxite, or oil. Except for most of its rice, it imports much of its food. Japan is richly endowed with human capital, however, and that makes all the difference.

The implications for the United States are equally striking. As capital, labor, and knowledge become more important than land in charting economic success, America can influence and possible even reshape its pattern of comparative advantage. The "new trade theory," articulated clearly by the economist Paul Krugman, focuses on path dependence, the so-called QWERTY effect of past choices. The QWERTY keyboard was not the arrangement of letter-coded keys that produced the fastest typing, except perhaps for left-handers. But, as the VHS videotape format became the standard for video recording even though other formats were technically better, the QWERTY keyboard became the standard for the typewriter (and computer) industry, and everyone else had to adapt to it. Nations that invested from the start in production facilities for the 16-kilobyte computer memory chip also had great advantages down the line in 4- and 16-megabyte chips.

Intervention at an early point in the chain of development can influence results later on, which suggests that the United States and other nations can and should deliberately alter their pattern of comparative advantage and choose their economic activity.

American college and graduate education, for example, has supported the decisive U.S. role in the international services industry in research and development, consulting, design, packaging, financing, and the marketing of new products. Mergers and acquisitions are American subspecialties that draw on the skills of financial analysts and attorneys. The American failure, rather, has been in the first 12 years of education. Unlike that of Germany and Japan (or even Taiwan, Korea, and Singapore), American elementary and secondary education falls well below the world standard.

Economics teaches that products should be valued according to their economic importance. For a long period, education was undervalued, socially and economically speaking, despite productivity studies by Edward Denison and others that showed its long-term importance to U.S. growth and innovation. Recent studies have underscored this importance. According to the World Bank, 64 percent of the world's wealth consists of human capital. But the social and economic valuation of kindergarten through 12th-grade education has still not appreciably increased. Educators, psychologists, and school boards debate how education should be structured, but Americans do not invest more money in it. Corporations have sought to upgrade the standards of teaching and learning in their regions, but localities and states have lagged behind, as has the federal government. Elementary and high school teachers should be rewarded as patient creators of high-vale capital in the United States and elsewhere. In Switzerland, elementary school teachers are paid around $70,000 per year, about the salary of a starting lawyer at a New York firm. In international economic competition, human capital has turned out to be at least as important as other varieties of capital. In spite of their reduced functions, states liberated from the confines of their geography have been able, with appropriate education, to transform their industrial and economic futures.

## The Reduced Danger of Conflict

As nations turn to the cultivation of human capital, what will a world of virtual states be like? Production for one company or country can now take place in many parts of the world. In the process of downsizing, corporations and nation-states will have to get used to reliance on others. Virtual corporations need other corporations' production facilities. Virtual nations need other states' production capabilities. As a result, economic relations between states will come to resemble nerves connecting heads in one place to bodies somewhere else. Naturally, producer nations will be working quickly to become the brains behind emerging industries elsewhere. But in time, few nations will have within their borders all the components of a technically advanced economic existence.

To server the connections between states would undermine the organic unit. States jointed in this way are therefore less likely to engage in conflict. In the past, international norms underlying the balance of power, the Concert of Europe, or even rule by the British Raj helped specify appropriate courses of action for parties in dispute. The international economy also rested partially on normative agreement. Free trade, open domestic economies, and, more recently, freedom of movement for capital were normative notions. In addition to specifying conditions for borrowing, the International Monetary Fund is a norm-setting agency that inculcates market economics in nations not fully ready to accept their international obligations.

Like national commercial strategies, these norms have been largely abstracted from the practices of successful nations. In the nineteenth century many countries emulated Great Britain and its precepts. In the British pantheon of virtues, free trade was a norm that could be extended to other nations without self-defeat. Success for one nation did not undermine the prospects for others. But the acquisition of empire did cause congestion for other nations on the paths to industrialization and growth. Once imperial Britain had taken the lion's share, there was little left for others. The inability of all nations to live up to the norms Britain established fomented conflict between them.

In a similar vein, Japan's current trading strategy could be emulated by many other countries. Its pacific principles and dependence on world markets and raw materials supplies have engendered greater economic cooperation among other countries. At the same time, Japan's insistence on maintaining a quasi-closed domestic economy and a foreign trade surplus cannot be successfully imitated by everyone; if some achieve the desired result, others necessarily will not. In this respect, Japan's recent practices and norms stand athwart progress and emulation by other nations.

President Clinton rightly argues that the newly capitalist developmental states, such as Korea and Taiwan, have simply modeled themselves on restrictionist Japan. If this precedent were extended to China, the results would endanger the long-term stability of the world economic and financial system. Accordingly, new norms calling for greater openness in trade, finance, and the movement of factors of production will be necessary to stabilize the international system. Appropriate norms reinforce economic incentives to reduce conflict between differentiated international units.

## Defusing the Population Bomb

So long as the international system of nation-states lasts, there will be conflict among its members. States see events from different perspectives, and competition and struggle between them are endemic. The question is how far conflicts will proceed. Within a domestic system, conflicts between individuals need not escalate to the use of physical force. Law and settlement procedures usually reduce outbreaks of hostility. In international relations, however, no sovereign, regnant authority can discipline feuding states. International law sets a standard, but it is not always obeyed. The great powers constitute the executive committee of nation-states and can intervene from time to time to set things right. But, as Bosnia shows, they often do not, and they virtually never intervene in the absence of shared norms and ideologies.

In these circumstances, the economic substructure of international relations becomes exceedingly important. That structure can either impel or retard conflicts between nation-states. When land is the major factor of production, the temptation to strike another nation is great. When the key elements of production are less tangible, the situation changes. The taking of real estate does not result in the acquisition of knowledge, and aggressors cannot seize the needed capital. Workers may flee from an invader. Wars of aggression and wars of punishment are losing their impact and justification.

Eventually, however, contend critics such as Paul Ehrlich, author of *The Population Bomb*, land will become important once again. Oil supplies will be depleted; the quantity of fertile land will decline; water will run dry. Population will rise relative to the supply of natural resources and food. This process, it is claimed, could return the world to the eighteenth and nineteenth centuries, with clashes over territory once again the engine of conflict. The natural resources on which the world currently relies may one day run out, but, as before, there will be substitutes. One sometimes forgets that in the 1840s whale oil, which was the most common fuel for lighting, became unavailable. The harnessing of global energy and the production of food does not depend on particular bits of fluid, soil, or rock. The question, rather, is how to release the energy contained in abundant matter.

But suppose the productive value of land does rise. Whether that rise would augur a return to territorial competition would depend on whether the value of land rises relative to financial capital, human capital, and information. Given the rapid technological development of recent years, the primacy of the latter seems more likely. Few perturbing trends have altered the historical tendency toward the growing intangibility of value in social and economic terms. In the 21st century it seems scarcely possible that this process would suddenly reverse itself, and land would yield a better return than knowledge.

Diminishing their command of real estate and productive assets, nations are downsizing, in functional if not in geographic terms. Small nations have attained peak efficiency and competitiveness, and even large nations have begun to think small. If durable access to assets elsewhere can be assured, the need to physically possess them diminishes. Norms are potent reinforcements of such arrangements. Free movement of capital and goods, substantial international and domestic investment, and high levels of technical education have been the recipe for success in the industrial world of the late twentieth century. Those who depended on others did better than those who depended only on themselves. Can the result be different in the future? Virtual states, corporate alliances, and essential trading relationships augur peaceful times. They may not solve domestic problems, but the economic bonds that link virtual and other nations will help ease security concerns.

## The Civic Crisis

Though peaceful in its international implications, the rise of the virtual state portends a crisis for democratic politics. Western democracies have traditionally believed that political reform, extension of suffrage, and economic restructuring could solve their problems. In the 21st century none of these measures can fully succeed. Domestic political change does not suffice because it has insufficient jurisdiction to deal with global problems. The people in a particular state cannot determine international outcomes by holding an election. Economic restructuring in one state does not necessarily affect others. And the political state is growing smaller, not larger.

If ethnic movements are victorious in Canada, Mexico, and elsewhere, they will divide the state into smaller entities. Even the powers of existing states are becoming circumscribed. In the United States, if Congress has its way, the federal government will lose authority. In response to such changes, the market fills the vacuum, gaining power.

As states downsize, malaise among working people is bound to spread. Employment may fluctuate and generally decline. President Clinton observed last year that the American public has fallen into a funk. The economy may temporarily be prosperous, but there is no guarantee that favorable conditions will last. The flow of international factors of production—technology, capital, and labor—will swamp the stock of economic power at home. The state will become just one of many players in the international marketplace and will have to negotiate directly with foreign factors of production to solve domestic economic problems. Countries must induce foreign capital to enter their domain. To keep such investment, national economic authorities will need to maintain low inflation, rising productivity, a strong currency, and a flexible and trained labor force. These demands will sometimes conflict with domestic interests that want more government spending, larger budget deficits, and more benefits. That conflict will result in continued domestic insecurity over jobs, welfare, and medical care. Unlike the remedies applied in the insulated and partly closed economies of the past, purely domestic policies can no longer solve these problems.

## The Necessity of Internationalization

The state can compensate for its deficient jurisdiction by seeking to influence economic factors abroad. The domestic state therefore must not only become a negotiating state but must also be internationalized. This is a lesson already learned in Europe, and well on the way to codification in East Asia. Among the world's major economies and polities, only the United States remains, despite its potent economic sector, essentially introverted politically and culturally. Compared with their counterparts in other nations, citizens born in the United States know fewer foreign languages, understand less about foreign cultures, and live abroad reluctantly, if at all. In recent years, many English industrial workers who could not find jobs migrated to Germany, learning the language to work there. They had few American imitators.

The virtual state is an agile entity operating in twin jurisdictions: abroad and at home. It is as prepared to mine gains overseas as in the domestic economy. But in large countries, internationalization operates differentially. Political and economic decision-makers have begun to recast their horizons, but middle managers and workers lag behind. They expect too much and give and learn too little. That is why the dawn of the virtual state must also be the sunrise of international education and training. The virtual state cannot satisfy all its citizens. The possibility of commanding economic power in the sense of effective state control has greatly declined. Displaced workers and businesspeople must be willing to look abroad for opportunities. In the United States, they can do this only if American education prepares the way.

---

### Notes

1. See, for example, Enzo R. Grilli and Maw Cheng Yang, "Primary Commodity Prices, Manufactured Goods Prices, and the Terms of Trade of Developing Countries: What the Long Run Shows," *The World Bank Economic Review*, 1988, Vol. 2, No. 1, pp. 1-47.

2. See José Ripoll, "The Future of Trade in International Services," *Center for International Relations Working Paper*, UCLA, January 1996.

3. Daniel Garstka, "Land and Economic Prowess" (unpublished mimeograph), UCLA, 1995; Deepak Lal, "Factor Endowments, Culture and Politics: On Economic Performance in the Long Run" (unpublished mimeograph), UCLA, 1996.

# Chapter 18

### ✳ ✳ ✳

## The Future of Diplomacy

Hans J. Morgenthau
Revised by Kenneth W. Thompson

*Hans J. Morgenthau, in this excerpt from his classic treatise, focuses on the future of diplomacy and how it can be revived. In discussing the promise of diplomacy, he prescribes nine rules—specifically, four fundamental rules for successfully executing diplomacy and five prerequisites of compromise. While compliance makes compromise possible, it does not assure its success; to give compromise a chance to succeed, the five other rules must be observed. One of his assertions is the idea that "as there can be no permanent peace without a world state, there can be no world state without the peace-preserving and community-building processes of diplomacy." Also, he suggests that the objective of war is simple and unconditional (to break the will of the enemy), while the objective of foreign policy is relative and conditional (to bend, not to break, the will of the other side). Do you agree with Morgenthau on these points? Are both war and diplomacy (or foreign policy) means of pursuing the same political objectives, as Clausewitz insisted?*

### How Can Diplomacy Be Revived?

The revival of diplomacy requires the elimination of the factors, or at least of some of their consequences, responsible for the decline of the traditional diplomatic practices. Priority in this respect belongs to the depreciation of

Hans J. Morgenthau, who died in 1980, was an Albert A. Michelson Distinguished Service Professor of Political Science and Modern History and a Director of the Center for the Study of American Foreign Policy, both at the University of Chicago. Educated at the Universities of Berlin, Frankfurt, and Munich, he taught and practiced law in Europe before going to the United States in 1937. Kenneth W. Thompson is the Director of the Miller Center of Public Affairs and the J. Wilson Newman Professor of Governance at the University of Virginia.

diplomacy and its corollary: diplomacy by parliamentary procedures. In so far as that depreciation is only the result of the depreciation of power politics, what we have said about the latter should suffice for the former. Diplomacy, however morally unattractive its business may seem to many, is nothing but a symptom of the struggle for power among sovereign nations, which try to maintain orderly and peaceful relations among themselves. If there were a way of banning the struggle for power from the international scene, diplomacy would disappear of itself. If order and anarchy, peace and war, were matters of no concern to the nations of the world, they could dispense with diplomacy, prepare for war, and hope for the best. If nations who are sovereign, who are supreme within their territories with no superior above them, want to preserve peace and order in their relations, they must try to persuade, negotiate, and exert pressure upon each other. That is to say, they must engage in, cultivate, and rely upon diplomatic procedures.

The new parliamentary diplomacy is no substitute for these procedures. On the contrary, it tends to aggravate rather than mitigate international conflicts and leaves the prospect for peace dimmed rather than brightened. Three essential qualities [or vices] of the new diplomacy are responsible for these unfortunate results: its publicity, its major votes, and its fragmentation of international issues. . . .

## The Promise of Diplomacy: Its Nine Rules[1]

Diplomacy could revive if it would part with these vices, which in recent years have well-nigh destroyed its usefulness, and if it would restore the techniques which have controlled the mutual relations of nations since time immemorial. By doing so, diplomacy would realize only one of the preconditions for the preservation of peace. The contribution of a revived diplomacy to the cause of peace would depend upon the methods and purposes of its use. The discussion of these uses is the last task we have set ourselves in this book.

### Four Fundamental Rules

***Diplomacy Must Be Divested of the Crusading Spirit***. This is the first of the rules that diplomacy can neglect only at the risk of war. In the words of William Graham Sumner:

> If you want war, nourish a doctrine. Doctrines are the most frightful tyrants to which men ever are subject, because doctrines get inside of a man's own reason and betray him against himself. Civilized men have done their fiercest fighting for doctrines. The reconquest of the Holy Sepulcher, "the balance of power," "no universal dominion," "trade follows the flag," "he who holds the land will hold the sea," "the throne and the altar," the revolution, the faith—these are the things for which men have given their lives. . . . Now when any doctrine arrives at that degree

of authority, the name of it is a club which any demagogue may swing over you at any time and apropos of anything. In order to describe a doctrine, we must have recourse to theological language. A doctrine is an article of faith. It is something which you are bound to believe, not because you have some rational grounds for believing it is true, but because you belong to such and such a church or denomination. . . . A policy in a state we can understand; for instance, it was the policy of the United States at the end of the eighteenth century to get the free navigation of the Mississippi to its mouth, even at the expense of war with Spain. That policy had reason and justice in it; it was founded in our interests; it had positive form and definite scope. A doctrine is an abstract principle; it is necessarily absolute in its scope and abstruse in its terms; it is a metaphysical assertion. It is never true, because it is absolute and the affairs of men are all conditioned and relative. . . . Now to turn back to politics, just think what an abomination in statecraft an abstract doctrine must be. Any politician or editor can, at any moment, put a new extension on it. The people acquiesce in the doctrine and applaud it because they hear the politicians and editors repeat it, and the politicians and editors repeat it because they think it is popular. So it grows. . . . It may mean anything or nothing, at any moment, and no one knows how it will be. You accede to it now, within the vague limits of what you suppose it to be; therefore, you will have to accede to it tomorrow when the same name is made to cover something which you never have heard or thought of. If you allow a political catchword to go on and grow, you will awaken some day to find it standing over you, the arbiter of your destiny, against which you are powerless, as men are powerless against delusions. . . . What can be more contrary to sound statesmanship and common sense than to put forth an abstract assertion which has no definite relation to any interest of ours now at stake, but which has in it any number of possibilities of producing complications which we cannot foresee, but which are sure to be embarrassing when they arise![2]

At the very beginning of colonial history, this conflict between self-interest and the crusading spirit was clearly recognized and decided in favor of the former by John Winthrop, the first governor of Massachusetts. In the words of Professor Edmund S. Morgan:

Winthrop had many more occasions to notice how self-righteousness extinguished charity. It also blinded men to realities. He knew that New England depended on the outside world in its new economy, and his heart was gladdened every time another ship splashed off the ways at Boston to carry New England codfish to markets where idolatrous Roman Catholics paid good money for them. He also knew, what a good foreign minister had to know, that righteousness endangered his community when it produced a blind and undiscriminating defiance to surrounding evils. Thus, when his colleagues refused to aid Rhode Island against the Indians, he remarked that it was an error in state policy, for though the Rhode Islanders were "desperately erroneous and in such distraction among themselves as portended their ruin, yet if the Indians should prevail against them, it would be a great advantage to the Indians, and danger to the whole country by the arms, etc., that would there be had, and by the loss of so many persons and so much cattle and other substance belonging to above 120 families. Or, if they should be forced to seek protection from the Dutch, who would be ready to accept them, it would be a great inconvenience to all the English to have so considerable a place in the power of strangers so potent as they are."[3]

The Wars of Religion have shown that the attempt to impose one's own religion as the only true one upon the rest of the world is as futile as it is costly. A century of almost unprecedented bloodshed, devastation, and barbarization was needed to convince the contestants that the two religions could live together in mutual toleration. After World War II, two political religions took the place of the two great Christian denominations of the sixteenth and seventeenth centuries. We asked, will the political religions of our time need the lesson of the Thirty Years' War, or will they rid themselves in time of the universalistic aspirations that inevitably issue in inconclusive war?

Upon the answer to that question depends the cause of peace. For only if it is answered in the affirmative can a moral consensus, emerging from shared convictions and common values, develop—a moral consensus within which a peace-preserving diplomacy will have a chance to grow. Only then will diplomacy have a chance to face the concrete political problems that require peaceful solution. If the objectives of foreign policy are not to be defined in terms of a world-embracing political religion, how are they to be defined? This is the fundamental problem to be solved once the crusading aspirations of nationalistic universalism have been discarded.

***The Objectives of Foreign Policy Must Be Defined in Terms of the National Interest and Must Be Supported with Adequate Power***. This is the second rule of a peace-preserving diplomacy. The national interest of a peace-loving nation can only be defined in terms of national security, and national security must be defined as integrity of the national territory and of its institutions. National security, then, is the irreducible minimum that diplomacy must defend with adequate power without compromise. But diplomacy must ever be alive to the radical transformation that national security has undergone under the impact of the nuclear age. Until the advent of that age, a nation could use its diplomacy to purchase its security at the expense of another nation. Today, short of a radical change in the atomic balance of power in favor of a particular nation, diplomacy, in order to make one nation secure from nuclear destruction, must make them all secure. With the national interest defined in such restrictive and transcendent terms, diplomacy must observe the third of its rules.

***Diplomacy Must Look at the Political Scene from the Point of View of Other Nations***. "Nothing is so fatal to a nation as an extreme of self-partiality, and the total want of consideration of what others will naturally hope or fear."[4] What are the national interests of other nations in terms of national security, and are they compatible with one's own? The definition of the national interest in terms of national security is easier, and the interests of the two opposing nations are more likely to be compatible, in a bipolar system than in any other system of the balance of power. The bipolar system, as we have seen, is more unsafe from the point of view of peace than any other, when both blocs are in competitive contact throughout the world and the ambition of both is fired by the crusading zeal of a universal mission. ". . . Vicinity, or nearness of situation, constitutes nations' natural enemies."[5]

Yet once they have defined their national interest in terms of national security, they can draw back from their outlying positions, located close to, or within, the sphere of national security of the other side, and retreat into their respective spheres, each self-contained within its orbit. Those outlying positions add nothing to national security; they are but liabilities, positions that cannot be held in case of war. Each bloc will be the more secure the wider it makes the distance that separates both spheres of national security. Each side can draw a line far distant from each other, making it understood that to touch or even to approach it means war. What, then, about the interjacent spaces, stretching between the two lines of demarcation? Here the fourth rule of diplomacy applies.

### Nations Must Be Willing to Compromise on All Issues That Are Not Vital to Them.

> All government, indeed every human benefit and enjoyment, every virtue and every prudent act, is founded on compromise and barter. We balance inconveniences; we give and take; we remit some rights, that we may enjoy others; and we choose rather to be happy citizens than subtle disputants. As we must give away some natural liberty, to enjoy civil advantages, so we must sacrifice some civil liberties, for the advantages to be derived from the communion and fellowship of a great empire. But, in all fair dealings, the thing bought must bear some proportion to the purchase paid. None will barter away the immediate jewel of his soul.[6]

Here diplomacy meets its most difficult task. For minds not beclouded by the crusading zeal of a political religion and capable of viewing the national interests of both sides with objectivity, the delimitation of these vital interests should not prove too difficult. Compromise on secondary issues is a different matter. Here the task is not to separate and define interests that by their very nature already tend toward separation and definition, but to keep in balance interests that touch each other at many points and may be intertwined beyond the possibility of separation. It is an immense task to allow the other side a certain influence in those interjacent spaces without allowing them to be absorbed into the orbit of the other side. It is hardly a less immense task to keep the other side's influence as small as possible in the regions close to one's own security zone without absorbing those regions into one's own orbit. For the performance of these tasks, no formula stands ready for automatic application. It is only through a continuous process of adaptation, supported both by firmness and self-restraint, that compromise on secondary issues can be made to work. It is, however, possible to indicate *a priori* what approaches will facilitate or hamper the success of policies of compromise.

First of all, it is worth noting to what extent the success of compromise—that is, compliance with the fourth rule—depends upon compliance with the other three rules, which in turn are similarly interdependent. As the compliance with the second rule depends upon the realization of the first, so the third rule must await its realization from compliance with the second. A nation can only take a rational view of its national interests after it has parted company with the crusading spirit of a political creed. A nation is able to consider the national interests of the other side with objectivity only after it has become secure in what it considers its own national interests. Compromise on any issue, however minor, is impossible so long as both sides are not secure in their national interests. Thus nations cannot hope to comply with the fourth rule if they are not willing to comply with the other three. Both morality and expediency require compliance with these four fundamental rules.

Compliance makes compromise possible, but it does not assure its success. To give compromise, made possible through compliance with the first three rules, a chance to succeed, five other rules must be observed.

### Five Prerequisites of Compromise

***Give Up the Shadow of Worthless Rights for the Substance of Real Advantage***. A diplomacy that thinks in legalistic and propagandistic terms is particularly tempted to insist upon the letter of the law, as it interprets the law, and to lose sight of the consequences such insistence may have for its own nation and for humanity. Since there are rights to be defended, this kind of diplomacy thinks that the issue cannot be compromised. Yet the choice that confronts the diplomat is not between legality and illegality, but between political wisdom and political folly. "The question with me," said Edmund Burke, "is not whether you have a right to render your people miserable, but whether it is not your interest to make them happy. It is not what a lawyer tells me I *may* do, but what humanity, reason and justice tell me I ought to do."[7]

***Never Put Yourself in a Position from Which You Cannot Retreat without Losing Face and from Which You Cannot Advance without Grave Risks***. The violation of this rule often results from disregard for the preceding one. A diplomacy that confounds the shadow of legal right with the actuality of political advantage is likely to find itself in a position where it may have a legal right, but no political business, to be. In other words, a nation may identify itself with a position, which it may or may not have a right to hold, regardless of the political consequences. And again compromise becomes a difficult matter. A nation cannot retreat from that position without incurring a serious loss of prestige. It cannot advance from that position without exposing itself to political risks, perhaps even the risk of war. That heedless rush into untenable positions and, more particularly, the stubborn refusal to extricate oneself from them in time is the earmark of incompetent diplomacy. Its classic examples are the policy of Napoleon III on the eve of the Franco-Prussian War of 1870 and the policies of Austria and Germany on the eve of the First World War. Its outstanding contemporary example is the American involvement in Indochina. These examples also show how closely the risk of war is allied with the violation of this rule.

***Never Allow a Weak Ally to Make Decisions for You.*** Strong nations that are oblivious to the preceding rules are particularly susceptible to violating this one. They lose their freedom of action by identifying their own national interests completely with those of the weak ally. Secure in the support of its powerful friend, the weak ally can choose the objectives and methods of its foreign policy to suit itself. The powerful nation then finds that it must support interests not its own and that it is unable to compromise on issues that are vital not to itself, but only to its ally.

The classic example of the violation of this rule is to be found in the way in which Turkey forced the hand of Great Britain and France on the eve of the Crimean War in 1853. The Concert of Europe had virtually agreed upon a compromise settling the conflict between Russia and Turkey, when Turkey, knowing that the Western powers would support it in a war with Russia, did its best to provoke that war and thus involved Great Britain and France in it against their will. Thus Turkey went far in deciding the issue of war and peace for Great Britain and France according to its own national interests. Great Britain and France had to accept that decision even though their national interests did not require war with Russia and they had almost succeeded in preventing its outbreak. They had surrendered their freedom of action to a weak ally, which used its control over their policies for its own purposes.

***The Armed Forces Are the Instrument of Foreign Policy, Not Its Master.*** No successful and no peaceful foreign policy is possible without observance of this rule. No nation can pursue a policy of compromise with the military determining the ends and means of foreign policy. The armed forces are instruments of war; foreign policy is an instrument of peace. It is true that the ultimate objectives of the conduct of war and of the conduct of foreign policy are identical: both serve the national interest. Both however, differ fundamentally in their immediate objective, in the means they employ, and in the modes of thought they bring to bear upon their respective tasks.

The objective of war is simple and unconditional: to break the will of the enemy. Its methods are equally simple and unconditional: to bring the greatest amount of violence to bear upon the most vulnerable spot in the enemy's armor. Consequently, the military leader must think in absolute terms. He lives in the present and in the immediate future. The sole question before him is how to win victories as cheaply and quickly as possible and how to avoid defeat.

The objective of foreign policy is relative and conditional: to bend, not to break, the will of the other side as far as necessary in order to safeguard one's own vital interests without hurting those of the other side. The methods of foreign policy are relative and conditional: not to advance by destroying the obstacles in one's way, but to retreat before them, to circumvent them, to maneuver around them, to soften and dissolve them slowly by means of persuasion, negotiation, and pressure. In consequence, the mind of the diplomat is complicated and subtle. It sees the issue in hand as a moment in history, and beyond the victory of tomorrow it anticipates the incalculable possibilities of the future. In the words of Bolingbroke;

> Here let me only say, that the glory of taking towns, and winning battles, is to be measured by the utility that results from those victories. Victories, that bring honour to the arms, may bring shame to the councils, of a nation. To win a battle, to take a town, is the glory of a general, and of an army.... But the glory of a nation is to proportion the ends she proposes, to her interest and her strength; the means she employs to the ends she proposes, and the vigour she exerts to both.[8]

To surrender the conduct of foreign affairs to the military, then, is to destroy the possibility of compromise and thus surrender the cause of peace. The military mind knows how to operate between the absolutes of victory and defeat. It knows nothing of that patient, intricate, and subtle maneuvering of diplomacy, whose main purpose is to avoid the absolutes of victory and defeat and meet the other side on the middle ground of negotiated compromise. A foreign policy conducted by military men according to the rules of the military art can only end in war, for "what we prepare for is what we shall get."[9]

For nations conscious of the potentialities of modern war, peace must be the goal of their foreign policies. Foreign policy must be conducted in such a way as to make the preservation of peace possible and not make the outbreak of war inevitable. In a society of sovereign nations, military force is a necessary instrument of foreign policy. Yet the instrument of foreign policy should not become the master of foreign policy. As war is fought in order to make peace possible, foreign policy should be conducted in order to make peace permanent. For the performance of both tasks, the subordination of the military under the civilian authorities which are constitutionally responsible for the conduct of foreign affairs is an indispensable prerequisite.

***The Government Is the Leader of Public Opinion, Not Its Slave.*** Those responsible for the conduct of foreign policy will not be able to comply with the foregoing principles of diplomacy if they do not keep this principle constantly in mind. As has been pointed out above in greater detail, the rational requirements of good foreign policy cannot from the outset count upon the support of a public opinion whose preferences are emotional rather than rational. This is bound to be particularly true of a foreign policy whose goal is compromise, and which, therefore, must concede some of the objectives of the other side and give up some of its own. Especially when foreign policy is conducted under conditions of democratic control and is inspired by the crusading zeal of a political religion, statesmen are always tempted to sacrifice the requirements of good foreign policy to the applause of the masses. On the other hand, the statesman who would defend the integrity of these requirements against even the slightest contamination with popular passion would seal his own doom as a political leader and, with it, the doom of his foreign policy, for he would lose the popular support which put and keeps him in power.

The statesman, then, is allowed neither to surrender to popular passions nor disregard them. He must strike a prudent balance between adapting himself to them and marshaling them to the support of his policies. In one word, he must lead. He must perform that highest feat of statesmanship: trimming his sails to the winds of popular passion while using them to carry the ship of state to the port of good foreign policy, on however roundabout and zigzag a course.

## Conclusion

The road to international peace which we have outlined cannot compete in inspirational qualities with the simple and fascinating formulae that for a century and a half have fired the imagination of a war-weary world. There is something spectacular in the radical simplicity of a formula that with one sweep seems to dispose of the problem of war once and for all. This has been the promise of such solutions as free trade, arbitration, disarmament, collective security, universal socialism, international government, and the world state. There is nothing spectacular, fascinating, or inspiring, at least for the people at large, in the business of diplomacy.

We have made the point, however, that these solutions, in so far as they deal with the real problem and not merely with some of its symptoms, presuppose the existence of an integrated international society, which actually does not exist. To bring into existence such an international society and keep it in being, the accommodating techniques of diplomacy are required. As the integration of domestic society and its peace develop from the unspectacular and almost unnoticed day-by-day operations of the techniques of accommodation and change, so the ultimate ideal of international life—that is, to transcend itself in a supranational society—must await its realization from the techniques of persuasion, negotiation, and pressure, which are the traditional instruments of diplomacy.

The reader who has followed us to this point may well ask: But has not diplomacy failed in preventing war in the past? To that legitimate question two answers can be given.

Diplomacy has failed many times, and it has succeeded many times, in its peace-preserving task. It has failed sometimes because nobody wanted it to succeed. We have seen how different in their objectives and methods the limited wars of the past have been from the total war of our time. When war was the normal activity of kings, the task of diplomacy was not to prevent it, but to bring it about at the most propitious moment.

On the other hand, when nations have used diplomacy for the purpose of preventing war, they have often succeeded. The outstanding example of a successful war-preventing diplomacy in modern times is the Congress of Berlin of 1878. By the peaceful means of an accommodating diplomacy, that Congress settled, or at least made susceptible of settlement, the issues that had separated Great Britain and Russia since the end of the Napoleonic Wars. During the better part of the nineteenth century, the conflict between Great Britain and Russia over the Balkans, the Dardanelles, and the Eastern Mediterranean hung like a suspended sword over the peace of the world. Yet, during the fifty years following the Crimean War, though hostilities between Great Britain and Russia threatened to break out time and again, they never actually did break out. The main credit for the preservation of peace must go to the techniques of an accommodating diplomacy which culminated in the Congress of Berlin. When British Prime Minister Disraeli returned from that Congress to London, he declared with pride that he was bringing home "peace . . . with honor." In fact, he had brought peace for later generations, too; for a century and a half there has been no war between Great Britain and Russia.

We have, however, recognized the precariousness of peace in a society of sovereign nations. The continuing success of diplomacy in preserving peace depends, as we have seen, upon extraordinary moral and intellectual qualities that all the leading participants must possess. A mistake in the evaluation of one of the elements of national power, made by one or the other of the leading statesmen, may spell the difference between peace and war. So may an accident spoiling a plan or a power calculation.

Diplomacy is the best means of preserving peace which a society of sovereign nations has to offer, but, especially under the conditions of contemporary world politics and of contemporary war, it is not good enough. It is only when nations have surrendered to a higher authority the means of destruction which modern technology has put in their hands—when they have given up their sovereignty—that international peace can be made as secure as domestic peace. Diplomacy can make peace more secure than it is today, and the world state can make peace more secure than it would be if nations were to abide by the rules of diplomacy. Yet, as there can be no permanent peace without a world state, there can be no world state without the peace-preserving and community-building processes of diplomacy. For the world state to be more than a dim vision, the accommodating processes of diplomacy, mitigating and minimizing conflicts, must be revived. Whatever one's conception of the ultimate state of international affairs may be, in the recognition of that need and in the demand that it be met, all men of good will can join. . . .

---

## Notes

1. We by no means intend to give here an exhaustive account of rules of diplomacy. We propose to discuss only those which seem to have a special bearing upon the contemporary situation.

2. "War," *Essays of William Graham Sumner* (New Haven: Yale University Press, 1934), Vol. 1, pp. 169 ff.

3. Edmund S. Morgan, *The Puritan Dilemma: The Story of John Winthrop* (Boston: Little, Brown & Co., 1958), pp. 189, 190.

4. Edmund Burke, "Remarks on the Policy of the Allies with Respect to France" (1793), *Works*, Vol. IV (Boston: Little, Brown, and Company, 1889), p. 447.

5. *The Federalist*, No. 6.

6. Edmund Burke, "Speech on the Conciliation with America," loc. cit., Vol. II, p. 169.

7. "Speech on Conciliation with the Colonies" (1775), *The Works of Edmund Burke* (Boston: Little, Brown, and Company, 1865), Vol. II, p. 140.

8. *Bolingbroke's Defence of the Treaty of Utrecht* (Cambridge University Press: 1932), p. 95.

9. William Graham Sumner, op. cit., p. 173.

# Chapter 19

## ✻ ✻ ✻

## Foreign Policy by Posse

Richard N. Haass

*Haass addresses four approaches (one unilateral and three multilateral) for dealing with foreign affairs. He examines each in turn by focusing on their respective strengths and weaknesses. First he deals with unilateralism and the tendency of the United States to go it alone in the world. He concludes that such a foreign policy emphasis is no longer realistic even though it is attractive in terms of domestic political support. He then examines formal alliances like NATO followed by support for, or creation of, powerful international institutions like a United Nations with its own standing military force. His final approach concerns ad hoc coalitions which he describes as foreign policy by posse. What are the strengths and weaknesses of the four alternatives and why does he tend to favor ad hoc coalitions? Are the approaches mutually exclusive or can they be used selectively and collectively to deal with the range of diplomatic, economic and security concerns faced by the United States now and into the 21st century?*

There is increasing consideration of (and, in some quarters, consternation about) what might be dubbed "the new unilateralism," the practice of the United States going it alone in the world. It merits attention. The 1989 U.S. invasion of Panama was a unilateral exercise, as for all intents and purposes were the interventions in Grenada and Haiti (at least in its initial phase). Sanctions against Cuba have become a mostly unilateral endeavor, as have those against Iran. The United States broke rank over NATO's enforcement of the Bosnian arms embargo, and Congress has tried to effect a unilateral abrogation of the embargo itself. Meanwhile, despite membership in the World Trade Organization (WTO), the Clinton administration chose to confront Japan unilaterally, and again to threaten sanctions, over the marketing of automobiles and their parts.

Richard N. Haass is director of national security programs and senior fellow at the Council on Foreign Relations.

The list could go on and no doubt will. Explaining why acting alone is as popular as it is in the United States is not all that hard, given the obvious advantages. It is much easier to act without having to gain the consent of others. No compromise is necessary and there is no one to slow you down. It is easier to keep secrets secret. And unilateralism has always been attractive to a people suspicious of the old world and wanting a free hand in dealing with matters closer to home.

Two features of the post-Cold War international environment—less automatic resistance from great power adversaries and less dependable assistance from erstwhile allies—also strengthen the temptation, and at times create the necessity, to act alone. The unilateralist impulse was strengthened further by both Somalia and Bosnia, two multilateral undertakings widely perceived as failures.

It should be recognized that on some occasions unilateral action is surely the best choice. This is especially so when interests are narrowly national, and when the logistical support of others is deemed unnecessary or undesirable, lest surprise be sacrificed or a friend embarrassed. Both Panama and Grenada fit this bill. Retaliating against state sponsorship of terror, as the United States did against Iraq in the wake of the failed attempt on the life of former President Bush, was something best done by the United States alone. In this latter circumstance, new technologies, such as ship-launched cruise missiles, provide opportunities for the United States to strike a limited set of targets with little or no third country role.

But in many instances, including the most significant ones, unilaterialism is neither wise nor sustainable. Most military interventions, for example, require either the indirect or direct support and participation of others. Access to bases, the right to overfly, intelligence support—all are usually necessary if an action is at all complicated or distant. Those operations that promise to be large in scale, or long-term, or both, need the active participation of others—their forces and equipment—for several reasons: to share the military burden, to distribute economic costs, and to assuage domestic political demands that the United States not assume a disproportionate share of the costs of acting in the world when the interests of others coincide with our own.

Burden sharing is increasingly relevant as a consideration in an era of flagging domestic support for defense and assistance budgets—and those budgets are all but certain to decline further in real terms over the next decade. Seen in the context of such increasing resource constraints, a penchant toward U.S. unilateralism would inevitably result in our progressively doing less overseas.

Economic burden-sharing apart, the support of others can also help politically. The endorsement of a course of action by the United Nations or a relevant regional body can add an aura of legitimacy and, in the eyes of some, legality to an undertaking. This can have several advantages: in generating domestic political support, in bringing about the military and economic participation of others, and in reducing resistance on the part of the target regime or its backers.

A pattern of seeking such international endorsement can also help inhibit intervention by those who would abuse their power. Russia, for one, might think twice before dispatching forces to its "near abroad" if it knew that the absence of a Security Council resolution endorsing its intervention made it more likely that criticism and even sanctions would follow.

Unilateralism on our part also carries the risk that it will encourage unilateralism by others. The best argument against unilateral abrogation of the Bosnian arms embargo is that it would encourage others to do the same with respect to, say, sanctions against Iraq. If we pay a price for multilateralism we also receive dividends; if we see an advantage for unilateralism we also must be sensitive to its costs.

Unilateral action in other realms—export controls and economic sanctions more generally come to mind—risks being feckless except in those circumstances where the U.S. component is so central that doing without or finding a substitute supplier is not a viable option for the target state. Increasingly, though, such U.S. dominance in the economic realm is rare, as others can provide comparable technologies, large markets, and substantial amounts of capital.

Thus, and despite its undeniable domestic political appeal, unilateralism is in most instances not a realistic foreign policy for this country. Putting aside those isolationists or minimalists who reject the need for any substantial foreign policy orientation, either because they discount the importance of overseas interests or want to focus attention overwhelmingly on domestic matters (or both), the real choice facing this country in the foreseeable future is not between unilateralism and multilateralism but among forms of the latter.

## Standing Alliances

There are three forms that a multilateral foreign policy can assume. The first type is the most familiar because it was often at the heart of U.S. foreign policy throughout the Cold War. It depends on formal alliances and other standing organizations as the principal vehicles for U.S. engagement in the world. A second approach is to create powerful international (and, in some cases, supranational) institutions, or to focus on making those that already exist—the United Nations, the World Court and others—more capable. A third approach is to build temporary coalitions to address specific challenges, be they problems or opportunities.

The traditional organizational approach that has characterized American foreign policy over the past half century was exemplified by NATO, although there were political and economic institutions to match. The North Atlantic Council was paramount in the political realm; in economic matters, the

International Monetary Fund and the OECD were created to help manage monetary coordination. The World Bank was given the task of promoting development. Although there was no counterpart trade body—the International Trade Organization was stillborn—there was the General Agreement on Tariffs and Trade (GATT), which provided rules of the road concerning government trade that served much the same purpose in favoring liberalization, and in offering a venue and process for dispute settlement.

Such institutionalism was possible because the international situation was, for all its potential dangers, essentially stable. If they are to function, standing alliances and other organizations require predictability, both as regards the source of problems and the friends and allies who can be counted upon to act in responding to them. There is time to consider scenarios and to prepare plans and capabilities for addressing them. NATO was made possible by the potential for a Soviet/Warsaw Pact attack on Western Europe, and the collective readiness of the United States, Canada, and NATO's European members to resist aggression in that location.

As useful as these institutions were, they had (and have) their limits. As associations of sovereign members, they were unable to force governments to do much of anything. France could not be compelled to remain in NATO's united military command. Several European governments balked at supporting the deployment of intermediate range missiles. Trade disputes festered. Chronic surplus and debtor states could not be forced to adjust their currencies or underlying economic policies. The need for consensus and voluntary adherence to collective decisions often became an explanation—or an excuse—for inaction.

Such standing bodies also tend not to deal well with non-core issues. NATO, for example, stood nearly helpless to contend with problems between its members—the conflict between Greece and Turkey comes to mind. It also had little to contribute to solving internal problems experienced by any of its members, or with challenges that could affect most or all members but fell outside the area covered by its charter. At the same time, formal organizations of any sort could not be successfully created and maintained in those regions of the world where friends and allies were few and/or weak, where perceptions of threat were not shared, and where scenarios were many but uncertain. The failure of CENTO (along with the Baghdad Pact before it) and SEATO provided demonstrations of how difficult it was to establish and maintain capable standing alliances, even in an international setting as highly regulated as the Cold War.

With the Cold War over, the limitations of standing alliances are even more obvious. They have become less relevant and at times counterproductive. Groups of countries that once shared common purposes now no longer do, or do so only in circumstances increasingly less common. NATO is again the classic case. The core mission—protecting members against a hostile external threat—has essentially disappeared. Meanwhile, NATO's unsuccessful attempts at undertaking ambitious new missions, as is the case in the former Yugoslavia, reveal a lack of consensus in the alliance. In this instance at least, the alliance has become an obstacle to effective action rather than its agent. Clearly, it would be better for NATO to concentrate on lesser but still important tasks: preserving a residual capacity to carry out its basic mission, integrating new members, and providing support for efforts undertaken by selected members in their individual capacities.

Western economic institutions are having a somewhat better time of it. The end to Cold War competition did not change the economic environment significantly. Nevertheless, they too are having trouble adapting to the emergence of massive pools of privately held funds that can overwhelm what governments or existing institutions do.

## The Supranational Way

A second form of multilateralism would go far beyond the initial and apparently abandoned impulse of the current administration—what was termed "assertive multilateralism"—to create supranational capabilities. In the security realm, it would involve creating a standing military force responsible to the Security Council and, in some circumstances, to the secretary-general. Such a force could be dispatched quickly to help prevent conflicts or (under Chapter VII of the UN Charter) to enforce Security Council resolutions. An expanded multilateralism of this sort could also seek to establish machinery (a strengthened World Court, for example) for resolving political disputes between states that would constitute arbitration, not just mediation. Economically, this form of multilateralism would require not simply rules regulating trade but mandatory dispute settlement mechanisms and strict monetary coordination.

There are obvious difficulties with multilateralism of this sort. National sovereignty may be much battered but it is still alive and kicking. Few governments (including, notably, our own) would be prepared to cede to some supranational agency or set of agencies, run by international civil servants, the independence governments enjoy in the political, economic, or military realms. Moreover, even if there were some desire to do so, building such organizational capacity (especially in the military sphere) would be a monumental undertaking, given the expense and the forces that would oppose it.

Less unrealistic but still problematic would be a scaled-down version of such multilateralism, one that would concentrate on trying to strengthen and make more independent existing international institutions. To some extent the United States has taken or is considering taking some modest steps in this direction, both in the form of efforts to create a stand-by force responsible to the Security Council and by agreeing to follow certain WTO procedures to resolve trade disputes.

The problem with even this more modest, sub-supranational form of interna-tionalism stems from the reality that we ourselves are not prepared (and rightly so) to give up our freedom of maneuver in those situations where we disagree and where important national interests are at stake. Given that others tend to feel the same, such multinational efforts are often no stronger than the weakest or most adamantly opposed member in possession of a veto. Again, sovereignty—not as an abstract norm but as a political reality—precludes almost any form of multilateralism that would override or take the place of domestic autonomy to a significant degree.

## Multilateralism that Makes Sense

There is a third approach to multilaterialism, one more informal in nature and more achievable in practice. It differs from the first in its rejection of reliance on standing, formal organizations, and differs from the second in eschewing interest in universal, supranational authorities. At its core is the idea of selected states and organizations coalescing for narrow tasks or purposes—and in most cases disbanding once the specific aim has been accomplished. Membership is available to those able and willing to participate, and this approach is thus sometimes referred to as "coalitions of the willing." Less formally it can be described as foreign policy by posse.

Examples of this approach are multiplying. The most famous cases, and in some ways the model for the idea, were Desert Shield and Desert Storm. Here, in response to a specific crisis, namely, the Iraqi invasion and occupation of Kuwait, the United States fashioned a multilateral coalition that over the course of the next seven months proved victorious on the battlefield. Like many inventions, it was born of necessity: there was no standing Gulf security organization to fall back upon, the UN lacked the capability, and it was too much for the United States alone to undertake.

The Gulf coalition was one in which tasks and roles differed according to both the desire and ability of governments to make a contribution. Some countries simply gave moral and political support by voting in one or another forum for action against Iraq. Others limited their participation to providing funds. In the military realm there was a wide disparity. The United States contributed more than a half million troops and equipment of all sorts. Some others, notably Great Britain and France, also committed sizable, balanced forces. Others, for political or military reasons or both, contributed much smaller forces and sometimes only for particular missions—say, sanctions enforcement or defense of rear areas.

The coalition that won the war disbanded as soon as it ended. But a more narrow coalition continues to work together in the war's aftermath to promote Iraqi compliance with various resolutions and to protect Iraqi citizens from their own government. The United States, Turkey, Great Britain, and France operate in and over Iraq's north to protect the Kurds. It is the United States, together with Great Britain, France, and several Gulf states, that maintain a no-fly zone over the predominantly Shi'a areas of Iraq's south. Both efforts are undertaken "pursuant to" authority judged to be implicit in Security Council resolutions in what amounts to a collective decision to act.

Other coalitions are longer standing. One set includes so-called supplier groups, i.e., those coalitions of states that agree not to provide designated technologies or capabilities to selected states in order to slow their efforts to develop certain military capacities. Right now there are supplier groups in the realm of nuclear, biological and chemical, and ballistic missile technologies. Membership of these groups obviously reflects relevance—only those who could provide such technologies are potential members—and a willingness to forgo exports. They operate much as cartels, with their effectiveness depending on the extent of their reach: that is, what it is they sanction and whether there are non-members ready and able to provide what they will not.

Ad hoc coalitions are also appearing in the economic sphere. The Mexican bailout is an interesting case. Viewing the potential failure of the Mexican economy as a major threat to U.S. and world economic health, and realizing that no existing institution or set of arrangements could provide the Mexican government the backing it required, the Clinton administration lashed together in early 1995 an ad hoc coalition that included, in addition to itself, the International Monetary Fund, the Bank for International Settlements, Canada, a consortium of Latin American governments, and several private banks. Although the private banks subsequently dropped out, the multi-billion dollar bail-out appears to have worked in allowing Mexico to weather the immediate crisis.

Diplomacy, too, increasingly turns to informal coalitions. The management of the Middle East peace process since the October 1991 Madrid Conference is coordinated by the United States (with Russia as nominal co-sponsor) that involves not only the immediate protagonists but also Egypt, the Gulf states, the European Union, and others. Similarly, diplomacy toward Bosnia—admittedly, not (yet) a shining example—is informally coordinated by a contact group consisting of the United States, Russia, France, Great Britain, and Germany. An earlier contact group, one that included the United States, Great Britain, France, Canada, and the then Federal Republic of Germany, was instrumental in helping to negotiate a political settlement in southern Africa in the 1980s.

An Asian example of foreign policy by posse is the informal coalition brought about by the October 1994 "Agreed Framework" between the United States and North Korea, which established the Korean Peninsula Energy Development Corporation (KEDO). The United States is in charge, with the Republic of Korea and Japan in principal supporting roles, and many other governments participating in lesser capacities. The purpose is to provide light water reactors and alternative energy (in this case, heavy fuel oil) to the North Koreans on economic terms they can afford and political terms they can accept.

What these and similar efforts have in common is that they tend to be U.S.-led groups that come together for a finite set of tasks. They are voluntary as regards membership participation in particular actions. Their charter is their own. They are often put together for a limited span of time. They tend to have little in the way of headquarters or permanent staff. They are better understood as an activity than an organization.

It is not difficult to imagine other applications, including a different approach to Bosnia. Rather than trying to force policy through a divided NATO or a UN with a different set of priorities, the United States would have been wiser to build a small coalition of like-minded states that would have been in a position credibly to threaten, and carry out as need be, military actions ranging from making the designated safe-areas safe to the so-called "lift and strike" option combining arms supplies to the Bosnians and attacks on Serbian positions. Some form of ad hoc coalition may prove useful in the future if, as seems likely, the NATO/UN phase of the conflict comes to an unhappy and unsuccessful end.

The United States will likely have to forge a small coalition to deal with North Korea's nuclear program if the current negotiated approach should come up short. This could prove the best way to tackle sanctions, in order to avoid the certain delay and possible Chinese veto in the Security Council that working through the UN would involve. It would be unavoidable if military action were to be taken. Indeed, given the controversial nature of preventive strikes, both as regards the act itself and the risk of retaliation against states near the target, it will almost always be necessary for the United States to create posses for such tasks. The same can be said of special sanctions regimes where something more formal or universal is simply not a realistic option, given the existence of opposition in the Security Council or among major trading partners of the target state. Indeed, the challenge for the United States in its policy toward Iran is to transform what is essentially a unilateral approach into something broader, if still ad hoc.

Obviously, the informal coalition approach is not without its drawbacks. By definition, such groups do not exist before the problem or crisis emerges, and they therefore offer no deterrent effect—although, if formed quickly enough, they can still provide a preventive or preemptive function. But informal coalitions take time to forge and not every protagonist will, like Saddam, provide months for a coalition to get up to speed. They will often lack clear political or legal authority and a means of reliable financing, the absence of which tends to detract from public and international support. The United States will more often than not have to act and provide the bulk of the impetus and resources. And, as is the case with any variant of multilateralism, informal coalitions constrain as well as facilitate. The Gulf War demonstrates that both strategic aims and tactical choices need to be negotiated among members of the coalition.

There are, however, important advantages. The United States has the inherent capacity to create posses where and when it chooses. They do not require much in the way of prior investment. Coalitions of the willing bring with them some of the advantages that derive from collective effort (resources, specialization, diplomatic co-support) without the need for consensus or prearranged authority. They also enjoy some measure of international legitimacy.

More than anything else, though, posses or coalitions of the willing (and able) constitute an approach to international engagement that reflects the basic personality and characteristics of the post-Cold War world. This is a time in history when there are: multiple great powers involved in relationships that resist clear definition and range from the cooperative to the competitive; a growing number of small and medium sovereign entities; proliferating regional and international bodies, as well as non-governmental organizations; an increasing diffusion of power in all forms; and new sorts of problems (or old problems on a new scale) for which institutions do not yet exist. What is needed as a result is an approach to foreign policy that is inherently flexible, one able to respond to unforeseen situations in unprecedented ways.

The posse approach thus offers a valuable supplement to a world in which regional and international institutions are limited to what they can usefully contribute. Moreover, posses come with the further advantage that they can become more structured and institutionalized if the need and consensus to move in that direction exists. The supplier groups already mentioned reflect this potential, as does the G-7, which over the years has evolved into a quasi-institution for helping to manage a diverse set of political and military, as well as economic, challenges. It may prove possible to adapt or expand the role of other regional or international institutions. Until then, posses can selectively draw on the available assets and resources of such organizations.

Again, though, there will be limits to what we can predict and prepare for. Hence, informal coalitions of the willing increasingly will offer the best vehicle for this country to act effectively in the world when it matters most. Indeed, the real question hanging over the future of this approach to multilateralism is not so much its utility as the willingness of the United States to lead and participate: a posse without a strong sheriff is far more likely to get itself into trouble than to accomplish something of value.

# Chapter 20

**\* \* \***

# The General Theory
# and Logic of Coercive Diplomacy

Alexander L. George

*Alexander L. George examines restrictions on coercive diplomacy and poses some questions that policymakers should ask before considering its use. In discussing the allure of coercive diplomacy, he notes that it offers the opportunity to alter another nation's objectives with less cost and a way around constraints on the use of force, but has the hazard that a strongly inspired target state may not concede. He believes that coercive diplomacy is different than deterrence and offers three types of applications along with four variants: ultimatum, tacit ultimatum, "gradual turning the screw," and "try-and-see." George also suggests that in some situations the way a sense of urgency of the demands is conveyed to the target state may have an impact the strategy's success. How do his theories apply to Bosnia and the use of sanctions by coalition? Did the U.S. effectively employ coercive diplomacy in Haiti? How might we determine whether coercive diplomacy is the best course of action for a situation? When are other measures more appropriate?*

In this part of the study\* I describe in some detail the *general, abstract theory* of coercive diplomacy which, properly understood, should be useful both to policymakers and scholars.

I emphasize that the abstract theory is not itself a strategy of coercive diplomacy. Rather, the abstract theory familiarizes policymakers with the

---

\* This article is Part I of the three part study, *Forceful Persuasion: Coercive Diplomacy as an Alternative to War* to which Alexander L. George refers. In this reprinting of Part I of the full monograph, references to other parts of the study are retained at the request of the United States Institute of Peace in order that our readers may be aware of the additional material available in the complete publication. The three parts in the original monograph are: Part One, "The General Theory and Logic of Coercive Diplomacy" (reproduced in this volume); Part Two, "The Practice of Coercive Diplomacy: Case Studies;" and Part Three, "Findings and Conclusions."

---

Alexander L. George is Professor Emeritus of International Relations at Stanford University.

---

general characteristics of coercive diplomacy and the logic on which its presumed efficacy rests. Therefore, it should be thought of as no more than an aid to enable policymakers to consider more carefully the possible use of strategy of coercive diplomacy in a particular situation. Part One of this study also provides policymakers with an indication of different variants of the strategy and a starting point for judging whether they can design a strategy that fits the configuration of the situation at hand. What the abstract theory does *not* do is provide policymakers with a basis for judging whether coercive diplomacy is likely to be effective in a particular situation. Rather, policymakers must turn to generic knowledge derived from study of a variety of past cases to make such judgments.

The abstract theory should also be useful to scholars who study past cases of coercive diplomacy in order to develop generic knowledge of the conditions and processes associated with success or failure of a strategy. The generic knowledge that can be gained from the seven historical cases analyzed in Part Two of this monograph is presented in Part Three.

Coercive diplomacy, or coercive persuasion as some might prefer to call it, is not an esoteric concept. Intimidation of one kind or another in order to get others to comply with one's wishes is an everyday occurrence in human affairs. And what we refer to as coercive diplomacy has often been employed in the long history of international conflict, sometimes successfully and sometimes not. The general idea of coercive diplomacy is to back one's demand on an adversary with a threat of punishment for noncompliance that he will consider credible and potent enough to persuade him to comply with the demand. Hence, it should be noted, the abstract theory of coercive diplomacy assumes pure rationality on the part of the opponent—an ability to receive all relevant information, evaluate it correctly, make proper judgments as to the credibility and potency of the threat, and see that it is in his interest to accede to the demand made on him. The abstract theory of coercive diplomacy, therefore, does not take into account the possibility of misperception and miscalculation or that an opponent's "rationality" is affected by psychological variables and by values, culture, and tradition that may differ from those of the coercive state. These possibilities are of critical importance and must receive careful attention whenever policymakers attempt to devise a strategy of coercive diplomacy in a particular situation against a particular opponent.

## The Concept of Coercive Diplomacy

First, we need to clarify how the concept of coercive diplomacy is being used in this study and to differentiate it from other ways threats are used as an instrument of policy.[1] In this study the term coercive diplomacy is restricted to *defensive* uses of the strategy—that is, efforts to persuade an opponent to stop and/or undo an action he is already embarked upon. Of course coercive threats can also be employed aggressively to persuade a victim to give up something of value without putting up resistance. Such offensive uses of coercive threats are better designated by the term "blackmail strategy." Coercive diplomacy also needs to be distinguished from deterrence, a strategy that employs threats to dissuade an adversary from undertaking a damaging action in the future. In contrast, coercive diplomacy is a response to an encroachment already undertaken. The term "compellance," which Thomas Schelling introduced into the literature over twenty years ago, is often employed to encompass both coercive diplomacy and blackmail. I prefer not to use that term for two reasons. First, it is useful to distinguish, as compellance does not, between defensive and offensive uses of coercive threats. Second, the concept of compellance implies exclusive or heavy reliance on coercive threats to influence an adversary, whereas I wish to emphasize the possibility of a more flexible diplomacy that can employ noncoercive persuasion and accommodation as well as coercive threats.

Coercive diplomacy does indeed offer an alternative to reliance on military action. It seeks to *persuade* an opponent to cease his aggression rather than bludgeon him into stopping. In contrast to the blunt use of force to repel an adversary, coercive diplomacy emphasizes the use of threats to punish the adversary if he does not comply with what is demanded of him. If force is used in coercive diplomacy, it consists of an exemplary use of quite limited force to persuade the opponent to back down. By "exemplary" I mean the use of just enough force of an appropriate kind to demonstrate resolution to protect one's interests and to establish the credibility of one's determination to use more force if necessary.[2] Even a relatively small exemplary action (for example, President Kennedy's order to U.S. "civilian advisers" in Laos in April 1961 to put on their uniforms) can have a disproportionately large coercive impact if it is coupled with a credible threat of additional action. The strategy of coercive diplomacy, however, does not require use of exemplary actions. The crisis may be satisfactorily resolved without an exemplary use of force; or the strategy of coercive diplomacy may be abandoned in favor of full-scale military operations without a preliminary use of exemplary force.

In employing coercive diplomacy, which may already include nonmilitary sanctions, one gives the adversary an opportunity to stop or back off before one resorts to military operations. Notice that either of two demands can be made on the adversary. He may be asked merely to *stop* what he is doing; or he may be asked to *undo* what he has done—that is, to reverse what he has managed to accomplish. The first type of demand generally asks less of the opponent and may be easier to accomplish in a particular situation than the second type. The use of threats (and of exemplary use of limited force) should be closely coordinated with appropriate communications to the opponent. Therefore, signaling, bargaining , and negotiating are important dimensions of coercive diplomacy, though their roles vary in different crises.

Coercive diplomacy is an attractive strategy insofar as it offers the possibility of achieving one's objective in a crisis economically, with little or no bloodshed, fewer political and psychological costs, and often with less risk of unwanted escalation than does traditional military strategy. But for this very reason coercive diplomacy can be a beguiling strategy. Particularly leaders of militarily powerful countries may be tempted sometimes to believe that they can, with little risk, intimidate weaker opponents to give up their gains and their objectives. But, of course, the militarily weaker side may be strongly motivated by what is at stake and refuse to back down, in effect calling the bluff of the coercing power. The latter must then decide whether to back off, accept a compromise settlement, or escalate to the use of military force to gain its objective. In addition, as the case studies will illustrate, a powerful country may encounter other constraints, risks, and uncertainties in attempting to make effective use of the strategy.

## Variants of Coercive Diplomacy Strategy

The general concept of coercive diplomacy, I suggest, contains a number of "empty boxes" (i.e., variables) that policymakers must fill in when constructing a particular strategy of coercive diplomacy to apply in a specific situation. Policymakers must decide (1) what to demand of the opponent; (2) whether and how to create a sense of urgency for compliance with the demand; (3) whether and what kind of punishment to threaten for noncompliance; and (4) whether to rely solely on the threat of punishment or also to offer conditional inducements of a positive character to secure acceptance of the demand.

Depending on how policymakers deal with these four components of the general model, significantly different variants of the strategy are possible. Let us identify first those variants of the strategy that stem from differences in how the first three variables are formulated.

The starkest variant of the strategy includes all three ingredients of a full-fledged ultimatum. A classic ultimatum has three components: (1) a demand on the opponent; (2) a time limit or sense of urgency for compliance with the demand; and (3) a threat of punishment for noncompliance that is both credible to the opponent and sufficiently potent to impress upon him that compliance is preferable. An ultimatum, although the starkest variant of coercive diplomacy, is not necessarily the most effective. There are often reasons why an ultimatum may be inappropriate, infeasible, or even highly risky in a particular situation. (I shall return to this point in Part Three.)

When an explicit time limit is not set forth but a sense of real urgency is conveyed by other means, one may refer to this variant of the strategy as a "tacit" ultimatum, which is not, for that reason, necessarily less potent. Similarly, when the threat of punishment is not specifically set forth but nonetheless is credibly conveyed by actions, one may refer to this variant also as a tacit ultimatum. Forgoing the delivery of an explicit ultimatum, a state may prefer to convey the gist of it by some combination of military preparation and stern warning.

Let us turn now to other variants of coercive diplomacy in which one of the three components of an ultimatum is diluted or absent. One variant is the "try-and-see" approach. In this version of the strategy, only the first element of an ultimatum—a clear demand—is conveyed; the coercing power does not announce a time limit or convey a strong sense of urgency for compliance. Instead, it takes one limited coercive threat or action and waits to see whether it will suffice to persuade the opponent before threatening or taking another step. There are several versions of the try-and-see approach, as will be evident in some of the case studies.

Somewhat stronger in coercive impact, although still falling well short of the ultimatum, is the variant that relies on a "gradual turning of the screw." It differs from the try-and-see approach in that a threat to step up pressure gradually is conveyed at the outset and is carried out incrementally. At the same time, the gradual turning of the screw differs from the ultimatum in that it lacks a sense of time urgency for compliance and relies on the threat of a gradual, incremental increase in coercive pressure rather than threatening large escalation to strong, decisive military action if the opponent does not comply. In practice, the analytical distinction between try-and-see and turning of the screw may be blurred if the policymaker wavers or behaves inconsistently.

Several observations about these variants of coercive diplomacy will be made later. When an ultimatum or tacit ultimatum is simply not appropriate or feasible, or may be considered premature or too risky, a try-and-see or turning of the screw approach may be judged to fit better the domestic political-diplomatic-military configuration of the conflict situation. It should be noted that, as happened in some of our historical cases, policymakers may shift from one variant of coercive diplomacy to another.

Thus far we have presented distinctions among four different forms that the strategy of coercive diplomacy may take: the ultimatum, tacit ultimatum, try-and-see, and gradual turning of the screw variants. While such distinctions are useful for some purposes, it would be misleading to assume that the form of the strategy alone determines the likelihood of success. Certainly from a formalistic standpoint the ultimatum is a stronger, or starker, variant than the try-and-see approach. But the coercive impact of any form of the strategy and whether it will be effective depends on other factors.

## Two Levels of Communication in Coercive Diplomacy

It is important to recognize coercive diplomacy often operates on two levels of communication: words and actions. In addition to what is said, significant nonverbal communication or signaling can occur via either military moves or political-diplomatic activities. Nonverbal communication often emerges from the structure and development of the situation. Coercive persuasion depends not merely or exclusively on whether all three components of a classic ultimatum are present in verbal messages to the opponent. The structure of the situation as it develops can enhance or weaken the impact of coercive threats. The actions taken or not taken during the crisis—for example, whether and what kind of military forces are deployed or alerted, whether the coercing power undertakes political and diplomatic preparations of the kind needed to carry out its threats of force—can reinforce verbal threats and make them more credible or can dilute and weaken the impact of even strong verbal threats.

Actions may reinforce strong words, or they may compensate for weak words when it is not possible or prudent to utter strong words. But, contrary to the conventional wisdom, actions do not always speak louder than words. However strong the actions, they may be perceived by the adversary as equivocal or as bluffs. Words, then, may be needed in some situations to clarify the meaning of the actions taken or to convey unalterable commitment and resolution. Similarly, of course, actions may be needed to avoid the possibility that threatening words may be dismissed as bluff.

We conclude, therefore, that the relationship between actions and words—the two levels of communication—is likely to be very important in employing the strategy of coercive diplomacy. But there is no single, simple way of stating what the relationship between words and actions must be to ensure the success of the strategy. Crises in which coercive diplomacy is employed are replete with opportunities for miscommunication and miscalculation. And this is another aspect of coercive diplomacy that can make it an elusive, problematical, and risky strategy.

## The Carrot-and-Stick Approach

The reader will have noted that the discussion of variants of coercive diplomacy thus far has focused exclusively, and much too narrowly, on the use of threats of punishment. We turn now to the fourth "empty box" or variable-component of the theory of coercive diplomacy—one that requires the policymaker to decide whether to rely solely on the threat of punishment or also to offer positive inducements. As in diplomacy more generally, the strategy of coercive diplomacy can use positive inducements and assurances as well as punitive threats to influence an adversary; when it does so it is often referred to as a strategy of "carrots and sticks." This approach greatly enhances the flexibility and adaptability of the strategy and gives the negotiation and bargaining dimensions of coercive diplomacy even greater prominence.

The policymaker must decide whether to rely exclusively or largely on the threat of punishment (as the United States and the United Nations coalition did in the Persian Gulf crisis) or also offer conditional positive inducements (as Kennedy finally did toward the end of the Cuban missile crisis). The carrot in such a strategy can be any of a variety of things the target of coercion values. And the magnitude and significance of the carrot can range from a seemingly trivial concession of a face-saving character to substantial concessions that bring about a settlement of the crisis through a genuine, balanced quid pro quo.

Whether coercive diplomacy will work in a particular case may depend on whether it relies solely on negative sanctions or combines threats with positive inducements. This point is of considerable practical as well as theoretical significance. Recognition that coercive diplomacy in principle can use a carrot-and-stick approach leaves open the question whether in practice the policymaker employing the strategy is willing or able to offer a positive inducement and, if so, to decide what conditional offer and concessions to make.

Nonetheless, the essential point remains: what the threatened stick cannot achieve by itself, unless it is a very formidable one, may possibly be achieved by combining it with a carrot. It should be said, too, that just as threats of punishment must be credible to the opponent, so must the positive inducements and reassurances offered be credible.

## The Central Task of Coercive Diplomacy

Let us turn now to the central task of a coercive strategy: to create in the opponent the expectation of costs of sufficient magnitude to erode his motivation to continue what he is doing. As already noted, success may depend on whether the initial coercive action or threat stands alone or is part of a broader credible threat to escalate pressure further if necessary.

How much of a threat, or combination of threat with positive inducement, is necessary to persuade an opponent to comply? The abstract, general theory of coercive diplomacy tells us that the answer depends very much on two variables: what one demands of the opponent and how strongly disinclined he is to comply with that demand. Of course, these two variables are not independent of each other, and the relationship between them must receive the careful attention of the side that is employing a strategy of coercive diplomacy. The critical point to remember is that the strength of the opponent's motivation not to comply is highly dependent on what is demanded of him. Thus, asking relatively little of the opponent makes it easier for him to permit himself to be coerced. Conversely, demanding a great deal will strengthen an opponent's resistance and make the task of coercing him more difficult. Demanding a great deal may mean not only requiring an opponent to give up the material gains he has or is about to achieve but also requiring him to pay the often-substantial psychological and political costs of compliance with the demand. Also critical, of course, is the adversary's perception of the costs to him, which may be significantly greater than what the coercing power believes it is demanding.

The general, abstract theory correctly emphasizes that what is demanded of the opponent and his motivation to resist are closely related. As will be seen in the case studies, the outcome of coercive diplomacy is extremely sensitive to the relative motivations of the two sides. Motivation, in turn, reflects the way they perceive the balance of interests engaged by the dispute. Motivation here refers to each side's conception of what is at stake in the dispute, the importance it attaches to the various interests engaged by the crisis, and what costs and risks it is willing to incur on behalf of these interests. The choice of the demand made on the opponent, therefore, is of considerable importance in shaping the relative motivation of the two sides. Not only does the demand influence the level of the other side's motivation, as already noted; the motivation of the coercing power will also vary depending on the nature and magnitude of the demand it makes on the opponent. In other words, there is often an important strategic dimension to the choice of the objective on behalf of which coercive diplomacy is employed. Quite simply, it affects the motivation of both sides and the balance of motivation between them.

According to the logic of the abstract model of coercive diplomacy, it is more likely to be successful if the objective selected—and the demand made—by the coercing power reflects only the most important of its interests. Such a choice is more likely to create an asymmetry of interests, and therefore an asymmetry of motivation, in its favor. Conversely, if the coercing power pursues ambitious objectives that do not reflect its vital or very important interests or makes demands that infringe on vital or very important interests of the adversary, the asymmetry of interests and the balance of motivation is likely to operate in favor of the adversary. (The importance of asymmetry of motivation will be seen in several of the historical cases. For example, in the Cuban missile crisis President Kennedy limited his demand to removal of the missiles, an objective which he then succeeded in persuading Khrushchev was more important to the United States than it was to the Soviet Union. Had Kennedy chosen more ambitious objectives, as some of his advisers urged—the elimination of Castro or the removal of Soviet influence from Cuba—Khrushchev's motivation to resist would have been greater, and quite possibly the variable of relative motivation would have operated in his favor. That is, confronted by such demands, Khrushchev might have been willing to accept greater risks to prevent Kennedy from achieving those objectives than Kennedy would have been willing to accept to achieve them.)

The general theory emphasizes still another dimension of this central task of coercive diplomacy. It is not enough that the policymaker feel confident that he has conveyed a threat of punishment for noncompliance with his demand that is potent and credible enough to convince the opponent to comply. Rather, it is the *target's* estimate of the credibility and potency of the threat that is critical. As in so much of coercive diplomacy, many of the critical variables are psychological ones having to do with the perceptions and judgment of the target. The possibility of misperceptions and miscalculations by the opponent is ever present and can determine the outcome.

The preceding discussion refines the general theory and logic of coercive diplomacy. It identifies four "empty boxes" or critical variables imbedded in the abstract model that the policymaker must deal with in formulating and implementing any particular strategy of coercive diplomacy. A typology of four different variants of the strategy is presented. Attention is directed to relationships between key variables of the strategy—what is demanded of the opponent and how strongly motivated he is to resist such demands—in order to emphasize that such relationships have much to do with the balance of interests and relative motivation of the two sides, which help determine the effectiveness of the strategy in a particular situation.

However, even as refined and reformulated in the present study, the abstract model of coercive diplomacy is not a textbook of "how-to-do-it" prescriptions. The task of "operationalizing" the theory remains. The policymaker must judge which variant of the strategy—or indeed whether any variant of it—can be made to work in the situation at hand. This task is difficult because it requires the policymaker to understand and deal with a number of additional contextual variables that the abstract theory does not take into account. Such variable are identified in the case studies and discussed in Part Three.

# Chapter 21

## ✴ ✴ ✴

## Sanctions

Kimberly Ann Elliott and Gary Clyde Hufbauer

*Kimberly Ann Elliott and Gary Clyde Hufbauer, in considering the coercive aspects of "economic statecraft," provide the purposes and an assessment of the effectiveness of economic sanctions. Despite the less than perfect success rate of sanctions, they are often the diplomatic tool of choice in situations where armed force would be inappropriate or diplomatic protest too weak. Sanctions can be used to punish, deter or to change behavior. The authors list five conditions for sanctions to be effective: modest goals; substantial existing trade between sender and target; a smaller "target country"; quick imposition of sanctions; and avoidance of high cost to the sender. Is this list of conditions complete? Is it overly restrictive and too limiting? Can the U.S. effectively impose sanctions if there has been a relative decline in its economic power?*

Throughout most of modern history, economic sanctions have preceded or accompanied war. Sanctions often have taken the form of a naval blockade intended to weaken the enemy during wartime. Only when the horrors of World War I prompted President Woodrow Wilson to call for new methods of dispute settlement were economic sanctions seriously considered as an alternative to war. Sanctions were incorporated as a tool of enforcement in each of the two collective security systems established in this century—the League of Nations between the two world wars and the United Nations since World War II. But individual countries, especially the United States, often use economic sanctions unilaterally.

### Purposes of Economic Sanctions

Students of international law frequently argue that only economic measures deployed against states that have violated international standards or obligations

Kimberly Ann Elliot is a research associate, and Gary Clyde Hufbauer a senior economist, with the Institute for International Economics in Washington, D.C.

may properly be classified as "sanctions." According to this view sanctions should be distinguished from national uses of economic power in pursuit of narrow national interests. But common usage of the term *economic sanctions* typically encompasses both types of actions. The broader meaning is used here. Specifically, economic sanctions are the deliberate, government-inspired withdrawal, or threat of withdrawal, of customary trade or financial relations. ("Customary" refers to the levels of trade or financial activity that would probably have occurred in the absence of sanctions.)

Although individual countries, as well as various ad hoc groups, have frequently imposed sanctions in response to perceived violations of international law, institutionally endorsed sanctions have been rare and have enjoyed mixed success. The League of Nations imposed or threatened to impose economic sanctions only four times in the twenties and thirties, twice successfully. But the league faded from history when its ineffectual response failed to deter Mussolini's conquest of Ethiopia in 1935 and 1936. The United Nations Security Council—divided because of the cold war—imposed sanctions only twice prior to the August 1990 embargo of Iraq. The first imposition was against Rhodesia beginning in 1966, the second an arms embargo against South Africa imposed in 1977. The British Commonwealth also imposed broader sanctions against South Africa (against the wishes of the United Kingdom).

The motives behind international uses of sanctions parallel the three basic purposes of national criminal law—to punish, to deter, and to rehabilitate. Like states that incarcerate criminals, international institutions that impose sanctions may find their hopes of rehabilitation unrealized, but they may be quite satisfied with whatever punishment and deterrence are accomplished.

Similarly, individual countries, particularly major powers, often impose economic sanctions even when the probability of forcing a change in the target country's policy is small. In addition to demonstrating resolve and signaling displeasure to the immediate transgressor and to other countries, politicians may also want to posture for their domestic constituencies. It is quite clear, for example, that U.S., European, and British Commonwealth sanctions against South Africa, as well as U.S., European, and Japanese sanctions against China in the wake of the T'ienanmen Square massacre, were designed principally to assuage domestic constituencies, to make a moral and historical statement, and to send a warning to future offenders of the international order. The effect on the specific target country was almost secondary. World leaders often decide that the most obvious alternatives to economic sanctions are unsatisfactory—military action would be too massive, and diplomatic protest too meager. Sanctions can provide a satisfying theatrical display, yet avoid the high costs of war. This is not to say that sanctions are costless, just that they are often less costly than the alternatives.

## Types of Sanctions

A "sender" country tries to inflict costs on its target in two main ways: (1) with trade sanctions that limit the target country's exports or restrict its imports, and (2) with financial sanctions that impede finance (including reducing aid). Governments that impose limits on a target country's exports intend to reduce its foreign sales and deprive it of foreign exchange. Governments impose limits on their own exports to deny critical goods to the target country. If the sender country is important in world markets, this may also cause the target to pay higher prices for substitute imports. When governments impose financial sanctions by interrupting commercial finance or by reducing or eliminating government loans to the target country's government, they intend to cause the target country to pay higher interest rates, and to scare away alternative creditors. When a poor country is the target, the government imposing the sanction can use the subsidy component of official financing or other development assistance to gain further leverage.

Total embargoes are rare. Most trade sanctions are selective, affecting only one or a few goods. Thus, the economy-wide impact of the sanction may be quite limited. Because sanctions are often unilateral, the trade may only be diverted rather than cut off. Whether import prices paid by (or export prices received by) the target country increase (or decrease) after the sanctions are applied depends on the market in question. If there are many alternative markets and suppliers, the effects on prices may be very modest and the economic impact of the sanctions will be negligible.

For example, Australia cut off shipments of uranium to France from 1983 to 1986 because of France's refusal to halt testing of nuclear weapons in the South Pacific. In 1984, however, the price of uranium oxide dropped nearly 50 percent. France was able to replace the lost supply, and at a price lower than the one specified in its contract with the Australian mine. Because Australia was unable to find alternative buyers for all the uranium intended for France, the Australian government ultimately paid Queensland Mines $26 million in 1985 and 1986 for uranium it had contracted to sell to France.

In contrast, financial sanctions are usually more difficult to evade. Because sanctions are typically intended to foster or exacerbate political or economic instability, alternative financing may be hard to find and is likely to carry a higher interest rate. Private banks and investors are easily scared off by the prospect that the target country will face a credit squeeze in the future. Moreover, many sanctions involve the suspension or termination of official development assistance to developing countries—large grants of money or concessional loans from one government to another—which may be irreplaceable.

Another important difference between trade sanctions and financial sanctions lies in who are hurt by each. The pain from trade sanctions, especially export controls, usually is diffused through the target country's population. Financial sanctions, on the other hand, are more likely to hit the pet projects or personal pockets of government officials who shape local policy. On the sender's side of the equation, an interruption of official aid or credit is unlikely to create the same political backlash from business firms and allies abroad as an interruption of private trade. Finally, financial sanctions, especially involving trade finance, may interrupt trade even without the imposition of explicit trade sanctions. In practice, however, financial and trade sanctions are usually used in some combination with one another.

The ultimate form of financial and trade control is a freeze of the target country's foreign assets, such as bank accounts held in the sender country. In addition to imposing a cost on the target country, a key goal of an assets freeze is to deny an invading country the full fruits of its aggression. Such measures were used against Japan for that purpose just before and during World War II. In the 1990 Middle East crisis, the United States and its allies froze Kuwait's assets to prevent Saddam Hussein from plundering them.

## Effectiveness of Sanctions

Senders usually have multiple goals and targets in mind when they impose sanctions, and simple punishment is rarely at the top of the list. Judging the effectiveness of sanctions requires sorting out the various goals sought, analyzing whether the type and scope of the sanction chosen was appropriate to the occasion, and determining the economic and political impact on the target country.

If governments that impose sanctions embrace contradictory goals, sanctions will usually be weak and ultimately ineffective. In such cases the country or group imposing sanctions will neither send a clear signal nor exert much influence on the target country. Thus, it may be the policy—not the instrument (sanctions)—that fails. For example, the Reagan and Bush administrations imposed economic sanctions against Panama beginning in 1987 in an effort to destabilize the Noriega regime. But because they wanted to avoid destroying their political allies in the Panamanian business and financial sectors, they imposed sanctions incrementally and then gradually weakened them with exemptions. In the end the sanctions proved inadequate, and military force was used to remove Noriega.

In many cases sanctions are imposed primarily for "signaling" purposes—either for the benefit of allies, other third parties, or a domestic audience.

If the sanctions are not carefully targeted or if they entail substantial costs for the sender country, however, the intended signal may not be received. It may be overwhelmed by a cacophony of protests from injured domestic parties, which may force a premature reversal of the policy. For example, American farmers howled with outrage when President Carter embargoed grain sales to the Soviet Union following the invasion of Afghanistan. The protests, buttressed by candidate Reagan's promise to lift the embargo if elected—which he did within three months of his inauguration—undermined the seriousness of intent that Carter wanted to convey. Efforts to extend sanctions extraterritorially may produce similar effects abroad. Thus, sanctions imposed for symbolic or signaling purposes must be carefully crafted if they are to convey the intended signal.

Sanctions intended to change the behavior or government of a target country are even more difficult to design. In most cases, sanctions must be imposed as quickly and comprehensively as possible. A strategy of "turning the screws" gives the target time to adjust by finding alternative suppliers or markets, by building new alliances, and by mobilizing domestic opinion in support of its policies. Great Britain, followed by the United Nations, adopted a slow and deliberate strategy in response to Ian Smith's "unilateral declaration of independence" in Rhodesia in 1965. Aided by hesitation and delays, the Smith regime was able to use import substitution, smuggling, and other circumvention techniques to fend off the inevitable for over a decade.

Overall, based on an analysis of 116 case studies, beginning with World War I and going through the UN embargo of Iraq, economic sanctions tend to be most effective at modifying the target country's behavior under the following conditions:

1. When the goal is relatively modest: winning the release of a political prisoner versus ending South Africa's apartheid system, for example. Less ambitious goals may be achieved with more modest sanctions; this also lessens the importance of multilateral cooperation, which is often difficult to obtain. Finally, if the stakes are small, there is less chance that a rival power will step in with offsetting assistance.

2. When the target is much smaller than the country imposing sanctions, economically weak and politically unstable. The average sender's economy in the 116 cases studied was 187 times larger than that of the average target.

3. When the sender and target are friendly toward one another and conduct substantial trade. The sender accounted for 28 percent of the average target's trade in cases of successful sanctions, but only 19 percent in failures.

4. When the sanctions are imposed quickly and decisively to maximize impact. The average cost to the target as a percentage of GNP in success cases was 2.4 percent and in failures was only 1.0 percent, while successful sanctions lasted an average of only 2.9 years versus 8.0 years for failures.

5. When the sender avoids high costs to itself.

It is obvious from this list that effective sanctions, in the sense of coercing a change in target country policy, will be achieved only rarely. Economic sanctions were relatively effective tools of foreign policy in the first two decades after World War II: they achieved their stated goals in nearly half the cases. The evolution of the world economy, however, has narrowed the circumstances in which unilateral economic leverage can be effectively applied. For multilateral sanctions, increasing economic interdependence is a double-edged sword. It increases the latent power of economic sanctions because countries are more dependent on international trade and financial flows. But it also means wider sources of supply and greater access to markets, and thus the possibility that a greater number of neutral countries can undermine the economic impact of a sanctions effort should they choose to do so.

## South Africa, Iraq, and the Future of Sanctions

What do the lessons of history tell us about the likely effectiveness of sanctions against Iraq and South Africa, and what do these cases portend for the future of sanctions as a tool of international diplomacy? Going against rule number one, both cases involved extremely difficult goals: forcing the removal of Iraqi troops from Kuwait in the first, and promoting the dismantling of the apartheid system in South Africa in the second. In the Iraq case, however, the level of international commitment and cooperation was unprecedented, trade and financial relations with Iraq were almost completely cut off, and the cost to the target probably approached half of GNP on an annual basis. Although the cost to the anti-Iraq coalition from boycotting Iraqi oil shipments could have been quite high, increased production of oil elsewhere within a few weeks lessened the impact. Thus, the embargo of Iraq had a high probability of achieving the stated UN goal of reversing Saddam Hussein's aggression, probably within a year to eighteen months, based on past history.

In the South Africa case, however, economic sanctions were applied piecemeal over a number of years, often halfheartedly, and at their height were far from comprehensive. The most significant sanctions, embodied in the U.S. Comprehensive Anti-Apartheid Act (CAAA) of 1986, were imposed only after Congress overrode a presidential veto, and administrative enforcement was reportedly weak. Even the CAAA, however, affected only some trade and financial relations, and except for the Nordic countries (Sweden, Norway, Finland, Iceland, and Denmark), other countries' sanctions were even less stringent. Thus, by the summer of 1991, the UN arms embargo had been in place for over a decade, an OPEC oil embargo for a similar number of years, and expanded U.S. sanctions for over five years. Yet the white government and the two major black opposition groups (the African National Congress and Inkatha)—though closer than previously—were still struggling to find common ground on which to begin constitutional negotiations. Assuming that reform is achieved and that South Africa does not degenerate into bloody civil war, sanctions will have made a modest contribution to the happy result.

The confluence of circumstances that resulted in the nearly unanimous condemnation and isolation of Iraq is unlikely to recur soon. Instead, future efforts at sanctions are likely to be plagued by the same economic, political, and diplomatic differences, both within and among countries, that long split the anti-apartheid coalition.

# Chapter 22

## ✱ ✱ ✱

## Strategy and Arms Control

Thomas C. Schelling and Morton H. Halperin

*In this brief excerpt from their classic book on arms control, Thomas C. Schelling and Morton H. Halperin established the conceptual basis for post-World War II arms control efforts. For Schelling and Halperin, the objective of arms control is to enhance global and regional stability through diplomatic efforts to reduce the likelihood of war, reduce the consequences of war if it occurs, and reduce the costs of preparing for war. What do you think of their discussion of the objectives of arms control? Should arms control be viewed as broadly as it is here? Do you agree that arms control should be focused more on incentives than on capabilities? Need arms control be seen as distinct from national security or national military strategy?*

### Introduction

This study is an attempt to identify the meaning of arms control in the era of modern weapons, and its role in the pursuit of national and international security. It is not an advertisement for arms control; it is as concerned with problems and difficulties, qualifications and limitations, as it is with opportunities and promises. It is an effort to fit arms control into our foreign and military policy, and to demonstrate how naturally it fits rather than how novel it is.

This is, however, a sympathetic exploration of arms control. We believe that arms control is a promising, but still only dimly perceived, enlargement of the

Thomas C. Schelling is Distinguished Professor of Economics and Public Affairs at the University of Maryland, College Park. He was previously the Lucius N. Littauer Professor of Political Economy, John F. Kennedy School of Government, and Professor of Economics, Harvard University.

Morton H. Halperin has served as a member of the staff of the National Security Council. He previously served as a Deputy Assistant Secretary of Defense and was the Director of the Center for National Security Studies, Washington, D.C.

scope of our military strategy. It rests essentially on the recognition that our military relation with potential enemies is not one of pure conflict and opposition, but involves strong elements of mutual interest in the avoidance of a war that neither side wants, in minimizing the costs and risks of the arms competition, and in curtailing the scope and violence of war in the event it occurs.

Particularly in the modern era, the purpose of military force is not simply to win wars. It is the responsibility of military force to deter aggression, while avoiding the kind of threat that may provoke desperate, preventive, or irrational military action on the part of other countries. It is the responsibility of military policies and postures to avoid the false alarms and misunderstandings that might lead to a war that both sides would deplore.

In short, while a nation's military force opposes the military force of potentially hostile nations, it also must collaborate, implicitly if not explicitly, in avoiding the kinds of crises in which withdrawal is intolerable for both sides, in avoiding false alarms and mistaken intentions, and in providing—along with its deterrent threat of resistance or retaliation in the event of unacceptable challenges—reassurance that restraint on the part of potential enemies will be matched by restraint on our own. It is the responsibility of military policy to recognize that, just as our own military establishment is largely a response to the military force that confronts us, foreign military establishments are to some extent a response to our own, and there can be a mutual interest in inducing and reciprocating arms restraint.

We use the term "arms control" rather than "disarmament." Our intention is simply to broaden the term. We mean to include all the forms of military cooperation between potential enemies in the interest of reducing the likelihood of war, its scope and violence if it occurs, and the political and economic costs of being prepared for it. The essential feature of arms control is the recognition of the common interest, of the possibility of reciprocation and cooperation even between potential enemies with respect to their military establishments. Whether the most promising areas of arms control involve reductions in certain kinds of military force, increases in certain kinds of military force, qualitative changes in weaponry, different modes of deployment, or arrangements superimposed on existing military systems, we prefer to treat as an open question.

If both sides can profit from improved military communications, from more expensive military forces that are less prone to accident, from expensive redeployments that minimize the danger of misinterpretation and false alarm, arms control may cost more not less. It may by some criteria seem to involve more armament not less. If we succeed in reducing the danger of certain kinds of war, and reciprocally deny ourselves certain apparent military advantages (of the kind that cancel out for the most part if both sides take advantage of them), and if in so doing we increase our military requirements for other dangers of warfare, the matter must be judged on its merits and not simply according to whether the sizes of armies go up or down. If it appears that the danger of accidental war can be reduced by improved intelligence about each other's military doctrines and modes of deployment, or by the provision of superior communication between governments in the event of military crisis, these may have value independently of whether military forces increase, decrease, or are unaffected.

This approach is not in opposition to "disarmament" in the more literal sense, involving the straightforward notion of simple reductions in military force, military manpower, military budgets, aggregate explosive power, and so forth. It is intended rather to include such disarmament in a broader concept. We do not, however, share the notion, implicit in many pleas for disarmament, that a reduction in the level of military forces is necessarily desirable if only it is "inspectable" and that it necessarily makes war less likely. The reader will find that most of the present study is concerned less with reducing national *capabilities* for destruction in the event of war than in reducing the *incentives* that may lead to war or that may cause war to be the more destructive in the event it occurs. We are particularly concerned with those incentives that arise from the character of modern weapons and the expectations they create.

An important premise underlying the point of view of this study is that a main determinant of the likelihood of war is the nature of present military technology and present military expectations. We and the Soviets are to some extent trapped by our military technology. Weapon developments of the last fifteen years, especially of the last seven or eight, have themselves been responsible for some of the most alarming aspects of the present strategic situation. They have enhanced the advantage, in the event war should come, of being the one to start it, or of responding instantly and vigorously to evidence that war may have started. They have inhumanly compressed the time available to make the most terrible decisions. They have almost eliminated the expectation that a general war either could or should be limited in scope or brought to a close by any process other than the sheer exhaustion of weapons on both sides. They have greatly reduced the confidence of either side that it can predict the weapons its enemy has or will have in the future. In these and other ways the evolution of military technology has exacerbated whatever propensities towards war are inherent in the political conflict between us and our potential enemies. And the greatly increased destructive power of weapons, while it may make both sides more cautious, may make the failure to control those propensities extremely costly.

Arms control can be thought of as an effort, by some kind of reciprocity or cooperation with our potential enemies, to minimize, to offset, to compensate or to deflate some of these characteristics of modern weapons and military expectations. In addition to what we can do unilaterally to improve our warning, to maintain close control over our forces, to make our forces more secure against attack, to avoid the need for precipitant decisions, to avoid accidents or the mistaken decisions that they might cause and to contain conflict once it starts, there may be opportunities to exchange facilities or understandings with our enemies, or to design and deploy our forces differently by agreement with our enemies who do likewise, in a way that enhances those aspects of technology that we like and that help to nullify those that we do not.

We say this to anticipate the objection that armaments are only a reflection of existing conflicts and not a cause of them. It is true that modern armaments and military plans are a response to basic international conflicts. It is also true that the size and character of military forces are an important determinant of national fears and anxieties, and of the military incentives of our potential enemies. There is a feedback between our military forces and the conflicts that they simultaneously reflect and influence. We have no expectation that by working on weaponry alone, or military deployments or expectations, we can eliminate the political, economic and ideological differences that genuinely underlie present international antagonisms. We do believe that much can be done through careful design of our military strategy, our weaponry, our military deployments and doctrines, to reduce the military danger of those hostilities to our security. We believe that, in addition to what can be accomplished unilaterally in this regard, there are actions and restraints for which the inducements are greater on each side if the other side reciprocates or leads the way. And we believe that something in the way of rules, traditions, and clearer expectations about each other's reactions and modes of behavior may reduce the likelihood of military action based on mistakes or misunderstanding.

What is striking is not how novel the methods and purposes of arms control are, and how different from the methods and purposes of national military policy; what is striking is how much overlap there is. There is hardly an objective of arms control to be described in this study that is not equally a continuing urgent objective of national military strategy—of our unilateral military plans and policies. What this study tries to do is to suggest those points at which these unilateral actions can be extended or supplemented through joint understandings with our potential enemies. In some cases the scope for such reciprocal actions seems substantial, in other cases very modest; but in all cases it seems worth taking into consideration. Since the dimension of military policy has traditionally been so little appreciated, we have felt it worth while to indicate many areas in which arms control may possibly prove helpful, even if we cannot yet perceive just where the promise lies.

We have also considered arms control to include the less formal, less institutionalized, less "negotiated" understandings and agreements. Some may object that there is no "control" when both sides simply abstain from an action which, if done by one party, yields an advantage but if done by both parties cancels out the advantages and raises risks all around. Our resolution of this semantic problem is to interpret "control" to mean induced or reciprocated "self-control," whether the inducements include negotiated treaties or just informal understandings and reciprocated restraints.

In surveying the possible areas in which arms control may play a role, we have tried to err on the generous side, doubting whether we can yet perceive all of the forms that arms control may take and the areas in which it may occur. In our discussion of the negotiation and administration of concrete agreements, we have been concerned to identify the difficulties, in the belief that these must be anticipated if experiments at arms control are to avoid unnecessary disappointment or disaster.

We have not stated what we believe to be the "ultimate goal" of arms control—whether it be a world disarmed, a world policed by a single benevolent military force or a world in which some military "balance of prudence" has taken the fear out of the "balance of fear." We should, however, acknowledge that we do not believe the problems of war and peace and international conflict are susceptible of any once-for-all solution. Something like eternal vigilance and determination would be required to keep peace in the world at any stage of disarmament, even total disarmament. International conflict, and the military forces that are their reflection, are not in our judgment simply unnatural growths in human society which, once removed, need never recur. Conflict of interest is a social phenomenon unlikely to disappear, and potential recourse to violence and damage will always suggest itself if the conflict gets out of hand. Man's capability for self-destruction cannot be eradicated—he knows too much! Keeping that capability under control— providing incentives to minimize recourse to violence—is the eternal challenge.

This is the objective of responsible military policy. And a conscious adjustment of our military forces and policies to take account of those of our potential enemies, in the common interest of restraining violence, is what we mean by arms control.

In the study that follows we are concerned mainly with the direct relation of arms control to the military environment. Arms control can also affect, for good or ill, our political relations with allies, neutrals and potential enemies. It can reduce tension or hostilities; it can reduce vigilance. It can strengthen alliances, collapse them, or make them unnecessary. It can create confidence and trust or create suspicion and irritation. It can lead to greater world organization and the rule of law or discredit them. And it evidently lends itself to the short-run competition in propaganda. . . .

# Chapter 23

## ✳ ✳ ✳

## Struggle for the Heartland:
## An Introduction to Geopolitics

Warren C. Robinson

*Warren C. Robinson provides a useful explanation of geopolitics. The specific goal of geopolitical analysis is to see a correlation between large geographical and historical generalizations and to find a formula expressing universal geographical causation in history. In effect, geopolitics is a theory explaining how and why wars occur, as well as why and how some nations are more likely than others to win their wars. Robinson notes its German roots and describes its impact on American strategists over the past century. He summarizes many different variants of this theory, noting that no major new geopolitical paradigm has emerged to extend or expand works that are now several decades old. In your judgment, which geopolitical insights are most helpful today? Least helpful? Would you agree with the assertion that nuclear weapons have made geopolitics as out of date as high button shoes? To what extent, if at all, can geopolitics help current strategists organize their thoughts and set priorities for the coming decade?*

G eopolitics is a wedding of politics and geography. The key assumption is that physical and situational conditions interact with political factors to produce the outcomes observed in the real world. Since it is clear, as Clausewitz pointed out, that war is politics carried on by other means, then questions of military or naval power must also be included as political factors. Geopolitics is very closely related to grand strategy, but the two are not quite interchangeable. Geopolitical analysis attempts to explain how a nation's people, institutions, leaders, resources and geographical situation all interact to lead it toward world greatness or mediocrity. Grand strategy, on the other hand, is an effort to optimize all these elements of national power to attain a specific political objective. The first is analytical in intent, while the second is prescriptive. In the realm of military affairs, geopolitics tries to explain how and why conflicts arise,

Warren C. Robinson is an expert on the history of geopolitics.

Reprinted by permission from *Strategy - Tactics*, March/April 1994, pp. 58-62. Copyright © 1994. Published by Decision Games.

and also how and why some nations are more likely to conquer and others to be the spoils of war. Grand strategy is about how any given nation can best play the cards nature and circumstances have dealt it.

Plato, Aristotle and other classical thinkers were unconscious pioneers of geopolitical analysis. They believed that wars arose between peoples because of competing economic claims on limited geographic areas and resources. They saw a potential for conflict as inherent in the existence of separate political entities but felt that most specific disputes follow from underlying economic factors, from geographical position or the lack of it, and competition for new areas. Political rivalry arises from geographical realities. This, in essence, may be called the "Geopolitical Theorem" and it can be found in the writings of many social theorists from Plato to the present. The modern version of the Theorem is broader but less purely deterministic than the Classical concept.

Geopolitics emerged as a distinct body of thought and writing in the late 19th Century. Its immediate roots lay in political geography, which had recently taken on a strongly German flavor with the dramatic rise of Prussia and the creation of a united German *Reich*. The term "geopolitics" seems to have been coined by the Swedish writer Rudolf Kjellen (1864–1922), but the first scholar to cross the boundary from political geography to true geopolitics and launch the field in its own right was the German academic Friedrich Ratzel (1844–1904). Ratzel was a synthesizer who took the geographical determinism propounded earlier by Friedrich List, Karl Ritter and Alexander Von Humboldt and combined them with the philosophical and political notions about world history and nationalism advanced by Heinrich Von Treitschke, George Hegel and Friedrich Nietzche. Ratzel fashioned his own theory of how and why nations grow, fight wars and achieve greatness or extinction, with geographical factors playing a key role in the process.

Ratzel created the agenda and identified the questions which became the core of geopolitics. The most famous German geopolitical theorist, Karl Haushofer, was a student of Ratzel and his work had a key impact on later non-German geopolitical writers such as Halford J. MacKinder and James Fairgrieve, as well as more purely strategic theorists such as Alfred T. Mahan and Homer Lea.

One of Ratzel's most seminal works, published in 1896, proposed a series of "laws" governing the territorial growth of states. Briefly, these saw the nation-state as based on a distinct *Kultur*. National expansion is an effort to spread this culture to other, frequently less advanced areas. Expansion is driven by the growing need for more area and more resources to fuel additional growth. The state's "frontier" areas are its cutting edge; as one nation-state attempts to expand it inevitably evokes a similar reaction from other peoples, even those less culturally advanced. "The general tendency toward territorial annexation and amalgamation," Ratzel concluded, "transmits the trend from state to state and increases in intensity."

Ratzel argued that the modern nation-state is essentially an organism with an innate "biological drive" to grow and absorb new areas. International politics becomes a Darwinian struggle in which only the "fittest" nations or cultures survive. Kjellen developed these notions at greater length and was sure that Imperial Germany was destined to emerge triumphant from the struggle for control of Europe. Thus, the felt need among leaders in Germany and the other newly industrializing states of 19th Century Europe for assured supplies of natural resources becomes cloaked in a theory of *Kultur* and *Geist* (spirit) driven by presumed historical and biological necessity. These vague, romantic, essentially irrational elements are an inescapable feature of German geopolitical writings.

Lenin clearly was familiar with these notions. His theory of imperialism also accepted the consensus view that war among modern states arose because of inescapable economic conflict. Lenin put a distinctly Marxist twist on the theory by arguing that there could be no winner of such a struggle and that the whole capitalist world system from which the conflict arose would soon collapse under the strain. While Communism was for decades widely feared, and has more recently been dismissed onto the rubbish pile of history, its roots in Western geopolitical theory are obvious.

Karl Haushofer (1869–1946) is probably the best known German geopolitician. A career German Army officer with a Ph.D. in geography from the University of Munich, he became a professor after the First World War. Haushofer wrote and lectured widely on geopolitical themes such as the desirability of national self-sufficiency (*autarky*), a nation's natural right to living space (*Lebensraum*) and resources to support its population, and the inevitable emergence of regional groupings of closely allied nations.

The impact of Germany's experiences in the First World War on Haushofer's approach is obvious. The soldier-turned-professor dabbled in politics and had contacts in Munich with the emerging Nationalist Socialist German Workers (Nazi) Party. He seems to have been in personal touch with Hitler himself through "deputy fuhrer" Rudolph Hess, who had been Haushofer's student at the University. After Hitler came to power, Haushofer was given the directorship of the newly-created Institute for Geopolitics in Munich. For a time Haushofer was seen as the evil genius behind Hitler's expansionary visions, but this now seems dubious. More likely he served as mere academic window dressing. Even so, Hitler may well have been influenced by some of Haushofer's writings. In particular, the notion of *Lebensraum* loomed large in the Fuhrer's thinking. But as a young man Hitler had read widely, and these same ideas were present already in Ratzel, Ritter and others that he probably read in the original or learned about second-hand.

Regardless of the true situation, Haushofer's links to Hitler helped to discredit the whole notion of geopolitics among many Western scholars. At the height of global war in 1943, the American scholar Derwent Whittlesey could write, "Geopolitics is a creation of militarism and a tool of war." This may seem a bit extreme today, but the desperate times certainly justified such a reaction. The term "geopolitics" still carries with it an overtone of opprobrium for many. Not surprisingly, no new generation of German disciples of Ratzel or Haushofer has emerged. Ironically, Haushofer later fell from Nazi grace and was actually imprisoned after the 1944 attempt on Hitler's life.

Geopolitics suffered from its German origins after 1945, but it promised useful insights in an era of superpower conflict. During the 1950s and 1960s geopolitical analysis was revived in both camps. English, French and American scholars drew upon half-forgotten scholarship produced in the decades around the turn of the 20th century. The tradition of grappling with geographic, economic and political forces at play against the backdrop of intense competition between blocs of nation-states seemed perfectly suited to fighting and winning the shadowy cold war, with its mixture of hard military realities and complicated political and economic maneuvering.

The result was a revival of geopolitical theories or paradigms. Some of the most notable old practitioners—MacKinder, for example—had been professional geographers, while others like Mahan had been military grand strategists. The American writer Homer Lea (1876–1912) was neither, which may explain why he was capable of crafting perhaps the most elaborate geopolitical theory of past and future world developments. Like the German writers, he saw world politics as a Darwinian struggle with inevitable conflicts which only the strongest, most unified nations were likely to survive. For Lea, England was the dominant power in the world circa 1900, and had been largely responsible for setting in motion throughout the world the changes leading to the grand struggle for world domination. Geographical factors mattered less than in the past because of rapid technological changes in both sea and land transport. The future would be a struggle for control of the world among England, Russia, Germany, and Japan.

Lea's assertions were breathtaking. The British empire was doomed and England along with it. Russia enjoyed a central, geographical position but the Germans and Japanese were superior in military and industrial strength. The U.S. weak and disunited, would fall under either German or Japanese control not long after the final dissolution of the British Empire. The North American continent might well be divided between the two! A world empire would ultimately be established by either Japan or Germany.

Lea's sweeping, often pessimistic geopolitical vision was widely read in the years prior to World War One and there is evidence that many world leaders respected his ideas. However, Lea created no school, had no disciples and his work lapsed into obscurity with the failure of the Great War to settle once and for all the ladder of dominance he outlined. Even so, the sheer drama Lea injected into often dry academic discussion permitted periodic revivals on a small scale. Following the Japanese attack on Pearl Harbor Lea's books were published in new editions. On occasion he is referred to today as the man who predicted the War in the Pacific—even though he got most of the details wrong.

Alfred T. Mahan's (1840–1914) work on the influence of sea-power has, on the other hand, remained influential for a full century. His starting point was detailed naval history, from which he drew important generalizations about grand strategy. Despite Mahan's preference for facts, which has certainly boosted his appeal among soldiers, his ideas rest on several key geographical insights or assumptions that add up to a major geopolitical theory.

Mahan enumerates several "principal conditions" affecting the sea power of nations. These include:

- Geographical Position
- Physical Conformation (natural productions and climate)
- Extent of Territory
- Population Size
- Character of the People
- Character of the Government (including national institutions)

Mahan's discussion of the last two conditions is pragmatic and common-sense, with none of the romantic, metaphysical overtones of the German writers. Mahan viewed national character from a distinctly American perspective: "All men seek gain and, more or less, love money; but the way in which gain is sought will have a marked effect upon the commercial fortunes and the history of the people inhabiting a country." As to the influence of the type of government, he writes: "In discussing the effects upon the development of a nation's sea power exerted by its government and institutions, it will be necessary to avoid a tendency to over-philosophize, to confine attention to obvious and immediate causes and their plain results, without prying too far beneath the surface for remote and ultimate influences." Both elements, national character and the type of government, arise from unique, situational factors in a nation's history. They do influence a nation's ability to become a sea power, but Mahan perceives no universal history or biological processes at work.

These "principal elements," Mahan felt, allowed him to reach conclusions regarding strategy which "belong to the unchangeable, or unchanging, order of things, remaining the same, in cause and effect, from age to age." Those nations which enjoyed natural geographical advantage for turning to the sea usually prospered. Those which deliberately chose to emphasize naval power over land power and gained control of the seas were always the winners in the major conflicts of history. Changes in naval technology resulted in changing tactics, but the underlying strategic importance of an oceanic orientation remained valid in all ages.

Scattered throughout Mahan's works is an appreciation of the importance of geographical factors. England's rise to control of the seas rested on her secure, insular position dominating the trade routes of most other European states, and her early conquest of the key control points of world trade—Gibraltar, Suez, Capetown and so on. This control gave England, in effect, "interior position" compared to her rivals and made it possible for her to fight wars cheaply and easily anywhere in the world she chose to. Oceanic transport was the most efficient means of travel in peace or war and control of the sea gave this advantage to England.

Mahan's books were enormously influential. Not only had he explained how and why England was the dominant world power in the last half of the 19th century, but also what other nations would have to do in order to catch up. Mahan provided a theoretical justification for the naval armaments race which began in the last decade of the 19th Century, and which saw not only Britain but the U.S., Imperial Germany, Japan, Russia and many other nations spend vast sums on fleets of the new armored steam-powered warships. Even such a traditionally continental power as Germany accepted Mahan's doctrine that only by taking to the sea could it become a world power capable of rivaling England. By exposing clearly the roots of England's world power, Mahan encouraged Germany and other nations to emulate her. Growing German naval power drove England to seek land-based continental alliances as a counterweight, and it was these entanglements that ultimately drew Britain (and everyone else) into World War One. Here is the clearest and probably the most important instance of the geopolitical view of world history actually affecting the course of events.

Political geography and geopolitics also emerged in England in the early part of this century. The British geographer Ellen Churchill Semple (1863–1932) was a student of Ratzel's. Along with James Fairgrieve (1870–1953) and Halford J. MacKinder (1861–1947), she attempted to explain world political and strategic developments in terms of underlying geographical forces. MacKinder is by far the best known of this group, on the strength of a simple but powerful paradigm he developed as a direct contradiction of Mahan's oceanic theorem. This is the famous *Heartland* thesis proposed in an article in 1904.

MacKinder started from a position of skepticism about the Mahan sea power thesis. England's world leadership was, after all, transitory. "Other empires have had their day and so may that of Britain. . . .The European phase of history is passing away as have passed the Fluviatile [civilizations of the Mesopotamian and Nile valleys] and Mediterranean [Greco-Roman] phases." European expansion and colonization had created a single world economy and also a single "closed political system," in the sense that major economic or political events *anywhere* in the world had immediate ramifications *everywhere* in the world. More fundamentally, the industrial revolution had also resulted in a transport revolution which had shifted the strategic balance in favor of land transport over sea transport. Railroads crisscrossed Europe and America, and would soon traverse Asia as well. Geographically, MacKinder argued, Asia and Europe constituted a single "world island" on which the vast majority of the world's resources and population were located. The other continents were smaller islands in the "world ocean."

The pivotal area of this world island was its "Heartland," a term borrowed from an earlier book by James Fairgrieve. This covered an area from the Volga Basin running east into Siberia and southward into Iran and Afghanistan. MacKinder perceived this region to be rich in people and resources, and hence in potential economic and political power.

The new land-based technologies seemed to be opening up these areas. (MacKinder undoubtedly was thinking of the then-new trans-Siberian railway and the railway construction underway in China and elsewhere in Asia.) This meant that the balance of world power would steadily shift into the Heartland. If and when a world empire developed, its stability and survival would have to be based on control of this region. This suggested Russia had an inherent advantage, but MacKinder accurately postulated a German *Drang nach Osten* (drive to the east) and penned the following famous aphorism:

> *Who rules East Europe commands the Heartland; who rules the Heartland commands the World-Island; Who rules the World-Island commands the World.*

The "Heartland Thesis" was the central paradigm of geopolitics for most of the inter-war period of the 1920s and 1930s. It almost certainly influenced the peacemakers at Versailles in 1919. The French in particular were anxious to keep both Russia and Germany out of Eastern Europe. In Germany, Haushofer enthusiastically embraced MacKinder's central tenet. Naturally, he was convinced that the "world island" would be controlled by a German-dominated coalition. Hitler's dream of conquering and colonizing Poland and Southern Russia owed as much to MacKinder's rationale as to Haushofer's less rigorous talk of breathing space. One reason France and Britain thought it worth the effort to guarantee Poland's sovereignty (at least on paper) was their concern that Germany would then gain "command over the Heartland" as MacKinder put it. The decision may also have been influenced by the estimate that Germany and Russia would inevitably fight a tremendous war for control of Eastern Europe and beyond. The West would need to play a role, but keep it limited so as to avoid the devastation that nearly everyone in the world outside the Nazi party believed would result from such a conflict. Some geopolitical gamblers may have sought to turn Hitler eastward and provoke the conflict, expecting bystander powers to "pick up the pieces" after the dust from the Fascist-Bolshevik showdown finally settled. Here might be an interesting twist on the so-called "Appeasement" policy! As late as 1942, the influential military journalist Major George Fielding Eliot wrote of the Heartland Thesis: "There is no escape from the logic of this conclusion and it is the most powerful, practical argument for intelligent international organization that could be presented."

MacKinder developed and refined his theory with admirable clarity and cogency for forty years. His precise delineation of the Heartland changed over time, but not the basic thesis. In 1943, after restating his thesis and reviewing world events in the intervening four decades, MacKinder set aside all false modesty and declared his academic position unassailable. "My concept of the Heartland . . .is more valid and useful today than it was either twenty or forty years ago." The grand old man of geopolitics outside Germany was willing to make one major but quiet modification. The year before the U.S. would successfully mount history's largest military invasions in Europe and the Pacific. MacKinder now saw the possibility of a second Heartland in North America. He also predicted that a powerful united Russia emerging triumphant from the Second World War would be a mighty contender for world domination.

One could argue that MacKinder's Heartland Thesis is a second instance of a geopolitical theory having a profound impact on real events through its effect on key policy-makers. As J.M. Keynes wrote: "The world is ruled by ideas and little else." He might have added that they rule for good or for ill. If humanity needed any reminder of that, the events of World War II and nearly a half century of ideological cold war certainly provided it. Yet there is no denying the fact that the past four decades have witnessed a heyday for geopolitics not matched since the decade preceding the Great War.

Mahan's theory dominated geopolitical thinking from roughly 1890 to 1920. MacKinder's theory was ascendant from roughly 1920 to around 1940. Both were based on particularized geographical and technological views of the world. Mahan saw the world as a series of trading posts tied together by oceanic highways which were cheaper and superior to land transport. MacKinder saw the world centering around a single resource- and population-rich Euro-Asian "island" that was becoming increasingly autonomous from oceanic concerns due to improvements in land transport.

Both theories were taken very seriously by academics until at least the 1960s, during the Cold War's most intense crises, and they are still discussed and debated. The only notable modification of the Heartland Thesis was proposed by the American academic Nicholas J. Spykman (1893–1943) who argued that the periphery of the Eurasian land mass, and in particular Western Europe, formed a "rimland" which if controlled by maritime powers effectively controlled the "world island" as well. Spykman coined an aphorism of his own: *"Who controls the Rimland controls the Heartland."*

Lea's theory drew upon the same basic foundations as Mahan's and MacKinder's, but he synthesized land and sea factors into a model all his own which actually reflected the unfolding world events during and just after World War Two better than either Mahan or MacKinder could.

The geopolitical tradition gave birth to one younger thinker who was first heard from in the midst of history's greatest war. The American James Burnham adapted many geopolitical concepts to the development of modern industrial states. In his controversial 1941 book *The Managerial Revolution*, he claimed that the world was gradually reorganizing itself into several superstates, each based on geopolitical areas with solid economic bases. These included the U.S., Germany and Japan along with their various dependencies. Each had control of one of the chief industrial regions of the world, which could serve as a springboard to expansion along military, political, and economic lines.

Burnham in turn influenced the thinking of the novelist and social critic George Orwell. One of the premises of Orwell's seminal dystopian story *1984* is that the world in the future will be organized into three super-states: Oceania (the Americas, Britain, Australia), Eurasia (Europe, Russia, Siberia), and Eastasia (Japan, Manchuria, China). All three will have sufficient resources to carry on an endless war with each other, but because of their geopolitical strengths none could ever be conquered.

A third major geopolitical theory has also been proposed, and it may yet emerge as the dominant geopolitical theorem of the future. This we can call the "air power dominance" theorem and proceeds in the first instance from the assumption that air power has attained such dominance in warfare as to make fleets and armies obsolete. This view was first propounded by novelists like H.G. Wells before World War One and after that conflict more systematically by Guilio Douhet (1869–1930), Billy Mitchell (1879–1936) and Alexander de Seversky (1894–1970). Wells' second effort at crystal-ball gazing, *Things To Come*, predicted the London Blitz to the year (1940) but like other air proponents he was too sanguine about the bombers always getting through and dropping poison gas and other biological agents. Although neither proved to be true, Wells' book and the companion film of the same name completed just prior to the outbreak of war in 1939 reflects the fear of civilization's destruction that overtook Europe (with the notable exception of Germany) years before nuclear weapons were invented.

Recent signs point to a revival of this school of thought in the U.S. military, particularly after the adoption of AirLand Battle doctrine in the 1980s and the incredible pyrotechnics associated with Operation Desert Storm in the Persian Gulf in early 1991. A more visionary projection of air power theory might conclude that air (and space) transportation of goods, people and weapons systems will become the norm to such an extent that distance, climate and geographical configuration will cease being major factors in interactions among nations and people. Perhaps an as yet unheralded writer is preparing a new aphorism: "Who controls the air, controls the Heartland, the World island, and all the Oceans as well." Seversky comes close to saying this and it seems the logical next step in the effect of changing transportation technology on geopolitical thinking.

In the purely military realm, the importance of air power has been clearly established. Fleets and armies can not operate safely or with any degree of success in the face of hostile air power unless accompanied by offsetting air power of their own. It is, however, still debatable that air power alone can actually win a major non-nuclear conflict without proper coordination with land and naval forces. Each new armed conflict in the last several decades has seemed to yield a slightly different answer, the Gulf War being the latest example. Even there, the pilots could not take and hold ground, and successive postmortems have consistently reduced the degree of credit given to "smart" bombs and guided munitions in the original Bomb Damage Assessments (BDAs).

In the early 1950s the U.S. actually announced a strategy which would have effectively relied upon air power alone to strike at a potential enemy. The enemy was the Soviet Union and the strategy was dubbed "massive retaliation." The doctrine was simply expressed; it embodied a promise to react fully to any hostile moves by the Soviet Union or its clients. As John Foster Dulles put it, the strategy would "depend primarily upon a great capacity to retaliate instantly by means and at places of our own choosing." Translated from "Cold War speak," this was generally understood to mean the nuclear-armed bombers of Strategic Air Command (SAC) would strike directly at Moscow and Leningrad, regardless of the degree of provocation.

Part of the underlying appeal of the doctrine was the belief that such a strategy would make a large, expensive military establishment on land and sea unnecessary. Dulles thought "it is now possible to get, and share, more basic security at less cost." This seemed to follow Seversky's earlier advice: "Our only hope is to make of our own heartland an invincible base from which we can project an offensive against any part of the world."

This strategy became untenable when the Soviet Union developed its own nuclear stockpile and intercontinental air strike capacity. By the late 1950s "deterrence" had become the operational doctrine, but this really meant that the nuclear strike ability possessed by both sides prevented action of any kind. Only actions that upset the rough balance, such as missiles in Cuba, could provoke a world-threatening crisis. Conventional army and naval forces regained their importance, at least in the far corners of the world where "brush fire" wars could be conducted without either superpower playing the "nuclear card."

This remained the underlying strategy for the balance of the Cold War Period. It was extended beyond the bounds of the earth with the rise of the "space race" in the late 1950s and 1960s. Both the U.S. and the USSR saw a necessity to gain "control" of orbital positions from which they could dominate the earth below with various surveillance and weapons systems. The much-maligned, now-abandoned "Star Wars" weapon-in-space initiative was a U.S. effort to gain a technological jump on the Soviets which could have implied a return to the "massive retaliation" doctrine. Like previous breakthroughs (missiles, multiple warheads, highly accurate targeting, throw weights), it did not produce a long-term decisive advantage. In fact, Star Wars has proven to be something of a technological bust. Military competition for space seems have abated with the end of the Cold War, but the respite is not likely to last much longer as most major powers develop space programs.

Perhaps the most interesting thing about the Cold War era is that no major new geopolitical theory or paradigm emerged to extend or replace the works of Mahan, MacKinder, and Burnham. Some writers saw the Cold War as essentially a struggle between a Mahan-type maritime strategy (the "free world") and a MacKinder-type heartland strategy (the "Communist bloc"). Spykman's Rimland Theorem fitted well with the notion of the NATO Alliance. In general, however, the over-arching threat of nuclear extermination effectively paralyzed geopolitical thinking in a fashion similar to that suffered by military planning in general. In any case, no good geopolitical interpretation of the Cold War has yet been produced.

There appears to be no central organizing geopolitical theorem guiding national strategies today. The Heartland notion seems quaint since the resource and population strength of this region (at least with 20th century technology) were vastly over-rated by MacKinder. Mahan's notion that control over the seas is the *sine qua non* for world power also seems untenable. How then, can one explain the rise of Japan, which thrives on world sea trade but exerts little if any physical control over it?

Leaving aside the nuclear option, which seems increasingly remote at least on a global scale in the post-Cold War world, air power has yet to establish its absolute dominance over space and geography. The "inevitable" world empire seems more distant than ever. The probable locus of future world power and even the likely geographical arenas of conflict in determining such a dominant nation or bloc are impossible to determine at this stage. Recent works attempting historical generalizations, such as Paul Kennedy's *Rise and Fall of the Great Powers*, propose some sort of organic "life-cycle" theory of national greatness with no grounding in geographical, economic or political realities. Confusion and uncertainty abound about the appropriate place of national advantage and the choice of a grand strategy. Policy makers need some new geopolitical theorem to help them organize global resources to move beyond the failures and limits of the past.

The role of near-orbital and outer space in future political developments must be a central feature of such a theory. This certainly moves beyond anything done by previous geopolitical analysts. One can imagine obscure academics at work producing paradigms to guide a future generation of statesmen confidently into the new era of international conflicts. Whether it is actually happening, or will soon commence, remains to be seen. Whatever happens, it is clear that changing times will demand new thinking. . . .

# Chapter 24

★ ★ ★

# The New World Order:
# Back to the Future

*The Economist*

*The Economist depicts the next phase of history as a "dance of the dinosaurs," which will likely be dominated by four powers: Europe, Russia, China, and the U.S. Europe has rather few options and cannot exercise much global strength until it achieves economic integration. Russia has vast economic potential and military clout, but must complete its post-communist transition. China is growing faster than any other great power, although it will be hampered by its huge population and lack of natural resources. The United States possesses an impressive array of advantages and options, but it must decide how it wishes to deal with the other powers and act accordingly. Japan is only a possible contender, as is a hypothetical (but potentially explosive) Muslim center of power. What are the strengths and the weaknesses of each one? Do you agree that the only alternative to this new world order is global anarchy? What role does The Economist suggest that the United States play in world affairs?*

So there is to be no new world order after all, says a chorus of disappointed voices as the curtain rises . . . on a scene of disorder in Russia, betrayal in Bosnia, terrorism in North Africa and nuclear poker-playing in North Korea. The voices are wrong. With one necessary proviso—that mankind avoids a new form of anarchy—there is going to be a new world order. It may not be the one you would have liked, or were hoping for after the defeat of communism and the slapping down of Saddam Hussein. But a reordering of the world's pattern of power, a new configuration of strong and weak, is almost certainly on the way.

Each period of history has produced its own pattern of relations, settled or otherwise, among the world's powers. It might be a near-monopoly, as the Roman

*The Economist* is a well known weekly publication with headquarters in London, U.K. Neither the editorials nor articles are identified by name of author.

empire was in the corner of the world the Romans knew, and the Middle Kingdom was for the Chinese until 150 years ago. (There has not yet been a near-monopoly in the real, whole world.) It might be a duopoly, as was more or less the case in the cold war, though duopolies seldom last long: when one side starts to get the better of the other, number two has nowhere to turn for help.

More usually, the order emerges from the interplay of three, four or five powers which create a shifting pattern of alliances and enmities among themselves. This is the dance of the dinosaurs. It is the way things were in most of Europe and Asia—the core of the historical world—for most of the time in the past few centuries, until 1945; and it is the way things are likely to be again now.

The new order may be more durable than earlier ones, or less durable; it may be sturdy, or wobbly; it may be kindly, or brutal. Most of its component parts may be democracies, or only a minority of them. But unless something happens to prevent any sort of order arising—which is to say unless anarchy takes over—a new world order is not something to be wished for or wished away. It is the next arrival on the conveyor-belt of history.

The four powers fairly certain to take part in the new pattern are the United States, China, Russia and Europe, in that order of probability. Then come two merely possible contenders: one is Japan, the other a hypothetical centre of power in the Muslim world (which, if it did come into being, could prove the most explosive of the lot).

Nobody else seems to qualify. It is unlikely that Africa or the Antipodes is going to produce a member of this dominant group. Latin America, even big Brazil, will probably stay under the eagle's wing of the United States for at least the next decade or two. India will be a power in its own neighborhood but its frail economy and its physical isolation between the Himalayas and the sea will almost certainly keep it out of the global competition. The only big question mark—the joker in the pack, the possible bringer of anarchy—is the proliferation factor: the danger that an unknown number of countries with no other claim to great power may prove able to equip themselves with nuclear or biological weapons of mass destruction, deliverable at a distance.

## Two Questions to Ask

To work out the various shapes the new pattern may take, it helps to ask two questions about the handful of big powers. The first is the up-or-down question. It is not hard to estimate the weight of the big powers in their relations with one another over the next few years—say, up to 2000. But how might those weights increase or diminish in the early part of the 21st century, and in response to what factors? Second, there is the who-with-whom question. On present evidence, which big powers are most likely to team up with one another, and which to go on glaring at each other?

As things stand now, the United States wields by far the most weight. Its economy is by the purchasing-power test roughly the same size as that of Western Europe . . . 260% the size of China's and 630% the size of poor Russia's. As a military power it is in a category of its own, not so much because of its nuclear weapons as because it is streets ahead of everybody else in its ability to use satellites, computers and stealth technology to aim ordinary, non-nuclear weapons with overwhelming precision. And, unlike the self-styled European Union (ex-European Community), America has a government capable of taking reasonably clear-cut decisions. It is not the world's "superpower" in the sense of having enough power to override everyone else, but it is manifestly *primus inter impares*.

Americans can hold on to this advantage for a while yet, if they want to. Their lead in military technology will probably go on growing for the next decade or more. Their economy has problems, but it is no longer fashionable to think that these are severe enough to paralyze American power.

The only thing which might bring about that paralysis is the Americans themselves. They, unlike the inhabitants of the Eurasian land-mass (who include all three of America's chief competitors), have an option of comfortable semi-retirement, of withdrawal into the cosy near-self-sufficiency of the Americas. They have shown a distinct interest in this option since the end of the cold war. If, at the close of the 20th century, it seems hard to believe that America might tiptoe out of the world, it is worth remembering that, at the start of the century, it was hard to imagine America tiptoeing in.

If Americans resist the temptation to withdraw, there is only one serious question to be asked about their side of the who-with-whom business. They will keep up their links with Europe, which is closest to them in political beliefs and practical interests. They are unlikely to make an ally of China, the power furthest from them on both those counts. The question is about Russia.

Many Americans are attracted by the idea of a Russia-America axis as the centre of a new world order, and are prepared to buy Russia's co-operation by giving it a free hand in the former Soviet Union. . . . There would be obvious problems. What would Europe think of letting Russian power seep back to the borders of Poland and Hungary? How could you make sure the seepage stopped there? But for Americans who want to stay involved in the world and yet to ration the amount of effort they need to put into it, a Russia-America axis has its appeal.

If America is the power with the widest range of choices, the narrowest belongs to Europe. The Europeans have not yet launched any coherent attack on the social costs that are weakening the competitiveness of their economies. They show no wish to spend the extra 2-3% of GDP per year needed to bring their armed forces anywhere near American levels of computer-and-satellite efficiency. Above all, it now seems clear that there will be no single European state with a coherent European foreign policy until well into the next century—if then. On the up-and-down scale, Europe is tilting down.

Europe also has the shortest list of prospective friends. [Several] years ago, after the fall of the Berlin Wall, there were Europeans who thought the time had at last come for an Atlantic-to-the-Urals deal with Russia. That idea looks a lot less attractive now that Russia seems condemned to a long period of political and economic turmoil; and Europeans would have difficulty in offering Russia the incentive—a resumption of control over the ex-Soviet Union—that some Americans are willing to offer for their own special relationship with Russia. A Europe-China axis is even more unlikely.

The Europeans' choice is stark. They can work with America in a new, outward-looking version of the Atlantic alliance, or they can drift off alone and wait for the squalls to hit them. . . .

Russia, on the face of it, looks better off; but appearances can be deceptive. Does Boris Yeltsin really hope for an alliance with America, and the global condominium that implies? Perhaps he does; but the odds are that even a half-confident America will come to see that such an arrangement is liable to be more trouble (in the resentment it causes elsewhere) than it is worth to America. It is just as hard to picture a coming together of Russia and the European Union, unless Europe is abandoned by America and has to accept Russia's terms. A new Russia-China alliance is almost inconceivable.

The hard fact is that no power is going to risk very much in its relations with Russia so long as that country's downward plunge goes on. On the up-down calculation, Russia's economic performance is much the worst of the big four. This has already weakened its armed forces, and will weaken them still further. Nor has Russia yet found the degree of political consensus needed to avoid continuing disorder and perhaps even disintegration. Russia's hope of being a force in the world ever again might seem even dimmer than Europe's, except for one thing. When Russians look westward into Europe, they feel envious; when Europeans look eastward to Russia, they feel nervous. That still gives Russia an edge.

Of the four main powers, the most indisputably upwardly-mobile is China. Even if the Chinese economy cannot sustain its . . . growth rate of the past [few] years, it promises to go on performing formidably well. This will before very long enable China to add a modern army, navy and air force to its existing nuclear armoury. In terms of world power, the measure of a country's economic success is not GDP per head (which for China's 1.2 billion people is bound to stay small for many years); rather, it is the ability to build up armed strength and to hearten the men who carry the guns with the confidence that their country is going up in the world. China has both those things within its grasp.

## Enter the Dragon

China may start to use its new self-confidence sooner than expected. [A short time ago] its prime minister said openly that, if America called for economic sanctions to prevent North Korea acquiring nuclear weapons, China would block the use of sanctions. The Chinese did not say this because they want a nuclear-armed Kim Il Sing; they must find that prospect as horrifying as everybody else does. They said it because they want to show they have the power to say No to the United States.

China's emergence could have a dramatic effect on the pattern of power. The Chinese believe that several of their neighbours—including Russia—sit on territory which really belongs to China. The present government in Beijing sees its adaptation of communism as a rival of the democracy to which most other countries now give at least lip-service. Even if that changes, and China goes democratic, it will still want to be the chief power in Asia, and one without whose consent America and Russia and Europe can do nothing important in that half of the world. At best it will be a lumberingly uncooperative partner in the dance of the powers; at worst, the disrupter who breaks up the whole dance.

So much for the four principals: on the two long shots. Japan ranks among them, despite its stunning wealth, because it will have trouble converting its splendidly high GDP-per-head into the more brutal currencies of international power. It is a small, vulnerable island lying between two great powers neither of which wishes to see it build up any very great armed strength.

The Chinese do not want an East Asian military competitor. The Americans would like some Japanese help in peacekeeping operations around the world, but would rather that they themselves remained the chief non-Chinese military power in Asia. There is no overwhelming demand for Japanese rearmament within Japan itself, and none at all from the smaller countries of the region—which makes Japan different from Germany, whose fellow Europeans urged it to rearm [over] 40 years ago. Unless these things change, Japan will stay economically big but militarily small. And a rueful look through history shows that a loaded gun generally counts for more than a fat purse.

The other long shot, an Islamic power, may never come into existence; but, if it did, it would doubtless give the gun priority over the purse. A new state created out of countries in the western part of the Muslim world, professing the principles of Islam, would have a clear-cut ideology in open competition with that of the modern West. If most of its people were Arabs, it would possess the further unifying force of a shared language. And it would have the power of oil, which could be denied to its adversaries or sold for buying the weapons with which to fight them.

This pugnacious new arrival would confront two ready-made enemies. One would be Europe, its centuries-old quarrel with western Islam still liable to flare up over places like Bosnia. Then would come Russia, whose border with Islam in central Asia remains a blur. It is by no means impossible that a new Islamic power would get into a fight with both Europe and Russia—and, if it did, it might look for an ally to China, which also has a border quarrel with Russia.

Finally, the joker: the proliferation factor. Proliferation could make it irrelevant to talk about any kind of order at all. If nuclear or biological weapons came into the possession of a half-dozen more countries—or a dozen more, or two dozen—any hope of a rule-governed world would almost certainly vanish.

Most of these new masters of mass destruction would have foreign-policy agendas of their own, which they could pursue without much fear of dissuasion by the countries that had once been the "big powers." The necessary bargaining and manoeuvring between America, China, Russia and Europe, which was hazardous enough before, would become impossibly complicated if each had to take this array of new missile-wielders into all its calculations. The world order would no longer be a delicate dance of four or five, but the stomping of a platoon's-worth of powers. . . . [I]t is a somber thought that the outcome of the . . . argument with North Korea may decide whether or not the scene is about to be thus transformed.

## The Likeliest Possibilities

So what are the likely patterns of this uneasy new world? There are many possible combinations and permutations, but several of them look pretty theoretical. (A Europe-China alliance to keep middle-man Russia under control? Hardly. A pairing of young America and China to keep oldsters Europe and Russia in their place? No.)

Let it be rather hopefully assumed that no mass proliferation of nuclear weapons takes place. Let it also be assumed, a little more confidently, that America stays engaged in the world, Russia stays wobbly but in one piece, and Europe fails to unite into a single state. In these circumstances, there are two main possibilities.

One is what will probably take place if China's arrival on the world-power stage happens soon and spectacularly, meaning within the next five or ten years and with an authoritarian Chinese government bent on carving out a place in the world for "socialism with Chinese characteristics." This will alarm next-door Russia, which occupies a large amount of territory taken from China 130-odd years ago.

The Russians, wanting the support of America and Europe against this new problem to the east, will become much more cooperative towards the West in foreign policy. Europe and America, also anxious about China, will be readier to help Russia without insisting very vigorously on Russian progress towards democracy and economic efficiency. The upshot will probably be a loose-wristed three-power alliance for the containment of China, while Japan—intimidated by China's growing power, and needing America's protection—stays modestly at sub-great-power level.

An explosive variant would be provided by the appearance of that new Islamic power. Fear of this would push Europe and Russia closer together. But the Islamic power might well find a natural ally in China, because China would share its dislike of Russia and would be a very practical partner in an exchange of oil for modern weapons. That combination would threaten Russia on two fronts, and the result could quite possibly be Russia's collapse. If you were looking for an apocalyptic scenario, this would be a candidate.

The kindlier—and, on the whole, likelier—alternative will prevail if China remains relatively unassertive and the new Islamic power never comes into being. Russia, free from external threat, will be able to concentrate on its long and difficult struggle towards a modern economy and a liberal political system. Russia would, in this case, be neither a formal ally nor an open adversary of Europe and America, just a prickly acquaintance emitting occasional cries of pain or rage.

A relatively mild China and a self-absorbed Russia would then give America and Europe, if they decided to work together, an opportunity to share the responsibilities of predominant power over the next two or three decades—not just in pursuit of their own interests, but also because they genuinely had something to offer the world.

Does it sound familiar? This was the opportunity many people thought had arrived a [few years] ago, after the formal collapse of the Soviet Union. The defeat of communism, followed by the defeat of Saddam Hussein, appeared to be ushering the Atlantic democracies into one of those rare periods of history when a lucky group of people finds itself possessed of a good idea, military strength and self-assurance all at the same time. But then the prospect seemed to fade, as the democracies failed to cope with the crises that hit them one-two-three in ex-Yugoslavia, Somalia and Haiti. Their performance in these three hard tests diminished the West in the world's estimation, and in its own.

But perhaps these disappointments were, in fact, no more than an uncommonly bumpy stretch of a much longer and generally smoother road. Perhaps Europe and America can now pull themselves together, literally and figuratively, for another attempt to seize the opportunity still lying ahead of them.

For they are, after all, the originators of the political idea that comes closest to exercising universal appeal in the modern world: democracy. People everywhere want the chance to eject bad or unpopular rulers peaceably from power. The machinery for that ejection may vary greatly from country to country. But the argument you hear from authoritarian politicians in East Asia and elsewhere—that their people do not want the power to eject, because they trust their rulers to rule them well—is self-serving nonsense. Nobody trusts the boss to be permanently perfect. Europe and America invented the idea that there should be an orderly way of getting rid of the boss who goes wrong. They can help to spread that idea wider, if they wish to do so.

Do they? The spreading of democracy—its "enlargement," in the Clinton administration's word—requires constant effort. It costs money and sometimes lives. The question is whether Europe and America can rediscover the will to make that effort. On the answer to that, the eventual shape of the new world order may depend.

# Chapter 25

## ★ ★ ★

## Pivotal States and U.S. Strategy

Robert S. Chase, Emily B. Hill and Paul Kennedy

*Robert S. Chase, Emily B. Hill and Paul Kennedy contend that the debate over the future of the international order is unlikely to be soon resolved. They agree with those who accept that America's national interest requires stability in important parts of the developing world. They suggest that there are "pivotal states" in each region of the globe whose fate is uncertain and whose future will profoundly affect their surrounding regions. Thus they conclude that a strategy of rigorously discriminate assistance focused on these "pivotal states" would benefit United States foreign policy in a number of ways. Among their reasons are a realistic use of limited resources, attention, and energies, including a pragmatic refocusing of foreign aid. As importantly, this sense of restraint would help counter a continuing isolationist mode among some Americans. Is there value in identifying these "pivotal states"? How would you modify the authors' list? Will this geopolitical focus provide the strategic benefit which the authors seek?*

### The New Dominoes

Half a decade after the collapse of the Soviet Union, American policymakers and intellectuals are still seeking new principles on which to base national strategy. The current debate over the future of the international order—including predictions of the "end of history," a "clash of civilizations," a "coming anarchy," or a "borderless world"—has failed to generate agreement on what shape U.S. policy should take. However, a single overarching framework may be inappropriate for understanding today's disorderly and decentralized world. America's security no longer hangs on the success or failure of containing communism. The challenges are more diffuse and numerous. As a priority, the

Robert S. Chase is a Ph.D. candidate in economics at Yale University. Emily B. Hill is a Ph.D. candidate in history at Yale University. Paul Kennedy is Professor of History at Yale University.

Reprinted by permission of *Foreign Affairs*, Vol. 75, No. 1, January/February 1996, pp. 33-51. Copyright © 1996 Council on Foreign Relations, Inc. Minor modifications to the text have been made.

United States must manage its delicate relationships with Europe, Japan, Russia, and China, the other major players in world affairs. However, America's national interest also requires stability in important parts of the developing world. Despite congressional pressure to reduce or eliminate overseas assistance, it is vital that America focus its efforts on a small number of countries whose fate is uncertain and whose future will profoundly affect their surrounding regions. These are the pivotal states.

The idea of a pivotal state—a hot spot that could not only determine the fate of its region but also affect international stability—has a distinguished pedigree reaching back to the British geographer Sir Halford Mackinder in the 1900s and earlier. The classic example of a pivotal state throughout the nineteenth century was Turkey, the epicenter of the so-called Eastern Question; because of Turkey's strategic position, the disintegration of the Ottoman Empire posed a perennial problem for British and Russian policymakers.

Twentieth-century American policymakers employed their own version of a pivotal states theory. Statesmen from Eisenhower and Acheson to Nixon and Kissinger continually referred to a country succumbing to communism as a potential "rotten apple in a barrel" or a "falling domino." Although the domino theory was never sufficiently discriminative—it worsened America's strategic overextension—its core was about supporting pivotal states to prevent their fall to communism and the consequent fall of neighboring states.

Because the U.S. obsession with faltering dominoes led to questionable policies from Vietnam to El Salvador, the theory now has a bad reputation. But the idea itself—that of identifying specific countries as more important than others, for both regional stability and American interests—is sensible. The United States should adopt a discriminative policy toward the developing world, concentrating its energies on pivotal states rather than spreading its attention and resources over the globe.

Indeed, the domino theory may now fit U.S. strategic needs better than it did during the Cold War. The new dominoes, or pivotal states, no longer need assistance against an external threat from a hostile political system; rather, the danger is that they will fall prey to internal disorder. A decade ago, when the main threat to American interests in the developing world was the possibility that nations would align with the Soviets, the United States faced a clear-cut enemy. This enemy captured the American imagination in a way that impending disorder does not. Yet chaos and instability may prove a greater and more insidious threat to American interests than communism ever was. With its migratory outflows, increasing conflict due to the breakdown of political structures, and disruptions in trade patterns, chaos undoubtedly affects bordering states. Reacting with interventionist measures only after a crisis in one state threatens an important region is simply too late. Further, Congress and the American public would likely not accept such actions, grave though the consequences might be to U.S. interests. Preventive assistance to pivotal states to reduce the chance of collapse would better serve American interests.

A strategy of rigorously discriminate assistance to the developing world would benefit American foreign policy in a number of ways. First, as the world's richest nation, with vast overseas holdings and the most to lost from global instability, the United States needs a conservative strategy. Like the British Empire in the nineteenth and early twentieth centuries, the interests of the United States lie in the status quo. Such a strategy places the highest importance on relations with the other great powers: decisions about the expansion of NATO or preserving amicable relations with Russia, China, Japan, and the major European powers must remain primary. The United States must also safeguard several special allies, such as Saudi Arabia, Kuwait, South Korea, and Israel, for strategic and domestic political reasons.

Second, a pivotal states policy would help U.S. policymakers deal with what Sir Michael Howard, in another context, nicely described as "the heavy and ominous breathing of a parsimonious and pacific electorate." American policymakers, themselves less and less willing to contemplate foreign obligations, are acutely aware that the public is extremely cautious about and even hostile toward overseas engagements. While the American public may not reject all such commitments, it does resist intervention in areas that appear peripheral to U.S. interests. A majority also believes, without knowing the relatively small percentages involved, that foreign aid is a major drain on the federal budget and often wasted through fraud, duplication, and high operating costs. Few U.S. politicians are willing to risk unpopularity by contesting such opinions, and many Republican critics have played to this mood by attacking government policies that imply commitments abroad. Statesmen responsible for outlining U.S. foreign policy might have a better chance of persuading a majority of Congress and the American public that a policy of selective engagement is both necessary and feasible.

Finally, a pivotal states strategy might help bridge the conceptual and political divide in the national debate between "old" and "new" security issues. The mainstream in policy circles still considers new security issues peripheral; conversely, those who focus on migration, overpopulation, or environmental degradation resist the realist emphasis on power and military and political security.

In truth, neither the old nor the new approach will suffice. The traditional realist stress on military and political security is simply inadequate—it does not pay sufficient attention to the new threats to American national interests. The threats to the pivotal states are not communism or aggression but rather overpopulation, migration, environmental degradation, ethnic conflict, and economic instability, all phenomena that traditional security forces find hard to address. The "dirty" industrialization of the developing world, unchecked population growth and attendant migratory pressures, the rise of powerful drug cartels, the flow of illegal arms, the eruption of ethnic conflict, the flourishing of terrorist groups, the spread of deadly new viruses, and turbulence in emerging markets—a laundry list of newer problems—must also concern Americans, if only because their spillover effects can hurt U.S. interests.

Yet the new interpretation of security, with its emphasis on holistic and global issues, is also inadequate. Those who point to such new threats to international stability often place secondary importance (if that) on U.S. interests; indeed, they are usually opposed to invoking the national interest to further their cause. For example, those who criticized the Clinton administration in the summer of 1994 for not becoming more engaged in the Rwandan crisis paid little attention to the relative insignificance of Rwanda's stability for American interests. The universal approach common to many advocates of global environmental protection or human rights, commendable in principle, does not discriminate between human rights abuses in Haiti, where proximity and internal instability made intervention possible and even necessary, and similar abuses in Somalia, where the United States had few concrete interests.

Furthermore, the new security approach cannot make a compelling case to the American public for an internationalist foreign policy. The public does not sense the danger in environmental and demographic pressures that erode stability over an extended period, even if current policies, or lack thereof, make this erosion inexorable and at some point irreversible. Finally, the global nature of the new security threats makes it tempting to downplay national governments as a means to achieving solutions.

A pivotal states strategy, in contrast, would encourage integration of new security issues into a traditional, state-centered framework and lend greater clarity to the making of foreign policy. This integration may make some long-term consequences of the new security threats more tangible and manageable. And it would confirm the importance of working chiefly through state governments to ensure stability while addressing the new security issues that make these states pivotal.

## How to Identify a Pivot

According to which criteria should the pivotal states be selected? A large population and an important geographical location are two requirements. Economic potential is also critical, as recognized by the U.S. Commerce Department's recent identification of the "big emerging markets" that offer the most promise to American business. Physical size is a necessary but not sufficient

The
Pivotal
States

condition: Zaire comprises an extensive tract, but its fate is not vital to the United States.

What really defines a pivotal state is its capacity to affect regional and international stability. A pivotal state is so important regionally that its collapse would spell transboundary mayhem: migration, communal violence, pollution, disease, and so on. A pivotal state's steady economic progress and stability, on the other hand, would bolster its region's economic vitality and political soundness and benefit American trade and investment.

For the present, the following should be considered pivotal states: Mexico and Brazil; Algeria, Egypt, and South Africa; Turkey; India and Pakistan; and Indonesia. These states' prospects vary widely. India's potential for success, for example, is considerably greater than Algeria's; Egypt's potential for chaos is greater than Brazil's. But all face a precarious future, and their success or failure will powerfully influence the future of surrounding areas and affect American interests. This theory of pivotal states must not become a mantra, as the domino

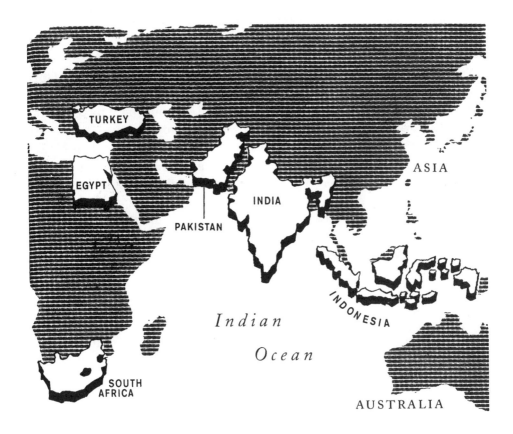

Ib Ohlsson for FOREIGN AFFAIRS

theory did, and the list of states could change. But the concept itself can provide a necessary and useful framework for revising American strategy toward the developing world.

## A World Turning on Pivots

To understand this idea in concrete terms, consider the Mexican peso crisis . . . [in January 1995]. Mexico's modernization has created strains between the central and local governments and difficulties with the unions and the poorest groups in the countryside, and it has damaged the environment. Like the other pivotal states, Mexico is delicately balanced between progress and turmoil.

Given the publicity and political debate surrounding the Clinton administration's rescue plan for Mexico, most Americans probably understood that their southern neighbor is special, even if they were disturbed by the means employed to rescue it. A collapse of the peso and the consequent ruin of the Mexican economy would have weakened the U.S. dollar, hurt exports, and caused convulsions throughout Latin America's Southern Cone Common Market and other emerging markets. Dramatically illustrating the potency of new security threats to the United States, economic devastation in Mexico would have increased the northward flow of illegal immigrants and further strained the United States' overstretched educational and social services. Violent social chaos in Mexico could spill over into this country. As many bankers remarked during the peso crisis, Mexico's troubles demonstrated the impossibility of separating "there" from "here."

Because of Mexico's proximity and its increasing links with the United States, American policymakers clearly needed to give it special attention. As evidenced by the North American Free Trade Agreement, they have. But other select states also require close American attention.

## Egypt

Egypt's location has historically made its stability and political alignment critical to both regional development and relationships between the great powers. In recent decades, its proximity to important oil regions and its involvement in the Arab-Israeli peace process, which is important for the prosperity of many industrialized countries, has enhanced its contribution to stability in the Middle East and North Africa. Furthermore, the government of President Muhammad Hosni Mubarak has provided a bulwark against perhaps the most significant long-term threat in the region—radical Islamic fundamentalism.

The collapse of the current Egyptian regime might damage American interests more than the Iranian revolution did. The Arab-Israeli peace process, the key plank of U.S. foreign policy in this region for the past 20 years, would suffer serious, perhaps irreparable, harm. An unstable Egypt would undermine the American diplomatic plan of isolating fundamentalist "rogue" states in the region and encourage extremist opposition to governments everywhere from Algeria to Turkey. The fall of the Mubarak government could well lead Saudi Arabia to reevaluate its pro-Western stance. Under such conditions, any reply of Operation Desert Storm or similar military intervention in the Middle East on behalf of friendly countries such as Kuwait or Jordan would be extremely difficult, if not impossible. Finally, the effect on oil and financial markets worldwide could be enormous.

Egypt's future is not only vital, but very uncertain. While some signs point to increasing prosperity and stability—birth rates have declined, the United States . . . forgave $7 billion of debt, and Egypt's international reserves reached $16 billion in 1995—the preponderance of evidence paints a dimmer picture.

Jealously guarding its power base and wary that further privatization would produce large numbers of resentful former state employees, the government fears losing control over the economy. Growth rates lurch fitfully upward, and although reform has improved most basic economic indicators, it has also widened the gap between rich and poor. Roughly one-third of the population now lives in poverty, up from 20-25 percent in 1990.

A harsh crackdown on fundamentalism has reduced the most serious short-term to the Mubarak regime, but a long-term solution may prove more elusive. The government's brutal attack on the fundamentalist movement may ultimately fuel Islam's cause by alienating the professional middle class; such a policy has already greatly strengthened the more moderate Muslim Brotherhood and radicalized the extremist fringe.

Environmental and population problems are growing. Despite the gradually decreasing birthrate, the population is increasing by about one million every nine months, straining the country's natural resources, and its forecast to reach about 94 million by 2025.

Recognizing Egypt's significance and fragility, successive U.S. administrations have made special provisions to maintain its stability. In 1995 Egypt received $2.4 billion from the U.S. government, making it the second-largest recipient of American assistance, after Israel. That allocation is primarily the result of the Camp David accords and confirms Egypt's continuing importance in U.S. Middle East policy. Current attempts by American isolationists to cut these funds should be strongly resisted. On the other hand, the U.S. government and Congress should seriously consider redirecting American aid. F-16 fighters can do little to help Egypt handle its internal difficulties, but assistance to improve infrastructure, education, and the social fabric would ease the country's troubles.

## Indonesia

While Egypt's prospects for stability are tenuous, Indonesia's future appears brighter. By exercising considerable control over the population and the economy for the last several decades, Indonesia's authoritarian regime has engineered dramatic economic growth, now expected to be about 7 percent annually for the rest of the decade. Poverty rates have dropped drastically, and a solid middle class has emerged. At first glance, Indonesia's development has been a startling success. However, the government now confronts strains generated by its own efforts.

Along with incomes, education levels, and health status, Indonesia's population is increasing dramatically. With the fourth-largest population in the world and an extra three million people added each year, the country is projected to reach 260 million inhabitants by 2025. The main island of Java, one of the most densely populated places on earth, can scarcely accommodate the new bodies. In response, the government is forcing many citizens to migrate to other islands. This resettlement program is the focal point for a host of other tensions concerning human rights and the treatment of minorities. The government's brutal handling of the separatist movement in East Timor continues to hinder its efforts to gain international respect. President Suharto's regime has made a point of cooperating with Chinese entrepreneurs to boost economic expansion, but ethnic differences remain entrenched. Finally, the government's favoring of specific businesses has produced deep-rooted corruption.

Because of the government's tight control, it can maintain stability even while pursuing these questionable approaches to handling its people. However, as a more sophisticated middle class emerges, Indonesians are less willing to accept the existing concentration of economic and political power. These opposing forces, one for continued central control and one for more dispersed political power, will clash when Suharto leaves office, probably after the 1998 elections.

A reasonable scenario for Indonesia would be the election of a government that shares power more broadly, with greater respect for human rights and press freedoms. The new regime would maintain Indonesia's openness to foreign trade and investment, and it would end favoritism toward certain companies. Better educated, better paid, and urbanized for a generation, Indonesians would have fewer children per family. Indonesia would continue its leadership role in the Association of Southeast Asian Nations (ASEAN) and the Asia-Pacific Economic Cooperation forum (APEC), helping foster regional growth and stability.

The possibility remains, however, that the transfer of power in Jakarta could trigger political and economic instability, as it did in 1965 at the end of President Sukarno's rule. A new regime might find it more difficult to overawe the people while privately profiting from the economy. Elements of the electorate could lash out in frustration. Riots would then jeopardize Indonesia's growth and regional leadership, and by that stage the United States could do nothing more than attempt to rescue its citizens from the chaos.

Instability in Indonesia would affect peace and prosperity across Southeast Asia. Its archipelago stretches across key shipping lanes, its oil and other businesses attract Japanese and U.S. investment, and its stable economic conditions and open trade policies set an example for ASEAN, APEC, and the region as a whole. If Indonesia, as Southeast Asia's fulcrum, falls into chaos, it is hard to envisage the region prospering. It is equally hard to imagine general distress if Indonesia booms economically and maintains political stability.

Despite the difficulty, the United States must have a strategy for encouraging Indonesia's stability. Part of this will involve close cooperation with Japan, which is by far the largest donor to Indonesian development. A more sensitive aspect of the strategy will be encouraging the regime to respect human rights and ethnic differences. The strategy also calls for calibrated pressure on Indonesia to decrease its widespread corruption, which in any case is required to achieve the country's full integration into the international business world.

## Brazil

Brazil borders every country in South America except Ecuador and Chile, and its physical size, complex society, and huge population of 155 million people are more than enough to qualify it as a pivotal state.

Brazil's economy appears to be recovering from its 1980s crisis, although the indicators for the future are inconsistent. President Fernando Henrique Cardoso's proposals for economic reform, which include deregulation and increased openness to foreign investment in key industries, have advanced in Brazil's congress. Many basic social and economic indexes point to a generally improving quality of life, including the highest industrial growth since the 1970s (6.4 percent in 1994), declining birth and death rates, increasing life expectancy, and an expanding urban infrastructure. In the longer term, however, Brazil must address extreme economic inequality, poor educational standards, and extensive malnutrition. These realities, together with a burgeoning current account deficit and post-peso crisis skittishness, help diminish investor confidence.

Were Brazil to founder, the consequences from both an environmental and an economic point of view would be grave. The Amazon basin contains the largest tropical rain forest in the world, boasting unequaled biodiversity. Apart from aesthetic regrets about its destruction, the practical consequences are serious. The array of plants and trees in the Amazon is an important source of natural pharmaceuticals; deforestation may also spread diseases as the natural hosts of viruses and bacteria are displaced to other regions.

A social and political collapse would directly affect significant U.S. economic interests and American investors. Brazil's fate is inextricably linked to that of the entire South American region, a region that before its debt and inflation crises in the 1970s bought large amounts of U.S. goods and is now potentially the fastest-growing market for American business over the decades to come. In sum, were Brazil to succeed in stabilizing over the long term, reducing the massive gap between its rich and poor, further opening its markets, and privatizing often inefficient state-run industries, it could be a powerful engine for the regional economy and a stimulus to U.S. prosperity. Were it to fail, Americans would feel the consequences.

## South Africa

Apartheid's end makes South Africa's transition particularly dramatic. So far, President Nelson Mandela's reconciliation government has set an inspiring example of respect for ethnic differences, good governance, and prudent nurturing of the country's economic potential. In contrast to other conflicts, in which different groups have treated each other with so much acrimony that they could not negotiate, the administration has successfully overcome some of its political divisions: it includes both former apartheid president Frederik Willem de Klerk and Zulu Chief Mangosuthu Buthelezi. Moreover, South Africa is blessed with a strong infrastructure, a sound currency, and vast natural resources. These assets make its economy larger and more vital than any other on the continent, accounting for a colossal 75 percent of the southern African region's economic output. No longer an international pariah, it is working to develop robust trade and financial links around the region and the globe. A hub for these connections, South Africa could stimulate growth throughout the southern cone of Africa.

There are indications, however, that South Africa could succumb to political instability, ethnic strife, and economic stagnation. Power-sharing at the cabinet level belies deep ethnic divisions. Any one of several fissures could collapse this collaboration, plunging the country into civil war. Afrikaner militias may grow increasingly intransigent, traditional tribal leaders could raise arms against their diminished influence, and when Mandela no longer leads the African National Congress, the party may abandon its commitment to ethnic reconciliation.

As Mandela's government struggles to improve black living standards and soothe ethnic tensions, the legacy of apartheid creates a peculiar dilemma. It will be had to meet understandable black expectations of equity in wages, education, and health, given the country's budget deficits and unstable tax base. As racial inequalities persist, blacks are likely to grow impatient. Yet if whites feel they are paying a disproportionate share for improved services for blacks, they might flee the country, taking with them the prospects for increased foreign direct investment.

While the primary threats to South Africa's stability are internal, its effectiveness in containing them will have repercussions beyond its borders. Even before apartheid ended, South Africa had enormous influence over the region's political and economic development, from supporting insurgencies throughout the "front-line states" to providing mining jobs for migrant workers from those same countries. If South Africa achieves the economic and political potential within its grasp, it will be a wellspring of regional political stability and economic growth. If it prospers, it can demonstrate to other ethnically tortured regions a path to stability through democratization, reconciliation, and steadily increasing living standards. Alternatively, if it fails to handle its many challenges, it will suck its neighbors into a whirlpool of self-defeating conflict.

Although controlling the sea-lanes around the Cape of Good Hope would be important, especially if widespread trouble were to erupt in the Middle

East, American strategic interests are not otherwise endangered in southern Africa. Yet because South Africa is the United States' largest trading partner in Africa and possesses vast economic potential, its fate would affect American trading and financial interests that have invested there. It would also destabilize key commodity prices, especially in the gold, diamond, and ore markets. More generally, instability in South Africa, as in Brazil and Indonesia, would cast a large shadow over confidence in emerging markets.

American policy toward South Africa should reflect its importance as a pivotal state. While recognizing South Africa's desire to solve its problems without external interference, the United States should promote South Africa's economic and political stability. Of $10.5 billion in American economic aid given in 1995, a mere one percent ($135 million) was for South Africa. A strategy that acknowledges this nation's importance to American interests would surely be less parsimonious.

## Algeria and Turkey

Algeria's geographical position make its political future of great concern to American allies in Europe, especially France and Spain. A civil war and the replacement of the present regime by extremists would affect the security of the Mediterranean sea-lanes, international oil and gas markets, and, as in the case of Egypt, the struggle between moderate and radical elements in the Islamic world. All the familiar pressures of rapid population growth and drift to the coastal cities, environmental damage, increasing dependence on food imports, and extremely high youth unemployment are evident. Levels of violence remain high as Algerian government forces struggle to crush the Islamist guerrilla movement.

While a moderate Islamist government might prove less disturbing than the West fears, a bloody civil war or the accession of a radical, anti-Western regime would be very serious. Spain, Italy, and France depend heavily on Algerian oil and gas and would sorely miss their investments, and the resulting turbulence in the energy markets would certainly affect American consumers. The flood of middle-class, secular Algerians attempting to escape the bloodshed and enter France or other parts of southern Europe would further test immigration policies of the European Union (EU). The effects on Algeria's neighbors, Morocco and Tunisia, would be even more severe and encourage radical Islamic elements everywhere. Could Egypt survive if Algeria, Morocco, Tunisia, and Muammar al-Qaddafi's Libya collaborated to achieve fundamentalist goals? Rumors of an Algerian atomic bomb are probably premature, but the collapse of the existing regime would undoubtedly reduce security in the entire western Mediterranean. All the more reason for the United States to buttress the efforts of the International Monetary Fund and for the Europeans to improve Algeria's well-being and encourage a political settlement.

Although Turkey is not as politically or economically fragile as Algeria, its strategic importance may be even greater. At a multifold crossroads between East and West, North and South, Christendom and Islam, Turkey has the potential to influence countries thousands of miles from the Bosporus. The southeast keystone of NATO during the Cold War and an early (if repeatedly postponed) applicant to enlarged EU membership, Turkey enjoys solid economic growth and middle-class prosperity. However, it also shows many of the difficulties that worry other pivotal states: population and environmental pressures, severe ethnic minority challenges, and the revival of radical Islamic fundamentalism, all of which test the country's young democratic institutions and assumptions. There are also a slew of external problems, ranging from bitter rivalries with Greece over Cyprus, various nearby islands' territorial boundaries, and Macedonia, on the developing quarrel with Syria and Iraq over control of the Euphrates water supply, to delicate relationships with the Muslim-dominated states of Central Asia. A prosperous, democratic, tolerant Turkey is a beacon for the entire region; a Turkey engulfed by civil wars and racial and religious hatreds, or nursing ambitions to interfere abroad, would hurt American interests in innumerable ways and concern everyone from pro-NATO strategists to friends of Israel.

## India and Pakistan

Considered separately, the challenges facing the two great states of South Asia are daunting enough. Each confronts a population surge that is forecast to take Pakistan's total (123 million in 1990) to 276 million by 2025, and India's (853 million in 1990) to a staggering 1.45 billion, thus equaling China's projected population. While such growth taxes rural environments by causing the farming of marginal lands, deforestation, and depletion of water resources, the urban population explosion is even more worrisome. With 46 percent of Pakistan's and 25 percent of India's population under 15 years old, according to 1990 census figures, tens of millions of young people enter the job market each year; the inadequate opportunities for them further strain the social fabric. All this forms an ominous backdrop to rising tensions, as militant Hindus and Muslims, together a full fifth of the population, challenge India's democratic traditions, and Islamic forces stoke nationalist passions across Pakistan.

The shared borders and deep-rooted rivalry of India and Pakistan place these pivotal states in a more precarious position than, for example, Brazil or South Africa. With three wars between then since each gained independence, each continues to arm against the other and quarrel fiercely over Kashmir, Pakistan's potential nuclear capabilities and missile programs, and other issues. This jostling fuels their mutual ethnic-cum-religious fears and could produce another bloody conflict that neither government could control. What effect a full-scale war would have on the Pakistan-China entente is hard to predict, but the impact of such a contest would likely spread from Kashmir into Afghanistan and farther afield, and Pakistan could find support in the Muslim world. For many reasons, and perhaps especially the nuclear weapons stakes, the United States has a vital interest in encouraging South Asia's internal stability and external peace.

Could this short list of important states in the developing and emerging-markets regions of the globe include others? Possibly. This selection of pivotal states is not carved in stone, and new candidates could emerge over the next decades. Having an exact list is less important than initiating a debate over why, from the standpoint of U.S. national interests, some states in the developing world are more important than others.

### Better Wise Than Wide

The United States needs a policy toward the developing world that does not spread American energies, attention, and resources too thinly across the globe, but rejects isolationist calls to write it off. This is a realistic policy, both strategically and politically. Strategically, it would permit the United States, as the country that can make the greatest contribution to world security, to focus on supporting pivotal states. Politically, given the jaundiced view of Americans and their representatives toward overseas engagements, a strategy of discrimination is the strongest argument against an even greater withdrawal from the developing world than is now threatened.

As the above case studies suggest, each pivotal state grapples with an intricate set of interrelated problems. In such an environment, the United States has few clear-cut ways to help pivotal states succeed. Therefore, it must develop a subtle, comprehensive strategy, encompassing all aspects of American interaction with each one. Those strategies should include appropriate focusing of U.S. Agency for International Development assistance, promoting trade and investment, strengthening relationships with the country's leaders, bolstering country-specific intelligence capabilities and foreign service expertise, and coordinating the actions of government agencies that can influence foreign policy. In short, the United States must use all the resources at its disposal to buttress the stability of key states around the globe, working to prevent calamity rather than react to it. Apart from avoiding a great-power war, nothing in foreign policy could be more important.

This focus on the pivotal states inevitably means that developing states not deemed pivotal would receive diminished attention, energy, and resources. This will seem unfair to many, since each of the pivotal states examined above enjoys a higher per capita GDP than extremely poor nations like Mali and Ethiopia. Ideally, U.S. assistance to the entire developing world would significantly increase, but that will not happen soon. A pragmatic refocusing of American aid is better than nothing at all being given to the developing world, which may happen if the isolationist mood intensifies.

Such a refocusing could improve the American public's confidence that its money can be used effectively abroad. Relative to what other states give for development, the American contribution is declining. By continuing to spread those resources across a broad swath of developing countries, the United States might further diminish the impact of its assistance in many countries. In contrast, concentrating on a few pivotal states would increase American influence in them and improve the chances of convincing the public to spend resources overseas.

Current patterns of assistance to developing and emerging countries do not reflect American global security interests and in many cases seem glaringly inconsistent with U.S. strategic priorities. While conceding that by far the largest amounts of American aid will go to Israel and Egypt, is it not curious that India, like South Africa, receives less than one percent of total U.S. assistance? Pakistan receives virtually nothing. Algeria receives nothing. Brazil is given one-fifth of the aid awarded to Bolivia. Turkey gets less than Ethiopia (although, like Egypt, Ankara is given a large amount of military assistance that is hard to explain in the post-Cold War environment). Surely this requires serious examination.

In changing these patterns, diplomatic and political objections will be inevitable. Questions will arise about countries not on the list, particularly when one of them faces a crisis. Some will plead that exceptions be made for states that have been encouraged to undertake internal political changes, like Haiti, El Salvador, and the Philippines. Foreign service professionals will caution against making this strategy part of the declared policy of the United States, for that could indicate likely American reactions in a crisis. The more critics raise these problems, the more controversial this idea will become.

However, the pivotal states strategy merits such a debate, and it is high time for such a policy discussion to begin. As Mackinder pointed out, democracies find it difficult to think strategically in times of peace. All the above-mentioned problems and reservations, far from weakening the case for helping pivotal states, point to the importance of identifying how better to order U.S. policies in different parts of the world. A debate over pivotal states would also provide a way of checking the extent to which American agencies already carry out a discriminative strategy and the degree to which they recognize that the traditional type of external threats are not the only sources of danger to countries important to U.S. interests.

Would this formula solve all of America's foreign policy challenges? By no means. Priority should always be given to managing relations with the other great powers. In view of the international convulsions of the past 10 years, who would be rash enough to predict American relations with Russia, Japan, and China a decade or more hence and the dire implications if they go badly? Yet even if those countries remain our primary concern, the developing world still needs a place in U.S. global strategy. By identifying pivotal states to Congress and the public and providing the greatest possible support to those countries, this strategy has a greater chance of coherence and predictability than vague and indiscriminate assurances of good will to all developing countries, large and small. America's concern about traditional security threats would then be joined by a heightened awareness of the newer, nonmilitary dangers to important countries in the developing world and the serious repercussions of their collapse. Whichever administration steers the United States into the next century, American priorities would be ordered, and its foreign policy toward the developing world would have a focus—that of supporting those pivotal states whose future affects the fate of much of the planet.

# Chapter 26

### ✱ ✱ ✱

# The Clash of Civilizations?

Samuel P. Huntington

*Samuel P. Huntington contends that international politics will no longer be domi-
nated by conflicts between nation states and ideologies, but instead by the clash
between civilizations. Specifically, he predicts that future conflicts will occur along
the cultural fault lines separating seven or eight major civilizations: Western,
Confucian, Japanese, Islamic, Hindu, Slavic-Orthodox, Latin American, and possibly African. He asserts that the West should strive to limit the military strength of
Confucian and Islamic states, as well as exploiting differences and conflicts among
them. Do you agree with Huntington's claim that the fault lines between civilizations
are replacing the political and ideological boundaries of the Cold War, as the flash
points for crisis and bloodshed? What are the implications of his thesis for Western
relations with Eastern Europe, Russia, and Japan? Would Huntington's strategy
actually solve the tensions between civilizations or just make them worse?*

### The Next Pattern of Conflict

World politics is entering a new phase, and intellectuals have not hesitated
to proliferate visions of what it will be—the end of history, the return of
traditional rivalries between nation states, and the decline of the nation state
from the conflicting pulls of tribalism and globalism, among others. Each of these
visions catches aspects of the emerging reality. Yet they all miss a crucial, indeed
a central, aspect of what global politics is likely to be in the coming years.

It is my hypothesis that the fundamental source of conflict in this new world
will not be primarily ideological or primarily economic. The great divisions
among humankind and the dominating source of conflict will be cultural. Nation

Samuel P. Huntington is the Eaton Professor of the Science of Government and
Director of the John M. Olin Institute for Strategic Studies at Harvard University. This
article is the product of the Olin Institute's project on "The Changing Security Environment and American National Interest."

Reprinted by permission of *Foreign Affairs*, Vol. 72, no. 3, Summer 1993, pp. 22-49.
Copyright © 1993 by the Council on Foreign Relations, Inc.

states will remain the most powerful actors in world affairs, but the principal conflicts of global politics will occur between nations and groups of different civilizations. The clash of civilizations will dominate global politics. The fault lines between civilizations will be the battle lines of the future.

Conflict between civilizations will be the latest phase in the evolution of conflict in the modern world. For a century and a half after the emergence of the modern international system with the Peace of Westphalia, the conflicts of the Western world were largely among princes—emperors, absolute monarchs and constitutional monarchs attempting to expand their bureaucracies, their armies, their mercantilist economic strength and, most important, the territory they ruled. In the process they created nation states, and beginning with the French Revolution the principal lines of conflict were between nations rather than princes. In 1793, as R. R. Palmer put it, "The wars of kings were over; the wars of peoples had begun." This nineteenth-century pattern lasted until the end of World War I. Then, as a result of the Russian Revolution and the reaction against it, the conflict of nations yielded to the conflict of ideologies, first among communism, fascism-Nazism and liberal democracy, and then between communism and liberal democracy. During the Cold War, this latter conflict became embodied in the struggle between the two superpowers, neither of which was a nation state in the classical European sense and each of which defined its identity in terms of its ideology.

These conflicts between princes, nation states and ideologies were primarily conflicts within Western civilization, "Western civil wars," as William Lind has labeled them. This was as true of the Cold War as it was of the world wars and the earlier wars of the seventeenth, eighteenth and nineteenth centuries. With the end of the Cold War, international politics moves out of its Western phase, and its centerpiece becomes the interaction between the West and non-Western civilizations and among non-Western civilizations. In the politics of civilizations, the peoples and governments of non-Western civilizations no longer remain the objects of history as targets of Western colonialism but join the West as movers and shapers of history.

## The Nature of Civilizations

During the Cold War the world was divided into the First, Second and Third Worlds. Those divisions are no longer relevant. It is far more meaningful now to group countries not in terms of their political or economic systems or in terms of their level of economic development but rather in terms of their culture and civilization.

What do we mean when we talk of a civilization? A civilization is a cultural entity. Villages, regions, ethnic groups, nationalities, religious groups, all have distinct cultures at different levels of cultural heterogeneity. The culture of a village in southern Italy may be different from that of a village in northern Italy, but both will share in a common Italian culture that distinguishes them from German villages. European communities, in turn, will share cultural features that distinguish them from Arab or Chinese communities. Arabs, Chinese and Westerners, however, are not part of any broader cultural entity. They constitute civilizations. A civilization is thus the highest cultural grouping of people and the broadest level of cultural identity people have short of that which distinguishes humans from other species. It is defined both by common objective elements, such as language, history, religion, customs, institutions, and by the subjective self-identification of people. People have levels of identity: a resident of Rome may define himself with varying degrees of intensity as a Roman, an Italian, a Catholic, a Christian, a European, a Westerner. The civilization to which he belongs is the broadest level of identification with which he intensely identifies. People can and do redefine their identities and, as a result, the composition and boundaries of civilizations change.

Civilizations may involve a large number of people, as with China ("a civilization pretending to be a state," as Lucian Pye put it), or a very small number of people, such as the Anglophone Caribbean. A civilization may include several nation states, as is the case with Western, Latin American and Arab civilizations, or only one, as is the case with Japanese civilization. Civilizations obviously blend and overlap, and may include subcivilizations. Western civilization has two major variants, European and North American, and Islam has its Arab, Turkic and Malay subdivisions. Civilizations are nonetheless meaningful entities, and while the lines between them are seldom sharp, they are real. Civilizations are dynamic; they rise and fall; they divide and merge. And, as any student of history knows, civilizations disappear and are buried in the sands of time.

Westerners tend to think of nation states as the principal actors in global affairs. They have been that, however, for only a few centuries. The broader reaches of human history have been the history of civilizations. In *A Study of History*, Arnold Toynbee identified 21 major civilizations; only six of them exist in the contemporary world.

## Why Civilizations Will Clash

Civilization identity will be increasingly important in the future, and the world will be shaped in large measure by the interactions among seven or eight major civilizations. These include Western, Confucian, Japanese, Islamic, Hindu, Slavic-Orthodox, Latin American and possibly African civilization. The most important conflicts of the future will occur along the cultural fault lines separating these civilizations from one another.

Why will this be the case?

First, differences among civilizations are not only real; they are basic. Civilizations are differentiated from each other by history, language, culture, tradition and, most important, religion. The people of different civilizations have different views on the relations between God and man, the individual and the group, the citizen and the state, parents and children, husband and wife, as well as differing views of the relative importance of rights and responsibilities, liberty and authority, equality and hierarchy. These differences are the product of centuries. They will not soon disappear. They are far more fundamental than differences among political ideologies and political regimes. Differences do not necessarily mean conflict, and conflict does not necessarily mean violence. Over the centuries, however, differences among civilizations have generated the most prolonged and the most violent conflicts.

Second, the world is becoming a smaller place. The interactions between peoples of different civilizations are increasing; these increasing interactions intensify civilization consciousness and awareness of differences between civilizations and commonalities within civilizations. North African immigration to France generates hostility among Frenchmen and at the same time increased receptivity to immigration by "good" European Catholic Poles. Americans react far more negatively to Japanese investment than to larger investments from Canada and European countries. Similarly, as Donald Horowitz has pointed out, "An Ibo may be ... an Owerri Ibo or an Onitsha Ibo in what was the Eastern region of Nigeria. In Lagos, he is simply an Ibo. In London, he is a Nigerian. In New York, he is an African." The interactions among peoples of different civilizations enhance the civilization-consciousness of people that, in turn, invigorates differences and animosities stretching or thought to stretch back deep into history.

Third, the processes of economic modernization and social change throughout the world are separating people from longstanding local identities. They also weaken the nation state as a source of identity. In much of the world religion has moved in to fill this gap, often in the form of movements that are labeled "fundamentalist." Such movements are found in Western Christianity, Judaism, Buddhism and Hinduism, as well as in Islam. In most countries and most religions the people active in fundamentalist movements are young, college-educated, middle-class technicians, professionals and business persons. The "unsecularization of the world," George Weigel has remarked, "is one of the dominant social facts of life in the late twentieth century." The revival of religion, "la revanche de Dieu," as Gilles Kepel labeled it, provides a basis for identity and commitment that transcends national boundaries and unites civilizations.

Fourth, the growth of civilization-consciousness is enhanced by the dual role of the West. On the one hand, the West is at a peak of power. At the same time, however, and perhaps as a result, a return to the roots phenomenon is occurring among non-Western civilizations. Increasingly one hears references to trends toward a turning inward and "Asianization" in Japan, the end of the Nehru legacy and the "Hinduization" of India, the failure of Western ideas of socialism and nationalism and hence "re-Islamization" of the Middle East, and now a debate over Westernization versus Russianization in Boris Yeltsin's country. A West at the peak of its power confronts non-Wests that increasingly have the desire, the will and the resources to shape the world in non-Western ways.

In the past, the elites of non-Western societies were usually the people who were most involved with the West, had been educated at Oxford, the Sorbonne or Sandhurst, and had absorbed Western attitudes and values. At the same time, the populace in non-Western countries often remained deeply imbued with the indigenous culture. Now, however, these relationships are being reversed. A de-Westernization and indigenization of elites is occurring in many non-Western countries at the same time that Western, usually American, cultures, styles and habits become more popular among the mass of the people.

Fifth, cultural characteristics and differences are less mutable and hence less easily compromised and resolved than political and economic ones. In the former Soviet Union, communists can become democrats, the rich can become poor and the poor rich, but Russians cannot become Estonians and Azeris cannot become Armenians. In class and ideological conflicts, the key question was "Which side are you on?" and people could and did choose sides and change sides. In conflicts between civilizations, the question is "What are you?" That is a given that cannot be changed. And as we know, from Bosnia to the Caucasus to the Sudan, the wrong answer to that question can mean a bullet in the head. Even more than ethnicity, religion discriminates sharply and exclusively among people. A person can be half-French and half-Arab and simultaneously even a citizen of two countries. It is more difficult to be half-Catholic and half-Muslim.

Finally, economic regionalism is increasing. The proportions of total trade that were intraregional rose between 1980 and 1989 from 51 percent to 59 percent in Europe, 33 percent to 37 percent in East Asia, and 32 percent to 36 percent in North America. The importance of regional economic blocs is likely to continue to increase in the future. On the one hand, successful economic regionalism will reinforce civilization-consciousness. On the other hand, economic regionalism may succeed only when it is rooted in a common civilization. The European Community rests on the shared foundation of European culture and Western Christianity. The success of the North American Free Trade Area depends on the convergence now underway of Mexican, Canadian and American cultures. Japan, in contrast, faces difficulties in creating a comparable economic entity in East Asia because Japan is a society and civilization unique to itself. However strong the trade and investment links Japan may develop with other East Asian countries, its cultural differences with those countries inhibit and perhaps preclude its promoting regional economic integration like that in Europe and North America.

Common culture, in contrast, is clearly facilitating the rapid expansion of the economic relations between the People's Republic of China and Hong Kong, Taiwan, Singapore and the overseas Chinese communities in other Asian countries. With the Cold War over, cultural commonalities increasingly overcome ideological differences, and mainland China and Taiwan move close together. If cultural commonality is a prerequisite for economic integration, the principal East Asian economic bloc of the future is likely to be centered on China. This bloc is, in fact, already coming into existence. As Murray Weidenbaum has observed,

> Despite the current Japanese dominance of the region, the Chinese-based economy of Asia is rapidly emerging as a new epicenter for industry, commerce and finance. This strategic area contains substantial amounts of technology and manufacturing capability (Taiwan), outstanding entrepreneurial, marketing and services acumen (Hong Kong), a fine communications network (Singapore), a tremendous pool of financial capital (all three), and very large endowments of land, resources and labor (mainland China).... From Guangzhou to Singapore, from Kuala Lumpur to Manila, this influential network—often based on extensions of the traditional clans—has been described as the backbone of the East Asian economy.[1]

Culture and religion also form the basis of the Economic Cooperation Organization, which brings together ten non-Arab Muslim countries: Iran, Pakistan, Turkey, Azerbaijan, Kazakhstan, Kyrgyzstan, Turkmenistan, Tadjikistan, Uzbekistan and Afghanistan. One impetus to the revival and expansion of this organization, founded originally in the 1960s by Turkey, Pakistan and Iran, is the realization by the leaders of several of these countries that they had no chance of admission to the European Community. Similarly, Caricom, the Central American Common Market and Mercosur rest on common cultural foundations. Efforts to build a broader Caribbean-Central American economic entity bridging the Anglo-Latin divide, however, have to date failed.

As people define their identity in ethnic and religious terms, they are likely to see an "us" versus "them" relation existing between themselves and people of different ethnicity or religion. The end of ideologically defined states in Eastern Europe and the former Soviet Union permits traditional ethnic identities and animosities to come to the fore. Differences in culture and religion create differences over policy issues, ranging from human rights to immigration to trade and commerce to the environment. Geographical propinquity gives rise to conflicting territorial claims from Bosnia to Mindanao. Most important, the efforts of the West to promote its values of democracy and liberalism as universal values, to maintain its military predominance and to advance its economic interests engender countering responses from other civilizations. Decreasingly able to mobilize support and form coalitions on the basis of ideology, governments and groups will increasingly attempt to mobilize support by appealing to common religion and civilization identity.

Western Christianity circa 1500 →

Orthodox Christianity and Islam →

RUSSIA

FINLAND

SWEDEN

ESTONIA

LATVIA

LITHUANIA

BELA-RUSSIA

POLAND

CZECH REP.

SLOVAKIA

UKRAINE

SLOVENIA

HUNG.

MOLD.

CROATIA

ROMANIA

BOSNIA

SERBIA

MONTE-NEGRO

MACEDONIA

BULGARIA

ALB.

ITALY

GREECE

Black Sea

N

TURKEY

0 — 200
MILES

Source: W. Wallace, THE TRANSFORMATION OF WESTERN EUROPE. London: Pinter, 1990. Map by Ib Ohlsson for FOREIGN AFFAIRS.

The clash of civilizations thus occurs at two levels. At the micro-level, adjacent groups along the fault lines between civilizations struggle, often violently, over the control of territory and each other. At the macro-level, states from different civilizations compete for relative military and economic power, struggle over the control of international institutions and third parties, and competitively promote their particular political and religious values.

## The Fault Lines Between Civilizations

The fault lines between civilizations are replacing the political and ideological boundaries of the Cold War as the flash points for crisis and bloodshed. The Cold War began when the Iron Curtain divided Europe politically and ideologically. The Cold War ended with the end of the Iron Curtain. As the ideological division of Europe has disappeared, the cultural division of Europe between Western Christianity, on the one hand, and Orthodox Christianity and Islam, on the other, has reemerged. The most significant dividing line in Europe, as William Wallace has suggested, may well be the eastern boundary of Western Christianity in the year 1500. This line runs along what are now the boundaries between Finland and Russia and between the Baltic states and Russia, cuts through Belarus and Ukraine separating the more Catholic western Ukraine from Orthodox eastern Ukraine, swings westward separating Transylvania from the rest of Romania, and then goes through Yugoslavia almost exactly along the line now separating Croatia and Slovenia from the rest of Yugoslavia. In the Balkans this line, of course, coincides with the historic boundary between the Hapsburg and Ottoman empires. The peoples to the north and west of this line are Protestant or Catholic; they shared the common experiences of European history—feudalism, the Renaissance, the Reformation, the Enlightenment, the French Revolution, the Industrial Revolution; they are generally economically better off than the peoples to the east; and they may now look forward to increasing involvement in a common European economy and to the consolidation of democratic political systems. The peoples to the east and south of this line are Orthodox or Muslim; they historically belonged to the Ottoman or Tsarist empires and were only lightly touched by the shaping events in the rest of Europe; they are generally less advanced economically; they seem much less likely to develop stable democratic political systems. The Velvet Curtain of culture has replaced the Iron Curtain of ideology as the most significant dividing line in Europe. As the events in Yugoslavia show, it is not only a line of difference; it is also at times a line of bloody conflict.

Conflict along the fault line between Western and Islamic civilizations has been going on for 1,300 years. After the founding of Islam, the Arab and Moorish surge west and north only ended at Tours in 732. From the eleventh to the thirteenth century the Crusaders attempted with temporary success to bring Christianity and Christian rule to the Holy Land. From the fourteenth to the seventeenth century, the Ottoman Turks reversed the balance, extended their sway over the Middle East and the Balkans, captured Constantinople, and twice laid siege to Vienna. In the nineteenth and early twentieth centuries as Ottoman power declined Britain, France, and Italy established Western control over most of North Africa and the Middle East.

After World War II, the West, in turn, began to retreat; the colonial empires disappeared; first Arab nationalism and then Islamic fundamentalism manifested themselves; the West became heavily dependent on the Persian Gulf countries for its energy; the oil-rich Muslim countries became money-rich and, when they wished to, weapons-rich. Several wars occurred between Arabs and Israel (created by the West). France fought a bloody and ruthless war in Algeria for most of the 1950s; British and French forces invaded Egypt in 1956; American forces went into Lebanon in 1958; subsequently American forces returned to Lebanon, attacked Libya, and engaged in various military encounters with Iran; Arab and Islamic terrorists, supported by at least three Middle Eastern governments, employed the weapon of the weak and bombed Western planes and installations and seized Western hostages. This warfare between Arabs and the West culminated in 1990, when the United States sent a massive army to the Persian Gulf to defend some Arab countries against aggression by another. In its aftermath NATO planning is increasingly directed to potential threats and instability along its "southern tier."

This centuries-old military interaction between the West and Islam is unlikely to decline. It could become more virulent. The Gulf War left some Arabs feeling proud that Saddam Hussein had attacked Israel and stood up to the West. It also left many feeling humiliated and resentful of the West's military presence in the Persian Gulf, the West's overwhelming military dominance, and their apparent inability to shape their own destiny. Many Arab countries, in addition to the oil exporters, are reaching levels of economic and social development where autocratic forms of government become inappropriate and efforts to introduce democracy become stronger. Some openings in Arab political systems have already occurred. The principal beneficiaries of these openings have been Islamist movements. In the Arab world, in short, Western democracy strengthens anti-Western political forces. This may be a passing phenomenon, but it surely complicates relations between Islamic countries and the West.

Those relations are also complicated by demography. The spectacular population growth in Arab countries, particularly in North Africa, has led to increased migration to Western Europe. The movement within Western Europe toward minimizing internal boundaries has sharpened political sensitivities with respect to this development. In Italy, France and Germany, racism is increasingly open, and political reactions and violence against Arab and Turkish migrants have become more intense and more widespread since 1990.

On both sides the interaction between Islam and the West is seen as a clash of civilizations. The West's "next confrontation," observes M. J. Akbar, an Indian Muslim author, "is definitely going to come from the Muslim world. It is in the sweep of the Islamic nations from the Maghreb to Pakistan that the struggle for a new world order will begin." Bernard Lewis comes to a similar conclusion:

> We are facing a mood and a movement far transcending the level of issues and policies and the governments that pursue them. This is no less than a clash of civilizations—the perhaps irrational but surely historic reaction of an ancient rival against our Judeo-Christian heritage, our secular present, and the worldwide expansion of both.[2]

Historically, the other great antagonistic interaction of Arab Islamic civilization has been with the pagan, animist, and now increasingly Christian black peoples to the south. In the past, this antagonism was epitomized in the image of Arab slave dealers and black slaves. It has been reflected in the on-going civil war in the Sudan between Arabs and blacks, the fighting in Chad between Libyan-supported insurgents and the government, the tensions between Orthodox Christians and Muslims in the Horn of Africa, and the political conflicts, recurring riots and communal violence between Muslims and Christians in Nigeria. The modernization of Africa and the spread of Christianity are likely to enhance the probability of violence along this fault line. Symptomatic of the intensification of this conflict was the Pope John Paul II's speech in Khartoum in February 1993 attacking the actions of the Sudan's Islamist government against the Christian minority there.

On the northern border of Islam, conflict has increasingly erupted between Orthodox and Muslim peoples, including the carnage of Bosnia and Sarajevo, the simmering violence between Serb and Albanian, the tenuous relations between Bulgarians and their Turkish minority, the violence between Ossetians and Ingush, the unremitting slaughter of each other by Armenians and Azeris, the tense relations between Russians and Muslims in Central Asia, and the deployment of Russian troops to protect Russian interests in the Caucasus and Central Asia. Religion reinforces the revival of ethnic identities and restimulates Russian fears about the security of their southern borders. This concern is well captured by Archie Roosevelt:

> Much of Russian history concerns the struggle between the Slavs and the Turkic peoples on their borders, which dates back to the foundation of the Russian state more than a thousand years ago. In the Slavs' millennium-long confrontation with their eastern neighbors lies the key to an understanding not only of Russian history, but Russian character. To understand Russian realities today one has to have a concept of the great Turkic ethnic group that has preoccupied Russians through the centuries.[3]

The conflict of civilizations is deeply rooted elsewhere in Asia. The historic clash between Muslim and Hindu in the subcontinent manifests itself now not only in the rivalry between Pakistan and India but also in intensifying religious strife within India between increasingly militant Hindu groups and India's substantial Muslim minority. The destruction of the Ayodhya mosque in December 1992 brought to the fore the issue of whether India will remain a secular democratic state or become a Hindu one. In East Asia, China has outstanding territorial disputes with most of its neighbors. It has pursued a ruthless policy toward the Buddhist people of Tibet, and it is pursuing an increasingly ruthless policy toward its Turkic-Muslim minority. With the Cold War over, the underlying differences between China and the United States have reasserted themselves in areas such as human rights, trade and weapons proliferation. These differences are unlikely to moderate. A "new cold war," Deng Xaioping reportedly asserted in 1991, is under way between China and America.

The same phrase has been applied to the increasingly difficult relations between Japan and the United States. Here cultural difference exacerbates economic conflict. People on each side allege racism on the other, but at least on the American side the antipathies are not racial but cultural. The basic values, attitudes, behavioral patterns of the two societies could hardly be more different. The economic issues between the United States and Europe are no less serious than those between the United States and Japan, but they do not have the same political salience and emotional intensity because the differences between

American culture and European culture are so much less than those between American civilization and Japanese civilization.

The interactions between civilizations vary greatly in the extent to which they are likely to be characterized by violence. Economic competition clearly predominates between the American and European subcivilizations of the West and between both of them and Japan. On the Eurasian continent, however, the proliferation of ethnic conflict, epitomized at the extreme in "ethnic cleansing," has not been totally random. It has been most frequent and most violent between groups belonging to different civilizations. In Eurasia the great historic fault lines between civilizations are once more aflame. This is particularly true along the boundaries of the crescent-shaped Islamic bloc of nations from the bulge of Africa to central Asia. Violence also occurs between Muslims, on the one hand, and Orthodox Serbs in the Balkans, Jews in Israel, Hindus in India, Buddhists in Burma and Catholics in the Philippines. Islam has bloody borders.

## Civilization Rallying: The Kin-Country Syndrome

Groups or states belonging to one civilization that become involved in war with people from a different civilization naturally try to rally support from other members of their own civilization. As the post-Cold War world evolves, civilization commonality, what H. D. S. Greenway has termed the "kin-country" syndrome, is replacing political ideology and traditional balance of power considerations as the principal basis for cooperation and coalitions. It can be seen gradually emerging in the post-Cold War conflicts in the Persian Gulf, the Caucasus and Bosnia. None of these was a full-scale war between civilizations, but each involved some elements of civilizational rallying, which seemed to become more important as the conflict continued and which may provide a foretaste of the future.

First, in the Gulf War one Arab state invaded another and then fought a coalition of Arab, Western and other states. While only a few Muslim governments overtly supported Saddam Hussein, many Arab elites privately cheered him on, and he was highly popular among large sections of the Arab publics. Islamic fundamentalist movements universally supported Iraq rather than the Western-backed governments of Kuwait and Saudi Arabia. Forswearing Arab nationalism, Saddam Hussein explicitly invoked an Islamic appeal. He and his supporters attempted to define the war as a war between civilizations. "It is not the world against Iraq," as Safar Al-Hawali, dean of Islamic Studies at the Umm Al-Qura University in Mecca, put it in a widely circulated tape. "It is the West against Islam." Ignoring the rivalry between Iran and Iraq, the chief Iranian religious leader, Ayatollah Ali Khamenei, called for a holy war against the West: "The struggle against American aggression, greed, plans and policies will be counted as a jihad, and anybody who is killed on that path is a martyr." "This is a war," King Hussein of Jordan argued, "against all Arabs and all Muslims and not against Iraq alone."

The rallying of substantial sections of Arab elites and publics behind Saddam Hussein caused those Arab governments in the anti-Iraq coalition to moderate their activities and temper their public statements. Arab governments opposed or distanced themselves from subsequent Western efforts to apply pressure on Iraq, including enforcement of a no-fly zone in the summer of 1992 and the bombing of Iraq in January 1993. The Western-Soviet-Turkish-Arab anti-Iraq coalition of 1990 had by 1993 become a coalition of almost only the West and Kuwait against Iraq.

Muslims contrasted Western actions against Iraq with the West's failure to protect Bosnians against Serbs and to impose sanctions on Israel for violating U.N. resolutions. The West, they alleged, was using a double standard. A world of clashing civilizations, however, is inevitably a world of double standards: people apply one standard to their kin-countries and a different standard to others.

Second, the kin-country syndrome also appeared in conflicts in the former Soviet Union. Armenian military successes in 1992 and 1993 stimulated Turkey to become increasingly supportive of its religious, ethnic and linguistic brethren in Azerbaijan. "We have a Turkish nation feeling the same sentiments as the Azerbaijanis," said one Turkish official in 1992. "We are under pressure. Our newspapers are full of the photos of atrocities and are asking us if we are still serious about pursuing our neutral policy. Maybe we should show Armenia that there's a big Turkey in the region." President Turgut Özal agreed, remarking that Turkey should at least "scare the Armenians a little bit." Turkey, Özal threatened again in 1993, would "show its fangs." Turkish Air Force jets flew reconnaissance flights along the Armenian border; Turkey suspended food shipments and air flights to Armenia; and Turkey and Iran announced they would not accept dismemberment of Azerbaijan. In the last years of its existence, the Soviet government supported Azerbaijan because its government was dominated by former communists. With the end of the Soviet Union, however, political considerations gave way to religious ones. Russian troops fought on the side of the Armenians, and Azerbaijan accused the "Russian government of turning 180 degrees" toward support for Christian Armenia.

Third, with respect to the fighting in the former Yugoslavia, Western publics manifested sympathy and support for the Bosnian Muslims and the horrors they suffered at the hands of the Serbs. Relatively little concern was expressed, however, over Croatian attacks on Muslims and participation in the dismemberment of Bosnia-Herzegovina. In the early stages of the Yugoslav breakup, Germany, in an unusual display of diplomatic initiative and muscle, induced the other 11 members of the European Community to follow its lead in recognizing Slovenia and Croatia. As a result of the pope's determination to provide strong backing to the two Catholic countries, the Vatican extended recognition even before the Community did. The United States followed the European lead. Thus the leading actors in Western civilization rallied behind their coreligionists. Subsequently Croatia was reported to be receiving substantial quantities of arms from Central European and other Western countries. Boris Yeltsin's government, on the other hand, attempted to pursue a middle course that would be sympathetic to the Orthodox Serbs but not alienate Russia from the West. Russian conservative and nationalist groups, however, including many legislators, attacked the government for not being more forthcoming in its support for the Serbs. By early 1993 several hundred Russians apparently were serving with the Serbian forces, and reports circulated of Russian arms being supplied to Serbia.

Islamic governments and groups, on the other hand, castigated the West for not coming to the defense of the Bosnians. Iranian leaders urged Muslims from all countries to provide help to Bosnia; in violation of the U.N. arms embargo, Iran supplied weapons and men for the Bosnians; Iranian-supported Lebanese groups sent guerrillas to train and organize the Bosnian forces. In 1993 up to 4,000 Muslims from over two dozen Islamic countries were reported to be fighting in Bosnia. The governments of Saudi Arabia and other countries felt under increasing pressure from fundamentalist groups in their own societies to provide more vigorous support for the Bosnians. By the end of 1992, Saudi Arabia had reportedly supplied substantial funding for weapons and supplies for the Bosnians, which significantly increased their military capabilities vis-à-vis the Serbs.

In the 1930s the Spanish Civil War provoked intervention from countries that politically were fascist, communist and democratic. In the 1990s the Yugoslav conflict is provoking intervention from countries that are Muslim, Orthodox and Western Christian. The parallel has not gone unnoticed. "The war in Bosnia-Herzegovina has become the emotional equivalent of the fight against fascism in the Spanish Civil War," one Saudi editor observed. "Those who died there are regarded as martyrs who tried to save their fellow Muslims."

Conflicts and violence will also occur between states and groups within the same civilization. Such conflicts, however, are likely to be less intense and less likely to expand than conflicts between civilizations. Common membership in a civilization reduces the probability of violence in situations where it might otherwise occur. In 1991 and 1992 many people were alarmed by the possibility of violent conflict between Russia and Ukraine over territory, particularly Crimea, the Black Sea fleet, nuclear weapons and economic issues. If civilization is what counts, however, the likelihood of violence between Ukrainians and Russians should be low. They are two Slavic, primarily Orthodox peoples who have had close relationships with each other for centuries. As of early 1993, despite all the reasons for conflict, the leaders of the two countries were effectively negotiating and defusing the issues between the two countries. While there has been serious fighting between Muslims and Christians elsewhere in the former Soviet Union and much tension and some fighting between Western and Orthodox Christians in the Baltic states, there has been virtually no violence between Russians and Ukrainians.

Civilization rallying to date has been limited, but it has been growing, and it clearly has the potential to spread much further. As the conflicts in the Persian Gulf, the Caucasus and Bosnia continued, the positions of nations and the cleavages between them increasingly were along civilizational lines. Populist politicians, religious leaders and the media have found it a potent means of arousing mass support and of pressuring hesitant governments. In the coming years, the local conflicts most likely to escalate into major wars will be those, as in Bosnia and the Caucasus, along the fault lines between civilizations. The next world war, if there is one, will be a war between civilizations.

## The West Versus the Rest

The West is now at an extraordinary peak of power in relation to other civilizations. Its superpower opponent has disappeared from the map. Military conflict among Western states is unthinkable, and Western military power is unrivaled. Apart from Japan, the West faces no economic challenge. It dominates international political and security institutions and with Japan international economic institutions. Global political and security issues are effectively settled by a directorate of the United States, Britain and France, world economic issues by a directorate of the United States, Germany and Japan, all of which maintain extraordinarily close relations with each other to the exclusion of lesser and largely non-Western countries. Decisions made at the U.N. Security Council or in the International Monetary Fund that reflect the interests of the West are presented to the world as reflecting the desires of the world community. The very phrase "the world community" has become the euphemistic collective noun (replacing "the Free World") to give global legitimacy to actions reflecting the interests of the United States and other Western powers.[4] Through the IMF and other international economic institutions, the West promotes its economic interests and imposes on other nations the economic policies it thinks appropriate. In any poll of non-Western peoples, the IMF undoubtedly would win the support of finance ministers and a few others, but get an overwhelmingly unfavorable rating from just about everyone else, who would agree with Georgy Arbatov's characterization of IMF officials as "neo-Bolsheviks who love expropriating other people's money, imposing undemocratic and alien rules of economic and political conduct and stifling economic freedom."

Western domination of the U.N. Security Council and its decisions, tempered only by occasional abstention by China, produced U.N. legitimation of the West's use of force to drive Iraq out of Kuwait and its elimination of Iraq's sophisticated weapons and capacity to produce such weapons. It also produced the quite unprecedented action by the United States, Britain and France in getting the Security Council to demand that Libya hand over the Pan Am 103 bombing suspects and then to impose sanctions when Libya refused. After defeating the largest Arab army, the West did not hesitate to throw its weight around in the Arab world. The West in effect is using international institutions, military power and economic resources to run the world in ways that will maintain Western predominance, protect Western interests and promote Western political and economic values.

That at least is the way in which non-Westerners see the new world, and there is a significant element of truth in their view. Differences in power and struggles for military, economic and institutional power are thus one source of conflict between the West and other civilizations. Differences in culture, that is basic values and beliefs, are a second source of conflict. V. S. Naipaul has argued that Western civilization is the "universal civilization" that "fits all men." At a superficial level much of Western culture has indeed permeated the rest of the world. At a more basic level, however, Western concepts differ fundamentally from those prevalent in other civilizations. Western ideas of individualism, liberalism, constitutionalism, human rights, equality, liberty, the rule of law, democracy, free markets, the separation of church and state, often have little resonance in Islamic, Confucian, Japanese, Hindu, Buddhist or Orthodox cultures. Western efforts to propagate such ideas produce instead a reaction against "human rights imperialism" and a reaffirmation of indigenous values, as can be seen in the support for religious fundamentalism by the younger generation in non-Western cultures. The very notion that there could be a "universal civilization" is a Western idea, directly at odds with the particularism of most Asian societies and their emphasis on what distinguishes one people from another. Indeed, the author of a review of 100 comparative studies of values in different societies concluded that "the values that are most important in the West are least important worldwide."[5] In the political realm, of course, these differences are most manifest in the efforts of the United States and other Western powers to induce other peoples to adopt Western ideas concerning democracy and human rights. Modern democratic government originated in the West. When it has developed in non-Western societies it has usually been the product of Western colonialism or imposition.

The central axis of world politics in the future is likely to be, in Kishore Mahbubani's phrase, the conflict between "the West and the Rest" and the responses of non-Western civilizations to Western power and values.[6] Those responses generally take one or a combination of three forms. At one extreme, non-Western states can, like Burma and North Korea, attempt to pursue a course of isolation, to insulate their societies from penetration or "corruption" by the

West, and, in effect, to opt out of participation in the Western-dominated global community. The costs of this course, however, are high, and few states have pursued it exclusively. A second alternative, the equivalent of "band-wagoning" in international relations theory, is to attempt to join the West and accept its values and institutions. The third alternative is to attempt to "balance" the West by developing economic and military power and cooperating with other non-Western societies against the West, while preserving indigenous values and institutions; in short, to modernize but not to Westernize.

## The Torn Countries

In the future, as people differentiate themselves by civilization, countries with large numbers of peoples of different civilizations, such as the Soviet Union and Yugoslavia, are candidates for dismemberment. Some other countries have a fair degree of cultural homogeneity but are divided over whether their society belongs to one civilization or another. These are torn countries. Their leaders typically with to pursue a bandwagoning strategy and to make their countries members of the West, but the history, culture and traditions of their countries are non-Western. The most obvious and prototypical torn country is Turkey. The late twentieth-century leaders of Turkey have followed in the Attatürk tradition and defined Turkey as a modern, secular, Western nation state. They allied Turkey with the West in NATO and in the Gulf War; they applied for membership in the European Community. At the same time, however, elements in Turkish society have supported an Islamic revival and have argued that Turkey is basically a Middle Eastern Muslim society. In addition, while the elite of Turkey has defined Turkey as a Western society, the elite of the West refuses to accept Turkey as such. Turkey will not become a member of the European Community, and the real reason, as President Özal said, "is that we are Muslim and they are Christian and they don't say that." Having rejected Mecca, and then being rejected by Brussels, where does Turkey look? Tashkent may be the answer. The end of the Soviet Union gives Turkey the opportunity to become the leader of a revived Turkic civilization involving seven countries from the borders of Greece to those of China. Encouraged by the West, Turkey is making strenuous efforts to carve out this new identity for itself.

During the past decade Mexico has assumed a position somewhat similar to that of Turkey. Just as Turkey abandoned its historic opposition to Europe and attempted to join Europe, Mexico has stopped defining itself by its opposition to the United States and is instead attempting to imitate the United States and to join it in the North American Free Trade Area. Mexican leaders are engaged in the great task of redefining Mexican identity and have introduced fundamental economic reforms that eventually will lead to fundamental political change. In 1991 a top advisor to President Carlos Salinas de Gortari described at length to me all the changes the Salinas government was making. When he finished, I remarked: "That's most impressive. It seems to me that basically you want to change Mexico from a Latin American country into a North American country." He looked at me with surprise and exclaimed: "Exactly! That's precisely what we are trying to do, but of course we could never say so publicly." As his remark indicates, in Mexico as in Turkey, significant elements in society resist the redefinition of their country's identity. In Turkey, European-oriented leaders have to make gestures to Islam (Özal's pilgrimage to Mecca); so also Mexico's North American-oriented leaders have to make gestures to those who hold Mexico to be a Latin American country (Salinas' Ibero-American Guadalajara summit).

Historically Turkey has been the most profoundly torn country. For the United States, Mexico is the most immediate torn country. Globally the most important torn country is Russia. The question of whether Russia is part of the West or the leader of a distinct Slavic-Orthodox civilization has been a recurring one in Russian history. That issue was obscured by the communist victory in Russia, which imported a Western ideology, adapted it to Russian conditions and then challenged the West in the name of that ideology. The dominance of communism shut off the historic debate over Westernization versus Russification. With communism discredited Russians once again face that question.

President Yeltsin is adopting Western principles and goals and seeking to make Russia a "normal" country and a part of the West. Yet both the Russian elite and the Russian public are divided on this issue. Among the more moderate dissenters, Sergei Stankevich argues that Russia should reject the "Atlanticist" course, which would lead it "to become European, to become a part of the world economy in rapid and organized fashion, to become the eighth member of the Seven, and to put particular emphasis on Germany and the United States as the two dominant members of the Atlantic alliance." While also rejecting an exclusively Eurasian policy, Stankevich nonetheless argues that Russia should give priority to the protection of Russians in other countries, emphasize its Turkic and Muslim connections, and promote "an appreciable redistribution of our resources, our options, our ties, and our interests in favor of Asia, of the eastern direction." People of this persuasion criticize Yeltsin for subordinating Russia's interests to those of the West, for reducing Russian military strength, for failing to support traditional friends such as Serbia, and for pushing economic and political reform in ways injurious to the Russian people. Indicative of this trend is the new popularity of the ideas of Petr Savitsky, who in the 1920s argued that Russia was a unique Eurasian civilization.[7] More extreme dissidents voice much more blatantly nationalist, anti-Western and anti-Semitic views, and urge Russia to redevelop its military strength and to establish closer ties with China and Muslim countries. The people of Russia are as divided as the elite. An opinion survey in European Russia in the spring of 1992 revealed that 40 percent of the public had positive attitudes toward the West and 36 percent had negative attitudes. As it has been for much of its history, Russia in the early 1990s is truly a torn country.

To redefine its civilization identity, a torn country must meet three requirements. First, its political and economic elite has to be generally supportive of and enthusiastic about this move. Second, its public has to be willing to acquiesce in the redefinition. Third, the dominant groups in the recipient civilization have to be willing to embrace the convert. All three requirements in large part exist with respect to Mexico. The first two in large part exist with respect to Turkey. It is not clear that any of them exist with respect to Russia's joining the West. The conflict between liberal democracy and Marxism-Leninism was between ideologies which, despite their major differences, ostensibly shared ultimate goals of freedom, equality and prosperity. A traditional, authoritarian, nationalist Russia could have quite different goals. A Western democrat could carry on an intellectual debate with a Soviet Marxist. It would be virtually impossible for him to do that with a Russian traditionalist. If, as the Russians stop behaving like Marxists, they reject liberal democracy and begin behaving like Russians but not like Westerners, the relations between Russia and the West could again become distant and conflictual.[8]

## The Confucian-Islamic Connection

The obstacles to non-Western countries joining the West vary considerably. They are least for Latin American and East European countries. They are greater for the Orthodox countries of the former Soviet Union. They are still greater for Muslim, Confucian, Hindu and Buddhist societies. Japan has established a unique position for itself as an associate member of the West: it is in the West in some respects but clearly not of the West in important dimensions. Those countries that for reason of culture and power do not wish to, or cannot, join the West compete with the West by developing their own economic, military and political power. They do this by promoting their internal development and by cooperating with other non-Western countries. The most prominent form of this cooperation is the Confucian-Islamic connection that has emerged to challenge Western interests, values and power.

Almost without exception, Western countries are reducing their military power; under Yeltsin's leadership so also is Russia. China, North Korea and several Middle Eastern states, however, are significantly expanding their military capabilities. They are doing this by the import of arms from Western and non-Western sources and by the development of indigenous arms industries. One result is the emergence of what Charles Krauthammer has called "Weapon States," and the Weapon States are not Western states. Another result is the redefinition of arms control, which is a Western concept and a Western goal.

During the Cold War the primary purpose of arms control was to establish a stable military balance between the United States and its allies and the Soviet Union and its allies. In the post-Cold War world the primary objective of arms control is to prevent the development by non-Western societies of military capabilities that could threaten Western interests. The West attempts to do this through international agreements, economic pressure and controls on the transfer of arms and weapons technologies.

The conflict between the West and the Confucian-Islamic states focuses largely, although not exclusively, on nuclear, chemical and biological weapons, ballistic missiles and other sophisticated means for delivering them, and the guidance, intelligence and other electronic capabilities for achieving that goal. The West promotes nonproliferation as a universal norm and nonproliferation treaties and inspections as means of realizing that norm. It also threatens a variety of sanctions against those who promote the spread of sophisticated weapons and proposes some benefits for those who do not. The attention of the West focuses, naturally, on nations that are actually or potentially hostile to the West.

The non-Western nations, on the other hand, assert their right to acquire and to deploy whatever weapons they think necessary for their security. They also have absorbed, to the full, the truth of the response of the Indian defense minister when asked what lesson he learned from the Gulf War: "Don't fight the United States unless you have nuclear weapons." Nuclear weapons, chemical weapons and missiles are viewed, probably erroneously, as the potential equalizer of superior Western conventional power. China, of course, already has nuclear weapons; Pakistan and India have the capability to deploy them. North Korea, Iran, Iraq, Libya and Algeria appear to be attempting to acquire them. A top Iranian official has declared that all Muslim states should acquire nuclear weapons, and in 1988 the president of Iran reportedly issued a directive calling for development of "offensive and defensive chemical, biological and radiological weapons."

Centrally important to the development of counter-West military capabilities is the sustained expansion of China's military power and its means to create military power. Buoyed by spectacular economic development, China is rapidly increasing its military spending and vigorously moving forward with the modernization of its armed forces. It is purchasing weapons from the former Soviet states; it is developing long-range missiles; in 1992 it tested a one-megaton nuclear device. It is developing power-projection capabilities, acquiring aerial refueling technology, and trying to purchase an aircraft carrier. Its military buildup and assertion of sovereignty over the South China Sea are provoking a multilateral regional arms race in East Asia. China is also a major exporter of arms and weapons technology. It has exported materials to Libya and Iraq that could be used to manufacture nuclear weapons and nerve gas. It has helped

Algeria build a reactor suitable for nuclear weapons research and production. China has sold to Iran nuclear technology that American officials believe could only be used to create weapons and apparently has shipped components of 300-mile-range missiles to Pakistan. North Korea has had a nuclear weapons program under way for some while and has sold advanced missiles and missile technology to Syria and Iran. The flow of weapons and weapons technology is generally from East Asia to the Middle East. There is, however, some movement in the reverse direction; China has received Stinger missiles from Pakistan.

A Confucian-Islamic military connection has thus come into being, designed to promote acquisition by its members of the weapons and weapons technologies needed to counter the military power of the West. It may or may not last. At present, however, it is, as Dave McCurdy has said, "a renegades' mutual support pact, run by the proliferators and their backers." A new form of arms competition is thus occurring between Islamic-Confucian states and the West. In an old-fashioned arms race, each side developed its own arms to balance or to achieve superiority against the other side. In this new form of arms competition, one side is developing its arms and the other side is attempting not to balance but to limit and prevent that arms build-up while at the same time reducing its own military capabilities.

## Implications for the West

This article does not argue that civilization identities will replace all other identities, that nation states will disappear, that each civilization will become a single coherent political entity, that groups within a civilization will not conflict with and even fight each other. This paper does set forth the hypotheses that differences between civilizations are real and important; civilization-consciousness is increasing; conflict between civilizations will supplant ideological and other forms of conflict as the dominant global form of conflict; international relations, historically a game played out within Western civilization, will increasingly be de-Westernized and become a game in which non-Western civilizations are actors and not simply objects; successful political, security and economic international institutions are more likely to develop within civilizations than across civilizations; conflicts between groups in different civilizations will be more frequent, more sustained and more violent than conflicts between groups in the same civilization; violent conflicts between groups in different civilizations are the most likely and most dangerous source of escalation that could lead to global wars; the paramount axis of world politics will be the relations between "the West and the Rest"; the elites in some torn non-Western countries will try to make their countries part of the West, but in most cases face major obstacles to accomplishing this; a central focus of conflict for the immediate future will be between the West and several Islamic-Confucian states.

This is not to advocate the desirability of conflicts between civilizations. It is to set forth descriptive hypotheses as to what the future may be like. If these are plausible hypotheses, however, it is necessary to consider their implications for Western policy. These implications should be divided between short-term advantage and long-term accommodation. In the short term it is clearly in the interest of the West to promote greater cooperation and unity within its own civilization, particularly between its European and North American components; to incorporate into the West societies in Eastern Europe and Latin America whose cultures are close to those of the West; to promote and maintain cooperative relations with Russia and Japan; to prevent escalation of local inter-civilization conflicts into major inter-civilization wars; to limit the expansion of the military strength of Confucian and Islamic states; to moderate the reduction of Western military capabilities and maintain military superiority in East and Southwest Asia; to exploit differences and conflicts among Confucian and Islamic states; to support in other civilizations groups sympathetic to Western values and interests; to strengthen international institutions that reflect and legitimate Western interests and values and to promote the involvement of non-Western states in those institutions.

In the longer term other measures would be called for. Western civilization is both Western and modern. Non-Western civilizations have attempted to become modern without becoming Western. To date only Japan has fully succeeded in this quest. Non-Western civilizations will continue to attempt to acquire the wealth, technology, skills, machines and weapons that are part of being modern. They will also attempt to reconcile this modernity with their traditional culture and values. Their economic and military strength relative to the West will increase. Hence the West will increasingly have to accommodate these non-Western modern civilizations whose power approaches that of the West but whose values and interests differ significantly from those of the West. This will require the West to maintain the economic and military power necessary to protect its interests in relation to these civilizations. It will also, however, require the West to develop a more profound understanding of the basic religious and philosophical assumptions underlying other civilizations and the ways in which people in those civilizations see their interests. It will require an effort to identify elements of commonality between Western and other civilizations. For the relevant future, there will be no universal civilization, but instead a world of different civilizations, each of which will have to learn to coexist with the others.

## Notes

1. Murray Weidenbaum, *Greater China: The Next Economic Superpower?*, St. Louis: Washington University Center for the Study of American Business, Contemporary Issues, Series 57, February 1993, pp. 2-3.

2. Bernard Lewis, "The Roots of Muslim Rage," *The Atlantic Monthly*, vol. 266, September 1990, p. 60; *Time*, June 15, 1992, pp. 24-28.

3. Archie Roosevelt, *For Lust of Knowing*, Boston: Little, Brown, 1988, pp. 332-333.

4. Almost invariably Western leaders claim they are acting on behalf of "the world community." One minor lapse occurred during the run-up to the Gulf War. In an interview on "Good Morning America," Dec. 21, 1990, British Prime Minister John Major referred to the actions "the West" was taking against Saddam Hussein. He quickly corrected himself and subsequently referred to "the world community." He was, however, right when he erred.

5. Harry C. Triandis, *The New York Times*, Dec. 25, 1990, p. 41, and "Cross-Cultural Studies of Individualism and Collectivism," Nebraska Symposium on Motivation, vol. 37, 1989, pp. 41-133.

6. Kishore Mahbubani, "The West and the Rest," *The National Interest*, Summer 1992, pp. 3-13.

7. Sergei Stankevich, "Russia in Search of Itself," *The National Interest*, Summer 1992, pp. 47-51; Daniel Schneider, "A Russian Movement Rejects Western Tilt," *Christian Science Monitor*, Feb. 5, 1993, pp. 5-7.

8. Owen Harries has pointed out that Australia is trying (unwisely in his view) to become a torn country in reverse. Although it has been a full member not only of the West but also of the ABCA military and intelligence core of the West, its current leaders are in effect proposing that it defect from the West, redefine itself as an Asian country and cultivate close ties with its neighbors. Australia's future, they argue, is with the dynamic economies of East Asia. But, as I have suggested, close economic cooperation normally requires a common cultural base. In addition, none of the three conditions necessary for a torn country to join another civilization is likely to exist in Australia's case.

# Chapter 27

**∗ ∗ ∗**

# The Coming Anarchy

Robert D. Kaplan

*Robert D. Kaplan presents an extremely pessimistic scenario of the future. He worries that scarcity, crime, overpopulation, tribalism, and disease are destroying the social fabric of the planet. Governments are becoming weaker in many regions. Some have effectively lost the ability to control events within their borders. Such a collapse of civil order and loss of sovereignty could call into question many traditional assumptions about the very nature of the international system. Although this process is most advanced in West Africa, he predicts that more comfortable countries will increasingly suffer the same fate. Do you agree with his warning that the world ignores the plight of this "dying region" at its own peril? What evidence supports his claim that the environment (i.e., diminishing natural resources) will become the national-security issue of the next century? Are his warnings overly pessimistic? What are the strategic implications for the U.S. of Kaplan's scenario?*

The Minister's eyes were like egg yolks, an aftereffect of some of the many illnesses, malaria especially, endemic in his country. There was also an irrefutable sadness in his eyes. He spoke in a slow and creaking voice, the voice of hope about to expire. Flame trees, coconut palms, and a ballpoint-blue Atlantic composed the background. None of it seemed beautiful, though. "In forty-five years I have never seen things so bad. We did not manage ourselves well after the British departed. But what we have now is something worse—the revenge of the poor, of the social failures, of the people least able to bring up children in a modern society." Then he referred to the recent coup in the West African country Sierra Leone. "The boys who took power in Sierra Leone come from houses like this." The Minister jabbed his finger at a corrugated metal shack teeming with children. "In three months these boys confiscated all the official Mercedes, Volvos, and BMWs and willfully wrecked them on the road." The

Robert D. Kaplan is a Contributing Editor to The Atlantic Monthly.

Extracts reprinted from *The Atlantic Monthly*, February 1994, by permission from the author Robert Kaplan. Copyright © 1994 Robert Kaplan as first published in *The Atlantic Monthly*.

Minister mentioned one of the coup's leaders, Solomon Anthony Joseph Musa, who shot the people who had paid for his schooling, "in order to erase the humiliation and mitigate the power his middle-class sponsors held over him."

Tyranny is nothing new in Sierra Leone or in the rest of West Africa. But it is now part and parcel of an increasing lawlessness that is far more significant than any coup, rebel incursion, or episodic experiment in democracy. Crime was what my friend—a top-ranking African official whose life would be threatened were I to identify him more precisely—really wanted to talk about. Crime is what makes West Africa a natural point of departure for my report on what the political character of our planet is likely to be in the twenty-first century.

The cities of West Africa at night are some of the unsafest places in the world. Streets are unlit; the police often lack gasoline for their vehicles; armed burglars, carjackers, and muggers proliferate. "The government in Sierra Leone has no writ after dark," says a foreign resident, shrugging. When I was in the capital, Freetown, last September, eight men armed with AK-47s broke into the house of an American man. They tied him up and stole everything of value. Forget Miami: direct flights between the United States and the Murtala Muhammed Airport, in neighboring Nigeria's largest city, Lagos, have been suspended by order of the U.S. Secretary of Transportation because of ineffective security at the terminal and its environs. A State Department report cited the airport for "extortion by law-enforcement and immigration officials." This is one of the few times that the U.S. government has embargoed a foreign airport for reasons that are linked purely to crime. In Abidjan, effectively the capital of the Côte d'Ivoire, or Ivory Coast, restaurants have stick- and gun-wielding guards who walk you the fifteen feet or so between your car and the entrance, giving you an eerie taste of what American cities might be like in the future. An Italian ambassador was killed by gunfire when robbers invaded an Abidjan restaurant. The family of the Nigerian ambassador was tied up and robbed at gunpoint in the ambassador's residence. After university students in the Ivory Coast caught bandits who had been plaguing their dorms, they executed them by hanging tires around their necks and setting the tires on fire. In one instance Ivorian policemen stood by and watched the "necklacings," afraid to intervene. Each time I went to the Abidjan bus terminal, groups of young men with restless, scanning eyes surrounded my taxi, putting their hands all over the windows, demanding "tips" for carrying my luggage even though I had only a rucksack. In cities in six West African countries I saw similar young men everywhere—hordes of them. They were like loose molecules in a very unstable social fluid, a fluid that was clearly on the verge of igniting.

"You see," my friend the Minister told me, "in the villages of Africa it is perfectly natural to feed at any table and lodge in any hut. But in the cities this communal existence no longer holds. You must pay for lodging and be invited for food. When young men find out that their relations cannot put them up, they become lost. They join other migrants and slip gradually into the criminal process."

"In the poor quarters of Arab North Africa," he continued, "there is much less crime, because Islam provides a social anchor: of education and indoctrination. Here in West Africa we have a lot of superficial Islam and superficial Christianity. Western religion is undermined by animist beliefs not suitable to a moral society, because they are based on irrational spirit power. Here spirits are used to wreak vengeance by one person against another, or one group against another." Many of the atrocities in the Liberian civil war have been tied to belief in *juju* spirits, and the BBC has reported, in its magazine *Focus on Africa*, that in the civil fighting in adjacent Sierra Leone, rebels were said to have "a young woman with them who would go to the front naked, always walking backwards and looking in a mirror to see where she was going. This made her invisible, so that she could cross to the army's positions and there bury charms . . . to improve the rebels' chances of success."

Finally my friend the Minister mentioned polygamy. Designed for a pastoral way of life, polygamy continues to thrive in sub-Saharan Africa even though it is increasingly uncommon in Arab North Africa. Most youths I met on the road in West Africa told me that they were from "extended" families, with a mother in one place and a father in another. Translated to an urban environment, loose family structures are largely responsible for the world's highest birth rates and the explosion of the HIV virus on the continent. Like the communalism and animism, they provide a weak shield against the corrosive social effects of life in cities. In those cities African culture is being redefined while desertification and deforestation—also tied to overpopulation—drive more and more African peasants out of the countryside.

## A Premonition of the Future

West Africa is becoming *the* symbol of worldwide demographic, environmental, and societal stress, in which criminal anarchy emerges as the real "strategic" danger. Disease, overpopulation, unprovoked crime, scarcity of resources, refugee migrations, the increasing erosion of nation-states and international borders, and the empowerment of private armies, security firms, and international drug cartels are now most tellingly demonstrated through a West African prism. West Africa provides an appropriate introduction to the issues, often extremely unpleasant to discuss, that will soon confront our civilization. To remap the political earth the way it will be a few decades hence—as I intend to do in this article—I find I must begin with West Africa.

There is no other place on the planet where political maps are so deceptive—where, in fact, they tell such lies—as in West Africa. Start with Sierra Leone. According to the map, it is a nation-state of defined borders, with a government in control of its territory. In truth the Sierra Leonian government, run by a twenty-seven-year-old army captain, Valentine Strasser, controls Freetown by day and by day also controls part of the rural interior. In the government's territory the national army is an unruly rabble threatening drivers and passengers at most checkpoints. In the other part of the country units of two separate armies from the war in Liberia have taken up residence, as has an army of Sierra Leonian rebels. The government force fighting the rebels is full of renegade commanders who have aligned themselves with disaffected village chiefs. A pre-modern formlessness governs the battlefield, evoking the wars in medieval Europe prior to the 1648 Peace of Westphalia, which ushered in the era of organized nation-states.

As a consequence, roughly 400,000 Sierra Leonians are internally displaced, 280,000 more have fled to neighboring Guinea, and another 100,000 have fled to Liberia, even as 400,000 Liberians have fled to Sierra Leone. The third largest city in Sierra Leone, Gondama, is a displaced-persons camp. With an additional 600,000 Liberians in Guinea and 250,000 in the Ivory Coast, the borders dividing these four countries have become largely meaningless. Even in quiet zones none of the governments except the Ivory Coast's maintains the schools, bridges, roads, and police forces in a manner necessary for functional sovereignty. The Koranko ethnic group in northeastern Sierra Leone does all its trading in Guinea. Sierra Leonian diamonds are more likely to be sold in Liberia than in Freetown. In the eastern provinces of Sierra Leone you can buy Liberian beer but not the local brand.

In Sierra Leone, as in Guinea, as in the Ivory Coast, as in Ghana, most of the primary rain forest and the secondary bush is being destroyed at an alarming rate. I saw convoys of trucks bearing majestic hardwood trunks to coastal ports. When Sierra Leone achieved its independence, in 1961, as much as 60 percent of the country was primary rain forest. Now six percent is. In the Ivory Coast the proportion has fallen from 38 percent to eight percent. The deforestation has led to soil erosion, which has led to more flooding and more mosquitoes. Virtually everyone in the West African interior has some form of malaria.

Sierra Leone is a microcosm of what is occurring, albeit in a more tempered and gradual manner, throughout West Africa and much of the underdeveloped world: the withering away of central governments, the rise of tribal and regional domains, the unchecked spread of disease, and the growing pervasiveness of war. West Africa is reverting to the Africa of the Victorian atlas. It consists now of a series of coastal trading posts, such as Freetown and Conakry, and an interior that, owing to violence, volatility, and disease, is again becoming, as Graham Greene once observed, "blank" and "unexplored." However, whereas Greene's vision implies a certain romance, as in the somnolent and charmingly seedy Freetown of his celebrated novel *The Heart of the Matter*, it is Thomas Malthus, the philosopher of demographic doomsday, who is now the prophet of West

Africa's future. And West Africa's future, eventually, will also be that of most of the rest of the world.

Consider "Chicago." I refer not to Chicago, Illinois, but to a slum district of Abidjan, which the young toughs in the area have named after the American city. ("Washington" is another poor section of Abidjan.) Although Sierra Leone is widely regarded as beyond salvage, the Ivory Coast has been considered an African success story, and Abidjan has been called "the Paris of West Africa." Success, however, was built on two artificial factors: the high price of cocoa, of which the Ivory Coast is the world's leading producer, and the talents of a French expatriate community, whose members have helped run the government and the private sector. The expanding cocoa economy made the Ivory Coast a magnet for migrant workers from all over West Africa: between a third and a half of the country's population is now non-Ivorian, and the figure could be as high as 75 percent in Abidjan. During the 1980s cocoa prices fell and the French began to leave. The skyscrapers of the Paris of West Africa are a façade. Perhaps 15 percent of Abidjan's population of three million people live in shantytowns like Chicago and Washington, and the vast majority live in places that are not much better. Not all of these places appear on any of the readily available maps. This is another indication of how political maps are the products of tired conventional wisdom and, in the Ivory Coast's case, of an elite that will ultimately be forced to relinquish power.

Chicago, like more and more of Abidjan, is a slum in the bush: a checkerwork of corrugated zinc roofs and walls made of cardboard and black plastic wrap. It is located in a gully teeming with coconut palms and oil palms, and is ravaged by flooding. Few residents have easy access to electricity, a sewage system, or a clean water supply. The crumbly red laterite earth crawls with foot-long lizards both inside and outside the shacks. Children defecate in a stream filled with garbage and pigs, droning with malarial mosquitoes. In this stream women do the washing. Young unemployed men spend their time drinking beer, palm wine, and gin while gambling on pinball games constructed out of rotting wood and rusty nails. These are the same youths who rob houses in more prosperous Ivorian neighborhoods at night. One man I met, Damba Tesele, came to Chicago from Burkina Faso in 1963. A cook by profession, he has four wives and thirty-two children, not one of whom has made it to high school. He has seen his shanty community destroyed by municipal authorities seven times since coming to the area. Each time he and his neighbors rebuild. Chicago is the latest incarnation.

Fifty-five percent of the Ivory Coast's population is urban, and the proportion is expected to reach 62 percent by 2000. The yearly net population growth is 3.6 percent. This means that the Ivory Coast's 13.5 million people will become 39 million by 2025, when much of the population will consist of urbanized peasants like those of Chicago. But don't count on the Ivory Coast's still existing then.

Chicago, which is more indicative of Africa's and the Third World's demographic present—and even more of the future—than any idyllic jungle scape of women balancing earthen jugs on their heads, illustrates why the Ivory Coast, once a model of Third World success, is becoming a case study in Third World catastrophe.

President Félix Houphouët-Boigny, who died last December at the age of about ninety, left behind a weak cluster of political parties and a leaden bureaucracy that discourages foreign investment. Because the military is small and the non-Ivorian population large, there is neither an obvious force to maintain order nor a sense of nationhood that would lessen the need for such enforcement. The economy has been shrinking since the mid-1980s. Though the French are working assiduously to preserve stability, the Ivory Coast faces a possibility worse than a coup: an anarchic implosion of criminal violence—an urbanized version of what has already happened in Somalia. Or it may become an African Yugoslavia, but one without mini-states to replace the whole.

Because the demographic reality of West Africa is a countryside draining into dense slums by the coast, ultimately the region's rulers will come to reflect the values of these shanty-towns. There are signs of this already in Sierra Leone—and in Togo, where the dictator Etienne Eyadema, in power since 1967, was nearly toppled in 1991, not by democrats but by thousands of youths whom the London-based magazine *West Africa* described as "Soweto-like stone-throwing adolescents." Their behavior may herald a regime more brutal than Eyadema's repressive one.

The fragility of these West African "countries" impressed itself on me when I took a series of bush taxis along the Gulf of Guinea, from the Togolese capital of Lomé, across Ghana, to Abidjan. The 400-mile journey required two full days of driving, because of stops at two border crossings and an additional eleven customs stations, at each of which my fellow passengers had their bags searched. I had to change money twice and repeatedly fill in currency-declaration forms. I had to bribe a Togolese immigration official with the equivalent of eighteen dollars before he would agree to put an exit stamp on my passport. Nevertheless, smuggling across these borders is rampant. *The London Observer* has reported that in 1992 the equivalent of $856 million left West Africa for Europe in the form of "hot cash" assumed to be laundered drug money. International cartels have discovered the utility of weak, financially strapped West African regimes.

The more fictitious the actual sovereignty, the more severe border authorities seem to be in trying to prove otherwise. Getting visas for these states can be as hard as crossing their borders. The Washington embassies of Sierra Leone and Guinea—the two poorest nations on earth, according to a 1993 United Nations report on "human development"—asked for letters from my bank (in lieu of prepaid round-trip tickets) and also personal references, in order to prove that I had sufficient means to sustain myself during my visits. I was reminded of my visa and currency hassles while traveling to the communist states of Eastern Europe, particularly East Germany and Czechoslovakia, before those states collapsed.

Ali A. Mazrui, the director of the Institute of Global Cultural Studies at the State University of New York at Binghamton, predicts that West Africa—indeed, the whole continent—is on the verge of large-scale border upheaval. Mazrui writes,

> In the 21st century France will be withdrawing from West Africa as she gets increasingly involved in the affairs [of Europe]. France's West African sphere of influence will be filled by Nigeria—a more natural hegemonic power. . . . It will be under those circumstances that Nigeria's own boundaries are likely to expand to incorporate the Republic of Niger (the Hausa link), the Republic of Benin (the Yoruba link) and conceivably Cameroon.

The future could be more tumultuous, and bloodier, than Mazrui dares to say. France *will* withdraw from former colonies like Benin, Togo, Niger, and the Ivory Coast, where it has been propping up local currencies. It will do so not only because its attention will be diverted to new challenges in Europe and Russia but also because younger French officials lack the older generation's emotional ties to the ex-colonies. However, even as Nigeria attempts to expand, it, too, is likely to split into several pieces. The State Department's Bureau of Intelligence and Research recently made the following points in an analysis of Nigeria:

> Prospects for a transition to civilian rule and democratization are slim. . . . The repressive apparatus of the state security service . . . will be difficult for any future civilian government to control. . . . The country is becoming increasingly ungovernable. . . . Ethnic and regional splits are deepening, a situation made worse by an increase in the number of states from 19 to 30 and a doubling in the number of local governing authorities; religious cleavages are more serious; Muslim fundamentalism and evangelical Christian militancy are on the rise; and northern Muslim anxiety over southern [Christian] control of the economy is intense . . . the will to keep Nigeria together is now very weak.

Given that oil-rich Nigeria is a bellwether for the region—its population of roughly 90 million equals the populations of all the other West African states combined—it is apparent that Africa faces cataclysms that could make the Ethiopian and Somalian famines pale in comparison. This is especially so because Nigeria's population, including that of its largest city, Lagos, whose crime, pollution, and overcrowding make it the cliché par excellence of Third World urban dysfunction, is set to double during the next twenty-five years, while the country continues to deplete its natural resources.

Part of West Africa's quandary is that although its population belts are horizontal, with habitation densities increasing as one travels south away from the Sahara and toward the tropical abundance of the Atlantic littoral, the borders erected by European colonialists are vertical, and therefore at cross-purposes with demography and topography. Satellite photos depict the same reality I experienced in the bush taxi: the Lomé-Abidjan coastal corridor—indeed, the entire stretch of coast from Abidjan eastward to Lagos—is one burgeoning megalopolis that by any rational economic and geographical standard should constitute a single sovereignty, rather than the five (the Ivory Coast, Ghana, Togo, Benin, and Nigeria) into which it is currently divided.

As many internal African borders begin to crumble, a more impenetrable boundary is being erected that threatens to isolate the continent as a whole: the wall of disease. Merely to visit West Africa in some degree of safety, I spent about $500 for a hepatitis B vaccination series and other disease prophylaxis. Africa may today be more dangerous in this regard than it was in 1862, before antibiotics, when the explorer Sir Richard Francis Burton described the health situation on the continent as "deadly, a Golgotha, a Jehannum." Of the approximately 12 million people worldwide whose blood is HIV-positive, 8 million are in Africa. In the capital of the Ivory Coast, whose modern road system only helps to spread the disease, 10 percent of the population is HIV-positive. And war and refugee movements help the virus break through to more-remote areas of Africa. Alan Greenberg, M.D., a representative of the Centers for Disease Control in Abidjan, explains that in Africa the HIV virus and tuberculosis are now "fast-forwarding each other." Of the approximately 4,000 newly diagnosed tuberculosis patients in Abidjan, 45 percent were also found to be HIV-positive. As African birth rates soar and slums proliferate, some experts worry that viral mutations and hybridizations might, just conceivably, result in a form of the AIDS virus that is easier to catch than the present strain.

It is malaria that is most responsible for the disease wall that threatens to separate Africa and other parts of the Third World from more-developed regions of the planet in the twenty-first century. Carried by mosquitoes, malaria, unlike AIDS, is easy to catch. Most people in sub-Saharan Africa have recurring bouts of the disease throughout their entire lives, and it is mutating into increasingly deadly forms. "The great gift of Malaria is utter apathy," wrote Sir Richard Burton, accurately portraying the situation in much of the Third World today. Visitors to malaria-afflicted parts of the planet are protected by a new drug, mefloquine, a side effect of which is vivid, even violent, dreams. But a strain of cerebral malaria resistant to mefloquine is now on the offensive. Consequently, defending oneself against malaria in Africa is becoming more and more like defending oneself against violent crime. You engage in "behavior modification": not going out at dusk, wearing mosquito repellent all the time.

And the cities keep growing. I got a general sense of the future while driving from the airport to downtown Conakry, the capital of Guinea. The forty-five-minute journey in heavy traffic was through one never-ending shanty-town: a nightmarish Dickensian spectacle to which Dickens himself would never have given credence. The corrugated metal shacks and scabrous walls were coated with black slime. Stores were built out of rusted shipping containers, junked cars, and jumbles of wire mesh. The streets were one long puddle of floating garbage. Mosquitoes and flies were everywhere. Children, many of whom had protruding bellies, seemed as numerous as ants. When the tide went out, dead rats and the skeletons of cars were exposed on the mucky beach. In twenty-eight years Guinea's population will double if growth goes on at current rates. Hardwood logging continues at a madcap speed, and people flee the Guinean countryside for Conakry. It seemed to me that here, as elsewhere in Africa and the Third World, man is challenging nature far beyond its limits, and nature is now beginning to take its revenge.

Africa may be as relevant to the future character of world politics as the Balkans were a hundred years ago, prior to the two Balkan wars and the First World War. Then the threat was the collapse of empires and the birth of nations based solely on tribe. Now the threat is more elemental: *nature unchecked*. Africa's immediate future could be very bad. The coming upheaval, in which foreign embassies are shut down, states collapse, and contact with the outside world takes place through dangerous, disease-ridden coastal trading posts, will loom large in the century we are entering. (Nine of twenty-one U.S. foreign-aid missions to be closed over the next three years are in Africa—a prologue to a consolidation of U.S. embassies themselves.) Precisely because much of Africa is set to go over the edge at a time when the Cold War has ended, when environmental and demographic stress in other parts of the globe is becoming critical, and when the post-First World War system of nation-states—not just in the Balkans but perhaps also in the Middle East—is about to be toppled, Africa suggests what war, borders, and ethnic politics will be like a few decades hence.

To understand the events of the next fifty years, then, one must understand environmental scarcity, cultural and racial clash, geographic destiny, and the transformation of war. The order in which I have named these is not accidental. Each concept except the first relies partly on the one or ones before it, meaning that the last two—new approaches to mapmaking and to warfare—are the most important. They are also the least understood. I will now look at each idea, drawing upon the work of specialists and also my own travel experiences in various parts of the globe besides Africa, in order to fill in the blanks of a new political atlas.

## The Environment as a Hostile Power

For a while the media will continue to ascribe riots and other violent upheavals abroad mainly to ethnic and religious conflict. But as these conflicts multiply, it will become apparent that something else is afoot, making more and more places like Nigeria, India, and Brazil ungovernable.

Mention "the environment" or "diminishing natural resources" in foreign-policy circles and you meet a brick wall of skepticism or boredom. To conservatives especially, the very terms seem flaky. Public-policy foundations have contributed to the lack of interest, by funding narrowly focused environmental studies replete with technical jargon which foreign-affairs experts just let pile up on their desks.

It is time to understand "the environment" for what it is: *the* national-security issue of the early twenty-first century. The political and strategic impact of surging populations, spreading disease, deforestation and soil erosion, water depletion, air pollution, and, possibly, rising sea levels in critical, overcrowded regions like the Nile Delta and Bangladesh—developments that will prompt mass migrations and, in turn, incite group conflicts—will be the core foreign-policy challenge from which most others will ultimately emanate, arousing the public and uniting assorted interests left over from the Cold War. In the twenty-first century water will be in dangerously short supply in such diverse locales as Saudi Arabia, Central Asia, and the southwestern United States. A war could erupt between Egypt and Ethiopia over Nile River water. Even in Europe tensions have arisen between Hungary and Slovakia over the damming of the Danube, a classic case of how environmental disputes fuse with ethnic and historical ones. The political scientist and erstwhile Clinton adviser Michael Mandelbaum has said, "We have a foreign policy today in the shape of a doughnut—lots of peripheral interest but nothing at the center." The environment, I will argue, is part of a terrifying array of problems that will define a new threat to our security, filling the hole in Mandelbaum's doughnut and allowing a post-Cold War foreign policy to emerge inexorably by need rather than by design.

Our Cold War foreign policy truly began with George F. Kennan's famous article, signed "X," published in *Foreign Affairs* in July of 1947, in which Kennan argued for a "firm and vigilant containment" of a Soviet Union that was imperially, rather than ideologically, motivated. It may be that our post-Cold War foreign policy will one day be seen to have had its beginnings in an even bolder and more detailed piece of written analysis: one that appeared in the journal *International Security*. The article, published in the fall of 1991 by Thomas Fraser Homer-Dixon, who is the head of the Peace and Conflict Studies Program at the University of Toronto, was titled "On the Threshold: Environmental Changes as Causes of Acute Conflict." Homer-Dixon has, more successfully than other analysts, integrated two hither-to separate fields—military-conflict studies and the study of the physical environment.

In Homer-Dixon's view, future wars and civil violence will often arise from scarcities of resources such as water, cropland, forests, and fish. Just as there will be environmentally driven wars and refugee flows, there will be environmentally induced praetorian regimes—or, as he puts it, "hard regimes." Countries with the highest probability of acquiring hard regimes, according to Homer-Dixon, are those that are threatened by a declining resource base yet also have "a history of state [read 'military'] strength." Candidates include Indonesia, Brazil, and, of course, Nigeria. Though each of these nations has exhibited democratizing tendencies of late, Homer-Dixon argues that such tendencies are likely to be superficial "epiphenomena" having nothing to do with long-term processes that include soaring populations and shrinking raw materials. Democracy is problematic; scarcity is more certain.

Indeed, the Saddam Husseins of the future will have more, not fewer, opportunities. In addition to engendering tribal strife, scarcer resources will place a great strain on many peoples who never had much of a democratic or institutional tradition to begin with. Over the next fifty years the earth's population will soar from 5.5 billion to more than nine billion. Though optimists have hopes for new resource technologies and free-market development in the global village, they fail to note that, as the National Academy of Sciences has pointed out, 95 percent of the population increase will be in the poorest regions of the world, where governments now—just look at Africa—show little ability to function, let alone to implement even marginal improvements. Homer-Dixon writes, ominously, "Neo-Malthusians may underestimate human adaptability in *today's* environmental-social system, but as time passes their analysis may become ever more compelling."

While a minority of the human population will be, as Francis Fukuyama would put it, sufficiently sheltered so as to enter a "post-historical" realm, living in cities and suburbs in which the environment has been mastered and ethnic animosities have been quelled by bourgeois prosperity, an increasingly large number of people will be stuck in history, living in shantytowns where attempts to rise above poverty, cultural dysfunction, and ethnic strife will be doomed by a lack of water to drink, soil to till, and space to survive in. In the developing world environmental stress will present people with a choice that is increasingly among totalitarianism (as in Iraq), fascist-tending mini-states (as in Serb-held Bosnia), and road-warrior cultures (as in Somalia). Homer-Dixon concludes that "as environmental degradation proceeds, the size of the potential social disruption will increase."

Tad Homer-Dixon is an unlikely Jeremiah. Today a boyish thirty-seven, he grew up amid the sylvan majesty of Vancouver Island, attending private day schools. His speech is calm, perfectly even, and crisply enunciated. There is nothing in his background or manner that would indicate a bent toward pessimism. A Canadian Anglican who spends his summers canoeing on the lakes of northern Ontario, and who talks about the benign mountains, black bears, and Douglas firs of his youth, he is the opposite of the intellectually severe neoconservative, the kind at home with conflict scenarios. Nor is he an environmentalist who opposes development. "My father was a logger who thought about ecologically safe forestry before others," he says. "He logged, planted, logged, and planted. He got out of the business just as the issue was being polarized by environmentalists. They hate changed ecosystems. But human beings, just by carrying seeds around, change the natural world." As an only child whose playground was a virtually untouched wilderness and seacoast, Homer-Dixon has a familiarity with the natural world that permits him to see a reality that most policy analysts—children of suburbia and city streets—are blind to.

"We need to bring nature back in," he argues. "We have to stop separating politics from the physical world—the climate, public health, and the environment." Quoting Daniel Deudney, another pioneering expert on the security aspects of the environment, Homer-Dixon says that "for too long we've been prisoners of 'social-social' theory, which assumes there are only social causes for social and political changes, rather than natural causes, too. This social-social mentality emerged with the Industrial Revolution, which separated us from nature. But nature is coming back with a vengeance, tied to population growth. It will have incredible security implications.

"Think of a stretch limo in the potholed streets of New York City, where homeless beggars live. Inside the limo are the air-conditioned post-industrial regions of North America, Europe, the emerging Pacific Rim, and a few other isolated places, with their trade summitry and computer-information highways. Outside is the rest of mankind, going in a completely different direction."

We are entering a bifurcated world. Part of the globe is inhabited by Hegel's and Fukuyama's Last Man, healthy, well fed, and pampered by technology. The other, larger, part is inhabited by Hobbes's First Man, condemned to a life that is "poor, nasty, brutish, and short." Although both parts will be threatened by environmental stress, the Last Man will be able to master it; the First Man will not.

The Last Man will adjust to the loss of underground water tables in the western United States. He will build dikes to save Cape Hatteras and the Chesapeake beaches from rising sea levels, even as the Maldive Islands, off the coast of India, sink into oblivion, and the shorelines of Egypt, Bangladesh, and Southeast Asia recede, driving tens of millions of people inland where there is no room for them, and thus sharpening ethnic divisions.

Homer-Dixon points to a world map of soil degradation in his Toronto office. "The darker the map color, the worse the degradation," he explains. The West African coast, the Middle East, the Indian subcontinent, China, and Central America have the darkest shades, signifying all manner of degradation, related to winds, chemicals, and water problems. "The worst degradation is generally where the population is highest. The population is generally highest where the soil is the best. So we're degrading earth's best soil."

China, in Homer-Dixon's view, is the quintessential example of environmental degradation. Its current economic "success" masks deeper problems. "China's fourteen percent growth rate does not mean it's going to be a world power. It means that coastal China, where the economic growth is taking place, is joining the rest of the Pacific Rim. The disparity with inland China is intensifying." Referring to the environmental research of his colleague, the Czech-born ecologist Vaclav Smil, Homer-Dixon explains how the per capita availability of arable land in interior China has rapidly declined at the same time that the quality of that land has been destroyed by deforestation, loss of topsoil, and salinization. He mentions the loss and contamination of water supplies, the exhaustion of wells, the plugging of irrigation systems and reservoirs with eroded silt, and a population of 1.54 billion by the year 2025: it is a misconception that China has gotten its population under control. Large-scale population movements are under way, from inland China to coastal China and from villages to cities, leading to a crime surge like the one in Africa and to growing regional disparities and conflicts in a land with a strong tradition of warlordism and a weak tradition of central government—again as in Africa. "We will probably see the center challenged and fractured, and China will not remain the same on the map," Homer-Dixon says.

Environmental scarcity will inflame existing hatreds and affect power relationships, at which we now look. . . .

## A New Kind of War

To appreciate fully the political and cartographic implications of postmodernism—an epoch of themeless juxtapositions, in which the classificatory grid of nation-states is going to be replaced by a jagged-glass pattern of city-states, shanty-states, nebulous and anarchic regionalisms—it is necessary to consider, finally, the whole question of war.

"Oh, what a relief to fight, to fight enemies who defend themselves, enemies who are awake!" André Malraux wrote in *Man's Fate*. I cannot think of a more suitable battle cry for many combatants in the early decades of the twenty-first century. The intense savagery of the fighting in such diverse cultural settings as Liberia, Bosnia, the Caucasus, and Sri Lanka—to say nothing of what obtains in American inner cities—indicates something very troubling that those of us inside the stretch limo, concerned with issues like middle-class entitlements and the future of interactive cable television, lack the stomach to contemplate. It is this: a large number of people on this planet, to whom the comfort and stability of a middle-class life is utterly unknown, find war and a barracks existence a step up rather than a step down.

"Just as it makes no sense to ask 'why people eat' or 'what they sleep for,'" writes Martin van Creveld, a military historian at the Hebrew University in Jerusalem, in *The Transformation of War*, "so fighting in many ways is not a means but an end. Throughout history, for every person who has expressed his horror of war there is another who found in it the most marvelous of all the experiences that are vouchsafed to man, even to the point that he later spent a lifetime boring his descendants by recounting his exploits." When I asked Pentagon officials about the nature of war in the twenty-first century, the answer I frequently got was "Read Van Creveld." The top brass are enamored of this historian not because his writings justify their existence but, rather, the opposite: Van Creveld warns them that huge state military machines like the Pentagon's are dinosaurs about to go extinct, and that something far more terrible awaits us.

The degree to which Van Creveld's *Transformation of War* complements Homer-Dixon's work on the environment, Huntington's thoughts on cultural clash, my own realizations in traveling by foot, bus, and bush taxi in more than sixty countries, and America's sobering comeuppances in intractable-culture zones like Haiti and Somalia is startling. The book begins by demolishing the notion that men don't like to fight. "By compelling the senses to focus themselves on the here and now," Van Creveld writes, war "can cause a man to take his leave of them." As anybody who has had experience with Chetniks in Serbia, "technicals" in Somalia, Tontons Macoutes in Haiti, or soldiers in Sierra Leone can tell you, in places where the Western Enlightenment has not penetrated and where there has always been mass poverty, people find liberation in violence. In Afghanistan and elsewhere, I vicariously experienced this phenomenon: worrying about mines and ambushes frees you from mundane details of daily existence. If my own experience is too subjective, there is a wealth of data showing the sheer frequency of war, especially in the developing world since the Second World War. Physical aggression is a part of being human. Only when people attain a certain economic, educational, and cultural standard is this trait tranquilized. In light of the fact that 95 percent of the earth's population growth will be in the poorest areas of the globe, the question is not whether there will be war (there will be a lot of it) but what kind of war. And who will fight whom?

Debunking the great military strategist Carl von Clausewitz, Van Creveld, who may be the most original thinker on war since that early-nineteenth-century Prussian, writes, "Clausewitz's ideas... were wholly rooted in the fact that, ever since 1648, war had been waged overwhelmingly by states." But, as Van Creveld explains, the period of nation-states and, therefore, of state conflict is now ending, and with it the clear "threefold division into government, army, and people" which state-directed wars enforce. Thus, to see the future, the first step is to look back to the past immediately prior to the birth of modernism—the wars in medieval Europe which began during the Reformation and reached their culmination in the Thirty Years' War.

Van Creveld writes,

> In all these struggles political, social, economic, and religious motives were hopelessly entangled. Since this was an age when armies consisted of mercenaries, all were also attended by swarms of military entrepreneurs. . . . Many of them paid little but lip service to the organizations for whom they had contracted to fight. Instead, they robbed the countryside on their own behalf. . . Given such conditions, any fine distinctions . . . between armies on the one hand and peoples on the other were bound to break down. Engulfed by war, civilians suffered terrible atrocities.

Back then, in other words, there was no "politics" as we have come to understand the term, just as there is less and less "politics" today in Liberia, Sierra Leone, Somalia, Sri Lanka, the Balkans, and the Caucasus, among other places.

Because, as Van Creveld notes, the radius of trust within tribal societies is narrowed to one's immediate family and guerrilla comrades, truces arranged with one Bosnian commander, say, may be broken immediately by another Bosnian commander. The plethora of short-lived ceasefires in the Balkans and the Caucasus constitute proof that we are no longer in a world where the old rules of state warfare apply. More evidence is provided by the destruction of medieval monuments in the Croatian port of Dubrovnik: when cultures, rather than states, fight, then cultural and religious monuments are weapons of war, making them fair game.

Also, war-making entities will no longer be restricted to a specific territory. Loose and shadowy organisms such as Islamic terrorist organizations suggest why borders will mean increasingly little and sedimentary layers of tribalistic identity and control will mean more. "From the vantage point of the present, there appears every prospect that religious . . . fanaticisms will play a larger role in the motivation of armed conflict" in the West than at any time "for the last 300 years," Van Creveld writes. This is why analysts like Michael Vlahos are closely monitoring religious cults. Vlahos says, "An ideology that challenges us may not take familiar form, like the old Nazis or Commies. It may not even engage us initially in ways that fit old threat markings." Van Creveld concludes, "Armed conflict will be waged by men on earth, not robots in space. It will have more in common with the struggles of primitive tribes than with large-scale conventional war." While another military historian, John Keegan, in his new book *A History of Warfare*, draws a more benign portrait of primitive man, it is important to point out that what Van Creveld really means is *re-primitivized* man: warrior societies operating at a time of unprecedented resource scarcity and planetary overcrowding.

Van Creveld's pre-Westphalian vision of worldwide low-intensity conflict is not a superficial "back to the future" scenario. First of all, technology will be used toward primitive ends. In Liberia the guerrilla leader Prince Johnson didn't just cut off the ears of President Samuel Doe before Doe was tortured to death in 1990—Johnson made a video of it, which has circulated throughout West Africa. In December of 1992, when plotters of a failed coup against the Strasser regime in Sierra Leone had their ears cut off at Freetown's Hamilton Beach prior to being killed, it was seen by many to be a copycat execution. Considering, as I've explained earlier, that the Strasser regime is not really a government and that Sierra Leone is not really a nation-state, listen closely to Van Creveld: "Once the legal monopoly of armed force, long claimed by the state, is wrested out of its hands, existing distinctions between war and crime will break down much as is already the case today in . . . Lebanon, Sri Lanka, El Salvador, Peru, or Colombia."

If crime and war become indistinguishable, then "national defense" may in the future be viewed as a local concept. As crime continues to grow in our cities and the ability of state governments and criminal-justice systems to protect their citizens diminishes, urban crime may, according to Van Creveld, "develop into low-intensity conflict by coalescing along racial, religious, social, and political lines." As small-scale violence multiplies at home and abroad, state armies will continue to shrink, being gradually replaced by a booming private security business, as in West Africa, and by urban mafias, especially in the former communist world, who may be better equipped than municipal police forces to grant physical protection to local inhabitants.

Future wars will be those of communal survival, aggravated or, in many cases, caused by environmental scarcity. These wars will be subnational, meaning that it will be hard for states and local governments to protect their own citizens physically. This is how many states will ultimately die. As state power fades—and with it the state's ability to help weaker groups within society, not to mention other states—peoples and cultures around the world will be thrown back upon their own strengths and weaknesses, with fewer equalizing mechanisms to protect them. Whereas the distant future will probably see the emergence of a racially hybrid, globalized man, the coming decades will see us more aware of our differences than of our similarities. To the average person, political values will mean less, personal security more. The belief that we are all equal is liable to be replaced by the overriding obsession of the ancient Greek travelers: Why the differences between peoples?

## The Last Map

In *Geography and the Human Spirit*, Anne Buttimer, a professor at University College, Dublin, recalls the work of an early-nineteenth-century German geographer, Carl Ritter, whose work implied "a divine plan for humanity" based on regionalism and a constant, living flow of forms. The map of the future, to the extent that a map is even possible, will represent a perverse twisting of Ritter's vision. Imagine cartography in three dimensions, as if in a hologram. In this hologram would be the overlapping sediments of group and other identities atop the merely two-dimensional color markings of city-states and the remaining nations, themselves confused in places by shadowy tentacles, hovering overhead, indicating the power of drug cartels, mafias, and private security agencies. Instead of borders, there would be moving "centers" of power, as in the Middle Ages. Many of these layers would be in motion. Replacing fixed and abrupt lines on a flat space would be a shifting pattern of buffer entities, like the Kurdish and Azeri buffer entities between Turkey and Iran, the Turkic Uighur buffer entity between Central Asia and Inner China (itself distinct from coastal China), and the Latino buffer entity replacing a precise U.S.-Mexican border. To this protean cartographic hologram one must add other factors, such as migrations of populations, explosions of birth rates, vectors of disease. Henceforward the map of the world will never be static. This future map—in a sense, the "Last Map"—will be an ever-mutating representation of chaos.

The Indian subcontinent offers examples of what is happening. For different reasons, both India and Pakistan are increasingly dysfunctional. The argument over democracy in these places is less and less relevant to the larger issue of governability. In India's case the question arises, Is one unwieldy bureaucracy in New Delhi the best available mechanism for promoting the lives of 866 million people of diverse languages, religions, and ethnic groups? In 1950, when the Indian population was much less than half as large and nation-building idealism was still strong, the argument for democracy was more impressive than it is now. Given that in 2025 India's population could be close to 1.5 billion, that much of its economy rests on a shrinking natural-resource base, including dramatically declining water levels, and that communal violence and urbanization are spiraling upward, it is difficult to imagine that the Indian state will survive the next century. India's oft-trumpeted Green Revolution has been achieved by overworking its croplands and depleting its watershed. Norman Myers, a British development consultant, worries that Indians have "been feeding themselves today by borrowing against their children's food sources."

Pakistan's problem is more basic still: like much of Africa, the country makes no geographic or demographic sense. It was founded as a homeland for the Muslims of the subcontinent, yet there are more subcontinental Muslims outside Pakistan than within it. Like Yugoslavia, Pakistan is a patchwork of ethnic groups, increasingly in violent conflict with one another. While the Western media gushes over the fact that the country has a woman Prime Minister, Benazir Bhutto, Karachi is becoming a subcontinental version of Lagos. In eight visits to Pakistan, I have never gotten a sense of a cohesive national identity. With as much as 65 percent of its land dependent on intensive irrigation, with wide-scale deforestation, and with a yearly population growth of 2.7 percent (which ensures that the amount of cultivated land per rural inhabitant will plummet), Pakistan is becoming a more and more desperate place. As irrigation in the Indus River basin intensifies to serve two growing populations, Muslim-Hindu strife over falling water tables may be unavoidable.

"India and Pakistan will probably fall apart," Homer-Dixon predicts. "Their secular governments have less and less legitimacy as well as less management ability over people and resources." Rather than one bold line dividing the subcontinent into two parts, the future will likely see a lot of thinner lines and smaller parts, with the ethnic entities of Pakhtunistan and Punjab gradually replacing Pakistan in the space between the Central Asian plateau and the heart of the subcontinent.

None of this even takes into account climatic change, which, if it occurs in the next century, will further erode the capacity of existing states to cope. India, for instance, receives 70 percent of its precipitation from the monsoon cycle, which planetary warming could disrupt.

Not only will the three-dimensional aspect of the Last Map be in constant motion, but its two-dimensional base may change too. The National Academy of Sciences reports that

> as many as one billion people, or 20 per cent of the world's population, live on lands likely to be inundated or dramatically changed by rising waters. . . . Low-lying countries in the developing world such as Egypt and Bangladesh, where rivers are large and the deltas extensive and densely populated, will be hardest hit. . . . Where the rivers are dammed, as in the case of the Nile, the effects . . . will be especially severe.

Egypt could be where climatic upheaval—to say nothing of the more immediate threat of increasing population—will incite religious upheaval in truly biblical fashion. Natural catastrophes, such as the October, 1992, Cairo earthquake, in which the government failed to deliver relief aid and slum residents were in many instances helped by their local mosques, can only strengthen the position of Islamic factions. In a statement about greenhouse warming which could refer to any of a variety of natural catastrophes, the environmental expert Jessica Tuchman Matthews warns that many of us underestimate the extent to which political systems, in affluent societies as well as in places like Egypt, "depend on the underpinning of natural systems." She adds, "The fact that one can move with ease from Vermont to Miami has nothing to say about the consequences of Vermont acquiring Miami's climate."

Indeed, it is not clear that the United States will survive the next century in exactly its present form. Because America is a multi-ethnic society, the nation-state has always been more fragile here than it is in more homogenous societies like Germany and Japan. James Kurth, in an article published in *The National Interest* in 1992, explains that whereas nation-state societies tend to be built around a mass-conscription army and a standardized public school system, "multicultural regimes" feature a high-tech, all-volunteer army (and, I would add, private schools that teach competing values), operating in a culture in which the international media and entertainment industry has more influence than the "national political class." In other words, a nation-state is a place where everyone has been educated along similar lines, where people take their cue from national leaders, and where everyone (every male, at least) has gone through the crucible of military service, making patriotism a simpler issue. Writing about his immigrant family in turn-of-the-century Chicago, Saul Bellow states, "The country took us over. It *was* a country then, not a collection of 'cultures.'"

During the Second World War and the decade following it, the United States reached its apogee as a classic nation-state. During the 1960s, as is now clear, America began a slow but unmistakable process of transformation. The signs hardly need belaboring: racial polarity, educational dysfunction, social fragmentation of many and various kinds. William Irwin Thompson, in *Passages About Earth: An Exploration of the New Planetary Culture*, writes, "The educational system that had worked on the Jew or the Irish could no longer work on the blacks; and when Jewish teachers in New York tried to take black children away from their parents exactly in the way they had been taken from theirs, they were shocked to encounter a violent affirmation of negritude."

Issues like West Africa could yet emerge as a new kind of foreign-policy issue, further eroding America's domestic peace. The spectacle of several West African nations collapsing at once could reinforce the worst racial stereotypes here at home. That is another reason why Africa matters. We must not kid ourselves: the sensitivity factor is higher than ever. The Washington, D.C., public school system is already experimenting with an Afrocentric curriculum. Summits between African leaders and prominent African-Americans are becoming frequent, as are Pollyanna-ish prognostications about multiparty elections in Africa that do not factor in crime, surging birth rates, and resource depletion. The Congressional Black Caucus was among those urging U.S. involvement in Somalia and in Haiti. At the *Los Angeles Times* minority staffers have protested against, among other things, what they allege to be the racist tone of the newspaper's Africa coverage, allegations that the editor of the "World Report" section, Dan Fisher, denies, saying essentially that Africa should be viewed through the same rigorous analytical lens as other parts of the world.

Africa may be marginal in terms of conventional late-twentieth-century conceptions of strategy, but in an age of cultural and racial clash, when national defense is increasingly local, Africa's distress will exert a destabilizing influence on the United States.

This and many other factors will make the United States less of a nation than it is today, even as it gains territory following the peaceful dissolution of Canada. Quebec, based on the bedrock of Roman Catholicism and Francophone ethnicity, could yet turn out to be North America's most cohesive and crime-free nation-state. (It may be a smaller Quebec, though, since aboriginal peoples may lop off northern parts of the province.) "Patriotism" will become increasingly regional as people in Alberta and Montana discover that they have far more in common with each other than they do with Ottawa or Washington, and Spanish-speakers in the Southwest discover a greater commonality with Mexico City. (*The Nine Nations of North America*, by Joel Garreau, a book about the continent's regionalization, is more relevant now than when it was published, in 1981.) As Washington's influence wanes, and with it the traditional symbols of American patriotism, North Americans will take psychological refuge in their insulated communities and cultures.

Returning from West Africa last fall was an illuminating ordeal. After leaving Abidjan, my Air Afrique flight landed in Dakar, Senegal, where all passengers had to disembark in order to go through another security check, this one demanded by U.S. authorities before they would permit the flight to set out for New York. Once we were in New York, despite the midnight hour, immigration officials at Kennedy Airport held up disembarkation by conducting quick interrogations of the aircraft's passengers—this was in addition to all the normal immigration and customs procedures. It was apparent that drug smuggling, disease, and other factors had contributed to the toughest security procedures I have ever encountered when returning from overseas.

Then, for the first time in over a month, I spotted businesspeople with attaché cases and laptop computers. When I had left New York for Abidjan, all the businesspeople were boarding planes for Seoul and Tokyo, which departed from gates near Air Afrique's. The only non-Africans off to West Africa had been relief workers in T-shirts and khakis. Although the borders within West Africa are increasingly unreal, those separating West Africa from the outside world are in various ways becoming more impenetrable.

But Afrocentrists are right in one respect: we ignore this dying region at our own risk. When the Berlin Wall was falling, in November of 1989, I happened to be in Kosovo, covering a riot between Serbs and Albanians. The future was in Kosovo, I told myself that night, not in Berlin. The same day that Yitzhak Rabin and Yasser Arafat clasped hands on the White House lawn, my Air Afrique plane was approaching Bamako, Mali, revealing corrugated-zinc shacks at the edge of an expanding desert. The real news wasn't at the White House, I realized. It was right below.

# Chapter 28
# An Overview of U.S. Military Strategy: Concepts and History

Mackubin Thomas Owens

*Mackubin Thomas Owens looks at the way in which U.S. strategy has guided force planning since the end of World War II. Military strategy describes how military means are applied to achieve national ends. To execute a military strategy, certain requirements must be met. To meet these requirements, military forces possessing the necessary capabilities are procured. This is a top-down approach in which strategy clearly drives force planning. Is this approach valid? What are the obstacles to this approach? How have the strategic requirements changed from the Cold War to the present? How have the "descriptors" of national military strategy changed over the past 50 years? Have changes in force structure matched changes in strategic requirements?*

"**S**trategy" is derived from *strategia*, the art of the general (*strategos*). Traditionally, the term has been used to describe the employment of military forces in war. For instance, B.H. Liddell-Hart defined strategy as "the art of distributing and applying military means to fulfill the ends of policy."[1]

It is, however, increasingly the practice to employ "strategy" more broadly, so that one can speak of *levels* of strategy in both peace and war.[2] Accordingly, strategy can be understood to apply not only to the application of force in wartime to achieve the goals of national policy, but also to the steps taken during peacetime to enhance national power in order to prevent war or win, should war become necessary.

This more expansive usage of strategy inevitably overlaps with the common meaning of "policy" which is defined as 1) the general overall goals and acceptable procedures that a nation might follow; and 2) the course of action selected from among alternatives in light of given conditions. In their military history of the United States, Allan Millett and Peter Maslowski define *defense policy* as "the sum of the assumptions, plans, programs, and actions taken by the citizens of the United States, principally through governmental action, to ensure the

Mackubin Thomas Owens is Professor of Strategy and Force Planning in the National Security Decision Making Department of the Naval War College and Editor-in-Chief of *Strategic Review*.

physical security of their lives, property, and way of life from external military attack and domestic insurrection."[3] For the purposes of this chapter, *policy* refers primarily to such broad national goals as interests and objectives; *strategy* to the alternative courses of actions designed to achieve those goals.

In general, strategy serves three purposes.[4] First, strategy *relates ends*, the goals of policy (interests and objectives) *to the limited means* available to achieve them. Both strategy and economics are concerned with the application of scarce means to achieve certain goals. But strategy implies an adversary who actively opposes the achievement of the ends.

Second, strategy *contributes to the clarification of the ends of policy by helping to establish priorities in the light of constrained resources*. Without establishing priorities among competing ends, all interests and all threats will appear equal. In the absence of strategy, planners will find themselves in the situation described by Frederick the Great: "He who attempts to defend too much defends nothing."

Finally, strategy *conceptualizes resources as means* in support of policy. Resources are not means until strategy provides some understanding of how they will be organized and employed. Defense budgets and manpower are resources. Strategy organizes these resources into divisions, wings, and fleets.

Strategy must answer the question: what plan will best achieve the ends of national security, given scarce resources for defense? The answer to this question serves as a guide to planning future military forces.

In theory, the strategy-force planning process is very logical: the planner first identifies national interests and the objectives necessary to achieve those interests. The planner then assesses the ability of adversaries to threaten those interests or to interfere with the achievement of national objectives. Next, the planner forges a strategy for employing the available means to counter the threats to the national interests and a budget to fund the capabilities required to implement the strategy.[5]

To execute any chosen strategy, certain strategic requirements must be fulfilled. These requirements determine the necessary military capabilities, which in turn drive the acquisition of forces and equipment. Thus, if there is a strategic requirement for a particular capability, then presumably the forces or equipment that provide that capability should be obtained.

Throughout the process, the planner must constantly evaluate any risk that may be created by a potential ends-means mismatch. Figure 1 is an attempt graphically to portray the elements of strategy making and strategic planning.

In practice, strategic decisions must always compete with the demands of domestic politics or what Samuel Huntington has called "structural decisions." These are choices "made in the currency of domestic politics." The most important structural decision concerns the "size and distribution of funds made available to the armed forces. . . ."[6] Fiscal constraints can never be ignored by the strategy maker or force planner. Indeed, political reality sometimes dictates that budgetary limits will constitute the primary influence on the development of strategy and force structure.

**Figure 1**

**Elements of Strategic and Force Planning**

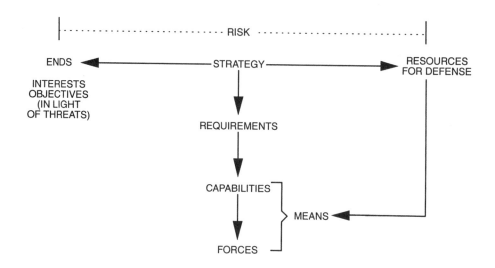

Although strategy can be simply described as the conceptual link between national ends and limited means in both war and peace, it cannot be reduced to a simple mechanical exercise. Rather, strategy is "a process, a constant adaptation to shifting conditions and circumstances in a world where chance, uncertainty, and ambiguity dominate." Clausewitz dismissed "principles, rules, or even systems" in strategic thinking. Strategy, on the contrary, "involves human passions, values, and beliefs, few of which are quantifiable."[7]

The strategic process is influenced by a number of recurring factors. Among the most important of these are geography; history; the nature of the political regime, including such elements as religion, ideology, culture, and political and military institutions; and economic and technological factors.[8]

Strategy is an indispensable element of national security. Without strategy, something else will fill the void. In war, service doctrines will dominate the conduct of operations if strategy is absent. This state of affairs is captured by Andrew Krepinevich's description of the Vietnam War: "a strategy of tactics."[9] In peacetime, defense planning comes to be dominated by Huntington's "structural decisions:" organizational imperatives, congressional politics, etc.

## Levels of Strategy

War and conflict can be divided into several levels. Clausewitz distinguished between tactics, "the use of armed forces in the engagement;" and strategy, "the use of engagements for the object of war."[10] A number of recent commentators have identified an intermediate level concerned with the planning and conduct of campaigns to achieve strategic goals within a theater of war, the "operational level of war."[11]

The central focus of this chapter is the strategic level of war and conflict, which in itself is subject to further subdivision. Writers often refer to grand strategy, military strategy, theater strategy, and service strategy.[12]

*Grand Strategy.* In its broadest sense, strategy is *grand* strategy. In the words of Edward Mead Earle:

> strategy is the art of controlling and utilizing the resources of a nation—or a coalition of nations—including its armed forces, to the end that its vital interests shall be effectively promoted and secured against enemies, actual, potential, or merely presumed. The highest type of strategy—sometimes called grand strategy—is that which so integrates the policies and armaments of the nation that resort to war is either rendered unnecessary or is undertaken with the maximum chance of victory.[13]

Grand strategy is thus intimately linked to national policy in that it is designed to bring to bear all the elements of national power—military, economic and diplomatic—in order to secure the nation's interests and objectives. Grand strategy can also refer to a nation's overarching approach to international affairs: isolationism or disengagement; cooperative or collective security; selective engagement; or primacy.[14] Finally, grand strategy can allude to a geopolitical orientation, e.g., "continental" or "maritime."[15] Whichever meaning is emphasized, the choice of a grand strategy has a major impact on the other levels of strategy and force structure.

*Military Strategy.* Military strategy is concerned with the employment of military power in peace and war. In peacetime, military strategy provides a guide to what Samuel Huntington calls "program decisions"—the strength of military forces, their composition and readiness, the number, type, and rate of development of weapons; and "posturing"—how military forces are deployed during peacetime to deter war (Clausewitz's "preparation for war"). In wartime, military strategy guides the employment of military force in pursuit of victory (Clausewitz's "war proper").[16]

A nation's approach to its security policy can take the form of either *strategic pluralism* or *strategic monism*. The former "...calls for a wide variety of military forces and weapons to meet a diversity of potential threats." In contrast, the latter refers to primary reliance on a single strategic concept, weapon, service, or region. Strategic monism "presupposes an ability to predict and control the actions of possible enemies."[17]

*Theater Strategy.* Theater strategy is really *operational planning* and *operational art*, the planning and conduct of campaigns. Both are aspects of the operational, not the strategic, level of war.

*Service Strategy.* Service strategy refers to what is more properly described as "doctrine" or a "strategic concept." Huntington defined the latter as "the fundamental element of a military service, . . . its role or purpose in implementing national policy." A service's strategic concept answers the "ultimate question: What function do you perform which obligates society to assume responsibility for your maintenance?"[18] When a single service is permitted to claim an independently decisive role for its own strategic concept, the result is usually some form of strategic monism.

The evolution of US strategy over the past fifty years illustrates the linkage among all these levels. More importantly, this evolution demonstrates the way in which strategy guides force planning. While defense budgets have fluctuated, sometime widely, resulting in strategy-force mismatches, there has been a more consistent relationship between strategy and force planning than some commentators have been willing to admit. By identifying what Henry Bartlett and Paul Holman have called strategic "descriptors," or key elements of a strategy, we can observe this relationship.[19]

## U.S. Policy and Grand Strategy for the Cold War

A nation's declaratory policy establishes the ends that it wishes to achieve in the world. Strategy and force structure logically flow from this policy. During the Cold War, "containment" was the declaratory policy of the United States. The primary objective of this policy was to protect U.S. national interests by deterring war while preventing the Soviet Union from dominating critical portions of the Eurasian continent, especially Western Europe, Northeast Asia and the Persian Gulf. In essence, Cold War U.S. policy embodied a global struggle for primacy with the USSR.

The geopolitical logic of containment was similar to that advanced in different ways by Sir Halford Mackinder and Nicholas Spykman,[20] a logic that the authors of NSC-68 and other documents underpinning containment apparently believed had not been fundamentally changed by the development of nuclear weapons.[21] This policy in turn led to the creation of a series of alliances designed to prevent the domination of the Eurasian "rimland" by the Soviet Union.

To meet the requirements established by this policy, the U.S. was obliged to commit substantial forces to the defense of allies on the Eurasian rimland. In the formulation of Sir Michael Howard, the U.S. had to make the "continental commitment" during the Cold War in order to prevent Soviet (and Chinese) hegemony over Europe, Northeast and Southeast Asia, and the Middle East.[22]

## Three Phases of U.S. Cold War Military Strategy

U.S. military strategy during the Cold War passed through three phases: Cold War Transition and NSC-68 (1945-1952), the New Look, (1952-1960); and Flexible Response, (1960-1989). While the particulars differed from phase to phase, all had three elements in common: dependence on unilateral nuclear deterrence; concurrent reliance on non-nuclear deterrence; and commitment to collective defense. With the exception of the New Look, the overall approach to U.S. Cold War military strategy can be characterized as strategic pluralism.[23]

***Cold War Transition and NSC-68.*** During the first phase, the U.S. attempted, in general, to pursue a balanced approach to deterrence. Although the 1948 Air Policy (Finletter) Commission declared that the threat of nuclear retaliation was the cornerstone of U.S. defense policy, in reality the U.S. lacked the nuclear capability to make good on this threat. This fact, as well as the assumption, made explicit by NSC-68, that the USSR would soon achieve nuclear parity with the U.S., led American policymakers to conclude that the nation must develop the capability to wage protracted conventional war.[24]

NSC-68, the corner-stone document of containment, developed four alternatives for the United States: continuing existing (inadequate) policies; retreating into unilateral isolationism; waging preventive war; increasing U.S./allied military strength in order to deter Soviet expansionism and war. The last alternative was the one preferred by the authors of the document, but they realized there was no public support for such an approach.[25] This situation changed in June of 1950 with the onset of the Korean War. This conflict made it possible for the U.S. to develop a force structure not only to wage war, but to pursue the long-range rearmament necessary to achieve strategic deterrence of the Soviet Union. Korea enabled the U.S. to close the gap between the rhetoric of containment and actual military capabilities.

***The New Look.*** The Korean War defense build-up was cut short by the election of Dwight Eisenhower, who was concerned that the pressure of defense spending to fight "proxy wars" such as the Korean conflict would fatally weaken the U.S. economy. Seeking "security with solvency," the Eisenhower administration put in place a version of strategic monism that de-emphasized conventional forces, stressing instead the deterrent and war-fighting potential of nuclear weapons. This New Look canceled the Korean War expansion plans, eliminating substantial Army, Navy and Air Force conventional capabilities. NSC 162/2 (October 1953), the top-secret statement of the New Look strategy, directed the Department of Defense to arm all service components with nuclear weapons.

NSC 162/2 declared that in the event of war with the USSR or China, "the United States will consider nuclear weapons to be as available for war as other munitions."[26] In 1954, Secretary of State John Foster Dulles announced that henceforth, the United States would rely on the threat of nuclear escalation to deter or stop Communist-inspired local wars. Articulating a nuclear weapons employment policy that came to be known as "massive retaliation," Dulles declared that Soviet adventurism would put at risk the very existence of the Soviet homeland, for the U.S. would "depend primarily upon a great capacity to retaliate, instantly, by means and at places of our own choosing. . . ."[27] The New Look is summarized in Figure 2.

---

**Figure 2**
**The New Look**

| | |
|---|---|
| **Policy -** | Containment of USSR |
| **Geographic Focus -** | Global |
| **Grand Strategy -** | Primacy |
| **Military Strategy -** | |
| **Descriptors -** | 1) Security with Solvency |
| | 2) Forward, Collective Defense |
| | 3) Massive Retaliation |
| **Required Capabilities -** | Deter/Defeat Soviet/Chinese Attack on U.S. and its allies |
| **Force Implications** | |
| **Nuclear Forces -** | Long-Range Bombers |
| | Medium-Range Bombers |
| | Emerging Long-and Medium-Range Ballistic Missiles |
| **Land Forces -** | Reduced Active Force Structure/Reliance on Reserves |
| | Theater and Tactical Nuclear Weapons |
| | Reassure Allies |
| **Maritime Forces -** | Sea Control |
| | Strike |
| | Emerging Deterrent (SLBM) |
| **Air Forces -** | Strategic Air Command (SAC) Dominant |
| | Reductions in Tactical Air Command (TAC) |

---

Its critics claimed that the New Look was deficient for a number of reasons. First of all, it was insufficiently vigorous and innovative in support of containment. Second, "massive retaliation" against the Soviet Union was not a credible response to proxy war, the form most often taken by communist aggression. Third, the focus on strategic nuclear air power to the exclusion of other capabilities resulted in strategic inflexibility: the U.S. largely lacked the ability to respond to threats at the lower end of the spectrum of conflict. The result was a mismatch between the declaratory policy of containment on the one hand and U.S. military strategy and force structure on the other.[28]

**Flexible Response.** The shortcomings of the New Look led the Kennedy administration to replace it with a strategy of Flexible Response. Flexible Response shifted away from a nearly exclusive reliance on unilateral nuclear deterrence, placing greater emphasis on shoring up the U.S.'s maritime alliances on the Eurasian rimlands, especially NATO, by means of forward conventional defense against a possible surprise attack by the Soviet Union and its satellites. Land and tactical forces, especially heavy land forces, resumed their place of importance. Formations were deployed in potentially threatened theaters, backed by rapid reinforcement forces, designed to be air and sea lifted to the crisis area in a matter of days.[29]

Flexible Response called for general purpose forces capable of simultaneously fighting 2½ wars: a Warsaw Pact attack in Europe, a Chinese-supported conflict in North or Southeast Asia, and an insurgency of some sort, most probably in the Caribbean region. As a result of the U.S. withdrawal from Vietnam and a diplomatic opening to China, this requirement was reduced to 1½ wars during the Nixon administration.[30]

Flexible Response called for responding to the Communist threat across the spectrum of conflict, from insurgency to central nuclear war. Although Flexible Response reemphasized conventional strategy and force structure, nuclear weapons continued to suffuse the strategy. The purpose of integrating nuclear and conventional strategy was to offset Soviet and Chinese manpower advantages by maintaining escalation dominance at all levels of conflict.

For the first time in its history, the United States maintained a large standing military establishment during peacetime with the industrial and technological infrastructure to support it. Each of the military services responded to the requirements of the U.S. Cold War policy and grand strategy by stressing a separate geographical or functional role for itself.

The primary focus of the U.S. Army was to defend Europe from a Warsaw Pact attack and to deter war on the Korean peninsula. The doctrine and procurement policies of the Army were largely formed by its perception of the Soviet ground threat: a mechanized attack in echelon supported by massive artillery and aviation bombardment, including the use of nuclear weapons.

The U.S. Air Force continued its orientation toward strategic bombing, especially the delivery of nuclear weapons against the Soviet homeland, but increased its focus on air superiority/deep strike in support of theater operations.

In the latter instance, the Air Force increasingly integrated its doctrine with that of the Army in order to defeat a massive Warsaw Pact offensive.

Naval power emphasized nuclear deterrence and sea control in support of the U.S. continental commitment to the defense of the Eurasian rimlands. Additionally, the U.S. Navy and Marine Corps had the primary functional responsibility for contingency response outside of NATO. The Maritime Strategy of the 1980s was the naval component of a grand strategy designed to deter the Soviet Union and defeat it as early as possible by conventional means if deterrence failed.

In reality, until the 1980s Flexible Response was more of an "atomic-intensive" defense policy than its creators originally envisoned. This was largely the legacy of Vietnam: as the counter-insurgency half-war there expanded to take on the foreign policy and force commitment of a major contingency, conventional forces, especially those committed to NATO, began to suffer. Flexible Response is summarized in Figure 3.

## Transition: The 1992 National Military Strategy

The collapse of the Soviet Union changed the character of the international security environment. No single power was now able to dominat Eurasia. Accordingly, the U.S. was in position to pursue a very different, "off-shore" grand strategy, similar to that followed by Britain until the twentieth-century German threat to Europe caused it to make its own continental commitment. This strategic approach placed primary reliance on "imperial policing" and was concerned with checking potential hegemons in those regions of importance to the nation.

By changing its grand strategy, the U.S. was able to rethink its military strategy, service strategies and force structure. It was in position to develop the CONUS-based force structure that had eluded planners since the end of World War II.[31] The process of shifting to this new grand strategy was well underway before the Iraqi invasion of Kuwait. On the eve of the invasion, President Bush outlined elements of this new strategy, which was fully developed and issued as the *National Military Strategy* in January 1992 (1992 NMS).[32]

While the U.S. Cold War military strategy had been a *global* strategy designed to counter the ability of the Soviet Union to threaten U.S. interests throughout the world, the 1992 NMS was a *regional* war-fighting strategy, the object of which was to employ, if necessary, overwhelming force to defeat aggressors in multiple simultaneous major regional conflicts (MRCs).[33] The descriptors (foundations) of the 1992 NMS were: *strategic deterrence and defense, forward presence, crisis response*, and *reconstitution* as shown in Figure 4. The 1992 NMS was designed to project power through joint littoral operations against regional threats. This required capability was supported by eight "strategic principles," including maritime and aerospace superiority, and strategic agility.[34]

---

**Figure 3**
**Flexible Response**

---

| | |
|---|---|
| **Policy -** | Containment of USSR |
| **Geographic Focus -** | Global |
| **Grand Strategy -** | Primacy |
| **Military Strategy** | |
| **Descriptors -** | 1) Nuclear/Conventional Integration |
| | 2) Collective Defense/Alliances |
| | 3) Forward Defense |
| | 4) Rapid Reinforcement |
| | 5) Mobilization Potential |
| | 6) Technological Superiority |
| **Required Capabilities -** | Plan for "2½ Wars" |
| | a) Deter/Defeat Soviet/Chinese Attack on U.S. and its Allies |
| | b) Control "Lesser Included Cases" (Contingencies) |
| **Force Implications -** | Nuclear Forces:  Triad |
| | Robust/High Readiness |
| | Countervalue/Counterforce |
| | Land Forces:  Forward Based |
| | Heavy |
| | NATO Emphasis |
| | Maritime Forces:  Deterrence |
| | Sea Control |
| | Deep Strike |
| | Non-NATO Contingencies |
| | Air Forces:  Surveillance/Counterstrike of USSR |
| | Air Superiority |
| | AirLand Battle/Follow-on Echelons |

---

The 1992 NMS postulated a top-down force planning approach. "The uncertain world we face requires us to deal effectively with the unknown and unexpected, and we have done so with flexible options and adaptive plans. The forces then are derived from the strategy—the forces needed to execute the strategy. . ." The resulting force structure was called the "Base Force," subdivided into four "conceptual force packages:" strategic forces, Pacific forces, Atlantic forces, and contingency forces; and four "supporting capabilities:" space, transportation, research and development, and reconstitution.[35]

Further force planning implications of the 1992 NMS included the Army's development of a contingency force with expeditionary capabilities; the Air Force's development of composite expeditionary wings; and the

Naval Service's emphasis on littoral expeditionary warfare. This was more fully articulated by the Navy Department's white paper, . . . *From the Sea.* The post-Cold War transitional strategy is summarized in Figure 4.

---

**Figure 4**
**U.S. Transitional Strategy (1992 NMS)**

| | |
|---|---|
| **Policy** - | Regional Stability/Deter Regional Aggression |
| **Geographic Focus** - | Critical Regions |
| **Grand Strategy** - | Selective Engagement |
| **Military Strategy** | |
| **Descriptors** - | 1) Strategic Deterrence/Defense |
| | 2) Forward Presence (vice Forward Defense) |
| | 3) Crisis Response |
| | 4) Reconstitution |
| **Required Capabilities** - | 1) Project Power Against Regional Threats |
| | 2) Fight/Win Multiple Regional Crises |
| | 3) Joint Littoral Operations |
| **Force Implications** - | "Base Force" |
| | Nuclear Forces:     Reduced Force Structure Declining Priority Slower Modernization |
| | Land Forces:     Expeditionary Global Flexibility |
| | Maritime Forces:     Littoral Expeditionary Presence/Crisis Response |
| | Air and Space Forces:     Recon/Strike System Information Warfare Air Superiority |

---

The 1992 NMS drew a great deal of criticism. Most critics, the most influential of whom was then-Chairman of the House Armed Services Committee, Les Aspin, contended that it did not go far enough because it did not sufficiently break with the Cold War era.

Aspin offered an alternative, building-block approach, based on "comparable, generalized judgments" about the U.S. forces required to meet a series of threats defined in terms of recent operations such as DESERT STORM and JUST CAUSE. The building blocks were supported by a "foundation block," a generalized set of capabilities including strategic nuclear forces, research and development (R&D), overseas forces "not directly tied to regional contingencies but providing U.S. presence," and special operating forces (Table 1). From the capabilities necessary to meet each more demanding strategic requirement, he derived four force-structure options.[36]

**Table 1**

**Aspin's Building Blocks**

| A | B | C | D |
|---|---|---|---|
| | | | Option C plus: |
| | | Option B plus: | — A Second Comfort-sized Operations |
| | Option A Plus: | — Rotation Base for Long-Term Deployments | — Additional Lift |
| — Basic Desert Storm | — Additional Regional contingency/Korea | — Panama-sized Contingency | — More Robust Contingency Forces |
| — Provide Comfort-type Humanitarian or Evacuation Action | — Additional Lift Prepositioning | | |
| — Lift/Prepositioning | | | |

**Defense Foundation**

| | | |
|---|---|---|
| — Strategic Nuclear Forces | — Overseas Presence/ Residual Soviet Threat | — Training/Operating Tempo |
| — Defense Forces for U.S. Territory | — R&D/Force Modernization | — Speical Operations Forces |
| | | — Industrial Base |

Rep. Les Aspin, Chairman, House Armed Services Committee, February, 1992.

## A Military Strategy to Support "Engagement and Enlargement:" The Bottom-Up Review

The Clinton Administration developed a national security strategy that melded elements of selective engagement and cooperative security. These principles were reflected in its National Security Strategy (NSS) of "Engagement and Enlargement," and the National Military Strategy document derived therefrom.[37]

Prior to issuing either its national security strategy or military strategy, the Clinton Department of Defense conducted a "Bottom-Up Review" (BUR).[38] Despite the fact that the BUR incorporated many of Les Aspin's criticisms of the 1992 NMS, the strategic assumptions of the BUR had much in common with those of its predecessor and its associated Base Force. However, the BUR proposed to meet the same strategic requirements with a budget of $104 billion less over five years and 180,000 fewer personnel than would have been provided had the Base Force been funded through FY1999.[39]

Because of its relationship to the BUR, and the fact that it is derived from a national security strategy based in part on selective engagement, the 1995 NMS shared some characteristics with its predecessor. It was still a regional strategy designed to avoid a continental commitment. It maintained an emphasis on fighting and winning two MRCs. One of its required capabilities was power projection.

But since the 1995 NMS mirrored the NSS's emphasis on cooperative security and a multilateral approach to security,[40] it was not primarily a war-fighting strategy, in contrast to its predecessor. As descriptors, *peacetime engagement* and *deterrence and conflict prevention* were placed on a par with *fight to win*. There was much more discussion of the former descriptors than of war fighting (Figure 5). The strategy emphasized "operations other than war" (OOTW). This has had important force planning implications for the Services (Figure 6).

**Figure 5**
**Elements of a Military Strategy of**
**"Flexible and Selective Engagement"**

## Toward the Quadrennial Defense Review and Beyond

There has been no shortage of criticisms of the BUR and the 1995 NMS. According to its detractors, the focus on fighting two-nearly simultaneous MRCs was misplaced because of the low probability that such a situation would ever confront the U.S.; that even in the unlikely event that it became necessary to fight two MRCs, the BUR force would be inadequate to the task; and finally, that the defense budget was too small to support even this inadequate force. Thus, the BUR represented either a policy-strategy mismatch, a strategy-force mismatch, a budget-force mismatch, or some combination of the three.

Others contended that, given the current security environment, the force structure rationalized by the BUR was too large and too oriented toward war-fighting; also the concurrent increase in OOTW starved the force of the funds for modernization that would be necessary for dealing with possible "peer competitors" in the future. They argued that the prevailing "threat trough" made it possible to reduce force structure in order to "recapitalize" forces for the future.[41]

---

**Figure 6**
**"Flexible and Selective Engagement"**

| | |
|---|---|
| **Policy -** | Regional Stability/Regional Cooperation |
| **Geographic Focus -** | Critical Regions |
| **Grand Strategy -** | Cooperative Security/Selective Engagement |
| **Military Strategy -** | |
| **Descriptors -** | 1) Peacetime Engagement |
| | 2) Conflict Prevention |
| | 3) War Fighting |
| **Required Capabilities -** | 1) Project Power Against Regional Aggressors |
| | 2) Fight/Win Two Nearly Simultaneous MRCs |
| | 3) Conduct Multilateral/Unilateral "OOTW" |
| | 4) Maintain Overseas Presence |
| | 5) Conduct Joint Littoral Operations |

| **Force Implications -** | | |
|---|---|---|
| | Nuclear Forces: | Much Smaller |
| | | Delayed Modernization |
| | Conventional Forces: | (All Components) |
| | | Expeditionary |
| | | Maintain Forces for Power Projection |
| | | Prepare to carry out OOTW |

---

*Joint Vision 2010*, a document issued by the Chairman of the Joint Chiefs of Staff, General John M. Shalikashvili is one response to the concern that the U.S. has not paid enough attention to dealing with a potential peer compeitor. This document contends that as a result of advancing technology trends, future battle space will become more lethal. In this environment, information superiority will become critical, transforming the traditonal functions of maneuver, strike, protection, and logistics. "These transformations will be so powerful that they become, in effect, new operational concepts: dominant maneuver; precision engagement; full dimensional protection; and focused logistics." [42]

As mandated by the 104th Congress, DOD has now embarked on its third strategy and force structure review since the end of the Cold War, the "Quadrennial Defense Review" (QDR). Debate associated with the QDR reflects the interplay among three broad categories of proposals: those advanced by the traditionalists or strategic pluralists, those by the strategic monists, and those by the "technophiles."[43]

The traditionalists argue for balanced forces capable of meeting threats across the spectrum of conflict. They contend that the geographic position of the U.S. and its global interests require a variety of forces, strategies, and weapons capable of carrying out, joint, expeditionary operations, in conjunction with allies if possible, but alone if necessary. In this view, the force structure established by the QDR should not be substantially smaller or differently balanced than the BUR force.

The "strategic monists" argue that the U.S. should invest in a single, strategically decisive capability. Strategic monism can be observed in the writings of several well-known defense analysts,[44] and in the position taken by some in the U.S. Air Force that the U.S. is now a continental air power rather than primarily a sea power. The crux of the argument advanced by this version of strategic monism is that air power (and increasingly, space power) is not only the *necessary*, but also the *sufficient* cause of strategic success in conflict, both today and tomorrow. Since the "air campaign" can achieve decisive victory independently of other arms, it rather than the "joint campaign" should be emphasized.

Closely related to the strategic monists are the "technophiles" who contend that the "revolution in military affairs" (RMA) has so completely changed the nature of warfare that many of the old verities no longer hold true. The technophiles argue that the U.S. must do whatever is necessary to ensure its dominance in military technology even if it means accepting a substantially reduced force structure.[45]

Both the technophiles and the strategic monists reject the U.S. post-war tradition of strategic pluralism. The question is whether advances in sensors, information technology, and precision strike have made strategic pluralism obsolete.

## Conclusion

Military strategy is designed to secure national interests and to attain the objectives of national policy by the application of force or threat of force. Military strategy is dynamic, changing as the factors that influence it change. Strategic requirements have evolved considerably since the end of World War II and with them, the descriptors of military strategy.

Reviewing the evolution of military strategy over the past 50 years illuminates the interrelationship of ends, means, and the security environment. Potential mismatches between ends and means create risks. If the risks resulting from an ends-means mismatch cannot be managed, ends must be reevaluated and scaled back, means must be increased, or the strategy must be adjusted.

Strategy making and strategic planning are critical components of defense policy. Without a coherent, rational strategy to guide force planning, structural factors such as bureaucratic and organizational imperatives dominate the allocation of resources for defense, leading to a sub-optimal result.

---

## Notes

1. B.H. Liddell Hart, *Strategy* (New York: Praeger, 1967), p. 335.

2. Paul Kennedy, ed., *Grand Strategies in War and Peace* (New Haven: Yale University Press, 1991); Edward N. Luttwak, *Strategy: The Logic of War and Peace* (Cambridge: Harvard University Press, 1987).

3. Allan R. Millett and Peter Maslowski, *For the Common Defense: A Military History of the United States of America* (New York: The Free Press, 1984. Revised and expanded, 1994), p. xiii.

4. I am indebted to Dr. Robert S. Wood, Dean of the Naval War College's Center for Naval Warfare Studies, for this formulation.

5. Cf. Robert P. Haffa, Jr., *Rational Methods, Prudent Choices: Planning US Forces* (Washington, DC: National Defense University Press, 1988), p. 5.

6. Samuel Huntington, *The Common Defense: Strategic Programs in National Politics* (New York: Columbia University Press, 1961), pp. 3-4. Huntington's strategic category corresponds to Graham Allison's "rational decision model," in which "[g]overnments select the action that will maximize strategic goals and objectives." Graham T. Allison, "Conceptual Models and the Cuban Missile Crisis," *American Political Science Review*, Vol. LXIII, No. 3, September 1969, p. 694. Huntington's structural category shares many of the attributes of Allison's "organizational" model, which sees the actor in national decisions as "a constellation of loosely allied organizations..." Allison, p. 699.

7. Williamson Murray and Mark Grimsley, "On Strategy," in Murray *et al*, eds., *The Making of Strategy: Rulers, States, and War* (Cambridge: Cambridge University Press, 1994), p.1; Carl von Clausewitz, *On War*, translated and edited by Michael Howard and Peter Paret (Princeton: Princeton University Press, 1976), pp. 134-136.

8. Murray and Grimsley, pp. 7-20.

9. Andrew F. Krepinevich, Jr., *The Army and Vietnam* (Baltimore: The Johns Hopkins University Press, 1986), pp. 164-193.

10. *On War*, p. 128.

11. Luttwak, *Strategy*, pp. 91-112, and "The Operational Level of War," *International Security*, Vol. 5, No. 3, Winter 1980-81; Allan R. Millett, Williamson Murray, and Kenneth Watman, "The Effectiveness of Military Organizations," in Millett and Murray, eds., *Military Effectiveness* (Boston: Allen and Unwin, 1988), Vol. 1, pp. 3, 12-19.

12. Cf. Luttwak, *Strategy*, pp. 69-189.

13. Edward Mead Earle, ed., *Makers of Modern Strategy* (Princeton: Princeton University Press, 1943), p.viii.

14. Barry R. Posen and Andrew L. Ross, "Competing Visions for US Grand Strategy," *International Security*, Vol. 21, No. 3, Winter 1996/97, pp. 5-53.

15. Mackubin Thomas Owens, "Toward a Maritime Grand Strategy: Paradigm for a New Security Environment," *Strategic Review*, Vol. XXI, No. 2, Spring 1993. Cf. Colin S. Gray, *The Geopolitics of Super Power* (Lexington: The University Press of Kentucky, 1988).

16. Huntington, p. 3; Clausewitz, *On War*, pp. 131-132.

17. On strategic pluralism and strategic monism, see Samuel P. Huntington, *The Soldier and the State* (Cambridge: Harvard University Press, 1957), pp. 400, 418-427; Huntington, *The Common Defense*, p. 264; Gordon W. Keiser, *The US Marine Corps and Defense Unification, 1944-47: The Politics of Survival* (Washington, DC: National Defense University Press, 1982), pp. 121-122; and Mackubin Thomas Owens, "The Hollow Promise of JCS Reform," *International Security*, Vol. 10, No. 3, Winter 1985/86, pp. 106-108.

18. Samuel Huntington, "National Policy and the Transoceanic Navy," United States Naval Institute *Proceedings*, Vol. 80, No. 5, May, 1954, p. 483.

19. Henry C. Bartlett and G. Paul Holman, Jr., "Strategy as a Guide to Force Planning," *Naval War College Review*, Vol. XLI, No. 4, Sequence 324, Autumn 1988, p. 15.

20. Sir Halford J. Mackinder, "The Round World and the Winning of the Peace," in *Democratic Ideals and Reality* (New York: Norton, 1962 [First Published, 1944]); Nicholas J. Spykman, *The Geography of the Peace* (New York: Harcourt and Brace, 1944).

21. For a discussion of the continuing relevance of geopolitics, see Colin Gray, *The Geopolitics of the Nuclear Era: Heartlands, Rimlands, and the Technological Revolution* (New York: Crane Russak, 1977), and "The Continued Primacy of Geography," *Orbis*, Vol. 40, No. 2, Spring 1996, pp. 247-259.

22. Sir Michael Howard, *The Continental Commitment: The Dilemma of British Defense Policy in the Era of the Two World Wars*, (London: The Ashfield Press, 1989 [First published 1972]). Cf. Owens, "Toward a Maritime Grand Strategy."

23. The best overviews of U.S. Cold War strategy are, among others, John Lewis Gaddis, *Strategies of Containment: A Critical Appraisal of Postwar American National Security Policy* (Oxford: Oxford University Press, 1982); Huntington, *The Common Defense*; and Millett and Maslowski, pp. 494-646. On the development of U.S. strategy from the end of World War II through the New Look, see Warner R. Schilling, Paul Y. Hammond, and Glenn H. Snyder, *Strategy, Politics, and Defense Budgets* (New York: Columbia University Press, 1962). On the genesis of Flexible Response, see William W. Kaufmann, *The McNamara Strategy* (New York: Harper & Row, 1964).

24. Millett and Maslowski, pp. 500-507.

25. Thomas H. Etzold and John Lewis Gaddis, eds., *Containment: Documents on American Policy and Strategy, 1945-1950* (New York: Columbia university Press, 1978), pp. 421-442.

26. Gaddis, p. 149.

27. Millett and Maslowski, pp. 531-552.

28. Millett and Maslowski, p. 553.

29. Millett and Maslowski, pp. 553-563.

30. Haffa, pp. 41-45; William Kaufmann, *Planning Conventional Forces 1950-1980* (Washington DC: The Brookings Institution, 1982), p. 8.

31. For the various attempts to create a CONUS-based, conventional and general purpose force structure, see Paul Y. Hammond, "NSC-68: Prologue to Rearmament," in Schilling *et al*, *Strategy, Politics, and Defense Budgets*; Kaufmann, *Planning Conventional Forces 1950-1980*; and Robert P. Haffa Jr., *The Half War: Planning US Rapid Deployment Forces to Meet a Limited Contingency, 1960-1983* (Boulder and London: Westview Press, 1984); Congressional Budget Office, *Rapid Deployment Forces: Policy and Budgetary Implications* (Washington DC: Government Printing Office, February 1983).

32. Colin L. Powell, *National Military Strategy of the United States* (Washington DC: Government Printing Office, January 1992).

33. *Ibid.*, pp. 1, 7.

34. *Ibid.*, pp. 6-10.

35. *Ibid.*, pp. 19-25.

36. Les Aspin, "An Approach to Sizing American Conventional Forces for the Post-Soviet Era: Four Illustrative Options," A Briefing to the House Armed Services Committee, February 25, 1992. For a critique of Aspin's approach in general, see James Winnefeld, *The Post-Cold War Force-Sizing Debate: Metaphors and Disconnects* (Santa Monica: RAND, 1992). For a critique of his approach applied to naval forces, see Mackubin T. Owens, "Why Planning Naval Forces is Different," *Defense Analysis*, April 1993; and Ronald O'Rourke, "Naval Forward Deployments and the Size of the Navy," Congressional Research Service, November 13, 1992.

37. Bill Clinton, *A National Security Strategy of Engagement and Enlargement* (Washington DC: Government Printing Office, July 1994); Gen. John Shalikashvili, *National Military Strategy of the United States of America: A Strategy of Flexible and Selective Engagement* (Washington DC: Government Printing Office, February 1995).

38. Les Aspin, Secretary of Defense, *Report of the Bottom-Up Review*, October 1993.

39. *Ibid.*, p. 107. Some critics contended that the reductions were in fact much greater: Cf. Senator John McCain, "Preserving International Stability in the Post-Cold War Era," *Strategic Review*, Vol. XXI, No. 3, Summer 1993 pp. 7-19.

40. *Engagement and Enlargement*, pp. 7, 13.

41. Critiques of the BUR include Larry Di Rita *et al*, *Thumbs Down to the Bottom-Up Review*, Heritage Backgrounder No. 957, September 24, 1993; Di Rita, *Clinton's Bankrupt National Security Strategy*, Heritage Backgrounder No. 1000, September 27, 1994; Mackubin Thomas Owens, "A Crash Course in Strategic Reality," *Strategic Review*, Vol. XXI, No. 4, Fall 1993; Dov Zakheim and Jeffrey M. Ranney, "Matching Defense Strategies to Resources: Challenges for the Clinton Administration," *International Security*, Vol. 18, No. 1, Summer 1993, pp. 51-78; Andrew F. Krepinevich, *The Bottom-Up Review: An Assessment* (Washington DC: Defense Budget Project, February 1994); Krepinevich, "The Clinton Defense Program: Assessing the Bottom-Up Review," *Strategic Review*, Vol. XXII, No. 2, Spring 1994; William T. Pendley, "Mortgaging the Future to the Present in Defense Policy: A Commentary on the Bottom-Up Review," *Strategic Review*, Vol. XXII, No. 2, Spring 1994; Don Snider, Daniel Goure, and Stephen A. Cambone, *Defense in the Late 1990s: Avoiding the Train Wreck* (Washington, DC: Center for Strategic and International Studies, 1995); Krepinevich, "The Clinton Defense Strategy," in Williamson Murray, ed., *Brassey's Mershon American Defense Annual, 1995-1996* (Washington, DC: Brassey's, 1995); and Owens, "Strategy and Resources: Trends in the US Defense Budget," in Murray, ed. Ibid.

42. Chairman of the Joint Chiefs of Staff, *Joint Vision 2010*, 1996. p. 19.

43. Owens, "How to Think About the Quadrennial Defense Review," *Strategic Review*, Vol. XXV, No. 1, Winter 1997.

44. Edward N. Luttwak, "Toward Post-Heroic Warfare," *Foreign Affairs,* May/June 1995; and Robert P. Haffa, "A 'New Look' at the Bottom-Up Review," *Strategic Review*, Vol. XXIV, No. 1, Winter 1996.

45. Some believe that *Joint Vision 2010* represents this approach. Cf. also Admiral William A. Owens, "The Emerging System of Systems," U.S. Naval Institute *Proceedings*, May 1995, pp. 35-39; Joseph S.Nye, Jr., and William A. Owens, "America's Information Edge," and Eliot A. Cohen, "A Revolution in Warfare," *Foreign Affairs*, Vol. 75, No. 2, March/April 1996. For critiques of the technophiles, see Mackubin Thomas Owens, "Planning for Future Conflict: Strategy vs. 'Fads,'" *Strategic Review*, Vol. XXIV, No. 3, Summer 1996; and the remarkable essay by Stephen Biddle, "Victory Misunderstood: What the Gulf War Tells Us About the Future of Conflict," *International Security*, Vol. 21, No. 2, Fall 1996.

* The author is grateful to his colleagues at the Naval War College, Henry C. Bartlett, G. Paul Holman, Jr. and Timothy Somes for their helpful comments on earlier drafts of this chapter.

# Chapter 29
# The Spectrum of Conflict:
# What Can It Do for Force Planners?

Henry C. Bartlett, G. Paul Holman, Jr. and Timothy E. Somes

*Henry C. Bartlett, G. Paul Holman and Timothy E. Somes explore the spectrum of conflict as a graphic tool to assist strategists and force planners. They first provide examples of this concept from various historic perspectives. They then discuss the use of the spectrum of conflict as a planning aid in setting priorities for the allocation of scarce resources. Stress is placed on the importance of analyzing an appropriate range of military missions, operations, and scenarios in terms of their relative destructiveness and likelihood for the time period under consideration. Finally they discuss the importance of applying this tool for several projected time periods. Throughout they emphasize that this approach can assist force planners in ensuring appropriate investment across the spectrum of conflict for each of several decades into the future. What are the strengths and pitfalls of the authors' concepts? How would you balance requirements across the spectrum of conflict, among different planning environments, with competing capabilities, and including multiple time horizons?*

P lanning the future size and composition of the United States military force structure is an arduous task. It consists of appraising the security needs of a nation, establishing military requirements, and selecting military forces within resource constraints. One graphic tool that can assist force planners is the "spectrum of conflict." This essay examines it in both theory and practice, proceeding step by step as the authors do in the classroom, examining its strengths and weaknesses, and showing how it can bolster security assessments. First providing

Henry C. Bartlett and Timothy E. Somes are professors of Strategy and Force Planning, National Security Decision Making Department of the Naval War College. G. Paul Holman, Jr. formerly a member of this department, is now a professor at the George C. Marshall Center, Garmisch, Germany. They teach and conduct research on global security issues, national military strategy and future military force requirements. Earlier versions of this article appeared in the *Naval War College Review,* Winter 1996, pp. 119-129; and in Strategy and Force Planning Faculty, eds., *Strategy and Force Planning*, Newport, RI: Naval War College Press, 1995, pp. 495-504.

An earlier version of this article appeared in the *Naval War College Review,* Vol. XLIX, No. 1, Winter 1996, pp. 119-129.

historical examples from Navy, Army and Joint Staff perspectives, the authors then explain the use of the spectrum of conflict from peace through nuclear war. An appropriate range of military missions, operations, and scenarios are analyzed for their relative destructiveness and likelihood of occurrence during the time period under consideration. What are the strengths and weaknesses of this concept? How would potential military tasks be prioritized for the coming decades? What degrees of destructiveness and likelihood can be associated with each one?

Figure 1

## The Spectrum of Conflict

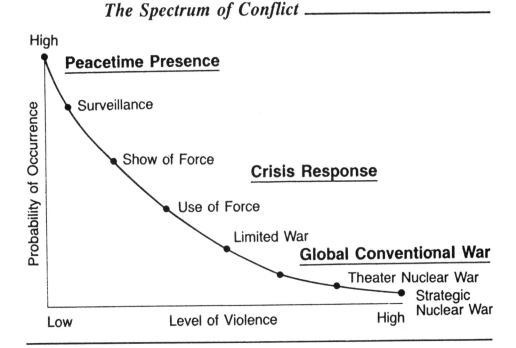

Comparing probabilities of occurrence and destructiveness of military operations is a natural part of the planning process, and when approached graphically, the resulting diagram is usually termed a spectrum of conflict. Although it has been used for objective analysis as well as programmatic advocacy, its significance and implications need to be fully explored. Instinctively, military strategists, force planners, and commanders think of a spectrum of operations, missions, and scenarios. Peacetime presence and nuclear war constitute two possible extremes. Between them lie many different forms of military activity—some more probable than others. For example, humanitarian assistance is much more likely to take place than two nearly simultaneous major regional conflicts. The operations more apt to occur are usually less destructive in scope and duration than conflicts at the other end of the spectrum.

## Historical Examples of the Spectrum of Conflict

The U.S. Navy used the spectrum of conflict (figure 1) to make a point in its famous *Maritime Strategy*, issued in 1986 during the waning years of the Cold War. It was intended to draw attention to the importance of the "lower levels of violence," particularly peacetime presence, "where navies are most often the key actors," even while the specter of war between NATO and the Soviet Union loomed large.[1]

The U.S. Army has long used the spectrum of conflict to explain its missions and operations. *The United States Army Posture Statement FY 90/91* depicted the spectrum as in figure 2.

**Figure 2**

## SPECTRUM OF CONFLICT

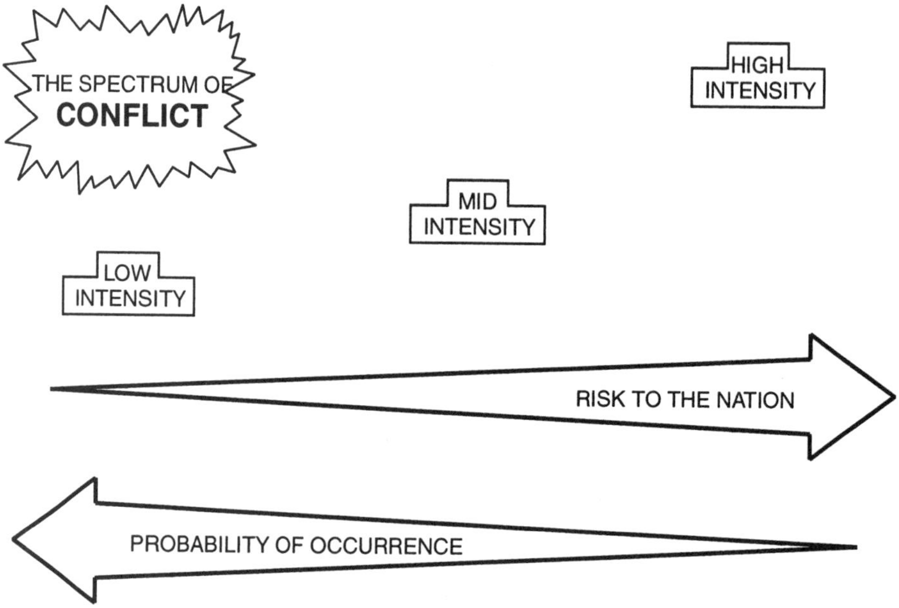

THE SPECTRUM OF **CONFLICT**

HIGH INTENSITY

MID INTENSITY

LOW INTENSITY

RISK TO THE NATION

PROBABILITY OF OCCURRENCE

Perhaps the most noteworthy aspect of this rendition is the way it aggregates Army operations into three major planning cases: low intensity, mid-intensity, and high intensity. It makes another distinction in weighing the "probability of occurrence" against "risk to the nation"—an inherently debatable factor—rather than referring to the more measurable attribute of destructiveness. The document carefully explains the importance of these concepts: "While the likelihood of U.S. involvement in a high intensity conflict is low, such a war would pose a high risk to the nation. Low intensity conflicts pose a smaller risk, but are much more likely to occur. Our Army must be prepared to fight and win across this entire spectrum of conflict."[2]

In 1993 General Gordon R. Sullivan, Chief of Staff of the Army, presented a more complicated version of the spectrum of conflict that reflected certain major debates over the Army's future.

> By 1991 the Army's capstone doctrinal manual, Field Manual 100-1, introduced the term 'peacetime engagement'. . . . [It] reintroduced the concept of 'hostilities short of war' to describe an increasingly important segment of the continuum of potential Army missions and employment. Many wanted to describe these missions as 'non-traditional,' but others recognized that the Army's historic role of serving the nation included a rich heritage of operations other than war.[3]

Sullivan's spectrum used two diverging axes to portray the likelihood and level of hostilities, with a smooth curve connecting the extreme cases of peacetime engagement and global nuclear war (figure 3). This depiction conveyed

**Figure 3**

LEVEL AND LIKELIHOOD OF HOSTILITIES

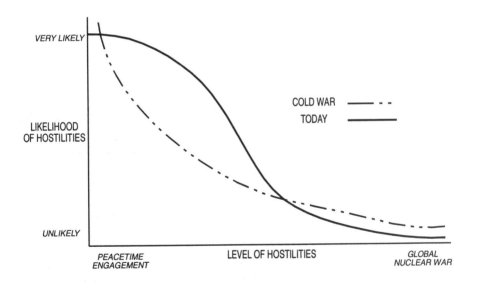

several assessments about the Army's future. In the aftermath of the Cold War, global nuclear war was deemed far less probable but still not out of the question. The term "peacetime engagement" was a notable change, but most important was the graphic judgment that more operations might take place at the lowest level of hostilities than during the Cold War.

A more complex version of the concept appeared in the 1991 *Joint Military Net Assessment (JMNA)* (figure 4). General Colin Powell, then Chairman of the

Joint Chiefs of Staff, explored implications for the entire force, rather than a single service, at a turning point in America's military history: "This assessment represents a first report of the transition from planning and programming principally for global war with the Soviet Union to planning and programming for the regional situations we expect to face in the 1990s."[4]

**Figure 4**

PROBABILITY OF OCCURRENCE

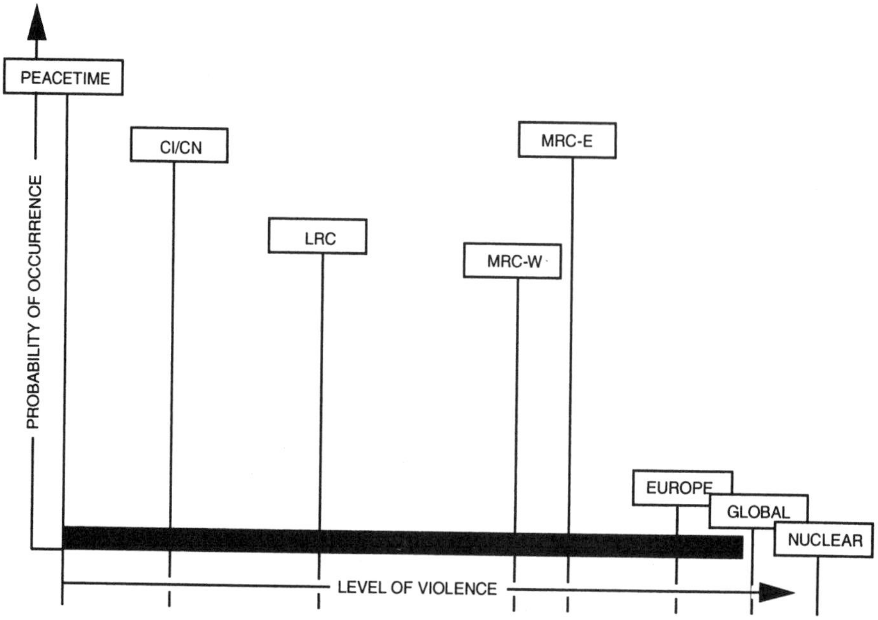

In this case, the spectrum of conflict is used to assess specific conflict scenarios, several of which are generic: peacetime engagement; counterinsurgency and counternarcotics (CI/CN); lesser regional contingencies (LRC); global; and nuclear. Others are more specific in terms of location: Major Regional Contingency-West (MRC-W for Korea); Major Regional Contingency-East (MRC-E for Southwest Asia); and war escalating from a European crisis.[5]

This depiction was built around the axes of "probability of occurrence" and "level of violence." Readers must assume that the point of origin is low (or perhaps zero) for the two axes, while the extremes are higher. The scenarios are labeled and plotted in reference to the two axes. Significantly, then, war in the view of the drafters is more likely to occur in Southwest Asia than in Korea, while war in Europe is doubtful. To convey another useful theme, the *JMNA* also portrays "consequences of failure" on a second vertical axis. Unfortunately, however, it does not provide the rationale for the consequences for failure (see figure 5). There are some scenarios, like nuclear war, that are intuitively obvious, but readers must decide for themselves why the consequences of failure would be so high for the peacetime scenario and so low for the CI/CN case.[6]

**Figure 5**
CONSEQUENCES OF FAILURE

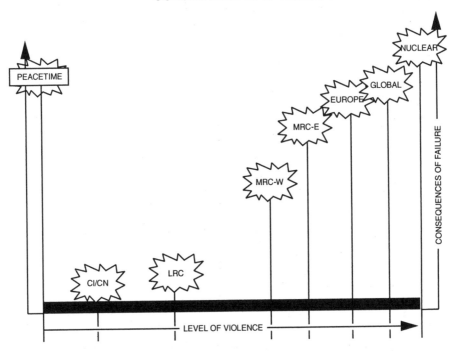

The *JMNA* did arrive at some important conclusions. Above all, "the spectrum of conflict, peace through nuclear war, has not changed; it continues to provide a method to overlay various scenarios."[7] The most destructive forms of conflict may have declined, but the consequences of failure would still be grave. Thus the spectrum of conflict served as a concise way to convey complex judgments about the post-Cold War world.

## Using the Spectrum of Conflict

As teachers of force planning, the authors begin by specifying the time period under consideration. An inevitable debate involves how far into the future we must look. The factors that drive this time horizon are both international and domestic. How soon, for example, could any country become a military peer competitor of the United States? At home, what are the lead times for procuring major weapon systems to replace aging force structure?

*Operations and Missions*. The second step is to list specific military tasks that dominate planning. An example appears in the *National Military Strategy of the*

*United States 1995*, which presents a summary graphic entitled "Achieving National Military Objectives." Three broad categories are identified: those that involve "peacetime engagement," those that include "deterrence and conflict prevention" and those that can be categorized as "fighting and winning" conflicts. Among the tasks in the first two categories are such operations as peacekeeping, counterdrug and counterterrorism , arms control, sanctions enforcement, peace enforcement and evacuation of noncombatants. The third category includes wartime power projection, countering weapons of mass destruction, force generation and winning the peace. Of significance are the twin foundation tasks of overseas presence and power projection.[8]

***Destructiveness (scope and duration).*** The next step is to plot relevant operations and missions along a horizontal axis, from the least to the most destructive. This defines the spectrum of conflict.[9] As the previous examples demonstrate, several other variables as well have been used to perform this task. Among them are "risk to the nation," "intensity of conflict," "level of hostilities," and "level of violence." All suffer from vagueness and subjectivity. A case in point is that most Americans probably believe that ethnic warfare in the Balkans poses little or no "risk to the nation"; yet many historians would disagree, reminding us that World War I began in Sarajevo and warning that American interests could well be jeopardized by another European conflict—especially one involving Greece, Russia, and Turkey. By the same token, mine warfare may present a low "level of violence" to strategic planners, but not to the commanding officer of an aircraft carrier.

The term *destructiveness* lends itself to measurement and tends to reduce misunderstanding. Force planners should estimate the destructiveness of any mission, operation, or scenario (for the time period under consideration) in the context of their country's national interests. They must take full account of the many assumptions and uncertainties that may skew their hypotheses. Specifically, we suggest that they evaluate hypothetical destructiveness in terms of its *scope* and *duration*. At the least, *scope* would involve such factors as lethality of weapons involved, number of forces engaged, and geographic expanse of the war. *Duration* is the estimated length of time a given conflict will last. Certain operational environments tend to lengthen wars, often belying the initial predictions of unwary strategists—jungles, mountains, and cities, for example, create sanctuaries for guerrillas while constraining conventional forces. Similarly, such large expanses as the Russian steppes permit the trading of space for time. In general, the duration of the conflict depends upon the intensity of historical animosity between the opponents, national will to bear the costs of war, physical geography, and rules of engagement—especially restrictive rules of engagement and attempts to control escalation, which have lengthened conflicts from Vietnam through Bosnia.

*Potential destructiveness* deserves more attention than it has received, especially during an era of ethnic conflict and collapsing states. Civil wars possess a deceptively different kind of destructiveness (combining both scope and duration) than do state-to-state conflicts, which may be why American forces have fared better against such governmental opponents as Grenada, Panama, and Iraq than against the guerrillas of Vietnam, the clans of Lebanon, and the warlords of Somalia.

Figure 6 is an illustrative spectrum of conflict for missions, operations, and scenarios. It includes not only the tasks specified in the National Military Strategy, but also a listing of more specific weapons of mass destruction cases (nuclear, chemical, and biological).

**Figure 6**

SPECTRUM OF MILITARY OPERATIONS,
MISSIONS & SCENARIOS
(1995 - 2005)

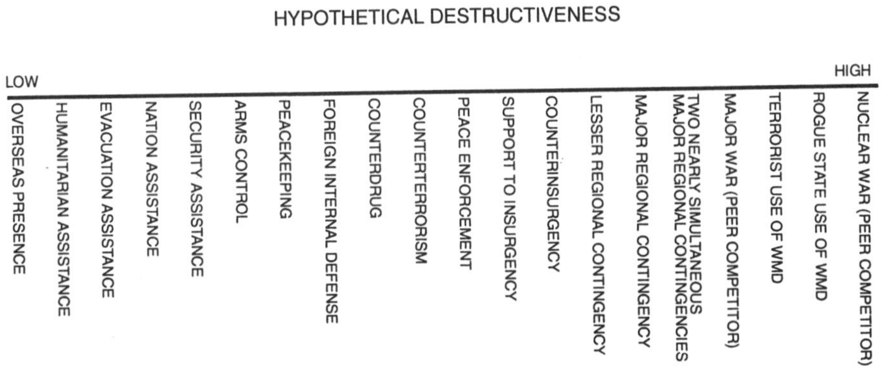

HYPOTHETICAL DESTRUCTIVENESS

LOW ... HIGH

OVERSEAS PRESENCE · HUMANITARIAN ASSISTANCE · EVACUATION ASSISTANCE · NATION ASSISTANCE · SECURITY ASSISTANCE · ARMS CONTROL · PEACEKEEPING · FOREIGN INTERNAL DEFENSE · COUNTERDRUG · COUNTERTERRORISM · PEACE ENFORCEMENT · SUPPORT TO INSURGENCY · COUNTERINSURGENCY · LESSER REGIONAL CONTINGENCY · MAJOR REGIONAL CONTINGENCY · TWO NEARLY SIMULTANEOUS MAJOR REGIONAL CONTINGENCIES · MAJOR WAR (PEER COMPETITOR) · TERRORIST USE OF WMD · ROGUE STATE USE OF WMD · NUCLEAR WAR (PEER COMPETITOR)

The unprecedented proliferation over the past several years of weapons-grade uranium and plutonium has increased the possibility of a nuclear incident, either by terrorists or by rogue states. Similarly, the rapid diffusion of chemical and biological capabilities has increased the chance of attack by other weapons of mass destruction. Such scenarios could be quite destructive, especially if they posit attacks on civilian population centers.

***Likelihood.*** The next step is to plot the estimated likelihood of occurrence for all these operations, missions, and scenarios against a vertical axis. Individual analysts and separate services or departments may disagree vociferously about the likelihood of different contingencies, just as they would over their relative destructiveness.[10] However, the usefulness of the spectrum of conflict lies in accentuating and debating both variables.

***Draw the Curve.*** Some analysts find it useful to connect the plotted points with a curve or line as shown in figures 1 and 3. However, there are pitfalls here. Drawing one smooth curve may oversimplify complex issues and conceal controversial judgments. As an example, "terrorist use of weapons of mass destruction" can range across the entire spectrum in terms of destructiveness and likelihood of occurrence. It could entail chemical attack against an isolated military unit, nuclear targeting of a civilian airport, or even contaminating New York City with a fearsome disease, such as anthrax. Consequently a scatter diagram plotting the points without a curve may be preferable, especially for analyzing a large number of operations, missions, and scenarios. If a curve is drawn, its shape is significant. At the least, it can have historical importance, showing differences in judgment from decade to decade. The smooth, asymptotic curve often plotted during the Cold War (figures 1 and 3) has changed considerably: not only will the military be conducting more operations at the lowest level of destructiveness, but the chance of operations other than war in the coming decade is almost a certainty. Moreover, there may be some important "spikes" upward or downward. Two MRCs, for example, seem much less likely than one, while the isolated use of weapons of mass destruction appears far more likely than global nuclear war.

***Focus on Major Planning Cases.*** The next step is to divide the spectrum into a few large categories. These broader sets of operations, missions, and scenarios are the major defense planning cases. Here again, experts may disagree on how to label them. There are those who think in terms of the intensity of conflict (low, medium, and high), while some stress technology (especially nuclear versus conventional conflict), and yet others use political circumstances as discriminators (such as war versus operations short of war).

As an example, the 1991 *JMNA* explains some important changes in how the Department of Defense thinks about the major planning cases. This document portrays these changes graphically (figure 7) and explains them with care:

> Previously, conventional force requirements were generated by focusing attention toward the right end of the spectrum, where the threat was large and the consequence of failure was great (depicted by the lightly shaded area on the graph). Consequently, our conventional force structure was large, heavy, and robust. However, more recently our focus has shifted to the left (depicted by the darker shaded area). . . . Today, the probability of occurrence for conventional conflicts at the right end of the spectrum is low, and warning time has so greatly increased, that these conflicts are no longer the central point of focus or the principal driver of requirements of forces. We find now, however, that the focus of attention and risk is the range of conflict scenarios where the probability of occurrence is greater and the consequences of failure are still high.[11]

Figure 7
PROBABILITY OF OCCURRENCE (IN BLOCKS)
AND CONSEQUENCES OF FAILURE (IN BURSTS)

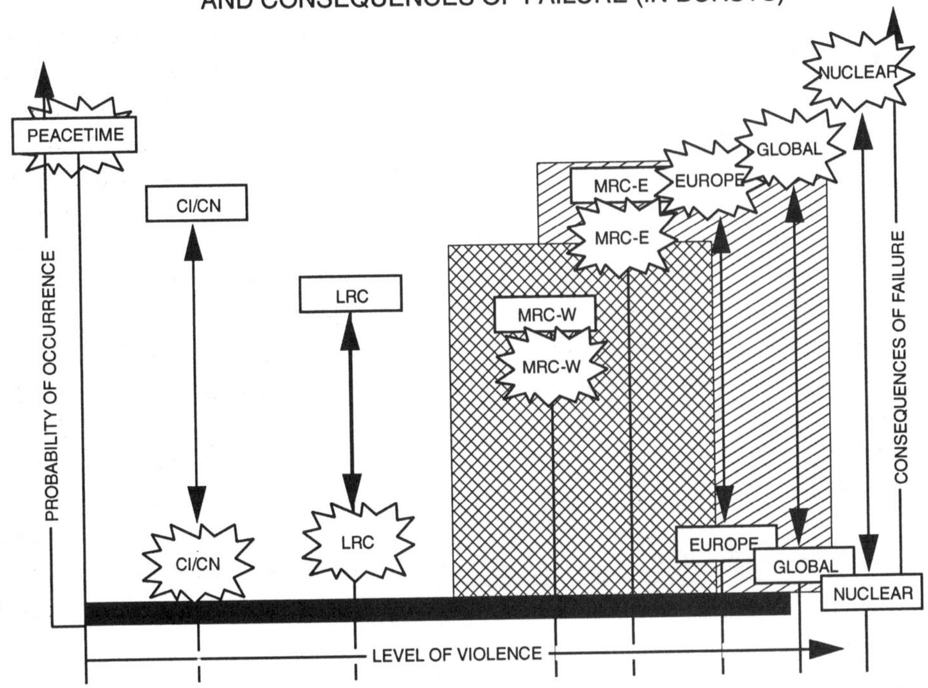

Recent events suggest the wisdom of dividing the spectrum into several major planning cases, such as "Operations Other Than War," "War," and "Weapons of Mass Destruction." Such a division can help strategists and force planners first to identify the common features among future missions, operations, and scenarios and then to set priorities for the allocation of scarce resources.[12] We do not mean that one case would take all available resources, or even most of them, nor do we mean that it would necessarily take the next available dollar, but rather that it should be considered first, using the criteria of destructiveness and likelihood as outlined above.

However, it will be no easy task to set such priorities. Some will argue that War (such as MRC-E and MRC-W) deserves the highest priority when preparing for the coming decade, while others would assign the greatest importance to Operations Other Than War. A few might even favor Weapons of Mass Destruction, particularly when rogue states are involved. In a period of constrained resources the ability to set priorities will continue to be crucial, and the spectrum of conflict can be a valuable aid.

## The Spectrum of Conflict and Multiple Planning Spaces

It is clear that the Cold War period was a more straight forward planning environment than the one force planners face in the late 1990s and early 21st century. Cold War planning focused on the basic NATO versus Soviet scenario where the implicit assumption was that the future would be an extension of the present. Threat based force requirements dominated, centered on the core components of nuclear, land, air and sea, with supporting elements such as strategic lift and space. Today the complexity of trying to anticipate a reasonable set of future conflict scenarios is exacerbated by a growing realization that a spectrum of conflict which adequately represents the planning challenges for one time period may not properly represent the problems strategists should anticipate in subsequent decades. Numerous radically different scenario proposals stridently demand that planners focus their attention on one sector of the spectrum vice another.

Figure 8

## SPECTRUM OF CAPABILITIES, ENVIRONMENTS AND TIME

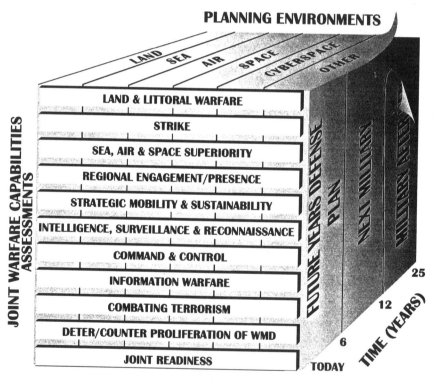

Among the efforts to deal with this vastly more complex security environment is the special attention being paid to capabilities based planning across a spectrum of mission tasks. The Joint Requirements Oversight Council (JROC) has created a set of Joint Warfighting Capabilities Assessment (JWCA) categories that encompass broad requirements as diverse as "land and littoral warfare," "sea, air, and space superiority," "information warfare,"

and "combating terrorism."[13] In a classic matrix approach, organizations within the U.S. military with specific expertise are planning across this spectrum of capabilities. This approach can be graphically represented as two sides of a cube as in figure 8. The front face illustrates the spectrum of capabilities encompassed by the JWCAs.[14] Unfolding the top face portrays a range of warfighting environments. Planners working from the perspective of one environment must look down through all the tasks, as well as across the other environments, to ensure future force choices adequately cover the spectrum of capabilities and the requirement for joint operations in all the environments.

Furthermore, it is now crucial to expand the time horizons planners consider. At least three seem appropriate to fully anticipate the complex array of future military force needs. As the third face of figure 8 unfolds, the near term planning horizon can be seen to be characterized by the six years encompassed in the U.S. Department of Defense's Future Years Defense Plan (FYDP), long the Pentagon's major planning horizon. However, most force structure investments take at least twice this period to enter the field. With the complex and changing nature of the security environment, planners are more consciously devoting attention to the "next military," that of twelve to fifteen years hence. Finally, there has been a ground swell of interest in a third major planning timeframe looking out a generation to what Professor Paul Bracken terms "The Military After Next." A particular emphasis is on the rise of a nation-state large and aggressive enough to constitute a "peer competitor."[15] The three time dimensions conveyed on the third face of the cube can be thought of as distinct planning "spaces" in which planners consider relationships among environments, capabilities and the spectrum of conflict. Furthermore, they must consider the relationship of one planning space to another in an effort to be adequately prepared for the future.

Multiple conceptual "visions" are a specific outgrowth of this widening appreciation for the need to plan across multiple time dimensions. Figure 9 suggests one method of combining several time horizons and the spectrum of conflict. The counter-intuitive reversal of the time periods looking back from 2025 is a deliberate effort to encourage planners to avoid thinking about the future as a slight modification of the present. Each time horizon may emphasize a different portion of the spectrum of conflict.

As an example, today's emphasis is on both operations other than war and regional contingencies (with one contigency being viewed as more likely than two). However, by 2010 the emphasis may be on operations other than war as the specter of regional conflicts lessens. On the other hand, 2025 may see the rise of a peer competitor intent on aggressively confronting U.S. core interests. This could heighten the possibility of a major war with renewed emphasis on weapons of mass destruction more reminiscent of the Cold War. As indicated by the publication of military documents such as *Joint Vision 2010* and the USAF Scientific Advisory Board's *New World Vistas* (an attempt to "see" at least three decades into the future), there is no substitute for vision when trying to think about the spectrum of use of military force in the murky future.[16]

**Figure 9**

# The Spectrum of Conflict Over Time

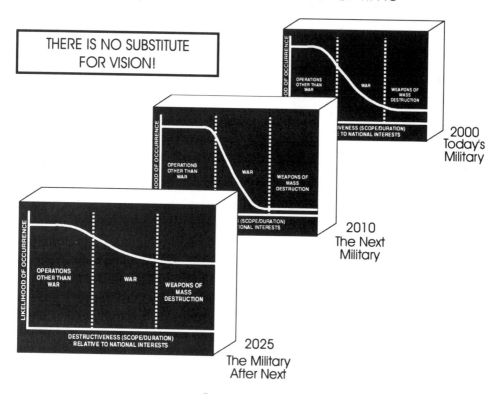

**Conclusion**

This essay began by showing U.S. Navy, U.S. Army and then Joint Staff versions of the "spectrum of conflict." Different variables were noted and different purposes were compared. The authors then suggested several steps for constructing a "spectrum of conflict." It has many important attributes that we believe can assist both strategists and force planners by: encouraging a comprehensive review of the operations, missions, and scenarios that a country's armed forces may encounter in the time period under analysis; examining them for completeness, relevance, and plausibility; stimulating debate over likelihood and destructiveness; facilitating aggregation into major planning cases; and setting priorities for the allocation of scarce resources.

This concept, however, does have some drawbacks. The term "spectrum of conflict" is itself a bit narrow and misleading. Perhaps "spectrum of military capabilities, missions, operations, and scenarios" would be more descriptive, albeit cumbersome. We continue to employ the term "spectrum of conflict" because of its wide acceptance. Unavoidably, the spectrum of conflict accentuates the utility of military power, as opposed to economic and political instruments for achieving national goals. It also reduces complex realities and relationships to stark, unqualified judgments, at the constant risk of oversimplification.

Perhaps most dangerously, the spectrum of conflict relies upon expert opinion about the future, in spite of the fact that such judgments have all too often been wrong. Political upheavals, for instance the collapse of the Soviet Union, altered Cold War formulations of the spectrum of conflict. By the same logic, technological progress (e.g., the mass production of nonlethal weapons) may reorient today's thinking about the probability and destructiveness of future operations, capabilities, missions and scenarios.

Such defects notwithstanding, national planners will surely continue to think in terms of a spectrum of conflict that extends from peace through nuclear war. They will also find it an excellent way to explain their decisions to the American people. Under the conditions the authors use in this essay, a major national goal will surely be to reduce the likelihood and the destructiveness of future conflict, while ensuring that should conflict arise, the nation can prevail. Achieving this goal will continue to require military capabilities across the spectrum of conflict for each new generation.

---

## Notes

1. Admiral James D. Watkins, U.S. Navy, "The Maritime Strategy," U.S. Naval Institute *Proceedings*, Special Edition, January 1986. It is of interest to note that in the late 1990s the U.S. Navy argues that forward (peacetime) presence is the most demanding in terms of defining the overall size of the Navy's force structure. This was not the case in 1986 when the demands of global conventional war (lower probability of occurrence) drove the rationale for a 600 ship navy. See in particular: The Honorable John H. Dalton, Secretary of the Navy, Admiral J. M. Boorda, USN, Chief of Naval Operations, and General Carl E. Mundy, Jr., USMC, Commandant of the Marine Corps, *Forward...From The Sea*, Department of the Navy, Washington, DC: (undated), p. 1; and Rear Admiral Philip A. Dur, U.S. Navy, "Presence: Forward, Ready, Engaged," in U.S. Naval Institute *Proceedings*, June 1994, pp. 41-44.

2. The Honorable John O. Marsh, Jr., and General Carl E. Vuono, *The United States Army Posture Statement FY 90/91*, Washington, DC: Department of the Army, 1990, p. 22.

3. Gordon R. Sullivan, *America's Army: Into the Twenty-first Century*, National Security Paper no. 14, Cambridge, Mass.: Institute for Foreign Policy Analysis in association with The Fletcher School of Law and Diplomacy, Tufts University, 1993, p. 6.

4. Chairman of the Joint Chiefs of Staff, *1991 Joint Military Net Assessment* [hereafter *JMNA*], Washington, DC: Department of Defense, March, 1991, pp. 1-5.

5. For the definition of MRC-E as standing for Southwest Asia (SWA) and MRC-W for Korea, see *JMNA*, pp. 9-2, 9-8.

6. For example, if one assumes that the most important military mission in peacetime is to deter nuclear war, then the consequences of failure would be high indeed. The low consequences of failure for CI/CN seem harder to justify. Vietnam was a case of counterinsurgency, but the outcome in Southeast Asia had devastating consequences for the country. Many authorities would also contend that the consequences of failure in the counternarcotics scenario are extremely serious.

7. *JMNA*, pp. 1-7.

8. John M. Shalikashvili, Chairman of the Joint Chiefs of Staff, *National Military Strategy of the United States 1995*, Washington, DC: U.S. Government Printing Office, 1995, p. 4.

9. According to the *Oxford American Dictionary*, New York: Avon Books, 1980, p. 656, a spectrum is "an entire range of related qualities or ideas."

10. We prefer the term "likelihood" to "probability" or "risk" (which connote a higher degree of statistical rigor than we believe to be achievable in national security matters).

11. *JMNA*, pp. 1-8.

12. During the Cold War, for example, the likelihood of nuclear war was judged by most experts to be low. However, the destructiveness of such a scenario demanded that strategists and force planners treat it as their highest priority. They needed confidence in the ability of the U.S. to deter the worst-case scenario—a surprise Soviet counterforce attack. Lacking that confidence, the nuclear planning case demanded additional resources to bolster deterrence. This case has declined sharply in priority over the past few years, and others have risen.

13. Refer to Office of the Chairman Joint Chiefs of Staff memorandum "Charter of the Joint Requirements Oversight Council," 7 February 1995; and Chairman of the Joint Chiefs of Staff Instruction 3137.01, "The Joint Warfighting Capabilities Assessment Process," 22 February 1996.

14. Joint Staff, *CINC Liason Office Newsletter*, Washington, DC: Joint Staff, November 1996 edition, p.3.

15. Paul Bracken, "The Military After Next," *The Washington Quarterly*, Autumn 1993, pp. 157-174.

16. John M. Shalikashvili, *Joint Vision 2010*, Chairman of the Joint Chiefs of Staff, Washington, DC: (undated, issued in 1996); and USAF Scientific Advisory Board, *New World Vistas: Air and Space Power for the 21st Century*, Washington, DC: 15 December 1995.

# Chapter 30

\* \* \*

# Toward Post-Heroic
# Warfare

Edward N. Luttwak

*A major problem for the United States is how to achieve its security interests in light of the American public's obvious distaste for casualties. Edward Luttwak's solution is a "new concept of war" that he labels "post-heroic warfare:" a return to a "pre-Napoleonic" style of military operations, epitomized by the careful, cautious strategy and tactics of the Roman Empire. "As far back as two millennia, the professional, salaried, pensioned, and career-minded citizen soldiers of the Roman legions routinely had to fight against warriors eager to die gloriously for tribe or religion." The preferred approach of the Romans was the siege. The modern version of the siege, according to Luttwak, would be the blackade or embargo, backed up by "patiently sustained air campaigns with sorties flown day after day, week after week." Is Luttwak correct about the "obsolescence" of total war? What are the strategic implications of Luttwak's call for a return to the eighteenth-century style of warfare so scathingly denounced by Clausewitz? What are the force planning implications? What are the advantages and disadvanatages of Luttwak's "new concept of war"?*

## The Obsolescence of Total War

Only one thing could possibly link the protracted warfare in the former Yugoslavia, the destruction of Grozny, and the recent border fighting between Ecuador and Peru. Once more, as in centuries past, wars are rather easily started and then fought without perceptible restraint. When belligerents see that no particular penalty is paid for opening fire first or using any and all means of warfare—even the wholesale destruction of cities by aerial or artillery bombardment—self-imposed restraints on the use of force are everywhere

Edward N. Luttwak is a Senior Fellow at the Center for Strategic and International Studies.

Reprinted by permission of Foreign Affairs, Vol. 74, No. 3, May/June 1995, pp. 109-122.

eroded. The border fighting between Ecuador and Peru had only just begun when tactical bombing was employed, as if it were no more consequential than one more infantry skirmish.

This new season of war is upon us as one more consequence of the passing of the Cold War. The latter induced or intensified a number of hot wars in the contested zones between each camp as each superpower provided allies and clients with weapons and expertise far beyond their own capacities. Thus the Middle East especially became something of a preferred battleground by proxy.

At the same time, however, the fear that escalation could eventually reach the nuclear level inhibited any direct combat whatsoever by the superpowers themselves in Europe or anywhere else, even on the smallest scale. Above all, the Cold War suppressed many potential shooting wars in a great part of the world because neither superpower would tolerate them within its own camp. Both, moreover, were notably vigilant in controlling the form and geographic scope of the wars they fought in Korea, Vietnam, and Afghanistan, and also the wars their allies and clients fought, again for fear of an escalation to direct clash and nuclear war.

The concept of war governing those encounters has long been so strongly entrenched that it is not even commonly recognized as particular, but rather is seen as the only possible concept for now and always. It envisages only wars fought for great national purposes that can evoke public fervor, by armed forces that represent the aroused nation rather than merely a body of professionals going about their business. Yet that is only one concept of war, as even casual readers of military history well know. Far from an eternal verity, the concept is a rather modern innovation, associated with a particular phase of fairly recent history. Before the French Revolution, most wars were fought for much less than imperative purposes that rarely evoked popular enthusiasm, with prudent strategies and tactics to conserve expensive professional forces. While no great purposes at hand could motivate the entire nation in war, there is much justification for some eighteenth-century warfare of our own, with modest purposes and casualty avoidance as the controlling norm.

## The New Culture of War

The Cold War culture of intense but controlled tension, which required disciplined constraints on the use of force, seems to have influenced even nonaligned nations such as India and Pakistan. To use force at all during the Cold War came to be seen almost everywhere as a very grave decision indeed, to be made only after the fullest deliberation, usually after all other means had been exhausted. Further decisions to escalate to regular infantry combat rather than deniable guerrilla operations, armored warfare and artillery support rather than infantry, aerial bombing rather than ground warfare were deemed worthy of distinct political decisions at the highest levels instead of being left, as in the past, to the discretion of military commanders. The latter complained, sometimes loudly, but they obeyed, thus affirming the new culture of restraint.

Restraint did not prevent 138 wars between 1945 and 1989, by the most expansive count, which killed as many as 23 million people. But in the previous 44 years, which included two world wars, many more were killed. In the absence of any restraint arising from strategic prudence, internal repression killed many more people over the years 1945-89 than all 138 wars combined.

Now that the Cold War no longer suppresses hot wars, the entire culture of disciplined restraint in the use of force is in dissolution. Except for Iraq's wars, the consequences have chiefly been manifest within the territories that had been Soviet, as well as Yugoslav. The protracted warfare, catastrophic destruction, and profuse atrocities of eastern Moldavia, the three Caucasian republics, parts of Central Asia, and lately Chechnya, Croatia, and Bosnia have certainly horrified and moved many Americans. But this diverse violence derives from the same postimperial devolution of epic, unprecedented scale or from purely localized sources. Hence one could still hope that the new readiness to start unrestrained wars would at least be geographically confined, if only within an area already vast.

The fighting between Ecuador and Peru, the mounting recklessness manifest between Greece and Turkey, and also perhaps Pakistan's increasing boldness over Kashmir suggest the more sinister possibility that a new, much less restrained culture of war is emerging and spreading far and wide. Nothing is now countering a number of perverse precedents. Aggression and willful escalation alike remain unpunished; victors remain in possession of their gains; the defeated are abandoned to their own devices. It was not so during the Cold War, when most antagonists had a superpower patron with its own reasons to control them, victors had their gains whittled down by superpower compacts, and the defeated were often assisted by whichever superpower was not aligned with the victor.

One may wonder what precedents the Ecuador-Peru fighting will set. Without knowing its map-changing results, one cannot assert that other dormant Latin American border disputes will be revived. But it would be most surprising if those disputes were not now undergoing some reappraisal, if only by politicians interested in defining ultranationalist stances for themselves. Moreover, some deceleration, if not an outright reversal, is certain to occur in the downward trend in military spending by many Latin American countries. That most positive development of recent years, which yielded important political and economic benefits, is now endangered. The Ecuador-Peru war could turn out far more costly for Latin America as a whole and indirectly for the United States too than its limited dimensions might suggest.

## The Meaning of "War"

Can the United States counter perverse precedents and the new culture of wars easily started and fought without restraint? Beyond diplomacy is the controversial remedy of armed intervention, with or without a multilateral framework, with or without foreign auxiliaries. But aside from its suitability in any particular setting (in some it is unimaginable), military force collides with the general refusal of the American public to sanction interventions in place after place without end.

That political given must be accepted, but it is contingent upon the cost in U.S. casualties of a particular concept of war and particular methods of intervention—the only concepts and methods the U.S. military establishment now offers. If these could be changed drastically to minimize the exposure of U.S. military personnel to the risks of combat, the response of public opinion to proposed military interventions should also change. The United States might then do more to dissuade aggression and escalation.

Much is implicit in American political discourse, the official manuals of the U.S. military services, and the popular understanding of the very word "war" when the United States is a protagonist. Quite naturally, the various Weinberger-Powell-Cheney doctrines, which set out to define several preconditions for any decision to send U.S. military forces into combat, are based squarely, tacitly, and without discussion on the same concept of war. While the three sets of preconditions differ in detail, they all require vital, fervor-arousing U.S. national interests to be clearly threatened, and that the United States employ forces powerful enough to win not only decisively but also quickly, before the fervor abates and the nation is no longer aroused.

War fought for grand purposes is yet another product of the French and American revolutions. With some chronological laxity, however, I here label it "Napoleonic" because grand purposes often imply the decisive employment of large forces in large operations, in true Napoleonic fashion. The concept originally emerged in reaction to the typical warfare of eighteenth-century Europe, ridiculed by Napoleon and systematically criticized by Carl von Clausewitz.

While fully recognizing that the cautious methods of the prior age of warfare were congruent with their times and the habitually modest aims of what were called "cabinet wars," Clausewitz was scathing in his descriptions. Demonstrative maneuvers meant to induce enemy withdrawals without firing a shot were readily called off if serious fighting ensued. Superior forces avoided battle if there was a risk of heavy casualties even in victory. Prolonged sieges were preferred to determined assaults and circumspect pursuits to all-out exploitation in the wake of battle victories. At the strategic level, elaborately prepared offensives had unambiguous objectives, promising campaigns were interrupted by early retreats into winter quarters merely to avoid further losses, and offensive performance was routinely sacrificed to the overriding priority of avoiding casualties and conserving forces for another day, with much effort expended to build and garrison linear defenses and fortifications.

Napoleon triumphed over such cautious military practices with bold strategic offensives powered by the mass and momentum of rapidly concentrated forces, and that was the kind of warfare that Clausewitz advocated. Envisaging only wars fought for great national purposes, and with the unification of Germany in mind, Clausewitz exposed the logical error of half-hearted, risk-avoiding methods likely in the long run to be more costly. To be sure, Clausewitz concurrently derived the strongest argument for strategic prudence from his insistence on the primacy of political considerations, but that did not affect his demonstration of the economy of tactical and operational boldness, a formula for efficacy that can easily become detached from its justifying context of correspondingly ambitious goals.

Complete with profound insights into the eternal mechanics and psychology of war, the teachings of Clausewitz remain unsurpassed. Along with parallel examples of the merits of risk-taking drawn from the successes of the great captains of history (a highly selective list that omits prudent victors, favoring Patton and Hannibal, for example, over Bradley or Fabius Cunctator), they pervade the professional discourse of U.S. service academies and war colleges and can easily be recognized in current field manuals and official doctrinal statements. Many such documents are prefaced by restatements of the principles of "war" (concentration, mass, momentum, etc.) that are actually in large part the Clausewitzian principles of Napoleonic war.

Both were fully appropriate to the circumstances of the two world wars and also of the Cold War as far as the planning of nonnuclear operations was concerned. Neither fits present circumstances, domestic or international. There are no threatening great powers on the current world scene, only a handful of quiescent rogue states, and many lesser wars and internal disorders that cannot arouse the nation, for none of them directly threatens the United States or its compelling interests. The preconditions of Napoleonic war-making, or for that matter of military interventions as specified in the Weinberger-Powell-Cheney doctrines, are therefore absent.

Yet its moral economy is damaged as the United States remains the attentive yet passive witness of aggressions replete with atrocities on the largest scale. Moreover, there is no doubt that the diffusion of the new culture of wars easily started and quickly escalated is damaging U.S. material interests. Commercial opportunities, not all of them small, are being lost every day wherever guns are firing, and many more could be lost in the future.

Given the performance of certain modern weapons, if military planning is appropriately modified to fully exploit their technical potential, it may be possible to emulate the casualty-avoiding methods of eighteenth-century warfare and thus conduct armed yet virtually bloodless interventions. To be sure, U.S. aims would have to be correspondingly modest and remain so, resisting all temptations to achieve more than partial, circumscribed, and often slow results as firmly as any good eighteenth-century general.

At present, by contrast, there is a profound contradiction between the prevailing military mentality, formed by the Napoleonic concept of war with its Clausewitzian adjuncts, and current exigencies. The Somalia intervention came to a sudden end after the bloody failure of a daring helicopter raid in true commando style—a normal occupational hazard of high-risk, high-payoff commando operations. But given the context at hand—a highly discretionary intervention in a country of the most marginal significance for American interests—any high-risk methods at all were completely inappropriate in principle. Nor was what happened the result of an error of judgment, still less of malfeasance. In accordance with the prevailing mentality, the senior military planners allowed a role in the Somalia undertaking to U.S. Special Operations Command, which naturally mounted its own kind of operations, which in turn inherently entailed the risk of casualties.

The casualties of war were not a decisive consideration, within reasonable limits, so long as the Napoleonic concept still applied. War fought for great purposes implies a willingness to accept casualties even in large numbers. Moreover, a certain tolerance for casualties was congruent with the demography of preindustrial and early industrial societies, whereby families had many children and losing some to disease was entirely normal. The loss of a youngster in combat, however tragic, was therefore fundamentally less unacceptable than for today's families, with their one, two, or at most three children. Each child is expected to survive into adulthood and embodies a great part of the family's emotional economy. Even in the past, the United States never had the supply of expendable soldiers that was the fuel of discretionary great power wars fought for colonial aggrandizement or yet more recondite motives. Still less is there such a supply of expendable lives at present, when all other low-birthrate, postindustrial societies refuse to sanction the casualties of any avoidable combat.

How, therefore, can armed forces, staffed by professional, salaried, pensioned, and career-minded military personnel who belong to a nation intolerant of casualties, cope with aggressors inflamed by nationalism or religious fanaticism? Yet to avoid combat and do nothing allows not only aggressive small powers such as Serbia, but even mere armed bands such as those of Somalia, to rampage or impose their victories at will.

Some view the dilemma as unprecedented and irresolvable. Actually it is neither. If we free ourselves from the Napoleonic concept to recognize the historical normality of eighteenth-century warfare, we can find many situations in which the same dilemma arose and was successfully overcome. As far back as two millennia, the professional, salaried, pensioned, and career-minded citizen-soldiers of the Roman legions routinely had to fight against warriors eager to die gloriously for tribe or religion. Already then, their superiors were far from indifferent to the casualties of combat, if only because trained troops were very costly and citizen manpower was very scarce. Augustus, famously, went to his grave still bitterly mourning the three legions Varus lost in Germany years before.

## The Roman Siege

The Romans relied on several remedies to minimize their troop losses while overcoming enemies from Britain to Mesopotamia. In the first place, it was their standard practice to avoid open-field combat, especially spontaneous engagements, if at all possible, even if their forces were clearly superior. Rather than face the uncertainties of time and place, which could result in an equally unpredictable casualty toll, the Romans routinely allowed their enemies to withdraw to positions of their own choosing, even if well fortified or naturally strong. Having thus turned a fluid situation into a far more controllable set-piece encounter, the Romans would gather forces and assemble equipment and supplies to commence systematic siege operations. Even then their first priority was not to breach enemy defenses but rather to build fairly elaborate fortifications to protect their besieging units, to minimize whatever casualties enemy sallies could inflict. Overall, the siege was the medium in which the Romans could best exploit both their technological superiority in siege craft and their logistic advantage, which normally enabled them patiently to outlast the food supplies of the besieged. A purposeful, calculated patience was a signal military virtue.

Trade embargoes and armed blockades, the modern equivalents of the Roman siege, are not tactical but strategic. But so long as the Napoleonic concept prevails, it is impossible to exploit their full capacity to achieve warlike results without the casualties of war. For the presumption of an aroused nation greatly discounts any results not rapidly achieved, while the effects of embargoes and blockades are cumulative rather than immediate and may be long delayed. Moreover, the Napoleonic concept only recognizes decisive results, while the effects of embargoes and blockades are usually partial rather than complete, even if very much worth having. For example, since 1990 those means have controlled the military resurgence of Saddam Hussein's Iraq. Its armed forces have not been allowed to recover from the equipment losses of 1991 and have instead been steadily weakened as imported weapons destroyed or worn out are not replaced. True, only direct oil exports by tanker or pipeline have been denied, but the lesser quantities Iraq has been able to send out overland have not been enough for rearmament. Nor does the imminent possibility that the United Nations will lift its prohibition on Iraqi oil exports alter the effective containment, without a more active use of force, of a serious threat. Incidentally (in this case), the decisive result that only an all-out war could have achieved would have been even more temporary and indecisive, for the complete destruction of Iraq's military strength would immediately have made containing Iran's threat that much harder.

Likewise, in the former Yugoslavia, amid the utter failure of every other diplomatic or military initiative of the United Nations, European Community, or NATO, only the denial of Serbian and Montenegrin imports and exports—notoriously incomplete though it has been—has had positive effects. In addition to the certain if unmeasurable impact on Serbian and Montenegrin war capabilities, the trade embargo has moderated the conduct of Belgrade's most immoderate leadership. The embargo dissuaded at least the more blatant forms of combat and logistic support for the Serb militias of Bosnia-Herzegovina, Slavonia, and Krajina and also induced whatever slight propensity has been shown to negotiate, if only in the hope of securing the lifting of the arms embargo. The prospect of perpetuating the embargo has almost certainly helped to avert an invasion of Macedonia, still now precariously vulnerable to Serb expansion aided and abetted by Greek malevolence.

Even by the most optimistic reckoning, those results are sadly inadequate. Nevertheless, without any cost in blood or treasure, the trade embargo has achieved much more than the expensive and ineffectual U.N. armed intervention or the tens of thousands of yet more expensive NATO air patrols over Bosnia, flown by heavily armed fighter-bombers that hardly ever fight or bomb, even as the carnage below them continues.

Against those two instances of at least partial success, in the entire record of blockades and embargoes, many outright failures can be cited. But quite a few of them only came to be considered failures because of the premise that results must be rapid to be at all worthwhile. It would take a new (or rather renewed) concept of war that esteems a calculated, purposeful patience to allow the full exploitation of embargoes and blockades, or of any slow and cumulative form of combat. As it is, the Napoleonic and Clausewitzian emphasis on sheer tempo and momentum unconsciously induces an almost compulsive sense of urgency, even when there are no truly imperative reasons to act quickly. British Field Marshal Bernard Law Montgomery was not the first nor the last general to achieve success where others had failed simply by insisting on thorough preparations where others had hurriedly improvised.

A compulsive sense of urgency was much in evidence during the first weeks of the 1991 Persian Gulf War, when the systematic air attack of strategic targets in Iraq was viewed with unconcealed impatience by many of the subordinate military commanders on the scene. News accounts duly conveyed their skepticism about the value of strategic bombing and their corresponding eagerness to see the air attack diverted to Iraqi army units and other tactical targets to open the way for a ground offensive as soon as possible.

The most senior officers resisted this upward pressure on the chain of command, which reflected no objective imperatives but only deeply rooted instinct as well as more obvious bureaucratic urges. But the pressure could not be completely denied. Well before strategic bombing was virtually stopped to provide air support for the ground campaign, which began on the 39th day of the war, many of the aircraft best suited to continue the methodical destruction of Iraqi research, development, production, and storage facilities for conventional and nonconventional weapons were instead diverted to attack some 4,000 individual armored vehicles.

The diversion of the air effort from strategic to tactical targets was to have unhappy consequences. In the aftermath, many important nuclear, biological, and chemical warfare installations remained undestroyed. For in spite of the great abundance of U.S. combat aircraft, less than 200 were fully equipped to attack strategic targets with precision weapons. That number, as it turned out, was simply too small to exhaust in less than 39 days a long list of targets, which included command and control, electrical supply, telecommunication, air defense, and oil refining and storage facilities, as well as air and naval bases, rail and road bridges, and any number of supply depots.

The same compulsive urgency almost certainly played some role in shaping the decision to launch the ground offensive on the 39th day of the war instead of, say, the 49th. By the former date the air campaign had thoroughly hollowed out Iraq's military strength, not least by cutting off most supplies to frontline units. Hence it cannot be argued that the decision to start the ground offensive sooner rather than later caused any more U.S. and allied casualties than the incidentals of war would in any case have claimed, the total number being so very small. But had the air campaign been prolonged just ten more days, 2,000 more sorties could have been flown against strategic targets. The novel instrument of precision air attack on a strategic scale, so slow in its methodical sequence but so effective in its cumulative results, so costly to acquire but so exceedingly economical in U.S. lives, was simply not allowed enough time to realize its full potential.

The central importance attributed in the immediate aftermath of the war to the swiftly victorious ground offensive was also suggestive of the dominant influence of the Napoleonic concept on civilian opinion. Though little more than a mopping-up operation, it resonated with the prevailing mentality much more than the air campaign because it was both rapidly executed and visibly decisive.

## Patient Air Power

The key professional argument advanced by the most senior U.S. military chiefs to reject all proposals to employ U.S. offensive air power in Bosnia rested on the implicit assumption that only rapid results are of value. After first noting that anything resembling area bombing would inevitably kill many civilians, the chiefs argued that the potential targets were simply too elusive, or too easily camouflaged in the rugged Bosnian terrain, to allow effective precision attacks. They took it for granted that any air operation would have to be swiftly concluded, or even amount to no more than a one-time attack. Any one precision air strike certainly can easily fail because the assigned targets are concealed by bad weather, are no longer where last spotted, or are successfully camouflaged. There is no doubt that weapons such as the 120-millimeter mortars much used by Serb militias to bombard Sarajevo can be quickly moved and readily camouflaged; even much more elaborate howitzers and field guns can be elusive targets.

But this argument utterly obscured the drastic difference between a one-time strike, or any brief operation for that matter, and a patiently sustained air campaign with sorties flown day after day, week after week. If one sorties fails because of dense clouds, the next one, or the one after that, will have clear visibility. If one sortie misses a howitzer just moved under cover, the next might spot another actually firing. If one sortie is called off because the target is too close to civilians, another can proceed to completion. What was the great hurry to finish an air operation quickly? The fighting in Bosnia continues even now, years after the use of U.S. air power was originally rejected on the grounds that nothing much could be achieved in a few days.

But of course the other presumption of the Napoleonic concept of war—that only decisive results are worth having—was even more consequential. As the most senior U.S. military chiefs correctly pointed out, air strikes alone could not end the war in the former Yugoslavia, nor save the Bosnian state from its enemies, nor safeguard civilians from rape, murder, or forcible deportation. Therefore, it was argued by implication, air power alone was useless. Actually it would be much worse than that because the Serb militias would immediately retaliate against U.N. troops, thereby causing the withdrawal of U.N. contingents from Bosnia, which might in turn force the United States to send its own troops.

Given the dubious assumption that U.N. troops were in fact usefully protecting vulnerable civilians, and the prior assessment that air attacks alone would be useless, the conclusion was inevitable. True, air attacks alone could not possibly end the war nor save Bosnia. But a sustained air campaign could most certainly have reduced the use of artillery against cities, a particularly devastating form of warfare. That would have sufficed to ameliorate a tragic situation and demonstrate the active concern of the United States—much less than a total remedy, but much more than nothing.

## Casualty-Free Warfare

A further aspect of Roman military practice is relevant for current acquisition policies as well as tactical doctrines. It is enough to recall images of legionary troops to see how far offensive performance was deliberately sacrificed to reduce casualties. The large rectangular shield, sturdy metal helmet, full breastplate, shoulder guard, and foot grieves were so heavy that they greatly restricted agility. Legionnaires were extremely well protected but could hardly chase enemies who ran away, nor even pursue them for long if they merely retreated at a quick pace. Moreover, to offset the great weight of armor, only a short stabbing sword was issued. The Romans evidently thought it much more important to minimize their own casualties than to maximize those of the enemy.

Much better materials than iron and leather are available today, but it is symptomatic of an entirely different order of priorities that till now very little research and development funding has been allocated to advanced body armor. In fact the best such items now available have been privately developed for sale to law enforcement agencies.

The modern equivalent of Roman fortifications is not to build walls or forts with modern techniques, but rather to emulate the underlying Roman priorities. That applies to weapons as much as tactics. Most notably, current cost-effectiveness criteria do not yet reflect the current sensitivity to casualties. In setting overall budget priorities, alternative force categories—ground, maritime, and air—are still evaluated by cost and combat performance, without treating casualty exposure as a coequal consideration. Yet the risk of suffering casualties is routinely the decisive constraint, while the exposure to casualties for different kinds of forces varies quite drastically, from the minimum of offensive air power to the maximum of army and marine infantry. Also revealing is the entire debate on stealth aircraft, which are specifically designed to evade radar and infrared detection. When judged very expensive, stealth planes are implicitly compared to non-stealth aircraft of equivalent range and payload, not always including the escorts the latter also require, which increase greatly the number of fliers at risk. Missing from such calculations is any measure of the overall foreign policy value of acquiring a means of casualty-free warfare by unescorted bomber, a weapon of circumscribed application but global reach. Casualty avoidance is not yet valued at current market prices.

Present circumstances call for even more than a new concept of war, but for a new mentality that would inject unheroic realism into military endeavor precisely to overcome excessive timidity in employing military means. A new post-Napoleonic and post-Clausewitzian concept of war would require not only a patient disposition, but also a modest one, so as to admit the desirability of partial results when doing more would be too costly in U.S. lives, and doing nothing is too damaging to world order and U.S. self-respect.

# Chapter 31

**\* \* \***

# Cavalry to Computer:
# The Pattern of Military Revolutions

Andrew F. Krepinevich

*Andrew Krepinevich states that military revolutions comprise four elements: technological change, systems development, operational innovation, and organizational adaption. He concludes, based on his examination of ten generally accepted examples of military revolutions since the fourteenth century, that technological advances typically underpin a military revolution, but alone do not constitute the revolution. His study of this subject suggests several other lessons about military revolutions: they are increasingly short-lived; asymmetrical strategic cultures produce different patterns of military innovation among nations; revolutions in warfare do not necessarily need the crucible of war to occur; not all, or even most militaries, recognize when a military revolution is taking place; and technologies that underpin these revolutions often first appear outside the military sector. Did the 1991 Gulf War herald a new revolution in military affairs as some have stated? Or as Krepinevich and others have suggested, are nations facing a revolution in military affairs whose nature, impact, and timing are not yet evident? If organizational change is an essential component of these revolutions will the U.S. military services inhibit, rather than foster, such modifications to traditional modes of operation? Such questions are increasing the level of interest, investment - and debate - about a potentially vital issue.*

Over the next several decades, the world is destined to experience a revolution in the character of warfare. Indeed, the way in which the United States and its allies won a quick and overwhelming victory in the Gulf War suggests to many that we are already in the early stages of such a military revolution. But if so, there is much more to come.

As it progresses, this revolution will have profound consequences for global and regional military balances, and thus for U.S. defense planning. In the past,

Andrew F. Krepinevich is director of the Center for Strategic and Budgetary Assessments and adjunct professor of strategic studies at Johns Hopkins SAIS.

military revolutions have induced major changes in both the nature of the peacetime competition between states and their military organizations, as well as in the ways wars are deterred, fought, and resolved. By changing radically the nature of the military competition in peace and war, military revolutions have changed the "rules of the game." In so doing, they have often dramatically devalued formerly dominant elements of military power, including weaponry, weapons platforms, and doctrines. Military organizations that did not adapt in a rapidly changing, highly competitive environment have declined, often quite quickly.

What is a military revolution? It is what occurs when the application of new technologies into a significant number of military systems combines with innovative operational concepts and organizational adaptation in a way that fundamentally alters the character and conduct of conflict. It does so by producing a dramatic increase—often an order of magnitude or greater—in the combat potential and military effectiveness of armed forces.

Military revolutions comprise four elements: technological change, systems development, operational innovation, and organizational adaptation. Each of these elements is in itself a necessary, but not a sufficient, condition for realizing the large gains in military effectiveness that characterize military revolutions. In particular, while advances in technology typically underwrite a military revolution, they alone do not constitute the revolution. The phenomenon is much broader in scope and consequence than technological innovation, however dramatic.

The transition from the Cold War period of warfare to a new military era that is now anticipated may take several decades—or it may arrive within the next ten or fifteen years. There is no common transition period from one military regime to another: the naval transition from wood and sail to the all big-gun dreadnoughts with their steel hulls and turbine engines took roughly half a century; the emergence of nuclear weapons, ballistic missile delivery systems, and associated doctrine and organizational structures took roughly fifteen years. The rate of transition is typically a function not only of the four elements noted above, but of the level of competition among the international system's major players, and the strategies the competitors choose to pursue in exploiting the potential of the emerging military revolution.

It may be argued that with recent transition periods of ten to twenty years, we are discussing a continuous military evolution rather than a revolution. But what is revolutionary is not the speed with which the entire shift from one military regime to another occurs, but rather *the recognition, over some relatively brief period, that the character of conflict has changed dramatically, requiring equally dramatic—if not radical—changes in military doctrine and organizations.* Just as water changes to ice only when the falling temperature reaches 32 degrees Fahrenheit, at some critical point the cumulative effects of technological advances and military innovation will invalidate former conceptual frameworks and demand a fundamental change in the accepted definitions and measurement of military effectiveness. When this occurs, military organizations will either move to adapt rapidly or find themselves at a severe competitive disadvantage.

## Ten Revolutions

There appear to have been as many as ten military revolutions since the fourteenth century. The Hundred Years' War (1337-1453) spawned two of them. The first was the so-called *Infantry Revolution*, which saw infantry displacing the dominant role of heavy cavalry on the battlefield.[1] During the period leading up to this military revolution, infantry typically employed tight formations of pole-arms and crossbowmen to protect the cavalry while it formed up for a charge. During the first half of the fourteenth century, however, the infantry—in the form of Swiss pikemen and English archers—emerged as a combat arm fully capable of winning battles, as was demonstrated at the battles of Laupen (1339) and Crecy (1346).[2] Following these engagements, major cavalry actions on the field of battle became increasingly rare.

Clifford Rogers cites several factors as responsible for the Infantry Revolution. One key factor was the development of the six-foot yew longbow, which gave archers a much enhanced ability to penetrate the armor of cavalrymen. It also gave archers both missile and range superiority over their adversaries. England, which developed a pool of yeoman archers over decades of warfare against the Scots and Welsh, established a significant competitive advantage over the formerly dominant army, that of the French, which failed to exploit the revolution until late in the fifteenth century.

But it was not the longbow alone that fueled the revolution. Once the ability of infantrymen to win battles was clearly established, tactical innovations followed. The English developed a tactical system based on integrating archers with dismounted men-at-arms. Interestingly, the dominance of infantry was given an additional boost by the fact that archers were far less expensive to equip and train than men-at-arms. Thus, Rogers points out, the tiny kingdom of Flanders, which was relatively quick in exploiting the revolution, was able to muster a larger army at Courtrai (1302) than the entire kingdom of France. Finally, the Infantry Revolution marked a sharp increase in casualties on the battlefield. Whereas formerly it had been important to capture knights for the purpose of realizing a ransom, common infantrymen neither held that value, nor did they share knightly notions of chivalry. Battles thus became more sanguinary affairs.

The Infantry Revolution was succeeded by the *Artillery Revolution*, which dramatically altered war in the latter period of the Hundred Years' War. Although Roger Bacon's recipe for gunpowder dates back to 1267, cannons only began to appear on the European battlefield in significant numbers some sixty years later. Even then, almost a full century passed before artillery began to effect a military revolution. During this period besieged cities typically surrendered due to a lack of supplies. In the 1420s, however, a major increase occurred in the number of besieged cities surrendering as a consequence of the besiegers' artillery fire fatally degrading the cities' defenses. In the span of a few decades, gunpowder artillery displaced the centuries-old dominance of the defense in siege warfare.

Several technological improvements underwrote the Artillery Revolution. One was the lengthening of gun barrels, which permitted substantial increases in accuracy and muzzle velocity, translating into an increase in range and destructive force (and also the rate of fire). Metallurgical breakthroughs reduced the cost of iron employed in fabricating gun barrels, reducing the overall cost of cannons by about a third. Finally, the "corning" of gunpowder made artillery more powerful and cheaper to use.[3] As one Italian observer noted, artillery could now "do in a few hours what...used to take days."[4] Unlike the Infantry Revolution, the Artillery Revolution was expensive to exploit. As early as 1442 the French government was spending over twice as much on its artillery arm as on more "traditional" military equipment.[5]

A kind of snowball effect developed. The richer states could exploit the Artillery Revolution to subdue their weaker neighbors (or internal powerful regional nobles), which in turn increased the resources available to exploit their advantage further. This phenomenon was a significant factor in the growth of centralized authority in France and Spain. Along with the changes in technologies that spawned the great improvements in artillery and changes in siege warfare, new military organizational elements, such as artillery siege trains, were formed to cement the revolution. Once this occurred, defenders could no longer rely on castles for protection. This led to further changes in military organizations and operations, as the defenders now had to abandon their fortified castles and garrison units and move the contest into the field. And, as Francesco Guicciardini wrote, "Whenever the open country was lost, the state was lost with it."

Military revolutions were not limited to land. The *Revolution of Sail and Shot* saw the character of conflict at sea change dramatically, as the great navies of the Western world moved from oar-driven galleys to sailing ships that could exploit the Artillery Revolution by mounting large guns. Galleys, being oar-driven, had to be relatively light, and, unlike ships propelled by sail, could not mount the heavy cannon that could shatter a ship's timbers, thus sinking enemy ships rather than merely discouraging boarding parties. Indeed, prior to the late fourteenth century, ship design had not improved significantly for two millennia, since the age of classical Greece. The French first mounted cannons on their sailing ships in 1494. But the death knell for the galley did not sound clearly until the Battle of Preveza, when Venetian galleasses won an overwhelming victory against Turkish galleys. The result was repeated at Lepanto in 1571.[6] By 1650 the warship had been transformed from a floating garrison of soldiers to an artillery platform.

The sixteenth century witnessed the onset of the *Fortress Revolution*, which involved the construction of a new style of defensive fortification employing lower, thicker walls featuring bastions, crownworks, ravelins, and hornworks, all of which were part of a defensive fortification system known as the *trace italienne*. As Geoffrey Parker observes, "normally the capture of a stronghold defended by the *trace italienne* required months, if not years." Static defenses thus effected a kind of "comeback" against the Artillery Revolution. However, as with artillery, the new fortification system was terribly expensive, a fact that limited its application and left considerable opportunity for operations in the field. This, in turn, shifted the focus back to infantry, where revolutionary developments permitted a new use of firepower; infantry moving beyond archers to the combination of artillery and musket fire on the battlefield in what might be termed the Gunpowder Revolution.

Muskets capable of piercing plate armor at a range of one hundred meters were introduced in the 1550s. The English abandoned longbows in the 1560s in favor of firearms. Finally, in the 1590s the Dutch "solved" the problem of muskets' slow rate of fire through a tactical innovation that saw them abandon the tight squares of pikemen in favor of drawing up their forces in a series of long lines. These linear tactics allowed for a nearly continuous stream of fire as one rank fired while the others retired to reload. Muskets were also attractive because they required little training in comparison to the years necessary to develop a competent archer (although linear tactics did require considerable drill). The large, tight squares of pikemen, which had proved so effective against cavalry, now became attractive targets for musket and artillery fire.

This revolution reached full flower in the campaigns of Gustavus Adolphus during the Thirty Years' War, which saw the melding of technology, military systems, operational concept, and new military organizations: a combination of pike, musketeers, cavalry and a large rapid-firing artillery component utilizing linear tactics—what has been described as the Swedish military system—yielded stunning success at Brietenfeld, Lutzen, Wittstock, Brietenfeld II, and Jankov.[7]

Linear tactics were perfected under the Prussian military system of Frederick the Great, who achieved significant improvements in the rate of fire, as well as major improvements in supply. But this refined system would be overturned by the *Napoleonic Revolution*.

The French were the first to exploit the potential for a military revolution that had been building for several decades prior to Napoleon's rise to prominence. During this period, thanks to the emerging Industrial Revolution, the French standardized their artillery calibers, carriages and equipment, and fabricated interchangeable parts. Other improvements in industrial processes allowed the French to reduce the weight of their cannon by 50 percent, thereby increasing their mobility while decreasing transport and manpower requirements dramatically.

The introduction of the *levée en masse* following the French Revolution helped to bring about another quantum leap in the size of field armies. Men proved much more willing to defend and fight for the nation than the crown. Consequently, France's revolutionary armies could endure privations, and attack almost regardless of the cost in men (since they could call upon the total resources of the nation). In battle, the individual could be relied upon; skirmishers and individually aimed fire could be integrated to great effect into the rolling volleys of artillery and musketry. Furthermore, armies became so large that they could now surround and isolate fortresses while retaining sufficient manpower to continue their advance and conduct field operations, thus largely negating the effects of the *trace italienne* and the Fortress Revolution.

The latter part of the eighteenth century also witnessed the creation of a new self-sufficient military organization—the division—and saw the growing importance of skirmishers in the form of light infantry, and cavalry as a reconnaissance, screening, and raiding force. A growing network of roads in Europe meant it was possible for an army to march in independent columns and yet concentrate quickly. Coordination was also improved through the availability of much more advanced cartographic surveys.

Napoleon's genius was to integrate the advances in technology, military systems, and military organizations (including his staff system) to realize a dramatic leap in military effectiveness over the military formations that existed only a short time before. Indeed, it took the other major military organizations of Europe at least a decade before they were able to compete effectively with the *Grande Armée* that Napoleon had fashioned to execute what one author has termed the "Napoleonic blitzkrieg."

Between the Napoleonic Wars and the American Civil War, the introduction of railroads and telegraphs, and the widespread rifling of muskets and artillery again dramatically transformed the character of warfare—the way in which military forces are organized, equipped, and employed to achieve maximum military effectiveness. The result was the *Land Warfare Revolution*. In the Civil War, both the Union and the Confederate forces used their rail nets to enhance greatly their strategic mobility and their ability to sustain large armies in the field for what, in the war's final year, was continuous campaigning. Their exploitation of the telegraph facilitated the rapid transmission of information between the political and military leadership and their commanders in the field, as well as among the field commanders themselves. The telegraph also dramatically enhanced the ability of military leaders to mass their forces quickly at the point of decision and to coordinate widely dispersed operations far more effectively than had been possible during the Napoleonic era.

The effects of rifling, which improved the range and accuracy of musketry and artillery, were not as quickly appreciated by the American military. Union and Confederate generals who clung to the tactics of the Napoleonic era exposed their men to fearful slaughter, as at Fredericksburg, Spotsylvania, and Gettysburg. The introduction of repeating rifles in significant numbers late in the conflict enabled the individual soldier to increase substantially the volume, range and accuracy of his fires over what had been possible only a generation or two earlier. One Confederate general is said to have observed that "had the Federal infantry been armed from the first with even the breechloaders available in 1861, the war would have been terminated within a year."[8] Still, both sides did adapt eventually.

The campaigns of 1864 and 1865 were marked by the proliferation of entrenchments and field fortifications. Indeed, by the time Sherman's men were marching from Atlanta to the sea in 1864, they lightened their packs by throwing away their bayonets—but they kept their shovels. Shelby Foote notes that the Confederate forces opposing Sherman had a saying that "Sherman's men march with a rifle in one hand and a spade in the other," while Union troops felt that "the rebs must carry their breastworks with them." Arguably, many of the major battles toward the war's end bore a greater resemblance to operations on the Western Front in the middle of World War I than they did to early Civil War battles like Shiloh or First Manassas.

Over the next fifty years this new military regime matured. The increases in the volume, range, and accuracy of fires were further enhanced by improvements in artillery design and manufacturing, and by the development of the machine gun. Again, military leaders who ignored, or who failed to see clearly, the changes in warfare brought about by technological advances and who failed to adapt risked their men and their cause. This myopia was induced partly by the fact that no large-scale fighting occurred among the great powers of Europe between 1871 and 1914. World War I provides numerous examples of this phenomenon, as the military regime that began with the mid-nineteenth century revolution in land warfare reached full maturity. One recalls here the mutiny of the French army after the futile and bloody Nivelle Offensive, the appalling casualties suffered by the British at the Somme and Passchendaele, and by the French and Germans at Verdun.

Just trailing this revolution in land warfare was the *Naval Revolution*. The Revolution of Sail and Shot had long since matured. The wooden ships that were powered by the wind and armed with short-range cannon that had dominated war at sea had not changed appreciably since the sixteenth century. But over the course of a few decades of rapid change from the mid-1800s to the first years of the twentieth century, these vessels gave way to metal-hulled ships powered by turbine engines and armed with long-range rifled artillery, dramatically transforming the character of war at sea. As persistent challengers to British naval mastery, the French consistently led the way early in the Naval Revolution.[9] In 1846 they pioneered the adoption of steam propulsion and screw propellers on auxiliary ships. In 1851 they launched the *Napoleon*, the first high-speed, steam-powered ship of the line. And in the late 1850s, France began constructing the first seagoing ironclad fleet. The British, however, quickly responded to these French innovations, taking the lead in applying these technologies. The mature phase of this revolutionary period found Britain attempting to sustain its position against a new challenger, Imperial Germany, by launching the first all-big gun battleship, *H.M.S. Dreadnought*, in 1906. This period also saw the introduction of the submarine and the development of the torpedo. Indeed the development of these two instruments of war led to the introduction in World War I of entirely new military operations—the submarine strategic blockade and commerce raiding, and anti-submarine warfare.

Toward that war's end, however, new operational concepts were developed to mitigate the effects of the dominant military systems and operational concepts. On land, massed frontal assaults preceded by long artillery preparations gave way to brief artillery preparation fires, infiltration tactics, and the use of the light machine gun as the dominant weapon of the German storm trooper assault. At sea, Great Britain and the United States established elaborate convoy operations to counter the U-boat threat that had transformed the nature of commerce raiding.

World War I both represented the mature stage of one military epoch, and presaged the rise of the *Interwar Revolutions in Mechanization, Aviation, and Information*. As the war progressed, the land forces of both the Allied and the Central powers found themselves employing new military systems based on dramatic advances in the fields of mechanization and radio. Following the war, improvements in internal combustion engines, aircraft design, and the exploitation of radio and radar made possible the *blitzkrieg*, carrier aviation, modern amphibious warfare, and strategic aerial bombardment. Entirely new kinds of military formations appeared, such as the panzer division, the carrier battlegroup, and the long-range bomber force. After a scant twenty years, the nature of conflict had changed dramatically, and those—like the British and the French—who failed to adapt suffered grievously.

Finally, in the mid-twentieth century, the *Nuclear Revolution* (especially after the coupling of nuclear warheads to ballistic missiles), brought the prospect of near-instantaneous and complete destruction of a state's economic and political fabric into the strategic equation. Here was a shift in technology so radical it convinced nearly all observers that a fundamental change in the character of warfare was at hand. Indeed, in the eyes of some observers, once nuclear weapons were stockpiled in significant numbers by the superpowers, they could no longer be employed effectively. Their only utility was in deterring war. Nevertheless, one also sees here the emergence of very different warfighting doctrines and military organizations among nuclear states (e.g., the U.S. nuclear submarine force; Soviet Strategic Rocket Forces).

## Seven Lessons

Reflecting on this record extending over seven centuries, it is possible to make some general observations about the character of military revolutions.

*First*, and to reiterate a point made earlier, emerging technologies only make military revolutions possible. To realize their full potential, these technologies typically must be incorporated within new processes and executed by new organizational structures. In the cases outlined above, all major military organizations fairly rapidly gained access to the emerging technologies. Failure to realize a great increase in military effectiveness typically resulted not so much from ignoring technological change as from a failure to create new operational concepts and build new organizations.

Perhaps the clearest example of the importance of organizational innovation occurred early in World War II. On the Western Front in 1940, British and French armored forces were roughly equal to the Germans' in size, and in quality. Both the allies and the Germans had modern aircraft and radios. In the interwar years, however, it was the German military that had identified both the operational concept to best integrate these new military systems and the organization needed to activate that concept. The result was a major increase in military effectiveness and the acquisition of a decisive comparative advantage. Germany defeated the allied forces and conquered France in six weeks. That victory was primarily due to the *intellectual* breakthroughs that led to new operational concepts and the organizational flexibility that allowed them to exploit these concepts.

A *second* lesson is that the competitive advantages of a military revolution are increasingly short-lived. Military organizations typically recognize the potentially great penalties for failing to maintain their competitive position. In early periods of military revolution, it was possible to maintain dominance for a relatively long period (witness the sluggish response of France to the Infantry Revolution and much of Europe to the Napoleonic Revolution). But since the Napoleonic era, it has been true that if a major military organization is to derive an advantage by having first access to new technologies it has to exploit those technologies quickly, before its major competitors copy or offset the advantage.

For example, the French innovations that sparked the nineteenth century Naval Revolution stimulated a furious British response that matched and then exceeded the French effort. Although the British were loath to introduce radical changes in ship design, they felt compelled to when faced with the French initiative, and retained a major advantage. What gave Britain its competitive advantage was its economic strength, its ability to tap into that strength through its financial system, and its ability to concentrate its resources on a naval competition in a way that France, a continental power, never could. As the revolution matured, France's fleeting opportunities evaporated.

By the end of the Naval Revolution, the tables were again turned. When the British launched *H.M.S. Dreadnought*, Germany quickly took up the British challenge, leading to the Anglo-German dreadnought arms race. Thus, the Royal Navy's lead in applying technologies to launch the first all-big-gun battleship designed to make all others "obsolete" produced only an ephemeral competitive advantage over Germany, and the other major navies of the world, which quickly constructed their own "dreadnoughts."

Indeed, in the last two centuries there do not seem to be any prolonged "monopolies" exercised by a single competitor in periods of military revolution. Fairly quickly, major powers who can afford the technology and who understand how to employ it, have it if they want it. Of course, one is immediately led to ask the question: Is "fairly quickly" quickly enough? After all, Admiral Alfred von Tirpitz, who directed Germany's naval buildup, viewed with alarm the period from 1906, when Britain launched *Dreadnought*, to 1910, when Germany's naval building program was able to offset partially the British advantage. It may be that although the period of competitive advantage appears to be fairly short there may be a potentially great advantage from being first, as the French discovered to their dismay and the Germans to their elation in the spring of 1940.

Having the initial competitive advantage in a period of military revolution—even if that advantage is considerable—is no guarantee of continued dominance, or even competitiveness. The list of military organizations that established an early lead, only to fall behind later, is long. Consider the history of the submarine: the French navy made much of the early progress in submarines in the late nineteenth century, but it was the Kaiser's navy that employed the new system to such devastating effect in World War I. In World War II, the United States quickly adopted many of Germany's innovations in mechanized air-land operations and in submarine commerce raiding. Or take military aircraft: the Americans were in the forefront of aviation in the first years of the twentieth century, but by the time of their entry into World War I had fallen substantially behind many European states. Or tanks: an American tank designed in the 1920s was adapted by the Soviets in the process of developing the T-34, one of the most effective tanks to emerge during World War II. The U.S. Army, on the other hand, was equipped during the war primarily with the inferior Sherman tank.

Even though monopolies may be fleeting, they are real and often decisive in war. The early years of World War II—in some respects like the Napoleonic era revolution in land warfare during the late eighteenth century—demonstrated what can happen when only one power is innovative and adaptive. In the run-up to that war, Germany proved far more adept than France, Britain, and Soviet Russia at operational and organizational innovation on land. Although the Soviet Union, Great Britain, and the United States caught up to Germany's blitzkrieg in the span of a few years, France was unable to adapt quickly enough in 1940 to avoid disaster, while Soviet Russia suffered enormous devastation at the hands of the German war machine.

A *third* lesson of history is that asymmetries in national objectives and strategic cultures, as well as limitations on resources and the potential number and strength of enemies, allow for niche, or specialist, competitors. This phenomenon seems to be characteristic of recent periods of military revolution, where technological change has been broadening and accelerating, offering a potentially rich menu of military innovation. Furthermore, the cost of competing imposes strong limitations on how a military organization will pursue the competition. Again, the best example of this phenomenon occurred during the Interwar Revolutions in Mechanization, Aviation, and Information. With one exception, the period was characterized by selective competition among the military organizations of the great powers. For example, for a time Germany, traditionally a land power, became dominant in mechanized air-land operations. Soviet Russia quickly joined that competition to survive. Japan, an island nation, competed in naval aviation and modern amphibious operations, while the British developed strong capabilities in strategic aerial bombardment, strategic defenses, and (arguably) modern amphibious operations. Only the United States had the resources to compete in every major area of the interwar military revolution (save strategic defenses, for which it had no need), while simultaneously positioning itself to exploit the coming military revolution in nuclear weapons. Clearly the level and sophistication of human and material assets, and the unique strategic circumstances faced by each competitor, shape how competitors approach and attempt to exploit the opportunities inherent in military revolutions.

*Fourth*, the historical record suggests that war and revolution in warfare are quite separate entities. True, it took the test of World War II to convince the world's major army organizations (and, one might add, much of the German army itself) that Germany's blitzkrieg concept could produce great advantages for its practitioners. The war also convinced the U.S. Navy and the Imperial Japanese Navy that aircraft carriers would be the new centerpiece of battle fleets, and convinced everyone to recognize the revolution in naval warfare brought on by the use of submarines. But a confirming war is not essential for military organizations to seize opportunities. For instance, the revolution in naval warfare in the late nineteenth century, from wood, sail, and cannon to steel, turbines, and rifled guns, was widely accepted in the absence of war. The introduction of nuclear weapons is another obvious example of broad acceptance by military organizations that the competitive environment had changed radically.

*Fifth*, though most militaries will be quick to recognize a competitor's advantage, there are no certainties. Not even war will guarantee that all military organizations will recognize and exploit a military revolution, or understand a revolution in all its dimensions. Thus, in the American Civil War, both sides were relatively quick in exploiting the dramatic gains in strategic mobility and command, control, and communications made possible by the railroad and telegraph. But years passed before either side clearly realized how drastically the appearance of rifled guns and muskets in large numbers had invalidated the Napoleonic battlefield tactics. Again, despite the experience of World War I the world's major naval powers tended to discount the effectiveness of strategic warfare conducted by submarines. And even after the German campaign in Poland alerted the world to the potential of the blitzkrieg, the French army remained remarkably, indeed fatally, resistant to innovation.

More than anything else, it is perceptions of future contingencies and likely enemies that determine whether and when there is full exploitation of the advantages offered by the military revolution. Having a single enemy or challenger may ease a military organization's problem by making it more manageable. For instance, Britain had three major kinds of naval contingencies to prepare for in the interwar period: a war against a major continental power in Europe; a "small war" involving its imperial possessions; and a war against Japan. Conversely, the world's two other major maritime powers, the United States and Japan, saw each other as by far their most prominent challenger, and organized their naval forces around a single contingency—a Pacific war. As it turned out, the Americans and the Japanese exploited the revolution in naval aviation far more proficiently than did the British, in part because of their ability to focus more precisely. In competing during a period of military revolution it is clearly advantageous to be able to identify not only the nature of future conflict but specific contingencies and competitors. But if that is not possible, a premium should be placed on possessing both sufficient organizational agility and resources to adapt quickly if or when the picture clarifies.

A *sixth* lesson is that technologies that underwrite a military revolution are often originally developed outside the military sector, and then "imported" and exploited for their military applications. Thus, in the early fourteenth century, the Artillery Revolution was fueled by the discovery that the method being used to cast church bells could also be used for casting artillery—so that, as Bernard Brodie observes, "the early founders, whose task had been to fashion bells which tolled the message of eternal peace...contributed unintentionally to the discovery of one of man's most terrible weapons." The development of the railroad and telegraph, which helped to effect the Revolution in Land Warfare, and the rise of the commercial automotive and aircraft industry which led to the Interwar Revolution, are other obvious examples. Indeed, all the military revolutions of the last two centuries are in a real sense spinoffs from the Industrial and Scientific Revolutions that have been central, defining processes of modern Western history.

That said, having a substantially inferior economic and industrial base need not be an absolute barrier to competition in a military revolution. During the interwar period the Imperial Japanese Navy developed a first-rate naval aviation capability and modern amphibious forces, which they employed to devastating effect in the early months of their war with the United States. The Japanese accomplished this with a gross national product that was less than 20 percent (and perhaps closer to 10 percent) of that of the United States, its major naval competitor in the Pacific. Again, following World War II, the Soviet Union, despite a German invasion that destroyed much of its most productive areas, developed with relative speed a nuclear weapon strike force to rival that of the United States. This was accomplished even though the Soviet Union's GNP was much lower than that of the United States, and it was burdened by war reconstruction costs and the maintenance of a far larger conventional military force. However, in neither case could this competitive posture be sustained indefinitely against a wealthier, equally determined rival.

In a sense, military revolutions may offer major opportunities for relatively small or "medium-sized" powers to steal a march on greater powers, or even for one great power to challenge an array of its peers. They do so by making it possible to substitute intellectual breakthroughs and organizational innovations for material resources. Examples are plentiful: Flanders exploiting the Infantry Revolution to challenge giant France; the Napoleonic Revolution that allowed France to challenge all of Europe; Germany's innovations (in mechanized air-land operations) during the Interwar Revolution against France, Britain, the Soviet Union, and the United States; and Japan exploiting the Interwar Revolution (in naval aviation) against the United States and Great Britain. Indeed, as Geoffrey Parker has argued, the West's global dominance from 1500-1800 is but an instance of this phenomenon writ large.

A *seventh* and last lesson is that a military revolution does not ineluctably imply a quantum leap in the cost of maintaining military forces. To take one example, the Infantry Revolution of the fourteenth century that replaced heavy cavalry with infantry archers and pikemen actually lowered the cost of maintaining forces. Also, the Nuclear Revolution has been comparatively cheap. While the ability to employ such weapons to achieve political ends has been much debated, the fact remains that nuclear weapons appeared to offer those who possess them considerable "bang for the buck."[10]

## The Current Revolution

Where are we now? Some believe that a revolution in warfare has already occurred, and cite the recent Gulf War as evidence. American military operations in that war, however, do not meet the historical criteria for revolutionary change. United States forces did not display any dramatic doctrinal changes in that war, nor any major new force structures or military organizations. One indication of how continuous with earlier practice the U.S. performance was is that during the U.S. "Linebacker" air operations in 1972, some nine thousand laser-guided bombs were dropped on Southeast Asia—roughly the same number as were dropped during the Gulf War. We are in a military revolution—but in its early stages.

What the Gulf War did was show us a glimpse of the potential influence of this revolution on military effectiveness. The Gulf War may be seen as a *precursor war*—an indication of the revolutionary potential of emerging technologies and new military systems. In this respect, it may be similar to the battle of Cambrai that took place on the Western Front in November 1917. There the British, for the first time, employed large numbers of planes and tanks in concert. They tried to integrate their operations, and those of the infantry and artillery, through the use of wireless communications. The British attack, spearheaded by nearly five hundred tanks, broke the German lines on a twelve kilometer front within hours.

This breakthrough was as surprising to the senior British leaders as the one-sided Desert Storm operation was to senior American Commanders. Indeed, the British had made no plans to exploit such a rapid rupture of the German front. In retrospect, one also realizes that the potential for far greater success at Cambrai was compromised by the immaturity of the new technologies and systems employed (tank breakdowns, limitations on aircraft bomb loads, and on wireless range, portability and reliability). To extend the analogy, we may be in the "early 1920s" with respect to this military revolution.

Where are we going? While precise prediction is out of the question, it is possible to speculate with some confidence on the current revolution's general path and nature. It appears certain that it will involve great increases in the ability of military organizations to detect, identify, track, and engage with a high degree of precision and lethality far more targets, over a far greater area, in a far shorter period of time, than was possible in the Cold War era. (No doubt it also will lead to systems and operations designed to degrade or offset these capabilities.) This aspect of the revolution will probably involve an improved ability to understand target *systems* and their relationship to operational and strategic objectives. The leverage obtained from such a capability is potentially enormous, since knowing *which* subset of targets to strike out of the many identified will be crucial to the effective employment of large numbers of precision weapons.

Furthermore, the growing importance of simulations—from computer-assisted design and manufacturing (CAD-CAM), to individual training simulators, to simulations of complex military operations involving high levels of systems and architecture integration—may witness a major increase in the ability of military organizations to extract the full potential of the human and material resources at their disposal.[11]

The transition rate to this revolution's mature stage will be a function of the level of military competition in the international system, the strategies for competition pursued by the competitors, and the four elements comprising a military revolution. It should also be appreciated that, as long as there are multiple competitors exploiting the potential of the emerging military revolution, the revolution itself will be likely to take several paths, if only because of the competitors' varying strategic goals, access to relevant resources, and strategic culture.

## What It Means For Us

Perhaps, as many believe, the United States and the world's other great powers have an opportunity unparalleled in this century to construct an international system that will provide a stable, enduring era of relative peace. Even if there is time and even if the opportunity is grasped, the question will remain: Will it last? Is it possible to avoid, or even forestall, a resumption of the great power competition that has been a staple of the international system since the rise of nation-states? If history is any indicator, the United States will, at some point, find itself again in a military competition, in the midst of both a geopolitical and a military revolution. What can the world's dominant military power learn from the general lessons of the West's prior military revolutions?

First, the United States should anticipate that one or more competitors seeking to exploit the coming rapid and dramatic increases in military potential may soon arise. Remembering that monopolies are transient, the United States should ponder how to avoid such a competition, or how to postpone it for as long as possible. Or how to win it if necessary.

Second, continued American technological and operational leadership is by no means assured. During the Interwar Revolution, Great Britain held an initial dominant position in mechanized air-land and naval aviation operations that was quickly forfeited. Even when countries will not be able to compete in the full spectrum of military capabilities, some of them, by specializing, will become formidable niche competitors.

Third, it is by no means certain that competitors will follow the same path as the United States. Different security requirements and objectives, strategic cultures, geostrategic postures, and economic situations will likely lead different competitors in different directions. While there are those who believe that, given our current advantage, this military revolution will only progress at a pace and direction that the United States decides to give it, history suggests that this is a dangerous delusion.

Fourth, it is not clear that the United States can rely on the cost of competition acting as an effective barrier to others. Although most military revolutions have raised the cost of "doing business," sometimes dramatically, there have been significant exceptions—and in terms of direct and initial costs the Nuclear Revolution is one of them, and, with proliferation very much at issue, this revolution is still very much with us. If much of the increase in military effectiveness in this emerging revolution stems from the so-called Information Revolution, which has dramatically lowered the cost of information-related technologies, competitors may find the barriers to competition relatively low. And given the history of military organizations adapting technologies initially developed in the commercial sector, the United States' ability to restrict access to these technologies, in the manner it attempted with nuclear fission and missile technologies, may be marginal at best.

In summary, the lessons of earlier revolutions seem to contradict much of the conventional wisdom with respect to the United States' prospective competitive military position. In a revolutionary epoch, long-term U.S. military dominance is not preordained. Indeed, one could argue that the prospects for continued U.S. dominance would be greater in a military regime that was entering early maturity, rather than in its early, most dynamic stages. If America wants to avoid or delay a resumption of military competition, it will have to identify a strategy for that purpose and pursue it energetically. If a competition cannot be avoided, the United States will begin with strong competitive advantages in terms of technology and military systems. As we have seen, however, it is typically those military organizations that are highly innovative and adaptive that seem to compete best in periods of military revolution. In those terms, it has yet to be clearly demonstrated that the United States military should be sanguine regarding its ability to respond effectively to the challenge that this revolution will likely pose.

## Notes

1. Clifford J. Rogers, "The Military Revolutions of the Hundred Years' War," *The Journal of Military History*, April 1993, pp. 241-78.

2. At the Battle of Crecy, for example, the French lost 1,542 knights and lords, and suffered over 10,000 casualties among crossbowmen and other support troops, while the English lost two knights, one squire, forty other men-at-arms and archers, and "a few dozen Welsh." Bernard and Fawn M. Brodie, *From Crossbow to H-Bomb* (Bloomington, IL: Indiana University Press, 1973), pp. 39-40.

3. "Corning" involves mixing wet powder and allowing it to dry into kernels. It is purported to have been three times as powerful as the sifted form, and considerably less expensive. Other improvements included the introduction of the two-wheel gun carriage, trunnions, and iron cannonballs. See Rogers pp. 269-71.

4. Guicciardini, Francesco, *History of Italy* (New York: Washington Square Press, 1964), p. 153.

5. Rogers also notes that, although the technology and military weapon system had been perfected, when military organizations failed either to restructure effectively, whether through a lack of funds or organizational

insight, they failed to achieve the benefits of a revolutionary increase in military effectiveness. For example, when the siege train was relatively weak, as was the case during the sieges of Guise (1424), Ferte-Bernard (1424), Torey Castle (1429), Chateau Gallard (1429), Laigny-sur-Marne (1432), and Harfleur (1440), the siege dragged on for from between three months to over a year.

6. Brodie, p. 64 and Geoffrey Parker, "The Western Way of War," lecture presented at the Johns Hopkins SAIS, February 17, 1994, p. 87. Parker goes on to note that the galley, while displaced as the centerpiece of naval warfare, did manage to survive, and even prevail on occasion, into the eighteenth century.

7. Gustavus Adolphus actually *increased* marginally the ratio of pike to shot when compared to the Dutch. However, he did it in such a way as to promote the integration of pike, shot, artillery, and cavalry into combined arms operations. See Michael Roberts, "The Military Revolution, 1560-1660," *Essays in Swedish History* (Minneapolis: University of Minnesota Press, 1967); Geoffrey Parker also argues that a third military revolution (or perhaps more accurately, a third element of the military revolution) involved the radical increase in the size of armies that occurred in the latter part of the seventeenth century, or, more precisely, between 1672 and 1710.

8. Brodie, p. 136. Shelby Foote observes that the Sharp repeating rifles employed by Union troops late in the war gave a cavalry force of 12,000 more firepower than an entire corps of infantry. See Foote, *The Civil War: A Narrative* (New York: Vintage Books, 1986), Vol. III, p. 872.

9. For a discussion of the early period of this revolution, see Bernard Brodie, *Sea Power in the Machine Age* (Princeton: Princeton University Press, 1942), pp. 48, 52, 66-68, 75-76, 195; Terrence R. Fehner, *National Responses to Technological Innovations in Weapon Systems, 1815 to the Present* (Rockville: History Associates Incorporated, 1986), pp. 7-14; and William H. McNeill, *The Pursuit of Power: Technology, Armed Force, and Society Since A.D. 1000* (Chicago: University of Chicago Press, 1982), pp. 227-28, 239, 291-92.

10. While this point is often made, its acceptance is far from universal. For example, the United States is just now beginning to face up to the enormous environmental costs associated with its nuclear weapons program. The cleanup costs are estimated to range from $150-200 billion over thirty years. The situation in the former Soviet states is considered to be far worse. See Government Accounting Office, *DoE Management: Consistent Cleanup Indemnification is Needed*, GAO/RCED-93-167 (Washington, DC: Government Accounting Office, July 1993). Still, it is not clear that long-term environmental costs will weigh heavily with the rulers of most of the countries that are now actively pursuing a nuclear capability.

11. For a more complete discussion, see Andrew F. Krepinevich, "La Révolution à Venir dans la Nature des Conflits: Une Perspective Americaine," in *Reflexions sur la Nature des Futurs Systèmes De Defense*, Alain Baer, ed., (Paris: Ecole Polytechnique, November 1993); and Andrew F. Krepinevich, "Une Révolution dans les Conflits: une Perspective Americaine," *Defense Nationale* (January 1994).

# Chapter 32

### * * *

# Force Planning, Military Revolutions and the Tyranny of Technology

Henry C. Bartlett, G. Paul Holman, Jr., and Timothy E. Somes

*It is the conventional wisdom that the United States is on the verge of a military revolution. But to constitute more than a fine cliché, the component parts and ultimate implications of a military revolution must be clearly understood. Perhaps the most important issue for strategists and force planners to understand is the place of technology in military revolutions. Henry C. Bartlett, G. Paul Holman and Timothy E. Somes contend that technology—for better or for worse—will dominate military revolutions. The U.S. military must identify, develop, and integrate critical emerging technologies, or face the risk that the next military revolution will take place elsewhere—perhaps in a country hostile to America. The first part of the article examines five historical examples of military revolutions that illustrate the link between technology and dramatic (although sometimes temporary) success on the battlefield. The second section examines several different ways to pursue technological innovation in order to stimulate a future military revolution. Is their emphasis on technology as a foundation for future military revolutions too restrictive? Should the U.S. Department of Defense emphasize research, development and limited production, rather than large scale procurement, lacking a fundamental threat to national security?*

The importance of technology in shaping military revolutions can be illustrated by five cases: the German Blitzkrieg in the opening campaigns of World War II; British air defense during the Battle of Britain; the German use of submarines in the Battle of the Atlantic; the United States-led war against

Dr. Henry C. Bartlett is a professor in the National Security Decision Making (NSDM) Department of the U.S. Naval War College. He served in the U.S. Air Force from 1955 to 1980, primarily in tactical aviation. Dr. G. Paul Holman is a professor at the George C. Marshall Center in Garmisch, Germany. He is an intelligence officer in the Air Force Reserve. Timothy E. Somes is a professor in the NSDM Department of the Naval War College. He retired as a Captain after thirty years in the U.S. Navy, during which time he served primarily in submarines.

Reprinted by permission from *Strategic Review*, Fall 1996, pp. 28-40. Copyright © 1996 by United States Strategic Institute.

Iraq; and the Atomic/Nuclear case. In the first four, the revolution was brief and specific. The last was much more general, covering several decades and combining two different but closely related revolutions.

Andrew F. Krepinevich's definition of a military revolution applies to these cases:[1]

[A military revolution] occurs when application of *new technologies* into a significant number of military systems combines with *innovative operational concepts* and *organizational adaptation* in a way that fundamentally alters the character and conduct of conflict. It does so by producing a dramatic increase—often an order of magnitude or greater—in the combat potential and military effectiveness of armed forces [emphasis added].[2]

These cases can be analyzed from two perspectives: by examining the strategic challenge that a military revolution was designed to meet, and the strategic, theater, and tactical requirements that had to be fulfilled (Matrix 1); and by looking at the near- and long-term effects of integrating technology, organization and operational concepts (Matrix 2).[3]

**Matrix 1**
**Background to Military Revolutions**

| Case | Challenge | Tactical Requirement | Theater Requirement | Strategic Requirement |
|---|---|---|---|---|
| German Blitzkrieg 1939-1941 | Achieve short war | Penetrate enemy lines Rapidly disrupt C⁴I | Paralyze decision-makers; Envelop and annihilate | Solve two-front dilemma |
| British Air Defense 1940 | Defeat German air attack; Forestall amphibious invasion | Stop Bombers | Economy of force | Threaten long war |
| German Submarine Campaign in WWII | Isolate Great Britain | Sink ships | Concentrate forces | Strangle British economy |
| U.S. Atomic/ Nuclear Weapons | Defeat Axis Deter USSR | Mass destruction; Assured delivery | Strategic bombardment; Massive retaliation; Flexible Response | End War/ Deter war |
| Desert Storm | Expel Iraq | Attack precisely | Disrupt entire target base simultaneously; Cause systemic failure | Stop Reverse Iraqi expansion |

*German Blitzkrieg*. The Blitzkrieg was a response to the challenge of winning campaigns quickly and sequentially  in order to preclude the strategic requirement to wage a protracted two-front war. Although tested against Poland in 1939, it was not fully proven until the fall of France in 1940. At the tactical level, a combined arms team of armor, infantry, and artillery rapidly penetrated the enemy front. Ground forces, assisted by aircraft, sowed confusion by attacking command elements and lines of communication, thus fulfilling the theater requirement to paralyze the enemy, allowing envelopment and annihilation of large but slow-reacting forces.

### Matrix 2
### Strategic Results of Military Revolutions

| Case | Technology | Organization | Operational Concepts | Effects Near-Term / Long-Term |
|------|-----------|--------------|---------------------|-------------------------------|
| German Blitzkrieg 1939-1941 | Tanks Trucks Aircraft Radios | Combined Arms | Offensive shock | Rapid collapse of Poland and France |
| | | | | Over-extension; Counter-revolution: Allies adapted to German innovations |
| British Air Defense 1940 | Radar Communications network Fighters | Incorporated scientists Began operations research Integrated air defense system | Concentrated forces | Battle of Britain won |
| | | | | Created concept of integrated air/missile defense |
| German Submarine Campaign in WWII | Submarines | Fushion of command, control, communications and intelligence | Wolfpack | U.K. almost strangled |
| | | | | Over-extension Counter-revolution: US and UK adjusted anti-submarine campaign |
| U.S. Atomic/ Nuclear Development | Bomb/Bomber, ICBM, SSBN (triad) | Manhattan Project; Strategic Air Cmd.; National mechanism for command, control, intelligence, and targeting | Offensive destruction; Strategic deterrence | Surrender of Japan; Nuclear arms race with USSR |
| | | | | Changed nature of war Counter-revolution: created incentive for proliferation |
| Desert Storm | Satellites Computers Stealth Precision munitions | Joint task force Informal networking | Near-simultaneous threater-wide offensive | Bloodless, rapid defeat of Iraq |
| | | | | Created model of future warfare Counter-revolution: rivals seek new breakthroughs |

The Blitzkrieg was rooted in the mature technological foundations of the internal combustion engine and Western heavy industry. German trucks, tanks, artillery, and aircraft were, at best, comparable and, in some cases, inferior, to enemy weapons. However, when coupled with improved radio communications, and integrated into the innovatively organized Panzer division, the result was a military revolution. The heart and soul of the Blitzkrieg was offensive shock, which allowed German forces to disrupt the decision process of enemy commanders. Spectacular victories were the result.[4]

The Blitzkrieg concept gave Germany near-term success in the early stages of World War II against Poland, France, the Soviet Union and the Allies in North Africa. However, it could not compensate for basic weaknesses in strategy. Ultimately, German forces became seriously over-extended, negating the power of the original concept.[5]

The Allies achieved their own counter-military revolution, denying Germany the strategic success it sought. The Soviet Union and Great Britain were able to reconstitute their military as the United States entered the war. Drawing on vast technological and industrial resources, they adapted German concepts to their own needs.

*British Air Defense*. In 1940, Great Britain faced its greatest threat since Napoleon. The British challenge was to defeat a German bomber offensive and forestall a subsequent amphibious invasion.[6]

Before the Battle of Britain, British force planners conducted a vigorous debate concerning the relative importance of offensive versus defensive measures.[7] Advocates of the offensive contended that the Royal Air Force should emphasize bombers for offensive strikes against German industrial centers. Their defensive-oriented opponents argued on behalf of fighters to defend the home islands, worrying that a "knock-out blow" would come from the skies, defeating Great Britain before her empire and allies could be mobilized for a long, global war.[8]

The battle for France in the spring of 1940 tilted this debate in the direction of the advocates of strategic defense. British bombers had proven to be ineffective against both armor and targets in the German rear, while attrition substantially reduced the number of Royal Air Force fighters sent to France. In spite of urgent French requests for more fighters, Churchill was persuaded to withhold his best air assets—such as the Spitfire squadrons—for the defense of England. This move proved critical to the subsequent defense of Great Britain, and thus to achieving the strategic requirement to maintain a base from which to prosecute a long war.

The Battle of Britain constituted a military revolution because it decisively changed the nature of air defense. The synthesis of radar, barrage balloons, guns, fighter aircraft, and communications (both radio and wire) was crucial for British success. All of these were developed before the war began. Of particular note was the tight secrecy surrounding radar, which became the decisive technology.[9]

The British also made radical changes in organizational structure. They integrated civilian scientists in operational headquarters as well as key staffs. These scientists were instrumental in founding the discipline of operations research.[10] Equally important, they helped create an integrated air defense system that included surveillance and warning, communications, and fighter aircraft organized into groups and sectors. This system ensured that British fighters were concentrated at the most critical point of attack. As a result, the Royal Air Force won the Battle of Britain, permitting the Allies to mobilize for the long war.

German air attacks did not cease. Indeed, they became more sophisticated with the advent of unmanned aerial vehicles (V-1), and ballistic missiles (V-2). Yet Nazi Germany's attempts to use its technological and industrial base to achieve a counter-revolution did not succeed. A major reason was the inability of Germany's own air defense system to counter the allied bombing campaign. To this day, the Battle of Britain stands as an important example of integrated air defense against prolonged air attack.

*German Submarine Campaign.* The German submarine campaign in the early part of World War II represented another military revolution. Berlin's challenge was to isolate Great Britain from its empire, allies, and resources. The German leadership hoped to strangle the British economy by sinking the vast numbers of commercial ships on which the country's economy depended, thus forcing it into submission.[11]

Based on his experiences in World War I, Admiral Karl Doenitz, the German U-boat commander, understood that submarines could revolutionize economic warfare. His theater objective required the concentration of submarines to defeat the convoy system. The inability to solve that tactical problem in the previous war had led to German failure. Drawing on advances in submarine technology, Doenitz developed a major operational innovation—the wolfpack. Rather than operating independently as lone raiders, German submarines worked together against the convoys. Radio transmissions tied German submarines into a tightly controlled network. Doenitz fused control, communications, and intelligence into a powerful shore-based operations center at Lorient, France, a major organizational breakthrough for a navy.[12]

The German submarine campaign peaked in the winter of 1943, with success close but elusive. By May 1943 the Anglo-American anti-submarine revolution, conceived out of desperation, had gained a powerful counter-momentum. The allies were sinking German submarines at such a rate that Doenitz was temporarily forced to pull them from the Atlantic. Although German technology continued to advance with such innovations as the snorkel and hydrogen-peroxide propulsion systems, Doenitz was never able to recover the initiative.

No one technology dominated the Anglo-American counter-revolution. Rather, it was a synthesis of many elements: convoying; rapid location of the wolfpacks through decryption of their messages with ULTRA; harassment by long-range aircraft; improvement of weapons and sensors such as sonar, radar and magnetic anomaly detection. The British and Americans also made good use of their massive resource base and scientific community. They devised better weapons and used operations research to improve tactics. The allies created their own fusion centers capable of faster processing of more data than the Germans. Never before had civilians made such a direct contribution to naval operations and tactics.[13]

*U.S. Atomic/Nuclear Development.* The Atomic Bomb marked the most dramatic military revolution in the 20th century. Although atomic fission was theoretically understood long before World War II and several countries had atomic programs in competition with the United States, it was the shock of Pearl Harbor that convinced American planners that the deadly competition with Germany and Japan would require extraordinary and innovative engineering applications of theories that had been germinating for decades. The dramatic climax of this effort occurred over Hiroshima and Nagasaki in August of 1945.

The crucial technology of the Atomic Revolution was the air delivered fission bomb. The organizational adaptation began as a highly secret, tightly controlled program, consisting mostly of civilian scientists. Their work introduced a weapon that changed the very concept of total war, theoretically permitting annihilation of entire countries.

The thrust of the subsequent Nuclear Revolution was less military and more political. The bomb, which first seemed to be the "ultimate weapon," soon became the "unusable weapon." It shifted the military focus from warfighting to deterring attacks from other nuclear powers by the threat of retaliation in kind. This concept of deterrence led to the creation of a robust "triad" of offensive forces built around long-range bombers and intercontinental ballistic missiles both land-based and submarine-launched, capable of surviving a surprise first strike.

Operational concepts were expanded to include flexible response, providing a range of options to prevent both conventional and theater war. Organizational adaptations included the integration of presidential authority directly into the procedures for targeting and employing nuclear assets through an array of specialized organizations such as the Strategic Air Command. This reliance upon strategic deterrence had the negative effect of a protracted arms race with the Soviet Union. First Moscow and then several other capitals followed the American example of building their own nuclear arsenals, perpetuating the nuclear revolution.

*Desert Storm.* Some question whether the 1991 Gulf War against Iraq constituted a military revolution on a par with the other cases. They see this war as an evolutionary application of late Cold War doctrine and technology that merely repeats Hitler's Blitzkrieg a bit faster.[14] But others disagree. They contend that Desert Storm was a manifestation of a concept developed by Soviet theorists of the 1980s: a modern military revolution built around a "reconnaissance-strike system" structured for rapid victory on a dense, deep armored battlefield.[15]

The coalition's stated challenge was to expel Iraq from Kuwait, preclude a further Iraqi incursion into Saudi Arabia and the Gulf states, protect sources of oil, reduce Saddam Hussein's financial and technical capabilities for building weapons of mass destruction, and reverse his expansionist ambitions. The tactical requirement called for precise attacks by air, land, and sea forces against such targets as command bunkers, radars, air defense headquarters, airfields, electrical power grids, bridges, and capabilities associated with weapons of mass destruction, while keeping collateral damage to the civilian population and historical and cultural features as low as possible. The theater requirement was to inflict systemic failure on Iraqi forces, thereby incapacitating their ability to fight effectively. Coalition air forces struck Iraq's strategic assets simultaneously, then attacked Iraqi ground forces. Subsequently, coalition land forces completed the rout of the Iraqi army. This campaign fulfilled its strategic requirement of immobilizing Iraq as an expansionist power.

Several aspects of the war with Iraq are truly revolutionary. Some of the technologies for Desert Storm were new. Others had matured significantly since previous combat employment. Space-based capabilities such as global positioning, ballistic missile launch warning, weather and communications satellites; precision-guided munitions; stealth aircraft and low-observable cruise missiles; secure communication systems; and networked computers all played crucial roles.

Organizationally, this was the first war fought by the Commander-in-Chief, Central Command, a unified commander created to deal with a Southwest Asia military problem. The dramatically successful prosecution of the war reinforced the trend toward greater integration of air, land, and sea forces as legislated by the U.S. Defense Reorganization Act of 1986.[16] Comprehensive joint scheduling and targeting of theater air assets by the Joint Forces Air Component Commander created an overall impact that significantly exceeded past experience.[17] Another important adaptation was informal, *ad hoc* dispersion of much of the support activity outside the theater. Stateside staffs directly supported their counterparts in the field using advances in information technology.[18]

These changes in technology and organization permitted a very ambitious concept of operations: a comprehensive, near-simultaneous, theater-wide offensive. The coalition possessed information dominance, giving commanders significant near-real-time knowledge while blinding the adversary. Iraq's inability to communicate, resupply, and maneuver caused systemic failure. The result was a nearly bloodless victory over Iraq. This fifth and final case of a military revolution provides an important model for force planners today. The United States hopes to improve upon its dramatic success in the Gulf; potential rivals seek to counter it.

Desert Storm ended too soon for Iraq to mount a counter-revolution. But American force planners have every reason to believe that potential adversaries are studying Desert Storm with care, looking for ways to counter American success and to achieve their own military revolutions.

## Countering the Military Revolution

Anyone wishing to understand military revolutions—let alone counter them—can profitably examine these five cases. Several generalizations about military revolutions can be gleaned from these examples.

The first is that technology, "makes possible the revolution . . . ,"[19] but only when integrated with organizational adaptation and operational innovation. As Krepinevich concludes, it was the synergistic effect of this triad that produced dramatic success on the battlefield.[20]

The second is that the interaction of peacetime innovation and wartime stress play crucial roles in shaping a military revolution. First, a climate of inventiveness and experimentation must be cultivated in peacetime.[21] Operational innovations generally follow technology, and organizational adaptation usually comes last. However, the final synthesis rarely occurs without the stimulus of extreme national stress. Hitler created such stress for Germany with his belief that war was necessary, imminent, and justified. The peril of Nazi rearmament forced Great Britain into initiatives which culminated in their own military revolutions. For the United States, first Pearl Harbor and then the Cold War created the stressful environments that resulted in the Atomic/Nuclear Revolution. Similarly, the fall of Kuwait prompted American planners to adapt NATO concepts and forces for use in the Gulf region.

The third is that revolutionary success is often short-lived. Just as German submarines were ultimately beaten by Anglo-American improvements in anti-submarine warfare, so German tanks were defeated after the Allies developed their own version of combined arms operations. Germany's enemies had time and the resources to launch their own aggressive counter-revolutions. It remains to be seen how long the revolutionary aspects of Desert Storm will last.

Of the cases covered, the only one in which the revolutionary effects still prevail is the Atomic/Nuclear Revolution. It established a technological tyranny over international relations that persists to this day.

*Organizational Revolutions*. Beyond these insights are cautions concerning military revolutions. One is that America's next adversary may seek a military revolution through organizational and operational changes using existing technologies—as opposed to technological innovation. Here, a particular threat is irregular or unconventional warfare, generally motivated by limited resource bases, but a sophisticated appreciation of how to politically leverage societies. Mao Tse-tung used guerrilla war (sometimes called people's war) to achieve dramatic victories on the battlefield by subjecting peasant populations to communist control.[22] Because Chinese Communist and Nationalist forces were roughly equal in technological sophistication, their civil war put a premium on organizational adaptation and operational innovation.

Mao's legacy of people's war provides a second cautionary lesson, posing a continuing challenge to the technologically advanced powers. Again and again, the mere possession of such technology failed to guarantee strategic success, let alone a military revolution. American forces in Vietnam had the world's finest technology, but the Vietnamese communists prevailed through organizational and operational concepts better suited to their culture, climate, and geography. The Soviets suffered their own Vietnam in Afghanistan once the technologically inferior Mujahideen guerrillas gained confidence and a degree of parity through the introduction of the Stinger missile.

Another way to counter American technology would be to conduct a protracted war of attrition. This might happen if America confronted a technologically equivalent power. There have been such wars in which neither side enjoyed technological superiority. World War I comes to mind, as does the Iran-Iraq War of the 1980s. In both cases, the opponents had rough parity in technology, organization, and operational concepts, dooming them to wars of attrition. Future enemies may also attempt to exploit America's revulsion against extended bloody wars, thus generating a loss of will comparable to that experienced in Vietnam.

The United States and other developed countries will encounter a range of different challenges in coming decades. At one end of the spectrum of conflict, sub-national and trans-national forces—such as guerrillas, terrorists, drug cartels, and insurgents—pose growing threats to U.S. national interests.[23] Technology will not put an end to such threats, but it can help to defeat them (assuming, of course, that we can field emerging technology faster than the opposition can buy it on the open market). Whenever American national interests require that forces be placed in harm's way, technology will be crucial—keeping casualties low, averting collateral damage, distinguishing friends from foes, and ending deployments quickly.

At the other end of the spectrum, countries which obtain nuclear weapons seem less likely to fight each other because of the risk of escalation. Yet, the nation-state is very much alive, and the divisions among states are still explosive in many regions (especially Eurasia and the Middle East).[24] Thus we regard state-to-state conflict as the most dangerous threat to U.S. national security—ranking well ahead of low-intensity conflict, drugs, terrorists, and intra-state conflicts. Indeed, it would be a great tragedy if the next military revolution were initiated against us by a peer competitor.

## Force Planners and Technology

As force planners prepare for the future, there is great utility in understanding the role of technology in previous military revolutions. In some cases, planners followed an evolutionary approach. They achieved a revolutionary impact by improving and integrating relatively old weapon systems (the fighter plane, tank, and submarine). In others, they used an explicitly revolutionary approach, launching intensive and highly secret programs to devise new weapons (radar, the atomic bomb, and stealth aircraft). Each approach can be further broken down, as in Matrix 3.

## Evolutionary Approaches

Evolutionary approaches build on existing technology. They are usually cheaper and more predictable than revolutionary approaches.

*The "Better Mousetrap": Platform Evolution.* We use the word "platform" in its most general sense to mean a single piece of military equipment (for example, a ship, an airplane, a missile, or a radar). In the simplest case of platform evolution, the platform in question is modified to achieve a more effective version. In more complex cases, the platform is adapted so that it can perform new missions or function in a more demanding environment.

The U.S. Navy's destroyers and cruisers constitute a current example. Over the past several decades these vessels have been transformed from anti-ship platforms using guns and torpedoes, through anti-submarine vessels using improved sensors and ASW weapons, to sophisticated fleet air defense and cruise missile platforms.[25]

In selecting an evolutionary approach, the force planner must remember the inherent weaknesses of the original platform. Although the evolutionary modifications may (or may not) be state-of-the-art, the basic platform is old. In the case of the destroyer/cruiser hull, it has inherited a vulnerability to mines, submarines, and a wide variety of anti-ship missiles.

*The "Melting Pot": System Evolution.* We use the word "system" to mean multiple related elements that are integrated in order to accomplish a common purpose. The goal is to solve a warfare problem by synthesizing several areas of technology. If successful, the result is a new, powerful synergy, yielding a truly revolutionary ability to cope with a difficult military challenge.[26]

**Matrix 3**
**Force Planning Approaches to Technology**

| Approaches | Drivers | Examples | Strengths | Weaknesses |
|---|---|---|---|---|
| EVOLUTIONARY APPROACHES | Build on existing technology | Improved plaforms or systems | Economy of effort | Rivals may overtake |
| Platform Evolution "Better Mousetrap" | Add capability | Destroyer/ Cruiser hulls | Efficient use of resources | Platform may be vulnerable |
| System Evolution "Melting Pot" | Integrate Technologies Synthesis of elements | Integrated Air Defense Force XXI "System of Systems" | Synergistic | Technologies and organizations are hard to integrate |
| User-driven Evolution "Bubble up" | Sensitize users | Gulf War Internet | Foster "Learning Organization" | Sub-optimization |
| REVOLUTIONARY APPROACHES | Develop entirely new technology Dominate state of the art | Develop radically different platforms and systems | Achieve major breakthroughts | Expense |
| Platform Revolution "Silver Bullet" | Build a dominant weapon/platform | Nuclear Weapon Ballistic Missile Nuclear-powered subs Stealth aircraft | Highly focused | Opportunity cost |
| System Revolution "Star Wars" | Create a vision Achieve global dominance | Strategic Defense Initiative | Holistic | Vision of war may be wrong Exacerbate arms race |
| Basic Research Revolution "Shotgun" | Pursue opportunities Deal with uncertainties Capitalize on civilian resource base | National Defense Laboratories Advanced Research Projects Agency Bell Laboratories | Emphasize basic science and technology Encourage originality and innovation | Military payoff is unclear |

Integrated air defense illustrates an evolutionary systems approach. It has evolved from localized protection (as in the Battle of Britain) to the theater-wide requirement of today. Elements of land, sea, air, and space technologies must all be synthesized to cope with the threat of aircraft, as well as cruise and ballistic missiles.

Another example is the U.S. Army's Force XXI concept. First, the "Louisiana Maneuvers" have created an innovative process for generating ideas. Innovations that could radically change the nature of war by leveraging "information-age" systems and technologies are then tested at "Battle Labs."[27] Perhaps the most important current example is the "system of systems" concept proposed by Admiral William A. Owens, USN, while he was Vice Chairman of the Joint Chiefs of Staff. The system of systems foresees a large, defined battlespace, which the U.S. commander would dominate through superior situational awareness, information warfare, space control, highly responsive command and control structures, dominant maneuver, and a wide array of precision strike systems.[28]

This "melting pot" approach adapts a variety of different technologies to achieve a synergism in which the final system is significantly more powerful than the sum of its parts. A major challenge for those using this approach is the difficulty of bringing together and integrating the many technologies, diverse organizations, and contending concepts within the boundaries of a reasonable expenditure of resources.

***"Bubble Up": A User-Driven Approach.*** This approach expects changes in current technology to "bubble up" from below, instead of being directed from above. A classic example is the new college campus. First, the students decide where to walk—then the sidewalks are built. The approach stresses individual initiative in the military establishment, as well as the ingenuity of the commercial marketplace. It uses resources already available, but permits, indeed encourages, future applications to be determined by innovative end-users.

An example is the informal use of computers and communications systems to create an information network during the 1990-91 Gulf War. Another powerful case is the Internet. Although initially established for limited, specialized use in research, the Internet has evolved into something far more creative and more ambitious than its original designers ever anticipated.

This approach is cheap and creative. It is especially effective in organizations that value flexibility, tolerate experimentation, and reward innovation—the characteristics of a learning organization.[29] However, it has some weaknesses. One is the risk of sub-optimization: solving minor problems that are not crucial to the mission. Another is the "not invented here" syndrome.

## Revolutionary Approaches

Revolutionary approaches seek to create entirely new, breakthrough technology. The "Holy Grail" of revolutionary approaches is a fundamentally different way to fight that enables one's forces to dominate the state of the art and swiftly achieve strategic success. However, such advances are invariably expensive, sometimes prohibitively so.

***The "Silver Bullet": Platform Revolution.*** This approach seeks to invent a dominant weapon or means of delivery. Perhaps the most striking example in modern times is the nuclear weapon. Initially created for strategic attack, it led to an entire family of weapons, a unique field of doctrine dedicated more to deterring war than to fighting it, and large numbers of specialized new organizations. These are the elements of a classic military revolution—a transformation so complete that it altered both military strategy and international relations. The nuclear revolution was then intensified by ballistic missiles and nuclear-powered submarines—both silver bullets in their own ways. Other examples include stealth aircraft and perhaps the U.S. Navy's proposed Arsenal Ship.[30]

This approach is highly focused. When successful, it can drive the next military revolution. However, it may easily draw funds away from other programs, some of which might also have had revolutionary implications. If unsuccessful, the opportunity costs are often large, as shown by the cancellation of the Navy's A-12 and AX stealth aircraft programs in the early 1990s.[31]

*"Star Wars": System Revolution*. Another revolutionary approach is to create a vision of future war and develop the technology to win it. The Reagan Administration's Strategic Defense Initiative was a prominent example. It began with a well defined military goal—to defend the continental United States with an anti-ballistic missile system. If the umbrella of planned sensors and shooters had been put into orbit, it might have radically altered future conflict by controlling access to space. This program funded a host of weapons development projects and basic research, but it did not come remotely close to achieving its declared military goals. Nevertheless, some authorities contend that the Strategic Defense Initiative did succeed in achieving its political goals by exacerbating Soviet economic stress and helping to end the communist system.[32]

This approach is both optimistic and holistic, seeking to integrate many different technologies. Service parochialism can be reduced by creating a dedicated, joint organization, while the potential contributions of allies and friendly countries can be taken into account. This approach creates intense competition among rival organizations, fostering a favorable environment for the desired breakthroughs.

However, the original vision may be wrong. Rivals may not attack as expected. For example, opponents of the Strategic Defense Initiative warned that an anti-ballistic missile system could not defend the United States against nuclear weapons delivered by commercial ships, low-flying aircraft, or even backpacks. Considering the vast opportunity costs, planned projects of this nature must be carefully balanced against the perceived risks.

*"Shotgun": Revolutionary Basic Research*. This approach encourages broad-based research and experimentation. Seed money stimulates a range of technological options in the hope that some will provide new military capabilities. The U.S. Defense Department's Advanced Research Projects Agency has

long excelled at funding "beyond state-of-the-art" projects. The National Defense Laboratories, such as Lawrence-Livermore and Los Alamos, have explored a broad spectrum of innovative technologies. A famous commercial example was Bell Laboratories.

This approach relies on a crucial American advantage—the world's largest resource base. Both governments and corporations—if they are powerful enough—can drive their rivals to compete on their own terms. An assumption underlying this approach is that the United States can make highly efficient use of its vast resources while keeping the competition reactive and inferior. Even clever adversaries can be confounded by this approach since they must react to several generations of American technology. The United States can take time to decide which weapons will have unquestioned superiority. This approach fosters originality and innovation through basic research. It can lead to significant innovations—when well funded—while preserving the defense industrial base.

This "shotgun" approach has some weaknesses. Its military payoff is uncertain, although "spin-off" to the commercial world may be significant. And its cost may also be high, relative to its potential military impact, because the planned research often tends to expand well  beyond the original focus. The challenge for planners using this approach is to balance potential dramatic discoveries against the risk of little useful return on investment of always limited resources.

## Conclusions

Technology imposes a tyranny—a harsh discipline, an external rigor—on any potential military revolution.[33] In most cases, a true military revolution requires technological innovation and integration. Therefore, force planners need a clear idea of how to approach technological development. It is helpful to distinguish between evolutionary and revolutionary approaches. Understanding both will help force planners as they strive to achieve a military revolution.

Many revolutionary approaches to force planning appear inappropriate today. No geopolitical rival threatens our national interests enough to justify a "Star Wars." Even the "Silver Bullet" approach should be scrutinized in terms of its risk of failure and subsequent opportunity costs. Consequently, force planners are driven toward utilizing "evolutionary approaches" in trying to stimulate a new military revolution. Future forces will require "better mouse-traps," while interoperability and jointness demand new "melting pots." Furthermore, the creativity and computer literacy of the younger generation will create solutions that "bubble up" from an information-intensive environment.

Other countries are working hard to create their own military revolutions, at a time when American support for basic research is dangerously low. Current thinking assumes that America's advantages in information processing, computers, and communications will drive the next revolution. Yet niche competitors will surely try to defeat that approach through less costly, but still dangerous revolutions, such as biological warfare.[34] This is why one revolutionary approach still has merit: the "Shotgun" approach of funding basic science and technology throughout the academic and industrial sectors.

Finally, force planners must understand that every military revolution creates a new dialectic. America's striking margin of victory in defeating Iraq guarantees that competitors are striving for their own revolution to overcome inferiority and avoid defeat. American force planners must assume that new challengers are exploring their own counter-revolutions; their intent is to dethrone America as the sole superpower.

There is a window of opportunity. The international security environment is relatively stable and peaceful. No major war looms on the horizon. However, history cautions that circumstances will change. In all likelihood the military instrument of national power will again be called upon as the ultimate guarantor of American national security. It is incumbent on today's national security leadership to ensure that time and resources are wisely used. Innovation and creativity must be encouraged. Scientific and technological investment must be adequately funded. If we maintain this focus, when a future time of national stress occurs, it will be the United States that prevails because it holds the high ground of the next military revolution.

---

## Notes

1. Throughout this article, we follow the example of Krepinevich in using the term "military revolution" as opposed to the older "military-technical revolution" or the more recent "revolution in military affairs" (RMA). "Revolution in military affairs" and "revolution in military-technical affairs" are of Soviet origin. Technology was one side of Soviet military doctrine, the other being political. For a historical treatment and selections from the Soviet press, see Harriet Fast Scott and William F. Scott, *The Soviet Art of War* (Boulder, CO: Westview Press, 1982), p. 123-156. James R. Fitzsimonds and Jan M. Van Tol provide an overview of the concept in "Revolution in Military Affairs," *Joint Force Quarterly*, Spring 1994, No. 4. For other recent reflections on this concept, see Jeffrey McKitrick, James Blackwell, Fred Littlepage, George Kraus, Richard Blanchfield, and Dale Hill, "The Revolution in Military Affairs," Chapter 3, Barry R. Schneider and Lawrence E. Grinter, eds., *Battlefield of the Future: 21st Century Warfare Issues*, Air War College, Studies in National Security No. 3, (Maxwell Air Force Base, AL: Air University Press, 1995), p. 65.

2. Andrew F. Krepinevich, "Cavalry to Computer: The Pattern of Military Revolutions," Chapter 44, Strategy and Force Planning Faculty, eds., *Strategy and Force Planning*, Newport, RI: Naval War College Press, 1995, p. 582. Reprinted from *The National Interest*, Fall 1994, pp. 30-42.

3. For a full explanation of the notion of "force planning approaches," see Henry C. Bartlett, G. Paul Holman, Jr., and Timothy E. Somes, "The Art of Strategy and Force Planning," Chapter 2, Strategy and Force Planning Faculty, Editors, *Strategy and Force Planning* (Newport, RI: Naval War College Press, 1995), especially pp. 20-25.

4. For a detailed analysis of the background and development of the Blitzkrieg concept between WWI and WWII, see Barry R. Posen, *The Sources of Military Doctrine: France, Britain, and Germany Between the World Wars* (Ithaca, NY: Cornell University Press, 1984), pp. 179-219.

5. For a detailed analysis of Germany's military overextension on the Russian front, see Combat Studies Institute Research Survey No. 5, *Standing Fast: German Defensive Doctrine on the Russian Front During World War II: Prewar to March 1943*, by Timothy A. Wray, (Fort Leavenworth, KS: U.S. Army Command and General Staff College, 1986).

6. Basil Collier, *The Defence of the United Kingdom*, as a part of J.R.M. Butler, ed., *History of the Second World War, United Kingdom Military Series*, p. 22. Chapter 2, pp. 1-48, "Retrenchment and Air Defense (1918-1932)," provides an official history of the development of the air defense system that culminated in the Battle of Britain.

7. Posen, Chapter 5, pp. 141-178.

8. Air Chief Marshal Sir Hugh C.T. Dowding, Royal Air Force, "Employment of the Fighter Command in Home Defence," *Naval War College Review*, Spring 1992, pp. 35-50. He hypothesized (p. 37) that a European dictator might begin a war by attacking British "aerodromes, his reserve storage depots, and his factories" and then "adopt any of the methods of frightfulness which are most likely to bring victory in the shortest possible time."

9. Air Ministry, *Air Publication 3368, The Origins and Development of Operational Research in the Royal Air Force* (London: Her Majesty's Stationary Office, 1963). "At the beginning of the Second World War our principal form of warning against attack was radar. At that time the Royal Air Force was superior to the German Air Force in everything but numbers. Radar offered the means to offset this disadvantage, and the evaluation of radar and the subsequent analysis of its impact on air tactics brought into existence an entirely new branch of applied science which became known as operational research. Its earliest exponents were therefore to be found at Headquarters Fighter Command, responsible for the air defence of Great Britain." (p. xviii)

10. The inventor of radar, Sir Robert Watson-Watt, defined operations research as follows: ". . . an investigation carried out, by scientific method, on actual operations, current, recent or impending, at the request of those responsible for the initiation or conduct of the operations, and explicitly directed to the better, more effective and more economical conduct of similar operations in the future." *The Origins and Development of Operational Research in the R.A.F.*, p. 9, quoting Sir Robert Watson-Watt, *Three Steps to Victory* (Odhams [U.K.], 1958), p. 203.

11. V.E. Tarrant, *The U-Boat Offensive 1914-1945* (Annapolis, MD: Naval Institute Press, 1981), provides an excellent synthesis of this military revolution. Of particular interest is the insight provided by looking at the German effort as a continuum from 1914 through 1945. See p. 81 for specifics of German strategic naval objectives at the start of World War II. See also Admiral Karl Doenitz, *Memoirs: Ten Years and Twenty Days*, Eng. trans. by R.H. Stevens, (New York: World Publishing Company, 1959), Chs. 1-4.

12. Tarrant, p. 94-98. See also Doenitz, pp. 18-24, 107, 128-143, and 152.

13. Tarrant, pp. 108-117. Doenitz, 315-341. See also Charles M. Sternhell and Alan M. Thorndike, OEG Report No. 51, *Antisubmarine Warfare in World War II*, (Washington, DC: Operations Evaluation Group, Office of the Chief of Naval Operations Navy Department, 1946), for a detailed discussion of the application of scientific and technical advice using operations analysis to create the counter-revolution in antisubmarine warfare. A recent review of this effort, including the importance of code-breaking (which was absent for reasons of classification until 1977) is contained in Montgomery C. Meigs, *Slide Rules and Submarines. American Scientists and Subsurface Warfare in World War II* (Washington, DC: National Defense University Press, 1990).

14. For example, Thomas A. Keaney and Eliot A. Cohen, *Gulf War: Air Power Survey. Summary Report*, (Washington, DC: 1993), p. 251: "It is probably too soon to conclude without reservation that we have entered a new era of warfare. But as we consider the war, some signposts of change surely stand out. . . . The ingredients for a transformation of war may well have become visible in the Gulf War, but if a revolution is to occur someone will have to make it."

15. Marshal N.V. Ogarkov, "Always in Readiness to Defend the Homeland," March 25, 1982. Cited by Jeffrey R. Cooper, *Another view of the Revolution in Military Affairs*, (Strategic Studies Institute, U.S. Army War College, Carlisle Barracks, PA, July 15, 1994), pp. 26-27.

16. Public Law 99-433-OCT. 1, 1986. Goldwater-Nichols Department of Defense Reorganization Act of 1986. Among other goals, it aimed ". . . to place clear responsibility on the commanders of the unified and specified combatant commands for the accomplishment of missions assigned to those commands and ensure that the authority of those commanders is fully commensurate with that responsibility. . ." p. 1.

17. For the early phases of planning the air war and the resulting controversies, see Michael R. Gordon and General Bernard E. Trainor, *The Generals' War*, (Boston, MA: Little, Brown and Co.), pp. 73-101 and pp. 178-202.

18. "One large organization innovation that did occur [as Keaney and Cohen point out on page 247]—unforeseen and by force of circumstances—was the dispersion of much command and control activity outside the theater. Officers in the basement of the Pentagon helped pick targets and plan attacks; staffs at Langley Air Force Base in Virginia managed CENTAF's spare parts accounts; Space Command provided warning of missile attacks against Israel and Saudi Arabia; meteorologists in the United States processed weather information for use within the theater."

19. This is the generally accepted view among American authorities. See Andrew W. Marshall, Director of the Office of Net Assessments, Office of the Secretary of Defense, Memorandum for the Record on "Some Thoughts on Military Revolutions—Second Version," August 23, 1993: ". . . there is often a misunderstanding about what one means by military revolution. The earlier terminology, referring to it as a military-technical revolution, is to be avoided because of the emphasis it puts on technology. Technology makes possible the revolution, but the revolution itself takes place only when new concepts of operation develop and, in many cases, new military organizations are created. There is also a tendency to talk about *the* military revolution. This could have the sense

that it is already here, already completed. I do not feel that this is the case. Probably we are just at the beginning, in which case the full nature of the changes in the character of warfare have not yet fully emerged. The referent of the phrase, 'the military revolution,' is therefore unclear and indeed should remain to some extent undefined for now. It would be better to speak about the *emerging* military revolution or the *potential* military revolution." (Emphasis in original.)

20. Krepinevich, p. 582.

21. Stephen Peter Rosen, *Winning the Next War: Innovation and the Modern Military*, (Ithaca, NY: Cornell University Press, 1991), stresses the importance of peacetime innovation, advocating intensive simulations of alternative concepts of operations (e.g., wargames) to educate the officer corps and explore future options.

22. For Mao's views on military strategy, see *Selected Military Writings of Mao Tse-tung*, (Peking: Foreign Languages Press, 1967).

23. Martin Van Creveld, remarks that, "Instead of war being conducted by states . . . almost all are now fought by organizations that do not have a clear territorial base and cannot be targeted by nuclear weapons, even when they are available. . . No more than an elephant can swat a swarm of gnats, is modern, conventional military technology capable of putting an end to low-intensity war." High Technology and the Transformation of War. Part II," *RUSI Journal*, December 1992, p. 63. Van Creveld explores these ideas more full in *Technology and War From 2000 B.C. to the Present* (New York: The Free Press, Macmillan, 1989).

24. "The Shape of the World: The nation-state is dead. Long live the nation-state," *The Economist*, December 23, 1995, pp. 15-18.

25. Thomas C. Hone, Douglas V. Smith, and Roger C. Easton, Jr., explore this issue in "Aegis—Evolutionary or Revolutionary Technology," Captain Bradd C. Hayes and Commander Douglas V. Smith, eds., "The Politics of Naval Innovation," Strategic Research Department Research Report 4-94, An Occasional Paper of the Center for Naval Warfare Studies, (Newport, RI: Naval War College, 1994), pp. 42-74. This case is especially interesting because the next step in platform evolution may incorporate Aegis Upper Tier for ballistic missile defense. At that point, it might be argued that the evolutionary process has culminated in a revolutionary change (theater ballistic missile defense from a mobile, flexible surface platform). See John H. Dalton, Secretary of the Navy, Admiral J.M. Boorda, Chief of Naval Operations, and General Carl E. Mundy, Jr., Commandant of the Marine Corps, *Forward. . .From the Sea*, (Washington, DC: Department of the Navy, 1995), p. 4.

26. An historical example of an evolutionary systems approach, beyond the cases cited in Matrix 3, occurred during the Cold War. NATO ground forces were out-numbered by Warsaw Pact forces arrayed in multiple echelons. NATO responded with rapid evolution in deep strike systems, such as Joint Strategic Attack Reconnaissance System (JSTARS) and Multiple Launch Rocket System (MLRS). Their radically improved capabilities permitted new organizational and operational concepts. AirLand Battle, in U.S. Army and Air Force terminology (or Follow-On Forces Attack in NATO terminology) was the ultimate result. Although designed for defending Europe against the Soviet Union, these weapons, systems, organizations, and operational concepts performed remarkably well against Iraq.

27. General Frederick M. Franks, Jr., "Battle Labs: Maintaining the Edge," (Ft. Monroe, VA: Headquarters, U.S. Army Training and Doctrine Command, May 1994). See also General Gordon R. Sullivan, *Military Review*, May-June 95, Vol. LXXV, No. 5, "Future Vision: A Vision for the Future," pp. 5-14; General Gordon R. Sullivan and Secretary of the Army Togo D. West, Jr., "America's Army of the 21st Century: Force XXI—Meeting the 21st Century Challenge," (Ft. Monroe, VA: Office of the Chief of Staff, Army, Jan. 15, 1995); and General William W. Hartzog, "Force XXI Operations. TRADOC Pamphlet 525-5," (Ft. Monroe, VA: United States Army Training and Doctrine Command, Aug. 1, 1994).

28. Admiral William A. Owens, "The Emerging System of Systems," U.S. Naval Institute Proceedings, May 1995, pp. 35-42. See also McKitrick, et al., "The Revolution in Military Affairs," p. 95.

29. Peter M. Senge, *The Fifth Discipline: The Art and Practice of the Learning Organization* (New York: Doubleday, 1990).

30. Some observers contend that the Arsenal Ship may revolutionize future littoral warfare by replacing the aircraft carrier. This 800 foot vessel may fire up to 500 very long-range cruise or ballistic missiles, long-range artillery shells, or rocket barrages to provide operational maneuver by fire from the sea. It would also have a very small crew (about 26) and be semi-submersible. Eric Schmitt, "Aircraft Carrier May Give Way to Missile Ship," *New York Times*, Sep. 3, 1995, p. 1 and 18.

31. See Congressional Budget Office, "DEF-20. Cancel the Navy's AX Aircraft," *Reducing the Deficit: Spending and Revenue Options. A Report to the Senate and House Committees on the Budget*, (Washington, DC: Government Printing Office, 1993), pp. 58-59. Also Ronald O'Rourke, "Navy Carrier-Based Fighter and Attack Aircraft: Modernization Options for Congress," CRS Report for Congress, Oct. 1, 1993, pp. CRS 9-10.

32. The Reagan Administration reportedly waged a secret economic war against the Soviet Union. National Security Decision Directive (NSDD) 75 changed the terms of the superpower relationship, aiming to alter the nature of the Soviet system, while NSDD 32 forged a multi-pronged effort to weaken Soviet control over Eastern Europe. The Strategic Defense Initiative played a major part in this strategy because of Soviet weaknesses in high technology, and one measure of its success "was the economic costs it would impose on Moscow." Peter Schweizer,

"Who Broke the Evil Empire?" *National Review*, May 30, 1994, p. 49. Ronald Reagan, *National Security Strategy of the United States*, (Washington, DC: The White House, January 1987), p. 4, lists the following as a national objective: "To force the Soviet Union to bear the brunt of its domestic economic shortcomings in order to discourage excessive Soviet military expenditures and global adventurism." See also Fred C. Ikle and Albert Wohlstetter, Co-Chairmen, *Discriminate Deterrence. Report of The Commission on Integrated Long-Term Strategy*, (Washington, DC: U.S. Government Printing Office, January 1988), which declared that "In combination with the USSR's growing ethnic tensions, economic failure might even trigger efforts by some parts of the Soviet empire to loosen their bonds." (p. 8) This commission treated anti-ballistic missile defenses as a crucial part of U.S. national security strategy. "Since we need to compete with the Soviet Union, we need to emphasize strategies for doing so more effectively—strategies that will continue to capitalize on our inherent advantages in technology, that maximize the return on our military investment, and that lower returns to the Soviets on their huge investment." (p. 40)

33. The essential role of technology in the creation of a military revolution leads to the title of this article. This tyranny, defined as "a rigorous condition imposed by some outside agency or force," in *Webster's Ninth New Collegiate Dictionary* (Springfield, MA: Merriam-Webster, Inc., 1983), is reality. Some may question this premise, or the desirability of being so dependent on technology, as a new military revolution is sought. Nevertheless, those who hope to avoid this tyranny must explain how to do so.

34. For a thoughtful analysis that links biological war to the military revolution, see the section on biological warfare issues in Barry R. Schneider and Lawrence E. Grinter, eds., *Battlefield of the Future: 21st Century Warfare Issues*, Air War College, Studies in National Security No. 3, (Maxwell Air Force Base, AL: Air University Press, 1995), pp. 201-266.

# Chapter 33

### ✳ ✳ ✳

# Warfare in the Information Age

### Bruce D. Berkowitz

*Bruce D. Berkowitz suggests that information warfare (IW)—the use of computers, communications networks and databases for military advantage—is drawing increased attention for at least two reasons: the United States vulnerability to IW attack; and the intriguing opportunities for developing new military strategies that information technologies appear to provide. Arraying a number of questions, scenarios, historic parallels and current issues, the author concludes that not only will defense against IW be difficult; as importantly, an effective plan for deterrence will be hard to pull off. But, he cautions, the biggest challenge in the expanding domain of information related strategic thinking will be the reconciliation of governmental secrecy with the realities of an open democracy. A "secret information system" is the ultimate oxymoron. Is information warfare likely to be the focus of the next revolution in military affairs? Should the U.S. Department of Defense create an Information Service responsible for all aspects of information related strategic offensive and defensive planning and future investment?*

Pentagon officials and defense analysts have a new topic to add to their list of post-Cold War concerns: information warfare, or IW, in the usual manner of military-speak. The term refers to the use of information systems—computers, communications networks, databases—for military advantage, either by the United States or by a variety of unfriendly parties.

IW is drawing increasing attention for at least two reasons. First, the United States is potentially vulnerable to IW attack. The United States, in civilian as well as military matters, is more dependent on electronic information systems than is anyone else in the world. In addition to the possibility that computer and communications systems might prove to be a vulnerable weak link for military forces, there is also a danger that hostile parties—countries, terrorist groups,

Bruce D. Berkowitz is an adjunct professor at Carnegie Mellon University. Based in Alexandria, Virginia, he consults frequently on national security issues.

religious sects, multinational corporations, and so on—could attack civilian information systems directly. Attacking these systems could be easier, less expensive, and certainly less risky than, say, sabotage, assassination, hijacking, or hostage-taking, and a quick cost-effectiveness calculation may make IW an aggressor's strategy of choice.

The second reason why the defense community is so intrigued with IW is that it may be as much an opportunity as it is a threat. The United States may be able to develop new military strategies using IW that are perfectly tailored to world conditions following the Cold War. Information technology is a U.S. strong suit, and military forces could use this know-how to improve our defense capabilities, perhaps dramatically, against hostile attack and to defeat any aggressors—and to accomplish both missions at the lowest possible cost. Indeed, U.S. military planners are already taking the first steps in this direction.

Yet, despite all of the attention that IW is receiving, several basic questions about information warfare remain to be resolved. These include:

● What is the actual IW threat, and how much should the United States worry about it? IW aficionados have suggested a number of scenarios in which IW might be used against us, but other observers think at least some of them are far-fetched.
● If the IW threats is real, what does the United States need to do in order to protect itself? Conversely, what must we do in order to make the most of the IW opportunity?
● As a practical matter, how should information warfare be integrated into overall U.S. defense planning? Will IW replace some military capabilities or merely supplement them? Should IW be considered "special," like atomic weapons or chemical weapons, and kept separate from other military forces, or should IW be part of the military's overall organization and planning process?
● What are the implications of IW for current concepts of offense, defense, coercion, and deterrence? For example, is it more difficult to deter an IW attack? Does information warfare automatically escalate to conventional warfare, or vice versa?
● What is the relationship between the military and civilian society in preparing for information warfare? Also, how can the nation protect democratic values—namely, freedom of expression and personal privacy—while taking the measures necessary to defend against an IW threat?

These are very basic issues. We have experience in dealing with similar questions in other areas of defense policy, but information warfare is in many ways quite different. So, if the world is indeed entering an Information Age and IW has the potential to improve, undermine, or just generally complicate U.S. military planning, we need to address such issues now.

## Origins of the Threat

Military weapons and military strategy usually reflect the politics, economy, and—most especially—the technology of any given society. Even the writers of scripture understood the technological relationship between plowshares and swords, and we take for granted the two-sided nature of nuclear power, long-range jet aircraft, and rockets. Thus, today's improvements in computers, communications, and other electronic data-processing systems that are driving economic growth and changing society are also changing military thinking and planning.

Armies have always used information technology—smoke signals in ancient days, telegraphs at the turn of the century, precision-guided munitions to-day—but until recently information systems were second in importance to "real" weapons, such as tanks, aircraft, and missiles. Today, information systems are so critical to military operations that it is often more effective to attack an opponent's information systems than to concentrate on destroying its military forces directly.

Also, because modern societies are themselves so dependent on information systems, often the most effective way to attack an opponent is to attack its civilian information infrastructure—commercial communications and broadcasting net-works, financial data systems, transportation control systems, and so on. Not only is this strategy more effective in crippling or hurting an opponent, but it often has some special advantages of its own, as will be seen.

Some recent books and films have raised the issue of information mayhem, although they may have exaggerated the dangers. High school students cannot phone into the U.S. military command-and-control system and launch a global thermonuclear strike (à la the 1984 movie *War Games*), and it would be hard for a band of international cyberterrorists to totally eradicate a woman's identity in the nation's computer systems (as in . . . [the] screen thriller *The Net*).

But consider some of the scenarios that the Department of Defense has studied:

• Approximately 95 percent of all military communications are routed through commercial lines. U.S. troops depend on these communications; in some cases, even highly sensitive intelligence data is transmitted in encrypted form through commercial systems. Although hostile countries may not be able to intercept and decipher the signals, they might be able to jam the civilian links cutting off U.S. forces or rendering useless numerous intelligence systems costing hundreds of millions of dollars.

• The United States buys most of the microchips used in military systems from commercial vendors, many of which are located in foreign countries. The chips are dispersed throughout a variety of weapons and perform a range of functions. Some experts are concerned that someone might tamper with these chips, causing the weapons to fail to perform when needed.

• One lesson of Operation Desert Storm is that it is unwise to provoke a full-scale conventional military conflict with the United States and its allies. A more subtle alternative might be to send several hundred promising students to school to become computer experts and covert hackers. Such a cadre could develop the training and tactics to systematically tamper with U.S. government and civilian computer systems. But unlike pranksters, they would play for keeps, maximizing the damage they cause and maintaining a low profile so that the damage is hard to detect.

● Some strategic thinkers believe that "economic warfare" between countries is the next area of international competition. This may or may not be so, but it is possible for government experts, skilled in covert action, to assist their countries' industries by well-designed dirty tricks. For example, a bogus "beta tester" could sabotage the market for a new software product by alleging on an Internet bulletin board that the prerelease version of the program has major problems.

● Modern military aircraft, such as the B-2 bomber and F-22 fighter, are designed without a single blueprint or drawing. Rather, they use computer-assisted design/computer-assisted manufacturing (CAD/CAM), in which all records and manufacturing instructions are maintained on electronic media and shared on a closed network. This makes it possible for plants across the country to share databases and to manufacture components that fit together with incredible precision. But it also makes these programs dependent on the reliability and security of the network, which might be compromised by an insider with access.

● Like many large-scale industrial operations today, the military uses "just-in-time" methods for mobilization. That is, to cut costs and improve efficiency, the military services trim stockpiles of spare parts and reserve equipment to the minimum, and they use computers to make sure that the right part or equipment is delivered precisely when needed to the specific user. If the computers go down, everything freezes.

● There is a hidden "data component" in virtually every U.S. weapon system deployed today; this component may be in the form of targeting information that must be uploaded into a munitions guidance system or a "signature" description that tells the guidance sensor what to look for on the battlefield (for example, the distinctive infrared emission that a particular type of tank produces from its exhaust). If this information is unavailable or corrupted, even the smartest bomb regresses into stupidity.

DOD and think tanks have in recent years been actively studying the national security threats that these and other IW scenarios present to U.S. security. But it is also important to remember that, in addition to the threat to military forces, many of these same vulnerabilities apply to commercial industry and the civilian infrastructure. Virtually all communications systems are computer-controlled. Virtually all aircraft and land vehicles have computer-based components. Most transportation systems—aircraft, railroads, urban transit—are directed by remote communications and computers. Thus, virtually all of these civilian systems are also vulnerable to IW attack and could become targets to unfriendly parties.

### The Changing Face of War

One way to understand the impact of IW on military thinking is to recall the evolution of mechanized warfare. Beginning in the mid-1800s, the Industrial Revolution made it possible to develop new weapons that were much more capable than anything produced before: mass-produced machine guns, steam-powered armored warships, long-range artillery capable of hitting targets from several miles away, and so on. The military also benefited from technology that had been developed mainly for civilian purposes, such as railroads and telegraphs, which vastly improved the ability of military forces to mobilize and to maneuver once they arrived at the battlefield. War became faster, longer-ranged, and more deadly. Just as important, new technology also created new targets. Military forces became critically dependent on their nation's industrial base—no factories, no mass-produced weapons, and no mass-produced weapons meant no victory. So, destroying a nation's industrial base became as important as destroying its army, if not more so.

The result was not just an adjustment in military thinking but a complete rethinking of how to wage war. Military planners began to understand that the faster, longer-range weapons offered the opportunity of leapfrogging the front lines on a battlefield in order to destroy an enemy's factories, railroads, and telegraph lines directly. A classic case in point is the progression from the invention of the airplane to the development of the entirely new doctrine of strategic bombing. Moreover, these military planners realized that such an expanded warfare plan was not only a possibility; in many cases, it was likely to be the dominant strategy.

Today's information revolution presents a similar situation. And just as new theories and doctrines were developed for industrial-age warfare, so have thinkers begun to develop a theory and doctrine of IW. As with mechanized warfare and strategic bombing, where it took awhile for military thinking to catch up with the technology, IW concepts have required a few years to mature. In fact, just as aircraft had been in use for almost three decades before the doctrine of strategic bombing was invented, the roots of IW also go back many years. For example, most of the tactics envisioned for attacking an opponent through its information systems—destruction, denial, exploitation, and deception—can be traced to classical military and intelligence fields, such as signals intelligence and cryptography, electronic countermeasures and jamming, "black" propaganda and disinformation, and measures for concealment and camouflage.

What stands clear today is that information technology has reached critical mass. Information systems are so vital to the military and civilian society that they can be the main targets in war, and they can also serve as the main means for conducting offensive operations. In effect, IW is really the dark side of the Information Age. The vulnerability of the military and society to IW attack is a direct result of the spread of information technology. Conversely, IW's potential as a weapon is a direct result of U.S. prowess in information technology.

Indeed, many of the problems of dealing with IW are linked to the nature of information technology itself. The most important feature may simply be the falling cost of information processing; since the 1950s, costs have declined at a rate of about 90 percent every five years, and most experts expect this trend to continue for the foreseeable future. One result is that information technology—and, with it, the ability to play in the IW game—is constantly becoming more available, and quite rapidly. Unlike nuclear weapons technology or aerospace weapons technology, which have been spreading steadily but slowly, the diffusion of IW technology is likely to accelerate. If a party cannot afford some form of information technology and IW capability today, it probably will be able to afford the technology tomorrow. This is evidenced in the spread of dedicated military electronic systems, but even more in the availability of commercial information technology such as computer networks, satellite and fiber-optic communications, cellular telephone systems, and so on. All of these can be used for hostile purposes, and all can be attacked by a hostile power.

A second feature of information technology that affects IW is that as the technology becomes cheaper and cheaper, it becomes less and less efficient to control information from a central authority. Indeed, one reason for the current increasing pressure in society to decentralize government, corporations, and other organizations is that low-cost information technology makes it affordable and feasible to decentralize. The demand and incentives for decentralization are following the technological opportunity.

This trend runs counter to several centuries of military tradition and experience, which are based on hierarchical command structures, rank, and centralized control. The new technology does not support the traditional military model. Also, the trend toward decentralized information systems changes the government's ability to interact with the commercial sector. As a result, national security officials and military planners must find new ways of issuing instructions and implementing policies.

## Dealing with Infowar

With these characteristics in mind, it is possible to discuss some specific issues and problems that the United States will face in dealing with information warfare.

The IW threat will grow because entry costs are low. As the cost of information technology falls, a greater number of foreign governments and nongovernment organizations will present a potential IW threat to the United States. Countries that could not match the United States and its Western allies in expensive modern weapons systems, such as tanks, aircraft, and warships, will be able to buy the computers and communications systems necessary to carry out IW.

One defining feature of the post-Cold War era has been that the single, large threat of the Soviet Union has been replaced by a greater number of lesser threats. The declining cost of information technology has facilitated this trend, and many of the new threats will take the form of IW. As a result, the U.S.

military will need to think about IW threats coming from a number of different directions.

To complicate matters further, each threat will probably be somewhat different. One terrorist group might like to fiddle with transportation control systems; another might be dedicated to compromising DOD databases. In the past, the United States has tailored its forces and plans to deal with the single Soviet threat, and has assumed that, if it could defeat the Soviet Union militarily, it could also deal with what the Pentagon calls "lesser included threats." In the IW world, threats are likely to be as varied as tailored software, and U.S. military forces will need to deal with each on its own terms.

There will be an international learning curve. Not only will more players engage in IW, they will steadily get better at it. Because information is so easily transferred, everyone can quickly learn from the IW mistakes that others make. For example, Desert Storm was essentially a situation in which one side fought a classical 20th-century conventional war while the other side fought a classical 21st-century IW war. The Iraqi army was not outgunned; indeed, it had a numerical edge, as well as the advantages of fighting from prepared defensive positions and its experience in battle gained during Iraq's decade-long war with Iran. The U.S. advantage was in information technology—intelligence, communications, precision-guided munitions, night vision equipment, stealth technology, and electronic countermeasures. As a result, the United States and its coalition partners were well-coordinated and could adjust their operations in real time, whereas Iraqi forces were isolated, disorganized, and blind.

It's unlikely future foes will repeat Iraq's mistakes and permit opponents such a free hand in the contest for what DOD has taken to calling "information superiority" on the battlefield. Indeed, a country or organization with even a rudimentary knowledge of IW could take countermeasures that can greatly reduce the U.S. advantage. The upshot is that the United States will have to work hard and persistently in order to maintain its present IW advantage. Also, because the U.S. advantage could potentially be tenuous and fleeting, it will be necessary to monitor the changing IW threat and develop the systems and expertise necessary to deal with it.

## The Changing Face of Deterrence

During the past 50 years, a well-developed body of theory about conventional and nuclear deterrence has accumulated. Although Star Wars advocates may quibble, most strategic thinkers would agree with U.S. military analyst Bernard Brodie, who noted in 1947 that it is hard to mount a foolproof defense against nuclear attack, so the more plausible strategy is to deter a nuclear attack through the threat of retaliation. Alas, the problem seems doubled for IW. So far, evidence suggests that not only will defense against IW be difficult; even an effective plan for deterrence will be hard to pull off.

One of the greatest difficulties in deterring a would-be IW threat is that an attacker may be anonymous. A country or nongovernmental group could tamper with U.S. communications and computer systems just enough to cause damage, but not enough so the perpetrator can be identified. To paraphrase a metaphor offered by Thomas Rona, a long-time IW thinker, we will be unlikely to find a smoking gun because our opponents will likely use smokeless powder. With no "attacker ID," it would be hard to determine who deserves retaliation, and without the threat of retaliation, deterrence usually fails. Indeed, a truly diabolical enemy would most likely adopt the strategy of an unseen parasite, quietly causing problems that would be attributed to normal glitches we routinely accept with software and information systems. (Have you tried installing OS-2 Warp or Windows 95 on your computer? Many people simply expect electronics to be difficult.)

Another problem for deterrence is that, even if an IW attack is identified, it may be difficult to develop an effective option for retaliation. As one DOD official has said, "What are we going to do, nuke them for turning off our TVs?" An IW attack may be just crippling and expensive, rather than lethal, so conventional retaliation (say, an airstrike) may be unpopular. On the other hand, because the United States is so dependent on information technology, we would likely come out on the losing end of a game of IW tit for tat. And mere diplomatic responses are likely to be ineffective.

Who will be responsible for IW? In the past, the usual response of the military to a new technology has been to assign responsibility for it to a new organization; for example, the Strategic Air Command (now simply Strategic Command) was created to assume responsibility for long-range bombers and missiles. Indeed, within DOD responsibility for information technologies has historically been assigned to specific organizations—the National Security Agency (NSA) in the case of signals intelligence and information systems security, the Central Intelligence Agency (CIA) in the case of covert operations such as black propaganda and covert political action, the National Reconnaissance Office (NRO) in the case of surveillance satellites, and so on.

Currently, each of the military services is developing an IW strategy to assist it in developing new weapons and doctrine, and commanders of U.S. military units deployed in the field are developing plans for IW in their theater of operation. DOD officials have mused—briefly—whether to consolidate responsibilities for IW in a single organization. Most have quickly concluded that this would not make sense. Not only would there be turf battles among existing organizations; such an organization would be inconsistent with the trend in which information systems are, in fact, becoming more decentralized.

Indeed, the more appropriate question may be why we need large operating organizations such as NSA and NRO when information systems are becoming cheaper, networked, and decentralized. It may soon be more efficient for military units to operate their own signals intelligence and even reconnaissance systems. There already is some movement in that direction; for example, Army and Navy units operate their own reconnaissance drone aircraft.

The objective should be to permit IW technology to spread throughout the DOD organization while ensuring that IW operations are coordinated so that they are consistent with national policy and the strategy of military commanders. At the same time, DOD needs to ensure that IW systems in the military can operate with each other and with those in the civilian world, without creating an unwieldy bureaucracy or body of specifications.

## Planning for IW "Civil Defense"

Planning for IW requires cooperation between the defense sector and the commercial sector. Civilian information systems are prime candidates for attack. So just as cities are targeted in strategic bombing, in future wars we can expect civilian information systems to be hacked, tapped, penetrated, bugged, and infected with computer viruses.

Another reason for cooperation is that DOD itself depends heavily on the civilian information infrastructure. As noted earlier, not only does the military use civilian information systems for "routine" activities such as mobilization; sometimes even the transmission of sensitive intelligence data is routed through commercial links. Obviously, it would be impossibly expensive for DOD to make the entire civilian information infrastructure secure to military standards. And even if it were affordable, the passwords, encryption systems, and other security measures would make it incredibly inconvenient for public use.

Moreover, the government's ability to control or influence the civilian information industry is limited. DOD lacks the leverage it has enjoyed in other situations. For example, the Air Force can influence the design of spacecraft because it is the largest operator of space systems, but DOD's share of the total computing and communications market is quite small compared with commercial users. Also, today's commercial information industry is often ahead of the defense industry in developing new technology. So, whereas DOD once could effectively create industry standards in order to enhance security though its leading-edge role in research and development and its buying power, standards are now being set by companies in the market. Add to this the burgeoning information industry worldwide and DOD's influence is diminished further.

The upshot is that DOD cannot use traditional-style directives or specifications to improve the ability to defend the nation against the IW threat. If it tries, no matter how well-intentioned, it will likely fail. As evidence, consider the recent Clipper Chip episode, in which the federal government tried to cajole and coerce the information industry to adopt a NSA-developed encryption system. The Clipper Chip was supposedly indecipherable, but critics claimed that any system designed by the government would permit the government to read messages using the code (in cryptography parlance, this is called "back door access"). According to the critics, the government's objective was to preserve the ability of NSA and law enforcement agencies to read encrypted communications that they intercepted.

Not only did the industry reject the Clipper Chip, but the government was unable to prevent private computer programmers from developing and illegally distributing their own encryption systems that the government supposedly could not crack or systems (such as SATAN) that can detect "back doors." The lesson of the Clipper Chip is that DOD must use a more sophisticated, less heavy-handed approach to get the civilian sector to take measures to protect itself against the IW threat. Because directives and standards usually will not work, DOD officials need to learn how to use incentive systems instead.

For example, simply informing industry and individuals that they could be IW targets will often lead them to adopt "street smart" information behavior to protect themselves from both foreign and domestic attack. DOD officials themselves have suggested that the government could encourage insurance companies to charge appropriately higher rates to corporations that did not take reasonable steps to protect their data or information systems (again, on the assumption that making the insurance companies aware of the damage an IW attack could cause will generally suffice). In cases in which DOD is critically dependent on a civilian information link, it may even make sense for the government to subsidize the civilian operators so that they adopt protective measures.

In other cases, the government may need to face the fact that some of its traditional activities will simply no longer be possible—for example, easily reading most transmissions that it intercepts. Instead, the government could concentrate on providing industry with the means to protect its information system. Indeed, in at least some cases it would seem that using the government's technical expertise to give U.S. industry an edge in the IW wars may do more for national security than collecting and decoding signals.

## Ensuring Democratic Control of IW Policy

Reconciling information security obviously collides with allowing easy access to information systems and freedom of expression. However, IW presents another problem for American democracy.

It is possible to imagine ways in which offensive IW tactics might cost less or be more effective than conventional military options; suffice it to say that almost all the tactics ascribed to our opponents could, at least potentially, be considered for adoption by the United States. Yet the defense community rarely discusses the offensive use of information warfare. The reason for this reticence is that, like intelligence plans and systems, IW options are easily compromised once the opponent learns about them. Even in the case of defensive IW, some government officials are reluctant to discuss the threat, thinking that raising attention to U.S. vulnerabilities will encourage new groups to target the United States.

The problem is that it will be hard to integrate IW into U.S. defense planning without building public support. Citizens will need to understand why the government is undertaking IW programs and how the programs may permit other military programs to be phased out. Without public discussion and under-standing of how IW capabilities might replace some conventional military systems, the nation may needlessly spend money for both conventional and IW programs. Secrecy also tends to increase costs by limiting competition and reducing the ability of DOD to draw on unclassified and commercial programs. One reason why commercial information technology is usually equal or superior to its military counterparts, and almost always less expensive, is that greater competition in the private sector forces innovation and pushes down prices.

Unless U.S. leaders deal with the problem of reconciling secrecy and democ-racy, IW will likely remain a marginal asset. In fact, the political system has considerable experience in dealing with such issues; nuclear weapons, intelli-gence operations, and covert action are all routinely reviewed by Congress and, at a more general level, are discussed in the public media. It seems reasonable that the nation can also have a public debate over the place of IW in U.S. defense policy without compromising the policy itself.

## Prescriptions for Preparedness

Dealing with the IW threat and especially with aggressive attackers who use IW as their main weapon against the United States will require new approaches. In most cases, it will probably be impossible to build a foolproof defense for the civilian information infrastructure. But it should be possible to prevent "cheap kills" by informing the general public and industry of the threat through formal and informal networks for government-civilian cooperation.

In the case of vital military communications links and computer systems, it may be possible to build hardened "point defenses," taking extra steps to thwart attackers. These could include, for example, building dedicated transmission lines for communications, isolating critical computers from all outside networks, and using hardware and software security systems that might be excessively expensive or inconvenient for commercial use but which are necessary for vital

DOD systems. These measures would also need to be repeated in the production of hardware and software, and in some cases dedicated production lines might be necessary for the most sensitive systems.

Yet, because defense and deterrence are both so difficult to achieve in IW, the best strategy to protect the most vital information systems may be stealth—keeping the very existence of such an information system a secret so that it does not become a target. Of course, "secret information system" is the ultimate oxymoron, which is another way of saying that such systems will also likely be among the most expensive, inefficient, and difficult to use.

The most challenging measures, though, are likely to be political, economic, and cultural. IW requires new concepts within DOD because traditional approaches to military planning and military command and control will not work for it. And the same is true across society, where the measures for countering the IW threat will often collide with the essential features of the democratic, free-market system that an IW policy is intended to protect.

# Chapter 34

### ✳ ✳ ✳

# Victory Misunderstood:
# What the Gulf War Tells Us
# about the Future of Conflict

Stephen Biddle

*Stephen Biddle concludes that a synergistic interaction between a major skill imbalance and new technology caused the radical outcome of the 1991 Gulf War. This explanation has important policy implications for net assessment, force planning and the defense budget. Most current net assessment and force planning methodologies focus on the numbers and technical characteristics of the weapons of two adversaries. By misunderstanding the role of skill in military outcomes, the author feels there is serious risk of nations misjudging other states' real military power, thus making major errors in estimates of the forces needed to meet future threats. Similarly, he asserts, arguments that modernization spending should be protected at the expense of training and readiness accounts overestimate the military value of technology per se, and underestimate the role of skill in determining the effects that any given technology will produce. He feels that his conclusions challenge the "new orthodoxy that we are embarked upon a 'revolution in military affairs.'" Is the increased focus on information warfare and military revolution based on a fundamental misreading of the Gulf War? If the author is correct, how can his conclusions be factored into force planning calculations?*

The standard explanations of the Gulf War's outcome are wrong. The orthodox view explains the war's one-sidedness in terms of the Coalition's strengths, especially its advanced technology, which is often held to have destroyed the Iraqis' equipment or broken their will without exposing Coalition forces to extensive close combat on the ground.[1] The main rival explanation

Stephen Biddle is a member of the research staff at the Institute for Defense Analyses (IDA), Alexandria, Virginia.

Stephen Biddle, "Victory Misunderstood: What the Gulf War Tells Us about the Future of Conflict," *International Security*, 21:2, Fall 1996, pp. 139-179. Copyright © 1996 by the President and Fellows of Harvard College and the Massachusetts Institute of Technology.

emphasizes Iraqi shortcomings, such as their weak morale, poor training and leadership, or numerical inferiority in the theater of war.[2] Both schools appeared within a few months of the cease-fire, and have changed surprisingly little since then.[3] The information base on the war's conduct, however, has changed substantially with the recent appearance of the first detailed official and semi-official independent histories of the war.[4] This new information, combined with the results of counterfactual analysis using new computer simulation techniques, undermines both schools' conclusions.

To account for what is now known, and in particular, for new details on the conduct of the ground campaign, I propose a new explanation based partly on a combination of pieces taken from both camps' arguments—but mostly on a different conception of *how* technology and skill affected the outcome. That is, I argue that a synergistic interaction between a major skill imbalance and new technology caused the radical outcome of 1991. In the Gulf War, Iraqi errors created opportunities for new Coalition technology to perform at proving-ground effectiveness levels and sweep actively resisting Iraqi Republican Guard units from the battlefield. Without the Iraqis' mistakes to provide openings, however, the outcome would have been far different in spite of the Coalition's technology, and Coalition casualties would likely have reached or exceeded prewar expectations. But without the new weapons, mistakes like the Iraqis' would not have enabled the Coalition to prevail with the historically low losses of the Gulf War. Many previous armies have displayed combat skills no better than Iraq's, but without producing results anything like those of 1991; only a powerful interaction between skill imbalance and new technology can explain the difference.

This new explanation has important policy implications for net assessment, force planning, and the defense budget. Most current net assessment and force planning methodologies focus on the numbers and technical characteristics of the two sides' weapons.[5] By misunderstanding the role of skill in military outcomes, such methods risk serious misjudgment of states' real military power, and major errors in estimates of the forces needed to meet future threats. Similarly, arguments that modernization spending should be protected at the expense of training and readiness accounts overestimate the military value of technology per se, and underestimate the role of skill in determining the effects that any given technology will produce.[6] While it is always better to have both newer weapons and higher skills, choices must often be made, and it would be a mistake to pay for faster modernization by accepting a less skilled military.

More broadly, this new explanation also challenges perhaps the most sweeping legacy of the war: the new orthodoxy that we are embarked upon a "revolution in military affairs." This thesis holds that precision air and missile strikes will dominate future warfare, and that the struggle for information supremacy will replace the breakthrough battle as the decisive issue for success.[7] I argue that this view is based on a fundamental misreading of the war, and that a proper understanding implies a very different pattern for the conflicts of the future.

To make this case, I first specify the outcome to be explained. I next describe the new information sources on which my analysis of this outcome is based. I then outline briefly the main events of the war, with particular emphasis on the ground campaign, and on a case study of a particular ground engagement (the "Battle of 73 Easting"). From this, I identify a number of important discrepancies between the record of the ground fighting and the implications of the main current explanations of the war's outcome. I then develop my alternative theory, and show how it provides a more satisfactory explanation of what we now know of the war's conduct. Finally, I discuss the implications of that alternative for policy and for scholarship in international security affairs.

## The War's Military Outcome and Its Legacy

While the Gulf War's disappointing political outcome has received much recent attention, my focus is on its military results, and in particular, the Coalition's ability to prevail with a historically low loss rate.

In less than six weeks, 795,000 Coalition troops destroyed a defending Iraqi army of hundreds of thousands, losing only 240 attackers.[8] This loss rate of fewer than one fatality per 3,000 soldiers was less than one tenth of the Israelis' loss rate in either the 1967 Six-Day War or the Bekaa Valley campaign in 1982, less than one twentieth of the Germans' in their blitzkriegs against Poland or France in 1939-40, and about one one-thousandth of the U.S. Marines' in the invasion of Tarawa in 1943.[9]

This unprecedentedly low loss rate came as a major surprise, despite great efforts before the war to predict losses. These efforts attracted many of the country's foremost scholars and policy analysts, and exploited the best available net assessment methods. The results were way off. All published results radically overestimated casualties: the best got no closer than a factor of three; the next best missed by a factor of six. The majority were off by more than an order of magnitude; official estimates were reportedly high by at least that much, while some official projections were reportedly off by more than a factor of 200.[10]

This unexpected and historically low loss rate has had important policy consequences. It has made the Gulf War a shaping event for defense planning in the 1990s in much the same way as the painful defeat in Vietnam came to shape U.S. planning in the 1980s. U.S. forces are now sized and structured against a Gulf War yardstick. New doctrines, weapons, and organizations are assessed in simulations of updated Gulf Wars. Acceptable casualty levels are judged against a 1991 benchmark.[11]

Before 1991, most planners expected future land wars to look like updated mid-century armored breakthrough battles, with air and missile forces playing mostly a supporting role by reducing the contestants' ability to push tanks forward into the decisive struggle at the point of attack.[12] Today, this traditional concept has almost disappeared, replaced by the new consensus that we are embarked upon a "revolution in military affairs" in which armored breakthroughs will be a thing of the past, and the struggle for information supremacy will be decisive. This sweeping policy legacy is a direct consequence of the extreme nature of the war's military outcome, and especially of the radically low Coalition loss rate. The reasons for this outcome are thus an important question for scholarship, and are my focus here.

## New Sources of Information

My explanation of this outcome draws heavily on two new sources of information on the conduct of the war: the Gulf War Air Power Survey and the 73 Easting Project.[13]

The Gulf War Air Power Survey (GWAPS) is an independent analysis commissioned by the U.S. Air Force and modeled on the post-World War II Strategic Bombing Survey. The GWAPS staff had exceptional access to people and information, and produced a detailed five-volume semi-official history of the air war.

The 73 Easting Project is a collaborative study conducted jointly by the independent Institute for Defense Analyses (IDA), the Defense Advanced Research Projects Agency (DARPA), and the U.S. Army. Its purpose was to develop a data base of unprecedented detail on the conduct of a single battle (the "Battle of 73 Easting"), then to use modern computer simulation technology to represent that data in a "virtual re-creation" of the minute-to-minute activities of each participating tank, armored vehicle, truck, or infantry team.[14] The resulting data provides an important resource in itself. But the unique strength of the 73 Easting analysis is the power that computer simulation provides to conduct controlled experiments by changing key characteristics of the historical event, then re-fighting the simulated battle and observing directly the effects on the putative outcome. This makes it possible to test alternative cause-and-effect hypotheses with especially thorough, systematic counterfactual analysis.[15]

Of course, simulation is not reality; as a counterfactual method, it cannot provide the realism of *ex post facto* observation of real events. A combination of simulation experimentation, deductive argument, and historical analysis by process tracing, however, compensates for the weakness of individual methods, and helps make the most of the available information base.

## Overview of Events

The war began with a massive six-week air campaign. This quickly crippled the Iraqi air defense system and destroyed key elements of the Iraqi command and control network. There followed more than a month of effectively uncontested, round-the-clock pounding of ground targets across Iraq and over the entire depth of the Kuwait Theater of Operations (KTO).

As the air war unfolded, Coalition ground forces secretly redeployed from east to west. By February 23, the Coalition had positioned two corps on the Iraqis' extreme right flank. The Iraqis were disposed with 26 conscript infantry divisions deployed forward in a prepared defensive belt. Behind them were 9 higher quality Army mechanized divisions, with 8 elite Republican Guard divisions located well to the rear.[16]

The Coalition ground invasion began on the morning of February 24, when lead elements of two U.S. Marine divisions entered the Iraqi defensive belt near the coastal highway. The main effort, however, was on the far left, where the Coalition VII and XVIII Corps soon followed with a massive single envelopment of the Iraqi forward defenses. This "left hook" quickly collapsed the right wing of the Iraqi defensive belt, and opened a clear path across the Iraqi rear toward the Republican Guard.

Progress was rapid. Iraqi conscript infantry offered little resistance and surrendered in large numbers as Coalition forces overran the forward defenses. By February 26, Kuwait City had been reached, and three heavy divisions of the Coalition VII Corps were massed for a direct assault on the Republican Guard.

Beginning on February 26, VII Corps drove through the Guard from west to east. Unlike the infantry at the border, however, the Guard fought back. By then the surviving Iraqis in the KTO were attempting to withdraw via Basra; perhaps three Guard and another three Army heavy divisions had been redeployed into blocking positions in an attempt to keep their retreat route open.[17] These units were in prepared defenses on familiar terrain, and the result was the heaviest fighting of the campaign as they met the Coalition's heaviest forces head on.

For some 41 hours, a series of battles was fought as VII Corps overran the Iraqi blocking force. Initial contact was made by the U.S. 2nd Armored Cavalry Regiment (ACR), which struck the Iraqi Tawakalna division on a stretch of mostly featureless desert near a map reference line called "73 Easting"; the ensuing engagement thus became known as the "Battle of 73 Easting." Advancing through a heavy sandstorm, the U.S. regiment was ordered to find the enemy, defeat any forward covering forces, determine the position and extent of the main defenses, and fix them in position for assault by the heavier forces advancing behind them. About 4 p.m. on the afternoon of February 26, the regiment's lead troop, under the command of Captain H.R. McMaster, made contact with the main Iraqi position.[18] Launching an immediate assault, McMaster's troop of 9 M1 tanks and 12 M3 Bradleys subsequently destroyed the entire defensive belt in front of them, hitting 37 Iraqi T-72s and 32 other armored vehicles in about 40 minutes. The adjoining troops immediately followed suit. Before stopping to regroup at around 5 p.m., this nominal scouting mission by three U.S. cavalry troops had overrun and wiped out an entire Republican Guard brigade. Subsequent Iraqi counterattacks were beaten off with heavy losses, leaving a total of 113 Iraqi armored vehicles destroyed at the cost of one U.S. Bradley lost and one crew member killed by Iraqi fire (with a second vehicle loss attributed to fratricide). Some 600 Iraqi casualties were removed from the battlefield.[19]

The other actions followed a similar pattern. The largest of these, the Battle of Medina Ridge, pitted the 2nd brigade of the U.S. 1st Armored against the 2nd brigade of the Medina Luminous division. In 40 minutes of fighting, the U.S. brigade annihilated the Iraqi armor in place, took 55 Iraqis prisoner, and killed another 340. No U.S. casualties were suffered.[20] At Objective Norfolk, two battalions of the U.S. 1st Infantry division destroyed more than 100 armored vehicles of the Iraqi Tawakalna and 12th Armored divisions with the loss of two U.S. Bradleys.[21] In the Battle for the Wadi Al Batin, a battalion of the U.S. 3rd Armored division wiped out an Iraqi brigade, killing more than 160 armored vehicles while losing less than a half dozen of its own.[22]

By the morning of February 27, the Iraqi blocking force had been effectively wiped out. In all, VII Corps destroyed as many as 1,350 Iraqi tanks, 1,224 armored troop carriers, 285 artillery pieces, 105 air defense systems and 1,229 trucks. VII Corps itself, by contrast, lost no more than 36 armored vehicles to enemy fire, and suffered a total of only 47 dead and 192 wounded.[23]

## Existing Explanations

What caused this result? The orthodox explanation focuses on Coalition strengths, and especially its superior technology. It holds that new surveillance, air defense suppression, stealth, and precision guidance systems gave Coalition aircraft total command of the skies and radical new lethality against Iraqi ground forces. This in turn enabled the Coalition to destroy the Iraqis' equipment and morale in a six-week air campaign without exposing itself to extensive close combat on the ground.[24] Some members of this school, however, emphasize the Coalition's advanced ground-force technology, such as the thermal sights, compound armor, and depleted uranium (DU) ammunition of the U.S. M1A1 tank, arguing that these enabled Coalition ground forces to strike with virtual immunity from well beyond the effective range of the out-gunned, out-armored Iraqi defenders.[25] Others hold that the Coalition's maneuver warfare concepts (aided significantly by new navigation and communications technologies) enabled it to outflank a static Iraqi defense via sweeping maneuvers conducted over trackless desert, thus ejecting the Iraqis from Kuwait without requiring a costly frontal assault.[26]

On the other hand, some critics have argued that Iraqi shortcomings, not Coalition strengths, were the main reason for the war's one-sidedness. In particular, some have argued that Coalition losses were so low because an unmotivated, dispirited Iraqi army simply did not fight back. As John Mueller recently put it, "The Americans gave a war and no one showed up." A related argument holds that the Iraqis were militarily incompetent, or hopelessly outnumbered.[27] If so, then the Gulf War was less a revolution than merely the "mother of all military anomalies."[28]

In fact, both schools are wrong. To show why, it will be useful to decompose these arguments into their main component pieces. I begin by assessing each component individually, after which I address simple combinations thereof.[29]

***Coalition Strengths***. The components of the "Coalition strengths" school are Coalition air technology, ground technology, and strategy.

*Air Technology.* For new air technology to have caused an unprecedentedly low Coalition loss rate by destroying the Iraqis' equipment or morale before the ground war is to imply that the number of surviving, willing Iraqi troops must also have been unprecedentedly low by February 24.[30] This was not so. The Iraqi armor force that survived the air campaign was still very large by historical standards, and many of these survivors fought back when attacked by Coalition ground forces.

It is now known that about 2000 Iraqi tanks and 2100 other armored vehicles survived the air campaign and were potentially available to resist the Coalition ground attack on February 24. Equipment attrition during the air campaign was highly variable. While some units suffered nearly 100 percent tank losses, others were virtually untouched. Overall, Iraqi tank attrition averaged about 48 percent, armored troop carrier losses were about 30 percent, and artillery losses were just under 60 percent. These were not uniformly distributed, however. In particular, the Republican Guard was significantly less hard-hit than the infantry and Army heavy divisions nearer the border—Guard tank losses, for example, came to less than 24 percent of their prewar KTO strength.[31]

Some of the surviving vehicles' crews surrendered without fighting, or after only token resistance, but others fought back. While the conscript infantry at the border lacked the will to fight (and may never have had it), the Republican Guard and at least some Army heavy divisions tried to resist the Coalition ground attack.

At 73 Easting, for example, 2nd ACR crews reported large volumes of small arms fire rattling off their vehicles during the assault, which means that Iraqi troops stayed at their weapons, returning fire, even as U.S. tanks passed within a few hundred meters of their positions (i.e., within small-arms range).[32] In fact, some Republican Guard infantry are known to have remained at their posts, concealed, until U.S. attackers had actually driven through their positions, only then emerging to fire short range antitank rockets at the vehicles from behind.[33] Heavy weapons fire was also received. Although large-caliber hits were rare, multiple Iraqi tank gun rounds were observed falling near U.S. vehicles.[34]

Perhaps most important, the Tawakalna division not only defended itself when attacked, but also counterattacked the 2nd ACR after being driven from its positions. After nightfall the Iraqis struck the northernmost of the three U.S. cavalry troops engaged, attacking in multiple, reinforced company-strength waves, and supported by dismounted infantry.[35] This assault was broken up long before it posed a serious threat. Moreover, even in the Tawakalna there is little evidence to suggest fanatical combat motivation: more than 200 prisoners surrendered themselves after the battle.[36]

Nevertheless, there is no evidence to suggest that the Iraqis gave up without fighting in 73 Easting. On the contrary, the readiness of Republican Guard counterattackers to advance at all under such withering fire is difficult to square with a conclusion that the Guard had lost the will to fight. The Tawakalna had ample opportunity to surrender or escape if it wished. Iraqi conscripts at the border had given up in the midst of U.S. assaults without suffering harm; if the Tawakalna had wanted, it too could surely have surrendered without fighting. Alternatively, when the 2nd ACR halted to consolidate, at least one other Iraqi battalion located within earshot of the battle had not yet been engaged; the halt offered this battalion an ideal opportunity to escape or surrender. Yet they stayed, fought, and were destroyed when the advance resumed after midnight. In fact, few prisoners on any part of the field were taken while their equipment was still operable; the great majority of those who surrendered did so only after the battle was over, when the Iraqis' armor had been destroyed and some 600 casualties had been suffered.[37]

Nor had the vehicles' crews deserted prior to the battle. The Tawakalna had moved on February 24 from its pre-invasion locations to occupy the blocking position from which it fought on February 26.[38] Vehicles lacking crews would not have been able to move and thus would not have been present on the 73 Easting battlefield. In fact, the entire Iraqi blocking force that opposed the VII Corps advance had redeployed into its battle positions only a few days before its destruction.[39] Though the Iraqi forces in the KTO as a whole were undoubtedly well under-strength by the time of the ground attack, the Guard and Army mechanized units that fought the VII Corps on February 26-28 had ample crews to man the equipment the VII Corps destroyed.

While we know more of the details for 73 Easting than for many of the war's battles, what we do know suggests that Iraqi behavior there was broadly representative of Guard and Army heavy divisions elsewhere as well. Reports of small arms fire striking Allied armor, for example, are widely distributed among accounts of the fighting on the 26th, 27th, and 28th, as are reports of Iraqi counterattacks, significant tank gun fire, and artillery action.[40] All suggest that the will to fight at 73 Easting was generally representative of the Iraqi blocking force, and possibly of other Iraqi units as well.

We will never know exactly how many of the Iraqis' surviving tanks fought back. We do know, however, that the great majority of Iraq's armor was concentrated in the higher quality units where Iraqi will to fight was greatest; the conscript infantry that gave up most readily was systematically under-equipped in heavy weapons and especially in armored vehicles.[41]

As a conservative lower bound on the number of actively resisting Iraqi tanks, one might count only those weapons in the remnants of five divisions from the Iraqi blocking force that are known to have resisted the VII Corps advance. These alone likely disposed of at least 600 surviving tanks and an additional 600 other armored vehicles on February 24.[42] A plausible range of active survivors might thus be 600 to 2000 Iraqi tanks, and 600 to 2100 other armored vehicles.

By contrast with these 1200 to 4100 Iraqi armored vehicles, the entire German army in Normandy had fewer than 500 tanks in July 1944. The Iraqi lower bound still had more tanks than the entire Israeli army in 1967. The upper bound had about as many as the entire Egyptian army in 1973.[43] If the Iraqis had inflicted only as many casualties per capita as the Arabs in 1967, the result would still have been radically higher Coalition losses.[44] Their inability to do so is thus hard to explain by pre-invasion losses of materiel or will power as a result of the air campaign.[45]

*Ground Technology.* Could the Coalition's combination of thermal sights, new armor, stabilized 120-mm guns, and depleted uranium ammunition explain unprecedentedly low Coalition losses? If so, this would imply that friendly forces in close combat *without* these technologies ought to have fared significantly worse than those equipped with them.

This was not so. Coalition ground force technology varied widely, but losses did not. The two U.S. Marine divisions, for example, were equipped mainly with 1960s-era M60A1 tanks with neither the thermal sights, 120-mm guns, DU ammunition, nor composite armor of the Army's M1A1s, yet the Marines suffered *fewer* tank losses than the Army against opposition that included Iraqi heavy divisions which fought back when attacked.[46] In fact, some of the Marines' heaviest fighting was by wheeled, thin-skinned, light armored vehicles (LAVs) such as those which defended against the Iraqi counterattack at the Burqan oil field.[47] The Army itself deployed thousands of lightly armored M2 and M3

Bradleys, and the British committed hundreds of similarly light Warrior troop carriers, all of which engaged in extensive close combat yet suffered very few losses.[48]

Second, a ground technology explanation implies that other battles between similarly equipped opponents should produce roughly similar results. Yet at the Army's National Training Center in the Mohave Desert, literally hundreds of battles have been fought between M1A1-equipped U.S. Army units and (simulated) T72-equipped OPFOR (or "opposition force") opponents, and the T72-equipped OPFOR almost always wins.[49]

*Coalition Strategy.* Others have argued that the Coalition's left hook strategy created the low loss rate by outflanking the Iraqis, forcing them to fight a war of maneuver for which they were ill-prepared.[50] But in fact, the key battles against the Republican Guard took the form of a corps-level frontal assault on a prepared positional defense from precisely the direction the Iraqis had anticipated when they established their blocking positions.[51] Moreover, the entire Marine offensive was a direct, frontal penetration of the Saddam line and the primary battle positions of the Iraqi heavy divisions to its rear.[52] Yet neither the VII Corps nor the Marines suffered heavily as a result.

**Iraqi Weaknesses.** The components of the "Iraqi weaknesses" school are Iraqi numerical inferiority and poor Iraqi troop skills and morale.

*Iraqi Numberical Inferiority.* Many have argued that Iraqi forces in the KTO were seriously understrength, and thus heavily outnumbered by their Coalition opponents.[53] While the Iraqis' actual manpower will probably never be known, it was surely much lower than initial estimates suggested.[54] As a result, the Coalition clearly outnumbered them in the theater overall. In principle, this might explain radically low losses in either of two ways. First, a large force-to-force ratio (or preponderance of attackers over defenders) might enable the attacker to overwhelm the defense so quickly as to quash or preempt effective return fire. Second, a low defensive force-to-space ratio (few defenders spread over a large area) might preclude the conduct of a "coherent" defense, denying the defender the benefits of positional warfare.

But while the *theater* force-to-force and force-to-space ratios may have been very disadvantageous for the Iraqis, the *local* imbalances in many of the key battles were much less so. In many important engagements the Iraqis enjoyed favorable local force ratios, yet still failed to inflict heavier losses. If either of these two mechanisms had been a powerful cause, it should have showed up here in heavier Coalition losses, but this was not so.[55]

At Medina Ridge, for example, a Republican Guard brigade conducted a prepared positional defense on a frontage of under 10 kilometers against an attack of roughly equal size.[56] Standard Western defensive frontages for brigade-size units are about 10-20 kilometers (or up to twice the Medina's), and parity is normally considered a very disadvantageous force-to-force ratio for an attack.[57] Yet the Medina brigade was annihilated by frontal assault without inflicting a single Coalition fatality. At 73 Easting, the Tawakalna's 18th brigade conducted a prepared positional defense on a 15-km front and was attacked frontally by a smaller force, yet the defenders destroyed only one of the attackers' 68 armored vehicles before losing essentially all of their own. If high local force-to-space and low local force-to-force ratios could still produce such low Coalition losses, then it is far from clear that numerical imbalance provides an adequate explanation.[58]

*Iraqi Troop Skills and Morale.* The other element of the "Iraqi shortcomings" argument is that Iraqi soldiers' skills and morale were very weak, while the Coalition's were very strong.[59] Iraqi morale was clearly much weaker, and they made many important errors in handling their forces. The Coalition's people were clearly superior soldiers. In fact, Iraqi mistakes are a necessary element of my explanation, as I argue in more detail below. But they are only a part of the story, and cannot explain the result by themselves.

To explain a historically unprecedented outcome this way is to imply that no prior war could have seen a skill imbalance as great. The Coalition's Gulf War loss rate was lower by at least a factor of ten than the Israelis' in the Six-Day War, or the British against the Italians in North Africa in 1941, or the Royal Marines against Argentine Army conscripts in 1982.[60] Of course, it is hard to measure skill differentials precisely.[61] But it is far from obvious that the difference between Coalition and Iraqi skills in 1991 dwarfs the imbalance between any of these armies. In each case the attacker enjoyed a major advantage in personnel quality and motivation, yet in no case were the attacker's losses anywhere near as low as during the Gulf War. Given this, it seems more likely that skill and motivation comprise only a part of a much larger picture. The challenge for analysis is to understand the complete picture, and how its pieces fit together.

**Simple Combinations of Causes.** How might such a larger picture fit together? One possibility is a simple linear combination of the causes described above. While there are too many possible combinations to address each individually, two general points should be made.

First, while much of the literature cites multiple causes, the analysis of causal mechanisms (or *how* the cited factors brought about the observed outcome) is almost always strictly univariate. That is, individual causes (and their effects) are described independently, providing no reason to expect the combination of several causes to yield more than just the sum of the parts taken individually.

Second, to explain the Gulf War, the sum of the parts must be large indeed. The Coalition loss rate was far lower than even very one-sided historical battles. To explain an order-of-magnitude difference in loss rates between

1991 and 1967 or 1982, for example, by a linear combination of contributing causes thus requires either a long list of contributors, or that at least some be very powerful.

The available information, however, provides little evidence to support such a conclusion. Each of the existing univariate explanations poses serious inconsistencies with the historical record. To explain, for example, the difference in attacker loss rate between the 1991 and 1967 Mideast wars by reference to the linear combination of 1991 air-induced attrition (or non-resistance); 1991 ground technology; skill or combat motivation; and Coalition numerical superiority is to imply that the latter three effects account for more than a factor of four in Iraqi combat performance relative to the Arabs' in 1967,[62] even though Coalition ground technology varied widely across the theater of war; the Arab-Israeli skill/motivation imbalance in 1967 was arguably as large as that of 1991 or nearly so; and many of the key engagements in 1991 were fought without meaningful local numerical advantages.

While such a possibility cannot be entirely ruled out, it is at least not obvious that the effects cited offer the necessary explanatory power in light of all that is now known. The case for an adequate explanation by simple linear combinations of causes is thus far from made.

But while an adequate *linear* combination may be hard to assemble given the limited strength of the component univariate pieces, nonlinear synergistic effects might enable a stronger explanation to be drawn from the same components, since nonlinear explanations permit the multivariate whole to be greater than the sum of its parts. An adequate nonlinear multivariate explanation, however, requires a new causal mechanism, and a demonstration that this mechanism is consistent with the observed events of the war.

## Synergistic Interaction of Skill and Technology

A synergistic interaction between technology and skill enables a more robust accounting on the basis of a smaller number of underlying causes. In particular, the evidence suggests that in the Gulf War, advanced technology raised the costs of defensive error dramatically relative to the consequences of similar mistakes in the past, making possible a radical reduction in attacker losses against an error-prone opponent.

To show how and why, I first describe in some detail a representative sampling of Iraqi mistakes. I then lay out a theory of how such mistakes might have combined with new technologies to create an unprecedented outcome. I close the section with a counterfactual analysis testing this theory against the 73 Easting data base.

*Iraqi Force Employment Mistakes.* The Iraqi military displayed very poor combat skills by contemporary Western standards. This can be illustrated by focusing on just three of their many tactical shortcomings.[63]

First, Iraqi defensive positions were very poorly prepared. The "Saddam line" at the Saudi border was haphazard at best (although given the poor quality of its conscript garrison, it is unclear how significant this was). More important for the outcome, the Republican Guard blocking positions were no better. Western armies dig their fighting positions into the earth below grade, and hide the soil removed in excavation. The Guard, on the other hand, simply piled sand into loose berms, or mounds, on the surface of the ground around combat vehicles and infantry positions.[64] This gave away the defenders' locations from literally thousands of meters away, as the berms were the only distinctive feature of an otherwise flat landscape, without providing any real protection against the fire this inevitably drew.[65] Loose piles of sand cannot stop modern high-velocity tank rounds. In fact, they barely slow them down. U.S. crews in 73 Easting reported seeing 120-mm tank rounds pass through Iraqi berms, through the Iraqi armored vehicle behind the berm, and off into the distance.[66] No U.S. tank crew would leave itself so exposed.

Republican Guard positions were also virtually devoid of anti-tank mines, ditches, wire entanglements, or any other attempts to delay or channel an attacker's progress.[67] In Western armies, units automatically begin preparing their positions as soon as they occupy them. If kept in place for more than a few hours, they begin to dig fighting positions, construct barriers and lay mines, with engineering assistance if available, but if not, then with the unit's own manpower. The Iraqi blocking positions had evidently been occupied for some time, yet they remained without even rudimentary countermobility preparations.[68] No U.S. unit would remain so inactive.

Second, the Republican Guard failed to coordinate the efforts of the different arms at its disposal. In particular, artillery support was almost wholly absent, both in defense against American assaults and in support of the Guard's own counterattacks. The Iraqis made some attempt to direct artillery against the advancing Americans, but proved unable either to adjust fire against moving targets (a difficult task) or even to deliver fire in mass against fixed points as Americans moved past them (an easier job).[69] The Iraqi counterattack at 73 Easting was executed with only a rudimentary attempt to suppress U.S. fire with artillery, or to screen the advance with artillery-delivered smoke.[70] Nor did the Iraqis make any attempt to scout the ACR's positions before the assault, to use engineers to create smoke or other obscuration, or to coordinate assault forces' movement with the use of overwatch elements to provide covering fire.[71]

Third, Iraqi covering forces systematically failed to alert their main defenses of the U.S. approach, allowing even Republican Guard units to be taken completely by surprise. Going back at least as far as World War I, all Western armies have used covering forces—whether observation posts, forward reconnaissance screens, or delaying positions—to provide warning to the main defenses that they are about to be attacked. Ideally, these covering forces serve other functions as well (such as stripping away the opponent's recon elements, slowing the attacker's movement, or channeling the assault), but the minimum function they must perform is to notify the main defense of an attacker's approach. This is not difficult. A one-word radio message is enough to sound the alarm. Even less can work if commanders agree in advance that failure to check in at specified times will be taken as warning of attack. The brevity of the message makes it virtually impossible to jam; the procedural backup of interpreting silence as warning means that even a dead observer can provide an alert.[72]

Yet at 73 Easting, for example, the Iraqi main position received no warning of the 2nd ACR's approach. A few observation posts were deployed well forward of the main defenses, but these were evidently destroyed without sending any messages, and without the local commander interpreting silence as evidence of attack.[73]

As a result, the Iraqi defenders were unready to meet the attack when it arrived. At a minimum, this slowed their reaction time in the initial exchange of fire. It may also have provided some U.S. attackers an opportunity to engage empty targets for the crucial opening minutes of the battle. Combat vehicles are rarely fully manned unless standing watch or otherwise on alert, which the Tawakalna as a formation was not. Thus it is likely that only a few on-watch vehicles were fully manned, while others would have been empty or manned by skeleton crews. In fact, there is evidence to suggest that many Iraqi crews interpreted the opening explosions of the battle as an air attack (they had received no warning of a ground advance); hence even some skeleton crews abandoned their vehicles to take cover in nearby air raid shelters at the very moment the ground attack began. As the attack's nature became clear, many of these crews attempted to remount, but by then dozens of Iraqi tanks and BMPs had already been destroyed, and by the time the remounting crews could get their weapons into action still more had been lost.[74]

By contrast, U.S. troops fought extremely well. At 73 Easting, for example, the 2nd ACR maintained a tight, efficient combat formation throughout an extended approach march, and did so in the midst of a sandstorm, in hostile territory, over unfamiliar terrain, and without significant losses to mechanical breakdown or logistical failure en route. Its crews' gunnery was exceptional, outperforming peacetime proving ground standards for both the M1 and the Bradley. The first three kills by Eagle troop were recorded in three shots by a single M1 over an interval of less than ten seconds.[75] As a whole, 182 of 215, or 85 percent, of the shots fired by 2nd ACR crews struck their targets at ranges of up to 2000 meters, under combat conditions.[76] Similar results were obtained by U.S. forces throughout the KTO.[77]

***The Price of Mistakes as a Function of the Opponents Technology.*** Mistakes are always damaging, and errors like poor position preparation, weak combined arms coordination, or failure to provide attack warning would hurt any twentieth-century defender. As technology has become more sophisticated, however, the consequences of such errors have progressively risen.

For example, against an attacker on foot armed with light machine guns of under 100 meters' effective range and supported only by artillery with little capability to adjust fire quickly, such defensive errors would be harmful but not necessarily catastrophic.[78] Against an armored attacker with an effective range of 500-1000 meters in daylight, and supported by aircraft dropping unguided bombs, the cost would be higher.[79] But against an attacker with all-weather, day/night thermal tank sights, stabilized 120-mm guns armed with DU ammunition effective on the first shot at 3000 meters, aircraft armed with precision-guided munitions (PGMs) and complete command of the sky, or attack helicopters with 5000-meter-range missiles capable of responding in minutes to a radio call from a forward observer, such slip-ups can very quickly be lethal to a very large number of defenders. If the defenders' mistakes are varied enough, and the attackers' suite of sophisticated technologies is diverse enough, then the number of ways in which defensive error can combine with decisive offensive exploitation becomes so wide as to enable a heterogeneous attack force, some of it sophisticated and some not, to find ways to prevail with very limited costs to any part of the offensive array.

While such interactions can dramatically increase weapon effectiveness, they can also imply very different roles, or mechanisms, by which specific systems influence outcomes. Perhaps the best example may be Coalition air technology. Most analyses have focused on its ability to destroy ground targets directly (and to influence Iraqi morale via direct attack of ground targets). Yet its *indirect* role in increasing Coalition *ground* force effectiveness—for example by increasing the cost of Iraqi covering force mistakes—may have been just as important and possibly broader in its impact.

Coalition air supremacy exposed Iraqi ground targets to continuous air attack. Many Iraqis survived these attacks, but responded by reducing vehicle manning levels: vehicles were known to be the primary air targets, and had virtually no capability against Coalition aircraft, hence many of the skeleton crews that might ordinarily have been left to stand watch were removed from Iraqi tanks and troop carriers. Moreover, weeks of unopposed air attack eventually bred a widespread assumption that all attacks were from the air, encouraging a reflex action of seeking cover in air raid shelters rather than in armored vehicles when under fire.[80] This greatly increased the effects of the Iraqis' failure to provide warning of ground force attack. It always hurts to be surprised. But when apparently invulnerable aircraft induce defenders to reduce vehicle manning levels, surprise takes on new significance: instead of partially manned weapons providing hasty covering fire while the remainder of their crews remount, empty vehicles now remain silent while their crews remain under cover trying to determine whether the attack is from the air (in which case they should stay put) or the ground (indicating they should remount).[81] The result was a powerful, but indirect, interaction effect of superior air technology and Iraqi error: by increasing the frequency with which targets would be unoccupied as a result of the Iraqis' failure to obtain warning, Coalition air technology increased friendly ground forces' ability to exploit Iraqi covering force mistakes.[82]

But while advanced technology has raised the cost of error dramatically, it has not affected well-handled defenses to nearly the same degree. While U.S. 120-mm guns with DU ammunition can perforate mounded dirt and destroy ill-prepared tanks from thousands of meters away, they cannot penetrate enough solid earth to harm a tank dug into the ground properly rather than perched on the surface. Thermal sights can identify exposed targets from tremendous distances at night, through dust, or in a sandstorm, but they cannot see targets that have been properly concealed below ground level. Air supremacy can induce defending tank crews to reduce manning levels, but if the defender's covering forces provide proper warning, then vehicles will be reoccupied before they can be overrun. In general, skillful handling of defending forces can thus often foreclose an attacker's best technological opportunities and thereby erode markedly the advantages of even very superior opposing weapons.

Even advanced technology and defensive error, however, cannot provide victory at very low losses unless the *attacker* is highly skilled. Opportunity is meaningless unless it can be exploited, and finding ways to exploit diverse and often idiosyncratic or unexpected defensive mistakes requires flexibility, initiative, and insight. The advanced weapons that provide the opportunity must be operated to their full potential, and such weapons often demand higher levels of training than do simpler systems. And mistakes can kill attackers, too. Even simple, hand-held antitank rockets fired from poorly prepared defensive positions can kill the most advanced tank if allowed a clear shot from the right direction at the right distance. Skilled offensive force employment is required if such opportunities are to be denied to the defense.

Offensive skill, defensive error, and advanced technology thus interact in a powerful, nonlinear way. Given an advanced technology attack, defensive error yields rapid, one-sided defeat, whereas the same mistakes against older technology would produce much less dramatic effects. Moreover, the combination of advanced technology and defensive error requires offensive skill to produce radically low losses: unskilled attackers may not find the right matches between defensive error and offensive technology, nor implement them without allowing defenders too many openings to kill attackers in the process. Each causal variable's effects thus change dramatically as a function of the others' presence or absence; contributing causes that are weak alone can be very powerful in interaction. This in turn enables an extreme outcome to be explained without having to pile up a long list of modest contributors.

By contrast with univariate or multivariate linear alternatives, this explanation can account for much of the new evidence on the conduct of the war. It explains, for example, how Coalition troops could fight through substantial, unbroken ground defenses without heavy losses; how a diverse array of Coalition weapons could prevail so one-sidedly against the Iraqis, when similar weapons cannot do so against the nearly error-free OPFOR at the National Training Center; how Coalition attackers could succeed even at modest local numerical advantages; and why historical skill mismatches (at lower levels of technological sophistication) have never provided such low offensive losses in the past. Finally, this explanation provides a causal mechanism by which a modest list of causes with modest power individually might combine to induce dramatic overall effects.

***Simulation Experiments.*** To explore the idea more fully, and from a different direction, I return to the 73 Easting Project, and in particular, to the computer simulations of the battle conducted by the Institute for Defense Analyses and the U.S. Army.[83] Many runs have been conducted in the course of the project; I concentrate here on a subset designed to examine the effects of technology and troop skills on casualty levels. In particular, these runs look at the interactions of:

- two of the Iraqi errors described above: poor defensive preparations, and failure of the covering forces to provide warning;

- two forms of the Coalition technological advantage described above: the thermal sights of the M1A1, and the air defense suppression systems that enabled Coalition aircraft to operate with impunity over the KTO; and

- one potential error in Coalition force employment that Coalition skill averted but that a less proficient force might have committed: a strung-out assault formation as a result of the 2nd ACR's extended approach march.

The runs are designed to contrast a base case corresponding to the historical technology, U.S. force employment, Iraqi unit dispositions, and the two Iraqi errors described above with a set of excursion cases (or scenarios with controlled variations from the base case), in which Iraqi errors are systematically corrected, Coalition technological advantage is systematically reduced, and Coalition skills are impaired.[84]

The results are summarized in Table 1, and illustrated graphically in Figure 1. They suggest four key observations.

*Technology Against an Error-Free Defense.* First, against an error-free defense, the 2nd ACR's technology overmatch did not provide victory at very low losses. Scenario A assumes that both of the Iraqi errors considered here are corrected—that is, that the above-ground revetments of the historical battle are entirely replaced with below-ground, turret-down positions from which the occupants move up to a hull-down posture upon acquiring a target;[85] and that functioning observation posts provide tactical warning of the attackers' approach. Coalition technology, Coalition skill, and all other aspects of the base case are held constant. As a consequence, simulated U.S. vehicle losses rise from only two in the base case to almost 50 (more than 70 percent of total U.S. strength), while Iraqi losses fall from 86 to about 30, even given the technological advantages of the M1A1, the effects of Coalition air supremacy, and the skilled handling of the U.S. attack.[86]

How is it that defensive error (and its absence) has such a large effect on attacker casualties here? The answer has to do with the way Iraqi errors play into the strengths of U.S. technology. Many have argued, for example, that thermal sights gave the United States an enormous range advantage over the Iraqis in the raging sandstorm of February 26.[87] For superior target acquisition range to be useful, however, there must be exposed targets to acquire. In the base case, the Iraqis' poorly constructed above-ground revetments guarantee this. In fact, the berms advertise the defenders' locations to attackers with advanced sights. In excursion scenario A, on the other hand, correct terrain preparation causes the Iraqis' vehicles to be concealed in turret-down positions unless their own crews see targets. At long range, where the thermal sight enables the attacker to see in spite of the sandstorm but where the defender's simple optics are blinded, the defenders (who see no targets) now remain concealed and the attackers have nothing to shoot at. Only when the attackers close the range and are seen do the defenders move into hull-down firing positions and become exposed. The net result is that the firefight takes place at much shorter range, and the long potential acquisition range of the thermal sight is negated.

Similarly, the Iraqis' failure to provide warning plays into the strengths of Coalition air technology. Advanced air defense suppression systems (together with the defeat of the Iraqi air force) afforded the Coalition air supremacy over the KTO. While this did not produce extensive direct air attrition to the Iraqi units that fought in 73 Easting, it did indirectly reduce their average manning levels. This potentially reduced their return fire in the critical opening minutes of the battle, and potentially enabled the attackers to kill undermanned Iraqi vehicles before they could be fully ready to fight. But to realize this potential required that the defenders be taken by surprise. If the main defenses had been warned in time, they could have regained full readiness

## Table 1
## Simulation Experiment Results

| Scenario | Key Features | U.S. Armored Vehicle Losses | | | Iraqi Armored Vehicle Losses | | | Loss Exchange Ratio (Iraqi: U.S. losses) |
| --- | --- | --- | --- | --- | --- | --- | --- | --- |
| | | Mean | Standard Error | Fractional Loss | Mean | Standard Error | Fractional Loss | |
| Base | Both Iraqi errors corrected | 2.00 | 0.94 | 0.03 | 85.80 | 3.46 | 0.77 | 42.90 |
| A | Iraqi berm error corrected | 48.30 | 4.30 | 0.71 | 31.20 | 5.98 | 0.28 | 0.65 |
| B | Iraqi warning error corrected | 5.30 | 1.83 | 0.08 | 57.20 | 4.24 | 0.51 | 10.79 |
| C | No U.S. thermal; Iraqi warning error corrected | 1.80 | 0.92 | 0.03 | 86.10 | 3.70 | 0.77 | 47.83 |
| D | No U.S. thermal; neither Iraqi error corrected | 39.10 | 2.18 | 0.58 | 38.30 | 3.23 | 0.34 | 0.98 |
| E | No U.S. thermal; neither Iraqi error corrected | 15.90 | 5.13 | 0.23 | 59.80 | 5.35 | 0.53 | 3.76 |
| F | No U.S. thermal, no U.S. air; neither Iraqi error corrected | 40.00 | 2.10 | 0.59 | 38.00 | 3.30 | 0.34 | 0.95 |
| G | U.S. formation strung out; neither Iraqi error corrected | 25.20 | 2.86 | 0.37 | 93.20 | 0.63 | 0.83 | 3.70 |

NOTES: Fractional loss provides the mean loss expressed as a fraction of the total vehicles available to that side at the beginning of the battle. For each scenario, ten runs were conducted; mean values provide arithmetic means for each set of ten runs.

**Figure 1**
**Simulation Experiment Results (73 Easting)**

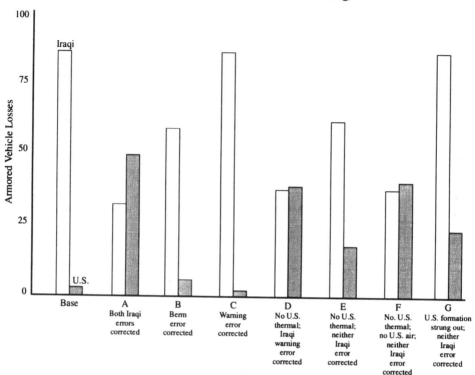

before meeting the attack, thus negating the indirect effects of Coalition air supremacy. In the historical battle (and the simulated base case), the Iraqi covering force's failure to send an alert prevented this. For many Tawakalna crews, their first warning appears to have been the destruction of their armor as the 2nd ACR opened fire. In excursion scenario A, however, adequate warning is provided, enabling all the defenders' vehicles to be manned and ready when the attacker appears. As a result, the indirect effects of air supremacy cannot be exploited and the outcome is a far less one-sided firefight in spite of the U.S. technological advantage.

*Technology Against an Almost Error-Free Defense.* A defense that is even slightly less than error-free is extremely vulnerable to an attacker with advanced technology. Excursion scenarios B and C assume that only one of the Iraqi errors is left uncorrected.[88] In excursion B, terrain preparation is remedied, but the covering force still fails to alert the defenses; in excursion C, the covering force performs properly but the defenses are still poorly prepared. In both excursion scenarios, the attacker annihilates the defender at losses little higher than those of the historical base case (in excursion B, 5 simulated U.S. vehicle losses rather than the 2 of the base case; and in excursion C, only about 2).

This is because the potential lethality of advanced weapons is so high that an opportunity to use even a part of the Coalition's technology suite at full capacity can be decisive in itself. The M1A1's thermal sight offered a potential range advantage of more than 1600 meters in the sandstorm of the historical battle. If poor Iraqi position preparation allows the 2nd ACR to exploit this advantage, then it does not matter whether the victims are also surprised or not: the range advantage alone is more than enough to annihilate the defense even if the defenders are ready to fight from the outset. Coalition air supremacy induced many Iraqis to leave their vehicles unoccupied. If the Iraqis allow themselves to be surprised in this state, then the resulting chance to engage empty or unready targets through the critical early minutes of the attack is decisive in it-self—whether the unready defenders are destroyed from 2000 meters away as they sit on the surface behind loose sand piles, or whether the shooting is done from point blank range against (unready) tanks that sit idly in better-dug, below-grade positions.

*Lesser Technology and the Consequences of Mistakes.* Less sophisticated or less diverse offensive technology reduces the consequences of a defender's mistakes. The simulation results suggest that the less advanced the attacker's technology, the more errors the defender can tolerate and still avert disaster. Conversely, the more advanced the attacker's technology, the more nearly perfect the defense must be to avoid catastrophe. If the simulated Coalition attacker enjoys the full technology advantage that the Coalition did in the actual battle, virtually error-free defensive employment is required for the Iraqis to avert disaster, as can be seen by comparing the base case with excursion scenarios A, B, and C. But if the attacker's technology advantage is reduced, the Iraqis can accept some degree of error and still impose heavy losses on the attacker. In excursion scenario D, for example, the attacker is denied the use of thermal sights, and it benefits only from the indirect effects of air supremacy, while the Iraqis commit only one of the two base case errors: they are assumed to obtain adequate warning, but they retain their problematic revetted vehicle positions. The resulting attacker casualties increase substantially relative to the historical base case (39 instead of 2).

But while the simulated Iraqis can tolerate somewhat more error against this lower-technology attack, they still cannot afford to make as many mistakes as the Iraqis actually did. In excursion scenario E, the attacker is again denied thermal sights, while the Iraqis commit both of the two base case errors; the resulting attacker losses are less than half the results that obtain when the Iraqis commit only one of the two errors (16 instead of 39).

If the Coalition technology advantage is reduced enough, however, then even a defense committing both base case errors can still impose severe costs on the attacker. In excursion scenario F, the attacker is denied both the thermal sight and air supremacy, while the Iraqis commit both errors assumed in the base case.

The resulting casualties are substantially higher than those of the historical base case (i.e., 40 instead of 2).

*Offensive Execution and Technology.* Without skillful offensive execution, even advanced technology and a poorly handled defense cannot ensure low offensive casualties. Excursion scenario G posits a less skillful U.S. advance to contact, where the concentrated, well-coordinated formation of the historical base case is replaced with a strung-out alternative typical of poorly trained units.[89] All other properties of the base case are held constant, including the attacker's technological advantages and the defender's force employment errors. Even given the historical technical edge and defensive errors, simulated U.S. losses in the excursion scenario rise by more than a factor of ten (from 2 to more than 25 vehicles killed).

The reason for this is that the edge provided by reduced defender manning levels and long-range offensive target acquisition cannot compensate for an inability to mass fires. To provide victory at very low losses under the conditions of 73 Easting, the attacker must destroy most or all of the defending vehicles before closing to within visual range of the surviving alerted defenders (and thus becoming exposed to accurate defensive fire). If the attacking formation is allowed to spread out during an extended approach march, however, as assumed in excursion scenario G, the result is a piecemeal commitment without the needed concentration. Arriving in penny packets, the attackers can still kill many defenders at long range, but they cannot kill enough to prevent survivors from extracting a toll as the small groups of attackers eventually come within visual range of the defenders.

**Implications of the Simulation Results.** Taken together, the counterfactuals suggest two broad implications for casualty causation in the Gulf War. First, the skill-technology synergy explanation is consistent with the simulation results. Where defensive error provided openings for offensive technology to exploit, the result was offensive victory by an outnumbered attacker at very low losses. But without defensive mistakes, advanced technology could not prevent radically higher attacker casualties. And without offensive skill, even advanced technology and defensive error proved insufficient to hold attacker casualties down to anything near Gulf War levels. Moreover (for a skilled attacker), the more advanced the attacker's technology, the graver were the consequences of a given defender mistake, and the fewer the mistakes the defender could afford to make without courting disaster. In these simulation runs, technology thus acted as a wedge, driving apart the real military capability of skilled and unskilled forces, increasing the premium on skilled combat performance, and raising the standards for acceptable levels of skill on the part of armies faced with an advanced technology opponent.

Second, the simulation results are inconsistent with the linear multivariate model implicit in the current literature. A linear relationship between casualties, technology, offensive skill, and defensive skill would imply that the marginal effect of any one contributing cause would be about the same regardless of the presence or absence of the others, and that the marginal effects of each would be roughly independent of its level (that is, there should be no diminishing or increasing marginal returns: given two technologies with roughly equal independent effects on casualties, the results of introducing or removing one should be about the same whether the other is present or not). Yet the value of the attackers' weapon technology varied radically with the presence or absence of defensive errors and offensive skill. The effects of either of the tested defensive errors varied radically as a function of whether the other was also present. In the presence of two defensive errors, either thermal sights or air supremacy produced about the same attacker losses, whereas with only one error present, the two technologies produced very different results. In these runs, the effects of the respective contributing causes thus do not simply cumulate linearly: they interact in a powerful, nonlinear manner.

## Conclusions

There are important discrepancies between the historical record and the existing explanations of the Coalition's low loss rate. Between 600 and 2000 surviving Iraqi tanks and 610-2100 other armored vehicles actively fought back when the VII Corps and 1st and 2nd Marine Divisions struck the Republican Guard and Iraqi Army heavy divisions beginning on February 26. These engagements were mostly frontal assaults at often very modest local numerical odds. Under such conditions, a defending force this size could be expected, given historical effectiveness levels, to inflict much higher losses than the Coalition actually suffered in 1991. Arguments explaining an unprecedented loss rate in terms of broken Iraqi will, air attrition of Iraqi ground equipment, Coalition strategy, or Iraqi numerical inferiority thus face a considerable burden of contradictory evidence.

Explanations focused on skill or land warfare technology per se encounter difficulties of their own. The former implies that the 1991 skill imbalance must have been of unprecedented magnitude, a conclusion for which no adequate supporting evidence has been advanced to date. The latter implies that technologically diverse Coalition ground forces should have suffered different casualty levels (and in particular, that U.S. Marine or Bradley-equipped Army units without the technological overmatch typically ascribed to the M1A1 should have suffered heavily), yet they did not. Similarly, such an explanation implies that technologically similar ground forces should produce roughly similar results, whereas a comparison of Gulf War and National Training Center experience suggests quite the opposite.

Simple linear combinations of these effects might provide a somewhat better explanation, but multivariate linear explanations are no better than the sum of their univariate parts, and those parts seem quite weak here. Moreover, several basic assumptions of any linear model (e.g., weak interaction effects among explanatory variables and constant marginal effects with respect to level) are at odds with the results of counterfactual analyses conducted on the 73 Easting data base.

To account more fully for these properties of the war's conduct and results, I have argued that a nonlinear synergistic interaction between these variables caused the radical outcome of 1991. In particular, the Coalition's advanced technology made it possible to exploit Iraqi mistakes with unprecedented severity, enabling entire Republican Guard divisions to be annihilated in close combat with minimal losses.

In this, the breadth of the Coalition's technology advantage and the scope and diversity of Iraqi mistakes created many different possibilities for decisive exploitation. The thermal sights and 120-mm guns of the 2nd ACR's M1A1s could wipe out Iraqi armor that had been left above ground in ill-conceived sand revetments; alternatively, the indirect effects of Coalition air supremacy could interact with the poor performance of Iraqi covering forces to enable a 1960s-era Marine Corps M60A1s to destroy Iraqi tanks unoccupied before their surprised crews could remount. Many other such combinations existed, many of which would probably have enabled the Coalition to recapture the KTO with modest losses. Against a technology advantage as broad and as deep as the Coalition enjoyed in 1991, the Iraqis would have needed a virtually error-free defensive battle to have avoided disaster—and the Iraqi defense was anything but error-free.

If the Iraqis had attained Western standards of organizational performance, however, this analysis suggests that the results would have been radically different, even given the Coalition's advanced technology and high troop skills. Without errors to exploit, modern technology cannot provide anything like the lethality seen in 1991.

This in turn suggests a broader hypothesis: that in general, late-twentieth century technology may be magnifying the effects of skill differentials on the battlefield. If so, then a given skill imbalance may be much more important today than in the past, but combat outcomes for comparably skilled opponents may be little changed by new weaponry. The main effect of new technology may thus be to act as a wedge, gradually driving apart the real military power of states that can field skilled military organizations and those that cannot, but without changing fundamentally the outcomes of wars between equally skilled armies.

*Implications for Policy.* Perhaps the Gulf War's broadest policy influence has been in persuading decision-makers that we may be on the verge of a revolution in military affairs brought about by the radical impact of new technology on warfare. If so, then such a revolution would imply a wide variety of changes in the way the United States should equip and operate its forces, as well as the conditions under which those forces should be committed to battle and the results they could be expected to obtain.

Counterarguments have been advanced. In particular, it has been argued that the desert terrain of the KTO, the poor strategic decision-making of Saddam Hussein, or other idiosyncratic features of the Gulf War mean that Desert Storm is not repeatable, and thus that predictions of a revolution in warfare are premature.[90]

The analysis presented here, however, suggests a different conclusion than either of these. That is, I would agree that the Gulf War does provide important evidence for understanding the future of warfare, but that its meaning has been misinterpreted.

In particular, the role played by skill differentials—and especially the role of opposing error—has been seriously misunderstood. Arguments that the Gulf War was merely idiosyncratic often focus on Iraqi mistakes, but typically imply either that these were somehow unique or anomalous, or that such errors are themselves sufficient to explain the Gulf War outcome. Neither is the case. Many past armies have fought with skills apparently no better than the Iraqis', and there seems little reason to suppose that this cannot happen again. In fact, it could be argued that Iraqi performance in 1991 was representative of at least an important subset of potential future U.S. opponents.[91] And the interaction between skill and technology is powerful enough that if a future opponent fights a major regional contingency with no greater skills than the Iraqis', then the United States could well prevail again with very low losses, even if the terrain or geo-political context were very different from those of 1991. In 1996, U.S. technology advantages are many, U.S. personnel are highly skilled and resourceful, and it is possible to imagine a variety of plausible opposing mistakes that such a combination could punish very severely even without the flat desert or elaborate Saudi Arabian logistical facilities of 1991.[92]

The Gulf War is thus not *sui generis*. But neither does it provide evidence that new technology (with or without doctrinal change) is creating a military revolution in which Gulf War-like results will become the norm for the major regional contingencies of the future. This is because no country can control the skills of its opponents, and these are likely to vary. Skills as low as the Iraqis' are probably more widespread than assumed by some; they are probably less widespread than needed for the Gulf War to provide a new paradigm for the future. If skill and technology interact as powerfully as suggested here, then skill variations are likely to become increasingly powerful drivers of military outcomes as technology advances, and this implies wider variance in future combat results, not a new pattern of quick, decisive results.

Rather than a revolution through information dominance and precision strike, what the Gulf War really suggests is thus a new ability to exploit mistakes. This, however, suggests very different policies. If new technology offered tremendous military power to any who acquired the new systems (and reformed their military doctrine to exploit them), this implies a powerful incentive for radical change: those who realize the full potential of the new era would enjoy enhanced security and influence, while those who do not do so would risk being left behind. This has led many "revolution" proponents to argue that the United States must, as quickly as possible, move away from such obsolescent "sunset systems" as heavy direct-fire ground forces, nonstealthy aircraft, or carrier battlegroups, and instead field a wholly new generation of deep precision-strike and information-warfare technologies. It is often argued that to do this, the United States should reorder near-term funding to preserve modernization (and redirect it away from incremental improvement of obsolescent weapon types), even at the expense of readiness or force structure. Similarly, it is argued that current operational concepts centered on outdated equipment risk the fate of French defensive doctrine at the hands of German blitzkrieg concepts in 1940, and that the U.S. military must therefore adopt radically new doctrinal and organizational ideas.[93]

But if, as I have argued, modern warfare provides increasing penalties for error but little ability to prevail cheaply over skilled enemies, then both the benefits of change and the costs of continuity are much lower. If so, then rapid modernization increases U.S. capabilities mostly where they are already very strong, against unskilled opponents, but offers little where they are not, against those with better skills. The practical benefits would thus be much smaller than often argued. Conversely, the threat to U.S. forces if potential opponents acquire such technologies and use them against the United States is also much smaller as long as the U.S. military retains the quality of its people and its organizations. If one's own skills are high, one is insulated to an important degree against variations in opposing technology, even if one's own weapons change only incrementally.

Thus one should be wary of proposals to protect modernization funding at the expense of training and readiness accounts. A less-skilled military is more dangerous than less-advanced technology.[94] The decay of today's combat skills would not only forfeit the ability to exploit current technical advantages against less-skilled opponents, but it would also enable future challengers to turn the tables by acquiring better technology themselves and using it to its full potential against inadequately skilled Americans. Neither is a risk worth taking.

The Gulf War's failure to provide evidence for a revolution in military affairs thus has important ramifications for modernization policy and defense budget priorities. It also affects net assessment and force planning more generally.

Force planning is often done by analogy, especially in the public literature, using planning yardsticks derived from apparently comparable military experience in the past. In recent years, the Gulf War has been the most widely used yardstick, and has influenced, explicitly or implicitly, even the most consequential official force planning analyses.[95] Yet the Gulf War outcome, and thus the adequacy of the forces used there, were powerfully influenced by the Iraqi military's limited skills. This creates two serious problems for force planners. First, requirements derived from a Gulf War yardstick could prove dangerously inadequate if applied against enemies more skilled than the Iraqis. But second, against unskilled enemies the Gulf force structure may *over*estimate future requirements: by the analysis above, it is at least plausible that a smaller Coalition force could still have prevailed at very low losses given the powerful interaction between skill and technology. Either way, for the Gulf War to provide a meaningful contribution to force planning requires a more discriminating treatment of opponents' skills than we have typically provided in the past; existing plans based on more conventional understandings of the war are potentially in serious error.

Most net assessments of foreign military capability turn on force size and weapon performance characteristics. The analysis above, however, suggests that neither feature provides much explanatory power for the actual combat outcome in 1991, at least not in the absence of a sound understanding of the skills of the organizations using them. This in turn suggests that net assessments carried out without such an understanding are subject to serious inaccuracies. Likewise, cost-effectiveness analyses of proposed weapon acquisitions can radically miscalculate the real military effectiveness of a new program if they do so without an explicit consideration of the interaction between the new system and the ways in which potential opponents might use their forces.

The Gulf War experience thus suggests that the global distribution of military skill and organizational performance is a pivotal issue for effective net assessment, weapon system cost-effectiveness analysis, and force planning, not to mention the debate over the prospects for revolutionary change in the nature of warfare itself. Yet the skills of national military organizations have not heretofore been the subject of systematic study. While anecdotal evaluations of individual armies have been compiled for generations, there have been few attempts to harness rigorous social scientific methods for the development of a deeper or more general understanding of the causes or distribution of such skills. And by contrast with the enormous effort, now spanning more than thirty years, to develop better understandings of the technical performance of weapons, the effort expended to date in understanding how those weapons interact with the skills of users and opponents to produce real combat results has been truly minuscule. A reallocation of intellectual effort is thus long overdue.

Of course, these conclusions are based on the technology of 1991 as observed in the Gulf War. The possibility cannot be excluded that future weapons might change the dynamics of battle in ways that render such conclusions invalid and bring about a revolution, perhaps of the type so often discussed. No analysis of the Gulf War can substitute for thoughtful speculation on the future. But the belief, now widespread, that radical change is upon us is based largely on the perceived experience of 1991, and that experience has been misread. Moreover, what we now know of the events of 1991 suggests that current net assessment and force planning methods may be significantly biased as a consequence of systematic misunderstanding of the role of skill in actual combat outcomes. The past can tell us only so much about the future, and it is always possible that it cannot tell us enough to provide a sound guide to current policy. But it is always a mistake to misunderstand the past, and we cannot possibly determine the proper relationship between current policy and recent history until we have got the history right.

This analysis was supported by the IDA Central Research Program. The views expressed are those of the author, however, and do not necessarily represent positions of IDA, its management, or sponsors. The author would like to thank Richard Betts, Tami Davis Biddle, Eliot Cohen, Steven David, Peter Feaver, Wade Hinkle, Marshall Hoyler, Christopher Jehn, Chaim Kaufmann, Michael Leonard, H.R. McMaster, Jesse Orlansky, Brad Roberts, Richard Swain, John Tillson, Robert Turrell, Victor Utgoff, Larry Welch, Caroline Ziemke, Robert Zirkle, and the members of the MIT DACS Program, the UNC Carolina Seminar, and the Triangle Universities Security Seminar for helpful comments on earlier drafts. Responsibility for any errors, however, remains the author's alone.

## Notes

1. See, e.g., William J. Perry, "Desert Storm and Deterrence," *Foreign Affairs, Vol.* 70, No. 4 (Fall 1991), pp. 66-82; Bobby R. Inman, Joseph S. Nye, Jr., William J. Perry, and Roger K. Smith, "U.S. Strategy After the Storm," in Joseph S. Nye, Jr., and Roger K. Smith, eds., *After the Storm: Lessons from the Gulf War* (New York: Madison Books for the Aspen Strategy Group, 1992), pp. 267-289; U.S. House Armed Services Committee, *Defense for a New Era: Lessons of the Persian Gulf War* (Washington, D.C.: U.S. Government Printing Office [U.S. GPO], 1992), hereafter cited as HASC, *Defense for a New Era.* Some have also explained the outcome in terms of superior Coalition military doctrine or strategic decision-making, or the training of Coalition troops, though these arguments have played a less central role. See, e.g., Lawrence Freedman and Efraim Karsh, *The Gulf Conflict, 1990-1991: Diplomacy and War in the New World Order* (Princeton, N.J.: Princeton University Press, 1993), p. 437; Norman Friedman, *Desert Victory: The War for Kuwait* (Annapolis, Md.: Naval Institute Press, 1991), pp. 235, 246, 252-253.

2. See, e.g., John Mueller, "The Perfect Enemy: Assessing the Gulf War," *Security Studies,* Vol. 5, No. 1 (Autumn 1995), pp. 77-117; Gregg Easterbrook, "Operation Desert Shill: A Sober Look at What Was Not Achieved in the War," *New Republic,* September 30, 1991, pp. 32ff; Michael J. Mazarr, Don M. Snider, and James A. Blackwell, Jr., *Desert Storm: The Gulf War and What We Learned* (Boulder, Colo.: Westview, 1993), pp. 113-117, 177-178.

3. Both originated in the extensive television coverage of the war, and the military briefings conducted during and shortly after the cease-fire. Among the earliest and most influential published versions of the orthodox technology explanation is Perry, "Desert Storm and Deterrence." Norman Schwarzkopf's famous observations on Saddam Hussein's strategic abilities were perhaps the earliest articulation of the "Iraqi shortcomings" school; see Easterbrook, "Operation Desert Shill."

4. See especially Eliot A. Cohen, Director, *Gulf War Air Power Survey* (Washington, D.C.: U.S. GPO, 1993), 5 vols. plus Summary Report, hereafter cited as *GW Air Power Survey;* Jesse Orlansky and Colonel Jack Thorpe, eds., *73 Easting: Lessons Learned from Desert Storm via Advanced Distributed Simulation Technology,* IDA D-1110 (Alexandria, Va.: Institute for Defense Analyses, 1992).

5. See, e.g., Paul K. Davis, ed., *New Challenges for Defense Planning: Rethinking How Much is Enough* (Santa Monica, Calif.: RAND, 1994); U. Candan et al., *Present NATO Practice in Land Wargaming*, STC-PP-252 (The Hague: SHAPE Technical Center, 1987); Wayne P. Hughes, Jr., ed., *Military Modeling* (Alexandria, Va.: Military Operations Research Society, 1984).

6. For arguments advocating protection of modernization accounts, see, e.g., Andrew Krepinevich, *The Bottom-Up Review: An Assessment* (Washington, D.C.: Defense Budget Project, February 1994), pp. 30-49; Daniel Goure, "Is There a Military-Technical Revolution in America's Future?" *Washington Quarterly*, Vol. 16, No. 4 (Autumn 1993), pp. 175-192, at pp. 188-190.

7. See, e.g., Andrew F. Krepinevich, "Cavalry to Computer: The Pattern of Military Revolutions," *National Interest*, No. 37 (Fall 1994), pp. 30-42, at p. 30; Alvin and Heidi Toffler, *War and Anti-War: Survival at the Dawn of the 21st Century* (Boston: Little, Brown and Co., 1993), p. 32; Michael J. Mazarr, Project Director, *The Military-Technical Revolution: A Structural Framework* (Washington, D.C.: Center for Strategic and International Studies, 1993), pp. 16-17; Commander James R. Fitzsimonds and Commander Jan M. Van Tol, "Revolutions in Military Affairs," *Joint Force Quarterly*, No. 4 (Spring 1994), pp. 24-31. This argument has gained an impressive range of adherents. See, e.g., Bradley Graham, "Battle Plans for a New Century," *Washington Post*, February 21, 1995, pp. 1ff; John Barry, "The Battle Over Warfare," *Newsweek*, December 5, 1994, pp. 27ff; Jeff Erlich, "One on One: Interview with Secretary of Defense William Perry," *Defense News*, May 1-7, 1995, p. 38; "Deutch Gets Report Card Letter on the Revolution in Military Affairs," *Inside the Navy*, October 24, 1994, p. 11.

8. Of the troops, 540,000 (and 148 of the fatalities) were Americans. Freedman and Karsh, *The Gulf Conflict*, p. 409. The exact count of Iraqi troops and equipment in Kuwait is unknown, but the lowest current estimates are of multiple hundreds of thousands of troops, multiple thousands of armored vehicles, and at least tens of thousands of artillery pieces. See discussion below.

9. Anthony H. Cordesman and Abraham R. Wagner, *The Lessons of Modern War*, Vol. I (Boulder, Colo.: Westview, 1990), pp. 15, 18, 150; Larry H. Addington, *The Patterns of War Since the Eighteenth Century* (Bloomington: Indiana University Press, 1984), pp. 182, 184, 237; Phillip Karber et al., *Assessing the Correlation of Forces: France 1940*, BDM/W-79-560-TR (McLean, Va.: BDM Corp., 1979), pp. 2-3; George Bruce, ed., *Harbottle's Dictionary of Battles*, 3rd ed. (New York: Van Nostrand Reinhold, 1981), p. 95.

10. See, e.g., *Crisis in the Persian Gulf: Sanctions, Diplomacy and War, Hearings Before the Committee on Armed Services, House of Representatives)*, House Armed Services Committee No. 101-57 (Washington, D.C.: U.S. GPO, 1991), pp. 448, 462, 463, 485, 917; "Defense Analysts: Limited War to Free Kuwait Could Cut Casualties by Over Half," *Inside The Army*, December 10, 1990, p. 11; "Air Strike on Iraq, the Favored Strategy, Means Big Risks for Both Sides," *New York Times*, October 23, 1990, p. A10. For reported prewar Defense Department estimates, see, e.g., Freedman and Karsh, *The Gulf Conflict*, p. 391; Michael Gordon and Bernard Trainor, *The Generals' War* (Boston: Little, Brown, 1995), pp. 132-133, 174; U.S. News and World Report, *Triumph Without Victory* (New York: Random House, 1992), pp. 129, 141; Bob Woodward, *The Commanders* (New York: Simon and Schuster, 1991), p. 349; Tom Matthews, "The Secret History of the War," *Newsweek*, March 18, 1991, p. 28ff.

11. See, e.g., Krepinevich, *The Bottom-Up Review*, pp. i, 22, 25-26, 49; Lawrence J. Korb, "The Impact of the Persian Gulf War on Military Budgets and Force Structure," in Nye and Smith, *After the Storm*, pp. 221-240; Inman, Nye, Perry, and Smith, "U.S. Strategy After the Storm," ibid., pp. 267-289, at p. 284; Representative Les Aspin, *An Approach to Sizing American Conventional Forces for the Post-Soviet Era: Four Illustrative Options* (Washington, D.C.: House Armed Services Committee, February 25, 1992); Christopher Bowie et al., *The New Calculus* (Santa Monica: RAND, 1993); Michael O'Hanlon, *Defense Planning for the Late 1990s* (Washington, D.C.: Brookings, 1995), e.g. pp. 30-32; Philip Finnegan, "War Emphasizes Stealth Need, Says Cheney," *Defense News*, February 11, 1991, p. 10; HASC, *Defense for a New Era*; John M. Collins, *Desert Shield and Desert Storm: Implications for Future U.S. Force Requirements* (Washington, D.C.: Congressional Research Service, 1991); Brigadier General Robert H. Scales et al., *Certain Victory: The United States Army in the Gulf War* (Washington, D.C.: Office of the Chief of Staff, U.S. Army, 1993), p. 364; Gordon and Trainor, *The Generals' War*, p. 470.

12. See, e.g., John J. Mearsheimer, "Numbers, Strategy, and the European Balance," *International Security*, Vol. 12, No. 4 (Spring 1988), pp. 174-185; Richard K. Betts, "Conventional Deterrence: Predictive Uncertainty and Policy Confidence," *World Politics*, Vol. 37 (January 1985), pp. 153-179; Seymour J. Deitchman, *Military Power and the Advance of Technology* (Boulder, Colo.: Westview, 1983).

13. I use these materials chiefly as data sources, from which I draw independent analytical conclusions with which neither project's staff might necessarily agree.

14. Data were collected using traditional documentary historical techniques, extensive engineering surveys of the battlefield immediately after the fighting, and exhaustive participant interviews, integrated using the simulation of the battle itself. Apparent discrepancies and data gaps were identified by representing all available information in the simulation and observing the results; these results were then shown to the participants in a three-dimensional, real-time visual display of the battle using the DARPA/IDA Simnet system. Simnet is a distributed network interconnecting large numbers of manned or unmanned individual-weapon simulators to create a single "virtual battlefield" on which the simulated weapons interact. It can be zoomed to follow individual combatants, or replayed as needed to review events in detail. Resolutions of contradictory or missing data were

then worked out by the battle participants and the analytic team in light of all known information, entered into the data base, and the process repeated. See Orlansky and Thorpe, *73 Easting*, pp. I-65-I-79; II-1-II-118.

15. I use counterfactual analysis as one of two means to provide variance and to help avoid the danger of indeterminacy that can otherwise affect a study of a single war. The first of these is a sub-unit analysis breaking the war into battles, sectors, or unit frontages with varying characteristics—in effect, changing the unit of analysis to create many separate events with varying properties. The second approach is to create variance experimentally via counterfactual simulations in which some properties of the historical battle are held constant while others are systematically varied. Taken together, these methods enable both a more incisive analysis of causation in the Gulf, and a better basis for drawing inferences from the experience of the Gulf to future wars under other conditions. The Army's Janus simulation was used for the counterfactual experiments discussed below because of its greater flexibility relative to Simnet and the reduced need for visual fidelity in counterfactual analysis. Janus is a stand-alone two-sided, interactive, stochastic combat simulation with resolution to individual weapon systems; for details, see Janus(A) 2.0 User's Manual (draft), Janus(A) 2.0 Model, prepared for the Department of the Army, HQ TRADOC Analysis Command ATRC-2D, Ft. Leavenworth, Kans., by TITAN Corporation, Ft. Leavenworth, Kans. On Janus' validity, see L. Ingber, H. Fujio, and M.F. Wehner, "Mathematical Comparison of Combat Computer Models to Exercise Data," *Mathematical and Computer Modeling*, Vol. 15, No. 1 (1991), pp. 65ff; L. Ingber, "Mathematical Comparison of Janus (T)," in S.E. Johnson and A.H. Lewis, eds., *The Science of Command and Control*, Part II (Washington, D.C.: AFCEA International Press, 1989), pp. 165-176. On theoretical indeterminacy and its avoidance, see Gary King, Robert O. Keohane, and Sidney Verba, *Designing Social Inquiry* (Princeton, N.J.: Princeton University Press, 1994), pp. 118-122, 220-221. On counterfactual analysis, see esp. James D. Fearon, "Counterfactuals and Hypothesis Testing in Political Science," *World Politics*, January 1991, pp. 169-195.

16. U.S. Department of Defense, *Conduct of the Persian Gulf War*, Final Report to Congress Pursuant to Title V of Public Law 102-25 (Washington, D.C.: U.S. GPO, April 1992), henceforth cited as DoD, *Conduct*, pp. 251-258.

17. These were the Tawakalna, Medina, and Adnan Republican Guard divisions, and the 52nd, 12th, and 10th Armored divisions; Scales, *Certain Victory*, pp. 232-236, 266; Richard M. Swain, *"Lucky War": Third Army in Desert Storm* (Ft. Leavenworth, Kans.: U.S. Army Command and General Staff College Press, 1994), pp. 244, 247; Gordon and Trainor, *The Generals' War*, p. 387; U.S. News, *Triumph Without Victory*, p. 335; Lieutenant Colonel Peter S. Kindsvatter, "VII Corps in the Gulf War: Ground Offensive," *Military Review*, February 1992, pp. 16-37, at 34.

18. U.S. armored cavalry regiments have three ground squadrons of three cavalry troops and one tank company each. Each troop is roughly equivalent to a reinforced tank or mechanized infantry company, and includes 20-30 armored vehicles. The three troops that fought at 73 Easting (G or "Ghost," E or "Eagle," and I or "Iron," as their radio call signs identified them) were assigned to two different squadrons (Ghost and Eagle in 2nd Squadron and Iron in 3rd). The Battle of 73 Easting per se thus pitted three U.S. cavalry troops (or less than half the 2nd ACR) against a brigade (the 18th) of the Tawakalna; Orlansky and Thorpe, *73 Easting*, pp. I-114, I-121-125.

19. Orlansky and Thorpe, *73 Easting*, pp. I-111 to I-136; Colonel Michael D. Krause, *The Battle of 73 Easting, 26 February 1991: A Historical Introduction to a Simulation* (Washington, D.C.: U.S. Army Center for Military History and the Defense Advanced Research Projects Agency [DARPA], August 27, 1991); J.R. Crooks et al., *73 Easting Re-Creation Data Book* (Westlake, Calif.: Illusion Engineering, Inc., 1992), IEI Report No. DA-MDA972-1-92, appendices, shoot history by vehicle for Eagle, Ghost, Iron Troops; "The Battle of 73 Easting," briefing slides prepared by Janus Gaming Division, TRADOC Analysis Command, White Sands, N.M., March 30, 1992 (henceforth TRAC brief), esp. slide 3 text, slide 16 text.

20. Scales, *Certain Victory*, pp. 292-300; Gordon and Trainor, *The Generals' War*, pp. 407-408; Rick Atkinson, *Crusade: The Untold Story of the Persian Gulf War* (Boston: Houghton Mifflin, 1993), pp. 465-467; U.S. News, *Triumph Without Victory*, pp. 377-386.

21. Scales, *Certain Victory*, pp. 282-284; U.S. News, *Triumph Without Victory*, pp. 357-370.

22. Scales, *Certain Victory*, pp. 267-270.

23. Kindsvatter, "VII Corps in the Gulf War," p. 17.

24. See, e.g., Gordon and Trainor, *The Generals' War*, p. 474; Perry, "Desert Storm and Deterrence," pp. 66-82; Inman, Nye, Perry, and Smith, "U.S. Strategy After the Storm," p. 284; HASC, *Defense for a New Era*, p. 7; Richard Hallion, *Storm Over Iraq: Airpower and the Gulf War* (Washington, D.C.: Smithsonian Press, 1992), pp. 241-268; Dilip Hiro, *Desert Shield to Desert Storm: The Second Gulf War* (New York: Routledge, 1992), pp. 320, 441.

25. See, e.g., Atkinson, *Crusade*, pp. 443-448, 467; U.S. News, *Triumph Without Victory*, p. 409; Scales, *Certain Victory*, pp. 364-367.

26. See, e.g., Freedman and Karsh, *The Gulf Conflict*, p. 437; Friedman, *Desert Victory*, pp. 235, 246, 252-253; James Blackwell, *Thunder in the Desert: The Strategy and Tactics of the Persian Gulf War* (New York: Bantam, 1991), pp. 220-223; Harry G. Summers, Jr., *On Strategy II: A Critical Analysis of the Gulf War* (New York: Dell, 1992), pp. 155, 265.

27. Mueller, "The Perfect Enemy," p. 106. See also Mazarr, Snider, and Blackwell, *Desert Storm*, pp. 113-117, 177-178; Jeffrey Record, *Hollow Victory* (Washington, D.C.: Brassey's, 1993), pp. 6, 135; James Pardew, "The Iraqi Army's Defeat in Kuwait," *Parameters*, Vol. 21, No. 4 (Winter 1991-92), pp. 17-23; Molly Moore, *A Woman At War: Storming Kuwait with the U.S. Marines* (New York: Charles Scribner's Sons, 1993), e.g. pp. 224, 275-276, 292, 302.

For explanations involving Iraqi numerical inferiority, see Easterbrook, "Operation Desert Shill," pp. 32ff; HASC, *Defense for a New Era*, p. 34; Mueller, "The Perfect Enemy," e.g., pp. 79-96.

28. Record, *Hollow Victory*, p. 85.

29. With few exceptions (e.g., Mueller, "The Perfect Enemy"), the Gulf War literature is largely journalistic in nature and intent. As a result, causal relationships are frequently only implicit. I thus do not attempt to falsify individual accounts, but rather address reasonable articulations of the main lines of debate, and determine by process tracing which of these (if any) offer significant explanatory power.

30. In principle, even historically large Iraqi armor residual could still produce unprecedently low Coalition losses if the *ratio* of Iraqi survivors to Coalition attackers were unprecedently low, or if the Iraqi loss *rate* were so high as to render their survivors ineffective (though numerous). Neither exception holds here. For the former, see the discussion under "Iraqi Numerical Inferiority" below. For the latter, the causal mechanism is typically held to be the loss of will to fight: Leonard Wainstein, *The Relationship of Battle Damage to Unit Combat Performance*, IDA P-1903, (Alexandria, Va.: Institute for Defense Analyses, 1986), pp. 1-2. As argued below, however, this cannot explain the result here.

31. *GW Air Power Survey*, Vol. II, Part II, pp. 170, 214, 218-219.

32. See, e.g., Krause, *73 Easting Historical Introduction*, pp. 11, 12, 13, 15, 16, 19, 21, 22; Lieutenant Colonel Douglas A. Macgregor, "Closing with the Enemy," *Military Review*, February 1993, pp. 64-71, at p. 65.

33. Krause, *73 Easting Historical Introduction*, p. 12; Second Lieutenant Richard M. Bohannon, "Dragon's Roar: 1-37 Armor in the Battle of 73 Easting," *Armor*, Vol. CI, No. 3 (May-June 1992), pp. 11-17, at p. 16.

34. 73 Easting Data Base. See also Krause, *73 Easting Historical Introduction*, pp. 12, 16, 17, 22.

35. In fact, some participants reported numerous small scale counterattacks at various points in the battle: see, e.g., Krause, *73 Easting Historical Introduction*, pp. 12, 16, 20, 22; also Lieutenant John Hillen, "2d Armored Cavalry: The Campaign to Liberate Kuwait," *Armor*, Vol. C, No. 4 (July-August 1991), pp. 8-12, at p. 11. Not all of these, however, can be unambiguously identified as deliberate attacks—confusion over the location of U.S. and Iraqi forces, for example, may account for some movements of small, isolated Iraqi units toward U.S. forces. The analysis above is conservative in crediting as a true counterattack only the action repelled by Ghost Troop after nightfall, which can be clearly distinguished as a deliberate counterattack by the behavior of the Iraqi units conducting the action (e.g., dismounting infantry, returning fire, and continuing to close with U.S. forces when taken under fire—such behavior is inconsistent with any interpretation other than deliberate counterattack): interview, Lieutenant Colonel Robert C. Turrell, USA (ret'd.), IDA, April 11, 1995. U.S. participants in the action were quite emphatic on this point. Krause, *73 Easting Historical Introduction*, p. 15.

36. Krause, *73 Easting Historical Introduction*, p. 14.

37. TRAC brief, slide 3 text, slide 16 text. In Eagle Troop's sector, for example, no Iraqis were taken prisoner until after the battle, when a U.S. psychological warfare team was brought forward to broadcast surrender appeals in Arabic. Personal communication, Major H.R. McMaster, USA, September 8, 1995.

38. Scales, *Certain Victory*, pp. 232-236; Swain, *Lucky War*, pp. 244, 247; Gordon and Trainor, *The Generals' War*, pp. 387-388.

39. Scales, *Certain Victory*, pp. 232-236.

40. See, e.g., Nigel Pearce, *The Shield and the Sabre: The Desert Rats in the Gulf, 1990-91* (London: Her Majesty's Stationery Office, 1992), pp. 101, 102, 166; Swain, *Lucky War*, pp. 247, 254; Gordon and Trainor, *The Generals' War*, e.g., pp. 359, 363-368; Atkinson, *Crusade*, pp. 441-481; U.S. News, *Triumph Without Victory*, e.g., pp. 332-398; Freedman and Karsh, *The Gulf Conflict*, p. 397.

41. *GW Air Power Survey*, Vol. II, Part II, p. 169.

42. The estimate is derived from standard vehicle counts for Republican Guard and Army heavy division organizations as found in Friedman, *Desert Victory*, p. 294; Major John Antal, "Iraq's Armored Fist," *Infantry*, Vol. 81, No. 1 (January-February 1991), pp. 27-30; and Richard Jupa and James Dingeman, "The Republican Guards," *Army*, Vol. 41, No. 3 (March 1991), pp. 54-62; average air attrition for Guard divisions as of February 23 as given by *GW Air Power Survey*, Summary Report, p. 106; specific air attrition for the 12th and 52nd Armored Divisions as derived from interviews with captured Iraqi officers and reported in *GW Air Power Survey*, Vol. II, Part II, p. 214; and Iraqi divisional dispositions as reported, e.g., in Gordon and Trainor, *The Generals' War*, p. 388. Note that although personnel and weapon strengths were significantly below nominally authorized levels in Iraqi infantry divisions, tank strength in Guard and Army Heavy divisions closely approximated nominal authorization; *GW Air Power Supply*, Vol. II, Part II, p. 388.

43. See, e.g., Martin Blumenson, *Breakout and Pursuit* (Washington, D.C.: Office of the Chief of Military History, 1961), p. 30; Cordesman and Wagner, *The Lessons of Modern War*, Vol. 1, pp. 15, 18.

44. In the 1967 Arab-Israeli War, an Arab defending army with 2,250 tanks killed about 300 Israeli tanks; while in mid-July 1944, a German force with only 230 tanks killed 500 British and Canadian tanks in defeating Operation Goodwood. Similar results for the February 24 Iraqi armored force would imply Coalition armor losses of perhaps 160 to 8000 vehicles, rather than the actual total of only 15 tanks and perhaps 25 other armored vehicles. For 1967 data, see Cordesman and Wagner, *The Lessons of Modern War*, Vol. 1, pp. 15-18; for coalition tank losses,

see DoD, *Conduct*, p. xiv; for ratio of, e.g., M1 to Bradley losses, see Kindsvatter, *VII Corps in the Gulf War*, p. 17; for more on Operation Goodwood, see Blumenson, *Breakout and Pursuit*, p. 193.

45. "Ironically, the loss of equipment, a key index of bomb damage assessment used during the war, was not decisive in any direct way. The Iraqi army did not run out of tanks, armored personnel carriers, or artillery." *GW Air Power Survey, Summary Report*, p. 117.

46. Marine tank losses were lower in both absolute terms and as a fraction of total strength. *Operation Desert Shield/Desert Storm, Hearings Before the Committee on Armed Services, United States Senate* (Washington, D.C.: U.S. GPO, 1991), S. Hrg. 102-326, hereafter cited as *Operation Desert Shield/Desert Storm*, pp. 79-80; U.S. Marine Corps Battlefield Assessment Team, *Armor/Antiarmor Operations in Southwest Asia*, Research Paper No. 92-0002 (Quantico, Va.: Marine Corps Research Center, July 1991), hereafter cited as USMC, *Armor/Antiarmor*, pp. v, 15. Note also that an Army brigade equipped with M1A1s (the "Tiger" brigade) was attached to support the Marine offensive, but most of the combat activity was borne by the Marine's organic M60A1s; ibid., p. A-2.

47. *Operation Desert Shield/Desert Storm*, pp. 66-68; Moore, *A Woman At War*, pp. 239-241, 245-248; Gordon and Trainor, *The Generals' War*, pp. 363-368.

48. The key ground force technology has, alternatively, been described as superior night-fighting equipment, which would pertain to Army M2s and M3s as well as M1s; see, e.g., Scales, *Certain Victory*, pp. 366-367. Marine LAVs and most Marine M60s, however, lacked thermal sights; the Army had loaned the Marines a small number of M60A3s with better night-vision equipment, but the great majority of Marine armor lacked this. Moore, *A Woman At War*, p. 200; DoD, *Conduct*, p. 747; Gordon and Trainor, *The Generals' War*, p. 359. Its absence did not cause heavier losses to the Marines. Moreover, not all the key ground battles were fought at night or in limited visibility conditions, yet daylight did not make the outcomes any less one-sided. See, e.g., Gordon and Trainor, *The Generals' War*, pp. 435-442. The U.S. Marines also used dismounted infantry, which lacked even the LAV's armor protection or weapon sights, in the initial assault of the ground campaign; *Operation Desert Shield/Desert Storm*, pp. 66-68.

49. See Lieutenant (P) John A. Nagl, "A Tale of Two Battles: Victorious in Iraq, An Experienced Armor Task Force Gets Waxed at the NTC," *Armor*, Vol. CI, No. 3 (May-June 1992), pp. 6-10. See also Daniel P. Bolger, *Dragons at War: 2-34 Infantry in the Mohave* (Novato, Calif.: Presidio Press, 1986).

50. See, e.g., Freedman and Karsh, *The Gulf Conflict*, p. 437; Friedman, *Desert Victory*, pp. 235, 246, 252-253; Blackwell, *Thunder in the Desert*, pp. 220-223; Summers, *On Strategy II*, pp. 155, 265.

51. See, e.g., Swain, *Lucky War*, pp. 244, 246. Many of the individual engagements that made up these actions were likewise simple frontal assaults. The Iraqi defenses at 73 Easting, for example, were oriented to meet an attack from the west; 2nd ACR's axis of advance was a straight line almost due west to due east. See Krause, *73 Easting Historical Introduction*, pp. 1-15; Orlansky and Thorpe, *73 Easting*, pp. I-121 to 136; 73 Easting data base. The Battles of Norfolk, Medina Ridge, and Wadi al Batin were also direct frontal assaults: see, e.g., Scales, *Certain Victory*, pp. 267-270, 282-284, 292-300; Gordon and Trainor, *The Generals' War*, pp. 407-408; Atkinson, *Crusade*, pp. 465-467; U.S. News, *Triumph Without Victory*, pp. 377-386. Even at the border, VII Corps did not completely avoid the need to confront prepared defenders head-on: the 1st Infantry division conducted a deliberate breach of the Iraqi barrier system on the extreme right of the "Saddam line." Scales, *Certain Victory*, pp. 224-232.

52. See, e.g., Gordon and Trainor, *The Generals' War*, pp. 341, 358.

53. See, e.g., Mueller, "The Perfect Enemy," e.g. pp. 79-96; Easterbrook, "Operation Desert Shill," pp. 32ff; HASC, *Defense for a New Era*, p. 34; Eliot A. Cohen, "Tales of the Desert: Searching for Context for the Persian Gulf War," *Foreign Affairs*, Vol. 73, No. 3 (May/June 1994), pp. 141-142, 143; Gordon and Trainor, *The Generals' War*, p. 469.

54. *GW Air Power Survey* estimates 200,000-220,000 Iraqi troops on the eve of the ground invasion; Vol. II, Part II, p. 220. Other estimates have ranged from a high of 547,000 (the wartime U.S. Central Command [CENTCOM] figure) to a low of 183,000; HASC, *Defense for a New Era*, pp. 29-34.

55. While local and theater ratios are usually different, the local conditions at the point of attack are the most important for casualty rates; the value of favorable theater ratios is the ability to create better local ones. See Biddle, *Determinants of Offensiveness and Defensiveness*, pp. 61-67. An explanation resting on the Coalition's favorable theater balance thus implies that this provided favorable local ratios at the key points, which were needed for the observed outcome. If the Coalition did just as well where local ratios were unfavorable, this poses serious problems for such an explanation.

56. Gordon and Trainor, *The Generals' War*, p. 407; U.S. News, *Triumph Without Victory*, p. 380.

57. For the upper bound frontage, see General John R. Galvin, "Some Thoughts on Conventional Arms Control," *Survival*, April 1989, pp. 99-107, at 103, and assuming, for the upper bound, three brigades abreast at Galvin's maximum divisional frontage. For the lower bound, see, e.g., Mearsheimer, "Numbers, Strategy and the European Balance," pp. 174-185, and assuming two brigades forward.

58. For other examples, see Nigel Pearce, *The Shield and the Sabre*, pp. 102, 110.

59. See, e.g., Mueller, "The Perfect Enemy," e.g., pp. 106-107; Mazarr, Snider, and Blackwell, *Desert Storm: The Gulf War and What We Learned*, pp. 113-117, 177-178; Record, *Hollow Victory*, pp. 6, 135; Pardew, "The Iraqi Army's Defeat in Kuwait," pp. 17-23; Moore, *A Woman At War*, e.g. pp. 224, 275-276, 292, 302.

60. Cordesman and Wagner, *The Lessons of Modern War*, Vol. I, pp. 15, 18; ibid., Vol. III, pp. 255-256, 261, 267; George Bruce, ed., *Harbottle's Dictionary of Battles*, p. 232.

61. In fact, no systematic attempt has yet been made to show that the 1991 skill differential was unusually large in historical terms. On the contrary: Mueller, for example, actually implies that the incompetence he ascribes to the Iraqis is typical of other defeated armies in previous Mideast wars ("The Perfect Enemy," p. 79n). While this seems quite plausible, it poses important difficulties for the "Iraqi incompetence" argument as an explanation of a historically unprecedented outcome.

62. In 1967, an Arab force with 2250 tanks killed about 300 Israeli tanks; in 1991, the active residual of Iraqi armor that remained after accounting for air-induced attrition numbered at least 600 tanks and 600 other armored vehicles, but killed only 15 Coalition tanks and perhaps 25 other Coalition armored vehicles. Of course, this is a crude comparison; weapons other than armored vehicles can kill tanks, for example. But to include non-armored-vehicle based antitank weapons would be to increase the difference to be explained by the latter three effects above, since such weapons' effectiveness has generally increased since 1967 (making the Iraqis' inability to kill more than 40 Coalition armored vehicles still more surprising). Likewise, to leave out tanks killed by Israeli aircraft in 1967 is conservative, as this overestimates the number of Arab tanks that survived to engage Israeli tanks, thereby reducing 1967 per capita Arab performance, and thus understating the difference between 1967 and 1991. For 1967 results, see Cordesman and Wagner, *The Lessons of Modern War*, Vol. 1, pp. 15, 18.

63. While the Iraqis made serious mistakes at all levels of war, their failings at the tactical level were both necessary and sufficient (together with new U.S. technology) to explain the resulting loss rate. Even given the Iraqis' strategic and operational errors, if their troops' tactical performance had been to Western standards then Coalition losses would probably have reached or exceeded prewar expectations, as the counterfactual analysis below suggests. But without better tactical performance, no improvements in strategy or operational art could have changed the Iraqis' fate much in a shooting war. Even outnumbered U.S. attackers annihilated dug-in, actively resisting Iraqi defenders by frontal assault in close combat; if the troops behind the triggers cannot kill targets under such conditions, it is hard to see what even virtuoso generalship could do to change the results.

64. Orlansky and Thorpe, *73 Easting*, p. I-54.

65. It was standard operating procedure in the 2nd ACR to fire at any berm, whether a target had been positively identified behind it or not. Robert Zirkle, "Memorandum for the Record: Information Obtained During West Point/IDA Janus 73 Easting Session, 8-10 April 1992," Institute for Defense Analyses, April 15, 1992, p. 2. On berms, see, e.g., TRAC brief, slide 10 text.

66. See, e.g., Orlansky and Thorpe, *73 Easting*, p. I-54; Peter Tsouras and Elmo C. Wright, Jr., "The Ground War," in Bruce W. Watson, ed., *Military Lessons of the Gulf War* (Novato, Calif.: Presidio Press, 1991), pp. 81-120; *Operation Desert Shield/Desert Storm*, p. 115. Solid earth in sufficient depth can stop any current tank gun, but this requires the tank to be dug into the ground, not perched above it behind piles of sand.

67. At 73 Easting, for example, no systematic minefields were found, nor were there any apparent attempts to erect barriers of any kind to slow U.S. movement through the engagement area. Zirkle, "Memorandum for the Record," pp. 1, 2.

68. Iraqi engineers had begun to prepare blocking positions in this area some two weeks prior to the battle (i.e., before the ground war began) in anticipation of a possible Coalition advance from the west; Scales, *Certain Victory*, pp. 233. The maneuver units that occupied these positions apparently neither expended significant labor themselves to further prepare the ground subsequent to its occupation, nor conducted training or operational rehearsals *in situ* (as any U.S. unit would). Orlansky and Thorpe, *73 Easting*, pp. I-54, 59. Iraqi infantry at the frontier were provided with much more extensive counter-mobility engineering, although these obstacles were often poorly constructed. See, e.g., DoD, *Conduct*, pp. 251-253; Murray Hammick, "Iraqi Obstacles and Defensive Positions," *International Defense Review*, Vol. 24, No. 9 (September 1991), pp. 989-991.

69. See, e.g., Krause, *73 Easting Historical Introduction*, p. 28; Scales, *Certain Victory*, pp. 117-118, 293; Atkinson, *Crusade*, p. 212; Robert H. Scales, Jr., "Accuracy Defeated Range in Artillery Duel," *International Defense Review*, May 1991, pp. 473-481.

70. Krause, *73 Easting Historical Introduction*, pp. 17-18. The Iraqis proved unable to implement evasive "shoot and scoot" tactics (wherein artillery relocates immediately after firing so as to avoid counterfire), and U.S. counterfire quickly silenced the Iraqis' one attempt to provide fire support. Orlansky and Thorpe, *73 Easting*, p. I-145.

71. Krause, *73 Easting Historical Introduction*, pp. 17-18.

72. See, e.g., Kenneth Macksey, *First Clash* (New York: Berkeley Books, 1988), p. 102.

73. A captured Iraqi lieutenant later reported that his first indication that he was under attack was when "the turret of the tank next to him blew off." Steve Vogel, "A Swift Kick: 2d ACR's Taming of the Guard," *Army Times*, August 5, 1991, pp. 10ff at p. 30; see also Krause, *73 Easting Historical Introduction*, p. 32.

74. Krause, *73 Easting Historical Introduction*, pp. 21, 32; Orlansky and Thorpe, *73 Easting*, p. 1-117; interview, Lieutenant Colonel Robert C. Turrell, USA (ret'd), IDA, April 11, 1995. In Ghost Troop's sector, for example, some 18 minutes elapsed between the time U.S. attackers made initial contact with the Tawakalna main line of resistance and the first observed return fire by the Iraqis; Krause, *73 Easting Historical Introduction*, p. 16. Properly-manned

defending vehicles would ordinarily return hostile fire immediately (indeed, defenders ordinarily get the first shot in tactical mechanized combat). Not all Tawakalna vehicles were empty, however; at least some 2nd ACR crews reported receiving Iraqi fire or observing tank turret movement from the beginning of the battle. Interview, Captain H.R. McMaster, USA, January 1994.

75. Krause, *73 Easting Historical Introduction,* pp. 11-12; personal communication, Major H.R. McMaster, USA, September 8, 1995. Another M1 in Eagle Troop killed two T72s and two BMPs with four shots in one minute: see IEI Report No. DA-MDA972-1-92, appendix, shoot history by vehicle for Eagle Troop, p. 4.

76. Ibid., appendices, shoot histories by troop.

77. See, e.g., Scales, *Certain Victory,* pp. 361-364.

78. Compare, for example, the mistakes by the British 3rd and 5th Armies in March 1918, which produced a German breakthrough and 40-mile exploitation, but did not destroy the Allied position in the theater (and still cost the Germans an estimated 250,000 casualties). Biddle, *The Determinants of Offensiveness and Defensiveness,* pp. 241-311.

79. See, e.g., the account of the Arab armies' defeat by the Israelis in 1967 in Chaim Herzog, *The Arab-Israeli Wars* (New York: Random House, 1982), pp. 143-192. Note, especially, the effects of Egyptian maldeployment, mistakes regarding terrain passability, and air force unreadiness; ibid., pp. 152, 157, 159, 161.

80. *GW Air Power Survey,* Summary Report, pp. 56, 117.

81. Considerable evidence suggests that this was widespread in the Gulf War. The Marine Corps, for example, has estimated that the majority of all Iraqi armored vehicles destroyed on the Marines' front were unoccupied when killed; USMC, *Armor/Antiarmor,* p. 18. Reports of Iraqi crews scrambling to remount their vehicles upon ground attack are common. In addition to 73 Easting, see, e.g., Steve Vogel, "Metal Rain: Old Ironsides and the Iraqis Who Wouldn't Back Down," *Army Times,* September 16, 1991, pp. 8ff, at p. 16: "Iraqi prisoners [taken at Medina Ridge] later said they thought the artillery was an air attack, and many had abandoned their vehicles for bomb shelters.... [thereafter] in their thermals, the U.S. crews could see Iraqi soldiers leaving their bunkers and reboarding tanks and BMP infantry fighting vehicles. 'A lot of them were mowed down trying to get back to their vehicles,' said [Major Chess] Harris, the 3d Brigade's executive officer." See also DoD, *Conduct,* pp. 139-140; Atkinson, *Crusade,* p. 466; Steve Vogel, "Hell Night: For the 2d Armored Division, It Was No Clean War," *Army Times,* October 7, 1991, pp. 8ff, at p. 15; Krause, *73 Easting Historical Introduction,* p. 19, describing 2nd ACR engagements prior to 73 Easting.

Of course, many Iraqis deserted (see, e.g., Gordon and Trainor, *The Generals' War,* p. 352); at least some kills of empty vehicles are doubtless attributable to desertion rather than the interaction of air attack and poor tactical warning. This cannot fully explain the results above, however—and in particular, desertion is likely to be a minor contributor to empty vehicle kills in the VII Corps action against the Iraqi blocking force, for three reasons. First, Iraqi attempts to remount vehicles were widely observed by U.S. troops. Second, Iraqi armor was concentrated in units whose will to fight was highest, and whose desertion rates were lowest (note, e.g., the absence of the Iraqi blocking force divisions from the list of high-desertion units given in ibid.). But third, and most important, much of the heaviest fighting involved Iraqi units that had moved into their battle positions within at most a day or two of the battles that destroyed them. Vehicles lacking crews could not have done this. Much of the war's armored ground combat thus involved Iraqi weapons whose crews were present at the battlefield.

82. Other indirect effects of Coalition air technology include reducing Iraqi command responsiveness by destroying command posts and communications systems, and complicating management of Iraqi ground maneuver through the constant threat of air attack, thus slowing major redeployments and encouraging them to fight from static positions. *GW Air Power Survey,* Summary Report, pp. 70-1, 99n, 116, 119; Orlansky and Thorpe, *73 Easting,* p. I-59. Each magnified the problems of poor Iraqi combat skills and created opportunities for Coalition ground forces even without killing Iraqi armor directly.

83. The 73 Easting Project has used two simulation systems, the IDA/DARPA Simnet, and the Army Janus model. Though Simnet has been the main vehicle for building and demonstrating the Project data base, both IDA and the Army have used Janus for complementary analyses. Janus offers quicker turn-around in exchange for simpler graphics and a somewhat more abstract user interface; it is thus less well suited for re-living the battle with its participants to establish the actual events, but better suited for running large numbers of counterfactual cases once the data base is complete. The analyses described here used Janus. For details, see W.M. Christenson and Robert Zirkle, *73 Easting Battle Replication,* IDA P-2770 (Alexandria, Va.: Institute for Defense Analyses, 1992).

84. This base case accurately represents the real battle's technology, dispositions, movements, and U.S. combat skills, but credits the Iraqis with much better skills than they actually displayed—even though it accounts for the two mistakes of poor position preparation and poor covering force performance. Janus assumes nominal (i.e., U.S.-quality) crew performance and unit behavior unless told otherwise; errors must be deliberately introduced to be considered. By introducing two such errors, the base case thus considers some, but far from all, of the Iraqis' actual mistakes (excluding, e.g., their poor tank gunnery, fire coordination, and vehicle maintenance). When the two introduced mistakes are removed, the result is thus very nearly an error-free Iraqi defense. The results are therefore treated as properties of error-free performance, but this does *not* imply that the Iraqis need only have

fixed their position engineering or covering force discipline to reap the benefits described. For the Republican Guard (much less Iraqi conscript infantry) to approach the performance credited them in the "no errors" case would have required much more sweeping reforms. In all excursion scenarios, historical deployments and movement tracks were retained (though in scenario G, some U.S. arrivals are delayed to create a strung-out U.S. formation). Neither U.S. nor Iraqi movements were predicated on the presence (or absence) of thermal sights, air supremacy, or poor Iraqi covering force discipline or position preparation—thus there is no reason to assume that these movements would have differed for any of the given excursion scenarios. At least one of the 2nd ACR's company grade officers has stated explicitly that his plan of maneuver would have been the same with or without the changes embodied in the excursion scenarios above. Interview, Captain H.R. McMaster, USA, January 1994. Finally, note that the mean base case simulation results—two U.S. vehicle losses—closely approximate the historical outcome: one. See Christenson and Zirkle, *73 Easting Battle Replication.*

85. In a "turret-down" or "turret-defilade" position, the entire vehicle is below grade, and is thus masked from opposing observation or fire; only the commander's hatch is above grade. Thus, a turret-down tank cannot fire its main gun (or be fired upon by opposing tanks), but the vehicle commander is able to search for targets by standing in the open hatch and scanning his surroundings with binoculars. In a "hull-down" or "hull-defilade" position, the vehicle's hull is below grade, but the turret is exposed. A hull-down tank can thus fire and be fired upon, though the defilade reduces the vehicle's vulnerability by reducing its presented area. In Western practice, prepared fighting positions for tanks are ordinarily dug as a ramp, connecting a deeper, turret-down position and a shallower, hull-down location; above-ground revetments are avoided. Headquarters, Department of the Army, *FM 5-103, Survivability* (Washington, D.C.: U.S. GPO, June 1985), pp. 4-14—4-15; Richard Simpkin, *Tank Warfare* (New York: Crane Russak, 1979), pp. 97, 112, 160, 167; Macksey, *First Clash*, p. 55.

86. The U.S. Army's simulation results differ with respect to variations in Iraqi defensive posture; this is because they assume only hull defilade, rather than a ramped, turret-to-hull defilade, position for the Iraqis: TRAC brief. In effect, the Army analysis thus assumes only partial improvement of Iraqi force employment—and as a consequence, the Army results much more closely resemble those obtained here for partial, but incomplete, improvement in defender skills.

87. See, e.g., Scales, *Certain Victory*, pp. 261-262; Atkinson, *Crusade*, p. 443; U.S. News, *Triumph Without Victory*, p. 409.

88. The Iraqis made many more mistakes in the actual battle than just the two considered here; the presence of only one error in excursion scenarios B and C thus implies a very dramatic (though still incomplete) improvement in Iraqi combat skills.

89. In particular, in this scenario 2nd ACR's actual, hybrid line-abreast—combat-vee formation (occupying a depth of 1500 meters for any given troop) was broken down into a straggling series of nine platoon-size lines abreast, separated in depth by three km each (and thus occupying a total of about 30 km depth for the ACR as a whole).

90. See, e.g., Record, *Hollow Victory*, pp. 71-85, 135-136; Inman, Nye, Perry, and Smith, "U.S. Strategy After the Storm," p. 57; Mazarr, Snider, and Blackwell, *Desert Storm: The Gulf War and What We Learned*, pp. 3-5, 113.

91. See Stephen Biddle and Robert Zirkle, "Technology, Civil-Military Relations, and Warfare in the Developing World," *Journal of Strategic Studies*, Vol. 19, No. 2 (Summer 1996), pp. 171-212; Stephen Biddle, "Recent Trends in Armor, Infantry and Artillery Technology," in W. Thomas Wander, ed., *The Diffusion of Advanced Weaponry* (Washington, D.C.: American Association for the Advancement of Science, 1994); Eliot Cohen, "Distant Battles: Modern War in the Third World," *International Security*, Vol. 10, No. 4 (Spring 1986), pp. 143-171.

92. For example, an offensive in mixed terrain using Soviet/East European-style tactics would require very skilled handling to avoid presenting decisive vulnerabilities to a skilled defender with advanced technology. Even where covering terrain is available, it is very hard to maintain the high operating tempos of standard Eastern military doctrine while keeping all necessary elements under cover. Improvising a lower-tempo offensive is itself no simple matter. While a highly skilled military might carry off either job, an unskilled or undisciplined one could easily produce congested roads full of easy PGM targets; command posts or ammunition dumps left too long in the open before finding concealment within reach of supported forces; or assault elements that spread out over varying terrain (presenting piecemeal attacks to sophisticated defenders), to cite just a few possibilities. Under such conditions, it is perfectly conceivable that a defender with advanced weapons could succeed at force levels supportable without a Saudi-scale logistical infrastructure.

93. See, e.g., Krepinevich, *The Bottom-Up Review*, pp. 30-49; Goure, "Is There a Military-Technical Revolution in America's Future?" pp. 175-192.

94. Some have argued that temporarily re-allocating funds from training to modernization would let U.S. forces recapitalize while threats are modest, then quickly re-establish combat skills later if and when needed. It is far from clear, however, that building a skilled organization is quicker than fielding new equipment. The determinants of organizational skill are poorly understood, making it especially risky to allow a highly competent military to decay now in the hopes that it can be quickly rebuilt later.

95. It has been argued, for example, that the Defense Department's 1993 "Bottom-Up Review" of U.S. force structure was strongly influenced by the Gulf War in its judgment of force adequacy and threat type: see, e.g.,

Krepinevich, *The Bottom-Up Review*, pp. i, 22, 25-26, 49; Krepinevich, "Recasting Military Roles and Missions," *Issues in Science and Technology*, Vol. 11, No. 3 (Spring 1995), pp. 41-48, at p. 44. For other force planning exercises using the Gulf War as a yardstick, see Aspin, *An Approach to Sizing American Conventional Forces;* Bowie et al., *New Calculus;* Korb, "The Impact of the Persian Gulf War on Military Budgets and Force Structure," pp. 221-240; Collins, *Desert Shield and Desert Storm: Implications for Future U.S. Force Requirements.*

# Chapter 35

## ✱ ✱ ✱

## Ensuring Future Victories Through Land Power Dominance: The U.S. Army Modernization Strategy

Major General Edward G. Anderson, III, U.S. Army
and Major Michael Linick, U.S. Army

*Major General Edward G. Anderson and Major Michael Linik observe that the U.S. Army's vision of the emerging strategic environment reflects the view that land power has returned to its dominant position in world affairs. But as the Army prepares to deal with this security environment, it must balance competing requirements, e.g. current operational readiness and future readiness. Over the past few years the Army has deliberately chosen to defer funding for modernization. But, contend Anderson and Linick, based on the assumption that the US currently possesses an overmatching technological advantage that will persist until approximately 2010, the Army now has a "window of opportunity" in modernization to exploit as it sees fit. This enables the Army to focus on a few high-payoff or previously under-resourced systems that will take the service to "Army XXI." The Army's resulting modernization strategy is based on three principles: the Army will be capabilities-based; because modernization objectives are so interdependent and interlinked, they must be balanced; and modernization is relative. Is this the right approach for the Army? Do the six components of the modernization strategy truly enable the Army to develop the priorities that should drive the service's investment program? What are the risks associated with the Army's modernization strategy?*

Major General Anderson is assigned to Headquarters, Department of the Army, where he is serving as the Assistant Deputy Chief of Staff for Operations and Plans, Force Development.

Major Linick is a former Staff Officer at Headquarters, Department of the Army, Office of the Deputy Chief of Staff for Operations and Plans, where he served as the focal point on the Army's modernization strategy. He is assigned to Headquarters, U.S. Army, Europe, Heidelberg Germany.

This article originally appeared in the *National Security Studies Quarterly*, Vol. II, Issue 4, Autumn 1996, pp. 1-18. Copyright © 1996 by the National Security Studies Quarterly Association.

The 1991 victory in Operation Desert Storm was the first time in modern history that the U.S. Army won the first battle of a war. That victory was the culmination of a modernization strategy and Army vision whose impetus came from the 1978 "Hollow Army" speech of then Chief of Staff General Edward C. Meyer. The Army [in the late 1990's] is faced with developing a strategy and vision that will ensure we still have that same dominance in the year 2010. To get there, we must develop a strategy and vision now, in an era of constrained resources, that will build us toward that future force—Army XXI.

Today's U.S. Army is the best in the world. Even though it is only the eighth largest, it is the envy of every other country. This standard was not easy to achieve; it required a lot of hard work and money. The Department of the Army is charged with the mission to man, train, equip, and sustain the country's primary ground combat forces. To accomplish this mission for the last 50 years, the "peacetime" Army has received between 22% and 24% of the Department of Defense (DOD) budget. There have been exceptions: traditionally, after years of peace and inability to recognize clearly identified threats, the Army has seen reduced funding and force structure. The consequence of these actions was always the same, tragic loss in battle (Kasserine Pass and Task Force Smith). The Army is once again undergoing fundamental peacetime change—along two axes. It is getting much smaller compared to its Cold War counterpart, an inevitable result based upon significant reduction of the communist threat. The Army is also undergoing reinvention, becoming more than just a smaller version of its Cold War self. During this downsizing and restructuring, the Army has again deferred vital modernization. This time it has been done during a period of more numerous operations and *increased reliance on land power*.

The Army's vision of the emerging strategic environment reflects the importance of land power dominance. In the context of the Cold War, the United States relied on a strategic triad of nuclear bombers, missiles, and submarines. The Army's role within this paradigm was to be prepared to defeat a known threat in a known theater, as well as being prepared to meet other conventional contingencies. One effect, however, of superpower confrontation was to limit the scope and number of those other contingencies.

In today's world, we must once again rely on a strategic triad, but this time one that is driven by conventional weapons and has as its key leg "Land Power Dominance." The end of true superpower confrontation has opened a Pandora's box of regional hot spots. Today's Army is becoming a force, as required by the National Security Strategy of Engagement and Enlargement, capable of being continually engaged in many operations involving many different missions around the world. While we are actively involved in peacetime engagement, deterrence, and conflict-prevention missions, the Army must maintain its core competency to fight and win when called on to do so. Finally, although there currently is no true "peer threat"—no nation or collective interest that can threaten out survival—we cannot afford to assume that one will not emerge in the foreseeable future.

The Army has become a very busy institution. Our business is to provide land power to support the National Military Strategy—and business is booming. Land power has become the key element of the National Military Strategy.

Since the end of the Cold War, the deployment of Army soldiers has increased by 300% while its size has decreased by 35%. We are now engaged in a wider variety of missions, and in a greater number of places, than ever before. The Army has provided the major component of military force for all major post-Cold War contingencies. Nearly 25% of the operational Army (120,000 out of 495,000) is forward deployed or operationally engaged right now.

Today we are faced with the challenge of balancing competing requirements. We must balance readiness against quality of life, and current operational readiness against future readiness. We must do this in an environment of constrained resources. With the move toward a balanced budget, managing those resources will become even more difficult. Maintaining the balance between current and future readiness requires, in essence, a program of risk management. We must examine the needs of the Army, and the country, in the short, medium, and long run. We must then decide on the best ways to manage or mitigate the difference between resources and requirements. Our priorities are not always Army programs: joint intelligence, joint theater missile defense, and strategic lift programs are high on the Army's priority list.

After virtually every military downsizing in U.S. history, its armed forces, particularly land forces, have suffered a loss in readiness. In managing the drawdown of the military since 1985, we have ensured that the force did not become the "Hollow Army" of the post-Vietnam era. The Army has identified six imperatives, which collectively must be maintained, resourced, and balanced, for the Army to remain trained and ready. These imperatives are: quality people, doctrine, leader development, training, force mix and design, and modern equipment.

Over the past few years we have deliberately chosen to defer the funding of one of these imperatives, acquiring modern equipment. The decision to take risk in this area was prudent and deliberate. During the drawdown the Army's budget dropped by over 40%. While our force structure also underwent a significant drop, from 18 divisions down to 10, our operational commitments, as discussed above, dramatically increased. The need for peak readiness dictated full funding of training and operations accounts. This meant a diversion of planned modernization funds. Concurrently, the increased tempo of operations was taking a higher than programmed useful life impact on Army equipment, thus shortening potential life-cycles and increasing the need for recapitalization.

The U.S. Army is doctrinally based. Implementing the doctrine requires *training, technical capabilities,* and *initiative.* Much has been written over the last few years about an on-going Revolution in Military Affairs (RMA). Though there is no one who can accurately predict where this RMA will lead, the Army has been active in attempting to understand it and developing ways to exploit it. Thus initiatives like the Louisiana Maneuvers Task Force and Force XXI are critical investments in the future of our doctrine and its corresponding effects on the types of organizations, soldiers, and leaders we will need in the future. Given all of this, it became clear that the one area in which the Army could best afford to accept risk, at least in the near-term, was in the area of modernization. That period, however, is coming to an end.

## The Window of Opportunity

Our current adversaries and competitors do not come close to having the capabilities that our Army now possesses. They are, however, attempting to incorporate them. It is only a question of time before we expect to see a peer threat emerge. We believe our current overmatching technology, even without significant modernization, will exist until approximately the year 2010. But this belief must be reexamined and revalidated on an annual basis. From now until then, we have a "Window of Opportunity" in modernization to exploit as we see fit. The Army's new modernization strategy can drive how we best take advantage of this window, but it is only viable if the projections in increases to Army acquisition funding materialize.

Funding projections show that we will not have the funding levels we need to modernize our forces across the full spectrum of our systems in the near to mid-term. So, we have chosen to accept some risk in this area. The Army is aggressively pursuing initiatives and efficiencies to harvest funds for modernization. We may also divert some funding from fielding new critical warfighting systems, extend the fielding times of some systems, and use the savings to fund some other, lower visibility, support systems, many of which have had modernization deferred for years. Although we must take some risk, the near-term represents a time period where we can best afford to prudently do so.

During this period, we can concentrate on certain systems, which we call our "Window of Opportunity" systems. By its nature, the window gives us the opportunity to truly focus on a few areas that will take us to Army XXI—enablers that provide high payoff or that have been under-resourced in the past. These systems are not "glamorous" and won't make headlines, but they will help rebalance the modernization objectives: soldier enhancements such as Land Warrior; command and control systems like Warfighter Information Network, Army Tactical Command and Control System, and Appliqué; logistic automation systems like Power Projection $C^4I$ and Defense Message System; night vision systems such as second-generation forward-looking infrared, thermal weapon sights, and night vision goggles; and Combat Support/Combat Service Support

(CS/CSS) systems like trucks, tactical quiet generators, and Logistics Over the Shore. We will have to defer major modernization of some of the "more glamorous," key warfighting systems until the beginning of the next century, focusing on prototype development and minor product improvements.

Of course, a key element to this approach is the assumption that a peer threat will not emerge until 2010-2015. An earlier, or later, peer threat emergence can affect the required timing for fielding new capabilities. This is clearly an area of great concern to us, so our modernization strategy provides for hedges against unfavorable changes in that assessment. Nevertheless, we believe we do have a window, and we intend to take advantage of it.

## Force XXI

Key to our ability to determine which systems are "Window of Opportunity" systems is a process called "Force XXI." This process attempts to distill the lessons from three different areas. *Operational experience*, from both real operations and from training exercises, provides information important to refining our force design, doctrine, training, and organization. *Operational concepts* represent attempts to develop innovative approaches to future Army doctrine. *Experimentation* allows us to use constructive, virtual, and live simulations to test progressive iterations of new concepts and technologies for land combat.

This construct of simulations occurs in a scheduled series of Army warfighting experiments, each focused on different aspects of the emerging doctrine of Decisive Operations. The live simulations are critical to ensure that what is developed through simulation can be executed by real soldiers. As part of our investment in this concept, we have designated an entire division, the 4th Infantry Division at Fort Hood, as the Experimental Force (EXFOR). This unit began testing Force XXI concepts at Battalion Task Force (Task Force XXI) level and will progress through division level.

The Force XXI process allows us to do the important scientific and intellectual ground work to ensure that as the window of opportunity closes, we have fielded the force necessary for battlefield dominance against any emerging threat. Though it has never been tied to the concept of a window of opportunity, the process will provide, through programs like Task Force XXI and the EXFOR, critical information for determining which systems to procure, which units to field them to, and how many units must have that equipment (thus setting appropriate procurement goals). It will also provide a picture of how the units of the future should be organized and manned.

This does not mean that we will not be developing and fielding new systems during the window of opportunity while we are deriving the lessons of Force XXI. We will. Force XXI has already played a role in helping the Army identify and verify that the "Window of Opportunity" systems mentioned earlier are our key enabling systems.

Force XXI serves another very important purpose. Force XXI not only gives us information about how to equip, organize, and deploy the army of the future, it is also a very important tool for helping us successfully plan, program, and defend the funding necessary for the modernization accounts to achieve that army. Force XXI assessments lead to key decisions and also demonstrate and validate our decisions in the eyes of the people who control the budgets, both inside and outside of the Army. Our modernization strategy, backed by the Force XXI process, provides a valuable tool in ensuring that our process for modernization is more widely understood and accepted.

## Developing a Strategy

In the 1980s, the Army fielded overwhelming technological superiority and then demonstrated this superiority through its "Big 5" in Operation Desert Storm. Those "Big 5" systems, the AH-64 Apache and UH-60 Blackhawk helicopters, the M1 Abrams tank and M2 Bradley infantry fighting vehicle, and the Patriot Missile system, were fielded in conjunction with another decision about risk. In their case the resources were not available to fully field all Army systems. We chose to concentrate our efforts on the "Big 5," at the expense of our truck fleet, our cargo helicopter fleet, and other non-high-dollar, non-high-profile, support system. Consequently, the Army is faced with the very pressing need to recapitalize fleets of support systems that in some cases are older than the soldiers who operate them.

At the same time, the "Big 5" are approaching the period in their life cycles where the Army must begin to either retire these weapons, develop their successors, or recapitialize the fleets by replacing older systems with new, like-but-improved capabilities. These five systems will begin to average 20 years of age by the year 2005. More importantly, for our premier combat systems, technology is rapidly changing. This means that even if the systems were still economical to operate as they age, they may no long be technologically capable of performing the missions required of them.

Of course we continue to improve them over time. We [are] fielding the M1A2 while conducting analysis for a completely new tank. The M2A3, Patriot PAC-3, UH-60L, and AH-64D are significantly improved versions over the original models, but eventually we will need to replace them with completely new systems having much greater capabilities. We cannot continue to add modifications to systems indefinitely; the cost is prohibitive relative to additional capability we can add to an existing platform.

In the mid 1980s we were building over 700 tanks a year, plus 100 attack helicopters and 400-600 Bradley fighting vehicles. Clearly those days are gone unless a peer threat emerges to push us to much higher levels of defense spending. For now, tank production averages from 90 to 120 a year, producing 72 attack helicopters per year may be beyond our reach, and upgrading 160 Bradleys per year is probably more than we can afford.

Today's challenge is to spend very limited dollars as wisely as we can. Where we used to spend $18 billion per year on procurement, we now have $6 billion. Buying fewer systems, however, greatly increases unit cost, so money is spent less efficiently. Much of the debate about defense funding in the recent budget debates in Congress has centered on the issue of modernization. There is a strong and growing acknowledgment that the modernization accounts of the armed forces have been allowed to decrease to a dangerous level and that the Army is in the most dangerous position of all the services. Adequately funding the Army's strategy requires a research, development, and acquisition (RDA) stable funding level of $15-20 billion per year, indexed to inflation.

In assuming risk in our modernization accounts, we believed that the money programmed in the later years of a Program Objective Memorandum (POM) cycle and in the extended planning period, would be sufficient to fix modernization. In essence, we wrote checks against the current modernization accounts to pay for other programs. Our belief was that an offsetting amount would be "deposited" into those modernization accounts in the out years. To date those deposits have proven illusory. But the $15-20 billion RDA requirement exists even as the country turns toward a balanced budget environment.

The challenge then is to break this paradigm. This requires a strategy that is capable of maintaining our fleets at acceptable ages. It must field equipment to the force in large enough quantities and short enough time periods to make that equipment decisive. We must find ways to make technology work for us, and get it into the force. And we must do so without the expectation that additional money will become available in the later years of the program.

Deciding, under these budget constraints, what systems to buy and in what quantity is no easy task. It requires a vision of how the Army expects to fight ten to 15 years from now. It requires the balancing of several different, competing priorities. And it, again, involves tough decisions about where and when to accept some risk. The Army's new Modernization Strategy lays out three principles which will underlie our decisionmaking in these areas. It consists of six components, which collectively will assist in answering the questions of what any how much to buy. It also addresses the questions of risk and how best to manage it over the next ten years.

## Principles of Modernization

*A Capabilities-Based Army.* The first principle of the Modernization Strategy is that the Army will be a capabilities-based Army. During the Cold War, determining whether or not the Army was modernized was easy. We measured ourselves against the single scenario of a Soviet invasion of Western Europe, and decided whether or not the Army, in conjunction with the other services, was sufficient to defeat that threat. The end of the Cold War ended the era of threat-based planning. In today's environment we face too wide an array of missions and too wide an array of potential adversaries to allow us to plan our force structure and design around any single one of them. Instead, the Army of the future must be designed to ensure it maintains certain critical capabilities that are necessary to meet its potential commitments.

The Army has been moving toward capabilities-based planning for the past few years. As with any major change in philosophy or doctrine, however, the new perspective has yet to be fully codified or implemented. We have recognized that the key capabilities we require have been captured within the five Army modernization objectives: (1) project and sustain the force; (2) protect the force; (3) win the information war; (4) conduct precision strike; and (5) dominate maneuver. Definition of these objectives begins to answer the question of how we expect to fight for the foreseeable future.

The objective of projecting and sustaining the force recognizes that:

> The Army is primarily a Continental U.S. (CONUS)-based force. Today's environment and future environments demand the capabilities to project CONUS-based forces quickly, and to sustain those forces for extended periods of time.[1]

For this, the Army requires rapid global force projection, power projection platforms with upgraded and improved rail and airheads in the United States, and the tactical mobility necessary for sustaining a force in a theater.

Under the objective of protecting the force, the Army recognizes that in the future:

> Military forces are most vulnerable during initial, forced entry into hostile areas. During the early stages of such operations, the systems required to protect forces are limited in availability. The potential for disruption of operations by theater ballistic and cruise missiles during this period is very high, and brings with it corresponding nuclear, biological, and chemical employment threats. The potential for fratricide still exists during any military operation and requires accurate situational awareness.[2]

Thus, the capability to protect the force from theater missiles and weapons of mass destruction, along with the reduction of fratricide, are the key capabilities required within this objective.

Winning the information war is the third of the modernization objectives:

> Information warfare capabilities harness advances in information technologies in order to collect, process, disseminate, and use information. The goal is to provide . . . the operational advantages of Information Dominance. Rapidly advancing

technology provides new opportunities for efficiently executing command and control responsibilities. At the same time, potential adversaries also have access to advanced technology to enhance their own command and control. Targeting and incapacitating the information systems of adversaries, while protecting our own, will allow deep and simultaneous attacks and lead to overmatching force and decisive victory.[3]

Winning the information war is the key to achieving the kind of situational awareness that will allow for the "astounding and unprecedented ability to amass and evaluate enormous quantities of information about any given battle arena . . . and the near instantaneous use of it."[4]

To take true advantage of the information advantage and situational awareness, the fourth modernization objective is to conduct precision strike. Thus the Army must:

> have [a] rapidly deployable capability to conduct deep attacks against the threat. To successfully attack targets with precision at extended ranges requires the capability to see deep, to find designated high-payoff targets, and then transmit that information/intelligence in near real time to firing units employing advanced weapons and munitions systems to destroy those targets.[5]

The ability to engage deep targets allows the ground commanders to effectively shape the battlefield. It also allows for the attrition of enemy forces without the necessity for direct fire combat. Once enemy forces have been attrited, either by organic deep fires or those of another service, and the battlefield has been shaped to support the ground commander's scheme, the Army is in a position to employ fifth modernization objective, dominating maneuver. This requires an Army that is able to control and dominate the fight in order to achieve swift, decisive victory with minimum casualties. Modernization of the maneuver force aims to make them more deployable, tailorable, and lethal. Maneuver forces must be able to get to the area of operations, and once there, they must have the versatility to function both in war and in military operations other than war (MOOTW).[6]

Taken together, these five modernization objectives frame the range of capabilities necessary to achieve the first principle of the Modernization Strategy, that the Army will be capabilities-based. The second principle is closely related: balancing the modernization objectives.

***Balancing the Modernization Objectives.*** Clearly, it does no good to be able to "dominate maneuver" if you cannot get the maneuver force into theater or sustain it when it gets there. Similarly, the Army would not choose to deploy a force which does not have the necessary protection against theater missiles and weapons of mass destruction. The reality is that the five modernization objectives are so interdependent and interlinked that it is critical to balance the funding of all five objectives. In fact, many systems provide critical pieces to more than one objective. The RAH-66 Comanche helicopter program, for example, will provide essential capabilities in both conducting precision strike and winning the information war, as well as playing a supporting role in the other three objectives.

This reality is embedded in our decision to move away from threat-based planning and into capabilities-based planning. We must ensure that, in deciding how to balance risk within the modernization accounts, we take risk in terms of how much of the force will have the suite of capabilities. This is a significant change from decisions about which capabilities we would field to the force. We must ensure the widest range of capabilities—and no group of three, or five, or seven systems will be able to do this. Instead, we must focus on full spectrum systems that provide significant capability across more than one modernization objective and across the widest spectrum of potential conflict. At the same time, we must resource certain systems which are not full spectrum, but which nevertheless provide critical capabilities. Some of these include tanks, fighting vehicles, and attack helicopters.

The nature of our peacetime engagement strategy also dictates the need for a balance. In many cases the capabilities required to effectively carry out our missions in environments short of war are not the same capabilities required to carry out the mission requirements of fighting a major regional contingency. We cannot afford to again assume risk the way we did with the "Big 5." That strategy was the correct one for the Cold War, but for the 1990s and beyond we must ensure a balanced approach to funding the five modernization objectives. But, critical to understanding the principle of balancing the modernization objectives is that it is *capabilities delivered—not dollars expended*—that must be balanced.

***Modernization is Relative.*** The third principle of the Modernization Strategy is that modernization is relative. This is true in two different contexts. First, in comparing our Army to our potential foes, we must maintain a relative warfighting advantage. *There is not, nor will there ever be, a definable end state to modernization.* The Modernization Strategy must, therefore, ensure that our Army maintains a relative technological edge over potential adversaries. This has historically been accomplished in two ways. One way is to produce premier systems. The "Big 5" represented the culmination of this method. The second way is to maintain our edge through our doctrine, soldiers, training, force mix, and leadership. If our Army were to maintain its current level of technology, it would still be an effective force capable of meeting the requirements placed upon it. However, a modernized force will achieve the required objective faster, and with fewer casualties.

The second aspect of the relativity of modernization is that if the equipment the Army receives has better capabilities than the equipment it turns in, it has been "modernized." This is true even if other, better, equipment exists. The Army's relative position has improved. Ideally, of course, everyone in the Army would receive the most technologically advanced version of a piece of equipment.

But the realities of the budget and acquisition process preclude this from happening.

In some sense we have always modernized the force this way. Using a "first to fight" principle, we have always had some units fielded with newer systems, while other units were waiting to receive that system. The length of their wait was a function of the budget and acquisition process, as well as the number of units that were to be equipped. This strategy recognizes this relative modernization as having value in the decisions about acquisition quantities and rates, not just as a factor of how well a program is funded.

## Components of the Modernization Strategy

There are six components to the Modernization Strategy:

(1) Priority Capability Enhancers;
(2) The Core Force;
(3) Refit, Replace, Retire ($R^3$);
(4) Modernization Tempo;
(5) Cascading;
(6) Initiatives and Efficiencies.

The concept behind them is to provide the Army's leadership a tool in developing the priorities and in making the decisions that will drive the Army's investment program, and our input into the budget process. Additionally, they provide a framework and rationale for explaining our decisionmaking process to the Secretary of Defense, the Joint Staff, and the Congress. Ultimately, the strategy is central to enlisting the necessary support for the Army's program.

*Priority Capability Enablers.* The first of these components involves the concept of identifying priority capability enablers. Simply put, a capability enabler is a system type that provides high leverage in achieving one or more of the five modernization objectives. For example, under the objectives of dominating maneuver and winning the information war, the Army can derive the need for the capability to "own the night." Thus, a capability enabler may be night vision devices (for individual soldiers) or night vision sights (for weapon systems). The key aspect of the priority capability enablers is that they define our priorities among the 300 or more competing systems that make up the force modernization program. In aggregate, these capability enablers provide balance among the five objectives.

The effect of this is to focus our effort on those systems which provide the highest leverage in modernizing the force. This is not to say that these are the only systems that will be resourced. It does, however, provide general guidance on prioritization among competitors for scarce RDA dollars.

***The Core Force.*** The second component is the definition of a core force. Designation of such a force is not entirely new. The Army has always had a program that gave priority for new equipment to the "first to fight" units and to our forward deployed units. The Army plan groups these units as our contingency response forces and our regional presence forces. Two other groupings of forces are the reinforcing forces and the strategic reserve.

Under the core force concept, the intent is to focus acquisition efforts on providing the entire suite of priority capability enablers to the core force (the contingency response and regional presence units), while ensuring that the reinforcing force maintains its ability to operate with the core force. This interpretability will be ensured by including the key command, control, communications, and intelligence ($C^3I$) systems in the fielding plan for the reinforcing forces.

This core force is one that, given those capability enablers, will be robust enough to meet a large portion of likely missions with overwhelming capability. It is a concept that accepts the fact that, while we would like to give all units the same range of capabilities, we cannot acquire and field systems fast enough, or in large enough quantities, to field all systems to all units quickly. However, it also acknowledges that there may not be a need for all units to have the same level of certain capabilities. Having a modular and tailorable Army will allow us to provide the combatant commanders with a mix of forces that will have the capabilities that they require to accomplish their missions.

The idea of a core force relies on the principle that modernization is relative and recognizes the impossibility of fielding all new equipment to the entire force in the current fiscal environment. Cutting off the authorized acquisition objective (AAO) for the capability enablers at the level of the core force does assume some risk, but the risk is deemed acceptable in order to modernize a greater portion of the total force. A smaller AAO for each of the priority enablers also brings with it overall program savings.

***Refit, Replace, Retire ($R^3$).*** The third component of the strategy examines individual systems and annually validates the system's usefulness against current Army needs and doctrine. For each system refit, replace, or retire ($R^3$) analysis is conducted. This process includes a revalidation of the requirement for the capability that the system provides, and an assessment of the timeframe for which that system will provide the necessary capabilities. The $R^3$ analysis examines the system in terms of its expected useful life, both mechanically and technologically, and determines for each a time period during which the system will need to be refitted, replaced, or retired. If a system will, at the end of this period, still provide the capability and technological overmatch necessary, the decision may be made to simply refit it, such as a factory rebuild or minor product improvement (the system could even be considered fit for its mission as is). An example of the refit process is conversion of M1 tanks into M1A2s.

If the system is judged to no longer possess required overmatching capabilities, the decision could be made to replace it, with either a major product improvement or a whole new system. The decision to discontinue use of M113 armored personnel carriers as the infantry squad vehicle and switch to the M2 Bradley is a typical replace decision. Finally, if the requirement for which the system was designed is overcome by doctrinal changes and/or other new systems, the decision could be made to retire the system. . . . The Army chief of staff made such a decision when he retired the M551 Sheridan. In doing so he recognized that precious dollars could better support airborne infantry if spent on C-17 delivered M1 tanks and hand-held Javelin missiles rather than on maintaining antiquated Sheridans.

*Modernization Tempo*. The next component of the strategy is to establish a modernization tempo for systems and programs. The "mod tempo" is established by using the $R^3$ point for a system to help set the desired production rates for new systems.

Further, the "mod tempo" is tied to the idea of a core force and includes an assessment of how much of the system we want to procure (the Army's Acquisition Objective [AAO]) and the efficiency with which the industrial base can provide it. For example, we may expect that any given model of tank will meet our warfighting requirements for a period of about eight to ten years without modification (its first $R^3$ point), and that our warfighting needs of the 21st century dictate a core force AAO for tanks of 1600. Given a cost-efficient rate of production of 150-200 tanks per year, and allowing time for retooling of the factory, it is possible to derive a "mod tempo" for tanks that says we can buy the full AAO every eight to ten years. Where low industrial capacity or lack of funds make it impossible to "buy out" the AAO within the time period desired to maintain our "mod tempo," we can decide to produce at an inefficient rate, work with industry to change the efficient rate, or allocate sufficient additional resources to achieve the efficient rate.

The combination of the "mod tempo" and the $R^3$ components provides an opportunity to provide specific "development tempo" guidance to the science and technology (S&T) and research and development (R&D) communities—setting target dates to develop new or improved capabilities. By projecting the $R^3$ points for a system, it is possible to focus and discipline the S&T and R&D processes. Improvements can be timed and resourced to come to fruition in conjunction with the beginning of a new cycle, and those that are not yet ready can be deferred to the beginning of the next cycle. Further, multiple improvements can be made simultaneously, and their development and fielding timed to ensure an effective synergy at the time of incorporation.

Using the tank as an example again, the S&T community would know that in eight to ten years the current tank will be refit, with minor upgrades. In 16-20 years it will be refit again, or replaced with an entirely new type of tank. In 24-30 years it will either be refit, replaced, or if its capabilities are merged into other systems, it will be retired. Working with the requirements community and the priority capability enablers, work can begin on all three timelines simultaneously, with a focused determination as to what will be expected and when.

The "mod tempo" also provides important information to the training, doctrine, and force structure communities. These communities can work in conjunction with the system developers along a set timeline to ensure that the impact of the modernization event can be smoothly incorporated into their processes and procedures.

*Cascading.* Institutionalizing the cascading of older equipment is the strategy's fifth component. Cascading takes equipment and displaces it to the next force segment. Thus, during each cycle the entire Army is modernized by the pipeline in at least a relative sense. This process allows units in the core force to always possess the Army's most modern equipment, while the reinforcing and strategic reserve forces receive relatively modern equipment in a short overall period of time. Again, modernization is relative.

This Army of tiered modernization is *not* to be confused with tiered readiness. As long as training and operating funds are maintained at sufficient levels for all units, the Army will be fully ready. This, in effect, is how the Army has always fought, with some units possessing more modern equipment than others, but all units trained to fight effectively with the equipment they have.

*Initiatives and Efficiencies.* Finally, the Army must make a commitment to seeking and gaining authority to harvest initiatives and efficiencies. This consists, in part, of divesting the Army of older equipment and reinvesting those gains, and other savings from operational resources, into the capital investment program. In like manner, systems in development must be terminated if other new systems or changes in doctrine eliminate their value on the battlefield. This maxim is especially pertinent in an era where military RDA cycles cover 20 years, while changes in technology and military thinking evolve much more quickly. This does not mean that the systems divested are not good systems, but only that their procurement or operations cost may not be affordable within the existing budget constraints, or there may be a less costly alternative for attaining the requisite capability.

Additional modernization-related initiatives and efficiencies cover a broad spectrum and involve activities such as maintaining efficient rates of production, reducing costs of depot operations, and accomplishing an efficient force design and doctrine through the Force XXI process. Key to the initiates and efficiencies component of this strategy is the Army's ability to harvest the savings generated by these efficiencies by being empowered to apply them towards the shortfalls identified in modernization funding.

*Summary.* No strategy is acceptable if it is severely underfunded. This modernization strategy, while efficient, is not cost free. It assumes that RDA accounts will grow relative to the Army's Table of Allowance (TOA). Reinvesting dollars, found within the Army TOA or from elsewhere in DOD, into modernization is necessary to ensure that near and far-term readiness remains in balance.

The Army can use these six components of the Modernization Strategy to effectively measure the costs of various investment programs. It can easily portray the ability of those alternative programs to meet the requirements of providing the core force with the right capability enablers at the right time. It will allow us to provide discipline and balanced decisions to the need for product improvements, new systems, or the retiring of old ones. And, it includes a commitment to find at least a portion of the money necessary from within the Army's current and projected TOA.

## Tough Choices

Having a strategy and a process provides a framework for decisionmaking. However, decisions must still be made, and the Army faces a series of tough choices. The central tenet of those choices is mitigation of risk. In this era of constrained budgets but increased operational activity, the implications of risk become proportionately greater. The Army must decide how best to balance the acquisition of modern equipment with the requirements of its other budget imperatives. Within the modernization program, the Army must decide how best to balance the acquisition of different modern systems and the capabilities they bring against the needs of Army XXI. The Army must balance its force capabilities to ensure the ability to perform the full spectrum of missions. These questions of balance require changes in the way we do business. And those changes bring with them additional risk.

The Army modernization strategy lays out the concepts of a core force and a modernization tempo. Each concept entails certain difficulties. The non-core force units will receive equipment cascaded from the core force. The core force must, therefore, be large enough to ensure that there is enough equipment to cascade. If one third of the total Army (active, Guard, and reserve) is in the core force, it follows there will be three levels of equipment modernization in the force. If the core force is only a fourth of the total force, then there will be four tiers of modernization. Of course, while it is cheaper to procure modern equipment for a smaller percentage of the force, unit costs are higher, and the cost to maintain and operate additional tiers of equipment may also be higher. Thus the first of the tough choices is how to size the core force. Inherent in this decision is the argument on whether to base the core force on warfighting needs or affordability. Army doctrine would argue for the former, but budget realities must be taken into account.

The Army funds over 300 different programs within its RDA budget. Prioritizing these, while deciding between our "Window of Opportunity" systems and our critical warfighting systems, is no easy task. Every system in development is based on a sound requirement and has its individual constituency within the Army, the Office of the Secretary of Defense, and the Congress. The second tough choice is deciding which of these systems are to be the priority capability enablers. This decision requires effective feedback from our Force XXI process. The choices must also be "sold" to these various constituencies. Inherent in this choice is the decision how deep into the force to field each capability enabler. Some enablers, like tanks, can be fielded to part of the force and cascaded. Other enablers, like some communication systems, must be fielded throughout the force in order to ensure command and control on the battlefield.

The third tough choice focuses on the question of how to manage the "mod tempos" of various systems. We could synchronize the tempo of many systems so they all coincide. Using this concept, the Army might take an entire division out of the ready force for a certain period and modernize it from top to bottom. This is similar to the way the Navy takes an aircraft carrier out of service for a year or two and completely refits it. However, the Army is not overstructured. Given our current operational requirements and constrained force structure, the option of modernizing an entire division simultaneously is not attractive. Therefore, we might need to ensure that systems meet their "mod tempo" milestones at different times. Using a more traditional approach to modernization, at any given time a division may have some of its units undergoing a partial modernization program, but the division as a whole is available for use.

Additional tough choices will emerge because ultimately, the Army is a member of a joint team. The increasing role of the Joint Staff, the Joint Requirements Oversight Council, and the Joint Warfighting Capabilities Assessments means that we must compete our choices with a wide variety of programs from other services and may also benefit from capabilities provided by other services.

## Conclusions

Much of the recent debate about defense funding has centered on the issue of modernization. There is a strong and growing acknowledgment that the modernization accounts of the armed forces have been allowed to drop to a dangerous level.

Given fiscal reality and the large number of competing priorities, the debate will continue. In developing and presenting its case for adequate and additional funding, the Army is guided by its emerging Modernization Strategy. This strategy is one that the Army firmly believes is central to its ability to ensure not only current operational readiness but also readiness against all potential threats for the foreseeable future.

Under Title 10 of the U.S. Code, the Department of the Army is charged with the mission to man, train, equip, and sustain the country's primary ground combat forces. In meeting the requirements of this mission, the Army's six imperatives, if achieved and properly balanced, will ensure our warfighting commanders-in-chief have a force readily available to accomplish any mission.

The Army's vision of the emerging strategic environment is one which stresses the importance of land power dominance. As the Secretary of Defense reported to Congress and the President [in 1996]:

> Today, our policy for managing post-Cold War dangers to our security rests on three basic lines of defense. The first line of defense is to prevent threats from emerging; the second is to deter threats that do emerge; and the third, if prevention and deterrence fail, is to defeat the threat to our security by using military force.[7]

[Former] Secretary of Defense William Perry mention[ed] the use of *military force* for the third line of defense, defeating threats, but the requirement to use *military forces* is a major part of achieving success in the first two lines of defense.

History has shown that a key aspect of deterrence and prevention is "troops on the ground." Whether the mission is peacekeeping, peacemaking, nation-building, reassurance, deterrence, humanitarian relief, or just military-to-military contact, it cannot be accomplished without the commitment of ground forces. Economic and political attempts at reassuring, deterring, supporting, or compelling are not complete without a credible ground force. Similarly, while warplanes and ships may be able to set the stage for a successful ground campaign, they cannot, by themselves, produce the ability to impose our will on an enemy force.

For the Army, there is a key question—what should that ground force look like? The Force XXI process has begun to lay the foundation for answering that question. The Modernization Strategy does not solve all Army modernization challenges. It requires both constant reassessment and the making of tough choices and tradeoffs. We know that the force conducting the ground campaign, compelling, reassuring, or deterring must be a modernized one.

---

## Notes

1. *The United States Army 1996 Modernization Plan*, Headquarters, Department of the Army, Washington DC, 1996, 23.

2. Ibid., 25.

3. Ibid., 27.

4. Eliot A. Cohen, "A Revolution in Warfare," *Foreign Affairs*, March/April 1996, 40.

5. *The United States Army 1996 Modernization Plan,* 30.

6. Ibid., 32.

7. William J. Perry, *Annual Report to the President and the Congress*, U.S. Government Printing Office, Washington, DC, March 1996, viii.

# Chapter 36

# * * *

# The End of Naval Strategy: Revolutionary Change and The Future of American Naval Power

Jan S. Breemer

*Jan Breemer states that two kinds of revolutionary change have historically altered the ways navies think about their functions: a "bottom-up" response to technological innovation and a "top-down" response to shifts in the international security environment. While the former is common, the latter is rare. The collapse of the Soviet Union and the end of the Cold War have precipitated a top-down revolution within the U.S. Navy, replacing the system that was created by the last such change in the thinking of the U.S. Navy a century ago. The bellwether of this revolution is the Navy Department's white paper, . . .From the Sea. That document was followed by Forward . . . From The Sea which updates and expands the strategic concept articulated in . . . From the Sea to address specifically the unique contributions of naval expeditionary forces in peacetime operations, in responding to crises, and in regional conflicts. Breemer argues this strategic concept shifts the U.S. Navy's strategic and doctrinal essence away from planning for war at sea toward support for joint operations on land. As such, if correct, it has revolutionary implications for the U.S. Navy's traditional self-image as the sole autonomous provider of oceanic security. Is Breemer's thesis correct? Or, as Professor Frank Uhlig of the Naval War College has written, is the first absolute of naval warfare to ensure that friendly shipping can flow and the second that hostile shipping cannot; only after which navies can risk landing armies on a hostile shore? Is the core essence of the U.S. Navy then, still control of the sea - or has it shifted irrevocably to projection of force from the sea?*

Two kinds of revolutionary change have historically altered the way navies think about their functions. The first, change "from-the-bottom-up," is

Dr. Jan S. Breemer is an Associate Professor of National Security Affairs at the Naval Postgraduate School in Monterey, CA. He publishes extensively on both historical and contemporary maritime strategic issues.

triggered by technological innovation, e.g., the airplane or the submarine. The response to technological change is at first confined to minor doctrinal adjustments in an effort to preserve the familiar doctrinal framework. As evidence accumulates that the new weapons do not abide by the old rules and that trying to make them fit is, in fact, counter-productive, strategic concepts and doctrine eventually undergo revolutionary change.

The second and less common revolutionary change follows a reverse course. The catalyst for this "top-down" revolution often is a systemic shift in the international security environment. Such a shift may be the result of the rise or fall of an opponent capable of challenging the continued relevance of the existing naval-strategic planning framework. If the gap between the new environment and the older naval strategic culture proves too wide to bridge by means of adjustments in force levels and force composition alone, the strategic culture must be changed in order to accommodate the environment.

The U.S. Navy last experienced a top-down revolution one century ago when it discarded coastal defense and commerce-raiding in favor of Mahan's vision of naval power as the struggle for command of the sea by battlefleets.[1] That vision, central to the Navy's professional culture since the birth of the "New Navy," is challenged today by the end of the Cold War and the demise of the Soviet naval menace. The Navy's white paper, *From the Sea*, was the service's response to this challenge; it gave notice that the service was about to go through the most fundamental top-down revolution since the birth of the "New Navy" one hundred years ago. As the Navy shifts its strategic and doctrinal essence away from planning for war at sea toward support for battle on land, it must come to grips with the revolutionary implications of this change for its traditional self-image as the sole, autonomous provider of oceanic security.

As part of this shift, the naval profession will need to radically reinterpret its role in national security. This paper proposes that, as part of this re-identification, the Navy adopt an narrow interpretation of its responsibilities for warfare on the littoral landmass and that it restructure its forces accordingly.

## Naval Power from the Sea: Once Again

In 1954 Samuel Huntington laid out the U.S. Navy's new "transoceanic" strategy for fighting the Cold War.[2] This "New Naval Doctrine," he wrote, recognized the "obvious fact that international power is now distributed not among a number of basically naval powers but rather between one nation and its allies which dominate the land masses of the globe and another nation and its allies which monopolize the world's oceans."[3] According to the author, the hostility between Western maritime power and Soviet continental predominance spelled the end of the Mahanian concept of seapower as the struggle between great fleets for command of the oceans. Instead, now that American naval power faced a continental rival without a fleet to speak of, it would fight its future battles away from the sea and on and over the opponent's "Littoral" land zone.[4]

Huntington also wrote that this transition had not come easily but only after an acute identity crisis that went to the "depths of the Navy's being."[5] That crisis centered on the question of what the world's most powerful fleet, armed with the Mahanian philosophy of the "decisive battle," was to do when it had no seagoing rival on the horizon, and when a strategic air force armed with nuclear bombs seemed to have "absolutely" replaced it as the nation's first line of defense. Huntington concluded that the Navy's determination to solve the crisis by looking beyond Mahan and switching its doctrinal focus away from blue water and toward the Eurasian landmass, proved its "flexibility and vigor" in adapting to new circumstances.

Forty years later, the Navy's ability to adapt to revolutionary change is again being tested.[6] This revolution is compelling the Navy to revise completely the way it has traditionally identified itself as a provider of national defense and international security. At the center of this revolution is the question of how an organization whose professional norms, values, and operating routines have customarily been identified with the Mahanian view of naval power, can accommodate itself to a security environment in which the struggle for "command of the sea" is no longer its *essential* charge.[7]

## Navies and "Bottom-Up" Change

Over the past 150 years or so, the face of naval power has been repeatedly and radically transformed by dramatic material changes.[8] Between 1860 and 1890, steam propulsion, iron and steel construction, and scientific gunnery turned fleets from collections of wooden sailing vessels with firepower not much different from Elizabethan days into "fighting machines" with unheard of destructive power.[9] Even before the naval profession had fully grasped the strategic and doctrinal implications of the new machine-age fleets, the submarine and the airplane unleashed a second material revolution. Next came the most controversial revolution of all, the impact of nuclear weapons on the character of naval power.[10]

Although very different in kind, these revolutions had one thing in common: they were *technological* transformations that, for a time at least, did not seem to threaten the blue water culture that dominated the naval profession. Autopropulsion, submarines, aircraft, and, albeit with greater difficulty, even the atomic bomb, could be "piggy-backed" to the customary vision of naval warfare as merely new and better ways for doing the old task of securing command of the sea.[11]

Attempts to graft large-scale technological change onto "old thinking" can only be a temporary expedient; new weapons demand their own operational culture and, along the way, ultimately revolutionize the very thinking about naval power. And it is in the "explosion of ideas," of course, not in the refinement of techniques or tactics, that the true revolutionary significance of a new weapon must be found.[12] When the dust has settled, the outcome may be a new doctrine, the emergence of new war-making "principles," or even, in the case of the atomic bomb, the rejection of the Clausewitzian concept of war as the pursuit of politics by other means.[13] Cultural change that has its roots in technological innovation takes place *from-the-bottom-up*.[14]

## Revolutionary Technological Change

Since the mid-nineteenth century, revolutionary changes from-the-bottom-up have thoroughly transformed our concept of naval power, of how it works, and how it relates to other forms of military force. Thus, the machine age fleets that were created in the Victorian era and whose controllability Mahan thought portended a much closer match between the (offensive) principles and the practice of war at sea, actually produced the opposite effect. The prospect of a truly annihilating sea battle made possible by modern gunnery also brought the sobering thought that a victory might well be of Pyrrhic proportions. The upshot for the naval strategy of World War I was that, rather than seeking to defeat the enemy in compliance with the "sounder military understanding of a navy,"[15] both the British and the Germans turned their "decisive battle" forces into fleets-in-being that waited for the other side to make a mistake that would place his forces at a disadvantage.[16]

The submarine and the airplane revolutionized thinking about sea power even more profoundly; both inventions vastly complicated the command of the sea concept. In the case of the submarine, World War I ended the notion that command of the sea could be gained through victory in one or more decisive battles between surface fleets. The submarine also undermined the view of naval warfare as one or a series of battles between massed fleets. This image was necessarily part and parcel of a war-fighting practice that insisted on the importance of concentration of forces. The submarine denied this principle; it fought alone and had to be defeated alone. This fact, plus the relative ease with which a submarine adversary could replace his losses, meant that the struggle for sea control would henceforth be a *campaign of exhaustion.*

The airplane further diluted the ship's monopoly on command of the sea; indeed, World War II demonstrated that just as the success of armies on land had come to depend on air superiority, so fleets could no longer aspire to command the sea without commanding the air. Even more important in the long run, aircraft (and later missiles) obliterated the dividing line that had always separated land warfare from sea warfare, and armies from navies. A few years before the Great War, Winston Churchill, then First Lord of the Admiralty, had sought to assure the Germans that, no matter how powerful the Royal Navy, it could not endanger a single continental hamlet.[17] He was correct then—or at least almost so. He could have added that the obverse was true as well: as long as armies were confined to *terra firma* not even the Kaiser's divisions could threaten the island kingdom's safety or its fleet. The airplane terminated this historical truism in World War II as naval aviation repeatedly struck inland, and land-based aviation became the fleet's most dangerous enemy. A corollary implication was that technology had conspired to create the *integrated* theater of war. In the past, the geography of warfare was necessarily divided between land and sea theaters; the only place the two intermingled was on the beach (hence the centuries-long controversy between armies and navies over who should be responsible for its defense), which usually occurred only momentarily during an amphibious landing. Air power *routinized* this crossover between the land and the sea.

Perhaps the most revolutionary consequence of the airplane for sea power was that, by the time of World War II, it had broken the later's historical monopoly on sea control. Land-based air power not only proved its "negative" ability to deny the opponent the use of the seas, but also the "positive" wherewithal to secure and keep the sea.[18] To be sure, there was another side to this coin as well. By embracing the airplane as its own, naval forces possessed, for the first time in history, the means to strike against land forces.[19] Yet, this development also contributed to the dilution of the old naval strategic concept that held that fleets existed solely to fight other fleets. In any case, the ability to strike inland gave navies merely a *competitive* capability; it was not clear that this compensated for the loss of the erstwhile *unique* ability to secure the seas.

Little remains to be said about the impact of nuclear weapons on naval strategic thought. It did not require the limited war theorists of the late 1950s to persuade naval officers that atomic warfare would not be business-as-usual. If the naval planners of World War I were deterred from all-out battle by the *cost* of victory, their nuclear successors were stymied by its apparent *impossibility*.

## "From the Top-Down"

While navies, along with other military forces, may stand on the brink of a new revolution "from the bottom up," a more fundamental challenge for naval power is the impending "top-down" revolution of naval roles and missions as articulated in *From the Sea* and reiterated in *Forward . . . From the Sea*. This revolution it more fundamental because it *overturns the very foundation of our modern concept of naval power and strategy*, that is to say, its *essential* preoccupation with command of the sea. Unlike the technology-induced changes of the past, this top-down revolution is dictated by the necessity for naval power to adapt to systemic changes in the international security environment. It calls for "a fundamental shift away from open-ocean warfighting *on* the sea toward joint operations conducted *from* the sea."[20]

Top-down revolutions that start with wholesale changes in military roles, doctrines and strategic concepts are rare.[21] The dynamics of the Navy's conversion to a blue water fleet one century ago were varied, but one was the expectation that the United States, along with the rest of the globe, was about to enter into a new "world order" of heightened competition very likely to embroil America in foreign conflicts.[22] The other top-down revolution has already been mentioned: the post-World War II period during which there was no prospective oceanic opponent, and the fleet appeared ready to step back from its Mahanian lineage and become "a navy oriented away from the oceans and towards the land masses on their far side."[23] But the doctrinal revolution that Huntington wrote about in 1954 was never quite consummated. True, for a while nuclear "power projection" took pride of place alongside sea control during the era of "massive retaliation." However, two events ensured that sea control would remain "*the* fundamental function of the U.S. Navy*," and that therefore naval power projection, though always available to a land campaign on a "collateral" basis, would continue to serve the ends of sea control first.[24]

The first event was the emergence of the Soviet submarine fleet. Contrary to Huntington's assertion, the size of this force and apparent intent to duplicate the onslaught of the U-boats of World War II, made anti-submarine warfare (ASW) a primary *sea control* mission.[25] Next came the emergence in the 1960s of a "real" Soviet fleet, complete with cruisers and aircraft carriers. For many Western observers this development signaled that traditional naval strategy had lost none of its relevance after all. Former U.S. Navy Secretary John Lehman thought so. Mahan's views, he wrote in 1981, "are being followed by the Soviet Union today," resulting in a blue water navy "patently Mahanian in design."[26]

There is irony in the fact that the progeny of Lehman's re-born naval strategy, the U.S. Navy's "Maritime Strategy," was rendered null and void by events in Eastern Europe and the Soviet Union at the very moment the strategy's goal of a "600-ship Navy" was about to be reached. Made public by the Navy and Marine Corps in 1986, the Maritime Strategy will probably be remembered as the highwater mark of "blue water" naval thinking in the post-war era.[27] When the Maritime Strategy's successor, *From the Sea*, was unveiled six years later, the 600-ship fleet target had already been reduced to 451, and further reductions continue as part of the Clinton Administration's program.[28] This kind of force cutting alone is more than sufficient grounds for a dramatic revision of the way the Navy has done business for the past 45 years. The real catalyst for change, however, rests with the revolutionary shift in the Navy's strategic culture embedded in *From the Sea*.

## From the Sea

The document's message is short and straightforward. It argues that, given the demise of the Soviet threat and therefore that of the specter of a far-ranging campaign for control of the transatlantic sea lines of communications, classic "sea control" need no longer be the Navy's first priority. In the words of then Acting Navy Secretary Sean O'Keefe, sea control has become "in some ways—a given" that the United States has "covered at this point."[29] It followed, reported the Commander-in-Chief of the newly-established U.S. Atlantic Command, that the Navy was now "permitted. . . to have a wider field of view and operational thought."[30] The focal point of this "wider field of view," says *From the Sea*, will be the so-called "littoral," or "near land" areas of the world oceans. Specifically, the document announces that the Navy will be reshaped into an instrument of crisis management and an "enabling" force on behalf of other military forces operating on the landward side of the littoral.

Using navies for purposes other than outright war at sea is not a novel development. On the contrary, sea battles and oceanic campaigns have historically been the exception, so that, other than preparing for the next "big" war, fleets have always spent most of their useful service life on "littoral" duties—showing the flag, suppressing piracy, intervening in local crises, etc. This was precisely the role of the Royal Navy for nearly one century after the defeat of Napoleon, and again after the two world wars.[31] The same has been true for the U.S. Navy since World War II.[32] Although its strategic concept, training and tactical routines, and weapons procurement were guided throughout by the scenario of a war at sea with the Soviet Union, its practical business has been to project its "moral effect" and shape events in the Third World.[33] The Navy has been more than happy to highlight its value as a naval-diplomatic and "crisis response" tool, but few of its officers took seriously the occasional suggestion that "presence" be elevated to an official function alongside sea control and that this be reflected in the make-up of the fleet.[34] However, the issuing of *Forward . . . From the Sea* acknowledges presence as a key stategic function.[35]

Given that intervention in local crises and conflicts has been the bread and butter of the navies of the major powers all along, it may be concluded that there is nothing unique or revolutionary about *From the Sea*. Nothing can be further from the truth. The document is without precedent in that *it explicitly defines littoral operations to contain crises or support land forces in "small" wars as the primary task for navies in the foreseeable future.* Never before has a major navy relegated sea control and the preparation for the next "big" war at sea to a secondary consideration. Even at the height of *Pax Britannica*, when successive generations of Royal Navy officers had never seen a sea fight, spending their careers instead "policing" the empire (oftentimes fighting native uprisings on *land*), the latter was never thought to be more than a passing collateral duty.

Throughout this period, ships were built and crews trained for "fleet action."[36] The same has been true for the principal blue water fleets after both world wars.

The reasons for this consistent mismatch between fleet theory and fleet practice were sound enough. During the era of *Pax Britannica*, Great Britain's Victorian navy had to keep a wary eye on France, its traditional rival across the Channel, and, to a lesser extent, the navies of Russia and the United States. After World War I, it took the Washington Naval Treaty of 1922 to break up the triangle of mutual suspicion over fleet building policies that had developed among the United States, Great Britain, and Japan.[37] And after World War II an increasingly powerful Soviet navy cast its shadow over the U.S. Navy's policing activities. It must be recalled that the crises and conflicts of the past 40 years usually had Cold War overtones, so that offsetting demonstrations of U.S. and Soviet naval power always carried the risk of escalation to full-scale war.[38]

Circumstances are entirely different today: for the first time in centuries, the world's largest fleet is without an actual or foreseeable competitor on the high sea. It can therefore focus its energies on "operations other than war at sea" without having to look over its shoulder for the next blue water challenge.[39] True, there still exists a very large Russian navy that, outwardly at least, still has all the material qualifications to endanger the seas. Nevertheless, despite the cautionary note that "intentions can change overnight," even the Navy's intelligence director acknowledged in 1992 that the main preoccupation of the former Soviet fleet was to "survive." With the exception of the ballistic missile submarines, its mission is no longer offensive, and will not become so for at least 20 years.[40] To paraphrase former Commander-in-Chief Atlantic Command, Admiral Miller, an ocean without challengers has forced the U.S. Navy to confront a "big change in operational culture."[41]

## The End of Naval Strategy

*From the Sea* writes the epitaph to the command of the sea "system" that has dominated naval thought since the late 16th century when, thanks to the growth of seaborne commerce and the development of warships capable of keeping the sea, "true naval war" replaced "cross-ravaging" as the main purpose of military power at sea.[42] For the next 300 years the fleets of the principal maritime powers fought by the unwritten rule that "nothing can be done of consequence in naval war till one side secures the control of the water area."[43] The rule was codified at the turn of this century in the great navalist writings of Corbett, Colomb, and Mahan.[44] Their body of writings also spelled out how navies went about securing command of the sea, i.e., *naval strategy*.[45]

Naval strategy is concerned, by definition, with the maneuvering of naval forces in order to win (or deny) command of the sea.[46] There have been very few sea wars in which the opposing strategies were purely naval and therefore command of the sea the sole issue.[47] In most conflicts with a large seagoing dimension, naval strategy and the struggle for command have been subordinated to a larger *maritime* strategy.[48] The distinction between "naval" and "maritime" strategy and the role of navies in both is often overlooked, but it is an important one. Corbett explained the relationship between the three in 1911: Maritime strategy, he wrote, pertained to the "principles which govern a war in which the sea is a substantial factor." This relationship is particularly important today. Calling it the "problem of coordination," Corbett stressed that the foremost principle of *maritime strategy* was "to determine the mutual relations of your army and navy in a plan of war."[49] In today's jargon this is called "jointness."

Corbett went on to explain that naval strategy was a sub-set of maritime strategy: it was concerned with how the fleet could best carry out the seagoing portion of the overarching maritime strategy. Naval tasks might include protection against invasion, blockading the enemy's ports, or projecting the army against enemy territory.[50] But no matter how varied the tasks, success or failure rested on a common prerequisite that was at the core of what Corbett called the "theory of naval war," namely to secure and exercise command of the sea.[51] There was nothing mysterious about this; command of the sea meant nothing more than control of the sea lines of communications, whether for military or commercial purposes.[52]

The implications were far-reaching, however. For one, wrote Corbett, the principles of naval strategy "should be found giving shape not only to strategy and tactics, but also to material, whatever methods and means of naval warfare may be in use at any given time."[53] In other words, if command of the sea is the fleet's foremost, indeed sole, naval (as opposed to maritime) strategic purpose, it follows that the capabilities required to command the sea will determine fleet size and structure, strategic orientation and tactical routines, and even ship and weapon characteristics. For another, since naval strategy was solely concerned with the contest for control of the maritime communications, it followed that once the latter was resolved, *"pure naval strategy comes to an end"*[54] (emphasis added). It was not that the successful fleet went out of business, but rather that winning (and keeping) command of the sea meant that the victorious fleet had fulfilled its naval purpose, had ceased to fight pure naval war, and could now turn all its attention to what Mahan called the "ulterior objects" of the nation's broader maritime (or continental) strategy. This is precisely where the U.S. Navy finds itself today and why *From the Sea* and *Forward . . . From the Sea* lay such great stress on the need for the Navy to satisfy the requirements of *national*, as opposed to naval, strategy.

## From Sea Control to Land Control

The history of sea warfare is full of instances in which fleets were used to fight a maritime strategy *sans* naval strategy. To reiterate: naval strategy is possible only if there is an opponent who is able and willing to contest the command of the sea; if there is not, the fleet is directly subordinate to the necessities of war on land. The Crimean War is an auspicious example. Shortly after war broke out in 1854, the Russians chose not to use their considerable fleet to oppose a threatened Anglo-French invasion at sea, but to turn their ships instead into floating coastal defense batteries. The Crimean peninsula was the center of hostilities, but the same policy was carried out in the Baltic and even in far away Petropavlovsk on the Pacific coast.[55] The result was allied command of the sea by default, which meant that the question before the naval commanders was not how to defeat the Russian fleet, but how to best influence events on land from-the-sea.

The use of a fleet to support land operations was known at the time of the Crimean war as a "conjunct" operation. One century later the term "combined operation" had come into vogue. Today's military planners speak of "joint" warfare. "Jointness" became the legislated *modus operandi* for the American military with the passage of the Goldwater-Nichols Department of Defense Act of 1986.[56] The reasons for its passage were perceived inefficiencies in the existing, service-focused command structure. The end of classic naval strategy reinforces the strategic logic of jointness. *From the Sea* acknowledges that the new strategic order—and therefore the service's institutional health—dictates that the Navy become a full-time player in land warfare. This is vastly different from naval power's conjunct or combined role in the past. Rather than a collateral and temporary association, a diversion, if you will, from the fleet's primary purpose *on* the sea. Jointness signifies a reverse order of priorities; it connotes *fusion* of effort in place of *ad hoc* arrangements and, most important, it subordinates all seagoing naval operations directly to events on land.

The Navy's new "battlespace" concept highlights the new primacy of land warfare in fleet operations. "Battlespace" is defined as the sea, air, and land areas that the Navy must dominate in order to conduct operations ashore; it encompasses the "area from the open ocean to the shore which must be controlled to support operations ashore," as well as the "area inland from shore that can be supported and defended directly from the sea."[57] What is important here is the pivotal role of operations on *land*: battlespace dominance matters for the ability of naval power to control military events *ashore*. Superficially, this may not sound terribly revolutionary; but it represents a 180 degrees reversal from the classic relationship between sea control and naval power projection. In the past, the Navy valued the ability to project power ashore primarily for its contribution to sea control—not to control operations on land. Admiral Holloway could therefore report, in 1977, that the "capability to project power was developed in naval forces largely as an adjunct to strategic sea control."[58] The battlespace concept overturns this hierarchy—battlespace dominance and power projection are now subordinate to naval (and joint!) *land control*!

## How Much Land Control?

During the "golden age" of navalism, when Mahan, Corbett, and others wrote their great works, naval thinkers carried on an endless debate over the exact meaning of "command of the sea." The question was whether a fleet should be strong enough to win "absolute" command, or whether it merely needed to be capable of establishing control at times and places as dictated by the nation's "ulterior objects" at the time. The answer was important, for on it depended how large (and expensive) a fleet should be built. The Navy's new strategic concept of land control poses a somewhat similar question—namely, *how much* land control should be the aim of warfare from the sea? Should it be sufficient to underwrite the Navy and Marine Corps' traditional, over-the-beach "enabling" role in order to "lay the doormat" for follow-on heavy Air Force and Army units; or should it include the wherewithal to conduct operations throughout the land theater of action, especially "deep strikes" by carrier aviation?[59] The signals so far are mixed.

Part of the problem has to do with the ambiguous definition of the word "littoral."[60] Many authorities, notably the former Chairman of the Joint Chiefs of Staff, have identified it with "coastal."[61] When still in office, Acting Navy Secretary O'Keefe seemed to agree, when he commented in an interview that *From the Sea* "focuses on the kinds of scenarios that call for shorter-range strike capabilities . . . pointed more toward close-air support missions."[62] The document itself, on the other hand, does not quite say that. The initial publication gave no details on how far inland the Navy's battlespace might reach, other than to say that it "expands and contracts and has limits."[63] A later (undated) version of the document is more explicit, however. It includes a map of the world that shows the "littoral region" as lying anywhere within the 650 nautical miles range of naval strike capabilities. The only areas of the world thus excluded are the very central portions of Canada, South America, Africa, and Siberia. Some question whether the Navy should stake out such a comprehensive land control claim.

## The Meaning of "Littoral"

There are at least three reasons for the Navy's land-control claim. First, it can be argued that a theater-wide strike capability is necessary to defeat enemy airplanes or missiles which threaten the "doormat" from rear areas hundreds of miles away. Next, the Navy may be "hedging" against an uncertain operational and organizational future. There is the long-standing argument that land bases for Air Force "strategic" bombers may not always be available.[64] *From the Sea* might also represent a transitional strategy, a stepping stone as it were, in a continuing debate over the future of separate military services. By claiming a broad land control role the Navy may be positioning itself for its share of a future unified service. Additionally, it makes perfect sense for a military organization, especially a Navy that has long been accustomed to operating self-sufficiently in all forms of warfare, to cast its mission "net" as widely as possible. Service mission responsibilities translate into budgets and joint command opportunities, and military organizations measure their "health" by both.

Equally weighty arguments can be advanced *against* "deep" littoral control. A Navy deep strike capability may not conflict with the *letter* of jointness, but it certainly tests its *spirit*.[65] It may also be wiser for the Navy to borrow from the economic theory of comparative advantage and focus its efforts on what it has always done best, i.e., amphibious forcible entry, instead of spreading its resources between "tactical" and "strategic" tasks and competing with the Air Force's strategic *forte*.[66] In fact, mission and burden allocation based on the idea of comparative advantage may hold the solution to a balanced yet joint-spirited Navy land control capability.

The theory of comparative advantage (sometimes called the "factor endowment" model for the particular natural and other "endowments" that give a nation a competitive edge in the production and export of certain goods) does not propose that nations will specialize in the production of endowed goods to the exclusion of all other, non-endowed, products. By the same token, even if it is agreed that naval air power can be used most cost-effectively for amphibious forcible entry (e.g., close air support, battlefield air interdiction, and general over-the-beach air superiority), it would still be worthwhile for it to keep *some* capacity for control of the "deep" littoral landmass. Why not make the Tomahawk cruise missile the Navy's deep strike "silver bullet?"[67] This would provide an on-call ability to strike against those enemy rear area targets that pose an immediate danger to the success of an expeditionary lodgment.

Conversely, deep targets whose control might be critical to the overall war effort but that do not threaten the amphibious doormat, would be left for follow-on land-based aircraft to deal with.[68] The reasoning behind this distribution of effort is clear: if sea-launched Tomahawks are not enough to contain the opponent's "strategic" threat, chances are that the contingency at hand is probably too large for assault from the sea alone.

In any event, an important task for today's naval planners is to consider the likelihood of "from the sea-only" contingencies that will require more than a few Tomahawk salvos. If the chances are high, it should next be asked whether those contingencies will be important enough to warrant the opportunity costs of a continued heavy investment in deep strike carrier aviation.

## Conclusion: A Dialectic of Sea Power?

When Huntington wrote about the Navy's new transoceanic doctrine, he commented how its adoption had come only after a crisis that went to "the depths of the Navy's being."[69] The Navy's uncertainty of purpose in the immediate post-World War II years pales in comparison with today's identity crisis. The crisis then was that the only potential opponent appeared immune to the pressure of seapower; today's problem is the absence altogether of an identifiable enemy.[70] Even this is only a part of the radically different security environment with which blue water naval power must come to grips. Equally unfamiliar phenomena include the prominence of "ethno-strife" as a source of armed conflict and intervention; the new legitimizing role of the United Nations in crisis and conflict management; and the heightened importance of multinational peacekeeping and peace enforcement operations. Collectively, these trends will no doubt create a very different "system" of sea warfare.[71]

There remains one concluding observation, or rather, question: how final is the end of naval strategy? What are the chances that naval power's landward orientation is a passing episode, and that its epicenter will be found at sea again? The answer seems to hinge on three factors. The first has to do with the historic interconnection between land-and seapower on the one hand, and between the offense and defense on the other. History reveals that landpowers threatened from the sea have always resorted to the sea themselves and aimed to ward off attack *on* the sea. The reason is simple: it is less destructive to the nation, and therefore cheaper in the long run, to defend oneself through offensive action away from home than by defending the beaches. That is why Sparta built a fleet to defeat the Athenians, why Rome took its military prowess onto the sea to fight Carthage, and why, 2000 years later, the Soviet Union pushed its strategic defenses onto the oceans. Taken in isolation, this trend suggests that a successful American strategy of intervention "from the sea" may eventually spur nations thus threatened to create their own seagoing countervailing capabilities, and contest *on* the sea the American ability to freely use the seas.

Whether or not this will happen depends on the second factor, the outcome of what Peter Schwartz has called a "critical uncertainty" about the existing international system.[72] Namely, few nations other than a united Europe, Japan, and China perhaps will have the financial and technical ability to counter American naval might at oceanic distances from their shores. The critical uncertainty concerns America's future relationship with Europe and Japan. If the global security environment continues to be defined by U.S. unipolarity and a (U.S.-led) "security community" among the major industrialized powers, the rise of competitors with enough resources to force U.S. naval power away from the littoral and defend itself on blue waters is unlikely.[73] This could happen, however, if, as has been claimed by some authors, U.S. unipolarity is bound to give way to balance of power competition, including possibly war, between the U.S., Europe, and/or Japan.[74]

Transatlantic or transpacific great power rivalry need not necessarily lead to a return of blue water strategy, at least not in its classic form. The third factor and second critical uncertainty is the evolution of technology, especially the range and endurance of aircraft and unmanned flying systems. While it is unlikely that aircraft will ever become more cost-effective than ships for the transportation of very large quantities of men and materiel, it is at least conceivable that improved design and more powerful engines will permit aircraft to reach out and compete for sea control across increasingly wider expanses of water. In that case, a future great power struggle for control of the "deep blue" may come in the form of power projection from opposing littorals.[75]

What is the likelihood of this scenario? Slim for the foreseeable future. This and the coming generation of naval officers will have to think about the uses and usefulness of naval force in an entirely different way than their predecessors. This shift of vision will be more difficult and more controversial than the Navy's last top-down revolution. The fleet's cultural transformation one century ago from "an alphabet of floating washtubs" to the "New American Navy" was easy, because centuries of fleet-against-fleet fighting had long produced a familiar bundle of ideas about the proper role of blue water fleets.[76] Mahan and his navalist *confreres* merely codified this experience. By contrast, the naval officer who must now be indoctrinated to fight for land control has very few historical lessons, let alone "principles," to consult. True, there is a long tradition of amphibious operations, but these were never central to the blue water culture or naval strategy *per se.*

It may be that the closest analogy to the Navy's doctrinal vacuum today is to be found in the period when fighting ships first turned from "cross-ravaging" to naval strategy on the sea. By the end of the 16th century, naval warfare had "settled into form," based on the idea that the best way to impose one's will on a seagoing opponent was to defeat his warfleet.[77] But it took most of the next century for this basic proposition to mature and become the centerpiece of a unique professional culture with a strategic code and tactical rules peculiar to war on the sea. Thus, the first naval "fighting instructions" were issued in the 1650s while, decades later, it was still common for fleets to be commanded by generals.[78] The Navy finds itself in somewhat similar circumstances: it has acknowledged the new shape of naval warfare, but it is still far from completing the necessary cultural transformation. This, more than anything else, is the challenge of the end of naval strategy.

---

### Notes

1. The terms "command of the sea" and "sea control" are used interchangeably throughout this paper, the sole difference between the two being that the second is of more recent origin. The author fully recognizes that

command of the sea (or sea control) is not a "generic" condition, that instead its geographic and temporal scope can vary greatly, depending on the particular military-strategic situation and the ultimate purpose of such command. It is also recognized that, strictly speaking, command is not peculiar to "blue water" operations, and that it may be just as necessary for "brown" water missions. This said though, it is clear that in the case of the U.S. Navy at least, its post-World War II concept of sea control has been defined by the specter of an oceanic struggle with the Soviet Union. See, *U.S. Navy Analysis of Congressional Budget Office Budget Issue Paper "General Purpose Forces: Navy,"* Report prepared for the Committee on Armed Services, House of Representatives, 95th Congress, 1st sess., (Washington, DC: U.S. Government Printing Office, 1977), p. 6.

2. Samuel P. Huntington, "National Policy and the Transoceanic Navy," U.S. Naval Institute *Proceedings*, May 1954, pp. 483–493.

3. *Ibid.*, pp. 488–489.

4. *Ibid.*, p. 490.

5. *Ibid.*, p. 484.

6. Department of the Navy, *From the Sea: Preparing the Naval Service for the 21st Century* (henceforth cited as *From the Sea*), (Washington, DC: September 1992). The document has been published in several editions, as well as in the November 1992 issue of the U.S. Naval Institute *Proceedings*, pp. 93-96. All subsequent references pertain to the September 1992 edition unless noted otherwise.

7. The term "essential charge" is adapted from Morton Halperin's "organizational essence," which he described as "the view held by the dominant group in the organization of what the missions and capabilities should be." The U.S. Navy's organizational essence, according to Halperin, is to maintain combat ships whose primary mission is to control the seas against enemies. Morton H. Halperin, *Bureaucratic Politics and Foreign Policy* (Washington, DC: The Brookings Institution, 1974), p. 28.

8. The best overall account of naval technological change during the 100 years leading up to World War II is Bernard Brodie's *Sea Power in the Machine Age* (Princeton, NJ: Princeton University Press, 1941).

9. *The Navy As a Fighting Machine* was the title of Rear-Admiral Bradley A. Fiske's book, published in 1916 (New York: Charles Scribner's Sons). Fiske, one of the "fathers" of modern gunnery in the U.S. Navy, wrote of the unprecedented firepower of the early 20th century battleship, how it could "whip an army of million men just as quickly as it could get hold of its component parts . . . , knock down all the buildings in New York afterward, smash all the cars, break down all the bridges and sink all the shipping." (p. 60).

10. Averting, not winning war, being the main purpose of the American military was Bernard Brodie's classic 1946 statement on the essence of nuclear deterrence.

11. Bernard Brodie is one of those who have observed that military organizations tend to have much less difficulty with accepting new weaponry than their adaptation, and will therefore often, to use Barry Posen's phrase, "graft new pieces of technology on to old doctrines." See Barnard Brodie, "Technological Change, Strategic Doctrine, and Political Outcomes." Klaus Knorr, ed., *Historical Dimensions of National Security Problems* (Lawrence: University Press of Kansas, 1976), p. 299. Cited in Barry R. Posen, *The Sources of Military Doctrine: France, Britain, and Germany Between the World Wars* (Ithaca, NY: Cornell University Press, 1984), p. 55.

12. Admiral of the Fleet Sir John Fisher's famous remark on the relevance of history was that, "in regard to the Navy . . . history is a record of exploded ideas." Cited in Paul M. Kennedy, "The Relevance of the Pre-War British and American Maritime Strategies to the First World War and Its Aftermath, 1898–1920." John B. Hattendorf and Robert S. Jordan, eds., *Maritime Strategy and the Balance of Power: Britain and America in the Twentieth Century* (New York: St. Martin's Press, 1989), p. 183.

13. Soviet military theoreticians, more so than their Western colleagues, stressed the materialist sources of change in the "principles" of war. For example, they concluded in the early 1950s that nuclear weapons had given rise to the principle of "surprise" as a new decisive factor in war.

14. Morris Janowitz's *The Professional Soldier* did not use the same term, but it was implied in his observation that there is a "cultural lag" between technological innovation and its adoption by the military. (New York: The Free Press of Glencoe, 1960), p. 25.

15. According to Mahan, writing in 1911, "Happily, the last twenty years has seen the conception of a navy 'for defense only' yield to sounder military understanding of the purposes of a navy; and that understanding, of the navy's proper office in offensive action, results as certainly in battleships as the defensive idea does in small vessels." Capt. A.T. Mahan, *Naval Strategy: Compared and Contrasted with the Principles and Practices of Military Operations on Land* (Boston: Little, Brown, and Co., 1911), pp. 151–152.

16. The charge that over-cautiousness and fear of excessive losses led pre-World War I Admiralty planners to forsake naval strategy's offensive principles and to rely instead on the deterrent effect of the Grand Fleet's superior numbers, was at the heart of the so-called "Jutland Scandal." For the view of one critic, see Arthur Hungerford Pollen, *The Navy in Battle* (London: Chatto & Windus, 1918), especially p. 55.

17. Winston S. Churchill, *The World Crisis, 1911–1918*, Vol. I (London: Odhams Press, Ltd., 1938), p. 76.

18. The best illustration, drawn from World War II, of how land-based airpower could dominate the struggle for command of the sea, was the ebb and flow of the Allied and Axis fortunes in the Mediterranean theater. Both sides sought to supply by sea their respective expeditionary forces in Africa; for both, success and failure depended

almost entirely on the control of the North African airfields. See, for example, Capt. S.W. Roskill, *The War at Sea 1939-1945, Vol. II; The Period of Balance* (London: Her Majesty's Stationary Office, 1956), p. 46.

19. In Congressional testimony in 1945, Navy Secretary James Forrestal told how, in a "struggle . . . unique in the history of war," U.S. naval aviation was fighting the Japanese land-based air force for air superiority over the Japanese islands. Cited in Vincent Davis, *Postwar Defense Policy and the U.S. Navy, 1943-1946* (Chapel Hill: University of North Carolina Press, 1966), p. 148.

20. *From the Sea*, p. 1.

21. Organizational theory offers an explanation why top-down revolutions are a sporadic occurrence, namely the tendency of organizations to be excessively rigid, incapable of purposeful adaptation, and constrained by inertia. For this view, see Michael T. Hannan and John H. Freeman, "The Population Ecology of Organizations," *American Journal of Sociology*, No. 82, 1977, pp. 929-964; and Herbert Kaufman, *The Limits of Organizational Change*. (University of Alabama Press, 1971). The author is indebted to Emily O. Goldman for directing him to this observation in her "Thinking About Strategy Absent the Enemy." Draft paper presented at the 1993 International Studies Association Annual Meeting, Acapulco, Mexico, March 23-28, 1993.

22. A report by the U.S. Navy's Policy Board in 1890 painted a remarkable degree of maritime security. The country had "no colonies, nor any apparent desire to acquire them;" its overseas commerce was largely carried in foreign vessels; exports competed with those of other nations in but a few overseas markets; and it was considered highly improbable that even the world's strongest naval power, Great Britain, could "detach all her effective navy from her own coast for distant operations" while she had to safeguard her own commerce. Nevertheless, the Board urged the immediate construction of 200 warships of all types because of "indications" that the country was entering an era of "commercial competition" in which it was "certain to reach out and obstruct the interests of foreign nations." In any case, the report continued, the opening of an Isthmian canal was bound to become a "fruitful source of danger." Cited in Harold and Margaret Sprout, *The Rise of American Naval Power 1776-1918* (Princeton: Princeton University Press, 1944), pp. 209-210.

23. Huntington, p. 488.

24. *U.S. Navy Analysis of Congressional Budget Office Budget Issue Paper, "General Purpose Forces: Navy,"* pp. 8, 12, 13-14.

25. Huntington thought that, because it was a defensive operation, anti-submarine warfare "can never become the primary mission of the Navy." It is also surprising that, writing in 1954 (when the scenario of a Soviet submarine assault against the Atlantic sea lines of communications had already gained wide credence), Huntington thought that the Navy only needed to be concerned with what he called submarine "raiding operations" against its combatants. Huntington, pp. 491-492.

26. John F. Lehman, Jr., "Rebirth of a U.S. Naval Strategy," *Strategic Review*, Summer 1981, p. 11.

27. The public version of the Maritime Strategy was published as a special supplement to the January 1986 U.S. Naval Institute *Proceedings*.

28. Secretary of Defense Les Aspin, *Report on the Bottom-Up Review* (Washington, DC: October 1993), p. 28.

29. "Be Careful What You Ask for . . ." Interview with Acting Secretary of the Navy Sean O'Keefe. U.S. Naval Institute *Proceedings*, January 1993, p. 73.

30. Interview with Admiral Paul David Miller, C-in-C U.S. Atlantic Command and Supreme Allied Commander Atlantic, *Jane's Defence Weekly*, March 13, 1993, p. 32.

31. For accounts of the British navy's "policing" activities in the 19th century, see C.J. Bartlett, *Great Britain and Sea Power 1815-1853* (Oxford: Clarendon Press, 1963), and by the same author, "The Mid-Victorian Reappraisal of Naval Policy" in K. Bourne and D.C. Watt, *Studies in International History* (Hamden: Archon Books, 1967), pp. 189-208. A good account of the Royal Navy's naval diplomatic and crisis management activities during the inter-world war years, especially in the Mediterranean, is Kenneth Edwards', *The Grey Diplomatists* (London: Rich & Gowan, 1938). See Eric Grove's *Vanguard to Trident: British Naval Policy Since World War II*. (Annapolis, MD: Naval Institute Press, 1987) for an account of the Royal Navy's "return to normalcy" in the first decade after World War II.

32. The standard—though now out-dated—account of the U.S. Navy's post-World War II crisis management activities is Barry M. Blechman and Stephen S. Kaplan, *Force Without War: U.S. Armed Forces As a Political Instrument* (Washington, DC: The Brookings Institution, 1978).

33. In a classic statement on naval suasion, Lord Palmerston, then Great Britain's foreign minister, wrote Prime Minister Melbourne in 1835 that he wanted to keep a fleet in the Mediterranean in spite of a threatening build-up of Russian naval power in the Baltic, because, "We want to act by the moral effect produced by the presence of our fleet, and the uncertainty in the minds of others, what the fleet may do; and thus to prevent the necessity of its having to act by force of arms." Cited in *Great Britain and Sea Power 1815-1853*, p. 107.

34. For example, a report by the Congressional Budget Office in 1978 recommended that the Navy build small V/STOL carriers for presence purposes "in less threatening Third World environment" so that the large-deck carriers could be held back for war with the Soviet Union. *U.S. Naval Forces: The Peacetime Presence Mission* (Washington, DC: U.S. Government Printing Office, December 1978). Writing a few years earlier, Admiral Stansfield Turner too wondered whether "the presence mission [is] becoming sufficiently important to warrant

building or designing forces for that purpose." "Missions of the U.S. Navy," *Naval War College Review*, September-October 1974, p. 16.

35. Department of the Navy, *Forward . . . From The Sea*,(Washington, DC: undated). In the forward to this document, signed by the Secretary of the Navy, Chief of Naval Operations and the Commandant of the Marine Corps, it is emphasized that *Forward . . . From The Sea* "Addresses specifically the unique contributions of naval expeditionary forces in peacetime operaitons, in responding to crises, and in regional conflicts." On page 4 the document goes on to stress, "the critical importance of a credible overseas presence is emphasized in the President's 1994 National Security Strategy: '. . . presence demonstrates our commitment to allies and friends, underwrites regional stability, gains U.S. familiarity with overseas operating environments, promotes training among the forces of friendly countries, and promotes timely initial response capabilities.' In peacetime U.S. naval forces build 'interoperability.'"

36. Writing at the end of the 19th century, one British naval author said of this period in his service's history that, compared with Trafalgar and "though notable enough," it "need not detain us." CDR Charles N. Robinson, *The British Fleet: The Growth, Achievements and Duties of the Navy of the Empire* (London: George Bell and Sons, 1895), p. 47.

37. For accounts of the post-World War I naval rivalry between the United States, Great Britain, and Japan see, for example, Hector C. Bywater, *Navies and Nations: A Review of Naval Developments Since the Great War* (Boston: Houghton Mifflin Co., 1927); Frederick Moore, *America's Naval Challenge* (New York: Macmillan Co., 1929); and Harold and Margaret Sprout, *Toward a New Order of Sea Power: American Naval Policy and the World Scene, 1918-1922* (Princeton: Princeton University Press, 1946).

38. The Jordanian crisis in September 1970 triggered a stand-off between the U.S. Sixth Fleet and the Soviet Mediterranean *eskadra* that prompted the Chairman of the Joint Chiefs of Staff to predict that if shooting started it would quickly spread to both the Atlantic and Pacific. Three years later, the commander of the Sixth Fleet, Vice Admiral Daniel Murphy, wrote how his fleet's confrontation with the Soviets at the height of the Arab-Israeli October War had set "the stage for the hitherto unlikely 'war at sea' scenario. . . ." Reported in Elmo R. Zumwalt, Jr., *On Watch* (New York: Quadrangle, 1976), pp. 297, 447.

39. The words "operations other than war at sea" are a liberal paraphrase of the U.S. Army's term "operations other than war." The Army defines the latter as including acts of violence and hostilities other than conventional combat ("war") between nation-states or coalitions of nation-states. *Preliminary Draft Field Manual FM100-5: Operations* (Washington, DC: U.S. Government Printing Office, August 21, 1992), pp. 5-1 through 5-6. Cited in Gen. Gordon R. Sullivan and Lt. Col. James M. Dubik, *Land Warfare in the 21st Century* (Carlisle, PA: U.S. Army War College, Strategic Studies Institute, February 1993), p. 9.

40. Statement of Rear Adm. Edward D. Shaefer, Jr., Director of Naval Intelligence, before the Seapower, Strategic, and Critical materials Subcommittee on Intelligence Issues (Washington, DC, February 5, 1992) p. 2, 8. Shaefer testified in 1992 that it might be another 20 years before a new Eurasian power might rise and challenge U.S. interests. He based his estimate on that he saw as a 20-year cycle in the fall and rise of Germany and the United States as great military powers in this century. If, on the other hand, the cyclical fortunes of Russian and Soviet naval power over the past 300 years is used as a clue, it may be 50 years before the world will see another Eurasian fleet to be reckoned with. For the history of the ups and downs of Russian naval aspirations, see Admiral of the Fleet of the Soviet Union S.G. Gorshkov, *The Sea Power of the State* (Annapolis, MD: Naval Institute Press, 1976), pp. 66-92; Fred T. Jane, *The Imperial Russian Navy*, 2d ed. (1904) (London: Conway Maritime Press, 1983), pp. 44-306; and Mairin Mitchell, *The Maritime History of Russia 1848-1948* (London: Sigwick and Jackson, 1948), pp. 310-339.

41. Interview with Admiral Paul David Miller, op. cit.

42. See Vice Adm. P.H. Colomb, *Naval War Warfare: Its Ruling Principles and Practice Theoretically Treated*, 2d edition, (London: W.H. Allen & Co., 1895), pp. 1-24. The author defined cross-ravaging as a "system of retaliatory expeditions attacking territory, destroying towns, burning property, and laying waste with fire and sword."

43. *Ibid.*, p. 21.

44. For the best single-volume study of the influence of Corbett, the Colomb brothers, Mahan, and others on turn-of-the-century naval thought, see Donald M. Schurman, *The Education of a Navy: The Development of British Naval Strategic Thought, 1867-1914* (London: Cassell, 1965).

45. The only competitive "system" of naval warfare was the French *jeune ecole* theory of *guerre de course* of the late 19th century. It too promoted the "blue water" use of naval power, but wanted to substitute raider warfare against enemy commerce for fleet-against-fleet battle.

46. Of course, this can only be the strategy of the stronger power; the "correct" strategy for the weaker fleet is to *deny* its opponent the use of the sea.

47. The most prominent, arguably sole, instances of pure opposing naval strategies are the Anglo-Dutch wars of 1652-1654 and 1665-1667. The third war between the two (1672), included a French land invasion of the United Republic, forcing the Dutch to divide their resources. Strictly speaking therefore, this was a *maritime* conflict.

48. Naval strategy can also be a subset of a continental strategy, the difference being that naval power makes a relatively smaller contribution to the continental belligerent's overall strategic purposes.

49. Sir Julian S. Corbett, *Some Principles of Maritime Strategy* (1911) (Annapolis: Naval Institute Press, 1972), pp. 13, 14.

50. British foreign minister Sir Edward Grey is credited with referring to the British army as "a projectile to be fired by the Navy." Cited in Samual R. Williamson, Jr., *The Politics of Grand Strategy: Britain and France Prepare for War, 1904-1914* (London: The Ashfield Press, 1990), p. 107.

51. In fairness to Corbett, it must be added that, unlike many of his contemporary navalists, he warned against deifying the importance for command of the sea as an absolute necessity. He wrote: "That this feature of naval warfare should be consecrated in a maxim is well, but when it is caricatured into a doctrine, as it sometimes is, that you cannot move a battalion overseas till you have entirely overthrown your enemy's fleet, it deserves gibbeting." Corbett, p. 101.

52. *Ibid.*, p. 90.

53. *Ibid.*, p. 110.

54. *Ibid.*, p. 87.

55. For an account of the little-known Pacific dimension of the Crimean war, see Barry M. Gough, *The Royal Navy and the Northwest Coast of North America, 1810-1914* (Vancouver: University of British Columbia Press, 1971), pp. 108-130.

56. *Goldwater-Nichols Department of Defense Reorganization Act of 1986*, Public Law 99-433, October 1, 1986.

57. *From the Sea*, pp. 3, 5.

58. *U.S. Navy Analysis of Congressional Budget Office Budget Issue Paper*. "General Purpose Forces: Navy," p. 4. Holloway drew a distinction between "strategic" and "tactical" sea control. The first, he said, involved sea control operations at some distance from the seagoing units to be protected, for example carrier air strikes or amphibious raids against enemy naval bases. He described "tactical" sea control as local self-defensive operations. Admiral Holloway deliberately stressed the primary sea control purpose of the Navy's aircraft carrier power projection capabilities in order to dispel the impression left by his predecessor, Admiral Elmo Zumwalt, that sea control and power projection forces entailed distinct capabilities and functions. The author is indebted to Capt. Peter Swartz, USN (Ret.) for leading him to this observation. For Zumwalt's claim that the Navy's "sea control forces" had been under funded to benefit its power projection fleet, see *On Watch*, p. 63.

59. Charles E. Myers, Jr. proposed that the sea services "should concentrate on being prepared to lay a doormat across any littoral and be ready to guarantee that it can be maintained. . . ." Myers thought that an area 20 miles inland or 400 square miles altogether should reasonably be the aim of the Navy's littoral land control aspiration. See his "Littoral Warfare: Back to the Future," U.S. Naval Institute *Proceedings*, November 1990, p. 54.

60. The word "littoral" comes from oceanography and technically includes only that part of the coast that falls dry between high and low tides.

61. See, for example, *Report on the Roles, Missions, and Functions of the Armed Forces of the United States*, p. III-17.

62. "Be Careful What You Ask For . . ." p. 74. O'Keefe added that the "long-range strike mission is one we still must be prepared for," but that the Navy could now rely more on the Air Force and cruise missiles.

63. *From the Sea*, p. 5.

64. This is a realistic concern. It should be noted, however, that there are some observers of the post-Cold War international scene who maintain that, as future contingencies will increasingly come in the form of U.N.-sponsored collective security actions, it will become relatively easier to find countries willing to host coalition land-based aircraft. *The Economist* thus wrote that, "The old cold-war excuse for dithering—'We can't let you in because the other superpower wouldn't like it'—no longer applies." *The Economist*, "Defence in the 21st Century," September 5, 1992, p. 15.

65. Jointness recognizes the advantages of different services owning complementary capabilities, but a key aim is to overcome redundancy and duplication of effort between the services.

66. For a discussion of "comparative advantage," applied to Service roles and missions, see Mackubin T. Owens, "After the Gulf War: The Marine Corps and the New National Military Strategy" in Force Planning Faculty, eds., *Fundamentals of Force Planning, Vol. II: Defense Planning Cases* (Newport: Naval War College Press, 1991), pp. 352-355. A legitimate analysis of the comparative advantage of sea- vs. land-based airpower in "tactical" and "strategic" roles would have to consider the relative cost of each in both roles.

67. For a similar recommendation, see Charles E. Myers, Jr., "Time to Fold 'Em." U.S. Naval Institute *Proceedings*, July 1991, pp. 37-41.

68. The distinction that is made here is analogous to the one between the commander's "area of influence" and "area of interest." The first is the geographical area in which a commander is directly capable of influencing operations through maneuver of fire support systems normally under his control. The second encompasses the commander's area of concern in general, including the area adjacent to his area of influence, which might be controlled by enemy forces that could jeopardize his mission. See, JCS Pub. 1-02. Cited in Department of the Navy, Headquarters, U.S. Marine Corps, FMFM 1: *Warfighting* (Washington, DC: March 6, 1989), p. 87.

69. Huntington, p. 484.

70. General Powell put it succinctly: "the real threat we now face is the threat of the unknown, the uncertain." *National Military Strategy of the United States*, (Washington, DC: January 1992), p. 4.

71. For example, if multinational crisis operations, whether sponsored by the U.N. or not, are going to be the wave of the future, U.S. national and Navy planners will need to become much more accustomed to the "culture" of coalition decision-making.

72. Peter Schwartz, *The Art of the Long View* (New York: Doubleday, 1991), pp. 105-123.

73. Barry Buzan, referencing Karl Deutsch and S.A. Burrell, has argued that the dominant feature of the post-Cold War security environment is a tacit "capitalist security community" among Europe, North America, Japan, and Australia. He defines such a community as a group of states that do not expect, or prepare for, the use of military force in their relations with each other. "New Patterns of Global Security in the Twenty-First Century" *International Affairs* (London), July 1991, pp. 16-18.

74. For an argument why U.S. unipolarity cannot last, see Christopher Layne, "The Unipolar Illusion: Why New Great Powers Will Rise," *International Security*, Spring 1993, pp. 5-51.

75. A 1982 report by the Naval Studies Board of the National Research Council forecast the technological feasibly of very high endurance aircraft with the ability to fly at 70,000 feet for two or three days. Naval Studies Board, *The Implication of Advancing Technology for Naval Aviation* (Washington, DC: National Academy Press, 1982), p. 29.

76. U.S. Representative John D. Long of Massachusetts has been credited with labeling the post-Civil War U.S. Navy "an alphabet of floating washtubs." Cited in Peter D. Karsten, *The Naval Aristocracy: United States Naval Officers from the 1840's to the 1920's—Mahan's Messmates*, Ph.D. dissertation, University of Wisconsin, 1968, p. 340. *The New America Navy* is the title of a 2-volume book written by John D. Long, who was Secretary of the Navy from 1897 to 1902 (New York: The Outlook Co., 1903).

77. Colomb, p. 25.

78. See Julian S. Corbett, *Fighting Instructions 1530-1816* (1905). Reprinted by Burt Franklin (New York), 1967.

# Chapter 37

* * *

# Presence:
# Forward, Ready, Engaged

Rear Admiral Philip A. Dur, U.S. Navy

*Admiral Philip Dur states that forward naval presence is the historic and enduring purpose of the Department of the Navy in the service of the United States. Indeed, he argues, it is the logic behind the American constitutional mandate that Congress maintain a navy. Critics who would build navies of a size strictly to deal with the requirements for potential conflict are overlooking this vital peacetime requirement. In linking naval force structure needs to regional political interests and specific peacetime military objectives, Admiral Dur provides a methodology for determining the types and numbers of ships, as well as other forces, which must be available to support this fundamental strategic goal. Naval forces—like all military forces—are built to fight and win wars. But their most important role by far, concludes Dur, is to be positioned to prevent them. Is the value of naval presence as important as Dur argues? Or is the utility of routinely deploying ships around the world vastly oversold as its many critics contend? If Dur is correct should peacetime forward presence requirements, which dictate a larger U.S. Navy than that determined to be necessary to fight regional conflicts, control the number of ships?*

Forward naval presence is the historic and enduring purpose of the Department of the Navy in the service of our maritime nation. Indeed, it is the logic behind our constitutional mandate that Congress maintain a navy. The overseas deployment of warships and embarked Marines literally dates from the infancy of the Republic. In the early 19th century, the maritime excursions against the Barbary pirates who preyed on U.S. merchantmen eventually were made a regular practice and organized into a Mediterranean Squadron. In the Pacific, early naval expeditions asserted our maritime interests in the waters off the contested coast of California and in the rich whaling grounds of the North

Admiral Dur was Director, Strategy and Policy Division, in the Office of the Chief of Naval Operations.

Pacific. The mid-19th century deployments to the Far East of Commodore Matthew Calbraith Perry strengthened America's diplomatic hand in the Pacific and were pivotal in opening Japan to world trade. The long-term result was the Asiatic Squadron.

This rich history notwithstanding, critics of a large and expensive fleet of carriers, amphibious ships, and surface combatants have long discounted the importance of presence and the Cold War commitments the fleet was said to serve. Prominent detractors of sea-based tactical aviation thundered that no one had ever invented a more expensive way of deploying tactical air power. Beginning with Secretary of Defense Robert S. McNamara and continuing through the end of the 1970s, repeated efforts were made to downsize the fleet and cut carrier procurement—but without publicly retrenching on commitments.

In the months leading up to the publication of the Bottom-Up Review, the RAND Corporation completed some modeling of the forces required for major regional contingencies in the Middle East and Far East. Requirements for two nearly simultaneous contingencies did not—in the opinion of former RAND analysts—justify a fleet much larger than the former House Armed Services Committee Chairman's "Option C," a fleet built around 11 active and deployable carriers.

It was not until the new defense team looked closely at requirements for overseas presence that the sizing criteria for major regional contingencies were recognized as inadequate if the Navy was to sustain a level of deployment activity approximating the tempo maintained since Desert Storm. While the Bottom-Up Review's force of 12 carriers, 2.5 Marine expeditionary brigade lift, and a somewhat fungible range of submarines and surface combatants remained the immediate force goals, the Navy and Marine Corps were challenged to demonstrate that these goals were justified by the demands of overseas presence. To that end, the Secretary of the Navy asked the Chief of Naval Operations and the Commandant of the Marine Corps to make an assessment of the forces required for the post-Cold War mission of forward naval presence.

## Why Forward Presence

On any given day, almost 20% of the U.S. Navy is deployed overseas, engaged in peacetime military operations. Additional ships and aircraft squadrons are preparing for deployment. All told, approximately 40% of the fleet is deployed or under way, preparing for deployment—every day. Keeping ships forward today requires supporting force structure at a time of significantly reduced defense spending. The returns will be measured in:

- Deterrence of aggression.
- Enhancement of regional stability.
- Improvement of interoperability with key allies.
- Readiness to provide a timely initial crisis response.

A consensus exists on the importance and propriety of these missions, but there are no accepted measures of effectiveness to gauge our success in meeting them. The challenge, therefore, is to develop a bridge that links the broadest national security interests and regional political objectives with the force structure required to service those interests and objectives.

The U.S. National Security Strategy of engagement, prevention, and partnership has an overarching goal of enlarging democracy and free markets by fostering stability and global security. Similarly, the National Military Strategy puts a high premium on deployed forces. Forward-deployed and forward-based naval forces are engaged in precisely those areas of the world where our most vital interests are concentrated—the Mediterranean and Middle East, Southwest Asia and the Persian Gulf, and the Western Pacific.

In cooperation with our friends and allies, forces are deployed near potential flashpoints to prevent the emergence of dangers to shared interests. Partnership is developed and enhanced when we promote interoperability at the operational and tactical levels with the naval, air, and ground forces of the most likely coalition partners. Exercises to practice this are the stock-in-trade of Navy and Marine units. In the most serious situations, our combat-ready forces help to deter aggression and, if deterrence fails, they provide the means for timely initial crisis response, should that become necessary. But naval presence must be more than a collection of ships on or over the horizon; deployed forces must embody credible combat capabilities if we are to be perceived as ready and determined to secure our interests and to secure them unilaterally, if we must.

A driving consideration in the case for forward-deployed naval forces is the demand from those responsible for promoting U.S. foreign policy, including U.S. diplomatic representatives and State Department officials. This must be coupled with the requirements from those responsible for ensuring military preparedness and the protection of U.S. and allied interests—the combatant commanders.

## Will Any Ship Do?

In 1973, former Secretary of Defense James Schlesinger wrote that "political justifications for military deployments, however relevant, rarely provide the basis for specific numbers and types of forces in a theater." Continuing, he argued that "a corporal's guard [might] be as effective as a division if our main purpose [were] merely to demonstrate a U.S. interest and presence in the area." Secretary Schlesinger was correct, in a sense: The force structure required for the presence role cannot be derived directly from the grand political objectives served by deployed naval forces. But, forces for presence must be shaped for combat, to provide credible assurance and to demonstrate serious resolve. The challenge is to translate strategic interests and regional political objectives into derivative military objectives for which we can define force structure. These objectives, in turn, must be sufficiently specific to develop listings of military tasks for which naval forces are organized, equipped, and trained.

The links between U.S. regional political interests and the force structure required for the forward presence mission are military objectives and supporting tasks. When interests and objectives are reduced to military tasks, the capabilities required to attain them can be specified and the force packages that embody those specific capabilities can be developed. The result is naval presence forces shaped for combat in the service of political objectives and national security interests.

## Force Structure Implications

Recently, sending naval formations forward for regular and extended deployments did not lead to arguments about force structure, because the aggregate force needed to meet the Soviet threat in the three principal maritime theaters of operations was more than adequate to meet our presence requirements. In short, the wartime force provided a large deployment base in peacetime. As we downsize the Navy, however, presence requirements no longer are a lesser-included case. In discussing the results of the Bottom-Up Review, former Secretary of Defense Les Aspin noted that "sizing our forces for two nearly simultaneous MRCs [major regional contingencies] provides a fairly large and robust force structure that can easily support other, smaller regional operations. However, our overseas presence needs can impose requirements for naval forces, especially aircraft carriers, that exceed those needed to win two [major regional contingencies]." The Navy-Marine Corps assessment of requirements to meet the demand for forward presence was a two-step process. A series of workshops to catalog relevant strategic and political interests by region was organized. Complementary military objectives and a list of military tasks then were derived and used to define capabilities and to develop force packages appropriate for each geographic region. The latter effort, undertaken with representatives of the Fleet commanders-in-chief and the unified commanders' staff, also was reviewed by representatives of other interested agencies, including the State Department and the Office of the Secretary of Defense.

Determining the appropriate force structure goes beyond determining the types of capabilities required within a theater. There is also the constancy—or rhythm—of presence measured by the extent of coverage and the frequency of deployments:

- Continuous Presence: Assigned forces within theater 100% of the time.
- Continuous Coverage: Assigned forces within theater 100% of the time or on explicit tethers.
- Periodic Presence: Assigned forces in theater less than 100% of the time, but on a planned and regularly recurring basis.

• Episodic Presence: Assigned forces deployed within or between theaters on an irregular or ad hoc basis.

In determining the rhythm of presence, the salience of the supported political interests as well as the immediacy of the danger to those interests must be considered. Clearly, this is a subjective area, and the political judgment of area "experts" who are well-versed in regional issues is needed to develop approximate answers to questions about coverage.

In Figure 1, both objectives derive from very important or salient interests, but the dangers to those interests are postulated as low in the northern flank and appreciably higher in the turbulent Mediterranean. The result is a demand for only periodic presence of a carrier battle group and amphibious ready group in the Norwegian Sea, but continuous (or nearly continuous) presence of these forces in the Mediterranean.

To illustrate how the interests-to-military-tasks methodology works: We postulate that one of the key political interests within the European theater is to maintain and foster U.S. leadership in NATO. In the opinion of the responsible commanders, the military objective associated with this political interest is a "credible U.S. naval combat force in situ." The credibility of the force is further defined by the capabilities needed to attain specific military tasks in support of this objective: (1) air defense/superiority, (2) intelligence/surveillance/command, control, and communications, (3) strike/surface fire, (4) sea-based theater ballistic missile defense, (5) amphibious warfare, (6) undersea warfare, and (7) sustainment.

These tasks require a force comprised of a carrier battle group and an amphibious ready group with an embarked special-operations-capable Marine expeditionary unit and supporting forces. Figure 2 shows the logic train that leads from postulation of an interest to derivation of a supporting military objective, military tasks, and, ultimately, the requisite capabilities and force packages.

As another example, among the most vital interests within the Central Command theater is the unimpeded flow of oil at fair market price. One important military objective that derives from this political interest is the protection of shipping. To service this single objective, a force must be capable of the following military tasks: (1) air defense/superiority, (2) littoral undersea warfare, (3) strike/surface fire, (4) intelligence/surveillance/command, control, and communications, (5) escort operations, (6) maritime interdiction operations, (7) mine countermeasures, and (8) gas/oil platform operations.

The force required for this objective includes five surface combatants (three Aegis), two mine-countermeasures ships, and supporting surveillance and logistics assets. While this force is adequate for this single objective, it is not adequate for the most demanding missions requiring capabilities for forcible entry.

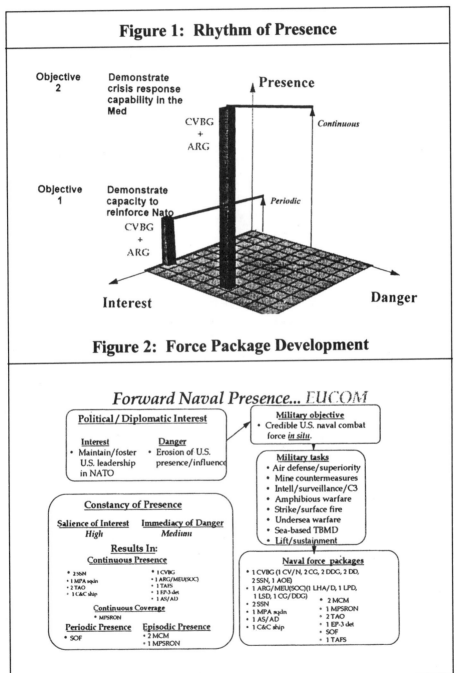

# Figure 1:  Rhythm of Presence

Objective 2 — Demonstrate crisis response capability in the Med

Presence

CVBG + ARG

*Continuous*

Objective 1 — Demonstrate capacity to reinforce Nato

CVBG + ARG

*Periodic*

Interest

Danger

# Figure 2:  Force Package Development

*Forward Naval Presence... EUCOM*

**Political / Diplomatic Interest**

**Interest**
• Maintain/foster U.S. leadership in NATO

**Danger**
• Erosion of U.S. presence/influence

**Military objective**
• Credible U.S. naval combat force *in situ*.

**Military tasks**
• Air defense/superiority
• Mine countermeasures
• Intell/surveillance/C3
• Amphibious warfare
• Strike/surface fire
• Undersea warfare
• Sea-based TBMD
• Lift/sustainment

**Constancy of Presence**

**Salience of Interest**
*High*

**Immediacy of Danger**
*Medium*

**Results In:**

**Continuous Presence**
• 2 SSN
• 1 MPA sqdn
• 2 TAO
• 1 C&C ship
• 1 CVBG
• 1 ARG/MEU(SOC)
• 1 TAFS
• 1 EP-3 det
• 1 AS/AD

**Continuous Coverage**
• MPSRON

**Periodic Presence**
• SOF

**Episodic Presence**
• 2 MCM
• 1 MPSRON

**Naval force packages**
• 1 CVBG (1 CV/N, 2 CG, 2 DDG, 2 DD, 2 SSN, 1 AOE)
• 1 ARG/MEU(SOC)(1 LHA/D, 1 LPD, 1 LSD, 1 CG/DDG)
• 2 SSN
• 1 MPA sqdn
• 1 AS/AD
• 1 C&C ship
• 2 MCM
• 1 MPSRON
• 2 TAO
• 1 EP-3 det
• SOF
• 1 TAFS

## Joint and Aggregate Regional Force Packages

In addition to developing naval force packages, this methodology can derive alternative joint force packages—using forces from the other services that can fulfill the required military tasks. Perfect matches are unlikely and some capability trade-offs will be necessary; nevertheless, by looking at discrete military tasks and then identifying the combat-ready units from the other services that are capable of accomplishing those tasks, we should be able to develop joint alternatives for at east some of the military objectives in each theater. For example, we can postulate that a key political interest within the European area of responsibility is the containment of religious and ethnic instability and conflict. One military objective that derives from this political interest is to support maritime interdiction and/or no-fly zones. The actual capabilities required in the force are defined by the specific military tasks that support this objective: (1) air defense/superiority, (2) intelligence/surveillance/command, control, and communications, (3) maritime inspection, (4) strike/surface fire, and (5) mine countermeasures.

With this list of tasks we can derive a naval force package and an alternative joint force package that meet the first three military tasks. The naval package includes a carrier, supporting surface combatants, and maritime patrol aircraft surveillance. The joint force package substitutes U.S. Air Force tactical and supporting aircraft—for air defense and superiority—and Army helicopters and special-operations forces to board and inspect suspect vessels attempting to circumvent the embargo. An important qualification and a limiting factor is also the governing issue:

> For there to be an effective complement or substitute for sea-based tactical air and ships to enforce the embargo, we need *physical access* to bases within the tactical reach of our military objectives as well as *prior understandings about the conditions governing the employment of forces* operating from foreign bases.

When these conditions are met—such as in the use of Incirlik, Turkey, to support operations in the northern no-fly zone in Iraq (Provide Comfort) or the use of Italian bases to support Deny Flight operations in Bosnia-Herzegovina—the complementarity of sea-based and land-based forces is nearly perfect.

Alternative combat-capable joint force packages clearly are an option that must be pursued to help bridge the gaps in naval presence that will result from the shrinking deployment base. However, when deploying land-based or ground units forward, host countries may attach conditions to the employment of these forces that could effectively limit their value. There is an obvious political advantage in not having to negotiate the conditions under which you use military force every time the objectives change. Therefore, when considering the full range of regional military objectives across a complex geographic area of responsibility—such as the Mediterranean—the capabilities embodied in the naval forces that service them must be seen as unique. They are mobile and flexible, ready and sustainable over time, and—most important—they are relatively independent of fixed foreign bases and conditions governing their use.

Once force packages for the specific military objectives in each region are defined, the next step is to determine which of those objectives are most demanding, in terms of force requirements. Those are termed "defining" military objectives. The force packages needed for this set of objectives are then aggregated by region to develop the forces necessary to meet the commanders-in-chief's (CinC's) demands for presence. The methodology assumes that forces sized to meet the defining objectives also serve the lesser-included objectives for each region.

To derive the force levels needed to sustain the demand in all the critical theaters, the individual CinC's needs are summed up and a model with accepted assumptions regarding length of deployment, transit speeds, turn-around ratios, maintenance requirements, etc., is used to derive force levels. Not surprisingly, the force levels needed to support the demands of all CinCs is larger than the programmed force today.

### Gaps in Presence and Political Risk

The process used to derive force structure can be reversed to measure the impact on interests if the deployment base is inadequate to meet the demand for forward-deployed forces. We can begin to better define the risk—in objectives which cannot be attained on short notice (e.g., timely initial crisis response) and, ultimately, in national interests that remain uncovered for varying periods of time.

Using carriers as an example, if the 12-carrier force level were to be further reduced to ten, the immediate result would be an 84-day gap in presence (as opposed to the 24-day gap required by a 12-carrier force) in both the Central Command and European Command theaters. Alternatively, we could absorb the impact in just one theater and accept either a 154-day gap in Central Command or a 186-day gap in the European Command. This absence of the carrier and her air wing would mean that certain military tasks—such as air superiority, surveillance, or strike—could not be met for long periods, thereby seriously affecting specific military objectives and the associated political interests (see Figure 3).

In the case of surface combatants, if force levels were reduced from 120 (the aggregate demand) to 105, the immediate impact would be a commensurate reduction in the number of combatants forward deployed to one or more of the theaters of operations. If the entire reduction were absorbed in the

Middle East Force, we would see a 50% decrease in our surface combatant presence there. Alternatively, we could reduce the number of combatants in the Mediterranean by three ships and abandon our stations in the Adriatic and curtail our participation in the Standing Naval Force Mediterranean. In any case, a reduction will be measured by important military objectives and political interests that will remain uncovered.

**Figure 3**
**Political Risk: The Price of Absence**

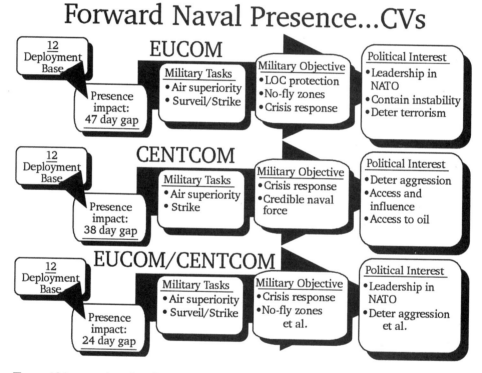

To avoid increasing the already heavy burden on our sailors and their families, the Joint Chiefs of Staff and the unified commanders have agreed to share the risks implicit in short-term gaps in forward presence by using "tethers." Tethers allow forces to operate outside the CinC area of responsibility but within an area defined by explicit response times. Accordingly, as the deployment base has declined, the demand for continuous presence of carriers and amphibious ready groups in the Mediterranean, the Indian Ocean, and the Western Pacific has been modified to provide a reasonable degree of coverage in these three areas. Only by the use of tethers is the current force structure adequate to meet the combat commanders' demand for forces without an unacceptable impact on the quality of life of Navy and Marine Corps personnel. The sharing of our principal combat-ready naval formations across adjacent forward theaters enables us to cover as many interests as possible within the limits of our deployment base and with due regard for the quality of life of our personnel. But this practice entails risks, and we need to understand what the possible consequences may be.

## Conclusion

Presence forces are shaped for combat. Forward-deployed naval forces provide the critical link between peacetime operations and the initial requirements for a developing crisis or major regional contingency. Their forcible entry capabilities provide the initial response and enabling capability for subsequent joint operations on a large scale in the event of conflict.

Our defense commitments and global interests require a robust forward naval presence. Forward presence has been a trademark of the Navy and Marine Corps, and its importance is likely to grow in the uncertain future. If we can identify specific national interests and regional objectives that can be advanced or protected by naval power, we can then determine the levels of forces necessary to secure those interests. Defining the forces we need for presence need not be guesswork.

Naval forces—like all elements of a military arsenal—are built to fight and win wars. But their most important role by far is to be positioned to prevent them. Sized and configured to meet military objectives, naval forces serve the nation's varied interests on a regular and continuous basis—in the littorals and on the open ocean, where U.S. economic security turns on free access in the world's markets and resources.

In this regard, the past really is prologue. Naval forces deployed forward will remain the front line in our transoceanic strategy.

# Chapter 38

* * *

# Operational Maneuver From the Sea: Building a Marine Corps for the 21st Century

General Charles C. Krulak, USMC

I n 1952 the 82nd Congress articulated a vision of the Marine Corps' future role in national security.

> [History] has fully demonstrated the vital need for the existence of a strong force in readiness. Such a force, versatile, fast-moving, and hard hitting, will constantly have a very powerful impact in relation to minor international disturbances. . . . Such a force can prevent the growth of potentially large conflagrations by prompt and vigorous action during their incipient stages. . . . The nation's shock troops must be the most ready when the nation is least ready . . . to provide a balanced force in readiness for a naval campaign and, at the same time, a ground and air striking force ready to suppress or contain international disturbances short of large scale war.

For the past 45 years, the Marine Corps has provided that force in readiness—in peace and in war. The task before us is to do so in the future. In this era of evolving national security interests, it is essential that we, as that "force in readiness," anticipate and adapt to changes looming on the horizon. In this light, allow me to describe the strategic environment that we see for the Marine Corps in the future: an operational concept flexible enough to meet the range of challenges to the national interest and programs necessary to make that concept a reality for the 21st century.

## Strategic Environment

In many ways our country's current situation mirrors the years immediately following the Second World War. Then as now, the United States stood alone as

General Krulak is the commandant of the United States Marine Corps.

This article originally appeared in the *National Security Studies Quarterly*, Vol. II, Issue 4, Autumn 1996, pp. 19-29. Copyright © 1996 by the National Security Studies Quarterly Association.

the world's military superpower—the only country capable of winning a war anywhere on the globe. But there are many new challenges in the emerging post-Cold War world. Just as we learned in the decade following the Second World War and are relearning during this decade, one decisive victory does not guarantee peace everywhere. It does not protect us from future threats nor relieve us of today's security obligations. The world has expectations of its victors.

With this historical perspective in mind and looking at future security requirements, we need to ask three questions. Why will we fight, where will we fight, and who will we fight? No one knows for certain the answers to these questions, nor are they the only concerns that we need to take into account, but they form a useful framework for thinking about the future.

Why will we fight? The historian Thucydides stated that a nation will fight for three reasons—security, ideology, or economics. That same philosophy is embodied in our current National Security Strategy and is expressed in the term "vital interest." Our National Security Strategy defines our most basic vital interests as the defense of our territory and citizens, the defense of our allies, and the preservation of our economic well-being. We will do whatever it takes to defend these interests, including the unilateral and decisive use of military power. With over 30% of the U.S. economy dependent upon overseas markets, any threat to the global economy will have a direct impact on our decision to deploy and commit military power beyond our shores in the 21st century.

This leads directly to the second question of *where* we might fight. U.S. foreign policy in the 20th century has been somewhat Eurocentric. As Secretary of State Warren Christopher said, *"Our health is in Asia, but our heart is in Europe."* Asia will not be our only vital interest, but maintaining stability there will be increasingly important to our foreign policy and security interests as we move into the 21st century.

Several indicators suggest a shift in geostrategic emphasis in U.S. foreign policy for the 21st century. By the year 2020, the global economic center of gravity will shift from the West to the East. Today in China and India, we are watching the emergence of two economic superpowers that together will have a major impact on the global economy. Both have burgeoning high-tech industries and a limitless pool of inexpensive labor that will compete with other manufacturing and service-based economies in the world.

By the year 2020, eight out of ten of the world's largest economies will be located along the Pacific and Indian Ocean rim. Today, 37% of U.S. overseas trade is with Asia, and U.S.-Pacific trade exceeds U.S.-European trade. By the year 2000, our Asian trade will be double our European trade. At the same time, economic growth will increase the ability of emerging nations to respond to perceived insecurity by obtaining military power, including high-tech weapons and weapons of mass destruction (WMD). This mix of super-heated economies, scarce resources, and readily available military arms is a basic and well-proven recipe for instability.

Three major implications arise from this shift to the East. First, these economies will require vast amounts of oil. This means access to Persian Gulf oil and clear sea lanes (the Straits of Hormuz and Mallaca) for its transport. Second, a combination of uneven population growth, arms proliferation, environmental pollution, finite natural resources, and long-standing rivalries will increase the likelihood of regional conflict as global competitors vie for advantage. Third, we know that our permanent overseas land-based presence, particularly along the Pacific-Indian Ocean-Persian Gulf littoral, is not likely to expand—for both domestic economic and international political reasons. Thus the only viable solution for maintaining presence in this region will be to maintain a robust naval power-projection capability.

As the global economy grows and becomes more interdependent, instability—anywhere—becomes less and less tolerable. That is why a continued credible forward presence is so vital. By underwriting stability, by providing the security foundation upon which economies can grow free from pressures to invest in massive military establishments, we help defuse issues that potentially lead to conflict. This is not just their gain but ours as well. We ultimately profit economically while enhancing regional security. Markets replace threats, and trading partners replace enemies. At the same time, geography will not change—the tyranny of distance in Asia remains. Distance equates to time, and time equates to political leverage. The more immediate our involvement, the more rapid and credible our response, the more we can influence events.

This leads us to consider the final question—*who* will we fight. This is a more difficult question today than during the Cold War. While a new peer-competitor could arise, it is unlikely to happen for the next decade or so. Our future opponents could range from a technologically savvy middle-income country to Chechen-like rebels. As old nation-states fall, new ones emerge. The fall of the Soviet Union, the disintegration of Yugoslavia, the tragedies in Somalia and Rwanda, and the conflict in Liberia all warn of the trend toward states "splintering" along ethnic, religious, or tribal lines. This trend suggests not just crises between states and within states but also a greater degree of instability—something we term "chaos."

The political dimensions of chaos are daunting, but combined with the proliferation of high-tech weapons throughout the world, chaos might well be as lethal as a clash between first rank military powers. In these increasingly lethal scenarios, warfare will be driven more by opposing mentalities and intellects than by a simple calculus of hardware and personnel. Instead of trying to match us tank for tank and plane for plane, fighting the kind of high-technology, industrial-age war that we saw in Desert Storm, they will target our vulnerabilities—ports, airfields, and Petroleum, Oil and Lubricants (POL)

Systems. They will target our information systems. Their militaries will neither possess nor employ the kinds of the "force structure" our systems are optimized to find and kill—massed armor, massed troops, and fixed communications and transportation systems. In short, they will seek to fight us where we are least able to bring our strength to bear. Our opponent will not be doctrinaire or predictable, and he will be lethal.

## Implications

Since the Civil War, we have had a very industrial approach to warfare—we emphasized killing "things" (people, tanks, aircraft, ships) efficiently. If we killed enough things, without losing too much ourselves, we won. However, in future conflicts, simply employing hardware and massing numbers of personnel will not be enough. We need to prepare for the complex, dynamic, asymmetric threats of the day after tomorrow, not simply design a force that can fight Desert Storm better. To defeat a thinking, flexible, lethal enemy, we must radically reduce our current vulnerabilities—key logistics nodes, command and control links, and so forth. To do this, we need to keep forward bases offshore wherever possible.

Ultimately, the issue is capabilities, not numbers of people or platforms. A narrowly defined threat will result in a narrow and ill-defined picture of the capabilities that we need for the future. We should not measure our future forces against one specific threat. We should not simply replace or modernize pieces of equipment. Instead, we must fundamentally alter the way we view warfare. We need to leap forward in our thinking, leap ahead organizationally, and leap over generations of hardware.

We need to be able to deal with "chaos in the littorals"—*all* forms of crisis and conflict. The forces we design for the day after tomorrow must be right for all operating environments. This includes the urban and jungle littorals, where information dominance and perfect sensor to shooter links are difficult to achieve. Our forces must be able to handle those things that technology alone cannot solve.

In the 21st century, if we are to live up to the mandate laid down by Congress in 1952, the Navy-Marine Corps team must field a more versatile, capable, and responsive naval power-projection capability. Uncertainty and the tyranny of distance will require the United States to field naval expeditionary forces that can execute missions ranging from humanitarian relief to high-intensity conflict. They must be capable of operations in terrain ranging from open ocean to Third World urban slums. The more immediate our ability to adequately respond, the more we can influence events. To do this we need a force that blends high-technology and maneuver warfare with the advantages of sea-basing. Anticipating these requirements, the Marine Corps has framed an operational concept for the future that we call Operational Maneuver from the Sea (OMFTS).

## Operational Concept

The heart of OMFTS is the maneuver of naval expeditionary forces at the operational level of warfare to exploit enemy weakness and deliver a decisive blow. The search for decisive effect is common to all forms of operational maneuver—whether on land, at sea, in the air or space, and in the littorals where land, sea, and air meet. What distinguishes OMFTS from all other types of operational maneuver is the extensive use of the *sea* as a means of gaining advantage—an avenue of friendly movement that is simultaneously a barrier to the enemy and a means for us to avoid disadvantageous engagements. This aspect of OMFTS makes use of, but is not limited to, such techniques as sea-based logistics, sea-based fire-support, and the use of the sea as a medium for tactical and operational movement.

The OMFTS concept:

1. Focuses on an operational objective;
2. Uses the sea as maneuver space;
3. Generates overwhelming tempo;
4. Pits strength against weakness;
5. Emphasizes flexibility, intelligence, and deception;
6. Integrates all organic, joint, and combined assets.

The capture of Seoul in 1950 was a classic example of an OMFTS. It was a joint operation—unified under a single commander—that flowed coherently from San Diego, Sasebo, and Pusan, *through* an amphibious assault at Inchon, *to key objectives well inland.* The Seoul operation focused on a critical North Korean vulnerability— the lines of support (and withdrawal) through the Han River Valley. The operation maintained this focus throughout, leading to the destruction of the North Korean Army and the liberation of South Korea. Had the operation focused simply on the conduct of an amphibious landing, it would have only generated an operationally insignificant tactical victory.

## Requirements

If OMFTS is the Marine Corps' operational concept for the 21st century, what capabilities must its force possess? For a force to conduct OMFTS it must be able to generate, inflict, or possess all or some of the following: simultaneous engagement, tempo, interchangeability, operational shock, operational depth, and mission depth.

*Simultaneous Engagement*. Simultaneous engagement is the capability to fight the whole battle as a single engagement, seeking to neutralize the enemy's capabilities through the simultaneous but selective application of force across their entire operational depth. This requires the employment of forces with multiple capabilities acting simultaneously, rather than in sequence. This includes the entire range of combat support and combat service support, plus specialized capabilities such as Civil Affairs Groups employed with Engineer Support Battalions. Simultaneous engagement of hostile forces across their entire operational depth not only is the quickest way to seize the initiative and control tempo, but also allows a force of limited size to achieve decisive results against a larger force. The ability of the force commander to see the battlefield (or "battlespace") in all its elements—as a single seamless area—is key. This applies to political dimensions as well as military aspects.

*Tempo*. Tempo is the rate at which actions and interactions occur within a campaign. Controlling or altering that rate is essential for maintaining the initiative. Standard thinking about tempo defaults to a first generation observe, orient, decide, act (OODA) loop, where we simply strike faster than a ponderous opponent or move around the battlespace more rapidly. Controlling tempo in the chaotic, urbanized battlefield will require far more than a quick deep strike against second echelon targets or rapid movement around the battlefield like Heinz Guderian. Instead, controlling tempo must be conceived in more subtle and multi-dimensional terms—broadening our thinking beyond simple force-on-force scenarios by actively attempting to alter the enemy's perceptions, as well as attack the entire depth and breadth of his capabilities.

*Interchangeability*. Each warfighting CINC or operational commander must have a tool kit of forces and resources necessary to execute the range of assigned and potential contingencies. Thus, our forces need more than just multi-role platforms, we need *multi-role organizations*. More importantly, they must be capable of operational thinking that is not bound by notions of capabilities that can only be applied in certain, set patterns. For example, we need to ask ourselves—what operations might an Amphibious Ready Group with a Marine Expeditionary Unit—Special Operations Capable [MEU (SOC)] perform beyond the conduct of amphibious landings and the 17 other standard MEU missions? How can our forces and resources be interchanged in order to create synergies of combat power? Stretching our thinking in this fashion will be critical to coping with the chaotic situations that will confront us in the future and is essential for the development of the flexibility and adaptability necessary to defeat the asymmetric threats we will encounter. It permits a committed expeditionary force to rapidly adapt as missions and tasks change.

*Operational Shock*. Operational shock is the end result of rapid, system-wide physical and psychological breakdown. We seek destruction or neutralization not only of our opponent's resources, but most importantly, his mind. If we succeed in achieving operational shock, the enemy becomes disoriented and is diverted from his objective. He loses functional decision making for force employment. The Germans achieved this at Sedan in 1940, when the speed with which Guderian's 19th Panzer Corps broke through the French defenses created panic—shutting down France's ability to respond coherently. In that case, news of the German advance—spread through the fire control nets—neutralized the very thing—artillery—that could have stopped the river crossing. We can also see this in the latter stages of the ground offensive during Desert Storm. The Iraqi command and control system disintegrated, and individual Iraqi units became so disoriented that they stopped functioning as military units, even though they had means at hand to resist.

*Operational Depth*. We must direct our efforts against the *operational depth* of the enemy. This is defined not just in terms of geographic distance but in terms of time and function as well. Operational depth allows commanders to sustain momentum and take advantage of all available resources in order to press the fight—attacking the enemy forces and capabilities simultaneously throughout the battlespace. The geographic operational depth that land forces normally operate is about 350 kilometers—Desert Storm was an example of this. Another example of operational depth is our recent experience in Somalia, where we operated *in depth* not only in terms of geography (the entire country), but also in terms of time (across two harvest seasons).

*Mission Depth.* As our forces encounter the "chaotic" situations of future contingencies—much like the Somalia, Liberia, or Bosnia that we have faced today—they will need to be able to operate not only across the geographical depth of a region but also across the spectrum of warfare and tasks at the same time. This requires the ability to adapt and shift mission focus as the problem evolves, changing "direction"—mission-wise— in mid-stride without losing momentum or effect. Mission depth is the ability to simultaneously conduct a range of missions across different levels of warfare. One illustration of this would be to consider the range of operational tasks Desert Storm forces might have faced if the assault into Iraq had continued after the liberation of Kuwait. We would likely have seen simultaneous missions from humanitarian efforts to full scale assault. The important thing to remember is that we must visualize the *whole* mission and potential follow-on missions—across the spectrum of war—and build our force composition accordingly.

## How Do We Plan to Get There

The Marine Corps is readying itself for OMFTS in the 21st century with three concurrent and inter-related efforts: we are making Marines; we are procuring and experimenting with advanced technologies; and we are institutionalizing innovation. Along the way we will continue to fight and win the nation's battles.

*People.* Before we talk about technology and equipment, we must talk about people. The Marine Corps' focus rests upon the enhancement of the individual Marine and his or her ability to win in combat. Therefore our most important OMFTS enhancement will be in the training of the individual Marine. Ultimately, people—not machines, define our success in war. Accordingly, we will equip our Marines, not man our equipment.

**Enhancing the Individual Marine.** Marines are the centerpiece of the Corps. All the technology and innovation in the world make little difference if we do not educate and train our Marines. On the battlefields of the 21st century, the junior enlisted Marine is going to have access to, and the need to use, more information than a battalion commander might today. We think that chaos in the littorals will require our Marines to be improvisers and innovators. This Marine must be comfortable with high-technology weapons and information systems and trained to know what to do with them. Above all else, the individual Marine must be a warrior without peer. We will leverage technology to provide demanding and realistic training for our Marines—allowing them to continually expand their warfighting envelope. *Team players, independent operators, chaos specialists—these Marines will need to be able to do it all.*

*Equipment.* The Marine Corps is aggressively pursuing new technologies to enhance our intelligence, information, communications, mobility, logistics, and fire-support systems so that we can effectively conduct OMFTS. Toward this end, the Marine Corps is involved in both development and procurement programs that will support this operational concept, several of which are described below. Because the Marine Corps is fundamentally a naval service, many of the items necessary to conduct OMFTS are traditional Navy procurement items, such as ships, aircraft, and naval surface fire-support.

**V-22 Osprey.** OMFTS requires the Marines to be able to strike from over the horizon and to project land forces deep into the enemy's interior. Our current medium-lift helicopter, the CH-46, does not have the range or lift capability to make this happen. The V-22 allows the OMFTS force to range throughout the entire operational depth of our opponent. For the first time our opponents will know that wherever they try to maneuver, our land forces will be within range, embarked upon V-22s flying from naval platforms. This capability facilitates tempo generation greater than our opponent and certainly will contribute to operational shock. The V-22 changes all the equations.

**Advanced Amphibious Assault Vehicle (AAAV).** The Navy and the Marine Corps developed the concept of over-the-horizon (OTH) assault to avoid enemy strengths, to exploit weaknesses, and to protect Navy ships from an increased land-based missile and sea-based mine threat. Together with the V-22, the AAAV will complete the amphibious portion of the OMFTS triad [V-22, AAAV, and the Landing Craft-Air-Cushion (LCAC)]. Each component of the triad is critical for the execution of the types of OTH assaults envisioned in OMFTS. The ability of the AAAV to swiftly transit from sea to land operations gives us a tremendous increase in the ability to apply force in operational depth. This capability will certainly aid in creating operational shock with our opponent. Think of these systems as you would combined-arms. Even if our opponent can counter one of our OMFTS systems, he will expose himself to exploitation by the other. The triad gives us offense in depth.

**Amphibious Shipping.** A Navy-Marine Corps power-projection force provides tremendous opportunity for maneuver. Sea-basing allows the Navy-Marine team to establish a "presence" that can serve either to deter a brewing conflict or, if conflict is unavoidable, to create a condition of operational shock upon our opponent. Additionally, unlike the aviation elements of power-projection, a sea-based force "controls the clock." The force that "controls the clock" gets to control operational tempo. Sea-basing also allows the land-force to reduce the vulnerabilities associated with land-based logistics depots. Using ships as mobile supply bases provides additional operational depth and a tempo advantage to the sea-based force. Additionally, with amphibious shipping, the Marine Air-Ground Task Force can conduct a simultaneous engagement through the use of V-22s, fixed-wing air support from short take-off, vertical landing (STOVL) joint strike fighters (JSF), and amphibious assault via LCACs and AAAVs. Without adequate amphibious shipping OMFTS is nonexistent.

**Joint Strike Fighter.** The JSF will bring a quantum increase in fire-support for OMFTS. Stealth technology combined with STOVL basing flexibility will allow the Marines to base this aircraft from a variety of platforms—able to strike critical deep targets and also provide close-air-support, suppress enemy air defenses, and conduct counter-air missions. Like the V-22, the JSF will give the Navy-Marine Corps power-projection force tremendous capabilities in operational depth, shock, and interchangeability, all of which create an operational dilemma for our opponent.

**Innovation.** Preparing the Marine Corps for the 21st century requires more than buying new equipment; it requires an institutional commitment to change. The accelerating rate of change in our operating environment requires us continuously to anticipate it, and adapt to our advantage. "Laminating" future technology on current doctrine and equipment is not the answer. To win in the 21st century, the Marine Corps must "steal a march" on the rate of global change.

**Sea Dragon.** One way to begin the process is to combine new technology with innovative new organizations, doctrine, and training. This is the starting point for one of our Corps' most important initiatives—the Warfighting Laboratory. Just as we used the Marine Corps Schools at Quantico, Virginia, to redefine the science and art of amphibious assault during the interwar years, so will the Warfighting Laboratory help us chart a course to master the challenges we see ahead in the 21st century. At the forefront of this effort is the testbed we call "Sea Dragon." Sea Dragon is not one particular innovation or idea, but rather a *commitment to innovation*. It is not a predetermined force structure or a predetermined operational technique, but a method of evaluating potential structures and techniques as well as training, education, and doctrinal ideas. It is a model for future thinking and an umbrella under which ideas are born, tested, bear fruit, or die. Perhaps best described as a "quest" for solutions to the problems of tomorrow, it is an overarching approach to developing a whole host of new tactical and operational techniques and thinking involving *both* Marine and Navy forces.

The concept is to combine various operational techniques with enabling technologies to produce a force that can deal with changing operating environments. Of course, we must assess the impact these new approaches will have on our training and education systems, as well as the logistics systems that support our operating forces. To do this we are forming a Special-Purpose Marine Air-Ground Task Force [Experimental] that can actually work through the ideas generated within the Warfighting Laboratory as part of the larger Marine Corps Combat Development Process. As the Warfighting Lab articulates its ideas and findings, it is important that we not lose sight of the overall idea. The only thing we *know* for certain is that the force we develop to fight tomorrow's battles will not look exactly like the force we pick to test our ideas today. By using Sea Dragon as a framework to think about and experiment for the future, we can prepare for the uncertainties that lie ahead.

Throughout its history, the Marine Corps has been at the forefront of military innovation with contributions such as close-air-support, amphibious vehicles, vertical assault, VSTOL and tilt-rotor aircraft, less-than lethal technologies, and unmanned air vehicles. The Marine Corps is our nation's force in readiness, ready to fight—anywhere—anytime. In order to survive and prosper in this environment we have had to innovate. To be successful at "innovating" we must be willing to accept the risks associated with change.

## Conclusion

The next century offers both challenge and opportunity. Combined with our exceptional Marines and sailors, the advanced technologies and flexible operational concepts we are developing today will enable us to meet the challenges of the 21st century.

Although no one can peer into the future and predict when or where our next conflict will arise, these trends—changing economic centers, the proliferation of advanced technologies and weapons of mass destruction, the emergence of non-state actors, and the rising importance of the Asia-Pacific littorals—all indicate that our next challenge will arise in regions that will demand the most of our naval expeditionary forces. Only naval forces give the United States the versatile capabilities required to project and sustain power over great distances. The programs and initiatives that we are putting into place today will guarantee a credible and capable naval force in readiness for the 21st century.

# Chapter 39

## ★ ★ ★

# The Influence of Space Power upon History

Colin S. Gray

*Colin S. Gray addresses the importance of space and its role in information warfare. The future of air power was clearly discernible in 1918; the future of space power is similarly discernible today, following the experience of Desert Storm. Space power, in common with sensible approaches to sea power and air power, can and should aspire to make the critical difference in war. Despite its growing importance, no comprehensive theory of space power has been formulated. How does Gray define space power? Why is it important for information warfare? How well does he support his thesis? What are the force planning implications of his strategic concepts?*

Countries that fail to adapt soon enough or well enough to the changing character of warfare are condemned either to fail or to succeed at unnecessary cost and loss of life. Space age information warfare, as deterrence or action, is not an opinion or a theory. Rather, it is a plainly emerging fact of the 1990s. The only live questions for policymakers and defense planners are: How rapidly will the United States adjust to this emerging fact? How thoroughly will it adjust? And taking due note of the limitations of space age information warfare, how prudently will it adjust? The future of space power and its actual meaning for particular conflicts are, of course, beyond precise prediction. What matters is to put a finger on a clearly identifiable trend (i.e., a trend toward information based war critically dependent on space systems), not on future details. Like history's "turning points" and "strategic moments," transformations of war are much easier to identify in the long perspective than they are contemporaneously.

Space age information warfare does not represent the first transformation of war in modern history, but only the most recent. The claims for space power

Dr. Colin S. Gray is professor of international politics and director of the Centre for Security-Studies at the University of Hull, Hull, United Kingdom.

Reprinted by permission from *Comparative Strategy*, Vol. 15, No. 4, October-December 1996, pp. 293-308. Copyright ©1996 Taylor & Francis.

advanced in this article are based on historical experience. *Space power* may be defined as the ability to use space while denying reliable use to any foe.

Space power is catalyzing a true transformation of war; it is a comprehensive change in the form and structure of armed conflict (of some armed conflicts, at least). Although the central claims for space power need to be expressed tersely and unambiguously, it also is necessary to recognize prudently the limitations of space systems and, no less, the limitations of the nonspace forces that space systems serve. Space power is not a panacea for terrestrial security ills. For this reason, the author will make every effort to offer the relevant significant caveats. These signs of caution are in the nature of significant footnotes, however. They do not undermine the validity of the thesis that a maturing space power is on—indeed is—the leading edge of a transformation of war.

The U.S. defense community at present is convulsed in debate over the reality and possible implications of a revolution in military affairs effected by the microchip. Popularized as "third wave" warfare by Alvin and Heidi Toffler, computer driven and dependent information age warfare is allegedly the wave of tomorrow's military effectiveness.[1] Information age warfare is not specific to any one geographical environment. The computer, indeed timely information processing and dissemination, will be valuable in most kinds of war in all environments. Emphatically, this is not to claim that the best "internetted" and siliconized armed forces always must defeat foes who are computer challenged. Intensity of political commitment, dispersion of forces, brute force (perhaps on the scale of weapons of mass destruction), and difficult terrain, can all degrade the effectiveness of state-of-the-art information age military machines.

The author's argument shifts focus from the familiar fixation upon computer hardware and software, and instead diverts attention to the environmentally specific application of information technologies to the geographical fourth dimension, space. This focus helps render more generally understandable some of the "techno-enthusiasm" for rapid information management. After all, combat is not waged by computer; it is waged by geographically specialized armed forces using computers and the output of computers. Also, this focus upon space helps correct for the problem that many computer minded people remain ignorant of the military effectiveness achievable by fusion of space systems and information technology. Space power is not synonymous with information age military prowess, but it is the prime provider for and the cutting edge of that prowess.

The form and structure of war and defense preparation change incrementally. New capabilities gradually transform the terms of deterrence and war, with no magic break point between one era and another. The fact remains, however, that the quality of deterrence and war can be radically altered by the cumulative availability of ever greater quantities of new military forces organized and directed to operate in pursuit of new operational concepts. The absence of a magic moment when the airplane, or the satellite, truly transforms the terms of war, should not be allowed to obscure the reality of transformation. Incrementalism in the emergence of new capabilities makes it difficult to recognize that quantity eventually changes quality.

Recognition of change is heightened, however, when a new form and structure to war progresses in strategic utility from the status of "important adjunct" toward "indispensable adjunct" and then toward possible "war winner." For example, 1936 (beginning with the invaluable experience offered by the Spanish civil war) to 1942 was a short period that registered a clear change in the terms of warfare, a change largely attributable to the emergence of newly potent air power as it began to lay claim to indispensable adjunct status. Figures 1 and 2, on the strategic utility respectively of air power and space power, suggest the potential value, though not necessarily the realized actual value, of those forms of military power reviewed on a historical continuum. It is useful to think about transformations of war taking place over a long time and occurring in four overlapping states. First, there are visions, and arguments about the sense in the visions, of what might be achievable. Second, there are experiments to give substance, or deny substance, to the visions in contention. Third, there is a period of extensive demonstration, far beyond experimentation, of potentialities. And finally, a more or less radical change in the terms of deterrence and war is confirmed by large-scale and undeniable experience, which invites thorough exploitation so as to be on the leading edge of contemporary military effectiveness.

## The Space Age of War

Progress in the evolution of warfare is irregular; occasional sudden leaps ahead are interspersed with decades or even centuries of marginal change. Signs of paradigmatic change in modern warfare are evident today. In comparatively recent history the American Civil War and, perhaps, the Russo-Japanese war (1904-1905) provide examples of particularly significant ruptures with the past. For all of its distinctiveness of terrain, issue, and foe, Desert Storm may well join such historic antecedents and come to be seen as the first "modern" war.

States prepare for and wage war according to their distinct natures. Modern postindustrial societies are information led across the board of economic and leisure activity. Collectively viewed, defense preparation and war comprise a social institution. Information age countries cannot help but incline toward the waging of information driven war. Of course, old habits, vested interests, and selective lack of investment may all contribute to such a military transformation occurring more slowly than it otherwise might, and perhaps more slowly than in a rival state.

Figure 1. The Strategic Utility of Air Power.

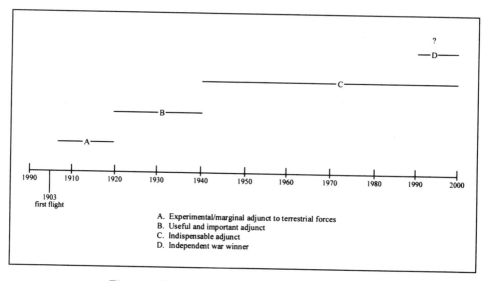

A. Experimental/marginal adjunct to terrestrial forces
B. Useful and important adjunct
C. Indispensable adjunct
D. Independent war winner

Figure 2. The Strategic Utility of Space Power.

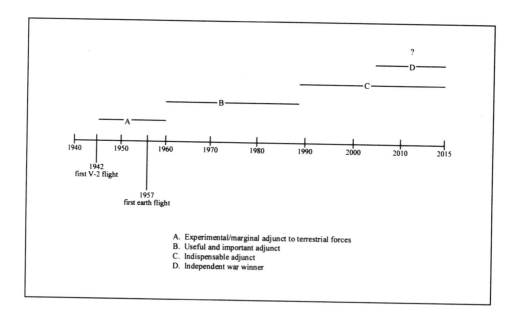

A. Experimental/marginal adjunct to terrestrial forces
B. Useful and important adjunct
C. Indispensable adjunct
D. Independent war winner

Rank ordering of the reasons for the demise of the former Soviet Union can be a subject only for speculative inquiry. Nonetheless, it is plausible to argue than an important reason for that demise was a systemic inability to innovate.

The Soviet ideology, economy, and especially the military, all exhibited aspects of the dinosaur. Soviet military leaders recognized the inability of their country to compete effectively with rival states on the frontier of the emerging information age. The new paradigm is information age warfare. Moreover, and perhaps less controversially, the new age of war is being propelled most directly by the quantity and quality of reliable, timely information of military value provided by space systems. Of course, warfare always has been led by information. No reader of Sun Tzu's *Art of War* could be in doubt on this point. Information is information, whether it is gathered by spies, cavalry, airplanes, or satellites.

Space systems are far from comprising the only means available for gathering information, but their pervasive influence and potential for augmenting, indeed multiplying, military prowess warrants their identification as at least the key coagent, along with the computer, to the transformation of war today. Again, quantity changes quality. Modern, information age forces may in principle have capabilities which, exploited together, provide the ability to wage a new form of warfare. Such modern forces can see over the hill to measure the enemy (an enemy already found over the hill by overhead observation), cheat time by the very rapid distribution and fusion of militarily usable information, employ superior information so that they can achieve by maneuver the annihilation of foes, and exploit precise knowledge in order to conduct war in a truly discriminate manner. One must think jointly and holistically to comprehend the total advantage secured by information age forces. Space age armed forces all have their military effectiveness augmented by space systems and each military organization functions synergistically to help the others perform more effectively. For example, a commentator may think that he or she is analyzing the military effectiveness of ground, naval, or air forces, but in fact he or she typically will be considering their prowess with a "value added" by precise navigational, inter alia, information from satellites.

Historically, transformations of the form and structure of war have had the most profound importance. When the terms of combat shift from a less effective to a more effective system of war, those who are left behind get beaten. The net effectiveness of armed forces may not be shifted radically, of course, if and when other, competing polities follow suit and also transform their ways of war.

Several historical transformations of war are noteworthy. From the fall of Rome to the present—approximately a 1,600-year span—at least seven new paradigms for the terms and structure of warfare can be identified.[2]

1. *Fifth Century Cavalry.* The heavy, mailed cavalry of Sassanian Persia, copied by the Byzantines, employing stirrups for the first time, ushered in a long period of advantage for soldiers who could fight on horseback.

2. *The "Military Revolution" of the Sixteenth and Seventeenth Centuries.*[3] The revolution in warfare that was led by the adoption of firearms for siege and open warfare took 250 years to complete.

3. *"Nation in Arms."* The idea of the citizen soldier found expression in the American Revolution in the 1770s, and especially, in the French Revolution in the 1790s.

4. *Industrial Age Mass Warfare.* This idea of the nation in arms also may be found in the concept of popular warfare, increasingly armed and sustained by industrially and agriculturally modern states, which helped fuel the "great wars," or total wars, of 1792-1815, 1914-18, and 1939-45.

5. *"Mechanized Warfare."* The advent of the paradigm of mechanized warfare may be fixed on the murderous year of 1916. That year witnessed the first use of the tank in battle (on the Somme), the first large-scale aerial battles (over Verdun), and a radical shift in the German modus operandi, characterized by the Hindenburg Program of mobilization for total war and the search for new methods in defense and offense to defeat a quantitatively superior foe committed to an attritional style of warfare.

6. *Nuclear Warfare.*[4] Since the mid-twentieth century, nuclear weapons have transformed the possible terms of combat, raised the casus belli, and cast a long shadow over great power, and even regional, security relations. The ironical strategic reality that nuclear weapons therefore have proved to be the one class of weapons not usable (which is not to say useful) in the nuclear age does not cast doubt on the claim for a nuclear "revolution."

7. *Information Age Warfare.* The 1980s, and especially the 1990s, are registering a still accelerating revolution in the quantity and quality of information available to military organizations at all levels (from planning staffs to tactical units).

Whether or not the emergence of air power warrants designation as a separate transformation of war is open to debate. The case for such designation is substantial, but may be argued.

The sheer complexity of war, and the interdependence of its many parts, has to mean that identification of a transformation of war always steers perilously close to comprising oversimplification of a messy reality. Transformations refer to generally dominant, organizing developments, but they proceed in company with older features on the historical landscape. The past transformations of war (from stirrup secured cavalry to nuclear covered forces) have not encompassed all aspects, even all important aspects, of war in their eras. War may be characterized by a dominant feature, yet it does not follow that contemporary war thereby can be explained completely.

As Carl von Clausewitz belatedly recognized after 1826, war is a rich basket of phenomena not easily captured by a master concept or dominant paradigm (i.e., by "absolute war").[5] Transformations of war generally are shared by several or more actual, or potentially, belligerent polities. Yet, an era can see different kinds of war. The arrival of the "nation in arms" in 1792 did not prevent the distinctly old-fashioned British army from defeating the French in campaign after campaign from 1809 to 1815. Mechanized warfare may have emerged in 1916-18, but in the deepest depths of the unusually cold Russian winter of 1941-42 it was not of much military utility; men on skis and Siberian horses were more important than tanks.

Advantage and potential disadvantage proceed hand in hand, both in life and in war. New sources of advantage bring new sources of vulnerability. Cavalry led armed forces can be wonderful instruments of military decision, but such armed forces are vulnerable to the unavailability of sufficient grass for the horses. Space age information warfare is the frontier of military effectiveness today and tomorrow, but if control of the "spaceways" is seriously contested, just how potent and reliable will our information led forces then be?

Officials can be so busy trying to peer into the future that they neglect the wisdom that they could garner from appreciation of the past. Just as it is naive and futile to argue the "whether" of nuclear weapons, because the nuclear age is a permanent fact, so also is it foolish to question the emerging reality of an information led transformation of war. But, too much of the current debate over information age warfare is focused upon the computer, and too little on how the information to be processed and deployed by the computer is gathered. Computers and their networks are only as valuable as their input. There is nothing militarily magical about computers per se. An important reason why computers can define an emerging era in defense preparation and war is that they draw directly on data gathered from the geostrategically unique vantage point of Earth's orbit. Although computers are key to the military value of spacecraft, it is the distinctive functioning of spacecraft—obeying the laws of orbital mechanics—which provides computers with the data most vital for information age warfare.

*Caveats*. It is important to avoid some potentially menacing errors. First, one must eschew exclusive claims for the value of space power for information warfare. No less critically, one should not hitch the future of space power exclusively to information warfare. The difference between a case convincingly stated, and one absurdly stated, can be perilously slim. Space forces provide generally superior flows of important information. But, is it sensible to tie space power tightly to the gathering and dissemination of information? If the United States ever is to consider seriously the development of "full-service" space forces (forces capable of logistic or weapons delivery), the information focus must be restricting. Space forces can provide more than information alone, and not only space forces provide information.

Second, proclamation of a transformation of war is independent of consideration of an enemy. When war is transformed, it can be transformed for all belligerents. A national lead is possible, indeed it is a fact for the United States today, but a permanent national lead is not certain. Moreover, even if (improbably) the United States alone can enjoy the benefits of space age information warfare for the next several decades, enemies will be motivated to find ways to restrict the domain of information led military advantage.

Third, a transformation in warfare is not effected by weapons, to say nothing of technologies, alone. For warfare to be transformed, as should be true for the consequences of space systems, the institutions that prepare for and wage war have to learn how to employ the new machines to good effect. And those machines must be available in numbers; and there is a need not only for mass, but also for critical mass. Above everything else perhaps, there is need for an authoritative vision of the future if the process of change is to be tolerably well managed. In the same way that the land and naval forces of the United States today pervasively "think air," so do they (and the air forces) urgently need to learn to "think space."[6]

Fourth, a plausible, commonsense argument for an emerging transformation of war, in favor of space power that yields superior information, cannot but be hurt by support in argument by dubious historical analogies. Peril lies in the possibility that choice of a poor historical analogy will allow critics to win an argument. If space age information warfare, for example, is deemed to have an analogy in the role of strategic air power anticipated in the 1930s, critics of space power may be handed the advantage by linking space to the much more contentious case of the value of strategic bombing in World War II.

Finally, a persuasive case for the transformation of war by the application of information age technologies can slide into the zone of snake oil salesmanship, unless enthusiastic advertisers exercise self-criticism. It is important to avoid the risk of overpromising. The reality of what space age information warfare offers in combat advantage is sufficiently significant, when properly understood, that there is no need to risk overstating an already good case. Proponents of mechanized land power, and especially of air power, provide negative object lessons for today's advocate of space power. From the 1920s to the present, some prophets of air power have asserted a gold standard for their favored instrument which translates as the opportunity and ability to wage and win wars independent of significant assistance from other, lesser forms of military power. Any form of military power (land, sea, air, nuclear, special operations) may have only adjunct roles in particular conflicts. Space warriors today should not compensate for their general underappreciation in the armed services by indulging in overstatement.

## Space Power

Space power, as mentioned above, refers simply to the ability to use space for military, civil, or commercial purposes and to deny the ability of an enemy to do the same. This functional, output oriented definition (tightly linked to the ability of the nation to control vital spaceways) is preferable to a strictly unilateral, descriptive usage and parallels common definitions of air power and sea power. Any concept which embraces the word "power" accepts the ambiguities of that difficult term.

Just as power in the air is power to use and to deny use of the air, so power is space similarly can be both positive and negative. The positive and negative benefits of space power are not identical. To be able to use space does not necessarily imply the ability to deny such use to an enemy, while the ability to deny use of space to an enemy certainly does not mean that, ipso facto, space can be used by friendly forces. Following the elegant example set by Alfred Thayer Mahan in the first chapter of *The Influence of Sea Power upon History, 1660-1783,*[7] it can be affirmed that space power has both "elements" and "conditions." The former comprise its vital constituent parts, the latter the context within which it will flourish or languish. Mahan speculated that mercantile trade, colonies, and a fighting navy were the elements most vital to a nation's sea power, while geographical position, physical conformation of national geography, extent of territory, numbers of population, national character, and character of the government constituted the six most important conditions influencing the growth of that sea power. A Mahanian analysis of the elements of, and conditions for, space power has yet to be undertaken.

"Star Trek" notwithstanding, the concept and reality of space power is unfamiliar to most people today; for that reason sea power and air power analogies are useful. Space power indeed is different, yet space power ought not be considered any more different from sea power and air power than these latter concepts are from each other. While respectful of the distinctiveness of each geographical environment, still it must be said that space power has begun the process of transforming the terms of war, just as did air power in the middle decades of this century. Space power must transform war in ways different from the overall accomplishment of air power, but a grasp of the latter bequeaths the beginning of understanding of the former. As each military revolution is "layered" on and pervades what persists from before, so the older military elements are altered. Space power augments the military effectiveness of air power, just as air power augmented the potency of sea power, and as air power and sea power worked synergistically and "jointly" to enable land power to terminate conflicts with territorially defined foes.

The military effectiveness of armed forces is influenced significantly by distinctive geographies. Technology advances, but the land, sea, air, and now space environments each shape military contributions unique to themselves. The logic of strategy, however, is common to armed forces in all environments. Space power has defining characteristics, identified below, but it is not governed by a distinctive strategic logic.

First, space is but the latest variant of the high ground that doctrine often advises military commanders to seize and hold. As with forces on all kinds of "high ground," space systems look down on friend and foe and are relatively difficult to reach and grasp. To attack up hill has never been easy; to attack up Earth's gravity well would continue that military condition. Second, the high ground of space is both global and of all but infinite military depth. The country or coalition that can operate at will in space is thereby able to operate from the highest of vantage points all over the world. And finally, space power, obedient to Keplerian astrodynamics, translates as satellites globally available as a regularly repeating, overhead presence.[8]

## Strategic Utility of Space Power

For all the uncertainties of the future, there is a possible analogy between 1918 vintage air power as a harbinger of air power in 1939-45, and 1991 vintage space power in Desert Storm and the use of space power in deterrence and war in the future. Analogy is a powerful tool that can, of course, do harm if applied uncritically. Several significant differences between the air power and space power cases have to be noted.

In 1918, the development and use of air power was unhindered by legal or customary regimes organized to serve the concept of "stability" by demilitarizing the air environment. Military planners in 1916-18 sought to apply the rapidly emerging technical possibilities of air power in ways most likely to generate strategic utility. The practical limits were formidable, but the constraints were not supplemented by the theory and practice of arms control. Also, it was relatively easier to use the air to practice air power in 1918, than it is to use earth's orbit to practice space power in the 1990s. The air is fundamentally more friendly to humans than is space. Next, there were fewer military alternatives to air power in 1918 than there are today to space power. The principal alternative to reconnaissance from the air in 1918 was reconnaissance by the cavalry, typically a nonalternative in the positional siege warfare on the western front. In the 1990s manned and unmanned air-breathing vehicles can do just about anything that space vehicles can do, only as a general rule (there are exceptions) they cannot do them anywhere nearly as well. Yet the fact that there are alternative ways of seeing over the hill, providing navigational assistance, and so forth, is important to the development of space power because it allows adaptably for specialization according to the principles of competitive advantage and a militarily prudent redundancy.

Finally, the entry level, and perhaps, the sustainment costs of new ventures in air power were relatively cheaper in 1916-18 than are costs today for new military space ventures. It may seem unfair, even misleading, yet it is realistic and important to compare air power in time of war (1918) with space power in time of peace. The author's argument is that the future of air power was clearly discernible in 1918 and that the future of space power is similarly discernible today, following the experience of Desert Storm.

In 1918 air power lacked the quality in unit effectiveness that could enable it, even in great quantity, to achieve decisive results under the governing military conditions of the day for war between great powers. Recall that the lack of strategic success in the war in the west, except eventually by attrition, derived from a lack of operational success attributable to two systemic tactical deficiencies. First, the armies of the period could not be commanded centrally in real time because they lacked tactical radio or other means of reliable communication. Second, contemporary armies lacked the mobility in attack to transform a "break-in" to an enemy's position into a true "breakthrough" that could be exploited to operational depths. The air power of 1918 certainly helped alleviate these deficiencies, but it could not offset them totally.

The future was demonstrated by air power in 1918. Air power performed strategic bombing, interdiction campaigns, close ground support, and it fought for air superiority and engaged in maritime reconnaissance and patrol. Air power also carried supplies to troops advancing in the field, spied behind enemy lines, and carried messages. Above all else, it observed events from the overhead flank. In 1918 air power did not demonstrate that it could win, or decide, a war, but it did demonstrate some potential toward achieving that. Whether or not there were significant operational limitations characteristic to air power itself, or limitations likely to be exploited by the foes of air power, remained to be seen.

In 1991, space power demonstrated that it could enable the combat arms of all kinds to be much more lethal than otherwise would be the case.[9] Space power showed that it enhanced the fighting power of all military elements prepared technically and doctrinally to exploit its services. Space power did not win, or decide, the Persian Gulf War, but then air power did not win, or decide, the Great War in 1918. The practical operational limitations upon a kind of power will always be disputable. After all, technological progress and better understanding of how to use new military capabilities properly should enhance the benefits to be derived from those capabilities. Land, sea, air, and now space, power nevertheless do have some characteristic systemic limitations.

Space power has distinctive limitations. The cost of transportation into orbit (i.e., launch costs) is a persisting limitation upon the pace of advance of military and commercial space systems. Next, laws of motion that must govern celestial bodies are a permanent constraint upon the flexibility with which space power can be employed. The laws of motion are the equivalent for space power of the landforms (maritime defiles) and weather conditions that restrict free passage of ships at sea. Also, it is in the very nature of space power to be distant from terrestrial events. Although it is that distance overhead that is militarily beneficial, still distance from Earth is a limitation of importance.

Although limits to the strategic value of space power cannot be estimated with confidence today, space plainly has the greatest near- and medium-term growth potential for military utility among all the geographically distinctive elements of power. The potential marginal return to scarce dollars expended is higher from investment in space than in the older forms of military power. Furthermore, land power, sea power, and air power are relatively mature, a maturity that must be assisted by the enabling value of space-exploiting information systems.

Two major classes of constraint on the evolution of space power should be emphasized. First, the persisting relatively high costs of space launch and operation have the necessary consequence of rewarding alternatives to space power. In peacetime, at least, cost-benefit analysis in the military field tends to focus more heavily on the certain dollar costs than on the uncertain benefits to the security of the nation. Second, the notion that weapons in space would be regarded differently from weapons on land, at sea, or in the air is a political reality that has the practical effect of inhibiting study of experimentation with space based weapons. It is a fact of long duration that the idea of space "weaponization" arouses unusual political opposition.

## The Totality of Conflict

Space power must always be useful, but its precise set of roles and its actual strategic utility will be distinctive to each class and case of conflict. Analogy makes this point easily. The wars in Afghanistan and the Falklands were contemporary events, but sea power was irrelevant in the former and all important in the latter. Superior air power could decide, albeit redundantly, which side would win the 1991 Persian Gulf War, but it could not decide the outcome of the low-intensity conflict waged throughout the 1980s in El Salvador. Because war is a whole enterprise with many parts working synergistically, plain evidence for the influence of this or that kind of military power can be difficult to find. If and when space power actually decides the course and outcome of a war, the proof most probably will lie in the combat prowess of land, sea, and air forces whose potency will have been augmented by information of all kinds gathered and disseminated by space systems.

Functioning in enabling, supporting, or adjunct roles, space power is manifested in satellite systems vital for communications, navigation by friendly forces (and their weapons) of all kinds, reconnaissance and surveillance, early warning of missile attack, and geodesy and meteorology. In addition, what one day may be called full-service space forces will themselves carry weapons for terrestrial bombardment as well as weapons designed to thwart the capabilities for long-range bombardment by foes.

Because of the distinctive strengths and limitations of each element of the armed forces, success or failure in deterrence and war itself must be a joint endeavor. Even though the outcome to a future war may, in some vital sense, plausibly be decided by space power, the fighting will be conducted largely on Earth. Humankind and the stakes of war are terrestrial in orientation. It follows necessarily that war must ultimately bear on terrestrial values. Exceptions to this prediction can be identified. For example, it is possible that if one state or coalition could secure and hold truly exclusive "command of space," the enemy might elect to surrender as a direct consequence (space might be blockaded against passage by an enemy's missiles).

Space power, in common with sensible approaches to sea power and air power, can and should aspire to make the critical strategic difference in war. But, it would not be sensible to aspire to the ability to wage and win wars independently by space oriented action. Long-standing military principles decree the general superiority of joint over single military element solutions to strategic problems.

Both sea power and air power have played extensive adjunct, and complementary, roles to land power.[10] Because mankind lives on the land and is politically organized into territorial polities, it is inevitable that belligerents usually need to come to grips with each other on the ground. If space power is to be described as playing an "adjunct" or supporting role, that role, therefore, has long-standing and distinguished precedents in the history of sea power and air power. If space forces are denied weaponization, and as a consequence, are unable directly to engage enemies on Earth, then a strictly adjunct status is mandated for them. Even if space forces are equipped with weapons to fight for space control, their overall roles in war still could be confined to those of an adjunct to land, sea, and air forces.

Systems that gather and provide information do not themselves fight the enemy. Ultra intelligence in World War II, whose potency as an enabling influence is beyond question, did not itself sink any submarines or destroy any aircraft, although it did empower tactical combat units to do those things. The NAVSTAR global positioning system (GPS) permits economies of force in mission planning, but NAVSTAR itself can put no weapons on target.[11] It is not always obvious where space power begins and ends when information from satellites augments the potency of naval, air, and terrestrial military operations.

Now this article will consider space power as the "leading edge" in a conflict. *Leading edge* has two meanings. First, it could refer to the military capability that most effectively takes the war to the enemy. Air power in Desert Storm is a classic example of leading edge, or "key force," military capability. Second, leading edge could refer to the capability that decides the outcome of a conflict, even if that capability is not itself of a combat kind (e.g., ultra intelligence) or is not itself more than a combat adjunct to other combat forces (e.g., typically naval forces enabling land forces to conclude a war on land).

As the leading edge of overall U.S. combat potency, space power will decide the course and outcome of some conflicts, even though space forces may not themselves be combat forces with offensive capabilities. To decide a conflict, a capability does not need to have a combat character itself. If it does have such a character, it certainly does not need to be able to conclude hostilities without the assistance of other kinds of forces. All that is claimed is that the leading edge military capability is the most potent source of military effectiveness.

In Desert Storm, space power demonstrated potential to achieve the status of leading edge in war. Whether or not that will occur soon depends on U.S. decisions with respect to the development of its space power for joint warfare and on the potency of those other armed forces that must exploit the advantages granted by space systems. The influence of space power, as of land, sea, and air power, will be characteristic of its unique geostrategic nature and specific to each particular class, perhaps even instance, of conflict. A leading edge capability for space power (indeed for air power) may be exploited much more readily in the open conditions of desert warfare or in war at sea than, for example, in heavily urban combat. Just because spacecraft can be present over all scenes of terrestrial conflict, it does not follow that they invariably must yield decisive military advantage.

## Von Clausewitz, Strategy, and Space Warfare

Most dimensions of national security are explained by too much theory. In the whole nuclear realm, for the most prominent case, theory has far outstripped evidence and common sense. Theories of sea and air power of dubious quality also have flourished. Today, space power suffers from an unusual malady—an acute shortage of space focused strategic theory and the lack of a binding concept to aid understanding of what it is all about. People of today, including many military professionals, remain less than enlightened on what space power is and does, how it works, and how it can and should function synergistically with other players in the joint military team.

Von Clausewitz had his limitations, but the level of his analysis renders his advice both timeless and generally environmentally nonspecific. In *On War*, the great man railed against scholastic theorizing, but he praised theory as properly understood and employed. He argued that theory is not a direct guide to action, but rather educates the mind so that some useful order can be imposed on an apparently disorderly universe. According to von Clausewitz,

> theory cannot equip the mind with formulas for solving problems, nor can it mark the narrow path on which the sole solution is supposed to lie by planting a hedge of principles on either side. But it can give the mind insight into the great mass of phenomena and of their relationships, then leave it free to rise into the higher realms of action.[12]

A theory of space power should help in recognizing and eliminating the weeds that grow from ignorance and labeling error as such when it appears; in showing how one thing is related to another, a point of no small importance given the complexity of war today; and in keeping the important issues and details separate from the unimportant.

Gresham's law (Sir Thomas Gresham) states that bad money drives good money out of circulation. The same phenomenon can apply to debate over ideas most suitable to explain space power. For example, fanciful claims for space power wreak political damage that balanced argument has great difficulty in offsetting. In the absence of a robust body of intellectually rigorous strategic theory, appeals to conceptual authority echo in a void. Space power needs to be integrated into the mainstream of strategic thought so that the joint reality of future conflict is expressed properly in the preparations that are made for it today. Unlike Mahan's unduly naval classic, *The Influence of Sea Power upon History, 1660-1783*, works of theory explaining space power should explore the interconnectedness of the different geographical environments. Space power is of little interest per se. The strategic interest lies in the consequences of its application for deterrence and the conduct of war as a whole.

Pending the arrival of a coherent theory of space power, one could do worse than reflect upon the meaning of von Clausewitz's ideas for the future of space age information warfare. A beginning to theory building for space power can be made with the following Clausewitzian ideas:

- War has a grammar of its own, but not a policy logic of its own.[13] War in space has its own distinctive characteristics that policy must know and respect, but that war has meaning only for the purposes of policy.
- Countries have "centers of gravity" key to their functioning.[14] A country's or a coalition's ability to wage war successfully can be negated if those centers of gravity are menaced, damaged, or taken. Space forces greatly enhance the ability of other kinds of military power to locate, threaten, harass, and destroy such centers.

- War is the realm of chance, uncertainty, and friction; the fog of war blinds the commander.[15] Space power assaults some of the friction that impairs terrestrial military performance, but is itself subject to the workings of friction.
- War is a unity.[16] Space power is an essential team player, and is probably due to become the team player who adds the greatest value for lethality in combat. Deterrence and war, however, will remain joint undertakings.
- Policymakers and military commanders need to understand what the military instrument can accomplish under particular conditions.[17] The emergence of space power adds to the burden of comprehension by the layman.
- As the "just war" tradition maintains, there needs to be a unity of character of political purpose with the scale and kinds of military means.[18] Contemplation of the practical military implications of a maturing space power has to accommodate appreciation of the value to high policy of an unprecedentedly discriminate military instrument.
- Success in battle flows from the achievement of overwhelming strength at the "decisive point."[19] This maxim can be difficult to apply in a theory of space power, yet it is basically as sound for space operations as it is for other kinds of military activity.
- Defense is the stronger form of waging war on land.[20] In space, defense probably is the stronger form of waging war in mid earth or high earth orbits, but probably not in low earth orbits. There is some safety in sheer distance (in many cases, equal to time).

In piecemeal fashion, many of the elements for a theory of space power have been collected via raids on the existing theories of sea power and air power. As stated already, space control is a direct borrowing, while discussion of blockade and choke points similarly have naval origins.[21] There is a large literature on space policy, space technology, antisatellite weapons, space based weapons for what used to be known as the Strategic Defense Initiative (SDI), and arms control for strategic "stability" in orbit.[22] There effectively is, however, no body of writing which attempts to explain what space power is and how it will work as a pervasive, albeit technologically dynamic, influence on strategic history in ways complementary to land, sea, and air power.[23] It is almost as if the defense and arms control community has been too busy debating the hot policy topic of the day to take the time to stand back and try to understand the character of broader subjects. After all, it is a rare historical event when a new geographical dimension is added to the environments in which, for which, and from which, human beings will fight. In the 1980s, debate over the SDI tended, like, Gresham's law, to drive out a broader discussion of strategy for space. In the 1990s, excitement over information warfare and a computer shaped revolution in war similarly appears to be attracting a great deal more attention than is the momentous trend toward the systematic operational military exploitation of space.

The development of air power was accelerated massively by the outbreak of the Great War only 11 years after the Wright brothers defeated gravity. Now that the cold war is over and truly first-class foes are temporarily out of sight, much of the urgency has departed from the debate about space power and strategy for war in space. That is understandable, but unfortunate, because the proliferation of missile (including space launch) prowess around the world, married to an electronic excellence far from confined to the United States, means that the space age of war is surely coming. Everything that is thought to be known about transformations of war, or revolutions in military affairs, shows that the side which has the services of a prescient and coherent vision of the military future enjoys a critical advantage as a consequence. If there is a plausible official U.S. vision of the strategic utility of, and the military requirements for, space power, that vision is indeed dim today.

## Space Control

*Space control*[24] is the concept that addresses the central issue of who can operate, and in what manner, in space. Nothing can be more fundamental than this in the argument about the influence of space power on future history. This concept has to be assigned master status. If space control is lost, or severely contested, almost everything else from among the country's ideas for the military use of spacecraft will be rendered irrelevant, at best.

Four conditions of control are possible. First, space control may be acquired and sustained either by default of challenge or by hard fighting. Second, the control described above may be enjoyed by an enemy. Third, space control may belong to a third party. Fourth, space may be contested and decided differently in different orbits.

All theories of space power must include treatment of space control. Unless theorists, including an official defense planner, can explain why and how their country will be at strategic liberty to derive military advantage from the use of space, their theory or defense plans must invite skepticism. History has left too many precedents of bold design for military campaigns that foundered for lack of reliable control over the most vital geographical environment. Consequently, there cannot be permissivity toward theorists of space power who neglect to come to grips with the issues of control. Although there will be periods of no contest for control of space in particular wars, there is no historical basis for a claim to the effect that space control will take care of itself, or really does not matter. Writing in June 1914, Sir George Aston speculated that "local command of the air will be fought for, even as we have battles to establish, for some purpose, the local command of the sea."[25] His thought can be adapted for today with the substitution of space for "air." Because of the laws of orbital motion, however, the "local command" of space will be global, though possibly restricted to orbits of particular shape and altitude.

The influence of space power upon history is already substantial and growing, and has the potential to yield decisive advantage. Where is the theory of space power? Where is the Mahan for the final frontier?

---

## Notes

1. See Alvin and Heidi Toffler, *War and Anti-War: Survival at the Dawn of the 21st Century* (Boston: Little, Brown, 1993), chap. 9. For an excellent cautious discussion, see Thomas A. Keaney and Eliot A. Cohen, *Gulf War Air Power Survey Summary Report* (Washington, D.C.: U.S. Government Printing Office, 1993), chap. 10; and Eliot A. Cohen, "The Mystique of U.S. Air Power," *Foreign Affairs* (January/February 1994): 109-24.

2. Andrew F. Krepinevich has identified no fewer than 10 military revolutions since the fourteenth century. In "Cavalry to Computer: The Pattern of Military Revolutions," *The National Interest* (Fall 1994): 30-42.

3. The proposition that there was a military revolution in early modern Europe remains a lively topic among historians long after its initial presentation. Recent entries into the cottage industry of early modern military revolution debate include Clifford J. Rogers, ed., *The Military Revolution Debate: Readings on the Military Transformation of Early Modern Europe* (Boulder, Colo.: Westview Press, 1995); and David Eltis, *The Military Revolution in Sixteenth-Century Europe* (London: Tauris Academic Studies, 1995). Andrew Ayton and J.L. Price, eds., *The Medieval Military Revolution: State, Society and Military Change in Early Modern Europe* (London: Tauris Academic Studies, 1995), helps demonstrate the generic popularity of the idea.

4. On this happily still theoretical subject, Robert Jervis, *The Meaning of the Nuclear Revolution: Statecraft and the Prospect of Armageddon* (Ithaca, N.Y.: Cornell University Press, 1989), remains outstanding.

5. Carl von Clausewitz, *On War*, Michael Howard and Peter Paret, eds. and trans. (Princeton, N.J.: Princeton University Press, 1976; first published 1832), book one chap. 1 and book eight chaps. 5-8.

6. This thought finds detailed explanation and exposition in Colin S. Gray, "Vision for Naval Space Strategy," *U.S. Naval Institute Proceedings* (March 1994): 63-68.

7. Alfred Thayer Mahan, *The Influence of Sea Power upon History, 1660-1783* (Boston: Little, Brown, 1890).

8. Johannes Kepler's three laws of planetary motion comprise the core principles of astrodynamics: his laws of motion also apply to earth satellites. Lightly adapted, Kepler's *First Law* states that the orbit of a satellite forms an ellipse with the center of the earth at one focus. The *Second Law* states that as a satellite moves around its orbit, an imaginary line (radius) joining it to the center of the earth sweeps out equal areas in equal amounts of time. Just as the First Law gives the shape and the inclination (relative to the plane of the equator) of an orbit, so the *Second Law* describes the speed of a satellite relative to its orbital position at any one point in time. Kepler's *Third Law*, again suitably rephrased, states that the square of the orbital period is proportional to the cube of the semi-major axis. In plain English, the period (which is to say the length of time a body takes to complete one revolution around the central body) of a satellite is dictated by the size, not by the shape, of its orbit. The major axis of an orbit passes through the longest diameter of the ellipse, and the minor axis through the shorter diameter. The semi-major axis is the parameter that equals half the distance of the major axis.

9. Secretary of Defense William J. Perry has written, most unobjectionably, that "[s]pace forces are fundamental to modern military operations. They are playing a central role in the ongoing revolution in warfare because of their unique capabilities for gathering, processing, and disseminating information. As demonstrated during the Persian Gulf War of 1991, space systems can directly influence the course and outcome of war. For example, space systems helped confer a decisive advantage upon United States and friendly forces in terms of combat timing, operational tempo, synchronization, maneuver, and the integrated application of fire power. These inherent strengths of space forces will contribute directly to the deterrent effectiveness of U.S. armed forces." *Annual Report to the President and the Congress* (Washington, D.C.: U.S. Government Printing Office, February 1995), p. 233.

10. For some historical perspective strongly supportive of the currently fashionable insistence on joint approaches to defense, see Charles E. Callwell, *Military Operations and Maritime Preponderance: Their Relations and Interdependence*, Colin S. Gray, ed. (Annapolis, Md.: Naval Institute Press, 1996; first pub. 1905); and George Aston, *Sea, Land, and Air Strategy: A Comparison* (London: John Murray, 1914).

11. The NAVSTAR global positioning system (GPS) comprises a minimum of 18 operational satellites (plus 3 spares) deployed in semisynchronous circular orbits in six orbital planes and is designed to allow friendly military users to secure unprecedented all-weather location (longitude, latitude, and altitude to within tens of feet) and

velocity information. The GPS tells friendly forces or weapons exactly where they are in relation to a precisely mapped (probably by satellite based sensors) enemy location.

12. Von Clausewitz, *On War*, p. 578.

13. Ibid., p. 605.

14. Ibid., pp. 595-97.

15. Ibid., pp. 119-21.

16. Ibid., p. 607.

17. Ibid.

18. Ibid., pp. 88, 579.

19. Ibid., p. 204.

20. Ibid., p. 359.

21. Space has its prospective choke points, just as do the maritime and land environments. Low earth orbit (LEO; 60-300 miles) and Geosynchronous orbit (GEO; 22,300 miles) are particularly attractive for, indeed are essential to, many military space missions (though not for navigation, for which semisynchronous polar orbits are most appropriate). There is a more specific choke point for any space launch into orbit in that every satellite must, obeying Kepler, pass over the precise antipode of its launch site in the course of its first revolution around the earth, regardless of the shape (i.e., eccentrically elliptical, or circular) or size of its orbit. Therefore, every launch site on Earth has its precisely precalculable antipodal choke point for the potential interception of satellites in orbit. Also, there are the Lagrange points, named after the eighteenth-century mathematician Joseph Lagrange, comprising five locations in space where offsetting (i.e., neutralizing) gravitational fields allow for satellite "parking" with the expenditure of relatively little energy to maintain station. Three of these points are on a line with the earth and the moon, while the other two are respectively 60° ahead of, and behind, the moon in its orbit. These are not the only possible choke points relevant to space warfare, but they are the leading candidates. This note has discussed the space equivalents to the Straits of Gibraltar, the Cape of Good Hope, the Cumberland Gap, and the Khyber Pass.

22. For example, Bhupendra Jasani, ed., *Space Weapons and International Security* (Oxford: Oxford University Press, 1987); and Kenneth N. Luongo and W. Thomas Wander, eds., *The Search for Security in Space* (Ithaca, N.Y.: Cornell University Press, 1989).

23. Honorable mention, however, is merited by David E. Lupton, *On Space Warfare: A Space Power Doctrine* (Maxwell Air Force Base, Ala.: Air University Press, June 1988).

24. A superior recent discussion is Steven Lambakis, "Space Control in Desert Storm and Beyond," *Orbis* (Summer 1995): 417-33.

25. Aston, *Sea, Land, and Air Strategy*, p. 268.

# Chapter 40

### ★ ★ ★

# The Army After Next

Colonel Robert B. Killebrew, U.S. Army

*Colonel Robert B. Killebrew describes a U.S. Army Training and Doctrine Command (TRADOC) process for thinking about and developing the "Army After Next" (AAN). It is oriented toward the year 2020 and would follow Force XXI which is focused on improving capabilities between now and the first decade of the 21st century. The process is based on five assumptions: (1) The Army's business is to win wars, not only battles and engagements; (2) The international system will continue to be geopolitically based for at least the next 30 years; (3) Most armies will continue to exist to fight other armies, (4) By 2025, at least one major security competitor to the United States will have emerged; and (5) The 'Western way of war' will probably remain sound for American warfare for at least the next 30 years. Advancing technologies will focus on the word faster— faster deployment, faster processing of information for faster decision making, faster firepower focused faster on fleeting targets, faster maneuver, faster finishing and decision. The AAN will avoid attrition warfare, be strategically mobile, focus on force protection and sustainment in bare-base theaters, and be expansible. How valid are the assumptions underpinning the AAN? What would you add or delete?*

The U.S. Army's Training and Doctrine Command (TRADOC) [has] initiated the "Army After Next" (AAN) project at Ft. Monroe, VA. . . . With its establishment, the Service has in place two major initiatives to guide the Army's thinking into the mid- and long-range future. "Force XXI," the field-testing, doctrinal development, and acquisition of information-age upgrades for the Army's current force, will prepare land fighting forces for the period from the present until about 2010. The AAN project, however, is a

---

Col. Bob Killebrew is Assistant Deputy Chief of Staff for Doctrine at U.S. Army Training and Doctrine Command. The views expressed in this article are solely the author's and do not necessarily reflect the views of the U.S. Army or the Deparment of Defense.

---

separate program, designed to take a conceptual look beyond Force XXI at the strategy, technology, organizations, and military art that might influence national defense and the Army beyond 2010. Not targeted at a specific date or force structure, it will constantly shift its aim ahead, examining new concepts and recommending options to the Army's laboratories and force development specialists.

## Why an "Army After Next"?

Why plan so far out? The Army considers the Force XXI process vital to maintaining battlefield dominance in the next decade. It essentially focuses on upgrading existing weaponry and organizations by applying information-based technology just arriving on the edge of practicality. The Army believes that by increasing the information and knowledge available to battlefield commanders, quantum improvements in combat effectiveness are possible. Of itself, the direction of Force XXI is a major move by the Army to capture emerging technology for the next decades. But Army planners believe that, even as doctrine writers and laboratories wrestle with the near-term future, three factors suggest the need to examine some even more fundamental long-term challenges.

*First*, for the Army, battlefield systems designed and bought during the modernization surge of the early '80s will approach the end of their useful service lives around 2010. Of course, existing systems can be rebuilt and upgraded. Either way, the Service faces a tough investment choice: to upgrade old systems, or to bet on new technology and organizational forms not yet invented. The staff officers working the AAN program at TRADOC point to the historic danger of keeping old fighting systems simply because of "sunk costs," citing the example of the French in the interwar years, when large stocks of WWI systems impeded modernizations in doctrines and equipment that were needed by the mid-30s.

*Second*, technology marches on. Advances in communications, weaponry, and other fields will inevitably make today's technologies less effective and more vulnerable. And with technological progress, organizational changes are (or should be) inevitable, as witnessed by the worldwide changes occurring today in information-based corporations. It is not proven that organizations and doctrines based on the M1A2 tank will be obsolete by 2020; it seems prudent, though, to forecast what effect emerging technologies and new organizations might have on the way the future Army fights.

*Third*, and most significant, the geopolitical world will change. Inevitably, Army planners feel, major competitors will emerge to challenge U.S. security interests. The nature of that competition should be anticipated and, to the extent possible, analyzed. Future competitors are virtually certain to take advantage of new technology, and an American army based on legacy systems—40-year-old tanks as an example—might not be adequate to deal with new challenges. Similar systems of the French (and the doctrines that bound them together) fell before the newer-model Wehrmacht of 1940.

## Approaching the Future—With Caution

In establishing AAN, the Army is taking some risks. The glamorous future is always more entertaining (and less expensive) than the difficult present. As long-range concepts begin to emerge from AAN, there is a danger that policy-makers will turn from the hard work and expense of fielding Force XXI units to the untested promise and undeveloped technologies of AAN. Shortcuts in fielding armies are seldom successful and often disastrous. Doctrinal development, human engineering, and technological change still take time. Old soldiers will remember the zip and glitter of the Pentomic era, with the flying jeeps and helmet radios that were never fielded, and the theoretical doctrines that briefed well but couldn't be executed. Unfortunately, the resources thus sidetracked in the late '50s and early '60s left the Army poorly prepared for Vietnam. The pattern of change in armies—even the U.S. Army, with its extensive network of schools and laboratories—is evolutionary, though the concepts may be revolutionary.

So in spite of every temptation to put Starship Troopers on multi-colored briefing charts, both national policymakers and programmers within the Army itself will have to resist the temptation to design the Army of 2020 in a few weeks. The AAN concept meets the Army's need for a low-key, deliberate, long-term evaluation process. The evaluation is based on a view of the nation's long-term security needs, evolving technology and the nature of war itself. There is no flashy AAN logo. AAN handoffs to the labs and combat developers will come only after extensive consideration and debate within and between TRADOC and the Army leadership.

In fact, AAN researchers know that 2025 is so far in the future, and the pace of change so rapid, that even with the best luck, the chances of accurately forecasting the world 30 years for now are remote. But, even so, the general outlines of future national security strategy can be predicted with some expec-tation of being partly right, and trends in technology and organizational theory can be examined.

By focusing so far in the future, AAN will attempt to remain aloof from budget, roles and missions, and force structure issues. Of course, this will be tough in today's defense environment. It will be particularly hard for the Army, a Service that feels itself in the cross-hairs of Defense budgeteers, and one that, as a legacy of the Cold War, has best understood strategy in terms of force structure. But long-term thinking is plainly needed, and not just by the Army. Although national military strategy is properly the purview of the Joint Staff, the Army and other services are clearly required by their Title 10 responsibilities to hypothesize long-term national needs in order to direct research and development of capabilities intrinsic to their warfare specialty. To the extent the services interlock their long-term development programs with one another and with the Joint Chiefs of Staff, the nation benefits and the kind of vicious roles and missions fights that characterized the early '50s can be avoided. AAN planners are working closely with the advanced planners of other services, as well as the joint community, to develop emerging theories of warfare for the early decades of the new century. The Joint Chiefs' new *Joint Vision 2010*, which speaks more to the timeframe of the Army's Force XXI than to the longer reach of the Army After Next, has been consulted and referenced extensively by the AAN staff, and many *JV 2010* concepts and phrases have found their way into AAN briefings and concept development.

The AAN program's DoD counterpart is centered in the Office of Net Assessment's Revolution in Military Affairs (RMA) program, where . . . [the] staff has broken the trail in many defense venues with thoughtful and far-ranging studies that challenge conventional military thinking. [B]oth the RMA and AAN efforts are proceeding roughly on the same azimuth, sharing in some cases the same contractors and databases, adapted where necessary for their separate missions. . . . [The Office of Net Assessment] tends to be slightly more technologically provocative, while the AAN team leans more toward the art of war.

The purpose of the AAN program, then, is not to develop the details of a new Army or to engage in budget wars, but to provide the army's senior leadership with a think tank in which the larger issues of long-term national strategy and future operational art can be debated and decided. Organized around an annual cycle, the program will deliver a paper to the CSA every June that will provide TRADOC's view of the long-range future and recommend R&D decisions. Six months later, TRADOC will conduct a Winter Wargame that will pose strategic military challenges the Army—and the nation—will likely face in the long-term future. The game will be inherently "joint" and focused at the strategic and operational level. . . . [The Army Chief of Staff] directive to ensure continuity of effort should allow for operational-level comparative analysis during each annual cycle, and strategic analysis over a multi-year cycle of games. . . .

## General Assumptions—So Far

Reflecting a general uneasiness that most "future" studies are unduly technologically driven at the expense of human factors, the program divides its research into four general areas—geopolitics, human and organizational behavior, technology, and the future art of war. To date, studies have centered around establishing the broad context for the US' likely security environment in 2025.

The results break into an interesting grouping of "most likely" assumptions about the future, some familiar, some radically different. Some of the more important are:

***The Army's business is to win wars, not only battles and engagements.*** The Army has an urgent need to understand future war in all its likely facets, from start to finish, small to large. It is remarkable how, in the few short years since the end of the draft in 1973 and the fall of the Berlin War, strategic debate about landpower has become foreshortened. To some policymakers, commitments to Somalia or Bosnia have become the *de facto* expression of land force requirements. In fact, peacekeeping deployments are probably the least demanding tasks for the Army in the years ahead, and they probably are no more a clue as to future warfare requirements than the Marine Corps expedition to Nicaragua in the '30s presaged World War II. To help the Army's leadership and AAN planners better grasp future war at its worst, the first Winter Wargame series will focus on a major war in 2020, in whatever form that takes, and the demands it will place on land forces as part of the joint team. The Army's sister services, as well as a number of civilian agencies of the US government, have been invited to play. Other, smaller excursions and wargames during the year will address future war in less intense forms.

***The international system will continue to be geopolitically based for at least the next 30 years.*** While drug lords and international crime cartels may continue to cause problems, nation-states will continue to be the most important actors on the international scene, and relations between states will continue to dominate security issues. Land *counts*—resources, populations, mountains, river deltas, cities, fields, homes. And the state will remain, at least for the foreseeable future, as the best organizer of resources and relationships that occur on the land even as certain parts of its authority and sovereignty may change. At least in the developed world, the state will adapt and survive, although some less viable states probably will go out of business.

***Most armies will continue to exist to fight other armies.*** While there have been some state armies whose function was not external conflict, most armies are—and will continue to be—focused on securing the state and its interests against the encroachments of other states. This is not to say that "lesser included offenses" are not important or will not demand attention and resources. Peacekeeping and its spin-offs will continue to evolve and involve military forces, as will the maintenance of law and order in some smaller developing countries. As the countries of eastern Europe emerge into the sunlight and establish their own security regimes, their armies are proving, through exercises and agreements, to be important instruments in providing reassurance and stability. But at the end of the day, the probability of state-on-state warfare will be the most serious *reaison d'être* of most military forces, certainly those of the major powers and those who feel themselves threatened by bellicose neighbors.

**By 2025, at least one major security competitor to the United States will have emerged.** While this point is generally accepted within the defense community, there has not been much depth so far to the thinking about what to do about it, or even what "competitor" means. Early on, the AAN staff rejected the term "peer" competitor, as currently used to denote a futuristic enemy with mirror-image capabilities of our own, because the term tended to camouflage the actual, likely strengths and weaknesses of our most probable competitors within the next 30 years. Language is important. "Major" is a term that, in the AAN world, means a competitor that will probably be able to challenge the U.S. in many dimensions of power—on land, sea, air, and space; economically; politically; and with the strategic depth and mass in populations and land surface to absorb military punishment as well as give it. There will certainly be other competitors, probably with the capability to attack the U.S. All but major competitors, however, can be addressed by specific methods—advanced counter-proliferation regimes, special or naval forces, counterterrorism, and so forth. Only a major competitor calls forth the entire range of national security capabilities.

There are at least two difficult aspects to the hypothesis of a major competitor. First, it is often difficult for the defense-intellectual community to come to grips with the idea of a major competitor without overlaying the kind of ideological divide that gripped the world during the Cold War. But in fact, granted the survival of the state system, some aspects of international competition in the early part of the 21st century may closely resemble the world in the first part of the 20th century. (Of course, there are many dissimilarities, the leading one being the continued existence of nuclear weapons in the hands of all potential major competitors. Perhaps even the Kaiser would have hesitated to mobilize in 1914 had they existed.)

Second, the management of multi-polar competition has the potential to become a separate and important field of study in and of itself. Certainly this century has provided three "case studies" of great-power competition, two of which led to war and one of which was resolved peacefully. The role of military forces in *preventing* conflict merits close study. Certainly there should be more options than displays of unpreparedness or bellicosity, both of which have been tried in the past 100 years. The AAN project is taking some first steps to study the management of international competition, but much more remains to be done in this area.

**The "Western way of war" will probably remain sound for American warfare for at least the next 30 years.** The science of war as embraced in

Joint Publication 3.0, as taught in U.S. war and staff colleges, and as embodied in the works of Clausewitz, Jomini, Corbett, Mahan, and Dohet remains generally sound. For the U.S., Clausewitz' "trinity" of the people, the government, and the army will remain the foundation of American security policy. But while the framework will be adequate, its application is liable to be much more difficult. Attacking an enemy's strategic center of gravity, for example, is liable to be much harder in a world where the enemy can hit back at one's own strategic vitals. In fact, one hypothesis is that future opponents may deliberately and rapidly escalate horizontally against US or allied "safe areas," to include homelands, to offset local weaknesses. To provide a practical illustration, current US strategic and operational controls—for example, boundaries between CinCdoms or current air-ground control measures—might provide opportunities for an enemy to exploit and bureaucratic obstacles to the rapid focus of American combat power.

Of particular interest, the "operational art" or the operational "level" of war will probably gain in importance, both as a way to focus tactical operations to achieve strategic ends, and as a lens through which the several U.S. military services will integrate their efforts. A going-in assumption of the AAN project is that the trend toward integration of multiservice combat functions will continue, and will be successful to such a point that, by 2020, fully integrated operations to very low levels will be the norm. The term "jointness" will have been relegated to the ash-heap of linguistic history. Front-line combat troops will direct airstrikes, naval guns and missiles will fire under the control of infantrymen, and the current procedural wrangles about "how deep is 'deep'?" will seem odd anachronisms.

## Future Technologies

Thus far, AAN's slant on advancing technologies can be summed up in one word—"faster." Faster deployment, faster processing of information for faster decision making, faster firepower focused faster on fleeting targets, faster maneuver, faster finishing and decision. While many promising new technologies are surfacing, there are several large points that are becoming embedded in the program thus far.

First, if one assumes that the "information revolution" will continue to be institutionalized by the services, by 2020 the use of advanced information technology will be routinely a part of military operations, like smokeless powder is today. What will the post-information "revolution" be? AAN planners are beginning to hypothesize that new sources of battlefield energy—for vehicles, as propellants in weapons, and for communications and other uses—will be the next major leap ahead for military forces, and will enable ground forces to cut logistical umbilical cords that today slow deployments and restrict maneuver. But such sources of battlefield energy do not exist today in a practical form. As opposed to the information revolution, which is generally a product of civilian technology, the "energy revolution" would have to be developed largely by the Army and DoD itself. It's difficult to estimate the true potential of cutting logistical ties. Oddly, it is a naval example that provides AAN planners their best guide. When the Navy put nuclear power into submarines, the thought was to merely develop a submarine that would be free of the need to surface to recharge batteries. No one envisioned the ultimate revolution, first in undersea than in naval warfare, that nuclear subs wrought. Some other points:

"Procurement agility" has emerged frequently as a strategic issue in AAN research. The issue is usually framed by the question, "In the future, will it be faster to be the developer of advanced technology or the buyer of off-the-shelf technology?" Allowing for differences in particular armies' ability to assimilate new equipment, and recalling that most new technology for land armies is easier, not harder, to train to, the answer almost always is off-the-shelf. This should give U.S. defense planners some pause. Unless present development-procurement cycles are shortened, it is not obvious that U.S. land forces will be the most advanced or best-equipped units on the battlefield in 2025, at least not in all particulars.

Finally, rapid strategic deployment continues to recur as a technology the future Army (and other services) will require. With the current success of the C-17 transport program and the ongoing construction and conversion of the Large Medium-Speed Roll On-Roll Off (LMSR) sealift fleet, the general shape of the Army's strategic mobility program has been set for the first decades of the new century. But interesting new technologies are beginning to emerge regarding ultra-fast-sealift (UFS) that suggests that speeds in excess of 50 knots, and perhaps as high as 100, might be possible. If such technologies can be made practicable, there might well be a niche for UFS as the Army's seven tip-of-the-spear fast sealift ships, procured in the early '80s, begin to approach the end of their service lives.

It is clear that there is a link between technological change and organizational behavior. In analyzing the future-technology landscape, an early AAN criticism of DoD's RMA was a dearth of human-factors studies, a shortcoming the RMA staff was aware of. Unfortunately for both programs, technological advances are relatively easily envisioned and quantified, but the organizational and human side of change is much harder to handle scientifically.

## An Outline of an Army

... TRADOC suggested that the Army After Next might be organized around the following characteristics, with the proviso that the ... work was sketchy and much more remains to be done.

First, the Army after Force XXI will have to be strategically mobile, dramatically improving on the Army's ability to deploy forces today or even in the Force XXI period. While sizable elements of the Army currently can deploy on very short notice via Air Force airlift or fast sealift ships, future demands will likely require a form of global maneuver that is considerably different from the fort-to-port model used today. Self-deployment of Army aviation assets, airdrop or airland of more tactically mobile forces, and fast sealift that can maneuver at sea to avoid space-based surveillance or precision attack may be required.

Second, the Army After Next must avoid attrition warfare. While the composition of future land forces won't be known for some time, it is a reasonable assumption that on a precision-dominated battlefield, losses of expensive materiel and highly trained personnel should be avoided. Some combination of precision fires and dominant maneuver should permit U.S. land forces to hit where they choose, and deny an enemy the opportunity to entrap U.S. forces in wearing and inconclusive combat.

Third, force protection and sustainment in bare-base theaters should be enhanced by the paths being blazed by Force XXI and technological advances in communications and materiel-handling capability. It's possible that the bulk of logistics and administrative support may be based *outside* the active theater of operations, beyond the reach of most threats, which would free up combat units to concentrate on active operations instead of security.

Finally, the future Army must be expansible. Expansibility, of course, is not an issue when dealing with the Somalias or Bosnias. But should the U.S. and its allies encounter an enemy with mass and depth of territory, two corps may not be enough for extended operations. Virtually no leading strategist today has defined what wartime expansion in the future might require, and leading experts' opinions vary widely.

# Chapter 41

## * * *

# The Next Naval Revolution

Reuven Leopold

*Reuven Leopold asserts that today, after 50 years or more during which carrier-born aircraft and nuclear-powered submarines dominated naval warfare, the surface warship is again poised to take center stage in future combat. Stand-off attack missiles and advances in combat systems functionality and connectivity are enabling the reemergence of the surface warship as a primary instrument of maritime warfare. Information and distance will be the hallmarks of this "next naval revolution." A vastly enlarged battlespace will be dominated by dramatically improved offensive and defensive capabilities of the future surface combatant. The author proposes three new warship designs-the arsenal ship, a new light combatant and a heavy, cooperative engagement master ship. These, combined with new systems and a return to building "technology demonstrators" before committing to building an entire class of ships, will be important components of this naval revolution. Do you think Leopold's arsenal ship and technology demonstrators are worth significant investment? Can the surface ship reemerge as the dominate naval platform?*

One hundred years ago the world's largest and most powerful navies had on their drawing boards a set of magnificent large surface warships. These were the battleships and heavy cruisers which were to dominate naval combat for more than quarter of a century. Although the concepts of aircraft and

Dr. Reuven Leopold is the President of SYNTEK, an international defence technology company in the Washington, D.C. area, and has been a member of the Executive Panel of the US Navy's Chief of Naval Operations for the past 15 years. Recently he chaired a Task Force examining future US Navy surface combatant designs in terms of both technology and the procurement process. Dr. Leopold was the US Navy's Senior Civilian Technical Director in charge of all surface ship and submarine designs. Classes designed under his technical direction included the CG-47 Ticonderoga class cruiser, the FFG-7 Oliver Hazard Perry class frigate, the LSD-41 Whidbey Island class dock landing ship, the DD-963 Spruance class destroyer, and the LHA-Tarawa amphibious assault ship.

submarines had already been invented, the technology to build them did not yet exist. Today, after 50 years or more during which carrier-borne aircraft and nuclear-powered submarines dominated naval warfare, the surface warship is again poised to take centre stage in future naval combat.

## Historical Perspective

Naval revolution is a by-product of emerging technologies, new threats, strategies, tactics and operational concepts. It is also influenced by new individual warship designs, which incorporate these new technologies. Over many centuries of naval combat, all of these factors have been subject to constant change. Strategy, tactics and public opinion have played key roles in naval warfare developments, but technology has clearly been the key enabler, and it continues to drive the next revolution.

Commanders have always had two main tactical priorities: locating the opponent's ships before being detected themselves; and increasing the range at which the enemy could be engaged. Distance and information have been paramount, as they translate into surprise and survivability. An attack can only be made with impunity if the opponent is without long-range detection and targeting capabilities, and does not have many long-range weapons.

Naval battles over the centuries have been subject to about a dozen major technological innovations that have enabled gradual changes in tactics and doctrine. In ancient times, the prime objective in battle was to reach and board an enemy's ship, and fight in hand-to-hand combat. It was not until 1750 that gunpowder enabled a metal ball to be thrown 600 metres from a ship, and this increased the distance between warring parties. However, the cannonball did not explode into small fragments which could injure large numbers of people and/or start major fires with the possible loss of the ship, so it was still necessary to board the ship to overcome the enemy.

The only equipment available 150 years ago was sails mounted on wooden hulls, and cannonballs that could travel only several hundred metres. However, in a very short period, navies have experienced tremendous advances. The first major innovation, introduced in the middle of the 19th century, was steam engines that turned fully submerged propellers housed at the stern of steel ships. Within a 20-year period (1866-1886), fast breaching mechanisms, cartridge cases of cannon calibre, hydraulic recoil mechanisms on pivot mountings and chemical propellants changed gun technology radically. However, without the telescope sights also introduced in the same period, the limitation of the human eyes aiming guns would still have restricted the fighting range to no more than 1.8km. With telescope sights, however, the range increased to about 7.5km. Within the next quarter of a century, by the First World War, battleships were able to increase the distance to about 13km. By the 1920s, battleships' guns—up to a calibre of 18 inches (on Japanese battleships)—were able to fire armour-piercing explosive projectiles weighing up to 2,700lb (1,215kg) to a distance of about 26km.

Submarines and aircraft developed in time for the First World War further widened the distance between the warring parties at sea. However, in retrospect, this First World War-vintage equipment was fairly primitive. It was the developments of the Second World War—radar, sonar and naval aircraft—that added "eyes and ears." Weapons could now be carried a considerable distance by air, and this increased further the distance between those engaged in naval warfare.

Anti-ship missiles fired from ships have been operational since the mid-1960s. However, even today, the longest missile reach is still under 100km. The only exception to this are those navies that have aircraft carriers, Tomahawk missiles or submarines-launched long-range ballistic missiles.

The next major naval warfare revolution will increase the distance between adversaries to as much as 1,000nm (1,850km). This will be enabled by:

- the explosive progress of information systems, sensors, communications and computing power, which will link systems and platforms. These include satellites, unmanned aerial vehicles (UAVs), land-based aircraft, naval aircraft (fixed and rotary wing), surface ships and submarines;
- the increased quality of integration of information, made possible by better and more secure signals. This allows surveillance, targeting, command and control platforms to be separate from the platforms that house the weapons themselves;
- the ability to fire new tactical ballistic and long-range cruise missiles from 500-1,000nm (925-1,850km) away;
- the feasibility of theatre ballistic missile defence from surface warships, allowing interception of ballistic missiles both within and beyond the atmosphere; and
- the fact that, as long as high explosives' power is a function of weight, the most cost-effective way of carrying large weapons, is by buoyancy (ships), not by dynamic lift (aircraft).

When this concept is perfected, surface warships could become magazines for weapons, commanded from army and marine forces located over 100nm (185km) inland. This will mean radical future changes in the heavy equipment of land forces.

Contrary to the belief of many, this naval revolution has not been achieved. It is only now that computing power, database structure, and systems design are reaching levels which will permit information integration of the numerous and complex elements involved in littoral naval warfare. Strategists, tacticians, and defence analysts can conceive new ways to fight wars, but they remain untested concepts until technology makes them possible.

Studies in innovation have shown that 75% of successful innovations stem from requirement pull, not technology push; but however strong the requirement pull, it cannot become reality without the physical availability of objects and, today, also software. Leonardo da Vinci conceived the helicopter in 1500, but not until the late 1940s did Igor Sikorsky build a modern helicopter. Jules Verne invented the concept of a submarine in the middle of the last century, but only in 1909 did John Holland build a modern submarine, and it took until the late 1950s for Adm Hyman Rickover to emulate successfully the Jules Verne concept with USS *Nautilus*, the first true submarine. The Technology had to catch up with the concept.

The situation is no different today. Operational concepts already exist for the 2010 timeframe, but systems have still to reach fruition.

Early this century, battleships and cruisers were the centrepiece of all navies. However, during the past half-century, surface combatants have been gradually relegated to a secondary role of escorting carrier task forces, replenishment groups, merchant ship convoys and amphibious task forces.

As long as 50 years ago, many respected observers predicted the demise of surface warships, believing they would be made obsolete by evolving modern technologies in surveillance, communications, weapon systems and the use of nuclear weapons at sea, which has fortunately never happened.

Field Marshal Bernard Montgomery said in 1945: "It seems to me that the day of the warship on the surface of the sea is over." The nuclear weapons scientist Edward Teller observed, in 1946: "If I project my mind into a time when not only we, but also a potential enemy, have plenty of atomic bombs, I would not put so many dollars and so many people into so good a target. Come to think of it, I would not put anything on the surface of the ocean . . . it's too good a target."

But things have turned out differently. Surface warships have continued to exist during the past 50 years, and are now poised to once again take on more significant roles. In fact, the future looks bright for surface warriors and warship designers; because of new weapon and electronic technologies, we now stand at the threshold of an unprecedented revolution in surface warfare and warship design.

Nevertheless, surface warships will not make the role of aircraft obsolete in the near future. Even if ship-launched missiles replace the need for strike aircraft in attacks against fixed targets, the problem of dealing with mobile targets is much more complex. Significant development remains in surveillance, targeting and precision weapons before the role of manned aircraft in such missions is threatened. In the near-term, carrier-based aircraft will have to be used against dispersed, mobile targets because of the time delay between targeting and getting a weapon to the target. The ability of an aircraft carrier to loiter in international waters in the vicinity of a potential threat also has a proven deterrence value. In addition, the aircraft themselves have major deterrence value in scenarios such as we have seen in NATO air operations over Bosnia and post Gulf War operations over no-fly zones in Iraq. It is hard to visualize such demonstrations from a surface combatant which stands off several hundred miles from shore.

Major innovations have occurred between the major conflicts of this century. The years between the two world wars ushered in the era of naval aviation—the innovation that changed the model for naval warfare from large surface-to-surface battles to engagements by naval aircraft.

During the Cold War, nuclear weapons were mounted on ballistic missiles, and have been a major deterrent for the past 50 years. The ability to hide these weapons deep underwater in vehicles with high mobility—thanks to nuclear power—has been perhaps the key to US nuclear deterrence.

The shift to littoral warfare is bringing the surface ship back in vogue. Novel operational concepts are emerging, in which the marines and even the army will rely more heavily on the navy for firepower and protection. Two major innovations will have a significant impact, particularly in littoral warfare: long-range precision strike; and theatre ballistic missile defence (TBMD).

Today, 50% of the world's population is located within 80km of the shore. By 2030, with the projected doubling of the population, 75% will live within 80km of the shore. Eighty percent of countries are not landlocked, and therefore have littoral borders. Eighty percent of the world's capitals are within 485km of a coastline; 125 cities with populations of over one million are within 485km of a coastline.

The concept of attacking land targets hundreds of miles into enemy territory from hundreds of miles at sea is not new. It was the US Navy's main reason for seeking new carriers during the Cold War. Then, however, the idea was to attack the targets with aircraft, which invariably exposed pilots to enemy fire and, in turn, to possible injury or capture.

Today, a new type of warfare is evolving: the sea-based reconnaissance/strike system. This has been made possible by technological advances—including wide-area surveillance, automated target identification, precision guidance, long-range target-seeking weapons, and reliable high-capacity communications. It consists of surveillance and targeting from space, from ship-based aircraft and from the ships themselves. The weapons are the sea-based Army Tactical Missile System (ATACMS) for the short-to-mid range (100-500nm [185-925km]) and tactical ballistic, as well as cruise (Tomahawk and future missiles) for the long range (up to 1,000nm [1,850km]). This system should produce decisive results with little risk to the lives of servicemen.

Meanwhile, the threat of tactical ballistic missiles is real and growing, in terms of the number and proliferation of weapons, and in their political and military effects. During the Gulf War, several Aegis ships actually tracked Scud missiles en route from Iraq to Saudi Arabia, but the vessels' weapons systems were not yet capable of engagement.

This is about to change. Naval forces are unique in the ability to provide the first on-scene capability. Insertion of marines and follow-on army and air force units requires protection form the sea against ballistic missiles. A navy therefore needs 1,000-1,500 weapons available at any one time. Thus, to carry out deep precision strike and TBMD, warships larger than the US Navy's latest DDG-51 Flight IIA destroyer are required, as these carry only about 100 weapons.

Next century warships must support a wide spectrum of multi-warfare missions and operations. The traditional sea control task is not disappearing, but will encompass the need to support forces ashore with firepower and precise munitions. Warships of the future will have to contend with faster missiles, with lower signatures and increased maneuverability in highly cluttered environments. Detecting and dealing with this threat at sea and over land will stress today's weapon systems. Ballistic missile defence for port cities, amphibious objective areas and early-entry land forces pose new mission requirements.

Combat systems of the future will provide the capability to project power ashore quickly, against fixed and mobile targets, at varying ranges, with great accuracy and intensity, and in coordination with other forces. This requires a faster reactive strike capability; near-seamless connectivity of disparate surveillance systems, including overhead systems; real-time and near real-time targeting systems; and missile payloads able to deal with a broad target set. Finding and destroying mines is another major challenge of future littoral warfare.

Re-targeting missiles in flight, based on real-time updates provided by UAVs and Joint Surveillance Systems, will be critical. A next-generation cruise missile can provide substantial warfighting improvements and operational flexibility from the sea. To conduct shore fire support operations, ships will be configured with advanced fire support missiles, guns and munitions, attack helicopters, and real-time battle damage assessment assets. They will also have a comprehensive, integrated real-time targeting system.

Future shipborne combat systems will be able to dominate air, surface and undersea battlespace. This requires a robust defence, capable of cooperative offensive operations with other naval, joint and allied systems; cooperative identification capabilities; and non-cooperative target identification support. The ability to detect, identify and engage all tracks at sufficient ranges, altitudes, and depths is vital.

Advances in solid state radar technology, development of sea-based theatre anti-tactical ballistic missile defence, and the addition of a force-wide cooperative engagement capability are essential to meet air dominance requirements. For surface warfare, future combat systems will provide organic, real-time, over-the-horizon targeting and engagement from close-in to extended ranges, fully integrated into the joint force. Undersea warfare requires the ability to detect and attack submarines in all acoustic environments. New detection systems, combined with active torpedo defence, will make this feasible. Remote minehunting systems will detect and avoid surface, moored, and bottom mines at all speeds.

Future combat systems will thus be fully integrated and inter-operable, functioning as a "systems of systems", based on open and distributed architectures. Surface combatants will participate in joint and coalition operations. The combat system of the future will provide an efficient infrastructure that supports the flow and use of information for all users. Sensor-to-shooter connectivity will be in place and functioning independent of target domain (surface, air, land) or of weapon required. An integrated shipwide architecture containing data displays, storage, data exchange, and computational capability is the essential ingredient, which will enable flexibility across a rapidly changing technology base.

## Future Force Architecture: A Vision for the US Navy

Thus, with the next warship designs, navies could revolutionise naval warfare to an unprecedented degree. Vulnerability could be much reduced by the greater stand-off, and by incorporating known platform stealth technologies. Operational costs could also be reduced through major reductions in the manpower required to operate future warships.

The principles of such a versatile fleet can be related to the US Navy, as it has a large surface warship fleet, with over 120 units.

The world is more complex than when the Soviet Union kept regional conflicts to a manageable affair. In the future, fleet commanders should have more options in the types of warship units available to them. They lose the cost-effective option if—as with the US Navy—the only warships available are destroyers and cruisers carrying the Aegis weapon system (CG-47 and DDG-51), which is all that will remain in 15 years or so with the retirement of the DD-963, DD-993 and FFG-7 classes.

Any navy which intends to engage in sophisticated offensive battles at sea in the future, should have units of radically different sizes and configurations, so that task force commanders can select the best combinations of ships for specific missions. The warship design process is in part an allocation process, through which the force structure architect—with the assistance of the ship designer—distributes resources (weapons, sensors, and integrating devices) to different platforms. This can create ships of 5,000 tons, 10,000 tons, 20,000 tons and larger. Of course, with only very large warships, any navy could afford only a very small fleet, which could not be everywhere it might want, or need, to be at any given time. Also, not all missions require the overwhelming power of an Aegis cruiser or destroyer. For example, the FFG-7 has limited warfighting ability compared to a fully battlegroup capable DDG. However, it is numerically the most popular warship design since the Second World War, having been built by the USA, Australia, Spain, and Taiwan.

If fleets are to be balanced to respond to the traditional open-ocean warfare role—and to the newly acquired littoral role—navies must build the next series of warships with a focus on the littoral mission. Some envision this mission to be one in which a variety of warships stand-off at least 300nm (555km) from hostile shores, almost immune to the traditional vulnerability of anything on the surface of the ocean located closer to the shores of a hostile nation. This set of warships will be able to reach deep inland with precision and without risking the life of a single pilot. With the addition of new offensive tactical ballistic missiles, surface warships may be able to engage designated targets extremely rapidly—perhaps within 10 minutes from 300nm (555km) away. Thus, with a variety of warheads under development—in addition to new ballistic missiles and advanced global positioning system (GPS) guided cruise missiles—future warships will become "buses" for munitions that can suppress enemy radars, burst bunkers buried deep underground, stop columns of advancing armour, and create havoc in the all-important logistic "tail" of an enemy.

Surface-to-air and surface-to-space missiles with endo- and exo-atmospheric warheads will be able to stop the Scud-type missiles that gave Coalition forces such a hard time during the Gulf War. Cooperative Engagement Capability (CEC) will permit the launching of missiles from ships, which are significantly less expensive in terms of ship cost per missile, and guide those missiles to their targets from platforms other than the ones from which they were launched.

One of the key features of littoral warfare is firepower, with targets estimated to be in the high hundreds to the low thousands. If existing warships can provide 50% of magazine capacity to inland fire support, as opposed to self- and fleet-defence, a navy would need 50 ships for one assault operation. At 30% magazine capacity dedicated to fire support (which is more likely), 80 ships would be needed.

It is unlikely that any fleet will be able to mass and maintain these numbers of warships, particularly for a single assault. An alternative approach is therefore needed: ships dedicated to carrying and launching long-range missiles into the littoral. These so-called arsenal ships would be large vessels, constructed for survivability and the ability to carry 500-1,000 missiles with no complex radar or control systems; their fire control and air defence would be provided by other warships via CEC. Their function would be: invasion stopping; long-range strike; fire support; and littoral battlespace dominance. To carry out these missions with a large number of missiles, each ship would have to displace about 20,000 tons.

A by-product of this concept is the elimination of the logistical chain required to land missiles and shells, which must then be distributed inland to individual army and air force units. Munitions fired from warships several hundred miles offshore obviate the need for such offloading.

The US Navy [is working] on a concept of operations document for the arsenal ship, which will address the question of how the arsenal ship should interface with the rest of the fleet; how it should be protected; the number of ships required; and how small the crew can be made. But whatever its precise configuration, size, and concept of operations, it appears increasingly likely that the US Navy will have such a ship in its fleet after the turn of the century.

Figure 1
A Notional Arsenal Ship

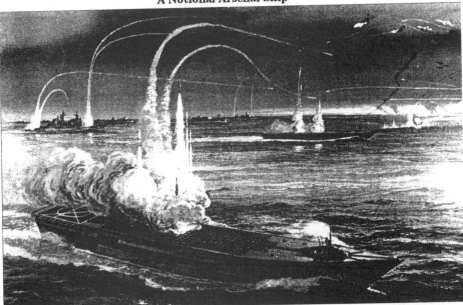

The US Navy's current warship production is limited to one class, the DDG-51 destroyer. While the DDG-51 is today's finest warship, it would make sense to have other options on the drawing board. From a standardization standpoint, a single type or size of warship fleet has its advantages, but a variety of capabilities and associated acquisition and operational costs provide options to force structure architects as well as fleet commanders. In addition to the arsenal ship, the following two warship concepts are representative designs for a future surface fleet:

● a relatively light warship of approximately 5,000t with a very low-signature profile; and
● A 25,000t, heavy combatant, power-projection (aviation-capable) capital warship that could act totally on its own in certain situations.

With these three new designs—the arsenal ship, the light combatant and heavy combatant—US fleet commanders will have the choice of task forces comprised of a combination of ship sizes of 5,000t, 10,000t, 20,000t, 25,000t, 40,000t, and 94,000t. Not every navy will have such a large choice—even after the substantial downsizing of the fleet, the US Navy is still larger than those of France, Germany, Italy, Japan, the Netherlands, Spain and the UK put together.

The light combatant's potential operations include:

● control of missiles to take out high-value targets, whether missiles are launched from the light combatant or from the Arsenal Ship using cooperative engagement capability;

- interdiction;
- naval gunfire support, using a future naval gun;
- intelligence gathering;
- helicopter operations in support of all mission areas using either ASW or attack helicopters; and
- escort operations.

The key innovative capabilities and features of a future light combatant will be:

**Figure 2**
**A Notional Future Light Combatant**

- a substantially more advanced combat system than current frigates;
- an advanced distributed computer system to allow the ship to be operated by a small crew with extremely high system redundancy, leading to significantly increased survivability;
- substantially improved seakeeping, thus increasing the helicopter operational envelope, provided through the use of an alternative hull form;
- a fully integrated electric drive and electrical distribution system; and
- passive and active signature control.

The heavy combatant provides through-deck ship short take-off and vertical landing (STOVL) capability It is stealthy, with modular weapons and sensors, including a multi-function radar and low probability intercept communications.

The heavy combatant would be the cooperative engagement master to the arsenal ship slave, to provide a robust launching platform for a deep precision strike capability. The US Navy has noting like this ship in its current inventory. In service, the heavy combatant would:

- provide real operational punch, when matched with the light combatant, creating the flexibility and balanced mix to the surface combatant force structure of the future;
- act as the centrepiece of an independent surface ship strike force, bringing ship and joint operations command and control capability;
- carry offensive firepower in land-attack missiles;
- capacity for 200-300 missiles; and
- provide battlespace superiority and serve as a launch platform for STOVL aircraft and UAVs.

**Figure 3**
**A Notional Future Heavy Combatant**

It is expected that the heavy combatant will incorporate the best advanced technologies, which hopefully would have been tested on a surface ship technology demonstrator developed and built prior to the design of the first operational fleet ship.

## Technology Demonstration

The history of surface warship design has reached a pivotal point, and navies must focus their research and development (R&D) efforts on systems, which will provide the capabilities of future warships as enumerated above. Also, navies must ensure that design decisions are not frozen too soon, before the newly developed systems become available. Last, but not least, the traditional lead ship concept for warship acquisition must be abandoned, to allow technology and operational demonstrators to be built first.

Innovations in naval warfare emerge from systems. New systems in turn depend on both new and tested technology. R&D generally nurtures scientific underpinnings and inventions and development of component technologies, but stops short of forming the systems that lead to warfare innovations.

Achieving innovation in warships and other new military systems requires that individual technological innovations be incorporated into systems. Systems must be synthesised into complete entity designs, and these designs need to be demonstrated in real, complete, and executable full-scale hardware—in full-up warships. Otherwise, most naval R&D programmes remain exercises in untested paper concepts and some interesting component and equipment improvements.

If revolutionary technologies, critical to new warship designs, are not fully tested prior to starting into critical stages of the acquisition cycle, it is highly unlikely that the programme will achieve the goal of being revolutionary.

What has differentiated the design and development of warships from other major military hardware is that for warships, navies rarely practise "fly before buy." Navies rarely build test-and-throw-away ships as they do with aircraft. In the case of warships, the first unit is expected to serve a full career, and the vessel's regular crew must play the same role as the test pilots of new aircraft. It is not usual to put out into the fleet one or two ships of a new design and wait for feedback from the fleet. But it should be.

With warships, the degree of difficulty is increased because of the high unit price. Navies have taken the approach of calling the first of a new design the lead ship. Unfortunately, however, just as the name implies, a lead ship is just that: the first in a large series production. Thus, the ship programme manager is charged with a certain schedule for delivering warships one after another, under fairly strict cost targets. This forces innovation and experimentation to take a back seat.

Why persist in doing it that way? Why build a new class of ship if it does not contain revolutionary improvements in performance resulting from new technologies that we know how to incorporate into newly created systems? Full-scale system demonstration is an approach which gives the naval community an opportunity to experiment with proposed systems in ways that go beyond simulations. Finally, tests help satisfy skeptics and build organisational confidence in specific innovations.

Therefore, a full-scale warship demonstrator programme has to be initiated before a commitment to build a whole new class. This is needed because the types of new systems, which will create the revolutionary new designs, are ones which permeate the whole ship. They include: drastic manning reduction, integrated power systems, stealth, and distributed computing.

It is hard to imagine a navy buying off on such major changes on the basis of simulation alone. Systems would have to be proven at sea before navies could accept these revolutionary new systems comprising the next warship design. The sweeping nature of the contemplated innovations entails a degree of risk only acceptable after a full-scale demonstration. Also, a full-scale demonstrator can serve as the basis for production cost reductions. Thus, technology maturation should be the pacing element for the development schedule of a new class of warships.

Navies should not rush into new design and build programmes. There is no point in using the same technologies that exist in current designs, or technologies with minor improvements, because numerous new technologies in various stages of development could enable revolutionary new features and systems. Table 1 shows the wide array of promising technologies, which could constitute the systems of future surface combatants. These could create the revolutionary new surface combatant designs—the hardware— which will enable the revolutionary naval warfare concepts of the future.

As it should be in a warship, the emphasis is on the combat systems side. Of the seven areas designated, only one—Hull, Mechanical & Electrical (HM&E)—impacts the platform, and the combat system. Nevertheless, such HM&E technologies as signature reduction, integrated power systems, modular production, fibreoptics, and new hullforms, along with manning reduction, are potent elements of the innovations expected for future warship designs.

### Table 1
### SYSTEMS ARCHITECTURE
Integrated computing networks, decision aids/algorithms, automated systems control

| Air/space superiority | Undersea warfare | Power projection |
|---|---|---|
| CEC | Shallow-water | Land-attack missiles |
| TBMD | sensors/weapons | NSFS [Naval Surface |
| Solid-state radars | Non-acoustic ASW | Fire Support] |
| Multi-mode missile | Advance tactical | guns/warheads |
| Multi-spectrum seekers | displays | Auto-target |
| | | recognition systems |
| **HM&E** | **Manpower** | **Joint C⁴I** |
| Signature reduction | Remote equipment | Secure wideband |
| Integrated power | monitoring | data links |
| systems | Fault-tolerant systems | Conformal antenna arrays |
| Modular production | Multi-function consoles | Wideband LPI |
| Radically new hull form | Condition-based | techniques |
| Fibreoptics | maintenance | IR sensors |
| | Autonomic principles | Offboard ECM |

## Summary

Whether attacking the land from the sea, or defending naval forces at sea or near land, or defending forces that have already landed ashore, future surface combatants will be the platform of choice to accomplish these tasks. Surface combatants will not do this job all by themselves, but will spearhead such operations.

If fleets are to be balanced so that they can respond to their traditional open-ocean warfare role and to their newly acquired mission in the littoral, navies must build their next series of warships with a focus on the littoral mission. Some envision this mission to be one in which a variety of warships stand-off at least 480km away. Thus, with a variety of warheads under development today, future warships will become "buses" for munitions delivered by new ballistic missiles as well as advanced GPS-guided cruise missiles, which can suppress enemy radars, burst bunkers buried deep underground, stop columns of advancing armour (remotely controllable TLAM [Tomahawk land attack missile], armed with a variety of anti-armour submunition weapons), and create havoc in the all-important logistic "tail" of ones foes.

Thus, new systems based on emerging technologies promise to provide the surface combatant of the 21st century with capabilities which guarantee its reemergence as a primary instrument of naval warfare. Information and distance will be the hallmarks of the next naval revolution. Information acquired, processed, fused, displayed, and disseminated will enable development of a coherent tactical picture, real-time targeting and battlespace dominance. A vastly enlarged battlespace will be dominated by the dramatically improved offensive and defensive capabilities of the future surface combatant and the tactics and doctrine which will employ them in exciting new ways.

Great ships—as great navies—are built by countries with strong global economies. As a rule, such countries seek global presence to support global economies and they build those ships that convincingly add to the effectiveness of their foreign policy interests. Because of this, there is a cautionary note to draw. In Paul Kennedy's words in his book *The Rise and Fall of British Naval Mastery* (1976), "the whole problem is whether a democracy is willing in peacetime to meet the calls of those who urge military readiness in case of war."

The modern surface warships described here will not reach their zenith unless people of one or more great countries clearly see the utility—indeed the revolutionary power—that comes from such a major investment in technology and steel. Only if such ships can be used to reduce regional conflicts effectively (witness the impact of Tomahawk on the Bosnian peace process), will we see new surface combatants achieve the prominence once held by the great sailing men-of-war, the battleships of a century ago, or the aircraft carriers and submarines of the last half-century.

In other words, the ascendancy of the surface combatant will occur not only because we have the technology, but because we have the global need for such ships and because we clearly see the success such ships bring in meeting these global needs. One does not build a warship in a vacuum. Warships and their embedded technology will shape policy, as Paul Kennedy recognized when speaking of the British fleet at an earlier date: "A great deal of this eagerness for battle can also be attributed to the superiority of British gunnery" (*Ibid*, p.

127). Thus, while the "art of the possible" determined by technology does influence policy, in the long run, political and economic interests of countries, along with resulting investment priorities in defence, will be the most essential ingredients in determining the future fleet structure of the world's navies.

# Chapter 42

\* \* \*

# New World Vistas: Air and Space Power for the 21st Century

USAF Scientific Advisory Board

*The Air Force Scientific Advisory Board draws parallels in this report to the board's first study fifty years ago. Then, it points out, emphasis on technology and capability, rather than assumptions about specific future geopolitical scenarios, served the nation well. This study, too, attempts to define capabilities and technologies that transcend particular missions and apply to all scenarios. The study's authors suggest that their recommendations do not fit into neat, well defined categories, but rather have technological threads that run through many future applications. Knowledge, control of information, space assets, accurate position and timing, material development and reduced cycle time are all themes in this report. One of their fundamental question is: "What are the discontinuous changes in the future and how are they enabled by technology?" Has the Board focused on the correct concepts and technologies for "The Future Force?" Do you agree with their recommendations for "What the Air Force Should Do?"*

In the fiftieth year of the Air Force Scientific Advisory Board, both the Air Force and the Nation are at the brink of a new era. Our Cold War adversary no longer exists, and we now face threats which are not precisely defined. The situation is further complicated by changing alliances as much as by the absence of well known adversaries. Armed conflict around the world shows us that the world is still a hostile place, but responses which may have been appropriate during the Cold War are no longer appropriate. There appears, however, to be even more widespread pressure for the United States to remain a stabilizing force throughout the globe. Our military forces are involved in dangerous

From USAF Scientific Advisory Board, *New World Vistas: Air and Space Power for the 21st Century*, Summary Volume, pp. iii-iv, 4-5, 8-14, 41, 57-62. (Washington, DC: Department of the Air Force, 15 December 1995). Portions of the text and some footnotes have been omitted.

Reprinted from "New World Vistas: Air & Space Power for the 21st Century," Summary Volume, USAF Scientific Advisory Board, 15 December 1995.

humanitarian and peacekeeping operations at an increasing rate, and anti-terrorist operations can be expected to increase as well. Although participation in these operations may require military action, we are expected to respond effectively with minimum injury and loss of life on both sides. Further, the domain of conflict is moving from earth into space and even into cyberspace. The balance of influence in the information domain has shifted from defense organizations to commercial organizations, and a similar shift will occur in space during the next decade. The crucial importance of detailed and timely knowledge and rapid communications to the successful pursuit of our new missions will demand creative use of commercial systems and technologies. This will produce an intimate intertwining of commercial and military applications to an extent not yet encountered. The intertwining will blur the distinction between threat and asset, offense and defense, and, even, friend and foe. Our future enemies, whoever they may be, will obtain knowledge and weapons better then those we have at present by making rather small investments. New sensor fusion and distributed processing capabilities will make operational distinctions such as onboard and offboard or space and ground obsolete. The rapid operation tempo enabled by complete and current knowledge, the operational demands generated by new missions, and the geographical constraints produced by a decreasing number of worldwide bases will require weapons system performance beyond that of existing systems. New technologies will permit improvement of existing systems, but new systems and new concepts will be needed to cope with the world of the 21st century.

There are strong analogies and contrasts between the world situation today and that at the time of the first Scientific Advisory Board study, *Toward New Horizons*, fifty years ago. We had won a devastating world war in 1945. In 1995, we have won the Cold War—a war less bloody, but one which always had the possibility of destroying most of civilization. In both cases, we eliminated the threat from a powerful enemy, but then and now we have understood that preparedness and technological superiority are the keys to national security. After 1945, the United States moved to establish bases and influence abroad, but in 1995 we are reducing our physical presence abroad while we attempt to maintain a moral presence. It was clear in 1945 that the technology gains of the first half of the twentieth century should be consolidated to create a superior, technology- and capability-based Air Force which could respond to threats not yet imagined. The world which emerged from the destruction of World War II could not have been predicted in 1945, but the emphasis on technology and capability rather than on assumptions about future geopolitical scenarios served us well as we entered the Cold War. In the intervening 50 years, we have treated increasingly specific problems related to the Soviet threat. Now, that threat has disappeared. It is appropriate to return to the idea that development of broad superior capabilities through application of new technology will maintain the United States Air Force as the most powerful and effective aerospace force in the world and will enable the Air Force to discharge its responsibilities as an equal partner with the other Services in the defense of the Nation.

These considerations and the broad applications of new, largely commercial, technologies which are now, or soon to be, possible have led us to present the conclusions of the participants of *New World Vistas* as an integrated, capability-based, report. Realization of these capabilities will permit future members of the Air Force of all ranks to know, to plan, to act, and to evaluate in the detail appropriate to their responsibilities. One should not doubt that the 21st century Air Force which will be enabled and, indeed, demanded by its new capabilities and responsibilities will hardly be similar to the Air Force of today. The changes will be as profound as those experienced by the Army in moving from horse to tank or by the Navy in converting from sail to steam. . . .

## Fundamental Considerations

We have attempted to define capabilities and technologies that transcend particular missions and apply to all scenarios. We have not divided our recommendations into neat, well-defined categories. We tried, but we found that the power of the technologies and concepts that we recommend is that each cuts across several fundamental capabilities. . . . For example, knowledge and control of information is necessary for all missions, whether in peace or war, logistics or combat. All missions depend on communications and reconnaissance and, therefore, increasingly on space assets. As space assets become increasingly important, space control becomes a necessary part of all missions. Throughout the Force, the necessity of accurate, absolute positioning and timing is apparent. The most efficient way to supply this service is through space assets such as an enhanced, countermeasure-immune Global Positioning System (GPS). A technological thread which runs through many future applications is materials development. Strong, lightweight materials and structures will enable many capabilities in space, aircraft, and weapons.

We know that reduced cycle time is a true force multiplier. It is characteristic of reduced cycle time that all components of the Force must operate at a higher tempo. If an airlifter is late with supplies, an attack mission will be delayed, and the choreography of an entire operation can be disrupted. The sensor systems that enable precision delivery of munitions can also be used in aircraft self protection. Technologies and functions will influence all capabilities. The Force will become so tightly integrated in function, and will be so tightly coupled to allies and the other services that boundaries between capabilities will become blurred if they exist at all.

For the purposes of *New World Vistas*, we have assumed that:

- The Air Force will have to fight at large distances from the United States. Some operations may be staged directly from the Continental United States (CONUS). Operations may persist for weeks or months, and they must be executed day and night in all weather.
- The site of the next conflict in unknown. The Air Force must be prepared to fight or to conduct mobility or special operations anywhere in the world on short notice.
- Weapons must be highly accurate, must minimize collateral damage, must minimize delivery and acquisition costs, and must enhance, and be enhance by, aircraft capabilities.
- Platforms that deliver weapons must be lethal and survivable. They must establish air superiority in areas that are heavily populated with surface to air missiles (SAM's), and they must carry the attack to all enemy targets, fixed and mobile.
- Adversaries may be organized national forces or terrorist groups.
- Targets may be fixed or mobile and may be well concealed. Target classes will span the range from personnel to armored vehicles and protected command centers and information systems. Operational geography will range from classical battlefields to cities and jungles.
- Adversary capabilities will steadily improve and will be difficult to anticipate. For example, the Air Force must be prepared to defend against improved SAM's, low observable aircraft, cruise missiles, directed energy weapons, and information attack.
- The Air Force must detect and destroy chemical, biological, and nuclear weapons and their production facilities.
- There will be peacetime missions in areas of local conflict. Aircraft must be protected against SAM's and ground fire by means other than offensive attack.
- Increasing the pace of operations increases the effectiveness of all operations.
- Cost will be equal in importance to capability.
- The number of people in the Air Force will decrease. Individual performance must be optimized. . . .

## The Future Force

What are the discontinuous changes of the future, and how are they enabled by technology? Both concepts and technologies are described in detail in subsequent volumes. In this volume we delineate the major features. We will set the stage for the discussions that follow by describing the Air Force that will be built from the concepts and technologies proposed.

***There will be a mix of inhabited and uninhabited aircraft.*** We use the term "uninhabited" rather than "unpiloted" or "unmanned" to distinguish the aircraft enabled by the new technologies from those now in operation or planned. The "unmanned" aircraft of the present have particular advantages such as cost or endurance, but they are either cruise missiles or reconnaissance vehicles. The "uninhabited" combat aircraft (UCAV) are new, high performance aircraft that are more effective for particular missions than are their inhabited counterparts.

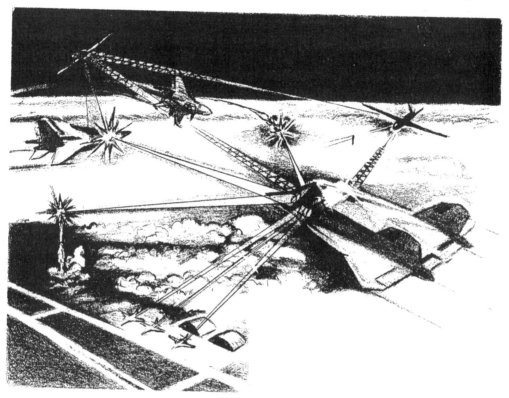

The UCAV is enabled by information technologies, but it enables the use of aircraft and weapon technologies that cannot be used in an aircraft that contains a human. There will be missions during the next three decades that will benefit from having a human present, but for many missions the uninhabited aircraft will provide capabilities far superior to those of its inhabited cousins. For example, shape and function will not be constrained by a cockpit, a human body, or an ejection seat. We believe that the design freedom generated will allow a reduction in radar cross section by at least 12 dB in the frequency bands currently addressed, compared to existing aircraft. A 12 dB reduction in aircraft cross section will reduce the effective range of enemy radar by a factor of two and area coverage by a factor of four. At this point we reach the limit of passive radar cross section reduction, and active methods must be developed. Also, reduction of infrared emissions is an important area where substantial improvements can be made. Other advantages of the UCAV will be described later. There is the possibility of extending UCAV performance into the hypersonic range to enable strikes from the CONUS on high value targets in minutes.

*Large and small aircraft will project weapons.* At present we think of large aircraft as bombers, tankers, surveillance aircraft, or air launched cruise missile (ALCM) launch platforms. In the future large aircraft will be the first to carry directed energy weapons, and their entry into combat as formidable tactical weapons will cause a discontinuous change in aerospace warfare. Eventually, after establishing their value aboard aircraft, directed energy weapons will move into space. Small UCAVs can be carried aboard and launched from large aircraft to provide intercontinental standoff capability.

Explosive weapons will be substantially more accurate than those of today, and explosive effectiveness per unit mass will be higher by at least a factor of ten than those of today. As a result, a sortie of the future can be ten times more effective than one of today. Weapon types will range from inexpensive enhanced accuracy weapons without sensors to GPS directed weapons with better than one foot accuracy to microsensor directed microexplosive systems that kill moving targets with grams of explosive.

*We must extend airlift capabilities.* The current generation of military airlifters and commercial transport aircraft will be useful for the next three decades, but replicating these aircraft with evolutionary upgrades will not provide the necessary capabilities. Even the addition of the Civil Reserve Air Fleet (CRAF) cannot provide enough airlift capacity for the future, and while commercial airlifters will form an important component of the future airlift fleet, their capabilities are limited, and they cannot be exchanged one for one with military airlifters. The future airlifter should be large ($10^6$ pounds gross takeoff weight), efficient (1.3-1.5 times current aircraft), and long range (12,000 nm). It should have point-of-use delivery capability through precision airdrop as a routine delivery process. Full airdrop capability will reduce theater infrastructure requirements for both the Air Force and the Army at forward locations. Rapid tempo of operations will require rapid resupply. As we take advantage of the operational possibilities enabled by technology, the Air Force of the future will be limited by logistics considerations just as surely as were the forces of Hannibal and Napoleon. We must pay close attention.

*The future force will become efficient and effective through the use of information systems to enhance U.S. operations and to confound the enemy.* The infancy of this capability is represented today in the F-22. Information and Space will become inextricably entwined. The Information/Space milieu will interact strongly with the air and ground components, and it is here that commercial technologies and systems will have the largest presence. Defense will not be a driver of important technologies in this area. Surveillance and reconnaissance will be done worldwide from commercial platforms, and international conglomerates may own some of those platforms. High resolution mapping services from space will be purchased. Worldwide weather monitoring will be possible, although current systems are not capable of adequate precision. Precise timing and positioning services will be provided by a new ultra precise, jam resistant Global Positioning System (GPS). Communication of information and instructions throughout the Force will be instantaneous over fiber and satellite networks. Computers and displays will be common, commercial units. Even avionics processors and data busses will be purchased off the shelf. As we improve the capabilities of information equipment, we should remember that the human is an integral part of the system. We must improve the capabilities of the human-machine interface as we improve the machine.

There is an area where development of defense information systems may diverge from development of commercial systems. Those are *systems used in Information Warfare (IW)*. The use of "information munitions" in offensive operations will become an essential component of warfare. The use of "information munitions" will, however, make unusual demands on software and equipment. At present, it appears as though Information Warfare is more of a "bag of tricks" than a system of warfare. As the technologies are better defined, this will change. We must constantly make IW more robust and more effective. Information Warfare has three components. One is the method, or core, of IW which uses computers and software to deceive and destroy enemy information systems. The second component is deployment. Deployment may be as simple as connecting to the Internet, or it may require special communication systems, high power microwave systems, special forces action, or surreptitious individual action. The final component is Defense. Defensive IW will be pursued by the commercial community because of the obvious effects that malicious mischief can have on commerce. The military problem is, however, likely to be different enough that some effort will be required. The commercial solutions should be monitored closely. It is the union of method, deployment, and defense which creates the Information Munition. These components must not become separated if maximum effectiveness is to be achieved.

*Space and space systems will become synonymous with effective operations*. In addition to government investment in military systems, U.S. companies will have large investments in space and information systems. The protection of our assets and the denial of capabilities to an enemy will be essential. The future Force will, eventually, contain space, ground, and airborne weapons that can project photon energy, kinetic energy, and information against space and ground assets. Many space and information weapons will destroy. Others will confuse the enemy and weave the "bodyguard of lies" that will protect our forces.

***Sensors and information sources will be widely distributed.*** Sensors onboard fighter aircraft will continue to be important, but they will form a progressively smaller part of the total information source for combat operations. Fighter-mounted sensors, too, will supply information to companion craft as often as they provide information to their bearer. There will be sensors functioning cooperatively aboard small, distributed satellite constellations, sensors aboard uninhabited reconnaissance aerial vehicles (URAVs), sensors aboard weapons, and sensors on the ground delivered by URAVs. We often speak glibly about enhancing capability through information, but we as often forget that information originates as data from active and passive sensors. The power of the new information systems will lie in their ability to correlate data automatically and rapidly from many sources to form a complete picture of the operational area, whether it be a battlefield or the site of a mobility operation. In particular, the accuracy of a single sensor and processor in identifying targets or threats is severely limited. Detection and identification probabilities increase rapidly with sensor diversity and the false alarm probability and error rates decrease correspondingly.

***Affordability restrictions demand caution at this point.*** For the technologist, the intellectual lure of ultra precise sensors and control systems aboard munitions flying at hypersonic speeds is seductive. But, sensors and control systems constitute a large fraction of the cost of a munition, and we see no substantial change to this situation in the future. We properly laud the improvement in capability generated by precision guided weapons. We sometimes forget, however, that Precision Guided Munitions (PGMs) do not always produce an increased operational advantage proportional to their increase cost. This situation can change as a result of reduced sensor costs in the future or as the result of reduced performance requirements. It will always be cheaper to carry reusable precision sensors aboard a reusable delivery platform and either to eliminate guidance and control on board the munitions entirely or to use rather inaccurate onboard systems. The trade between munition precision and platform precision will, of course, depend on the survivability of the platform at appropriate release distances and the dependence of cost on munition accuracy. It may be possible to reduce the cost of precision delivery by building reusable, close approach delivery platforms that have precision positioning and sensing systems, reproducible weapon release, and wind measuring equipment onboard. Munitions can be built with low drag coefficients. Significant cost reduction will result from the reuse of sensors and processors. The munition can either have no guidance or can have simple inertial or GPS guidance and low precision controls. This option favors the low observable UCAV for attack of mobile and protected targets.

***Finally, the loop must be closed.*** The operational components of the Air Force must plan together, function together, command and be commanded, exchange information, and assess results collegially with each other, other services, and allies. Planning and directing must be done in parallel rather than in series to sustain high rate operations. Plans must be analyzed continuously at all levels by simulation. We refer to the construct that makes this possible as a complete "internetting of nodes" and as a seamless "operation across networks." A node can be an airplane, a general, an Army private, a tank, or a UCAV. A collaborating network may be operated by the U.S. Army or by an allied command. Internetting provides for the nearly direct connection of one of the nodes to any other node. Communication channel, processor, and terminal considerations determine the fundamental physical limitations, but with the exception or radio frequency (RF) channels, these limitations are vanishing as practical limitations to the internetting process. Even RF data channel capacities are increasing as the result of new compression algorithms and error correction schemes. Major difficulties remain, however, in establishing priorities for information transfer and in maintaining adequate security. Capture of nodes must not compromise system integrity. Elimination of these difficulties will be neither easy nor inexpensive. *We must solve the important security problems before the full impact of information sciences can be realized.*

This low resolution snapshot of the Force was intended to give the reader an idea of the extensive enhancement and integration of capabilities that will be possible in future decades. We hope that the applications of the new technologies are so profound that they are obvious and compelling, and we hope that they stimulate the reader to create personally pleasing combinations of capabilities. For example, improved stealth provides higher effectiveness against both aircraft and SAMs in establishing air superiority. Improved aircraft performance, say through UCAVs will increase survivability in high threat areas. Together, stealth and performance will reduce the reliance on electronic countermeasures with an accompanying reduction in cost and system volatility, and when directed by offboard information and passive sensors, they have the surprise value of a silent force. Large airlifters with point of use delivery capability can provide the military equivalent of "just in time" supply from CONUS, if necessary, with cost reductions and efficiency increases that are as large as those realized by commercial industries. Accompanied by airlifters carrying UCAVs and directed energy weapons for self defense, the airlifter fleet will become a survivable offensive weapon system in high threat areas. Distributed space systems can revisit areas of interest at rates not now possible. Distributed space sensors can operate cooperatively with staring sensors aboard Uninhabited Reconnaissance Air Vehicles (URAVs), which continuously monitor important targets, to optimize the collection and use of intelligence information.

*A word about the application of commercial technologies is appropriate.* No one doubts that many commercial technologies are applicable to military problems and that their use can reduce system costs and improve utility. There are, however, obligations concomitant with their use. Commercial technologies accompany commercial practices. We must be prepared to change requirements and operating procedures to agree with commercial practice if we are to make efficient use of commercial technology. *In the fields* of space, communications, *and information, the time from concept to deployment must be no longer than two years. Information systems should be replaced in five years.* Many processes can be improved by an injection of commercial practice, but the price paid for the improvement will be uncertainty in ultimate performance and survivability. Replacement of damaged units will become more acceptable than hardening to reduce cost. A program development culture that generates continuous improvement from humble beginnings rather than ultimate initial performance will be demanded. The new development culture will require an operational culture that can accept less than optimum performance today in exchange for rapid improvement tomorrow. We must demand reduced cycle time in procurement just as we will demand it in execution. . . .

## Revolutionary Concepts in Context

The word "revolutionary" is in common use, and overuse, today. *New World Vistas* proposes concepts that we believe to be revolutionary. The word has been used to mean many things, and it is useful to put the term into a context within which we can discuss new technologies and their use. The word is frequently used to identify a "silver bullet"—a single concept or device that will immediately produce the ascendancy of the user's forces over those of the user's adversaries. The world is not like that. Science, technology, and military inventions are not like that. Nearly always, it is the evolutionary follow-on of a new concept that produces a revolution in capability. For example, the nuclear weapon was the most revolutionary weapon ever invented. It not only changed the nature of warfare but also it changed the nature of all interactions among nations, and it changed the way all science was viewed by the public. The first two nuclear weapons, however useful as a demonstration of the principle, would not, had they been duplicated many times, have had that affect. It was the evolutionary development the thermonuclear weapon from the fission weapon coupled with the evolution of the ICBM from the V-2 that produced the profound effects on society. Frequently, too, it is the association of well-known principles in an innovative way that produces the revolutionary result. The geometric arrangement of junction voltages between semiconductors in an unusual way produced a transistor. The evolutionary development of Complimentary Metal-Oxide Semiconductor (CMOS) and integrated circuits has led to the information revolution.

Thus, we can seldom expect to produce truly revolutionary effects with the first manifestation of a new technology. In recognition of this fact, demonstrations should not include all aspects of a new technology. Smaller steps should be taken to minimize the total cost and to permit more flexibility. The first attempt to apply new concepts is a necessary, but not sufficient step. In military systems, the second step in the development of a radically new concept must be determined after operational deployment. The warfighters will use the system in innovative ways not described in the manuals, and it is this experience that will define the path to revolution.

We should keep some general guidelines in mind:

- The relationship between revolutionary and evolutionary concepts is complex and complementary.
- Revolutionary ideas often point the way to later applications which are far more useful than the original idea.
- Early applications of revolutionary concepts should not be required to be complete and final weapons systems.
- Identification and development of revolutionary concepts require intuition, innovation, and acceptance of substantial risk.
- We must be prepared for a failure rate greater than 50 percent.
- Most revolutionary ideas will be opposed by a majority of decision makers.
- We must remember that science and science fiction are related only superficially. . . .

### What the Air Force Should Do

*Global Awareness.* A future goal of the Air Force should be to know at all times the relevant global military situation given the existing political and economic conditions and the state of military conflict. Such awareness should be in near real time (in time enough to understand and act) and with near real perfect knowledge (knowledge good enough to make good decisions in the time available to decide and act). This is the idea of Global Awareness. Some will argue, and we do not disagree, that this is or is not a part of Information Warfare. In this regard, we recognize the importance of Information Warfare in the future and that much of what we present . . . is Information Warfare said another way. The key technologies to make Global Awareness possible lie in the right mix and integration of sensors, communications, and processing to collect data and convert it into information and knowledge in a meaningful time frame over the area of interest. . . . A top level list of the relevant technologies are outlined without comment as follows:

- Clusters of cooperating satellites
  - Precision station keeping
  - Autonomous satellite operations
  - Signal processing for sparse apertures
- Laser cross and down links
- Precise global positioning, time transfer, and mapping
- Large, sensitive focal plane arrays and associated read out
- Radiation resistant satellites and components
- Spectral sensing at all relevant wavelengths
- Active sensors
  - Large light weight antennas
  - High efficiency radio frequency sources
  - High energy lasers
- Micro-electro-mechanical systems
- Communications and networking
- Automated fusion
- Automated target recognition

*Dynamic Planning and Execution Control*. The first step toward acquisition of Dynamic Planning and Execution Control capability is to *make this idea or concept part of Air Force and Joint Doctrine*. Next is to *pursue a joint architecture* definition to implement the doctrine. The concept of Dynamic Planning and Execution Control is to exploit the Global Awareness acquired through the technologies just listed above. As such, this idea will make possible the most efficient use of the mobility, power projection, space operations and people associated with the military capabilities of the United States. The attainment of relevant Global Awareness and its exploitation through Dynamic Planning and Execution Control will be a high leverage capability to win America's future wars quickly, decisively, with minimum or no human losses (on both sides). As with Global Awareness . . . this topic is replete with information warfare aspects and can be viewed in that context as well as in the functional categories used for this presentation. The following technologies summary applies to support Dynamic Planning and Execution Control:

- Support for Planning. Faster than real time interactive, predictive, continuous running simulations for planning and mission rehearsal will be the driving technology for planning future employment of air and space power.
- Support to mission execution. Execution of the plan is where the true flexibility and speed of employment of air and space power will be realized. Technologies which permit near real time changes and updates to on-board databases as well as other planning and situational awareness databases will be key. Rapid capture of information from onboard sensors, including the crew, into these databases will also be very important. Finally, concurrent faster than real time simulations for near real time mission execution, planning, and attack will insure we remain inside any enemy's timeline for action.

*Global Mobility in War and Peace*. The United States military has a long tradition of going where necessary in the world to conduct military and peaceful operations. Such a capability will perhaps be even more important in the 21st century. The Air Force brings speed and reach to the global mobility equation. The current introduction of the C-17 will serve the country well as we enter the next millennium. The following technology areas are recommended to make a difference in the use of the C-17 and after the C-17.

- *Point of Use Delivery*. The idea here is that supplies delivered by aerial transport should be delivered directly to where they are to be used without landing the transport aircraft. Delivery of medical supplies beside the hospitals, food directly to the soldier or feeding facility, and weapon system load and reload ammunition to the weapon in its firing position are possible examples. Secure dependable communications, precision airdrop, multi-spectral sensors for weather and intelligence, intransit visibility of cargo, aircraft situational awareness and aircraft self protection are the key technologies.
- *Low Cost Precision Airdrop*. A key driver in making "point of use delivery" possible will be the need for a low cost way to dispense air cargo in modules, containers, or pallets with appropriate guidance, control and arresting mechanisms. A proper balance of expendable and reusable components is needed to achieve the results within a reasonable cost.
- *The "Million Pound" Airlifter*. Thinking needs to begin now for the next generation airlifter. High lift over drag wing/airframe design and testing needs to begin. Engineered materials, high temperature engine components, composite fabrication and fastening, and next generation material for airframe and skin are needed.

*Projection of Lethal and Sublethal Power*. The four major technology directions that the Air Force should pursue to project lethal and sublethal power in the 21st century are as follows. . . .

- *Uninhabited Combat Aerial Vehicles (UCAV)*. As this technology is developed it will offer potential for significantly more capable weapon systems at lower cost. Such vehicles serendipitously accommodate the probably inexorable trend of American society which are more and more expecting no human losses during U.S. military operations. The technologies to realize the UCAV include new high efficiency, high supersonic engines; advanced structures; avionics, control systems, and observables; very high altitude/low speed cruise, very small/miniaturized "micro-air vehicles"; very high dynamic pressure cruise vehicles; intelligent signal and data processing; secure and possibly redundant control data links; control science and applications for mission and vehicle management of a complex, highly coupled system, control criteria to achieve optimal performance based on that used for missile control; and human/machine interface for off board air vehicle control.
- *High Power Microwave and High Power Laser Directed Energy Weapons*. Speed of light weapons with the full spectrum of capability to deny, disrupt, degrade and/or destroy will leap past and could eventually replace many traditional explosive driven weapons and self protection countermeasure systems. There are five innovative technologies required for "energy frugal" practical directed energy weapons. They are large, light-weight optics, HPM antennas using thin membrane

fabrication; high-power short-wavelength solid-state lasers; high average-power phase conjugation; new approaches to adaptive optics and phased arrays of diode lasers.

- *Stealth-the Next Plateau.* Active radio frequency and next generation passive infrared stealth capability will replace what we have today with another quantum leap forward in vehicle survivability.
- *Hypersonic Air Breathing Platforms/Vehicles.* Even with the tremendous increase in space operations in the future there will continue to be a major place for air breathing platforms/vehicles. Time is now, always has been, and even more so in the information age future, will be of the essence in military operations especially those of the Air Force. All distances on the earth are fixed. If the Air Force is to execute faster than an enemy in the 21st century, then to reduce time, the only alternative is to go faster. Hypersonic air breathing flight is as natural as supersonic flight. Advanced cycle, dual mode ramjet/scramjet engines and high temperature, lighter weight materials which allow for long range, long endurance, high altitude supercruise are the enabling technologies.

**Space Operations.** Space Operations will grow rapidly as a factor in United States military capabilities limited primarily by affordable access. Space operations already contribute much to global observation and global situational awareness. Space control and projection of force from space technologies will become as important in the 21st century as space becomes more available to many countries of the world.

- *Access to Space.* Affordable access to space will require many advances in technology. Such technology includes lower mass of the components for power, energy storage and conversion, attitude control, propulsion, large-thrust, high-specific impulse chemical propulsion, multi-functional structures that integrate spacecraft bus functions into the structure of the spacecraft itself, high temperature materials, ultra-light-weight integrated cryogenic structures and miniaturized sensors.
- *Global Observation and Situational Awareness.* Sensors, the conversion of sensor data to information and knowledge, the necessary communications to move the data, information and knowledge when and where needed are necessary for global observation and situational awareness. Although such activity may be conducted in both the air and space medium, the use of space will continue to grow and begin to dominate in the 21st century. The technical trades and costs associated with global observation and situational awareness from either air or space will have to be made as the decisions to replace or improve current capabilities are faced. In the mean time, there are many technologies needed regardless of whether the job is done from air or space. These technologies are outlined in the previous section on Global Awareness.
- *Space Control Technologies.* The Air Force must begin to think and bring forward the technologies necessary for space control. Capabilities to defend our own space based resources and to disrupt, degrade, deny or destroy that of the enemy will be needed sooner or later in the 21st century. The technologies needed to protect our space resources from enemies include high thrust, high specific impulse electric propulsion, large constellations of low cost satellites with distributed functionality

or networking across the system and autonomous guidance and navigation.

• *Force Projection from Space.* The laser directed energy weapon mentioned above in the "Projection of Lethal and Sub-lethal Power" section may be employed from space. Alternatively, the laser can be ground based with directing mirrors deployed in space. Short wavelength, electric lasers along with large optics and antenna technology will be needed. In addition, for space deployment of the laser, large electrical prime power such as nuclear or power beaming along with power storage in advanced capacitors or secondary advanced flywheels will need to be pursued. The sensor, communications and autonomous guidance and navigation technology needs mentioned above will contribute to force projection from space.

*People*. There can be no question as we enter the 21st century that the idea of the individual's central importance will continue to be a driving force in our culture. As such, the expectation of the American people (perhaps unrealistic but nonetheless powerful) is that there should be almost no casualties during the conduct of military operations. In addition to the capabilities and technologies mentioned above, attention must be paid to the technologies which will improve the human part of the military capability equation. Those entrusted with the defense of our country must be well trained, able to control and work with machines and information systems in the most efficient way and be mentally physically superior within moral and ethical bounds to any enemy. The five human-related technology areas that will allow significant improvements in human performance are summarized as follows.

• *Training.* Training can be significantly improved and made less expensive through personnel selection and classification technologies which more closely match skills and aptitudes to the task. In addition, interactive individual and group training using virtual reality and other distributed interactive simulation where appropriate will be the training technologies of the 21st century.

• *Human/Machine System Fusion.* Voice recognition and voice generation, gesture recognition and response, multi-lingual translation and generation and brain control of computer technologies will all contribute to making sure that the human is not the limiting factor in rapid exploitation of Global Awareness through Dynamic Planning and Execution Control.

• *Operational.* In order to better understand, design and operate the weapon systems of the next century a more detailed understanding of the human is needed. Technologies associated with cognitive and non-cognitive models of the human learner and of the instructional process are needed. Such understanding not only will help with the training needs listed above, but will make possible the most cost effective human machine fusion in such areas as displays and controls, brain control of computers, etc.

• *Biological.* Technologies which temporarily enhance human performance and provide for emergency mission extension should be developed. The technologies should be brought forward into capabilities under the social and ethical standards of our country and leave no short or long term after effects. It is expected these capabilities will only be used on the most difficult and dangerous missions. We owe with proper controls, such capability to our people who must do the military job just as much as we do the best tank, ship or aircraft if we truly believe that wars are best fought to win quickly, decisively and with no or minimum human losses.

• *Scientific and Technical Personnel Management.* Air Force leadership from the days of General Hap Arnold to the current Chief and the Secretary recognize that science and technology is the life force of our country's air and space capability. We must have a path for more scientific and technical officers to attain the highest positions in our Air Force. . . .

# Chapter 43

## * * *

## America's Information Edge

Joseph S. Nye, Jr. and William A. Owens

*Joseph S. Nye, Jr., and William A. Owens assert that more than ever before knowledge is power. The United States is the one country that can best lead the information revolution; consequently, it will continue to be more powerful than any other. Dominating as it does important communications and information processing technologies, this advantage can help deter or defeat traditional military threats at relatively low cost. However, contend the authors, information's "soft-power" edge—the attraction of American democracy and free markets—is equally important as a force multiplier, often replacing more traditional tools of American statecraft. A strategy based on the United States' information edge has some prerequisites. These include adequate funding of related technologies, appropriate sharing of information, and the maintenance of diplomatic and public broadcast channels. Most important is the preservation of the kind of healthy democracy at home that is at the heart of America's soft power appeal around the world. Is "soft power" as important to a nation desiring an "information edge" as the power associated with military systems? If the authors are correct, what are the implications for strategists and military force planners?*

### The Power Resource of the Future

K nowledge, more than ever before, is power. The one country that can best lead the information revolution will be more powerful than any other. For the foreseeable future, the country is the United States. America has apparent strength in military power and economic production. Yet its more subtle comparative advantage is its ability to collect, process, act upon, and disseminate

Joseph S. Nye, Jr., former Chairman of the National Intelligence Council and Assistant Secretary of Defense for International Affairs in the Clinton administration, is Dean of the John F. Kennedy School of Government at Harvard University. Admiral William A. Owens is former Vice Chairman of the Joint Chiefs of Staff in the Clinton administration.

Reprinted by permission of *Foreign Affairs*, Vol. 75, No. 2, March/April 1996, pp. 20-36.
Copyright © 1996 by the Council of Foreign Relations, Inc.

information, an edge that will almost certainly grow over the next decade. This advantage stems from Cold War investments and America's open society, thanks to which it dominates important communications and information processing technologies—space-based surveillance, direct broadcasting, high-speed computers—and has an unparalleled ability to integrate complex information systems.

This information advantage can help deter or defeat traditional military threats at relatively low cost. In a world in which the meaning of containment, the nuclear umbrella, and conventional deterrence have changed, the information advantage can strengthen the intellectual link between U.S. foreign policy and military power and offer new ways of maintaining leadership in alliances and ad hoc coalitions.

The information edge is equally important as a force multiplier of American diplomacy, including "soft power"—the attraction of American democracy and free markets.[1] The United States can use its information resources to engage China, Russia, and other powerful states in security dialogues to prevent them from becoming hostile. At the same time, its information edge can help prevent states like Iran and Iraq, already hostile, from becoming powerful. Moreover, it can bolster new democracies and communicate directly with those living under undemocratic regimes. This advantage is also important in efforts to prevent and resolve regional conflicts and deal with prominent post-Cold War dangers, including international crime, terrorism, proliferation of weapons of mass destruction, and damage to the global environment.

Yet two conceptual problems prevent the United States from realizing its potential. The first is that outmoded thinking clouds the appreciation of information as power. Traditional measures of military force, gross national product, population, energy, land, and minerals have continued to dominate discussions of the balance of power. These power resources still matter, and American leadership continues to depend on them as well as on the information edge. But these measures failed to anticipate the demise of the Soviet Union, and they are an equally poor means of forecasting for the exercise of American leadership into the next century.

In assessing power in the information age, the importance of technology, education, and institutional flexibility has risen, whereas that of geography, population, and raw materials has fallen. Japan adapted to these changes through growth in the 1980s far better than by pursuing territorial conquest in the 1930s. In neglecting information, traditional measures of the balance of power have failed to anticipate the key developments of the last decade: the Soviet Union's fall, Japan's rise, and the continuing prominence of the United States.

The second conceptual problem has been a failure to grasp the nature of information. It is easy to trace and forecast the growth of capabilities to process and exchange information. The information revolution, for example, clearly is in its formative stages, but one can foresee that the next step will involve the convergence of key technologies, such as digitization, computers, telephones, televisions, and precise global positioning. But to capture the implications of growing information capabilities, particularly the interactions among them, is far more difficult. Information power is also hard to categorize because it cuts across all other military, economic, social, and political power resources, in some cases diminishing the strength, in others multiplying it.

The United States must adjust its defense and foreign policy strategy to reflect its growing, comparative advantage in information resources. Part of this adjustment will entail purging conceptual vestige. Some of the lingering Cold War inhibitions on sharing intelligence, for example, keep the United States from seizing new opportunities. Some of the adjustment will require innovation in existing institutions. Information agencies need not remain Cold War relics, as some in Congress describe them, but should be used as instruments that can be more powerful, cost effective, and flexible than ever before. Likewise, the artificially sharp distinction between military and political assets has kept the United States from suppressing hate propaganda that has incited ethnic conflicts.

## Military Capability and Information

The character of U.S. military forces is changing, perhaps much more rapidly than most appreciate, for, driven by the information revolution, a revolution in military affairs is at hand. This American-led revolution stems from advances in several technologies and, more important, from the ability to tie these developments together and build the doctrines, strategies, and tactics that take advantage of their technical potential.

ISR is the acronym for intelligence collection, surveillance, and reconnaissance. Advanced C4I refers to technologies and systems that provide command, control, communications, and computer processing. Perhaps the best-known advance is precision force, thanks to the videotapes on precision-guided munitions used in Operation Desert Storm. The latter is a broader concept than some imagine, for it refers to a general ability to use deadly violence with greater speed, range, and precision.

In part because of past investments, in part serendipitously, the United States leads other nations in each of these areas, and its rate of improvement will increase dramatically over the next decade. Sensors, for example, will give real-time continuous surveillance in all types of weather over large geographical areas. Fusing and processing information—making sense of the vast amount of data that can be gathered—will give U.S. forces what is called dominant battlespace knowledge, a wide asymmetry between what Americans and opponents know. With that, the United States will be able to prevail militarily, whether the arena is a triple-canopy jungle, an urban area, or similar to Desert Storm. Improvements in command-and-control systems and in other communications technologies—already funded and entering service—posit leaps in the ability to transfer information, imagery, and other data to operating forces in forms that are immediately usable. In short, the United States is integrating the technical advances of ISR, C4I, and precision force. The emerging result is a system of systems that represents a qualitative change in U.S. military capabilities.

These technologies provide the ability to gather, sort, process, transfer, and display information about highly complex events that occur in wide geographic areas. However, this is important for more than fighting wars. In a rapidly changing world, information about what is occurring becomes a central commodity of international relations, just as the threat and use of military force was seen as the central power resource in an international system overshadowed by the potential clash of superpowers.

There has been an explosion of information. Yet some kinds of information—the accurate, timely, and comprehensible sort—are more valuable than others. Graphic video images of Rwandan refugees fleeing the horror of tribal hatreds may generate worldwide sympathy and demands for action. But precise knowledge of how many refugees are moving where, how, and under what conditions is critical for effective action.

Military information on the disposition, activity, and capabilities of military forces still ranks high in importance because military force is still perceived as the final arbiter of disagreements. More to the point, concerns that military force may be used still figure prominently in what states do.

The growing interdependence of the world does not necessarily establish greater harmony. It does, however, make military force a matter of interest to audiences outside the local theater. The direct use of military force no longer calls up the specter of escalation to global nuclear holocaust, but it remains a costly and dangerous activity. The Gulf War raised the price of oil worldwide. Russian military operations in Chechnya have influenced the political actions of Muslims from North Africa to Indonesia. The armed conflict in Bosnia colors the character and future of NATO and the United Nations. Military force tears the fabric of new interrelationships and conditions the political and economic behavior of nearly all nations. These considerations suggest a general framework within which the emerging military capabilities of the United States can be linked to its foreign policy.

The concept of deterrence undergirding the emerging American military system of systems envisions a military strong enough to thwart any foreign military action without incurring a commensurate military risk or cost. Those who contemplate a military clash with the United States will have to face the prospect that it will be able to halt and reverse any hostile action, with low risk to U.S. forces.

The United States will not necessarily be able to deter or coerce every adversary. Deterrence and coercion depend on an imbalance of will as well as capabilities, and when a conflict involves interests absolutely vital to an adversary but peripheral to the United States, an opponent may not yield short of a complete American victory battle. Still, the relationship between willpower and capabilities is reciprocal. Superior battlefield awareness cannot reduce the risk of casualties to zero, but it can keep that risk low enough to maintain the American public's support for the use of force. The ability to inflict high military costs in the early phases of a conflict can undermine an adversary's will, unity, and hope that it can prevail. Because the United States will be able to dominate in battle, it has to be prepared for efforts to test or undermine its resolve off the battlefield with terror and propaganda. But military force can deter the use of those instruments as well.

## The Information Umbrella

The information technologies driving America's emerging military capabilities may change classic deterrence theory. Threatening to use military force is not something Americans will do automatically or easily and has always had some undesirable side effects. In an era in which soft power increasingly influences international affairs, threats and the image of arrogance and belligerence that tends to go with them undercut an image of reason, democracy, and open dialogue.

America's emerging military capabilities—particularly those that provide much more real-time understanding of what is taking place in a large geographical area—can help blunt this paradox. They offer, for example, far greater pre-crisis transparency. If the United States is willing to share this transparency, it will be better able to build opposing coalitions before aggression has occurred. But the effect may be more general, for all nations now operate in an ambiguous world, a context that is not entirely benign or soothing.

In this setting, the emerging U.S. capabilities suggest leverage with friends similar to what extended nuclear deterrence once offered. The nuclear umbrella provided a cooperative structure, linking the United States in a mutually beneficial way to a wide range of friends, allies, and neutral nations. It was a logical response to the central issue of international relations—the threat of Soviet aggression. Now the central issue is ambiguity about the type and degree of threats, and the basis for cooperation is the capacity to clarify and cut through that ambiguity.

The set of fuzzy guidelines and meanings the Cold War once provided has been replaced by a deeper ambiguity regarding international events. Because nearly all nations viewed the international system through Cold War lenses, they shared much the same understanding. To nations throughout the world, the character and complexities of a civil war in the Balkans would have been far less important than the fact of disruption there because the event itself could have triggered a military confrontation between NATO and the Warsaw Pact. Details on the clashes between Chinese and Soviet border guards did not really matter; what counted was that a split had appeared in one of the world's great coalitions. Now the details of events seem to count more. With the organizing framework of the Cold War gone, the implications are harder to categorize, and all nations want to know more about what is happening and why to help them decide how much it matters and what they should do about it. Coalition leadership for the foreseeable future will proceed less from the military capacity to crush any opponent and more from the ability quickly to reduce the ambiguity of violent situations, to respond flexibly, and to use force, where necessary, with precision and accuracy.

The core of these capabilities—dominant situational knowledge—is fungible and divisible. The United States can share all or part of its knowledge with whomever it chooses. Sharing would empower recipients to make better decisions in a less-than-benign world, and should they decide to fight, they could achieve the same kind of military dominance as the United States.

These capabilities point to what might be called an information umbrella. Like extended nuclear deterrence, they could form the foundation for a mutually beneficial relationship. The United States would provide situational awareness, particularly regarding military matters of interest to other nations. Other nations, because they could share this information about an event or crisis, would be more inclined to work with the United States.

The beginning of such a relationship already exist. They were begun in the Falklands conflict and are being developed today in the Balkans. At present, the United States provides the bulk of the situational awareness available to the Implementation Force, the U.N. Protection Force, NATO members, and other nations involved in or concerned with the conflict there. It is possible to envision a similar central information role for the United States in other crises or potential military confrontations, from clarifying developments in the Spratly Islands to cutting through the ambiguity and confusion surrounding humanitarian operations in Cambodia and Rwanda. Accurate, real-time, situational awareness is the key to reaching agreement within coalitions on what to do and is essential to the effective use of military forces, whatever their roles and missions. As its capacity to provide this kind of information increases, America will increasingly be viewed as the natural coalition leader, not just because it happens to be the strongest but because it can provide the most important input for good decisions and effective action for other coalition members. Just as nuclear dominance was the key to coalition leadership in the old era, information dominance will be the key in the information age.

All this implies selectively sharing U.S. dominant battlespace knowledge, advanced C4I, and precision force. Old-era thinking might recoil from such a prospect, and it would have to overcome long-established prejudices against being open and generous with what might broadly be called intelligence. In the past, two presumptions supported this reluctance: first, that proving too much of the best information risked disclosing and perhaps even losing the sources and methods used in obtaining it, and second, that sharing information would disclose what the United States did not know and reduce its status as a superpower.

These assumptions are now even more questionable than before. The United States is no longer in a zero-sum game that makes any disclosure of capabilities a potential loss for itself and a gain for an implacable opponent. The character of this growing prowess is different. For one thing, the disparity between the United States and other nations is quite marked. U.S. investment in ISR—particularly the high-leverage space-based aspects of this set of systems—exceeds that of all other nations combined, and America leads by a considerable margin in C4I and precision force as well. It has already begun, systematically, to assemble the new system of systems and is well down the revolutionary path, while most nations have not yet even realized a revolution in military affairs is under way.

Some other nations could match what the United States will achieve, albeit not as early. The revolution is driven by technologies available worldwide. Digitization, computer processing, precise global positioning, and systems integration—the technological bases on which the rest of the new capabilities depend—are available to any nation with the money and the will to use them systematically to improve military capabilities. Exploiting these technologies can be expensive. But more important, there is no particular incentive for those nations to seek the system of systems the United States is building—so long as they believe they are not threatened by it. This is the emerging symbiosis among nations, for whether another nation decides to make a race out of the information revolution depends on how the United States uses its lead. If America does not share its knowledge, it will add incentives to match it. Selectively sharing these abilities is therefore not only the route of coalition leadership but the key to maintaining U.S. military superiority.

## The Soft Side of Information Power

The information age has revolutionized not only military affairs but the instruments of soft power and the opportunities to apply them. One of the ironies of the twentieth century is that Marxist theorists, as well as their critics, such as George Orwell, correctly noted that technological developments can profoundly shape societies and governments, but both groups misconstrued how. Technological and economic change have for the most part proved to be pluralizing forces conducive to the formation of free markets rather than repressive forces enhancing centralized power.

One of the driving factors in the remarkable change in the Soviet Union was that Mikhail Gorbachev and other Soviet leaders understood that the Soviet economy could not advance from the extensive, or industrial, to the intensive, or postindustrial, stage of development unless they loosened constraints on everything from computers to xerox machines—technologies that can also disseminate diverse political ideas. China tried to resist this tide, attempting to limit the use of fax machines after the 1989 Tiananmen Square massacre, in which they were a key means of communication between protesters and the outside world, but the effort failed. Now not only fax machines but satellite dishes have proliferated in China, and the government itself has begun wiring Internet connections and plans to install the equivalent of an entire Baby Bell's worth of telephone lines each year.

This new political and technological landscape is ready-made for the United States to capitalize on its formidable tools of soft power, to project the appeal of its ideals, ideology, culture, economic model, and social and political institutions, and to take advantage of its international business and telecommunications networks. American popular culture, with its libertarian and egalitarian currents, dominates film, television, and electronic communications. American higher education draws some 450,000 foreign students each year. Not all aspects of American culture are attractive, of course, particularly to conservative Muslims. Nonetheless, American leadership in the information revolution has generally increased global awareness of and openness to American ideas and values.

In this information-rich environment, those responsible for four vital tasks can draw on America's comparative advantage in information and soft power resources. These tasks are aiding democratic transitions in the remaining communist and authoritarian states, preventing backsliding in new and fragile democracies, preempting and resolving regional conflicts, and addressing the threats of terrorism, international crime, proliferation of weapons of mass destruction, and damage to the global environment. Each requires close coordination of the military and diplomatic components of America's foreign policy.

*Engaging Undemocratic States and Aiding Democratic Transitions.*
Numerous undemocratic regimes survived the Cold War, including not only communist states such as China and Cuba but a variety of unelected governments formed by authoritarians or dominant social, ethnic, religious, or familial groups. Ominously, some of these governments have attempted to acquire

nuclear weapons, among them Libya, Iran, Iraq, and North Korea. U.S. policies toward these countries are tailored to their respective circumstances and international behavior. The United States should continue selectively to engage those states, such as China, that show promise of joining the international community, while working to contain those regimes, like Iraq's, that offer no such hope. Whether seeking to engage or isolate undemocratic regimes, in every case the United States should engage the people, keeping them informed on world events and helping them prepare to build democratic market societies when the opportunity arises.

Organizations such as the U.S. Information Agency are vital to the task of aiding democratic transitions. Again China is instructive. USIA's international broadcasting arm, the Voice of America, has in the last few years become the primary news source for 60 percent of the educated Chinese. America's increasing technical ability to communicate with the public in foreign countries, literally over the heads of their rulers via satellite, provides a great opportunity to foster democracy. It is ironic to find Congress debating whether to dismantle USIA just when its potential is greatly expanding.

***Protecting New Democracies.*** Democratic states have emerged from the communist Soviet bloc and authoritarian regimes in other regions, such as Latin America, where for the first time every country but Cuba has an elected government. A major task for the United States is preventing their reversion to authoritarianism. Protecting and enlarging the community of market democracies serves U.S. security, political, and economic interests. Capitalist democracies are better trading partners and rarely fight one another.

An important program here is the International Military Education and Training Program. Begun in the 1950s, IMET has trained more than half a million high-level foreign officers in American military methods and democratic civil-military relations. With the end of the Cold War, the program has been expanded to deal with the needs of new democracies and emphasizes training civilians to oversee military organizations and budgets. With an annual budget less than $50 million, IMET is quite cost-effective. Two similar Defense Department efforts are the Marshall Center in Garmisch, Germany, and the Asia-Pacific Center for Security Studies in Hawaii, which train both military and civilian students and promote contacts among the parliaments, executives, and military organizations of new democracies.

***Preventing and Resolving Regional Conflicts.*** Communal conflicts, or conflicts over competing ethnic, religious, or national identities, often escalate as a result of propaganda campaigns by demagogic leaders, particularly those who want to divert attention from their own failings, establish their nationalist credentials, or seize power. Yet in developing countries, telephones, television, and other forms of telecommunication are rapidly growing, creating an opening for information campaigns by USIA and other agencies to undermine the artificial resolve and unity created by ethno-nationalist propaganda. At times, U.S. military technology may be used to suppress or jam broadcasts that incite violence, while USIA can provide unbiased reportage and expose false reports. U.S. air strikes on Serb communications facilities, for example, had the added benefit of making the transmission of Serbian propaganda more difficult.

The negotiation of the Bosnian peace agreement at Dayton, Ohio, last fall illustrated a diplomatic dimension of information power. The United States succeeded in getting an agreement where for years other negotiating parties had failed in part because of its superior information assets. The ability to monitor the actions of all parties in the field helped provide confidence that the agreement could be verified, while detailed maps of Bosnia reduced potential misunderstandings. The American-designed three-dimensional virtual reality maps also undoubtedly helped the negotiating parties in drawing cease-fire lines and resolving whether vehicles traveling various roads could be targeted with direct-fire weapons, and generally demonstrated the capacity of U.S. troops to understand the terrain in Bosnia as well as or better than any of the local military groups.

Information campaigns to expose propaganda earlier in the Rwandan conflict might have mitigated the tragedy. Rwanda has only 14,000 phones but some 500,000 radios. A few simple measures, such as suppressing extremist Hutu radio broadcasts that called for attacks on civilians, or broadcasting Voice of America (VOA) reports that exposed the true actions and goals of those who sought to hijack the government and incite genocide, might have contained or averted the killing.

Such cases point to the need for closer coordination between the USIA and the Department of Defense in identifying hateful radio or television transmissions that are inciting violence and in taking steps to suppress them and provide better information. In some instances the United States might share intelligence with parties to a dispute to reassure them that the other side is not preparing an offensive or cheating on arms control or other agreements.

***Crime, Terrorism, Proliferation, and the Environment***. The fourth task is to focus U.S. information technology on international terrorism, international crime, drug smuggling, proliferation of weapons of mass destruction, and the global environment. The [former] director of the CIA, John M. Deutch, has focused his agency's efforts on the first four of these, while the State Department's new Office of Global Affairs has taken the lead on global environmental issues. Information has always been the best means of preventing and countering terrorist attacks, and the United States can bring the same kind of information processing capabilities to bear abroad that the FBI used domestically to capture and convict the terrorists who bombed the World Trade Center. On international crime and drug smuggling, various U.S. agencies, including the CIA, FBI, Defense Intelligence Agency, and Department of Defense, have begun working more closely with one another and their foreign counterparts to pool their information and resources. Such efforts can help the United States defeat adversaries on and off the battlefield.

The United States has used its information resources to uncover North Korea's nuclear weapons program and negotiate a detailed agreement for its dismantlement, to discover Russian and Chinese nuclear cooperation with Iran quickly and discourage it, to bolster U.N. inspections of Iraqi nuclear facilities, and to help safeguard enriched uranium supplies throughout the former Soviet republics. And mounting evidence on environmental dangers such as global warming and ozone depletion, much of it gathered and disseminated by American scientists and U.S. government agencies, has helped other states understand these problems and can now begin to point the way to cost-effective remedies.

## The Market Will Not Suffice

Many of the efforts in these four overarching tasks have been ignored or disdained by some who have clung to narrow Cold War notions of U.S. security and of the roles of various agencies in pursuing it. Some in Congress, for example, have been reluctant to support any defense spending that does not directly involve U.S. combat troops and equipment. However, defense by other means is relatively inexpensive. Programs like the Partnership for Peace, USIA, IMET, the Marshall Center, the Asia-Pacific Center, the military-to-military dialogues sponsored by the U.S. unified command, and the Defense Ministerial of the Americas constitute only a tiny fraction of the defense budget. Although it is impossible to quantify these programs' contributions, we are convinced they are highly cost-effective in serving U.S. security needs. Similarly, USIA's achievements, like those of IMET and other instruments of soft power, should be more appreciated. USIA's seminal contribution of keeping the idea of democracy alive in the Soviet bloc during the Cold War could be a mere prologue.

Some argue that the slow, diffuse, and subtle process of winning hearts and minds can be met by nongovernmental news organizations. These organizations, as well as the millions of private individuals who communicate with friends and colleagues abroad, have done much to disseminate news and information globally. Yet the U.S. government should not abdicate the agenda-setting function to the media because the market and private individuals cannot fulfill all the information needs of American foreign policy. The Voice of America, for example, broadcasts in 48 languages and has an audience tens of millions greater than CNN, which broadcasts only in English. The station's role in China illustrates the problem of market failure: one of the reasons it is the leading source of news for educated Chinese is that Rupert Murdoch ended his broadcasting of the BBC World Service Television News in China, reportedly to win a commercial concession from the Chinese communist government. In addition, VOA can broadcast in languages such as Serbo-Croatian, which are spoken in a geographic area too small to be more than a commercial niche market but crucial for foreign policy. Nonetheless, current budget cuts could force VOA to drop its broadcasting in as many as 20 languages.

The market will not find a private means to suppress radio broadcasts like those of the perpetrators of genocide in Rwanda. There is no economic incentive for breaking through foreign efforts to jam broadcasts or compiling detailed reports on communal violence in the 30 or so ongoing conflicts that rarely make the front page. Left to itself, the market is likely to continue to have a highly uneven pattern of access to the Internet. Of the 15,000 networks on the global Internet in early 1994, only 42 were in Muslim countries, and 29 of these were in Turkey and Indonesia. In response, USIA and the U.S. Agency for International Development have worked to improve global access to the Internet.

## The Coming American Century

The premature end of what *Time* magazine founder Henry Luce termed the American century has been declared more than once by disciples of decline. In truth, the 21st century, not the twentieth, will turn out to be the period of America's greatest preeminence. Information is the new coin of the international realm, and the United States is better positioned than any other country to multiply the potency of its hard and soft power resources through information. This does not mean that the United States can act unilaterally, much less coercively to achieve its international goals. The beauty of information as a power resource is that, while it can enhance the effectiveness of raw military power, it ineluctably democratizes societies. The communist and authoritarian regimes that hoped to maintain their centralized authority while still reaping the economic and military benefits of information technologies discovered they had signed a Faustian bargain.

The United States can increase the effectiveness of its military forces and make the world safe for soft power, America's inherent comparative advantage. Yet a strategy based on America's information advantage and soft power has some prerequisites. The necessary defense technologies and programs, ISR, C4I, and precision force, must be adequately funded. This does not require a bigger defense budget, but it does mean the Defense Department, which is inclined to accelerate and expand these capabilities, should be granted flexibility in setting funding priorities within its budgetary top line. Congressional imposition of programs opposed by the military and civilian leaders in the Defense Department—such as the requirement to buy more B-2 aircraft at a cost of billions of dollars—detract from that flexibility and retard the military leverage that can be gained by completing the revolution in military affairs. Channels to parlay these new military capabilities into alliances and coalitions must be supported: military-to-military contacts, IMET, and the Marshall and Asia-Pacific Centers. Information is often public good, but it is not a free one. Constraints on the sharing of system-of-systems capabilities and the selective transfer of intelligence, imagery, and the entire range of America's growing ISR capabilities should be loosened.

Diplomatic and public broadcasting channels through which information resources and advantages can be applied must be maintained. The USIA, VOA and other information agencies need adequate funding. The Cold War legislation authorizing the USIA, which has changed little since the early 1950s, draws too sharp a line in barring USIA from disseminating information domestically. For example, while USIA should continue to be prohibited from targeting its programs at domestic audiences, Congress has discouraged USIA even from advertising its Internet sites in journals that reach domestic as well as foreign audiences. Congress should instead actively support USIA's efforts to exploit new technologies, including the agency's new Electronic Media Team, which is working to set up World Wide Web home pages on democratization and the creation and functioning of free markets.

The final and most fundamental requirement is the preservation of the kind of nation that is at the heart of America's soft power appeal. In recent years this most valuable foreign policy asset has been endangered by the growing international perception of America as a society riven by crime, violence, drug abuse, racial tension, family breakdown, fiscal irresponsibility, political gridlock, and increasingly acrimonious political discourse in which extreme points of view make the biggest headlines. America's foreign and domestic policies are inextricably intertwined. A healthy democracy at home, made accessible around the world through modern communications, can foster the enlargement of the peaceful community of democracies, which is ultimately the best guarantee of a secure, free, and prosperous world.

---

## Note

1. "Soft power" is the ability to achieve desired outcomes in international affairs through attraction rather than coercion. It works by convincing others to follow, or getting them to agree to, norms and institutions that produce the desired behavior. Soft power can rest on the appeal of one's ideas or the ability to set the agenda in ways that shape the preferences of others. If a state can make its power legitimate in the perception of others and establish international institutions that encourage them to channel or limit their activities, it may not need to expend as many of its costly traditional economic or military resources. See Joseph S. Nye, Jr., *Bound to Lead: The Changing Nature of American Power*, Basic Books, 1990.

# Chapter 44

## * * *

## The Military After Next

Paul Bracken

*Paul Bracken uses an attention-getting title, "The Military After Next," to suggest that U.S. military force planning and structure are implicitly focused on the problems of today, by which he means the next few years. He argues that focusing on the military after next will break away from this tunnel vision. He identifies three specific problems for the military after next: (1) sustaining an advantage over competitors (particularly potential peer competitors); (2) understanding the immense distances that future militaries will face; and (3) determining how to assure sustainable U.S. military advantage by emphasizing organizational learning. Are Bracken's issues valid and as important as he suggests? Are militaries institutionally incapable of planning for a future as distant in time and as vague as that Bracken hypothesizes? What fundamental strategic and force structuring initiatives are needed to ensure that the U.S. is preparing to field the proper "military after next?"*

An important element is missing from the debate now taking place over U.S. national security policy. In the enthusiasm for identifying and examining new kinds of security issues—the economy, the environment, human rights, and so on—the oldest source of security, military power, has seemingly disappeared. The military posture for the next 20 years is conceptualized implicitly in terms of problems of *today*, rather than in terms of deeper forces that reflect both the changing character of war and the military transformation taking place in the world. Immediate U.S. problems are characterized by deep military budget cuts, regional contingencies, "messy" operations (such as Yugoslavia), and a substantial military capacity inherited as a legacy from the Cold War. All of these are worthy of attention. But if anything is certain, it is that in 20 years the current budget crisis, the regional strategy, and even Yugoslavia will be forgotten as new

Paul Bracken is professor of political science and of international business at Yale University.

Paul Bracken, "The Military After Next," *The Washington Quarterly*, 16:4 (Autumn 1993), pp. 157-174. Copyright © 1993 by the Center for Strategic and International Studies (CSIS) and the Massachusetts Institute of Technology.

problems of national security and international order appear. The focus on the immediate means that a larger, more important question is not being asked: How should planners redesign the U.S. military for an entirely new operational environment, taking account of revolutionary changes in military technology and the possible appearance of entirely new kinds of competitors? There is not enough fresh thinking on this question, thinking that starts with a clean sheet of paper and examines the revolutionary impact of technology on U.S. strategy and force structure.

This article does not criticize the current security debate as much as it ignores it in order to redirect attention to the costs of strategic tunnel vision. Unless there is a far more sober approach it is likely that organizational inertia will produce what is referred to here as "the next military"—a military that is essentially no more than an improved version of the current one. The next military will emphasize fine tuning of existing operational strategies for air and land battle, superaccurate bombing, marginal improvements in weapon ranges, and making the whole thing smaller in cost and size. It is not likely to be well matched to the future security environment.

This article promotes the use of a new and different concept, "the military after next," to break away from tunnel vision. This is the military that will be built *after* the next military and will reflect fundamental changes in the nature of warfare and the security environment. It is offered as a powerful technique by which to judge whether current plans and debates are far enough ahead of today's problems, and whether U.S. armed forces will incorporate innovations in operations technology, new architecture, and radically different doctrines in ways that will make those innovations a real part of the forces designed. The military after next is a benchmark for analyzing force and strategy development plans in a way that raises important questions that are otherwise missing from the debate.

Today's problems are urgent, but they are not necessarily important for national and international security. Although many disorders have followed the collapse of the Communist bloc, the United States is in a period without vital threats to itself or its allies. It is true that if danger is defined broadly enough there is a crisis. Defining national security in such broad terms, however, undermines the central foundations of national security and its relationship to the nation-state. In addition, even if these new definitions of security are correct in some technical sense, they are unlikely to have the power to catalyze public support for action.

The United States is at a position in its national history when there are few vital threats to its security, but when warfare is fundamentally changing, as much as it has at any time in this century. This Indian summer in national security should be used to explore fundamentally different ways of structuring the military that are not driven by the current stream of problems stemming from various regional dangers. The concept of the military after next focuses attention back to innovation, exploration of radically different operational concepts, and other issues that are important for the future. Myopically recreating a military that is a marginal improvement of the current one, or one that is different but still shaped by immediate pressures, has large opportunity costs. It could effectively remove the United States as a serious military actor from major parts of the world, because its forces will be scaled to the world of the 1980s at a time when rapid changes are taking place in both international relations and the nature of war itself.

This article first describes the military after next concept, then analyzes three critical problems in terms of this framework.

## The Military After Next

The next U.S. military is the one that current trends will produce 10 years from now. Much of it already exists. Not much innovation or replacement will occur during this period, but the military will be modified in various ways. National policy will have some influence on how it is organized, trained, and equipped. Some new technologies will be developed and fielded, offering improved performance in certain areas. Doctrine will change, not dramatically but to reflect the experience of recent military actions. In short, the next military is the one arising out of current trends and recent experience.

Strategies are easier to change than institutions. What the next military concept focuses attention on are those institutional factors that are relatively slow to change. This very inertia makes them more predictable than strategy. Despite wide-ranging debates over such national policies as isolationism versus internationalism, when it comes to what actually gets fielded in 10 years—what the force looks like and what it can do—more prosaic factors are as important as national policy. Institutional characteristics, such as operational concepts, use of technology, and the way the military organization goes about its business, take many years to change, whereas national strategy can change in a moment. Just think how many strategies the United States has had over the last few years alone. Flexible response, forward defense (now called forward positioning), cooperative security, the regional strategy, and many others have at one time or another been the strategies the U.S. military was ostensibly designed to support.

Most observers understand that when it comes to shaping military forces, a number of factors matter, not just strategy from the top. The U.S. military could not possibly reshape itself to deal with the changes in policy and strategy that take place with every new administration, and frequently more often than that. The idea of the next military is intended to capture this broader range of institutional, doctrinal, and technical trends, the collection of microissues that collectively describe what a military force is capable of accomplishing. This is often easier to predict than the next strategy.

Because most of the decisions shaping the next military arise out of a search for solutions to immediate problems, its outlines are already clear. It is likely that reduced budgets will encourage the services to protect force structure, that is, the number of divisions, air squadrons, and ships retained in active roles. Acquisition will be postponed or deferred indefinitely to free up resources for this force structure. The reason is not entirely bureaucratic; it also reflects the view that whatever the strategy of the United States may be there is a certain floor below which its forces just should not go. Below that level, according to this argument, the nation is unable to undertake any of a broad range of strategies.

Another predictable feature of the next military is its doctrine. This doctrine is likely to perpetuate current concepts rather than explore fundamentally new ways of doing things. Current land, air, and sea doctrine proved effective in Desert Storm, and the contingency scenarios of highest bureaucratic interest involve other opponents on the same scale as Iraq. Geographic tailoring may be required to deal with North Korea, Iraq (again), or a Russian move into Lithuania or Poland, but the doctrines of Desert Storm could be modified appropriately.[1] The scale of these opponents dictates the level of effort needed to deal with them. The kinds of competitors faced and the level of effort shape doctrine. The next U.S. military as reflected in official plans roughly calls for a deployable 10-division field army, 20 air wings, and about 10 aircraft carriers.[2] Current structures are to be maintained, that is, the organization of forces into divisions, squadrons, and naval task forces is to remain the same. Given that these are the relatively fixed factors of the debate, it would be highly surprising if major new doctrinal improvisation occurred, or if radically new experiments in organization were considered.

Yet another reason for staying with current military doctrine is that technology is one of the biggest drivers of doctrinal change. In the current environment, not much new military technology is going to be bought. The United States is not about to introduce into the forces anything as radical as the atomic bomb, the intercontinental ballistic missile, or the nuclear-powered aircraft carrier. Without this stimulus, innovation will seem more like pipe dreaming than force planning. It may produce interesting ideas, but because none of these would ever be funded they are likely to be considered a waste of time.

The next military, if official plans are carried out, will be a marginally improved reproduction of the current one, regardless of what new strategies and policies are imposed upon it. In the next military, enemy tanks will be killed at 3,000 meters rather than 2,500, aircraft loiter times will increase by 10 percent, and aircraft carriers will improve their all-weather attack capability. If the current pressure to refocus on lower-intensity threats and peacekeeping is pursued instead, then the next military will have fewer heavy forces, such as tank divisions and bombers, and relatively more light mobile forces trained in border protection, low-intensity conflict, and counterterrorism. In either case there will be a strong tendency to defer or avoid revolutionary changes in favor of incremental ones. Innovation will be confined to programs closely aligned with strategy. The need to rigorously justify nearly all programs means that only the most defensible will be considered—and this means the immediate ones because these are conceived of as most likely to be needed.

The next military will be blind to changes in the international environment beyond those that reinforce its own conception of itself. It will fix its attention on current technologies to such a degree that the enabling power of new technologies will not be seen, as has happened to many military institutions in history. Locking in current force structures, concepts, technologies, and doctrine will have an unintended adverse impact on innovation, perception of the world, incentives, and sense of priority. This applies to all institutions, not just the military, and it is one of the gravest dangers overlooked in the current security debate. The United States is moving from its position during the Cold War, when it probably devoted too much attention to innovation and technology, to one at the other extreme, where these factors are neglected for the reasons described above. What is badly needed is a way to change this state of affairs, to introduce tolerance for innovation, experimentation, and for doing things differently in a budget-constrained world.

The military after next is the one that future trends will produce 20 years from now.[3] Much of it does not exist today. The large inherited military legacy from the Cold War will be gone. Innovation in technology and replacement of outdated equipment will be major issues. Revolutionary modifications from current practice will be more likely than they appear today. National strategy will hardly reflect the imperatives of the downsizing of the early 1990s, regional threats like Iraq, or messy situations like Yugoslavia. Doctrine is as likely to change in ways today considered inconceivable as it is to change incrementally. In short, the military after next is the one arising from trends and decisions that reflect the technology and international security environment of the next century.

The argument of this article is that, instead of allowing immediate pressures to completely shape the military, it is important to look beyond these pressures to longer-term forces that will affect the military after next and to think through how these should affect today's decisions. This means identifying what the longer-term forces are and creating a system to assess their meaning for strategy and organization. Part of today's military planning should examine the potential to go beyond immediate problems to consider revolutionary changes in military technology, operational doctrines, and new forms of organization.

This article does not claim that long-term predictions about the future security environment should directly guide today's force planning, nor that revolutionary new kinds of military forces should be built or acquired. There is hardly enough confidence in any one scenario to justify the former. In the current security environment revolutionary new kinds of forces are not needed because the United States can handle most problems with its current forces.

But this might not be true in the future. And the problem today is that the planning time horizon is in danger of fixating on the immediate and urgent, to the detriment of the long term and important. The current defense budget has, to its credit, included a small increase in research and development spending. And each of the services has a research group looking at future military structures. But it is not clear that these desirable activities will survive in an environment of budget pressure and immediate crises. If they do not, and if these activities are not expanded, the United States will put itself out of the business of being the predominant military power in Europe, Asia, and elsewhere if it conceptualizes its problem as cutting its defense programs only up to the point at which they do not completely squander the cold war military legacy it inherited. Conceiving military power only in terms of force sizing against immediate threats, while reducing or even eliminating research and development on new operational concepts and technologies, will incur the opportunity cost of not keeping up with others as their military potential evolves. Eliminating the learning mechanisms, which are the parts of the U.S. defense organization critical for innovation and change, exemplifies a dangerous level of tunnel vision. It will result in the military after next looking like the next military, a reproduction of the victorious forces of Desert Storm with self-referential performance standards.

There is always a tension between the short and long term, incremental and revolutionary change, cost saving and new programs, and preservation of existing forces and experimentation with new ones. But today the United States has skewed its policies to the first in each of these categories. The places where longer-term considerations have traditionally been the greatest—in the services, the war colleges, and other places of organizational learning—will either be put out of business altogether, or reined in to reflect the demands and needs of current policy. This would be a disaster for U.S. national security, akin to the U.S. government telling the army and navy in the 1920s and 1930s that thinking about the future of warfare was unneeded, did not conform to national policy, and wasted resources.

This is especially unfortunate for a number of reasons peculiar to what is happening in technology and the world. In the military sphere it is likely that changes in the nature of warfare brought on by the enabling power of new technologies combined with fundamental changes in doctrine, employment concepts, and force structures will alter the character of warfare to a degree witnessed only in periods of military revolution. That is, military potential may be about to vault from one technical era to the next, as it did between the

Napoleonic era and the Franco-Prussian War, or between the two world wars. It is not common to think about national security in such terms. Usually, policy goals are formulated and then force structure implications derived from them. History is not so clear in its causal relationships, however, and radically new improvements in military capacities can have their own impact on international relations. The point is not that new opportunities should be embraced blindly, but that they should be carefully studied and evaluated for what they could mean for the United States, something that is not being done in the current environment of focusing on the immediate problem. Conventional military thinking has an aversion to the logic of military revolution that is understandable but is nonetheless dangerous in its consequences.

The underlying forces behind radically new military capacities are the rapid advance in computers and communications and the rapidly declining cost of both. These forces have already worked to change big corporate organizations in ways not seen since the creation of the mass bureaucracy in the nineteenth century. This article asserts only that changes of comparable magnitude will occur in the military. The most fundamental notions of hierarchy, span of control, response time, and centralization are being reevaluated, and it is difficult to imagine that the transformation seen in other big organizations will not produce a similarly dramatic impact in the military sphere. For the United States to be removed from this development, for whatever reason, would be detrimental to the national interest.

The high performance of U.S. forces in Desert Storm demonstrates the benefits of a fundamental rethinking of military processes.[4] In retrospect, the experience of Desert Storm will be seen as one of the earliest experiments in a new kind of warfare based on redesigns in military process that occurred in the decade before that conflict, namely changed flows of work and information in the forces, which led to operations that were much more interconnected, quick-reacting, and flexible. It is true that no opponent today can challenge the United States on this level of war, but using this as an argument to halt learning and innovation is a mistake. It is imperative that innovation not be stopped in its tracks because of budget pressures and immediate demands that do not at present necessitate more advanced capacities than the United States now possesses.

The military after next is the continuation of developments displayed in the Persian Gulf War and carried on over the years rather than frozen in place. It requires process redesign in the rest of the defense establishment, not just in the combat forces. At the moment the United States has highly capable field forces but a defense macrostructure that resists change and is overly departmentalized with each service maintaining independent support, depot, intelligence, and logistic centers. Linkage and integration of this superstructure with the field forces has not even begun. In Desert Storm the field forces were horizontally linked with one another. Now a remodeled defense superstructure needs to be vertically linked with the high-performing field forces. The current security debate treats these high performing field forces and the defense superstructure as separate, independent problems. This is extremely shortsighted, for it encourages a deep disconnect between the policy and execution levels of action. Their relationship is likely to go almost completely unanalyzed as budgeteers focus on logistics, administration, intelligence, and other functions, as if analysis of any one of these makes sense in isolation from another. This artificial separation follows from the accounting system used in defense analysis: the Planning, Programming, and Budgeting System (PPBS)—a system designed in and for the Cold War to stabilize a defense effort for long-term minimum cost containment. Integration of the different parts of the defense establishment is akin to the organizational transformation taking place in the corporate world. The trend there is to link cross-functional areas into a seamless unit. This development alone should cause a great deal of comparable rethinking in defense.

Another reason for keeping up with innovative technical developments is that the immediate security problems facing the United States are not that important in relative terms. None compares with those facing the nation in the 1940s or during the Cold War. Most are pressing and even urgent, but what happens in Yugoslavia or Lithuania is not of great concern to the United States. It would be a mistake to dismiss these problems out of hand, but to exaggerate their significance would also be wrong. In fact, an averaging strategy is probably what the United States will actually pursue during the next 10 years as far as intervention goes. Some crises will be ignored, others will be acted upon. None is likely to matter in the larger calculus of national interest relative to the emergence of new competitors, a subject to which we now turn. What will matter is whether or not the United States exploits the period when no vital threats to its security exist to modernize its forces and to stay in the forefront of what technology can and cannot do. In short, this is a time for thinking and learning about the military after next.

## Sustaining Competitive Advantage: The First Problem

The first problem for the military after next is to sustain an advantage over competitors at a time when their military capacities are growing, and when U.S. military resources are declining. The United States has been a major military actor in the world since World War II, but as other nations build up their military as the U.S. military declines or stays the same, various regional power balances are shifting against the United States. To some degree, the adverse consequences of this can be offset by improved diplomacy, greater reliance on collective security, allies, and perhaps changes in the currency of international relations. That is, military power may be of declining importance. But this assumption is certainly a dangerous foundation for military planning, and it is a dangerous one for U.S. foreign policy more generally.

International order is not self-policing. It depends on state power—including military power—to shape and protect the underlying political and economic arrangements that sustain it. A declining use of force as an element in relations among the great powers in the early post-cold war era tells us only that force has not been necessary or possible, given the current threats and distribution of power capacities. It does not tell us that force has lost its utility. Conditions can change. New power distributions are not only possible, but given the growing wealth in many countries and their adoption of new military technologies, they are likely. This development has the potential for upsetting the currently tranquil relations among the strong powers of the world. It is this world that the military after next must consider as its competitive environment.

What does it mean to "consider" such a question? First, it means that to be a relevant actor—to stay in the game—the military after next must be designed to operate in a very different environment than that which exists today. The U.S. military of the late nineteenth century was irrelevant to shaping the security environments in Europe during the rise of Prussia and in Asia during a period of colonial expansion. Something similar could happen again early in the next century, once the cold war legacy has worn away. Second, U.S. military strength and preparedness can help to deter and stabilize transitions in this new environment. By remaining a factor, the United States may help to prevent some of the worst outcomes. Several nations now have great wealth that they can direct into different paths of development. The history of the nation-state teaches that military power is one principal avenue of its development. The two have gone hand in hand. This may change in benign ways, but it is more likely to do so with an underwriter that has the capacity to shape some of the transitions.

The United States could be faced with a more hostile world, but the greater problem lies with changes to the ordering of military power as it exists today. I distinguish among "A," "B," and "C" competitors. "A" nations are peer competitors, or major regional competitors with which the United States may have to deal. These are nations that could seek regional hegemony backed up with military power. In this century Germany, Japan, and the Soviet Union have been "A" class competitors. Each of these had a potential for excess influence on the Eurasian land mass and thus threatening U.S. allies. But more important, they posed strong indirect dangers by denying the United States access to key areas there.

"B" competitors are mid-level developing states with modernized conventional forces (much like Iraq in 1990), with the possibility of Model T nuclear, chemical, and biological (NBC) forces. The existing Middle Eastern states fall into the "B" class. Today, nations like Pakistan and India are also in this category, measured by their military potential.

"C" competitors are militarily ineffectual nations with complex or complicated security problems: ethnic civil war (Yugoslavia), insurgency (Peru), terrorism (Egypt), civil disorder (Somalia), or infiltration (narcotics flows). These pose many complicated military demands on the United States, both in tactics and in political interaction. Some can be managed as long as U.S. casualties are kept low. Others represent political problems that defy military solution.

Although today the United States is the world's only military superpower, a new ordering of potential competitors could arise through "graduations" and "demotions" among these categories over the next two decades that will change this ranking.

There are major differences in dealing with the different categories. This framework is more useful than the more standard one, which posits the number of wars that can be waged at the same time. Not nearly enough attention is paid to potential new peer competitors, because U.S. security policy is unconsciously focused on Iraq-scale contingencies to the exclusion of others.

Although there may be no mathematically rigorous dividing line among the different classes of competitors, there nonetheless are distinctions worth making. Some nations, notably in Asia, are becoming wealthy in the sense of being able to devote relatively large amounts of money to military modernization without economic disruption. "A" countries would have little difficulty in 2012 building a military with the rough potential of a 1960 Strategic Air Command (SAC). Assuming even that such a SAC would not pose insurmountable dangers to the U.S. homeland, it undoubtedly would pose large dangers to its neighbors. For larger "A" states there would be little economic barrier to such an achievement. For this reason, the term competitor is not restricted to outright military opponents. An emergent "A" state might not have any adverse bearing on the United States, but might so upset the power balance as to reshape regional expectations. The rise of Prussia in the 1870s did not pose any immediate direct problem for the United States, yet the United States was affected by the upsetting effects of that rise on the European order.

If one or more "A" scale competitors emerged in Asia, and if the United States continued with its present Asian military strategy, it is hard to see how Japan could maintain its present foreign policy course. Although today the U.S.-Japan security tie is seen in psychological terms, or more precisely in terms that compel no one to count numbers or draw up scenarios, the appearance of "A" powers in Asia would change this. Even the psychological linkage would have many complicated and problematic aspects, much more so even than the North Atlantic Treaty Organization (NATO) linkage that connected the United States to the defense of Europe.

The geographic size of countries on the list is also relevant to U.S. competitive advantage. With current operational concepts, the United States is geared to attack targets set in a country roughly the size of Iraq. With projected budget cuts even this concept might not be supportable, but in any case it will certainly not grow under current guidance. More will be said about this later.

The interesting question is to what extent countries could graduate from "B" to "A" status by skillfully manipulating appropriate training, the disciplined administration and development of forces and operational concepts, and the international availability of advanced military technologies. So far this has really only occurred with respect to "B" states dealing with one another. Iraq could exploit its military prowess to hold off a larger Iran in the 1980s, but against the United States this proved impossible. Yet the Iraqi example may be just one point on a learning curve, with different "B" nations possessing a differential capacity to climb this curve. "B" countries that expand their military capacity on the cheap by acquiring nuclear, chemical, or biological weapons, rather than developing general military capabilities in many areas, may be an especially important subcategory in the future. Past some point they would graduate to "A" status, and this might even be a goal sought for its own sake. It would be very important to understand the character and shape of this learning curve and what makes advancing on it more and less difficult.

The biggest unanalyzed problem facing the United States is sustaining its military and strategic competitive advantage over potential "A" competitors. Nothing lasts forever. This is as true of U.S. military superiority as anything else. Time, the denominator of military power, will whittle away at U.S. superiority and render the cold war military legacy obsolete. It is not hard to see how this could happen, even if the exact details of where or when are impossible to predict. It is clear that economic and technology dynamics make it possible for nations to develop forces that could pose a danger to U.S. strategic interests, and that along with U.S. cutbacks newly emergent "A" powers are a real possibility. But it is hard to see why there is so little attempt to acknowledge the need to maintain U.S. competitive advantage in shaping future U.S. military organization, that is, the military after next. It may well be that pressing demands foreclose this as a major factor in short-term planning. But there is no good reason why it should be dropped altogether from influencing the military after next. It bears directly on tomorrow's force and strategy thinking.

"A" competitors need to be looked at in terms of economic power and their ability to eventually adapt modern military technology, not to their entire military, but to certain pieces of it. Here, the high rates of economic growth in Asia are noteworthy. Asia has the largest military organizations in the world if the unit of measure is numbers of troops. The question then arises, what are the consequences of the conversion of these rapidly growing economies to efficient military use? That most Asian armies are technically obsolete only makes the question more interesting. A small amount of advanced technology, with changed operational concepts, could transform these outdated infantry hierarchies into organizations capable of using technology to project power long distances from their borders.

New competitors may compete on very different terms, and in ways very different from what the United States now anticipates. Unless transnational organizations like the United Nations (UN) successfully recreate the world system in a new peaceful form, the diffusion of advanced technology and the continued organization of the world into the nation-state system mean that eventually some country will press its military advantage for political gain that will hurt either the United States directly or one of its key allies. Such a country will also learn—from the United States, from its own exercises, and from the failures of others. Failure is a particularly compelling learning mechanism. The lack of success of the Argentines in the Falklands and the Iraqis in Kuwait could be interpreted in terms of the inability of these countries to administer modern forces to maximum effect. Or these failures could be seen as the catalysts for innovation and new thinking in other nations, much as the crises of the early Cold War taught both Americans and Soviets much about the character of their bilateral competition. It would certainly be presumptuous to infer that only the advanced states could master modern military technology.

Yet even debating the question in such terms biases the answer. The difficulties for the United States will lie less in either the ability of these rising powers to muster numbers of advanced weapons or their administrative mastery over them, than in the development of entirely new operational concepts, perhaps founded on new technologies, which will pose the largest problems for maintaining the U.S. competitive advantage. The Soviet Union was a well-understood opponent. Any changes there were known well in advance. But this will be less true for future competitors of the United States, who will not challenge it everywhere as the Soviets did but only where they already have strong advantages. The United States, after all, could not deal with what was at best a "B" competitor in Vietnam, which exploited such an advantage with a very different concept of operations from what the Americans expected.

History suggests that competition in the future is likely to be no different from competition in the past, when competitors actually knew little about each other until the competition was well advanced. The nineteenth-century Russian czar and his general staff completely missed the significance of the capacities of the western maritime powers for amphibious attack and disruption until western forces landed in the Crimea. Until then Imperial Russia had been secure in its landlocked cocoon. Now it learned that what worked against Napoleon would fail against powers using fundamentally different strategic concepts.

Today's problem can be stated clearly: With the growing economic capacity of many large countries, what will happen when large, wealthy (in terms of gross national product [GNP]) nations convert 10 to 20 percent of their product into modern forces that will use strategic concepts never used before? The way to deal with such competitors cannot be based on existing U.S. operational doctrines, which are designed for "B" type powers. This is a line of thinking not generally considered by planners today. Instead, U.S. security policy is shaped on "likely" scenarios, without regard for the nation's need to remain a dominant military actor regardless of the contingencies it faces.

A relationship between the military after next concept and the "A," "B," "C" scale of competitors is shown in Figure 1. Suppose it is possible to represent the important features of U.S. military organization by a circle. Then at present the U.S. military is represented by 1. Ranged against it is a spectrum of competitors, represented by types "A," "B," and "C" on the horizontal axis. The formal U.S. Department of Defense plan of the Regional Strategy and Multiple Regional Contingencies provides a mechanism for shaping the next military,[5] and if these plans are left alone will drive the military to state 2 in the figure. The military in state 2 is designed to deal with regional type "B" competitors, principally Iraq, North Korea, or a weakened Russia. Some people and groups are, however, dissatisfied with this state of affairs and want to intervene and divert the military toward state 3 to deal with a messy set of type "C" problems. Intervention in Somalia and possible interventions in Bosnia and other countries are examples of such problems. State 3 represents the state of the U.S. military as it confronts both immediate threats for the current military to deal with and future ones for the next military to manage.

The current debate about the next military concerns whether it should more resemble state 2 or state 3. Informal pressures, political demands, and some bureaucratic forces are pulling toward state 3, while the Pentagon's formal apparatus is resisting this, holding out for state 2. Interestingly, those in the Pentagon advocating state 2 see working toward it less as an immutable ideal than as a way to resist what they believe are the undesirable consequences of reshaping the military for various kinds of low-intensity conflicts, peacekeeping, and civil policing.

Virtually no one is considering states 4, 5, and 6—where the next military will face competition from its peers or from major regional competitors that can adversely affect U.S. interest in key regions. This is terra incognita, and there appears to be little recognition of how this potential scenario clashes with most thinking found in U.S. national security policy debates. A great controversy arose in 1992 over a leaked Defense Planning Guidance (DPG) study issued by the Pentagon that called for the United States to maintain its military dominance over competitors and allies. It reportedly advocated a policy that would prevent any military superpower from emerging anywhere in Eurasia, an objective to be achieved through U.S.-led alliances and coalitions.[6] Regardless of how this document was distorted by the press, or its impolitic language, it appeared to

Figure 1.
SUSTAINING U.S. COMPETITIVE ADVANTAGE

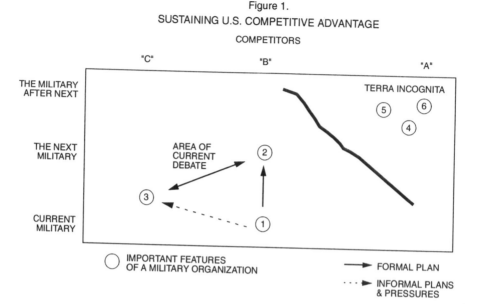

assume that this policy could be achieved with a military of Desert Storm vintage. If anything is certain, it is that if the United States pursues its current formal directives, or if it goes off in any one of a number of different directions reflected in the current security debate, it will be unable to do so.

The U.S. failure will stem from several causes: the military capacity of Eurasian states is growing; U.S. forward deployments are headed for levels that will be both ridiculously low and irrelevant to the security situation of their regions of deployment; and budget travails will mean that although force structure will be preserved, it will only be with an organization locked into the operational concepts and structures of the 1980s. As technology spreads, and as at least some states in Eurasia shift resources from inefficient defense and their economy into efficient defense expenditures, the regional balance of military power will change, even as the United States for too long celebrates its Desert Storm victory as a harbinger of a new world order.

U.S. national security policy risks being stuck in the middle. It will not come to grips with the implications of new peer competitors of class "A" scale, and it will avoid the politically messy world of the "C" situations. The compromise, clearly, is to consider only type "B" competitors: easy and small enough to take on with the inherited military and doctrine left over from the Cold War, and not so politically difficult as the lower-intensity conflicts that represent a Vietnam-like quagmire to many analysts. The problem with much of the military debate is that it offers the promise of managing, or at least dealing with, even large powerful competitors with no more than the conceptual apparatus of a military designed for "B" opponents. This is the tunnel vision that characterizes the current debate. The air and naval power based in Japan and 35,000 troops in South Korea would bear no obvious military deterrent value to the emergence of an "A" competitor in Asia, save perhaps for maintaining a tenuous psychological linkage to the United States. Yet the Defense Planning Guidance implicitly suggests that this way of operating will be as relevant in the future as it has been in the past.

The strategic problem for the United States is that continuing to operate as it has in the past makes no sense except during the brief interim period of a few years in which the U.S. cold war military legacy is worked off against "B" competitors. The current military, and even the next military, might be designed to this end, but not the military after next. Developing a military force takes a long time; the planning and design stages alone take over a decade. If U.S. defense executives are to avoid the tunnel vision of immediate problems and pressures they need to include in their current planning a thorough reassessment of organizational, management, and technological opportunities open to them. As for the military after next, it will seem so far away that it is not likely to appear in immediate plans. If, however, research and development is to influence the potentially most important U.S. security problems, the military after next is the one that more people should be thinking about.

### Distance: The Second Problem

A second need is to understand the immense distances that the military after next may operate in. The problem with the next military is not that it will not perform well at what it does. The U.S. military could land a 10-division field army against India, the People's Republic of China (PRC), or Pakistan and support it for weeks while prosecuting a vigorous air campaign. Current AirLand Battle concepts are likely to tear through the first wave of counterattacks. The next U.S. military, depicted by state 2 in figure 1, might be able to operate even longer in this environment. The problem, of course, is that the scale of military operations anticipated in the future so dwarfs that of operations against Iraq that such operations would be strategically meaningless. AirLand Battle, the way U.S. forces use space, their logistics, and other support needs have to be matched to a far larger scale to deal with "A" type powers, even as U.S. forward bases are being reduced in number.

The effects of distance and scale on operational concepts were clearly seen in World War II. The German Army attacked to the west in 1940 with 141 divisions, only 10 of which were armored Panzer units. By concentrating 9 Panzer divisions at the focal point of the battle they were able to split the Allies in two, despite being outnumbered in tanks overall 3,505 to 2,445. Most analysts draw the correct conclusion that by using their armor in an unexpected way, the Germans outmaneuvered the allies and quickly broke down the defense.

But there is another lesson. Against Russia the Germans used 156 divisions, with 29 Panzer units. But the scale and shape of the eastern front was so much larger than the western that the concentration tactic could not work there. European Russia resembles a funnel, widening as one goes east. As German units charged into Russia, the length of the front doubled from 800 to 1,500 miles. The frail road and rail net compounded problems. In short, the operational space in the East was so different from that in the West that the operational concept that worked in one failed in the other. This resulted in a precipitous "demodernization" of war for the Germans, for which they had no technical or operational counter.[7]

In an analogous way, many high-technology U.S. concepts designed for use against "B" competitors will not work against "A" competitors because distance and scale will be so vast. Most recent U.S. military innovations were stimulated by the need to counter Soviet land attack in Europe but were still reliant on forward bases for support. Operations at a greater distance from bases, or against opponents lacking the high connectivity of Soviet forces, might look very different. Operations in Eurasia especially call for entirely new concepts of operations, not greater numbers of weapons. It is in this area especially that strategic thinking is being neglected. U.S. planners have an automatic tendency to view problems as requiring more resources for their solution, but what figure 1 suggests is that, for managing in a world with new peer competitors, thinking would be better directed toward operational research—changing concepts of operations and organization—than toward budgets and force levels. Asian military institutions are now changing from agrarian peasant infantry hierarchies to more advanced outward-looking forces using technology to project power over distance.[8] The United States became a military power in Asia in 1898, following the Battle of Manila Harbor. Given the military changes believed to be taking place there, and a U.S. intention to focus its military on "B" or "C" powers, the twenty-first century could see the United States being essentially out of the military picture in this dynamic region. Although better diplomacy, reliance on international organizations and cooperation, and other actions can perhaps compensate for the U.S. secular decline as an Asian military power, it is by no means clear that this change will not also be accompanied by troubling strategic consequences well short of military action.

The military after next cannot be looked at exclusively in terms of technology or political forecasts. These have to be compared to the scale of operations needed for maintaining competitive advantage, even against "A" competitors.

## Organizational Learning: The Third Problem

The argument so far calls for far greater consideration of longer-term trends in force and strategy design. The question of how exactly to achieve this remains. Details of what the military after next should look like are intentionally left out of this article for one simple reason. No one knows what they are. It is impossible to design this force now. Instead, what is needed is a learning process that will produce the design. This is a long-term, evolutionary project, one that requires a different approach to defense management than during the Cold War.

What is not needed are defense budget increases to take account of potential new "A" scale competitors. Nor is preservation of existing cold war force structure necessary, beyond what is prudent for immediate security requirements. What is needed is a reorientation of strategic thinking into an area that has not yet received it. The best way to preserve U.S. competitive advantage is to recognize that the only source of sustainable advantage is learning to come to grips with the new problems and demands. This is *organizational* learning, which will be reflected in the capacities of the U.S. military working with allies to deal with these problems.

The emphasis in this article on organizational learning, rather than pursuit of the correct strategy, is carefully considered to reflect the transience of strategy discussions. As argued above, strategies are easier to change than institutions. What is needed is institutional learning, learning that shows up in the procedures, operational concepts, training, and reflexive responses contained in the military after next. This is very different from individual learning, where people learn how to do things better. Individual learning is a prerequisite for organizational learning. But it is not sufficient, because making a complex organization do new things requires different kinds of behavior and habit than those needed to change only an individual.

One way to accomplish this organizational learning is to encourage innovation in the formal learning parts of the defense establishment designed to foster innovations and new thinking. New concepts will be worked out and tested in the services, war colleges, operational testing centers, laboratories, and new distributed simulation and gaming networks. These centers need support and protection from immediate pressures. This is a shift from recent power distribution in the defense structure of the United States. The Goldwater-Nichols legislation increased the authority of the Joint Chiefs of Staff and unified and specified commands. They now have greater authority over budgets, strategy, and planning. Although this change is not a bad thing, it is time to ask if it needs to be slowed down or reversed. Units with operational authority are subject to the greatest immediate pressures. This increases incentives to solve tomorrow morning's problems.

Short-term pressures drive out long-term planning, every time. This is true in every organization. The only way to get around this problem is to bolster the independence of the learning parts of defense. This can be accomplished by supporting them, and by leaving them alone.

As simple as this sounds, it is difficult because it interferes with the basic administrative systems of the Department of Defense. One of the most insidious effects of PPBS has been its reinforcement of the principle that military organizations succeed primarily through an ability to reduce diversity and ambiguity. Every major decision is mapped on to a cost benefit calculus. Each service is pressured to come up with precise estimates of kill probabilities against threats under unknown conditions. Service staff organizations have even been changed to mirror the organization of the military staff tasked with immediate responses. Goldwater-Nichols carried this idea to its logical conclusion. Against a well-defined threat—the Soviet Union—it could be argued that all of these attempts to reduce diversity, whether to subordinate everything to a single unique concept of jointness or to conduct one grand optimization of different command capabilities, made sense. In the emerging security environment, its relevance is less evident. For its unintended effect is to force strategic thinking into one single vision of where national security policy is headed. In this framework, it makes perfect sense to assure continued success by making only slight changes to current strategies, structures, and skills.

Instead of this almost static approach, defense management needs to stimulate a constantly shifting tension between opposites: between coherence and dissonance, jointness and independence, centralization and de-centralization, hard and soft decisions, and among "A," "B," and "C" competitors. This is so different from standard conceptions of good defense management that it first appears to fly in the face of basic military principles. But nothing could be further from the truth. The single best example of this fact is the success in organizational learning of the U.S. military in the interwar period. During this period the army and navy developed entirely new concepts of operations that went on to prove successful in World War II. The navy, in particular, deserves special mention here, because its learning centers focused on "A" scale threats at a time—the 1920s and early 1930s—when this went against national policy and sentiment, particularly because there were no obvious threats to American vital interests.

Take the experience of the U.S. Naval War College at Newport as an example.[9] During the 1920s and early 1930s, Newport developed the operational concepts of carrier task force operations and amphibious island-hopping tactics in the Pacific. During this early period, all planning was done essentially on paper, or more precisely in the war gaming center at Newport. This prescient thinking took place at a time when Japan was not an enemy of the United States, when overall military budgets were less than 1 percent of GNP, when the force structure needed to execute the concepts did not exist, and when the national sentiment was to avoid foreign entanglements. The essential reason why it could occur at Newport was that this institution was protected and insulated from external immediate pressures. It was supported, and its oddball activities tolerated, by senior managers who understood that to reduce diversity would be very dangerous in such an uncertain strategic environment.

Had there been a modern rigorous review of Newport's activities in this period it is certain that its eccentric activities would have been brought into conformance with official policy. Yet doing this would have destroyed the institution's contributions to thinking about what, for them, was the military after next. The United States today faces the same situation. Newport's budget in the 1930s was tiny. The budgets needed to support research on the outlines of the military after next are correspondingly small. The nerve needed to support, and protect, independent thinking in the services, however, is not small.

One way to encourage organizational learning, then, is to strengthen independence and tolerance for diversity within the services, war colleges, laboratories, and simulation centers. Another way is to change the basic approach to defense management inherited from the PPBS. To the extent that the United States is actually in a period of military revolution, it is a revolution whose benefits will appear less in broad policy areas than in fundamental redesign of flows of work and information in the combat forces, and between these and the defense macrostructure that is supposed to support and assist them. In this framework, the job of senior defense managers changes from deciding what programs to fund to rethinking military processes. Since the advent of the Department of Defense's PPBS, the role of senior defense executives has been to function as if they were really running a miniature capital market, rationing scarce resources among many different competing programs. In order to rationalize this process, a specialized accounting system was devised to place all programs in a common measurement system. The tools of operations research and systems analysis forced disparate activities into this overall resource allocation framework.

This framework has been criticized above, but another of its defects is that nearly all analysis takes the existing programming categories for granted. Categories such as strategic operations, conventional operations, and command, control, and intelligence rigidly define the business of the Pentagon. The PPBS created incentives to make programs look attractive in terms of the specialized PPBS accounting system, but this unintentionally reduces the likelihood of innovations not susceptible to measurement in this system. Changes in operational concepts, linkages across functional areas (e.g., logistics with operations), and changes in basic military processes have taken place in the PPBS era but only by resisting or circumventing the PPB system.

In management jargon, *reengineering needs to replace reprogramming*. With new information technologies, organizations are changed not by changing budgets within existing categories—reprogramming in the jargon of the PPBS—but by analyzing to see if these categories make sense in the first place. Reengineering has been defined as "the fundamental rethinking and radical redesign of business processes to achieve dramatic performance improvements in critical areas of performance," and it is a useful new concept for defense executives to become familiar with.[10] In the past, an organization would acquire computers to automate the way it did things. Now, it looks at how to do things differently. Paving over a zigzagging cow path gives a zigzagging paved road. But first straightening out the road, and then paving it, gives a superhighway. What the Naval War College of the 1930s did was to reengineer the force to deal with a new scale of competition. They designed the work and information flows in carrier and amphibious attack. The result was a new superhighway that led to victory at Midway and the Coral Sea.

## Conclusion

The thinking in this article is not likely to be popular, but it deals with a problem that is badly in need of attention. Unless current conceptions are changed and a more sober attitude to long-term military planning becomes important in the debate over national security, the United States risks being left out of a fundamental change in the character of warfare. At the same time, changes in the security environment suggest that the United States will become essentially an irrelevant military actor in many important parts of the world. Although the United States could defeat any power in a head-to-head showdown for global supremacy, this is the least likely form of competition it will face. Far more likely and important are situations in which it must deal with new peer competitors, and one important element—not the only one, to be sure—in such situations is having military forces matched to the scale of the problem.

This scale is defined as much in terms of operational and strategic concepts as it is in terms of force structure and budgets. At present, no peer competitors are clearly emerging to confront the United States, and it would be foolish and wasteful to begin a rearmament program to meet them. But it is by no means too soon to conceptualize what they potentially mean for the United States. The learning parts of the defense establishment must be supported and insulated so that they can experiment with new concepts—and this will cost very little. It is certainly possible, and desirable, that new approaches to international order reflected in, for instance, a revitalized United Nations and an increased interest in economic over military development will prove effective in making the need for any large military program obsolete. Statesmanship unassisted by military power may obviate the need for any of what is proposed here. But the outcome of even the most well-meaning, high-minded, and intelligent decisions can be disastrous, and it is not premature for national security planners to begin to consider some of the possibilities that could follow.

---

### Notes

1. These scenarios are taken from Pentagon planning as described in Barton Gellman, "Pentagon War Scenario Spotlights Russia," *Washington Post*, February 20, 1992, p. A-1.

2. Michael R. Gordon, "Cuts Force Review of War Strategies," *New York Times*, May 30, 1993, p. 1.

3. An analogous approach is taken to change in manufacturing in Robert Malpas, "The Plant After Next," *Harvard Business Review* 61 (July-August 1983), pp. 122-130.

4. See U.S. Department of Defense, *Conduct of the Persian Gulf War*, Report to Congress (Washington, D.C., April 1992).

5. The Regional Strategy was officially described in *National Security Strategy of the United States*, issued from the White House in August 1991 by President George Bush. It was described in greater detail by General Colin L. Powell in Joint Chiefs of Staff, *National Military Strategy of the United States* (Washington, D.C.: GPO, 1991).

6. Accounts of the DPG study and the associated controversy are in Patrick E. Taylor, "Pentagon Drops Goal of Blocking New Superpowers," *New York Times*, May 24, 1992, p. 1; and Barton Gellman, "Keeping the U.S. First; Pentagon Would Preclude a Rival Superpower," *Washington Post*, March 11, 1992, p. A-1. See also Francis Fukuyama, "The Beginnings of Foreign Policy," *New Republic*, August 17 and 24, 1992, pp. 24-32.

7. See Omer Bartov, *Hitler's Army* (New York, N.Y.: Oxford University Press, 1992), pp. 12-28.

8. This is the thesis of my book *Asian Military Institutions*, in process.

9. See Michael Vlahos, *The Blue Sword* (Newport, R.I.: Naval War College Press, 1980) for a detailed account of the Naval War College and the American strategic mission in the period from 1919 to 1941.

10. Michael Hammer and James Champy, *Reengineering the Corporation* (New York, N.Y.: Harper, 1993), p. 32.

# Strategy and Force Planning Faculty
## Naval War College

Dr. Henry C. Bartlett is a graduate of the Naval War College and holds D.B.A., M.B.A., and B.S. degrees from Indiana University. He served in the U.S. Air Force from 1955 to 1980, primarily in tactical aviation. His research interests include strategy and force planning, defense economics, Eurasian security affairs, technology and innovation, and war gaming. He is the author and co-author of numerous published articles about strategy and force planning.

Captain Michael J. Filkins, USNR, is a Naval Aviator and has spent his entire career in Maritime Patrol aviation (VP). His career highlights include tours on the staff of Commander, Naval Air Reserve Force as the VP Program Manager, a major staff tour with Director, Air Warfare (N-88) in Washington, and Commanding Officer of Patrol Squadron 65. He holds a M.A. in national security and strategic studies from the Naval War College (1995), a M.S. in systems engineering from the Naval Postgraduate School (1985), and a B.S. in biology from Michigan State University (1973).

Dr. Richmond M. Lloyd is Director of the Strategy and Force Planning course and holds the Theodore Roosevelt Chair of Economics. He received a Ph.D. in business administration from the University of Rochester, has a M.B.A. from the University of Chicago, and a B.S. in mechanical engineering from the University of Rochester. His current research and teaching interests include strategy and force planning, defense and international economics, and logistics.

Lieutenant Colonel James J. Maye is an Army infantry officer with extensive experience in both light and air assault infantry operations. He served as the commandant of the U.S. Army Northern Warfare Training Center in Alaska. He graduated with distinction from the Naval War College in 1996. In addition to a M.A. from the Naval War College he holds a M.S. from the University of Kentucky and B.S. from the United States Military Academy. He has taught on the faculty of both the U.S. Army Command and General Staff College and Military Academy.

Colonel Kevin E. McHugh holds the Alan B. Shepard Military Chair of Space Warfare. An Air Force fighter and instructor pilot, with time in the F-106, T-38, and T-37, he last served as Deputy Commander of the 47th Operations Group and as Commander of the 84th Flying Training Squadron. Prior to that, he was the Assistant Air Attaché to Canada from 1986 to 1989. He graduated with distinction from the Naval War College in 1994, with a M.A. in national security and strategic studies. He also earned a M.S. in chemistry from Michigan State University and a B.S. from the Air Force Academy, where he was commissioned in 1973.

Dr. Mackubin T. Owens, Jr., received a regular Marine Corps commission in 1968. He transferred to the Marine Corps Reserve in 1978 and earned his Ph.D. in politics from the University of Dallas in 1982. He also holds a M.A. in economics from Oklahoma University. He has served as National Security Advisor to Senator Bob Kasten and as Director of Legislative Affairs for the Nuclear Weapons Programs of the U.S. Department of Energy. He is Editor-in-Chief of the defense quarterly, *Strategic Review* and Adjunct Professor of International Relations at Boston University. His has published numerous articles on grand strategy, economics and national security, maritime strategy and force structure, defense organization, civil-military relations, and the congressional role in national security.

Ambassador Lauralee M. Peters, a career officer of the U.S. Foreign Service, served as U.S. Ambassador to Sierra Leone from 1992 to 1995. She also served overseas in Vietnam, Thailand, Pakistan, and Paraguay. As an economic officer she specialized in international finance and development issues. Her current research interests include humanitarian assistance, preventive diplomacy, and collapsing nations. She graduated with highest honors from the University of Kansas, did three years of graduate work there, and has trained at the Foreign Service Institute of the Department of State.

Dr. Andrew L. Ross earned his Ph.D. and M.A. in government from Cornell University. Prior to joining the faculty of the NSDM Department in 1989, he taught in the political science departments of the University of Illinois and the University of Kentucky, held research fellowships at Harvard and Princeton, and worked as an analyst at the U.S. Arms Control and Disarmament Agency and the RAND Corporation. He has published numerous works on grand strategy, strategic planning, regional security, weapons proliferation, the international arms market, and defense industrialization.

Professor Timothy E. Somes is a graduate with highest distinction of the Naval War College. He holds a M.A. in international relations from Salve Regina University as well as a B.S. in engineering from Tufts University. Captain Somes was chairman of the Naval War College's Joint Military Operations department for a number of years before retirement. A thirty year veteran of the Cold War, his over twenty years at sea on nuclear ballistic and nuclear attack submarines included many years in command and post-command billets. Lecturing widely on naval force planning issues, Professor Somes co-authors frequent articles on an array of strategy and force planning topics.

Lieutenant Colonel James A. Stevens is an Air Force fighter and instructor Weapons System Officer, with experience in the F-111. He graduated from the Army War College in 1995. He has served as Base Commander, Chief of Airborne Command Element for Operation Provide Comfort, Chief of Operations and Training at Incirlik AB, Turkey during Desert Storm, Assistant Ops Officer, Flight Commander, Executive Officer, and F-15E Manufacturing Manager. He holds a M.S. in contracting and manufacturing from the Air Force Institute of Technology, a M.B.A. in finance from Eastern New Mexico University, and a B.S. in industrial management from Georgia Institute of Technology.

Mr. David W. Swindle is a Special Agent with the Naval Criminal Investigative Service (NCIS) with extensive experience in counterintelligence, specifically espionage investigations. Prior to his assignment to the faculty of the Naval War College, he was the Deputy Assistant Director for Technical Services, NCIS Headquarters, Washington, D.C. He holds a M.A. in national security and strategic studies from the Naval War College, a M.A. in government from Georgetown University, and a B.S. in finance from the University of Alabama.

*U.S. Government Printing Office:  1997 — 501-364